INFORMAL REASONING AND EDUCATION

edited by

JAMES F. VOSS
Learning Research and Development Center
University of Pittsburgh

DAVID N. PERKINS
Harvard University

JUDITH W. SEGAL
United States Department of Education
Washington, D.C.

LEA LAWRENCE ERLBAUM ASSOCIATES, PUBLISHERS
1991   Hillsdale, New Jersey   Hove and London

Lawrence Erlbaum Associates, Inc., Publishers
365 Broadway
Hillsdale, New Jersey 07642

Library of Congress Cataloging-in-Publication Data

Informal reasoning and education / edited by James F. Voss, David N. Perkins, Judith W. Segal.
    p. cm.
    Includes bibliographical references and index.
    ISBN 0-8058-0208-8.—ISBN 0-8058-0209-6 (pbk.)
    1. Thought and thinking—Study and teaching. 2. Reasoning—Study and teaching. I. Voss, James F., 1930– . II. Perkins, David N.
III. Segal, Judith W.
LB1590.3.I54 1990
370.15′24—dc20   90-43491
                                                CIP

Printed in the United States of America
10 9 8 7 6 5 4 3 2 1

Contents

PART II: Modes and Models of Informal Reasoning

PART III: Informal Reasoning and Instruction

PREFACE

TEACHING REASONING:
THE CHALLENGE FACING OUR SCHOOLS

Reasoning has long been considered one of the highest forms of mental activity. Indeed, it plays an important role in virtually all areas of life, including the vocational, the civic, the social, and the academic. People who are good reasoners generally excel, or so it is believed.

Although reasoning has always been held in high esteem, many would argue that it is even more important to success in daily life now than ever before. We live in a highly complex and rapidly changing technological environment. Information about complicated issues fill the pages of our newspapers, demanding a high level of reasoning proficiency on the part of all citizens. The workplace is also changing in ways that place greater demands on reasoning. Recent trend data suggest that, in the economy of the future, a substantially larger segment of the workforce can expect to encounter challenging reasoning requirements than do so today. Offering evidence in support of this point, the Hudson Institute (1987) reported that the fastest growing occupations in the United States require a high level of proficiency in reasoning. By contrast, occupations that are declining in size require a low level of proficiency. Using current economic statistics to predict the skill requirements of the labor force in the year 2000, occupations that are now in the middle of the skill requirement distribution for mathematics, language, and reasoning proficiency will become the least skilled occupations of the future.

Because reasoning plays such an important role in our lives, it is not surprising that educators have always aimed to teach children how to reason. The official documents of school districts throughout the United States now often contain language that affirms such aspirations (Sizer, 1985). Although reasoning has never achieved the status of an academic subject that consumes a specific block of instructional time, many of the activities associated with learning academic subjects have also always been considered useful in fostering proficiency in reasoning. These include opportunities to read and interpret texts, develop written and oral arguments, and solve problems. In this sense, although our schools do not teach it as a separate subject, students are assumed to receive instruction in reasoning as a byproduct of instruction in other subjects.

Yet, when we look more closely at the school curriculum, we find that not all of the courses offered make challenging reasoning demands. Students who choose the most difficult courses encounter such demands on a frequent basis, whereas those who choose the least difficult ones encounter them rarely, if at all. This, in turn, has led some educational observers to argue that, although our schools express a commitment to teaching students how to reason, they do not view this commitment as extending to all students.

In a historical overview of the evolution of American secondary education, Powell, Farrar, and Cohen (1985) indicated that a crucial turning point in our schools' interpretation of this commitment occurred during the first half of this century. Our secondary schools then faced the enormous challenge of expanding from selective institutions, designed to train an intellectual elite, to mass institutions, offering an education to all young people. Confronted with the need to educate a much more varied student population, they responded by adding to the school curriculum many new and intellectually undemanding courses. A college placement track was retained for intellectually able and ambitious students, while less demanding vocational and general tracks were added for other students. Once established, this pattern of providing courses at varying levels of academic difficulty became a standard feature of the curriculum. As a result, over the years, large numbers of students have found themselves receiving educations that have entailed few, if any, reasoning demands. The persistence of this situation has led many to conclude that, although we have succeeded in making secondary education available to all young people, we have never seriously accepted the challenge of teaching all members of this diverse population how to become competent thinkers and reasoners (see also Resnick, 1987).

Altogether, over the past several years, a diverse array of stakeholders in the educational process have echoed concern about the school's lack of success in teaching reasoning. Included among them are: school teachers, school administrators and the professional organizations that represent them, government agencies responsible for administering educational programs at the state and national levels, and other groups that have an important influence on educational policy (Bennett, 1988; Marzano et al., 1988; National Commission on Excellence in Education, 1983; National Governors' Association, 1986; Reich, 1989).

Their concern is buttressed by data from a variety of reports and assessments.

For example, in recent reports of the National Assessment of Educational Progress (NAEP), students have been found to perform well on tasks that demand routine basic skills, but poorly on tasks that demand complex higher order skills. Data from reading assessments indicate that, although almost all students eventually learn how to comprehend short, uncomplicated passages of text conveying information about familiar phenomena, large numbers of students, even at older ages, experience difficulty with longer and more complicated passages and with passages that convey specialized information (NAEP, 1985). Similarly, data from mathematics assessments indicate that almost all students eventually learn how to perform basic calculation operations and solve simple word problems, but large numbers of students, even at older ages, experience difficulty applying mathematical concepts and operations to nonroutine situations (NAEP, 1988). Data from writing assessments tell a similar story. Large numbers of students, even at older ages, experience difficulty with complex writing tasks, such as building and evaluating arguments (NAEP, 1986).

As researchers follow recent graduates into the workplace, additional grounds for concern about the quality of their reasoning emerges. A National Academy of Sciences Panel, examining the performance of high school graduates in working situations, reported that many graduates lack the ability to draw correct inferences from written, pictorial, or mathematical information, to develop alternatives and reach conclusions, and to express their ideas intelligibly and effectively (National Academy of Sciences, 1984).

Studies of the instructional programs offered by schools provide yet further grounds for concern. Several recent studies of American high schools, involving visits to classrooms along with extensive interviews with students, teachers, and parents, have presented a dismal picture of the frequency with which students actually encounter demands for reasoning in the course of engaging in daily classroom activities (Boyer, 1983; Goodlad, 1984; Sizer, 1985). The enormous diversity of courses available in the typical American high school has led one set of observers (Powell et al., 1985) to characterize it as a "shopping mall" that seeks to accommodate a vast heterogeneity in clientele by providing a broad spectrum of products. Included among the course offerings available in American high schools are some that make strenuous reasoning demands and many others in which it is possible to achieve a passing grade simply by memorizing the information highlighted by the teacher and/or text. A small minority of students (those seeking admission to highly select colleges) opt for the more demanding courses, but the vast majority, to avoid academic engagement, select the ones that make minimal reasoning demands.

Other fine-grained studies of instructional materials and activities reinforce the view emerging from such global studies. Applebee (chapter 20 in this volume), for example, has looked closely at the nature of school writing assignments. He has found that, in most classrooms, writing represents an opportunity for assessing the factual knowledge students have acquired, rather than an opportunity for fostering the development of reasoning skills. More specifically, he reports that school writing assignments are typically both so broad, in terms of the topics assigned, and so confining, in terms of the time allotted, that they permit only one coping strategy. Students respond by regurgitating the material from the text for the course, rather than by attempting to integrate and draw implications from it.

School mathematics problems provide additional opportunities for teaching students how to reason. Again, however, recent studies support the conclusion that these opportunities are not being used to advantage. Stigler and Baranes (1988), for example, conducted a cross-cultural comparison of mathematics instruction at the elementary school level in the United States and Japan. Their data suggest that mathematics problems serve different instructional purposes in Japanese classrooms than in American ones. In Japanese classrooms, problems provide opportunities for promoting proficiency in mathematical reasoning, whereas in American classrooms, they provide opportunities for promoting fluency in the execution of mathematical procedures. In particular, Stigler and Baranes noted that the typical Japanese mathematics lesson focuses on only two or three problems, discussing them from many angles and exploring underlying principles and implications. In contrast, the comparable American lesson covers more problems but treats them in a way that makes minimal demands on reasoning. The lesson usually begins with the teacher offering a brief explanation of a new procedure. Following this, the children are asked to solve many similar problems, each of which requires use of the procedure just taught. (See chapter 16 in this volume, by Schoenfeld, for a discussion of the role that problems play in American mathematics instruction.)

In addition to writing assignments and math problems, textbooks represent a third instructional tool that might serve as a stimulus for prompting children to engage in reasoning. Beck (1989), among others, has recently been studying the way in which content is presented in school textbooks. Beck has conducted a careful analysis of several social studies textbook programs for elementary school. Again, however, her analysis documents many lost opportunities for encouraging children to engage in reasoning. Like others who, in recent years, have reported a "dumbing down" of school textbooks, Beck found that content is typically presented in the form of descriptions of isolated facts and events. What is lacking is a sufficiently well integrated supporting context to enable the students to grasp the underlying relationships. For example, she found that the American Revolution is depicted in these texts as a series of disparate events, without the connecting explanations that would permit readers to grasp the factors that caused one event to lead to another. Again, as in the case of school mathematics problems and writing assignments, the curriculum offers a set of arbitrary facts and procedures that must be memorized, rather than a rich body of knowledge that can be explored and understood.

As a set, the studies just discussed paint a vivid picture of a disturbing state of affairs. They indicate that large numbers of students complete their years of secondary schooling without having acquired sufficient proficiency in reasoning to cope with citizenship and work responsibilities in an increasingly complex world. They further indicate that instruction, as it occurs on a daily basis in American classrooms, provides few opportunities for students to acquire such proficiency. Not surprisingly, this state of affairs has not gone unnoticed. To the contrary, it has generated considerable concern, and many experimental efforts to explore ways of improving instruction in reasoning have recently been initiated.

It was in the context of these many concerns that the Office of Research, Office of Educational Research and Improvement, United States Department of Education sponsored a conference on the topic of informal reasoning, which was held at the Learning Research and Development Center of the University of Pittsburgh in March 1987. Nothing in this volume, however, should be assumed to represent the views of the United States Department of Education.

GOALS OF THIS VOLUME

As educators take on the challenge of improving instruction in reasoning, they will find that the knowledge base on which they can draw is only now emerging. If they turn to the psychological research literature for insight into the nature of reasoning as it occurs in classrooms and in much of everyday life, they will find some useful information, but numerous questions, as well. The fact is that, until recently, the phenomenon of contextualized reasoning, as opposed to abstract mathematical or logical reasoning, has received very little theoretical attention from psychologists. Although interest in this topic is now growing, the studies undertaken to date have been limited to a narrow range of reasoning situations. As a result, although we have come to understand the reasoning demands that arise in these situations, we continue to know very little about reasoning as it occurs in many other important everyday contexts, both at school and at work. Similarly, if educators turn to the instructional literature for advice on methods that can be used to improve children's reasoning, they will again find some useful information along with major questions about reasoning that is contextualized and knowledge-rich. The NAEP data indicate that, with sufficient schooling, our very best students do eventually become proficient reasoners—although, even with this population, many would argue that there is room for improvement. Indeed, a selection process may be operating such that the better reasoners are the individuals who pursue advanced schooling. The practical methods that have evolved over the years for working with highly able students represent one resource that can be consulted in developing ideas about extending instruction to a wider population. However, as we begin to work with a more varied population, we may find that we need to do more than widely implement existing methods. Less able individuals encounter greater difficulty in achieving proficiency in reasoning than do more able individuals, and thus require more extensive forms of instruction.

From time to time, major curriculum reform efforts have been mounted in the hope of encouraging our schools to adopt more powerful methods for teaching reasoning (see Cuban's chapter, 23, in this volume). One particularly extensive effort occurred during the 1960s. Educators, working in collaboration with disciplinary scholars, developed new curricula for many of the subjects taught at the elementary and secondary school levels. These curricula, unlike more conventional ones, sought to teach students not only the content associated with particular academic disciplines, but also the forms of reasoning that experts use in working with this content. Many promising methods for teaching reasoning were built into these curricula. The underlying goal was practical: to produce widespread changes in the instruction that students experience on an everyday basis in American classrooms. Measured against this goal, the effort was not successful. Neither the curricula nor the methods for teaching reasoning that were built into them are currently in widespread usage. Although this work did not lead to practical improvements in instruction, it did deepen our understanding of the complexities associated with teaching reasoning in ordinary classroom settings (see chapters 19 and 23 in this volume, by Newmann and Cuban).

More recently, in addition to a new wave of large-scale curriculum development projects, a theoretically based research literature on instruction in reasoning has begun to emerge. The research has three foci: exploring the feasibility of extending instruction to a wider population, identifying effective instructional methods, and understanding why certain approaches work. As a set, these studies offer grounds for optimism. In particular, we can point to examples that have produced substantial and enduring improvements in reasoning with varied student populations, across many carefully controlled studies (e.g., Brown & Palincsar, 1987). One distinguishing feature of such successful efforts is that they are grounded in a rich body of data from modern psychological research on the processes used by competent individuals in coping with the reasoning situation in question. Although these results are encouraging, they are only a beginning. Much additional research is needed both to determine whether success can be achieved in other research on reasoning and to explore what is involved in moving such interventions from experimental settings into more widespread instructional usage.

The goal of this volume is to extend the research on reasoning in directions that will create a firmer knowledge base for instruction. To accomplish this goal, the chapters that follow focus on informal reasoning, that is, on modes of thinking not restricted to rules of logic and mathematics, but to include inferential processes such as argumentation, which occur in classrooms as well as non-classroom situations. They seek to elucidate the nature of such reasoning, and to consider how it can be taught in classroom settings.

THE NATURE OF REASONING

What is informal reasoning? This question itself may be approached informally or formally—that is, either by delineating the types of situations in which such reasoning occurs or by specifying the properties that define it. Informally, informal reasoning refers to reasoning that occurs when a person is deciding which car to buy, which political candidate to vote for, or how to persuade a colleague to adopt a particular position with respect to some burning issue. Informal reasoning involves inferences, justifications of beliefs, and explanations for observations. Informal reasoning is found in virtually all professional, business, and other working contexts, in medical diagnoses, in legal arguments, in foreign policies, in management decision making, and in repairing cars. Children, as well as adults, reason informally. Informal reasoning, typically, is deliberate. In other words, informal reasoning pervades all facets of life.

Formally, informal reasoning may be viewed in relation to logic and to the use of the tasks of formal logic in experimentation. Formal logic has as its primary unit of analysis the argument, a formal argument typically consisting of two premises and a conclusion. A conclusion is valid if it follows from the premises in a manner that is consistent with the rules of logic. In addition, evaluation usually takes place by converting the premises and conclusion to symbolic form, as "All A are B." The examination of validity is thus content-free. Interestingly, in the study of reasoning, psychologists have almost exclusively employed tasks of formal logic, with individuals being asked to judge the validity of syllogisms or to examine the validity of an argument of propositional logic. It is, moreover, reasoning involving the use of the tasks of formal logic and of tasks in formalized systems such as mathematics that may be termed formal reasoning. (See chapter 15, by Nickerson, in this volume.)

Informal logic is also concerned with arguments; however, in informal logic, the arguments are typically inductive, or at least nondeductive, depending on one's definition of induction. Again, there is the question of whether a conclusion follows from premises, but there is also the question of the extent to which one or more reasons provide support for the conclusion. Thus, assume that a person asserts, "This country needs a Republican president in 1992. The Republican party's fiscal policies are better for the economic growth of the country than are the fiscal policies of the Democrats." The first sentence is a conclusion, or a claim, and the second sentence is a reason that is stated to support the conclusion. The quality of the argument is not determined in terms of a set of rules that indicates whether the conclusion is or is not valid; instead, the quality is judged in terms of *soundness*, soundness referring to (a) whether the reason providing support is acceptable or true, (b) the extent to which the reason supports the conclusion, and (c) the extent to which an individual takes into account reasons that support the contradiction of the conclusion (i.e., the counterarguments). Thus, a person may not agree that (a) the fiscal policies of the Republican party are better for the growth of the country, (b) that this statement, even if true, constitutes strong support for the conclusion, and (c) that the argument takes into account reasons that would support the conclusion that a Democrat should be elected in 1992. When an argument is evaluated in terms of soundness, the contents of the assertions are important, and the conclusion and reasons are not evaluated solely in symbolic form, as they are in formal logic.

There are, of course, many variations of the informal argument. There is the standard form of providing a conclusion and reasons that support the conclusion. An argument may be causal: John stopped at the light because it was red. An argument may be conditional: If tariffs are imposed on imports, then, in the long run, the economy will suffer. Finally, arguments may, of course, involve a number of supporting and opposing reasons, although typically the attempt is made to refute the counterarguments.

Informal reasoning may thus be considered reasoning that takes place in what may broadly be termed situations that involve the use of various forms of argument. Thus, although we generally do not think of our everyday mental activity as dealing with tasks of informal logic, thinking is so constituted. Considering informal reasoning formally, we arrive at essentially the same point as when we considered the matter informally; that is, informal reasoning consists of the reasoning performed in nondeductive situations that are essentially the everyday situations of life and work, including the academic and professional disciplines. Phrased another way, informal reasoning basically derives from Aristotle's rhetoric, not Aristotle's logic.

THE CONTENTS OF THIS VOLUME: AN OVERVIEW

This volume is organized into three sections. Part I, entitled "Contexts for Informal Reasoning," samples many different contexts in which informal reasoning can be observed. The goal is to understand the demands and difficulties that individuals encounter as they engage in reasoning across a broad range of situations that are characteristic of everyday life. Tweney describes the reasoning strategies used by scientists in exploring problems that are at the frontiers of human knowledge. Turning to medicine, Christensen and Elstein describe the reasoning engaged in by physicians in seeking to diagnose the nature of illnesses. In additional chapters, Voss discusses reasoning as it is found in the field of international relations, and Lawrence explores the nature of the reasoning engaged in by judges and jurors in reaching decisions on court cases. Perkins, Faraday, and Bushey discuss informal reasoning in everyday experience, and Miller-Jones considers reasoning as it is found in inner-city children. In the final chapter of this section, Johnson and Blair, as discussants, comment on the chapters and further explore the meaning of the term *informal reasoning*.

Part II, entitled "Modes and Models of Informal Reasoning," looks across the many contexts in which informal reasoning can be observed to identify its distinguishing characteristics. In particular, the chapters in this section explore: (a) the different forms that informal reasoning can assume; (b) its underlying mechanisms and processes; (c) how it is influenced by and differs from related skills, such as rhetoric and formal logic, and (d) how it develops in children.

Salmon opens the section with a challenge to the purity of formal argument, showing that formal argument applied to realistic situations involves considerable accompanying informal reasoning. Then, Baron discloses misconceptions that people hold about good argument and urges that sounder beliefs about argument need to be cultivated to enhance people's reasoning. Rissland presents a discussion of how examples are used to facilitate the reasoning process. Leland takes people's informal reasoning to task from another perspective: departures from normative standards for inferences that involve probabilities and values. Williams explores how people mix up issues of rhetorical form with matters of good reasoning.

Turning to a developmental perspective, Keil examines the dependence of reasoning on domain-specific causal theories that children evolve, and Stein and Miller discuss how children first develop concepts of argument in the context of social disputes, not truth testing. In the commentary, Nickerson returns to the continuing issue of the nature of informal versus formal reasoning in light of this set of chapters.

Part III, entitled "Informal Reasoning and Instruction," focuses on the problem of teaching reasoning in classroom settings. As a set, the chapters address four issues: (a) they consider how reasoning takes place in the academic content domains taught at the elementary and secondary school levels; (b) they describe the nature of current content area instruction and consider its advantages and limitations with respect to fostering proficiency in reasoning; (c) they explore opportunities and methods for improving instruction; and (d) they identify barriers that prevent teachers from engaging in more powerful forms of instruction.

Teachers seeking to incorporate instruction in reasoning into content area courses face challenges that are unique to their particular content areas as well as challenges that are shared with other content areas. Several of the authors featured in Section III describe domain-specific challenges. Schoenfeld considers opportunities for fostering informal reasoning in mathematics. Clement explores ways in which teachers can work with analogies and extreme cases to deepen their students' understanding of physics. O'Reilly describes a set of instructional materials that he has developed for teaching informal reasoning in history. Newmann considers the nature of higher order thinking in social studies and identifies barriers to its instruction.

Other authors in Section III consider challenges with respect to instruction in reasoning that all teachers encounter, regardless of their individual content domains. Applebee considers ways of using writing as a vehicle for improving reasoning, and Swartz explores possibilities for improving school textbooks. Norris discusses the use of multiple-choice tests as devices for assessing proficiency in reasoning, and Cuban, as discussant for this section, further identifies the nature of barriers to instruction in reasoning.

CONCLUSION

Since World War II, the world has grown smaller. Not only is economic interdependence greater today, but technology and communication have made the flow of news and ideas more rapid than ever before. The academic disciplines, although highly specialized, have benefited from the interdisciplinary exchange of ideas. It is in this spirit that the present volume was conceived; the nature of informal reasoning is not only of central interest to a variety of academic and practical disciplines; it plays a critical role in the life of any thoughtful human. It is to the improvement of such reasoning, for everyone, that this volume is dedicated.

REFERENCES

Beck, I. L., McKeown, M. G., & Gromoll, E. W. (1989). Learning from social studies texts. *Cognition and Instruction, 6,* 99–158.

Bennett, W. (1988). *American education: Making it work.* Washington, DC: Government Printing Office.

Boyer, E. (1983). *High school: A report on secondary education in America.* New York: Harper and Row.

Brown, A. L., & Palincsar, A. S. (1987). Reciprocal teaching of comprehension strategies: A natural history of one program for enhancing learning. In J. D. Day & J. G. Borkowski (Eds.), *Intelligence and exceptionality: New directions for theory, assessment, and instructional practices.* (pp. 81–132). Norwood, NJ: Ablex Publishing Co.

Goodlad, J. I. (1984). *A place called school: Prospects for the future.* New York: McGraw-Hill.

Hudson Institute. (1987). *Workforce 2000: Work and workers for the 21st century.* Indianapolis, IN: W. B. Johnston & A. E. Pacher.

Marzano, R. J., Brandt, R. S., Hughes, C. S., Jones, B. F., Presseisen, B. Z., Rankin, S. C. & Suhor, C. (1988). Dimensions of thinking: A framework for curriculum and instruction. Alexandria, VA: ASCD.

National Academy of Sciences. (1984). *High schools and the changing workplace: The employers' view.* Washington, DC: National Academy Press.

National Assessment of Educational Progress. (1985). *The reading report card: Progress toward excellence in our schools.* Princeton, NJ: Educational Testing Service.

National Assessment of Educational Progress. (1986). *The writing report card: Writing achievement in our schools.* Princeton, NJ: Educational Testing Service.

National Assessment of Educational Progress. (1988). *The mathematics report card: Are we measuring up?* Princeton, NJ: Educational Testing Service.

National Commission on Excellence in Education. (1983). *A nation at risk.* Washington, DC: Government Printing.

National Governors' Association. (1986). *Time for results: The governors' 1991 report on education*. Washington, DC: Center for Policy Research and Analysis.

Powell, A. G., Farrar, E., & Cohen, D. K. (1985). *The shopping mall high school*. Boston, MA: Houghton Mifflin Co.

Reich, R. B. (1989). Must economic vigor mean making do with less. *NEA Today, 7*, 13–19.

Resnick, L. B. (1987). *Education and learning to think*. Washington, DC: National Academy Press.

Sizer, T. R. (1985). *Horace's compromise: The dilemma of the American high school*. Boston, MA: Houghton Mifflin Co.

Stigler, J. W., & Baranes, R. (1988). Culture and mathematics learning. *Review of Research in Education, 15*, 253–306.

James F. Voss
David N. Perkins
Judith W. Segal

I CONTEXTS FOR INFORMAL REASONING

1 Informal Reasoning in Science

Ryan D. Tweney
Bowling Green State University

That informal reasoning plays a large role in scientific inquiry is a point that is relatively undisputed among scholars and scientists studying science itself. At least since Kuhn's *Scientific Revolutions* (1962/1970), inquiry into the nature of science has acknowledged that science does not rely exclusively, or even primarily, on formal modes of reasoning. Although the results of science are frequently expressed in the formal language of mathematics and with heavy reliance on inferential logic, few current scholars expect results to originate in formal ways. Recently, there has been a great tendency to ascribe certain very irrational processes to science: Kekulé's dream, for example, or the lucky accidents of Fleming. On this view, science can begin to seem a very arbitrary process indeed (see, e.g., Austin's 1978 book, *Chase, Chance, and Creativity: The Lucky Art of Novelty,* the subtitle of which leaves no doubt about its message!)

In fact, however, the point can be stretched too far. Although we may all agree that luck, dreams, and wild associations play a role in science, this is not the same as ascribing such irrationality to all scientific thought. Although it is not formal, the informal reasoning that occurs in science *is* rational, in the sense that it is goal-directed, sometimes highly systematic, and fully justifiable on pragmatic grounds. Baron (1985) has even argued that we can create normative schemes of informal reasoning. Perkins (1981) has argued that many of the processes underlying creative thought correspond to rather ordinary processes of thought applied in novel contexts. I hope to show in this chapter that the further analysis of informal reasoning in science has potentially great explanatory power for an understanding of scientific thought.

In another context (Tweney, 1989), I have argued that understanding complex, real-world thought requires moving beyond the rather narrow laboratory research that has characterized much of cognitive psychology and must include, also, an effort to apply the generalizations of cognitive psychology to the interpretive understanding of complex thought in vivo. Such an approach requires closer attention to case studies of scientific thinking than is customary in recent psychology (see also Wallace & Gruber, 1989). Although there is now a greater willingness to deal with idiographic materials in cognitive work, most of the descriptive base is still depersonalized. We do not, in general, know much of the life of the subjects in the ordinary study of, say, problem solving. There may be an incredibly detailed analysis of an hour's worth of cognition, but rarely are ties made between the results of the analysis and anything else that may or may not be knowable about the "subject"—whose very identity still hides behind that jargonized term.

As an alternative approach, I offer a case study based on the thinking of the English physicist Michael Faraday (1791–1867). Because he kept extensive diaries and notes, we have, perhaps, more raw material for such an analysis than for any other scientist. If a plausible account of Faraday's thought is possible, and if it reveals in more detail how informal reasoning processes are manifest in science, then the effort should exemplify one of the main themes of this volume of essays and support my claim about the importance of case study analysis. Cognition of the sort we are describing occurs in persons, and we neglect the uniqueness of the cognizer at our peril (see Gruber, 1974, for a similar claim).

FARADAY'S SCIENTIFIC ACHIEVEMENTS

Faraday is important in the history of science primarily for his empirical and theoretical investigations into the nature of electricity and magnetism. He is sometimes regarded as the first true field theorist in the line of thinking that leads to relativity and quantum theory (Einstein & Infeld, 1938). A brilliant experimentalist, Faraday published the results of thousands of experiments and kept records of literally tens of thousands conducted during his career. As a theorist, he was the first to present a cogent field theory as a genuine alternative to 18th century interpretations of Newtonian theory. Whereas the Newtonian universe consisted of hard material objects ("billiard balls" on an atomic scale), acting upon each other at a distance, via forces whose nature was not explained, Faraday's universe was filled with forces only and dispensed to a large degree with matter as a primary physical reality. For Faraday, the Newtonian "billiard ball" atoms were instead conceived of as centers of force. The mystery of action-at-a-distance was replaced by imponderable but real lines of force that reach out from the centers to fill all space (Williams, 1966). In Faraday's account, matter is a stage on which the primary reality, namely forces, acts.

Ultimately, Faraday was able to ground his conception of lines of force on a number of empirical phenomena: the patterned arrangement of iron filings in a magnetic field, the conversion of electric currents into magnetic forces and vice versa, the quantitative relationships governing the forces on a magnetic needle placed near a current-carrying wire, and so on. Faraday never developed his theory in formal mathematical terms (a task carried out by others, most notably, James Clerk Maxwell [1831–1874]), nor did he succeed in grounding all aspects of his theory empirically. Thus, for example, he never succeeded in verifying his strong belief that gravity was somehow related to electrical and magnetic phenomena; as a result, his system never fully exorcised action-at-a-distance from physics. Nevertheless, Faraday's theory was so rich in empirical consequences and so compelling as an alternate world view, that he fully deserves the revolutionary status sometimes accorded him.

In his research, Faraday consciously moved from vague construals to formal concepts and precise quantitative laws, pursuing experimental demonstrations of striking simplicity (rather than mathematical formalisms) to convince the scientific community of the rightness of his views (Gooding, 1985). Showing some of the ways in which he did this is the major focus of this chapter.

FARADAY THE PERSON

Before we can know how he reasoned, we must know a few things about Faraday. He has been the subject of a number of excellent biographical studies, most notably those of Tyndall (1868), Thompson (1898), Williams (1965), and, most recently, the studies in the collection edited by Gooding and James (1985). Several crucial aspects of Faraday's cognitive style are revealed in these studies: his reliance on visual imagery, the presuppositions that he brought to science, the social effects of the research of his contemporaries (and the way he utilized their results), and so on.

Especially striking for our purpose is the heavy reliance that Faraday placed on manipulation as a source of knowledge. Experimentation was his royal road to truth and the final test of all of his ideas. Although he held very strong beliefs about the nature of the physical world, he was always careful to distinguish between what he believed to be true and what he could demonstrate to be true via experiment; if something were true, then it should lead to ways of acting on the world in tangible and fruitful fashion. Faraday's epistemology was procedural in a very basic sense (Tweney, 1987b; see also Gooding, 1985, and Gooding, 1990). His epistemology coincided neatly with his force-centered ontology. Just as forces were, for him, the primary physical reality (a "push–pull" universe), so also was manipulation the primary means of getting knowledge (a "push–pull" view of truth).

Both his epistemology and his ontology have early origins in Faraday's intellectual development. Born poor, he received only a little formal schooling before being apprenticed to a bookbinder. While learning his trade, Faraday read some of the books that he bound, most notably an *Encyclopedia Britannica* article on electricity (Tytler, 1797) and a popular work, Jane Marcet's *Conversations on Chemistry* (1809). He later identified Marcet's book as an early source for his reliance on experimentation; when he tried her experiments, they actually worked as she said they would! As he later wrote, "I felt that I had got hold of an anchor in chemical knowledge and clung *fast* to it" (Letter to De La Rive, October 2, 1858, in Williams, 1971, p. 912).

Faraday's self-education in science, itself a fascinating tale, is not detailed here. Suffice it to say that, by 1813, when he was plucked from the binding trade to serve as bottle washer, amaneuensis, and gofer for the eminent scientist Sir Humphry Davy (1778–1829), Faraday had already acquired a basic knowledge of science. Bright and hard-working, his role in Davy's lab expanded quickly. His first scientific paper was published only 3 years later (Faraday, 1816a), and, only 5 years after, he caused a sensation in the scientific community by discovering that a current-carrying wire could be made to revolve in a magnetic field (Faraday, 1821).

The force-centered view that characterizes Faraday's physical theory can be seen in embryonic form in some of his earliest notebooks. In an 1816 commonplace book, he copied out the following quote from Laplace: "The true march of Philosophy consists in rising by the path of Induction and calculation from phenomena to laws and from laws to forces" (Faraday, 1816b, p. 335). Although we can discount the "Induction and calculation" part of the quote (fairly standard boilerplate for the times), it is significant that Faraday approvingly noted the explanatory role of forces in physical science. In the same notebook, Faraday speculated on the meaning of action-at-a-distance formulations and queried whether or not electrostatic induction could be seen as an example of action-at-a-distance. Beginning in the same year, he gave a series of lectures on chemistry (Faraday, 1816–1818). Force concepts also played a major role in these lectures, although, at the beginning, he stuck to a basically Newtonian view of matter.

In another context, I have traced the development of his force schema after 1816 (Tweney, 1985). The important point here is that this schema evolved slowly and continuously across the years, but without altering the fundamental point: that forces are central and that matter is secondary, something to be explained by forces rather than as an ultimate reality in itself. It is not surprising, therefore, that an interest in magnetic and electrical phenomena is present in his very earliest notes (Faraday, 1809–1810). Finally, we must acknowledge the central influence of Davy on Faraday's conceptualizations. Heavily influenced by Coleridge, Davy was a neo-Kantian and himself an advocate of the importance of electrical forces in the composition of matter. In fact, Davy was the first to see the significance of the phenomena of electrolytic decomposition (Davy, 1812; Forgan, 1980).

It is also important to note the religious roots of Faraday's views (Cantor,

1985). A devout Sandemanian, Faraday was a fundamentalist who believed that God had made it possible to "read the book of nature" but that doing so required enormous effort with no guarantee that the right answers would be attained. God would not deceive, but neither was God's nature an open book! Further, the human desire for knowledge was sometimes hindered by human weakness, by pride, conceit, and sloth. Out of this view, Faraday drew a kind of humility that was of great usefulness to his scientific work. Alert to the possibility of self-deception, he was consciously aware of the danger of confirmation bias and of the need to avoid it by deliberate attempts to disconfirm. Such views supported his reliance on experiment as the test of truth. Moreover, as Cantor (1985) has noted, Faraday's distrust of mathematical formulations in science (there are *no* mathematical equations of any sort in any of his papers) stem also from religious grounds. Sandemanians relied on numbers as signs of God's will, using, for example, simple lotteries to determine church seating. But they eschewed any transformations of these numbers—one could not weight the lots, for example—because this amounted to a distortion of God's message. In the same way, Faraday relied heavily on quantification but never used abstract formalisms to distort the message of the quantified relationships. Instead of algebra, he relied on a kind of intuitive geometry, a visual depiction of physical reality manifested in careful diagrams and verbal descriptions for the mind's eye (Maxwell, 1855; Gooding & Tweney, in preparation).

In sum, then, we can see that Faraday's approach to science was structured by his characteristics as a person. The product of a specific cultural, social, and historical context, his unique background and education in science further shaped the way he thought. Although unsurprising in itself, this point serves to introduce the more specific question of exactly how he carried out his research and what kinds of informal reasoning were manifest within it.

FARADAY'S EXPERIMENTAL SCIENCE: A SPECIFIC EXAMPLE

To illustrate the role of informal reasoning in Faraday's experimental work, I focus on one episode, a series of experiments carried out from August to November of 1831, in which Faraday explored the properties of his newest discovery, electromagnetic induction (Faraday, 1832, is the first published report). By passing a current through a coil of wire, he found that currents were induced in another coil placed a short distance away. Because the current in the first coil was known to generate magnetic forces (Oersted, 1820), this was the first demonstration of the conversion of magnetic forces into electrical forces. The induced currents were transient; they could be observed only at the instant when the current in the first coil was turned on or turned off. Having found this much, what did he do then?

Between August 29, 1831 and the first presentation of his results to the Royal Society on November 4, 1831, Faraday carried out 134 experiments to explore his discovery (see his published diary records for these dates in Faraday, 1932–1936, volume 1). In the course of these experiments, he determined the spatial relationships among the induced and inducing forces, established that ordinary bar magnets as well as electromagnets could induce currents, confirmed that the induced currents had many of the properties of ordinary battery currents, explored the effect of different substances, intensities, and geometries on the observed effects, and conducted experiments that related his discovery to prior findings (e.g., his rotation experiments of 1821 and certain effects found by Arago). It is possible to see the series as an extended problem-solving episode in which numerous subgoals are pursued in the service of the overall goal of learning more about the new phenomenon.

Because Faraday kept extensive diary records, it is possible to trace the many twists and turns of his thought and his experimental practice. The twists and turns are not surprising, given that there was no clearly defined single goal that Faraday was attempting to reach. The problem space was an ill-defined one, and thus of a kind that creates problems for analysis (Ericsson & Simon, 1984; Voss, Greene, Post, & Penner, 1983). In fact, Faraday's progress during the series can be analyzed at several different levels, depending on the particular aspect that we wish to emphasize.

The ideal example here would be a protocol analysis that abstracts out a minimal set of states and operators sufficient to capture Faraday's diary record and simple enough to permit us to get some sense of his overall strategies. Of course, a diary record is not like a think-aloud protocol, so the ideal is not attainable in the strictest sense. Further, a good deal of the critical information is non-verbal—manipulation of apparatus, observation of "noisy" data, etc. Thus, critical information is not apparent in the diary and must be reconstructed (Gooding, 1989). Even so, by modifying some of the procedures of the usual analysis, something analogous to protocol analysis is possible, and this, in turn, reveals some of the characteristics of the series (Tweney & Hoffner, 1987). In brief, we can regard the series as directed toward producing new empirical observations. By coding each perceptual statement and each would-be perceptual statement (hypotheses, analogies, etc.) as *states* in the Newell and Simon (1972) sense, we can then search for *operators* that transform one state into another. Doing this for the 1831 series of experiments results in surprisingly few operators, as Table 1.1 shows, although they are admittedly of fairly wide scope. Notice the preponderance of DO operators, reflecting the fact that this is, after all, an experimental diary. But notice, also, how closely the remaining operators reflect the informality of the underlying thought that structures the series. Comparisons (a kind of "noticing") are frequent, as are analogies. Formal logical statements (HYP operators exclusively in this record) are much less frequent and occur only near the end of the series.

TABLE 1.1
Operators

In all of the following, (X) is a brief description of the content upon which the operator acts.

DO: (X)
        Any statement of a physical activity, for example,
            DO: Make apparatus/substance/etc.
            DO: Test apparatus/substance/etc.
            DO: Adjust apparatus/substance/etc.
            DO: Connect apparatus/etc.

OBSERVE: (X)
        Any statement of a perceived attribute or relationship among attributes.

INFER: (X)
        Any statement of an inferred (i.e., not perceived) attribute or relationship.

STATE GOAL: (X)
        Any statement of a purpose or goal, for example a sought-for relationship.

COMPARE: (X, Y)
        Any statement of a quantitative or qualitative comparison between two attributes, relationships, conclusions, experiments, etc.

REASON: (X because Y)
        Any statement of a reason for, or a justification of, an activity. N.B.; X must be an *activity.*

JUSTIFY: (X because Y)
        Any statement of a reason for, or a justification of, an observable. N.B.; Y must be an *inference.*

ANALOGY: (X as if Y)
        Any comparison which involves an analogical or metaphorical comparison.

NAME: (X = X′)
        Any labeling of an activity, entity, or observation.

IF (X) THEN (Y)
        Any statement of a conditional relationship.

HYP [IF (X) THEN (Y)]
        Any statement of a hypothetical conditional.

STATE CONCLUSIONS
        Any statement of a conclusion as to the correctness or incorrectness of a hypothesis.

Something like a problem behavior graph can be constructed from this analysis, as is shown in Fig. 1.1. The graph was prepared by coding each state as a node and connecting the nodes by lines representing a sequence of one or more operators. States move rightward only when a new empirical phenomenon is registered. States that involve no new knowledge or involve hypothetical knowledge (analogies, for instance) always move downward. Whenever Faraday recorded a finding that he later regarded as spurious, the line backs up to the last reliable node. Hence the little "branches" that move rightward from the main stem of the graph are blind alleys. Although the diagram sacrifices a good deal of

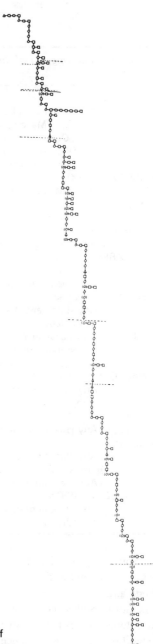

FIG. 1.1.   A protocol analysis of
a portion of Faraday's diary.

the detail of the diary record, it permits us to see one overriding characteristic, the fact that Faraday spent very little time or effort on things that did not work as he expected them to. He seemed unwilling to pursue avenues that did not quickly produce positive results.

A glance through the pages of Newell and Simon's *Human Problem Solving* (1972) reveals how starkly different this diagram is from those obtained in the more commonly studied laboratory situations. Whereas Faraday's diary protocol produces a nearly branchless but generally progressive single trunk, Newell and Simon usually found heavily foliated structures, even when there was a generally progressive movement. We are, of course, looking at a special case and would not necessarily expect to see a similar structure elsewhere, not even necessarily in other parts of Faraday's diary. In particular, his extensive attempts to demonstrate a relationship between gravity and electricity show extensive back-ups, insofar as Faraday was repeatedly finding results that he thought confirmed his supposition but that turned out to be artifactual (Faraday, 1851 summarized his failures). Even so, the disparity between the present analysis and the more usual findings is striking.

This disparity reveals an important point about the role of informal reasoning in science. From a formal point of view, a failure to explore potentially disconfirming evidence is a serious lapse. Popper, after all, advocated the active *pursuit* of disconfirming evidence (see his 1934/1959 book, as well as Platt, 1964; Tweney, Doherty, & Mynatt, 1981). Yet, in the context of what Faraday was attempting here, his strategy makes perfect sense. One ought to ignore unproductive avenues of exploration if there are other alternatives that can be explored. Had Faraday further pursued the blind alleys, he might simply have distracted himself. This is not to say that he was unaware of the power of disconfirmation; as noted earlier, he was well aware of its value. But he had a strong sense of when it should be invoked and when it should be ignored. During the early stages of exploration of a new phenomenon, it is best set aside.

We can contrast Faraday's strategy in this regard with that of Ampère (1775–1836), the noted French physicist who inadvertently discovered electromagnetic induction in 1822 but failed to publish his finding. According to Williams (1986), the finding was seen by Ampère as damaging to his current theoretical views about the nature of the relation between electricity and magnetism; he therefore failed to see the significance of his result, assumed it was due to an unknown artifact, and "buried" the result. Ampère's thinking betrays a much less sophisticated sense of the role of disconfirmation than we find in Faraday. The roots of Faraday's actions in this regard, as we have suggested earlier, can be found in the unique circumstances of his life and thought. Ampère, unlike Faraday, was devoted to the power of formal mathematical analyses in science. Unlike Faraday, he was centrally committed to a Newtonian view of force and matter, but, in this instance at least, the glory of discovery was not for him.

INFORMAL REASONING IN FARADAY'S
THEORETICAL VIEWS

Although Faraday displayed a good deal of informal reasoning in his experimentation, does it necessarily follow that his theoretical ideas were shaped in similar ways? After all, theory is, in a sense, the final product of scientific thinking. Just because Faraday eschewed formal mathematics, it does not follow that he eschewed the logical constraints proper to theory. In fact, there is little evidence that Faraday used logical constraints except in the process of putting his ideas into their final publishable form. Here, too, we see his reliance on informal methods of inference.

Faraday's theorizing has been the subject of a number of excellent recent studies, most notably those of Gooding (1981, 1982), Miller (1984), and Nersessian (1984, 1985). The focus has been the careful explication of his developing field theory. Whereas earlier studies (e.g., Berkson, 1974) were concerned primarily with the question of when he *first* can be said to have had a true field theory, this issue is really a matter of the definition of field theory (Nersessian, 1985). More to the point, all of the cited studies provide us with good reason to believe that Faraday's theorizing was informal.

Nersessian (1984), for example, has shown that Faraday's evolving sense of the importance of lines of force was heavily dependent on analogies with other "line-like" phenomena, for example, light rays and the spreading rings that move outward from a stone dropped in water. She has argued that these analogies were used heuristically by Faraday both concretely, to provide visualizable images, and abstractly, as a source of similarities that operate to link an unfamiliar domain with a better understood domain. Neither use was formal in any sense. In a similar argument, Gooding (1985) has shown how certain visualizable images played a central role in Faraday's thought, and that he sought to transform these images into concretely verifiable hypotheses by doing experiments. Faraday used experiments in part for their power to create perceptions, not merely as tools to verify or discover new laws. As a result, it would be incorrect to regard Faraday as having formally developed his theory by deducing consequences that were then tested to see if they confirmed or disconfirmed the theory. Instead, experimentation played a productive role in the creation of theoretical concepts while remaining the ultimate test of those concepts.

Consider briefly a global view of Faraday's theory. By the end of his career, he had satisfied himself that lines of force were real but imponderable entities, the primary reality of physical matter. He remained puzzled about the nature of gravity but convinced that someday it would be shown to fit the general picture he advocated. Faraday was not particularly successful in selling his ideas to other scientists at the time. For the most part, they relied on notions of a material ether to preserve the Newtonian view and regarded Faraday's lines of force as merely a convenient representation. Maxwell, himself an ether theorist, took Faraday's scheme as a starting point. By setting up a mechanical analogy between electrical and magnetic phenomena and the mechanical properties of fluid flow, he was able to create a mathematical formalism that allowed him to push the consequences of Faraday's discoveries into a new realm of empirical predictions (most notably, the hypothesis that electromagnetic radiation should exist, as was verified later by Hertz). Maxwell, like Faraday, reasoned informally (Nersessian, 1984; Wise, 1979). Although he showed great respect for Faraday's ideas (e.g., Maxwell, 1855), Maxwell's worldview was substantially different. Yet this difference did not prevent him from drawing—informally—from the earlier conceptions. In retrospect, of course, Maxwell's presuppositions about the physical universe seem less accurate than Faraday's, insofar as the Einsteinian worldview completely removed the ether notion from physics, and quantum theory looks more like Faraday's centers of force notion of matter than Maxwell's billiard ball notion. In a sense, Faraday guessed right, and Maxwell did not.

THE NATURE OF INFORMAL REASONING

If there is a lesson in all this, it is that the use of informal reasoning never guarantees success. What it does guarantee, at least in the hands of its greatest practitioners, is a continual flow of changing conceptions, some of which will retrospectively look right and some of which will not. What distinguishes the life of science from other kinds of intellectual endeavor resides elsewhere, in, say, the willingness of science to constrain its ideas by empirical consequences (imagine a religious system that attempted to do the same!). Once this constraint is accepted, scientific thinking is prevented, in the long run at least, from the worst excesses of confirmation bias, and it is opened to a gradually evolving and hopefully progressive series of changes in worldview. We can have faith in the ultimate outcome even as we acknowledge the informal, even irrational, sources.

In a larger sense, the centrality of informal reasoning in science suggests that we should not be surprised to see it in other domains as well–indeed, that is a major theme of this book. In education in particular, we ought not expect the best learning to occur in formal contexts of reasoning. Yet, as I have shown elsewhere (Tweney, 1987a), our science texts are excessively formal, emphasizing rigid definitions and formal deductions and downplaying informal reasoning. Had Faraday tried to read nature's book with such an approach, it is likely that he would not have advanced beyond bottle washing in Davy's lab! Faraday learned by doing and considered himself to be "In Nature's school" (see Gooding, 1985, p. 106) and Nature's school, as we have seen, rewards informal reasoning.

ACKNOWLEDGMENTS

Grateful acknowledgement is made to the staffs of the Institution of Electrical Engineers, London, England, and to the Royal Institution of Great Britain for permitting access to archival materials and for many assistances, large and small, during the course of this research. This work was supported in part by a grant from the Faculty Research Committee, Bowling Green State University.

REFERENCES

Austin, J. H. (1978). *Chase, chance, and creativity: The lucky art of novelty*. New York: Columbia University Press.

Baron, J. (1985). *Rationality and intelligence*. Cambridge: Cambridge University Press.

Berkson, W. (1974). *Fields of force: The development of a world view from Faraday to Einstein*. New York: Halsted Press.

Cantor, G. N. (1985). Reading the book of nature: The relation between Faraday's religion and his science. In D. Gooding & F. A. J. L. James (Eds.), *Faraday rediscovered: Essays on the life and work of Michael Faraday, 1791–1867* (pp. 69–82). New York/London: Stockton/Macmillan.

Davy. H. (1812). *Elements of chemical philosophy, Part 1, Volume 1*. London: J. Johnson.

Einstein, A., & Infeld, L. (1938). *The evolution of modern physics*. New York: Simon & Schuster.

Ericsson, K. A. & Simon, H. A. (1984). *Protocol analysis: Verbal reports as data*. Cambridge, MA: MIT Press.

Faraday, M. (1809–1810). *A philosophical miscellany*. Unpublished manuscript, Royal Institution of Great Britain, London, England.

Faraday, M. (1816–1818). *Chemistry lectures*. Unpublished manuscript, Institution of Electrical Engineers, London, England.

Faraday, M. (1816a). Analysis of the native caustic lime. *Quarterly Journal of Science, 1*, 261–262.

Faraday. M. (1816b). *Common-Place Book . . . .* Unpublished manuscript, Institution of Electrical Engineers, London, England.

Faraday, M. (1821). On some new electro-magnetical motions, and on the theory of magnetism. *Quarterly Journal of Science, 12*, 74–96.

Faraday, M. (1832). Series I. On the induction of electrical currents. . . .*Philosophical Transactions, 122*, 125–162. Based on a paper read November 24, 1831. (Reprinted in Faraday, 1839–1855, Vol. 1).

Faraday, M. (1839–1855). *Experimental researches in electricity*. (Vols. 1–3). London: R. & J. E. Taylor.

Faraday, M. (1851). Series XXIV. On the possible relation of gravity to electricity. *Philosophical Transactions, 1–122*. (Reprinted in Faraday 1839–1855, vol. 3.)

Faraday, M. (1932–1936). *Faraday's Diary . . . 1820–1862 . . .* (Vols. 1–7). London: Bell. (Edited by T. Martin).

Forgan, S. (Ed.). (1980). *Science and the sons of genius: Studies on Humphry Davy*. London: Science Reviews Ltd.

Gooding, D. (1981). Final steps to the field theory: Faraday's study of magnetic phenomena, 1845–1850. *Historical Studies in the Physical Sciences, 11*, 235–275.

Gooding, D. (1982). A convergence of opinion on the divergence of lines: Faraday and Thomson's discussion of diamagnetism. *Notes and Records of the Royal Society of London, 39*, 229–244.

Gooding, D. (1985). "In nature's school:" Faraday as an experimentalist. In D. Gooding & F. A. J. L. James (Eds.), *Faraday rediscovered: Essays on the life and work of Michael Faraday, 1791–1867* (pp. 105–136). New York/London: Stockton/Macmillan.

Gooding, D. (1989). "Magnetic curves" and the magnetic field: Experimentation and representation in the history of a theory. In D. Gooding, T. Pinch, & S. Schaffer (Eds.), *The uses of experiment: Studies in the natural sciences* (pp. 183–224). Cambridge: Cambridge University Press.

Gooding, D. (1990). *The making of meaning.* Dordrecht: Martinus Nijhoff.

Gooding, D., & James, F. A. J. L. (Eds.). (1985). *Faraday rediscovered: Essays on the life and work of Michael Faraday, 1791–1867.* New York/London: Stockton/Macmillan.

Gooding, D., & Tweney, R. D. (in preparation). *Mathematical thinking about experimental matters: Faraday as a mathematical philosopher.*

Gruber, H. E. (1974). *Darwin on man: A psychological study of scientific creativity.* New York: Dutton. (2nd ed., 1981, University of Chicago Press.)

Kuhn, T. (1962/1970). *The structure of scientific revolutions* (2nd ed.). Chicago: University of Chicago Press.

Marcet, J. (1809/1814). *Conversations on chemistry* (3rd. ed.). New Haven: Sydney's Press.

Maxwell, J. C. (1855). On Faraday's lines of force. *Transactions of the Cambridge Philosophical Society, 10,* 27–83.

Miller, A. I. (1984). *Imagery in scientific thought: Creating 20th century physics.* Boston: Birkhauser.

Nersessian, N. (1984). *Faraday to Einstein: Constructing meaning in scientific theories.* Dordrecht: Martinus Nijhoff.

Nersessian, N. (1985). Faraday's field concept. In D. Gooding & F. A. J. L. James (Eds.), *Faraday rediscovered: Essays on the life and work of Michael Faraday, 1791–1867* (pp. 175–188). New York/London: Stockton/Macmillan.

Newell, A., & Simon, H. A. (1972). *Human problem solving.* Englewood Cliffs, NJ: Prentice-Hall.

Oersted, H. C. (1820). Experiments on the effect of a current of electricity on the magnetic needle. *Annals of Philosophy, 16,* 273–276.

Perkins, D. N. (1981). *The mind's best work.* Cambridge, MA: Harvard University Press.

Platt, J. R. (1964). Strong inference. *Science, 146,* 347–353.

Popper, K. R. (1934/1959). *The logic of scientific discovery.* London: Hutchinson.

Thompson, S. P. (1898). *Michael Faraday: His life and work.* London: Cassell.

Tweney, R. D. (1985). Faraday's discovery of induction: A cognitive approach. In D. Gooding & F. A. J. L. James (Eds.), *Faraday rediscovered: Essays on the life and work of Michael Faraday, 1791–1867* (pp. 189–210). New York/London: Stockton/Macmillan.

Tweney, R. D. (1987a). *What is scientific thinking?* Paper presented at the annual meeting of the American Educational Research Association, Washington, DC. (ERIC Document Reproduction Service No. ED 283 675)

Tweney, R. D. (1987b). Procedural representation in Michael Faraday's scientific thought. In A. Fine & P. Machaner (Eds.), *PSA 1986* (Vol. 2, pp. 336–346). East Lansing, MI: Philosophy of Science Association.

Tweney, R. D. (1989). A framework for the cognitive analysis of science. In B. Gholson, A. Houts, R. A. Neimayer, & W. Shadish (Eds.), *Psychology of science and metascience* (pp. 342–366). Cambridge, England: Cambridge University Press.

Tweney, R. D., Doherty, M. E., & Mynatt, C. R. (Eds.). (1981). *On scientific thinking.* New York: Columbia University Press.

Tweney, R. D., & Hoffner, C. E. (1987). Understanding the microstructure of science: An example. *Proceedings of the Cognitive Science Society, Ninth Annual Meeting* (pp. 677–681). Hillsdale, NJ: Lawrence Erlbaum Associates.

Tyndall, J. (1868). *Faraday as a discoverer*. London: Longmans Green.

Tytler, J. (1797). Electricity. In *Encyclopedia Britannica*, (3rd ed., Vol. 4). Edinburgh: A. Bell & C. Macfarquhar.

Voss, J. F., Greene, T. R., Post, T. A., & Penner, B. C. (1983). Problem-solving skill in the social sciences. In G. Bower (Ed.). *The psychology of learning and motivation* (Vol. 17, pp. 165–213). New York: Academic Press.

Wallace, D. B., & Gruber, H. E. (Eds.). (1989). *Creative people at work: Twelve cognitive case studies*. New York: Oxford University Press.

Williams, L. P. (1965). *Michael Faraday: A biography*. New York: Basic Books.

Williams, L. P. (1966). *The origins of field theory*. New York: Random House.

Williams, L. P. (Ed.). (1971). *The selected correspondence of Michael Faraday* (Vols. 1 and 2). Cambridge: Cambridge University Press.

Williams, L. P. (1986). Why Ampère did not discover electromagnetic induction. *American Journal of Physics, 54,* 306–311.

Wise, M. N. (1979). The mutual embrace of electricity and magnetism. *Science, 203,* 1310–1318.

2 Informal Reasoning in the Medical Profession

Caryn Christensen
Arthur S. Elstein
University of Illinois at Chicago

Consider this case: A 37-year-old male bartender had been well until he developed increasing pain in his left knee, which became hot and swollen. A few days later, pain, swelling, and heat developed in his left wrist and right knee. Examination revealed swelling, heat, and effusion in both knees and left wrist. There were no deformities. His liver was enlarged 2 cm below the costal margin. The complete blood count was normal. There were excess pus cells in his urine. His fever was 100°F. (Adapted from Arkes, Saville, Wortmann, & Harkness, 1981).

Even with this limited amount of information, the process of clinical reasoning begins, for the physician must consider at least some of the following questions: Based on the information available, what diagnostic possibilities should be considered? What additional tests or laboratory studies should be ordered at this time? Does this problem require urgent management, or can it be explored in a more leisurely fashion over the next week? Should the patient be hospitalized or evaluated as an outpatient? Does he have adequate health insurance to cover inpatient care if it is needed? These questions, and others like them, will be answered by most physicians without the aid of formal mathematics, decision analysis, symbolic logic, Venn diagrams, or computerized consultation. In short, physicians will employ informal reasoning techniques. A chain of reasoning will be rapidly executed, not all the steps involved will be explicit, and the activity will depend more on some well-mastered, overlearned, sometimes elaborate mental models of structure, function, and causation than on formal mathematics, statistics, and logic, although principles of logical inference may be invoked if a colleague or student requests an explanation of some aspect of the clinician's thinking.

In order to better understand this elaborate process, in this chapter we explore informal reasoning in the medical profession by (a) describing briefly the environment of medical decision making from a psychological standpoint; (b) reviewing, selectively, the work of information-processing and behavioral-decision researchers concerning the process and products of everyday clinical reasoning; and (c) identifying methods, based on these two programs of research, for improving clinical judgment.

THE MEDICAL ENVIRONMENT

Medical decisions are complex for several reasons. First, the subject matter, that is, the prevention, diagnosis, and cure of medical pathology, is extremely complicated. New diseases appear (most dramatically, AIDS) that create novel problems, just as old diseases fade from the scene (e.g., diptheria). In addition, rapid advances in health care technology have vastly increased the range of diagnostic and therapeutic options, so physicians can now make choices where previously little could be done. Finally, the potential costs, risks, and benefits of medical interventions can be very high. Quality of life, and sometimes life itself, may be at stake, although most clinical situations are not that dramatic. It is not surprising that good reasoning is difficult under such circumstances.

Within this complex environment, patient management includes a series of decisions with interrelated goals. As the opening clinical vignette suggests, (a) decisions must be made about what patient information to observe and obtain, (b) the information must be assessed and inferences made in order to arrive at a diagnosis, and (c) treatment and management plans must be instituted. Although these goals are usually pursued sequentially (data collection, followed by diagnosis, then treatment) the dynamic nature of medical practice sometimes requires that goals be pursued simultaneously. For example, an emergency room physician may have to provide life-sustaining treatment with only a minimal examination of the patient. As a case progresses, a patient may develop complications or new symptoms and thereby require reassessment or rediagnosis. Because clinical decision making is always complex and is often dynamic, it is quite difficult to study comprehensively.[1]

Clinical decisions are characterized also by uncertainty. Clinical and laboratory data are usually probabilistically related to the presence of a particular disease. Most laboratory tests are subject to errors, including false positives, a positive test result for a nondiseased patient, and false negatives, a negative test result for a diseased patient (Weinstein & Fineberg, 1980). In addition, in situations where

---

[1]Some psychological researchers have been criticized for focusing more on explaining the processes of information collection and diagnosis than on explaining how treatment decisions are made (McGuire, 1985). Others involved in studies that have focused on treatment selection have been criticized for using overly simplified clinical situations that do not provide enough flexibility for variability in data collection and problem structuring to emerge.

no tried-and-true treatment is available, the effects of treatment for any given patient are also uncertain. Even when a diagnosis can be made with certainty and a preferred treatment is well established, the treatment may still not succeed. It is also difficult to identify, prior to treatment, those who will suffer serious side effects; the occurrence of drug reactions and postsurgical complications are also probabilistic events. Finally, some medical situations can be said to involve uncertainty about probabilistic relationships. A clinician may believe that a procedure will be successful for 70% of the patients treated but may be unsure about the 70% estimate and believe, rather, that the estimate might range anywhere from 50% to 90%. This extra uncertainty is referred to as ambiguity (Curley, Eraker, & Yates, 1984; Einhorn & Hogarth, 1986).

Another characteristic of clinical decision making is the need to make value judgments about the risks and benefits of possible actions (Pauker & Kassirer, 1987; Weinstein & Fineberg, 1980). For example, estrogen replacement therapy (ERT) has been shown to alleviate menopausal symptoms and prevent the development of osteoporosis (Weiss, Ore, Ballard, Williams, & Daling, 1980). However, ERT has also been associated with an increased incidence of endometrial carcinoma (Zeil & Finkel, 1975). What risk of cancer are we willing to tolerate in order to achieve relief of menopausal symptoms and prevent fractures from osteoporosis? What values would people place on outcomes in these categories? As another example of a therapeutic trade-off, consider a 65-year-old woman, with a recently diagnosed breast cancer, who has just had a mild heart attack (MI). How should the increased risk of a second, possibly fatal MI be balanced against the possible risks of delaying surgery? How much more attractive do other treatment options become? Such value judgments and trade-offs underlie almost all clinical decisions, although the issues are much more explicit in cases where treatments are clearly risky and only probably effective.

Finally, we cannot pretend that clinical decisions are made in a vacuum. Clinical decisions are evaluated in light of professional standards and ethics. Every hospital has procedural guidelines and formalized policies. Where explicit policies are lacking, implicit policies fill the gap. For administrators and policy analysts, actions should benefit the patient *and* be cost-effective. Again, clinicians are confronted with multiple—and perhaps conflicting—goals.

THE PREPARATION OF CLINICIANS

A long program of classroom study, field experience, and supervised practice, generally with increasing specialization, is required before a physician assumes independent responsibility for patient care and clinical decision making. Medical students spend approximately the first 2 years of medical school acquiring an extensive body of basic science knowledge. This knowledge, mostly in the areas of anatomy, physiology, microbiology, pharmacology, and pathology, must subsequently be applied appropriately to clinical problems. For novice clinicians, the application of basic knowledge in clinical practice can be quite difficult. For example, Balla (1980) investigated the ability of medical students to use their knowledge of neuroanatomy to solve clinical problems 6 months after completing their neuroanatomy exams. Some students experienced difficulties because they had forgotten the necessary information in the period since they had been tested. Even those who could access relevant facts about neuroanatomy could not necessarily apply them correctly to the problems. Basic knowledge, as it is learned in medical school, is not easy to tie to clinical practice. Expert neurologists found it easier to apply basic principles to clinical cases, perhaps because they had more practice accessing similar basic knowledge for past cases or because they had highly organized knowledge structures, in which clinical and basic science information were integrated. Expert–novice differences in knowledge structure in clinical medicine is an area of continuing cognitive research.

The training of physicians, however, consists of more than classroom instruction in biological sciences. Practical knowledge of principles and procedures is also accumulated during a lengthy supervised clinical apprenticeship organized in clerkships, internships, residencies, and fellowships. This method of learning is essentially a case-study approach that is supplemented by seminars, conferences, and reading. Such learning by examples is quite valuable where future problems are likely to be similar to those that are encountered during training. When problems deviate significantly from those that are routinely found, however, the cognitive burden placed on the clinician increases greatly. To the degree that textbook and case-based knowledge are applicable to new clinical problems, they will be useful; but when the gap between the clinician's knowledge base and a new problem is very large, cognitive demands increase, as does the possibility of errors and biases (Neisser, 1976).

Several related features seem to be quite characteristic of clinical education in medicine and the other health professions: (a) learning and understanding, as well as technical proficiency, must be based on practical experience with cases; (b) it is hoped that general principles and strategies will be abstracted to be applied subsequently to a broader range of cases than those seen, so that the student has not simply learned a set of recipes; (c) usually, less generalization takes place than is hoped for (so-called case specificity first identified by Elstein, Shulman, & Sprafka, 1978); and (d) abstract, theoretical statements of principles are not judged to be as useful as gaining additional practical experience through caring for, reading about, or listening to discussions of more cases. Consequently, clinical training programs are lengthy and stress patient care responsibilities as the essential route by which the needed knowledge structures and generalizations will be built up. The desired relation between clinical experience and a comprehensive conceptual model is acquired gradually (cf. Feltovich & Patel, 1984). Through repeated experiences, physicians gradually acquire proficiency in the techniques of performing a physical examination smoothly and in the cognitive task of recognizing crucial features in complex and often muddied stories.

One strategy that may be used by experts to manage complex medical cases is to cluster clinical findings into larger sets, known as diagnoses, problem formulations, or working hypotheses. In the clinical vignette at the beginning of this chapter, for example, early hypotheses would help the clinician cluster and remember the crucial features and would also suggest what additional information should be obtained to confirm or refute each alternative hypothesis. Such a process would be consistent with findings from studies of chess players that indicate that masters better remembered the positions of pieces because they grouped them into chunks or strategic units (deGroot, 1965; Simon & Chase, 1973; Simon, 1974). Chess experts were proposed to have a large differentiated store of memory models, acquired through experience, that enabled them to recognize familiar board patterns (Chase & Simon, 1973). Presumably, experienced clinicians have the ability to create and store similar chunks of diagnostic information (Kassirer & Gorry, 1978).

Chunking is one example of a simplification strategy that may enable physicians to cope with the enormous demands of the clinical environment. Simplifying complex cognitive tasks is a necessary and natural method of dealing with our surroundings. We are not yet certain, however, under what conditions intuitive methods of cognitive simplification are truly useful in the clinical domain and when formal decision support will be helpful. To answer this question, we must try to assess the accuracy of informal clinical judgment and consider the possible significance of disparate views of decision making.

RESEARCH ON INFORMAL CLINICAL REASONING

Research in clinical reasoning can generally be divided into two schools or traditions, the information processing school and the decision making or judgment/decision making (JDM) school. Their underlying assumptions, methods, and some research conclusions differ, but both camps seem to agree on certain major points. They each seek to understand clinical reasoning in order to improve decisions among practicing clinicians (often through the development of decision aids and supports) and to develop educational programs for training novice clinicians. They also agree that individuals have limited cognitive capacities and that, in order to deal with the complex environment of medicine, information must be selectively attended to and simplified. It is when we move beyond these very basic premises that the information processing and JDM schools begin to part company.

Information Processing

Information processing theory is primarily concerned with the mechanisms, structure, and processes that people employ in operating on environmental stimuli. Problem-solving behavior is viewed as an interaction between an information-processing system (the problem solver) and the task environment (Newell & Simon, 1972). In complex tasks, such as clinical diagnosis, extensive task requirements may lead to "cognitive strain" (Bruner, Goodnow, & Austin, 1956) that can be overcome by the use of short cuts or heuristics that both reduce the amount of information to be held in working memory and simplify the task in some organized fashion (for example, by clustering symptoms into potential diagnoses or syndromes).

The information-processing approach rests on close analysis of protocols obtained from the problem solvers (i.e., the expert clinicians), as they solve diagnostic problems or make therapeutic decisions. The adequacy of the theoretical formulation of the problem-solving process can then be tested by comparison with more general cognitive principles, to see if the clinical formulation is consistent with them, by comparison with the clinical judgment of experienced clinicians, and by resort to computer simulation (Feltovich, Johnson, Miller, & Swanson, 1984; Johnson, 1983; Kunz, Shortliffe, Buchanan, & Feigenbaum, 1984; Miller, Pople, & Myers, 1982; Shortliffe, 1976). For this last test, the theory of clinical reasoning is written as a computer program, and, if the program performs like the clinician, it can be said to be a sufficient representation of the reasoning process.

In addition, the problem representations, or protocols, of experts are often compared with those of novices. Information-processing researchers assume that by capturing experts' informal process, either in the form of causal flowcharts (Patel & Groen, 1986) or in the form of computerized expert systems (Clancey, 1984), we may come to understand the art of clinical reasoning and teach it more effectively. Because the reasoning of experts is obviously superior to that of novices and because it is the best example of actual clinical reasoning that can be found, it merits modeling. This assumption reflects the optimistic attitude toward human reasoning that underlies the information-processing approach. Even though skilled informal reasoning is susceptible to "bounded rationality" (Newell & Simon, 1972), such limited processing still leads to decisions that "satisfice" (Simon, 1974), precisely because the practitioners of the art are skilled. That is, even though decisions may be suboptimal (from the standpoint of a normative theory), because they are based on selected information processed in a simplified representation of the task and limited by the constraints of working memory (bounded rationality), the decisions of experts are, for all practical purposes, adequate, and they satisfy the demands of the task (i.e., they satisfice). This optimism regarding human reasoning is not shared by the JDM group.

One strength of the protocol analysis approach is its rather broad scope. Although researchers must choose a specific problem domain within which to work, protocol studies still attend to a wide variety of factors. According to Balla (1985), "information processing may be seen as a gathering and translation of present data into terms referable to past experience and theoretical knowledge" (p. 17). That is, clinical problem solving involves the encoding of new information in light of a clinician's past knowledge to produce a particular problem space or problem representation. This is obviously a complex cognitive task.

But then, attempts at analyzing these interactive processes are fraught with difficulties. Clearly, in order to understand real-life judgment, we must consider the factors that come into play in real situations. Yet, if we try to capture many of the complexities of clinical reasoning at once, we may be left with elaborate schematic models or complicated representations that are nearly incomprehensible. Furthermore, the precise methodological steps between protocol collection and the conclusions of protocol analysis can appear elusive or ambiguous to those who were not personally involved in the research. Such difficulties arise whenever we try to capture the complexities of real-life tasks. One way to minimize these problems is to formulate the results of protocol analysis as a set of hypotheses to be tested in more controlled studies.

Early studies of clinical reasoning within the information-processing framework employed either trained actors, serving as simulated patients, or descriptive case vignettes (Barrows, Feightner, Neufeld, & Norman, 1982; Elstein, Shulman & Sprafka, 1978; Johnson et al., 1981). Clinicians provided concurrent or retrospective verbal protocols as they proceeded through diagnostic work-ups. Analyses of these early protocols revealed that clinicians used early case cues to generate a limited number of tentative hypotheses. These early hypotheses served to direct information gathering and were modified in light of new data. Diagnosis was, therefore, thought to be a hypothesis-testing procedure. Further research also indicated that experts differed from novices in the quality but not the number of their early hypotheses (Barrows, et al., 1982).

More recent information-processing studies have been aimed at acquiring a deeper understanding of expert reasoning. A series of studies in pediatric cardiology (Feltovich et al., 1984; Feltovich & Patel, 1984) explored the organization of the knowledge base of expert and novice physicians. In one study, subjects thought aloud as they diagnosed six unfolding cases. Protocol analysis indicated that the knowledge base of experts was highly organized into clusters, according to principles of pathology. Other studies in radiology (Lesgold, 1984; Lesgold, Feltovich, Glaser, & Wang, 1981; Lesgold, Rubinson, Feltovich, Glaser, Klopfer, & Wang, 1988) provided information that has led to an intriguing theory regarding the development of clinical reasoning skills. Based on these studies, Feltovich & Patel (1984) described the skills of novices, intermediates, and experts in interpreting x-ray films:

> Novices learn a set of text-book medical conditions and rules of interpretation connecting film features to these interpretive models. As they diagnose more films, intermediates learn that these simple, direct rules at times lead to error . . . This leads to a period in which the student tries to understand the underlying basis of interpretive rules, in the principles of anatomy and pathophysiology responsible for the appearance of a particular film. This kind of deeper processing analysis is

cognitively taxing and places high demands on available mental processing resources, sometimes leading to error. High levels of expertise are then achieved when the contextual considerations focused on by the intermediate are compiled within cognitively efficient direct associational rules of interpretation (productions). Understanding which the intermediate strives for through focused, deliberate effort and model building is then accounted for implicitly within the structure of the rules of interpretation that experts use. (p. 9)

According to Feltovich and Patel, experts construct models or problems representations of a case based on major pathophysiological principles and operate according to performance rules in which basic biomedical issues are embedded.

Patel (Patel, 1984; Patel & Groen, 1986) has used another technique, propositional analysis, to examine expert and novice protocols. Propositional analysis is usually applied in studies of text comprehension. In Patel's studies, the text is a clinical vignette. In a recent study by Patel and Groen (1986), subjects read case studies and were then asked to provide a free-recall protocol, describe the underlying pathology of the case, and offer a diagnosis. Propositional analysis was used to obtain a *recall frame* and a *pathophysiology frame*. Comparison of these frames produced an understanding of the problem-solving process and of the underlying data base. Patel and Groen found that, "all of the experts with accurate diagnosis used bottom-up forward reasoning whereas the experts with inaccurate diagnoses used at least some top-down backward reasoning" (1986, p. 107).

Another growing area of information processing research is the development and study of expert systems. Researchers interested in the knowledge structures and production rules of experts have joined with those working in artificial intelligence to produce systems such as MYCIN (Shortliffe, 1976), NEOMYCIN (Clancey & Lestinger, 1984), and INTERNIST (Miller et al., 1982). Expert systems are intended to emulate human performance and have, at times, been shown to perform as well as medical specialists within a fairly narrow domain (Yu et al., 1979). These systems are based on diagnostic rules gleaned from expert reasoning. Expert systems are a promising area of research. Presently, developed systems exist for only a limited number of specific clinical problems (for example, NEOMYCIN performs clinical diagnosis in the area of meningitis).

Behavioral Decision Theory

Behavioral decision theory differs from information processing theory in a number of ways. Both schools maintain that people use simplification strategies or heuristics when confronting complex clinical dilemmas. Yet, Judgment and Decision Making (JDM) researchers believe that these heuristics are not always helpful. The JDM literature is filled with illustrations of the suboptimal decision making that results from the use of heuristics (Hogarth, 1980; Nisbett & Ross, 1980). Hence, the terms *heuristics* and *biases* have become practically synonymous in the JDM field, and researchers have largely ignored the early caution of Kahneman and Tversky (1974) that cognitive heuristics such as representativeness are generally quite useful and only occasionally biased. Usually, JDM research psychologists have been more interested in the instances of bias than in demonstrating the general usefulness of the heuristics. (For an exception, see Christensen-Szalanski's 1986 critique of this experimental literature.) In addition, both experts and novices are believed to be equally susceptible to biases and errors (Balla, Iansek, & Elstein, 1985; J. Christensen-Szalanski, Beck, C. Christensen-Szalanski, & Koepsell, 1983). This view of human reasoning is certainly less optimistic than the views of the information-processing researchers.

Informal decision making, whether undertaken by experts or novices, often appears suboptimal in JDM work because it is compared with the decisions produced by normative statistical models. In medicine, mathematical techniques can be used to produce a set of cue weights designed to maximize diagnostic accuracy or to select the action that will maximize expected utility. There is a great deal of evidence indicating that intuitive decisions, both in clinical medicine and in other domains, deviate significantly from those of normative models (Elstein et al., 1986; Goldberg, 1970; Hogarth, 1980; Kahneman, Slovic, & Tversky, 1982; Kern & Doherty, 1982; Meehl, 1954; Politser, 1981). Such deviations are considered irrational.

JDM researchers are interested in (a) developing descriptive models that illustrate how people really make decisions, (b) developing normative models that prescribe how decisions should be made, and (c) isolating the factors that produce discrepancies between normative (prescriptive) decisions and intuitive or informal decisions. Unlike information-processing work, which focuses only on informal reasoning, JDM work examines informal and formal decisions. By focusing on the descriptive–prescriptive distinction, researchers are reminded to think about how people actually make decisions *and* about how they might make better decisions.

Most applications of decision theory to clinical judgment have been prescriptive in nature, with less attention focusing on comparisons to actual human judgment (cf. Kassirer, Moskowitz, Lau, & Pauker, 1987, for a recent review with over 225 citations, mainly prescriptive studies). The general form of these studies is that a model of the clinical situation is constructed, relevant probabilities are obtained from the literature or by clinical judgment when necessary, utilities are assessed or survival data are obtained, and the strategy that maximizes expected utility or expected survival is identified. The probabilistic nature of clinical decision making lends itself to such an approach. Although it may be difficult to convince clinicians to follow the prescribed decisions of a normative model, decision analysis can be used to enhance a clinician's understanding of a clinical problem. The acts of identifying possible actions and outcomes and translating hunches and attitudes into probabilities and utilities should help clarify many complicated situations.

Recent JDM work in clinical judgment has shifted away from the goal of developing prescriptive models toward the goal of documenting the prevalence of cognitive biases within the medical domain. To accomplish this goal, research in cognitive psychology, originally performed with contrived experimental tasks, is often modified to accommodate clinical problems. In contrast to the thinking-aloud procedure used in information processing research, JDM research usually employs short, highly structured case vignettes that require a brief response from the subject. We review only a few of the cognitive biases found in clinical reasoning.

1. *Neglect of Base Rates.*   To predict whether a patient suffers from a particular disease, given a test result, the accuracy of the test and the prevalence of the disease within the population must both be considered. Bayes's theorem is the formal rule for combining these quantities correctly. In order to test physicians' abilities to combine such data, Schwartz, Gorry, Kassirer, and Essig (1973) asked physicians and medical students to consider information about a test for cancer. The test is supposedly positive in 95 of 100 patients with cancer and negative in 95 of 100 people without cancer. In the population, 5 people in 1,000 have undetected cancer. Subjects were asked to predict the possibility of cancer for a randomly selected person with a positive test result. The correct prediction is 9%. Most subjects gave estimates above 50%. These inflated predictions reflect a neglect of base rate information. Subjects failed to account correctly for the prevalence of the disease in the population. Numerous subsequent studies have demonstrated the inappropriate use of base rate information in predicting the presence of a disease for a given patient (Balla, Elstein, & Gates, 1983; Balla et al., 1985; Berwick, Fineberg, & Weinstein, 1981; Borak & Veilleux, 1982; Casscells, Schoenberger, & Graboys, 1978; Eddy, 1982; Politser, 1984).

2. *Anchoring.*   Some clinical judgments are influenced by anchoring, the tendency to stick with an early diagnosis and ignore contradictory evidence. Balla (1982) found that both experts and novices were influenced by anchoring when responding to a vignette about a patient with a possible cardiac problem. Early cues favored cardiac syncope; later cues did not. Most people failed to appropriately adjust their early diagnoses in light of the later, opposing evidence.

3. *Hindsight Bias.*   We have all found ourselves reacting to new information with the feeling that we "knew it all along." This bias is reflected in the tendency to assign higher probabilities to an outcome after hearing that the outcome occurred than we would assign if the outcome remained unknown. Hence, people believe that what they know in hindsight is, in fact, the same as what they

believed in foresight. This hindsight bias encourages overconfidence and may impede learning. To assess the hindsight bias in the clinical domain, Arkes, Saville, Wortman, and Harkness (1981) presented two groups of practicing clinicians with a hypothetical case and asked them to assign probabilities to each of four possible diagnoses. The control group assigned probabilities without knowing which was true. Each of four hindsight groups assigned probabilities after learning that one of the possible diagnoses was correct. Analysis of probabilities revealed that the hindsight bias was exhibited by the two groups of clinicians who had been told that the least plausible diagnoses were true. These results can be considered qualified evidence of the existence of the hindsight bias in clinical reasoning.

4. *Framing.*   Kahneman and Tversky (1974, 1979) have developed prospect theory as a descriptive model of decision making under uncertainty. One of the propositions of prospect theory is that decisions are influenced by the presentation or framing of actions and outcomes. For instance, the same clinical outcome can be framed as a loss (10% chance of mortality) or as a complementary gain (90% chance of survival). Furthermore, according to prospect theory, people respond differently to losses than to equivalent gains. McNeil, Pauker, Sox, and Tversky (1982) found support for these propositions among patients and physicians who were asked about alternative treatments for lung cancer. Treatment choices were influenced by whether the possible outcomes were framed as losses (probability of mortality) or as complementary gains (probability of survival).

5. *Regret.*   To make accurate clinical decisions, all possible outcomes must be taken into account. There are times, however, when clinicians overweight certain attributes of the clinical problem. Some clinical decisions may be guided by regret minimization. The physician chooses the action that will avoid the most dreaded outcome. For example, Iansek, Elstein, and Balla (1983) compared neurosurgeons' decision making in a case of congenital arteriovenous malformation with the decisions recommended by a normative model. Most neurosurgeons favored surgery, whereas the decision analysis indicated that medical management of possible seizures was a superior strategy, inasmuch as surgery could take place in the future, if the need arose. Regret minimization would explain these results if physicians were trying to avoid the worst possible outcome of death due to hemorrhage.

Beyond work on such biases, an important focus of JDM research is the development of debiasing techniques. These techniques include warnings and admonitions, a variety of forms of feedback, and organized systems for presenting information. Unfortunately, researchers have been far more successful in demonstrating biases than in finding successful methods for eliminating them (Fischhoff, 1982).

COMPARISON OF APPROACHES

How do information processing and JDM work compare?

1. There is a basic difference in attitudes regarding the ability of people to reason correctly. In information-processing research, heuristics are beneficial shortcuts, and experts are viewed as competent decision makers. In the JDM view, heuristics lead to biases, and experts and novices alike may be viewed as suboptimal decision makers.

2. In light of their optimism concerning human reasoning, it is perfectly logical for information-processing researchers to use the expert decision maker as the prototype of correct reasoning and attempt to build systems to model expert behavior. The goal of education, then, is to teach novices the strategies used by experts. By contrast, JDM researchers cite evidence showing that both novices and experts are susceptible to biases. Therefore, the expert system will also be fallible. The goal of education, therefore, is to teach the normative principles of statistical decision theory and to raise the awareness of novice clinicians about the prevalence of cognitive biases.

3. The conflicting attitudes of information-processing and JDM researchers regarding the strengths and weaknesses of human reasoning are reflected in differing research programs. Information-processing research focuses on informal reasoning. Studies explore problem solving, knowledge representations and the development of expert systems. JDM research focuses on formal and informal reasoning. Researchers construct normative and descriptive models, explore the differences between these models, and document the prevalence of cognitive biases.

4. Information-processing work is mostly descriptive in nature. JDM work explicitly maintains the descriptive–prescriptive distinction.

5. The types of reasoning investigated by the two groups also differ. Information-processing research employs production rules, semantic networks, and computer programs to capture causal relationships. It argues that, to understand clinical reasoning, we must understand how clinicians think about the underlying causes of disease and resulting clinical findings. In contrast, the normative model of decision theory concentrates on risks, benefits, and forecasting.

6. Finally, information-processing researchers attempt to produce entire models of human performance or expert systems intended to emulate human reasoning. This is an analysis of judgment at a rather macroscopic level. JDM research usually focuses instead on only one particular facet of the reasoning process at a time (for example, a study of the influence of base rates on diagnosis).

7. It should be noted that the discrepancy between the information-processing and JDM views of intuitive reasoning is based not only on different views of ideal performance (the normative model or the judgments of other experts), but also on

the type of tasks employed in research. In JDM research, experts are often asked to undertake novel tasks, such as encoding their knowledge in probabilities, revising these probabilities, quantifying preferences, or combining abstract quantities. It is, perhaps, not surprising that clinicians have difficulties with these tasks. Information-processing research, by contrast, usually requires clinicians to provide structure or interpretation in qualitative (not quantitative) terms for a familiar problem. Prior knowledge and experience are very helpful in such tasks and, therefore, intuitive reasoning appears to be quite powerful.

In light of the findings of both research approaches, how do we rate the accuracy of intuitive reasoning within the medical domain? At this time, we might say, "It depends." It depends on whether we believe that the strategies that most physicians use to deal with the enormous complexities of the clinical environment produce optimal or suboptimal decisions. To further complicate the matter, our perception of optimal and suboptimal decision making also depends on the confidence we have in the normative model. Experts perform better than novices in many tasks, yet they appear equally suboptimal when compared to statistical models. Because our assessment of judgmental accuracy and the over-all quality of clinical decisions is dependent on the research that we examine, perhaps, rather than debating whether or not clinicians make good decisions, we should focus on the methods proposed by information-processing and JDM researchers to help clinicians make better decisions.

IMPROVING CLINICAL REASONING

Research-based knowledge about informal clinical reasoning may be used to teach new physicians or to assist their more experienced counterparts. Methods for improving clinical reasoning depend, again, on which school of research we examine. The theoretical underpinnings of information-processing research imply that experienced physicians can produce adequate reasoning because clinical experience results in the acquisition of an organized body of domain specific knowledge that is (a) tightly organized around principles of pathology; (b) dense, in the sense that activation of one hypothesis produces activation of related ones; and (c) flexible, in the sense that experts can recognize a slight deviation from a prototype as being an instance of the same underlying disease (Feltovich & Patel, 1984).

In light of this characterization of expertise, the educational task becomes trying to find methods of helping novice clinicians develop expert knowledge representations. At this point, the only surefire method of acquiring such expertise is through clinical experience. Research is needed to determine what kinds of training or what types of collateral classroom experiences can accerate acquisition of expert knowledge structures. Because it appears that clinical case work is an integral step in the development of expert knowledge structures, the mixture of didactic and experiential learning that takes place in traditional medical school programs seems to contain the basic elements needed. Researchers may, however, be able to identify new techniques, formats, or materials that facilitate the proper integration of basic science knowledge and case experience. Problem-based curricula have been offered as an alternative to traditional programs, and they appear to be a logical extension of information processing findings, although evaluators have not shown that such programs produce physicians who are better problem solvers than those from traditional medical schools (Schmidt, Dauphinee, & Patel, 1987).

Another possible strategy, based on information-processing work, is to try to help students develop an expert knowledge structure by explicitly demonstrating the deep and complex principles employed by experts. Such principles, however, might be overwhelming for the novice clinician. Clancey (1984), for instance, tried to teach the expert rules of the MYCIN system to medical students. Because students did not really comprehend how or why the rules applied, they had to learn them by rote. Operating by rules without understanding is not a useful method of clinical reasoning. Clearly, other methods of developing expert knowledge structures need to be explored.

Information-processing research also suggests that clinical judgment can be improved with the use of expert systems and computerized decision supports. Such supports must be user-acceptable and efficient enough to improve decisions without adding to the substantial time and effort demanded of clinicians. Presently, expert systems exist for a limited number of clinical problems, and they have not gained widespread clinical acceptance. There seems to be more potential for their role in clinical instruction and training than as aids to the decision making of seasoned clinicians (deDombal, 1984; Kleinmuntz & Elstein, 1987).

In light of JDM work, what can we teach novice clinicians and their more experienced counterparts? Because JDM research stresses the problems that both novices and experts have in weighting, combining, and integrating information, it follows that improving a novice's knowledge base or structure will not necessarily sharpen his or her reasoning. Decisions may be improved by the use of formal techniques or models and perhaps by implementing strategies that will help physicians avoid or overcome biases. To implement these strategies, several problems need to be addressed. First, clinicians will not use decision analysis unless convinced of its value. This may be difficult, because the decisions recommended by formal models often seem counterintuitive. That is, there are decisions in which people would rather not maximize expected utility. Clinicians, who are trained to attend to the idiosyncracies of the individual case, may find it difficult to categorize a given patient as a member of a larger population and to apply probabilities. (Only if a case is unique should base rates be ignored.) Uncertainty (embodied in probabilities) is also difficult to tolerate. If someone uses a decision rule that is correct 93% of the time (perhaps because it is based on an imperfect laboratory test), errors will result 7% of the time. This error rate may seem unacceptable, even if unaided decisions produce even more errors. Einhorn (1986) recently reminded us that, in using a prescriptive model, we must "accept error to avoid more error" (p. 1). Some clinicians may be unwilling to accept any error at all (Arkes, Dawes, & Christensen, 1986).

Although some clinicians may remain skeptical regarding prescriptive models, there are several situations where the use of formal techniques should not be particularly controversial. First, most clinicians realize that the process of evaluating test results and combining test information with prevalence data in order to determine a diagnosis can be difficult. Therefore, physicians should be motivated to use Bayes theorem. There are also several noncontroversial applications of decision analysis within medicine. It can be useful when conflicts arise within the medical community or when conflicts arise between the recommendations of a physician and the desires of a patient. Constructing a formal model and making implicit values explicit helps clarify points of conflict. In addition, decision analysis (and the underlying Expected Utility model) may be easier to implement when dealing with public policy questions, because such decisions are intended to benefit as many people as possible in the long run (policy makers wish to maximize expected utility. Finally, decision analysis is a powerful teaching tool. It forces students to explore their values and their knowledge of treatment options, possible outcomes, and probabilistic relationships.

What should medical educators do in light of JDM research? First, they need to teach formal techniques, probably at a time when students can tie this knowledge to clinical experiences (during clerkships and internships, rather than during basic science instruction). Second, they need to foster an awareness of common errors in clinical judgment. Students who are aware of their cognitive processes and limitations can try to avoid biases. For example, a physician who knows that the framing of outcomes as probability of survival or probability of mortality may affect choices can make an effort to consider multiple frames or to present multiple frames to a patient who is facing a treatment decision. Third, students need to be exposed to software and decision aids that will enable them to use formal techniques. These aids stand a better chance of being accepted by current students, who are becoming more familiar with the use of computers than past generations. Finally, teaching formal techniques is useless without an environment that supports the use of prescriptive models. There has been a steady, albeit rather slow, growth of interest in formal techniques, yet more physicians need to be involved.

Broader acceptance of formal techniques may be facilitated by several types of research. First, JDM researchers need to understand more about why physicians are often resistant to the use of formal techniques. This implies continued exploration of the prescriptive–descriptive problem. They may also need to determine what types of problems require formal analysis. There are many common problems when pattern matching yields a correct diagnosis and treatment routines provide adequate care. Formal techniques may not significantly improve clinical reasoning in these well-understood domains, but it may be more helpful with more controversial questions. If we can identify the appropriate uses of prescriptive techniques and make them readily available, medical educators can begin to model their use, and physicians and patients alike will reap the benefits.

CONCLUSION

Research in clinical decision making has produced a substantial understanding of informal reasoning and several plausible suggestions for improving the accuracy of clinical judgment. Information-processing research has been particularly valuable in its contribution to the understanding of knowledge representations, knowledge structures, and the intuitive strategies of clinical experts. The translation of this line of work into viable decision support systems has, because of its complexity, progressed rather slowly. JDM work has consistently demonstrated discrepancies between intuitive clinical decisions and those produced by normative models and has begun to explore the extent of judgment errors due to heuristics or biases. In general, attempts at debiasing have not been particularly successful. If we believe that errors in clinical judgment are frequent or serious, decision analysis may be called for. In any case, clinicians should spend time examining their own decisions and judgmental processes. With their help, we can acquire a deeper understanding of intuitive clinical reasoning, promote educational programming that develops the skills necessary for accurate decision making, and construct decision supports that improve judgment without increasing the burdens placed on the clinician.

REFERENCES

Arkes, H. R., Dawes, R. M., & Christensen, C. (1986). Factors influencing the use of a decision rule in a probabilistic task. *Organizational Behavior and Human Decision Processes, 37,* 93–110.

Arkes, H., Saville, P. D., Wortman, R. L., & Harkness, A. (1981). Hindsight bias among physicians weighing likelihood of diagnosis. *Journal of Applied Psychology, 66,* 252–254.

Balla, J. (1980). Logical thinking and the diagnostic process. *Methods of Information in Medicine, 19,* 88–92.

Balla, J. (1982). The use of critical cues and prior probability in decision making. *Methods of Information in Medicine, 21,* 9–14.

Balla, J. (1985). *The diagnostic process.* New York: Cambridge University Press.

Balla, J., Elstein, A. S., & Gates, P. (1983). Effects of prevalence and test diagnosticity upon clinical judgment of probability. *Methods of Information in Medicine, 22,* 25–28.

Balla, J., Iansek, R., & Elstein, A. S. (1985). Bayesian diagnosis in the presence of pre-existing disease. *Lancet, 8424,* 326–329.

Barrows, H. S., Feightner, J. W., Neufeld, V. R., & Norman, G. R. (1982). The clinical reasoning of randomly selected physicians in general medicine. *Clinical and Investigative Medicine, 5,* 49–55.

Berwick, D. M., Fineberg, H. V., & Weinstein, M. C. (1981). When doctors meet numbers. *American Journal of Medicine, 71,* 991–998.

Borak, J., & Veilleux, S. (1982). Errors of intuitive logic among physicians. *Social Science and Medicine, 299,* 999–1001.

Bruner, J. S., Goodnow, J. J., & Austin, G. A. (1956). *A study of thinking.* New York: Wiley & Sons.

Casscells, W., Schoenberger, A., & Graboys, T. B. (1978). Interpretation by physicians of clinical laboratory results. *The New England Journal of Medicine, 299,* 999–1001.

Chase, W. G. & Simon, H. A. (1973). Perception in chess. *Cognitive Psychology, 1,* 55–81.

Christensen-Szalanski, J. J. (1986). Improving the practical utility of judgment research. In B. Brehmer, H. Jungermann, P. Lourens, & E. G. Sevon (Eds.), *New directions in research on decision making* (pp. 383–410). New York: Elsevier Science Publishing.

Christensen-Szalanski, J. J., Beck, D. E., Christensen-Szalanski, C. M., & Koepsell, T. P. (1983). Effects of expertise and experience on risk judgments. *Journal of Applied Psychology, 68,* 278–284.

Clancey, W. J. (1984). *Acquiring, representing and evaluating a computer model of diagnostic strategy.* Unpublished manuscript, Stanford University, Stanford, CA.

Clancey, W. J., & Lestinger, R. (1981). Neomycin: Reconfiguring a rule-based expert system for application to teaching. In *Proceedings of the Seventh International Joint Conference on Artificial Intelligence* (Vol. 7, pp. 829–836).

Curly, S. P., Eraker, S. A., & Yates, J. F. (1984). An investigation of patient's reactions to therapeutic uncertainty. *Medical Decision Making, 4,* 501–511.

deDombal, F. T. (1984). Clinical decision making and the computer: Consultant, expert, or just another test? *British Journal of Health Care Computing, 1,* 7–10.

deGroot, A. D. (1965). *Thought and choice in chess.* The Hague, Netherlands: Mouton.

Eddy, D. M. (1982). Probabilistic reasoning in clinical medicine: Problems and opportunities. In D. Kahneman, P. Slovic, & A. Tversky (Eds.), *Judgment under certainty: Heuristics and biases* (pp. 249–267). New York: Cambridge University Press.

Einhorn, H. J. (1986). Accepting error to make less error. *Journal of Personality Assessment, 50,* 387–395.

Einhorn, H. J., & Hogarth, R. M. (1986). Decision making under ambiguity. *Journal of Business, 59,* S225–S250.

Elstein, A. S., Holzman, G. B., Ravitch, M. M., Metheny, W. A., Holmes, M. M., Hoppe, R. B., Rothert, M. L., & Rovner, D. R. (1986). Comparison of physician's decisions regarding estrogen replacement therapy for menopausal women and decisions derived from a decision analytic model. *American Journal of Medicine, 80,* 246–258.

Elstein, A. S., Shulman, L., & Sprafka, S. (1978). *Medical problem solving.* Cambridge, MA: Harvard University Press.

Feltovich, P. J., Johnson, P. E., Moller, J. H., & Swanson, D. B. (1984). LCS: The role and development of medical knowledge in diagnostic expertise. In W. J. Clancey & E. H. Shortliffe (Eds.), *Readings in medical artificial intelligence: The first decade* (pp. 275–319). Reading, MA: Addison Wesley.

Feltovich, P. J., & Patel, V. (1984, March). *The pursuit of understanding in clinical reasoning.* Paper presented at the meeting of the American Educational Research Association, New Orleans, LA.

Fischhoff, B. (1982). Debiasing. In D. Kahneman, P. Slovic, & A. Tversky (Eds.), *Judgment under uncertainty: Heuristics and biases.* New York: Cambridge University Press.

Goldberg, L. R. (1970). Man versus model of man: A rationale, plus some evidence, for a method of improving on clinical inference. *Psychological Bulletin, 73,* 422–432.

Hogarth, R. M. (1980). *Judgment and choice.* New York: Wiley & Sons.

Iansek, R., Elstein, A. S., & Balla, J. (1983). Application of decision analysis to cerebral arteriovenous malformation. *Lancet, 21,* 1132–1135.

Johnson, P. E. (1983). What kind of expert should a system be? *Journal of Medicine and Philosophy, 8,* 77–97.

Johnson, R. E., Duran, A. S., Hassebrock, R., Molle, J., Prietulla, M., Feltovich, P. J., & Swanson, D. (1981). Expertise and error in diagnostic reasoning. *Cognitive Science, 5,* 235–283.

Kahneman, D., Slovic, P., & Tversky, A. (1982). *Judgment under uncertainty: Heuristics and biases.* New York: Cambridge University Press.

Kahneman, D., & Tversky, A. (1974). Judgment under uncertainty: Heuristics and biases. *Science, 184,* 1124–1131.

Kahneman, D., & Tversky, A. (1979). Prospect theory: An analysis of decisions under risk. *Econometrica, 47,* 263–291.

Kassirer, J. P., & Gorry, G. A. (1978). Clinical problem solving: A behavioral analysis. *Annals of Internal Medicine, 89,* 245–255.

Kassirer, J. P., Moskowitz, A. J., Lau, J., & Pauker, S. G. (1987). Decision analysis: A progress report. *Annals of Internal Medicine, 106,* 275–291.

Kern, L., & Doherty, M. E. (1982). Pseudodiagnosticity in an idealized medical problem-solving environment. *Journal of Medical Education, 57,* 100–104.

Kleinmuntz, B., & Elstein, A. S. (1987). Computer modeling of clinical judgment. *Critical Reviews in Medical Informatics, 1,* 209–228.

Kunz, J. C., Shortliffe, E. H., Buchanan, B. G., & Feigenbaum, E. A. (1984). Computer-assisted decision making in medicine. *The Journal of Medicine and Philosophy, 9,* 135–160.

Lesgold, A. M. (1984). Acquiring expertise. In J. R. Anderson & S. M. Kosslyn (Eds.), *Tutorials in learning and memory: Essays in honor of Gordon Bower.* New York: W. H. Freeman.

Lesgold, A. M., Rubinson, H., Feltovich, P. J., Glaser, R., Klopfer, D., & Wang, Y. (1988). Expertise in complex skills: Diagnosing x-ray pictures. In M. T. H. Chi, R. Glaser, & M. Farr (Eds.), *The nature of expertise* (pp. 311–342). Hillsdale, NJ: Lawrence Erlbaum Associates.

McGuire, C. (1985). Medical problem solving: A critique of the literature. *Journal of Medical Education, 60,* 587–595.

McNeil, B. J., Pauker, S. G., Sox, H. C., & Tversky, A. (1982). On the elicitation of preferences for alternative therapies. *New England Journal of Medicine, 306,* 1259–1262.

Meehl, P. E. (1954). *Clinical versus statistical prediction: A theoretical analysis and review of the evidence.* Minneapolis, MN: University of Minnesota Press.

Miller, R. A., Pople, H. E., & Myers, J. D. (1982). Internist-I, an experimental computer-based diagnostic consultation for general internal medicine. *The New England Journal of Medicine, 307,* 468–476.

Neisser, U. (1976). *Cognition and reality.* New York: W. H. Freeman.

Newell, A., & Simon, H. (1972). *Human problem solving.* Englewood Cliffs, NJ: Prentice-Hall.

Nisbett, R. E., & Ross, L. (1980). *Human inference: Strategies and shortcomings of social judgment.* Englewood Cliffs, NJ: Prentice-Hall.

Patel, V. L. (1984). Expert diagnostic reasoning: An interactive process of case comprehension. *Professions Education Research Notes, 5,* 7–11.

Patel, V., & Groen, G. J. (1986). Knowledge based solution strategies in medical reasoning. *Cognitive Science, 10,* 91–116.

Pauker, S. G., & Kassirer, J. P. (1987). Decision analysis. *New England Journal of Medicine, 316,* 250–258.

Politser, P. E. (1981). Decision analysis and clinical judgment: A re-evaluation. *Medical Decision Making, 1,* 361–389.

Politser, P. E. (1984). Explanations of statistical concepts: Can they penetrate the haze of Bayes? *Methods of Information in Medicine, 23,* 99–108.

Schmidt, H. G., Dauphinee, W. D., & Patel, V. (1987). Comparing the effects of problem-based and conventional curricula in an international sample. *Journal of Medical Education, 62,* 305–315.

Schwartz, W. B., Gorry, G. A., Kassirer, J. P., & Essig, A. (1973). Decision analysis and clinical judgment. *American Journal of Medicine, 55,* 459–472.

Shortliffe, E. H. (1976). *Computer based medical consultation: Mycin.* New York: American Elsevier Publishing.

Simon, H. A. (1974). How big is a chunk? In H. A. Simon (Ed.), *Models of thought.* New Haven, CT: Yale University Press.

Simon, H. A., & Chase, W. G. (1973). Perception in chess.

Weinstein, M. C., & Fineberg, H. V., Elstein, A. S., Frazier, H. S. Neuhauser, D., Neutra, R. R., & McNeil, B. J. (1980). *Clinical decision analysis.* New York: Sanders.

Weiss, N. S., Ore, C. L., Ballard, J. H., Williams, A. R., & Daling, J. R. (1980). Decreased risk of fractures of the hip and lower forearms with postmenopausal use of estrogen. *New England Journal of Medicine, 303,* 1195–1198.

Yu, V. L., Fagan, L. M., Waith, S. M., Clancey, W. J., Scott, A. C., Hannigan, J. F., Blum, R. L., Buchanan, B. G., & Cohen, S. N. (1979). Antimicrobial selection by computer: A blinded evaluation by infectious disease experts. *JAMA, 242,* 1279–1282.

Ziel, H. K., & Finkel, W. D. (1975). Increased risk of endometrial carcinoma among users of conjugated estrogen. *New England Journal of Medicine, 19,* 88–92.

3 Informal Reasoning and International Relations

James F. Voss
University of Pittsburgh

This chapter is concerned with informal reasoning in the domain of international relations, a specialized field of the social sciences. The study of informal reasoning in this domain raises interesting theoretical issues for cognitive science (as well, perhaps, as a few eyebrows), but it also has potential significance elsewhere. In recent years, a number of specialists in international relations have become increasingly concerned with the role of cognitive processes in shaping foreign policy decisions (e.g., Bonham & Shapiro, 1977; Chan & Sylvan, 1984; O. R. Holsti, 1976; Mandel, 1986; Pruitt, 1965). The argument is that, because governments consist of people, the process of understanding the decisions made by a particular government must take into account cognitive and affective components of the decision makers. Thus, the study of informal reasoning in international relations may, in addition to expanding scientific inquiry in informal reasoning, aid in the development of an interdisciplinary field that has the potential to impact on decision making as found in international relations.

In addition to considering informal reasoning within the context of international relations, this chapter is concerned with the issue of instruction in informal reasoning, especially as found in social sciences. Reasoning in international relations may be viewed as a special case of reasoning in the social sciences, and the study of the more specific domain may help to show how instruction may be improved in the general social science case. The chapter, therefore, has two central objectives: to explore the nature of informal reasoning in international relations and to consider how instruction could help enhance the quality of informal reasoning in the social sciences generally. In the first section, the international relations context is discussed, with the contents primarily serving as a setting for the following section. In the second section, interpretation and reasoning in international relations are considered, and the findings of a number of studies are reported. The third section addresses the question of how instruction may facilitate reasoning in the social sciences.

THE CONTEXT
OF INTERNATIONAL RELATIONS

One approach to the study of international relations originated in the 5th century, B.C., with the writings of Thucydides on the Peloponnesian wars. Later writers focused on how statesmen wield power rather than on the relationships among nations per se, with Machiavelli's (1532/1980) 16th century treatise, *The Prince,* being, to this day, the classic portrayal. In the 18th and 19th centuries, various writings, especially diplomatic memoirs, described the intricacies of international agreements, international law, and military strategy. Only in the early 20th century did the field assume a character that could be considered distinct from the parent disciplines of history, political theory and political economy, diplomatic relations, and so forth. Since then, courses in international relations have included international law in relation to warfare, neutrality, the economy, and a host of related issues. (See K. J. Holsti, 1977, for an overview of the history of the field.)

The field of international relations, as it is understood today, has largely developed since World War II. The postwar period produced profound increases in international trade, including the increased development of multinational corporations; in communications, with greater international exposure occurring because of media access and ease of travel; and in the number of issues of mutual concern, particularly those emerging from modern technology and the development of nuclear weapons.

The field of international relations is rather loosely organized; specializations range from the study of problems and issues of international interaction, such as international law, narcotics control, and/or trade, to government in particular areas of the world, like Eastern Europe or Central America. Individuals who are called "strategists" now take in growing numbers of those concerned with the issues of nuclear war and, in particular, deterrence theory. Finally, there are theorists who deal with more global issues, such as the basic motives involved in the actions of countries.

The Cognition–International Relations Interface

The dominating theory of the field of international relations assumes a realist position (cf. Morgenthau, 1966). Those who subscribe to it maintain that the primary aim of a state is the exercise of power, an emphasis that minimizes the role of the individual decision maker within the state. This does not mean that the realist denies the importance of the individual decision maker; instead, the realist suggests that the beliefs of particular elites contribute only a small percentage of the variance to the decision-making process. O. R. Holsti (1976), in considering the realist position, listed three arguments that trouble those who question the importance of cognition in the analysis of international relations: First, foreign policy making occurs in a bureaucratic context, and the bureaucracy places strong constraints on individual decision makers. Second, foreign policy decisions are grounded in long-standing ideologies and institutions that shape the process. Third, the international system itself limits what individual decision makers can do. Thus, in general, Holsti's overview of this line of thinking reveals emphasis on conditions over which the decision maker has little control.

In contrast, a number of scholars have argued—as O. R. Holsti ultimately did—that the cognitive, affective, and motivational character of a country's elite must be taken into account if the actions of the country's government are to be explained (e.g., Bonham & Shapiro, 1977; Chan & Sylvan, 1984; George, 1980; O. R. Holsti, 1976; Pruitt, 1965). The argument is that, although the constraints on decision making posed by external factors are substantial, in most cases policy is also a function of the cognitive and affective characteristics of the leadership. Whether the Soviet Union is perceived by American decision makers as aggressive or reactive will, it is argued, influence how they interpret the actions of the Soviet Union and how they decide to respond to a particular situation that involves the Soviet Union.

The argument that characteristics of decision makers help to explain the decision-making process is requisite to the idea that cognitive psychology can be of considerable importance to the analysis of international relations. Chan and Sylvan (1984), for example, argued that the study of foreign policy decision making has changed in recent years because (a) the concept that nation states are monolithic is highly questionable, that is, that nations have a simple, highly cohesive, ruling elite; (b) the idea that government decision makers function as rational actors is suspect; (c) the leaders of countries differ in their views of reality with each having his or her own perspective; and (d) the "billiard ball" view of international relations exaggerates determinism. These objections, according to Chan and Sylvan, argue for the study of the leaderships' cognitive characteristics in the analysis of foreign policy decision making.

O. R. Holsti (1976) has suggested that international relations analysis involving cognitive processes may be especially useful under particular conditions. Such conditions include: (a) various nonroutine situations, especially those that require more than the application of rules, as when decisions are made at the highest level of government in the process of long-range policy planning; (b) those in which circumstances are highly ambiguous; (c) those where there is substantial information overload for the decision maker; and (d) those where there are likely to be unanticipated events. Taken as a whole, Holsti's position suggests that cognitive analysis is likely to be important in virtually any situation in which there is not a standard operating procedure.

REASONING IN INTERNATIONAL RELATIONS

Within the conditions of today's world, assume that a particular country, X, takes some type of significant overt action. If one assumes the position of an analyst or group of analysts of the United States government, one is confronted with the need to interpret that action and to determine what, if anything, should be done in response. The processes of interpretation and decision making usually involve a number of people and a series of steps, but for our purposes the first concerns are to delineate the interpretive and decision-making components. These components are, of course, not independent, but the literature does tend to focus on either interpretive or decision-making activity. A third, brief discussion focuses on the topic of argumentation, especially as studied in the international relations context.

The Interpretive Process

The interpretation of the action of country X is an inferential process, inasmuch as one must infer the intention of country X and derive the possible implications of the action. Indeed, this task is certainly fundamental to the study of international relations. It is clear that the action of country X did not occur in a vacuum; government analysts quite likely had beliefs about country X before the action took place, and these beliefs provided for a set of expectations. The particular action, thus, may or may not have been in agreement with the expectations. If the action was in line with the expectations, the interpretation of the action will tend to support the existing beliefs about country X. However, if the action is not in agreement with expectations, then the need for interpretation increases; under such conditions, the interpretive process may involve the use of mechanisms that provide an acceptable interpretation of the action while preserving the beliefs and perceptions about country X. Such mechanisms include denial, bolstering, rationalizing, differentiation, and stopping thinking (cf. Abelson, 1963).

In his book, *Perception and Misperception,* Jervis (1976) provided a number of interesting examples of how expectations have influenced the interpretive process. For example, Admiral Kimmel, fleet commander at Pearl harbor before the Japanese attack of December 7, 1941, was notified that the Japanese had ordered missions in allied territories to burn their code books, an action that perhaps should have alerted Kimmel to the possibility of an impending attack. However, Kimmel believed that the Japanese were going to invade Southeast Asia, and he found the action of burning code books to be consistent with this belief. Similarly, when the commanding officer at Pearl Harbor was warned by Washington, DC officials of an enemy threat, he interpreted the message as suggesting possible sabotage, an issue that had been of concern at Pearl Harbor, and not as a warning about a possible air strike, which was unanticipated.

But with an event such as the North Korean invasion of South Korea or the

Soviet invasion of Afghanistan, by what processes do analysts arrive at an interpretation? Sometimes, of course, one is suggested immediately and is accepted; at other times, however, an interpretation is not forthcoming and/or a simple one is not accepted. When an interpretation is needed, it becomes necessary to conduct a search for an appropriate one, the search involving that of one's own memory and/or that of other resources, including other people's interpretations and various relevant documents. Moreover, such a search typically involves the use of heuristics, such as those described by Newell (1980) as weak problem-solving methods or those described by Tversky and Kahneman (1974). A number of such heuristics are now considered.

Generate-and-Test.   The generate-and-test method, one of the most frequently employed heuristics, consists of generating interpretations and/or scenarios and testing their validity. This process, although acknowledged to be important, has received little psychological study, so some comments are in order.

Let us assume that an interpretation is being sought for the Soviet invasion of Afghanistan and, further, that someone suggests that "This is just another example of Soviet expansionism." Assume, however, that another person suggests that "The Soviet Union was afraid of a takeover of the Afghanistan government by Moslems." Yet another person may assert that "It is not expansionism per se but taking a step that allows the Soviet Union to move closer to obtaining a warm-water port." Given such interpretations, which, if any, is (are) correct?

The first of the interpretations suggests that an individual may infer why the Soviets invaded Afghanistan by invoking a belief-based categorization about the Soviet actions in the Afghanistan situation. Such an inference is not necessarily thought through; the idea that this Soviet invasion is "just another example of Soviet expansionism" would likely be generated when an individual believes that expansionism is a characteristic of Soviet foreign policy. Moreover, the individual would likely support this belief by pointing to Czechoslovakia, Vietnam, and possibly Nicaragua, depending on the extent of the belief. The Afghanistan invasion, thus, is essentially classified as another instance for generalization from a particular concept. Furthermore, the individual would not likely examine the Afghanistan invasion and state the reasons why the invasion should be viewed as a case of expansionism (confirming evidence) and why it should not be (disconfirming evidence).

Another person interpreting the invasion may generate a number of alternatives, as for example, by asserting that the Soviets were afraid that a Moslem government would come into power in Afghanistan, or that the Soviets wanted a warm-water port. These alternatives would likely be generated by another heuristic, means–ends analysis, in which an individual considers the present state of affairs and the goal and tries to generate a reason that would explain the goal. "The Soviet goal was the control of Afghanistan. Why would they do that?"

The generation of an interpretation via a belief-based categorization or via means–ends analysis are but two of a number of heuristics that may be employed. One other example is analogy, in which case an individual may assert that the Soviet Union invaded Afghanistan because, analogous to the United States' invasion of Vietnam, the Soviet Union wanted to establish a strong government to prevent a takeover by what could be a hostile government.

Turning to the "test" or evaluation phase of the generate-and-test method, it is hypothesized that there are two types of evaluation, *belief evaluation* and *reasoned evaluation*. Belief evaluation takes place when an individual examines an interpretation by comparing it for consistency to one or more other beliefs; reasoned evaluation takes place when the individual reviews the proposition in terms of its support and disconfirming evidence (i.e., the pros and cons). Both methods have a characteristic that is quite important—namely, that a criterion exists against which the proposition is evaluated. In the case of belief evaluation, the criterion is another belief or set of beliefs; in the case of reasoned evaluation, the criterion is soundness.

The concept of belief evaluation is related to the principle of immediate implication, as stated by Harman (1986). This principle is "That P is immediately implied by things one believes can be a reason to believe P" (p. 21). Thus, in the case of the Soviet invasion of Afghanistan, that proposition is implied by a belief that the Soviet Union is expansionistic, and hence the proposition will be believed. On the other hand, a person who believed that the Soviet Union is not expansionistic would likely not agree with the proposition. An important aspect of belief evaluation is that it does not involve the evaluation of the particular proposition in terms of the comparison of pro and con reasons; the justification of the proposition is via agreement with a belief and not via the consideration of pro and con evidence regarding the proposition.

Reasoned evaluation, as previously noted, attempts to determine soundness. Assume that an individual has generated an interpretation of the Afghanistan invasion, such as "The Soviets invaded Afghanistan because they did not want a Moslem government in power." To evaluate this interpretation, a person would state one or more supporting reasons. Soundness is then judged in terms of the reason's acceptability, its strength in corroborating the conclusion, and its endurance in the face of any disconfirming evidence (cf. Angell, 1964). Thus, assume that the individual states that Moslems were about to overthrow the Afghanistan government and that having a Moslem fundamentalist state on its border would be a threat to the Soviet Union because (a) the Soviet Union has a relatively large Moslem population and because (b) the Moslem government would be hostile. The argument, therefore, would be evaluated in terms of the acceptability or accuracy of these statements, the strength of their support of the conclusion, and the impact of disconfirming evidence. A person could call the conclusion into question by noting, for example, that a Moslem government should not be a threat to the Soviets because, with their military superiority, the

Soviets could invade Afghanistan and overthrow the Moslem government if it so desired.

In sum, the generate-and-test procedure for interpretation of an action entails a generate phase that involves the use of one or more heuristics in reaching the interpretation and a test phase that involves justification of that interpretation by belief or by argument. One may, of course, question whether beliefs are grounds for justification. However, justification by belief is not uncommon, and the assumption is generally made that a person using justification by belief could, in turn, conduct a reasoned evaluation of the belief. But this is a matter of conjecture; in fact, people have many beliefs that they never have tried to justify.

Analogy. Another frequently employed method of developing an interpretation of an event or series of events is the use of analogy. Indeed, the use of historical analogy in the international relations context has been of considerable interest. For example, when President Truman was asked why he felt it necessary to resist the North Korean invasion, he replied that he did not want "another Munich." Truman did not, of course, mean that North Korea posed the type of threat that Germany posed before World War II. Instead, the Korean invasion was interpreted as being an initial move on the part of a Soviet-dominated communist bloc and that failure to act in Korea could be followed by other aggressive acts in other areas of the world, such as Berlin (cf. Paige, 1968; 1970). Similarly, research by Gilovich (1981) and by Read (1983, 1984) suggests that differing perceptions of the United States policy in Central America may be related to the extent to which an individual views the Central American situation as analogous to that of Munich or that of Vietnam.

Probably the most extensive analysis of the use of historical analogy in the context of international relations is that of Neustadt and May (1986). Interestingly, these authors concluded that, more often than not, analogy fails to provide a satisfactory interpretation when used in the international context, because a number of conditions in the existing situation do not map well onto the historical situation. To avoid overgeneralization from historical episodes, Neustadt and May suggested that, when using analogy in analyzing an existing set of conditions, individuals should list precisely what is known, what is unclear, and what is presumed before assuming that a situation has a counterpart in the past. Such an exercise is aimed at helping to define objectives and determine the nature of the decision to be made. Similarly, with respect to analogies between two current situations, it is important to list the specific likenesses and differences in the two situations. This activity helps tease out assumptions as well as make explicit auxiliary hypotheses (Salmon, 1984).

Analogy has been studied quite closely and extensively by cognitive scientists in recent years. Gentner (1983), for example, has argued that analogies are drawn via a mapping process in which an argument and its predicate in one case map onto another argument–predicate relationship. This position, thus, emphasizes that syntactical relationships, rather than surface structures, are critical to analogical thinking.

Use of Base Rates.   Before providing an interpretation for the action of a country, one determines whether action should be taken seriously, that is, whether it can essentially be ignored or whether it should be interpreted. Tversky and Kahneman (1982), in their research on biases and heuristics, have reported that in a number of situations, individuals tend to disregard the base rate of an event, relying more strongly on the event's probability per se. In their widely cited taxicab problem, for example, individuals were told that a particular town had 70% blue and 30% green cabs. An accident occurred, and a witness said that the cab was green, and, when tested under the conditions of the accident, the individual was 80% accurate in identifying a cab as green. When asked to estimate the probability that the cab involved in the accident was green, individuals tended to ignore the base rates of 30% and 70%. Instead, they responded that the cab was green with an 80% likelihood. Individuals do tend to take the base rate into account, however, when there is a causal connection between the base rate and the event that is perceived.

Jervis (1986) provided an interesting analysis of the base rate issue in the international relations context. He argued that, in the foreign policy context, individuals tend to neglect the individual case and are biased in favor of the base rate, the opposite of the effect that is characteristic of reports of studies in other domains. Thus, if the action of country *X* is not in agreement with one's expectations, the tendency is to disregard the action and, instead, maintain one's beliefs, that is, to adhere to the base rate. Jervis also argued that, within the international relations context, the individual case is considered of greater importance only in new situations, when one's beliefs and prior expectations have not been sufficiently developed.

A possible reason for the ignoring of the base rates in the Tversky and Kahneman tasks and the bias in favor of base rates in the Jervis analysis is that the former used laboratory tasks that did not involve long-standing beliefs of the participants. However, in the international relations perspective, individuals usually have long-standing beliefs about other countries and the motivation of their leadership. Moreover, these beliefs include causal attributions; it is assumed that the leadership makes decisions that cause actions that are directed toward goals to which that leadership aspires.

Confirmation Bias and Learning.   An influence on the reasoning process, beyond that of the heuristics used, that shapes the interpretation of an event is expectations; expectations often produce a confirmation bias, that is, predisposition to seek information that will support an existing hypothesis rather than information that may disconfirm it (e.g., Einhorn & Hogarth, 1978; Tweney & Doherty, 1983). Because expectations play such an important role, moreover,

Klayman and Ha (1987) pointed out that the goal of disconfirmation per se should be set aside initially in determining the means by which disconfirmation is sought. Specifically, the authors argued that, in some cases, direct testing for disconfirming evidence is a method that must be used. In others, testing for disconfirmation requires seeking confirming evidence. The important point, however, is that individuals tend to seek evidence—whether confirming or disconfirming—that supports their interpretations.

Examples of confirmation bias are abundant, especially in relation to a person's interpretation of his or her own actions. If a government takes an action to produce a desired effect and that effect is forthcoming, the outcome is interpreted as indicative of the action's success. Indeed, in late 1987 and early 1988, actions by Nicaragua that were in agreement with the peace plan developed by other Central American countries were interpreted by administration officials as giving evidence of the success of United States support for the Contras; these officials argued that such support has produced the change in Nicaragua's position. In this case, confirmation bias involved interpreting subsequent events in a way that lent support to a well-entrenched hypothesis. An excellent analysis of the reasons for such judgments has been developed by Einhorn and Hogarth (1978).

The occurrence of confirmation bias and the failure to seek counterfactual information raises an interesting question for international relations, namely, whether, over time, learning can take place (cf. Einhorn & Hogarth, 1981; Etheredge, 1985). Specifically, if individuals working in an international context seek information that tends to confirm their expectations and if outcomes are interpreted in terms of their existing beliefs, then there is relatively little opportunity to revise those beliefs on the basis of new evidence. Indeed, the feedback that is received will be interpreted in terms of existing expectations.

Two interesting examples of the learning issue are provided by O. R. Holsti (1967) and by O. R. Holsti and Rosenau (1977). In the first, Holsti analyzed many speeches of John Foster Dulles, as well as his written work, and concluded that Dulles maintained a reasonably well-defined belief system about the Soviet Union that essentially differentiated the people and the government. Holsti presented evidence indicating the extent to which Dulles went to interpret information in a way that would sustain this belief structure. In other words, learning, in the sense of change of belief, was not demonstrated. The Holsti and Rosenau (1977) study involved conducting an extensive survey on Americans who were leaders in 10 occupational fields. The questionnaire first obtained information about belief structures along a more or less "hawk–dove" dimension. Subsequent questions dealt with how the individuals felt about American involvement in Vietnam and what went wrong in Vietnam. The results provided strong evidence that what an individual felt about the lessons learned from Vietnam was a function of the person's beliefs. Thus, the more "hawkish" person tended to provide answers indicating that the United States learned that it should have used more force, whereas the more "dovish" person provided answers indicating that the United States underestimated the Vietnamese motivations. Thus, what was learned was, in fact, a function of the person's beliefs.

The issue of whether learning can take place in the international context has been examined in detail by Etheredge (1985). Basically, he has argued that learning has been blocked in the analysis of United States foreign policy by (a) the repeated use of policies in historically similar situations, (b) a mentality that essentially prohibits an evaluation of particular concepts of national security, and (c) common errors in perception and judgment. Etheredge also suggested that the system of government is well developed for checks and balances and for feedback as far as domestic issues are concerned but not with respect to foreign policy. Feedback is difficult to obtain in the latter case, because, for example, citizens of Central American countries do not get to vote on American aid programs or on the American presence in their countries. Therefore, a type of historic mental model of countries and their governments is maintained that changes little over time and that includes misperceptions.

An Experimental Study.   In the discussion of the interpretative process, belief justification and reasoned justification were described. Recently, we conducted an experiment on the role of these two modes of evaluation as they related to a person's agreement or disagreement with particular propositions. Individuals were first assessed with respect to their knowledge of and attitude toward the Soviet Union, and, subsequently, they rated 20 statements pertaining to the Soviet Union to indicate the extent of their agreement or disagreement with each. Then, the individuals were presented again with each statement and were asked to list all pro and con reasons they could think of with respect to the particular statement. After doing this, they rated the strength of each argument on a scale of 1 to 10.

Analyses indicated significant correlations of the agree–disagree judgments with measures of the pro and con arguments; for example, a measure of mean pro strength rating minus mean con strength rating correlated significantly with the agree–disagree rating. Thus, it was found that relative pro and con strength was related to relative agreement or disagreement with the statement. Additional regression analyses conducted on an item basis, however, revealed that, using the agree–disagree judgment as a target variable, both relative pro–con strength and attitude yielded significant predictions of the agree–disagree ratings. Moreover, the particular analysis yielded results suggesting that relative strength of justification, as reflected in the pro–con reasons and the attitude per se, are independent. The idea that attitudinal components and reasoned justification may conceivably develop independently has interesting implications. For example, it suggests that sometimes we may have a belief without being able to state much support for it, but on other occasions we may weight pros and cons in order to establish a belief (cf. Zajonc, Pietromonaco, & Bargh, 1982).

In sum, the interpretive process may be viewed as involving the use of a variety of heuristics in seeking information from which interpretations are inferred and subsequently tested. Evaluation of the interpretation, moreover, takes place in relation to criteria involving belief justification and/or reasoned justification. As such, the process is susceptible to biases based on one's beliefs and expectations.

Reasoning and the Decision Process

The topic of decision making is, of course, extremely broad, and much has been written concerning decision making in international relations (e.g., Allison, 1971; Bonham & Shapiro, 1977; Snyder & Diesing, 1977). In this section, the structure of the decision process and its relation to informal reasoning are considered.

Structure of the Decision Process.   The classical rational choice model of decision theory states that decision making proceeds by considering the choices in the situation, the probability of the alternative outcomes for each choice, and the value or utility associated with each outcome. The choices then may be given a preference order by examining the probability of the alternative outcomes combined with the weightings of value with each alternative. The preferred outcome is then chosen according to a decision rule (cf. Hogarth, 1980; Lee, 1971). The model thus assumes that the decision maker has knowledge of the possible alternatives and their probabilities, knowledge of the outcomes of the alternatives, the ability to weight the various outcomes, and the ability to select the preferred decision, given some decision rule, as well as to order the alternatives in terms of preference.

The rational choice model has received criticism, principally because individuals often do not know all of the alternatives and they often do not know and/or cannot evaluate the outcomes of particular alternatives. Simon (1983; 1985) has proposed another model that acknowledges that decision makers do not consider all alternatives but consider alternatives only until particular constraints are met, the decision then being made. This process is referred to as *satisficing.* The position further maintains that, within constraints and processing limitations, the human has "bounded rationality." As noted by Snyder and Diesing (1977), the differences between the classic and satisficing models go well beyond their accounts of alternative generation. An important difference concerns assumptions regarding values: Specifically, the classical model holds that the values assigned to the outcomes of alternatives are homogeneous, in the sense that they may be compared to each other and one may be judged as more important than the other. The Simon position, however, assumes heterogenity of values, because the outcomes of alternative choices are not comparable. Thus, the decision makers in the Simon model arrive at a conclusion by evaluating an alternative with respect to some set of criteria and not by direct comparison with all other alternatives. In addition, the Simon model emphasizes that people satisfice because of the human limitations in working memory capacity. Proponents of the rational choice model admit to satisficing, but do so with a cost–benefit argument, that is, sometimes the cost of considering additional alternatives is greater than the likely benefit.

Within the international relations context, one of the most extensive studies done on decision making was that of Allison (1971), who examined the extensive records on the decision-making process that took place during the Cuban missile crisis. In using the accounts of John Kennedy's ExCom group, Allison examined the data in relation to two models in addition to the classical decision model: the organizational model and a bureaucratic model. The organizational model emphasizes the operation of group decision making, such as coalition formation. The bureaucratic model holds that a person's position on issues is a function of the individual's role in government, a frequently used paraphrase of the model being "Where you stand depends on where you sit." Specific responsibilities are thus presumed to constrain decision makers' options; in the course of the decision process, individuals are presumed to bargain and negotiate among themselves.

Allison's analysis suggested that no one model explained the decision process that occurred. The classical model provided an analysis that, in part, was found to be inconsistent with the discussion that led to the decision. In addition, although the organizational and bureaucratic models were each supported by evidence, neither provided an adequate description of the process. Indeed, in a general sense, the reasoning that took place in the decision process involved statements based on beliefs, the generation of inferences with respect to Soviet intentions, and the generation of possible United States actions, which were evaluated (generate-and-test) with respect to constraints and outcomes. Analogy was also used, as with Bobby Kennedy's remark to his brother about not going down in history as another Tojo.

The Decision Process in Problem Solving.   The information-processing model of problem solving (Newell & Simon, 1972) can accommodate most decision-making situations as ill-structured problems (cf. Voss, Greene, Post, & Penner, 1983), problems that are characteristic of social sciences. In well-structured problems, the givens, goal, and constraints are present in the problem statement, or they are readily accessible, whereas in ill-structured problems, the givens, goal, and constraints are only minimally stated. Moreover, well-structured problems typically have solutions that are agreed on by individuals working in that domain, whereas ill-structured problems usually do not. (See Reitman, 1965, Simon, 1973, and Voss & Post, 1988, for discussions of the well-structured/ill-structured distinction.)

The information-processing analysis of the solving of ill-structured problems in, say, history or political science (cf. Voss, Tyler, & Yengo, 1983; Voss et al., 1983) indicates that the individuals who are knowledgeable in a particular domain tend to approach ill-structured problems by first developing a representation of the problem and then stating a solution. Developing a representation involves isolating possible causes of the problem and, when appropriate, developing an argument that justifies attributions of causality. The solution offered is typically relatively abstract, and, most importantly, the statement of the solution is usually followed by supporting arguments. The arguments typically emphasize why the solution will work and address possible deficiencies of the solution and how such deficiencies may be resolved. Indeed, the structure of the solution has the form of classical rhetoric.

If one approaches the Cuban Missile crisis situation as an ill-structured problem, then the account described by Allison (1971) suggests that the discussion involved developing representations of the problem and generating and evaluating alternative actions in relation to the respective representations. Interestingly, the generating and evaluating of alternatives may be viewed as a generate-and-test process, with the particular alternatives presumed to be a function of the specific representation under consideration. Similarly, the evaluation of alternatives took place in relation to constraints, the constraints consisting of varying beliefs about the influence of germane foreign and/or domestic circumstances as well as the strength of pro and con reasons employed to evaluate particular components.

Without unpacking the argument in full detail, the analysis of the decision process as an example of the solving of an ill-structured problem leads to the conclusion that the mechanisms involved are essentially those described in relation to interpretation. Specifically, in the case of interpretation, individuals generate information that will provide a representation of the event that requires interpretation, and, in doing so, they use a variety of heuristics. The representation, in a sense, constitutes a tentative solution. Then, the representation is evaluated by comparison to some criterion or criteria. Similarly, the problem solution is evaluated by showing why it will work (pros) and providing a rationale for dealing with its difficulties (cons).

Applying the preceding argument more directly to decision making, the representation of the problem essentially defines the situation in which the decision is to be made. Moreover, the nature of the representation will act to constrain the alternatives that may be generated in the decision situation. This is the case because the particular representation will have been generated by an analysis that defines a particular cause or set of causes; the specific set of causes will, to some extent, dictate which alternatives are to be generated and which do not seem reasonable to generate, that is, constrain the set of alternatives. Then, in the evaluation of the alternatives, the previously described heuristics are used to evaluate the alternatives, once again evaluating them in relation to a particular criterion or set of criteria.

The difficulty in evaluating alternatives, of course, occurs when each of a given set has particular costs and benefits and one must choose one alternative.

But again, in this case, heuristics are employed in refining the criterion, and the goals that are most cogent receive priority. Much decision making, indeed, occurs through the consideration of alternatives by a process that is designed to reduce the choice to one, more or less obvious, possibility. Moreover, when this occurs, it is difficult to determine when and how the decision was actually made, because it *emerges*—at no point do the decision maker(s) "make" the decision. This description takes satisficing into account as the outcome of constraint mechanisms. Such constraints operate in conjunction with those imposed by the nature of the problem representation that was developed.

In sum, by using concepts that are developed in analyses of the solution of ill-structured problems, the processes of decision making can be considered to be essentially those employed in the interpretation process, with three components of primary importance: the individual's knowledge base, the use of heuristics, and the establishment of criteria.

Argumentation

As indicated in the previous subsection (The Decision Process in Problem Solving), much of the reasoning that takes place follows the structure of classical rhetoric. Viewed in this way, an interesting question that arises is how argumentation and justification take place in the context of international relations. One study on this topic (Axelrod, 1977) consisted of examining the written accounts of negotiation meetings that occasioned considerable argumentation. Axelrod was interested in the extent to which a debate model held; that is, did the negotiators state pro and refute con arguments and attack the other side's arguments?

Axelrod (1977) did an extensive analysis of the conversations that took place in three, quite different negotiation contexts. One meeting involved a British ad hoc committee discussing the continued British occupation of Persia; the second involved a number of Japanese officials discussing Japanese defense policy; and the third was the Hitler-Chamberlain meeting at Munich. Axelrod found a number of interesting results, with findings varying little across the three situations. First, presentation of evidence in support of statements was infrequent, with less than 6% of the statements providing such support. Second, causal statements were infrequent, ranging from 1% to 4%. Third, attacks on another's statements were infrequent such that, with 300–500 relationships expressed, in each of the three settings only 1.5% to 6% expressed disagreement. Fourth, mutually supportive causal statements were rare—less than a percent. Fifth, even when unstated inferences are included, the results did not change much. Sixth, 16% to 21% of the statements were emphasized as "the truth" or "of importance." This finding suggests that the negotiations did not so much involve trying to persuade the opponent or refute the opponent's argument but instead the negotiator wanted to be sure that the other side knew what the negotiator felt was important.

From these and other results, Axelrod concluded that the debate model does not hold in such negotiation settings. He suggested that, instead, an argument evolves in which someone's presenting a new approach to the problem can be the most influential factor. These results are of considerable interest, for they suggest that reasoning, when considered in relation to a goal (even a vaguely defined goal), consists not only of weighing pros and cons but also of a process that proceeds until the issue is resolved, an impasse is acknowledged, a need for more information becomes clear, or some other form of closure is reached.

Another study, conducted by Levi and Tetlock (1980), involved use of a measure termed *cognitive complexity*. Cognitive complexity refers to the differentiation and integration of concept usage in a sample of text, complexity being judged on a scale of one to seven. Levi and Tetlock had access to the accounts of meetings held by the Japanese high command during the year before the bombing of Pearl Harbor. There were two types of meetings: liaison and imperial. The former included only the high command, whereas the latter included the high command with the emperor. The authors were testing the hypothesis that increased stress, presumed to occur as the date of Pearl Harbor came closer, decreased cognitive complexity.

Although results did not support the hypothesis, another finding was particularly interesting, namely, that cognitive complexity was greater in the imperial meetings than in the liaison meetings. Looking at the contexts, the authors suggested that in the liaison meetings, there was little justification of statements, but in the meetings with the emperor, the members of the high command needed to explain their decisions, thereby producing greater cognitive complexity. An implication of the results is that, apparently, less justification took place in meetings in which the decisions were actually made than in meetings in which the decisions needed to be communicated and justified.

The Axelrod (1977) and the Levi and Tetlock (1980) studies, taken with the preceding discussion, suggest that the individual reasoning that takes place by a weighting of pros and cons has interesting limitations in accounts of decision making. Weighing the relative strength of pro and con arguments may appear in the course of the argument, but each of the respective pro and con arguments has a weighting that is based on individual beliefs as they relate to the particular situation—beliefs that may vary considerably from person to person. Thus, beliefs play a role in the weighting process. Furthermore, the Axelrod data point to the possibility that persuasion, as typical in a debate model, may not be the form in which it most often occurs; instead, the process likely involves individuals' stressing points and stating positions, with the comparing and contrasting of differing positions essentially leading to a new, quite possibly acceptable, solution, a more or less dialectical process. Indeed, as noted, Axelrod suggested that issues are likely resolved not primarily by persuasion but by developing a new solution which, quite frequently, emerges in the discussion process. The account of the Cuban Missile crisis also supports this concept.

Another point about justification of positions that has interesting implications is that individuals in a negotiation process may not justify their conclusions by presenting supportive arguments because they do not want to expose their reasons, thereby potentially inviting refutation. As someone once commented about a decision, "he was so sure he did not want to do it that he offered no reason."

Summary Comments

Informal reasoning, as observed in the context of international relations, reveals peculiarities that suggest the following tentative conclusions:

1. The reasoning is informal in nature, with individuals generating inferences that lead to conclusions and generating beliefs and/or reasons to support conclusions.

2. During the course of such reasoning, individuals use heuristics to obtain the information that is used in the processing.

3. Two factors of special importance to reasoning in this context are a person's beliefs and a person's conclusions.

Moreover, the evidence suggests that both components are susceptible to formulations and biases related to the way in which issues are approached, which again may be influenced by beliefs and justification. Given these conclusions, we now turn to the issue of instruction.

INSTRUCTION IN INFORMAL REASONING
WITH SPECIAL REFERENCE TO SOCIAL SCIENCE

When instruction is studied in the context of mathematics or the natural sciences, the focus tends to be not on content, per se, but on the manner in which it is presented. In the area of social sciences and social studies, however, there is a much greater concern with what should—or for that matter, what should not—be taught. Moreover, a recent study (e.g., Ravitch & Finn, 1987) has raised serious questions regarding the relative paucity of high school graduates' social science knowledge. Although United States History is required in virtually all secondary schools in the United States, and a course such as World Cultures or World History is required in many, there is much less consistency in the other social sciences courses. Similarly, the goals of the elementary social science/social studies curriculum are unclear; the goals often are considered in relation not only to the subject matter per se but also to the development of the somewhat nebulous concept of citizenship. (See Barth & Shermis, 1970, for a discussion of the development of the social science curriculum.)

The remainder of this section is concerned with three questions:

1. What role does and/or should informal reasoning play in social science instruction?

2. What constraints limit improvement in social science instruction?

3. What actions are necessary to improve social science instruction, especially in relation to the use of informal reasoning?

Informal Reasoning in Social Science Instruction

One of the concepts that is implicit in contemporary instruction is that learning consists of acquiring subject matter. The subject matter is regarded as knowledge that is declarative in nature or is procedural, as in the solving of problems. One of the aspects of learning that is often not considered is the ability to utilize what has been acquired, and it is this aspect that is most important to the informal reasoning required in social science domains. As studies of international relations show, informal reasoning takes place when a person has a particular goal, such as interpretation or decision making and needs to utilize information in accomplishing this goal. Under these conditions, heuristics are employed to seek out and evaluate ideas, interpretations, solutions, and possible decisions.

What seems to be needed in social science instruction, if it is to facilitate skill in informal reasoning, is experience in the utilization of the knowledge that is to be acquired. Such experience could take many forms and would lend itself to the creative teaching. Taking a position on an issue and defending it would be valuable experience, as would be interpreting actions, solving problems, and making decisions. But, to provide such experience, a change in orientation is required. We accept as given that, in mathematics and science, learning to solve problems is fundamental. However, in social sciences, such an orientation is not present. A primary reason for learning social science subject matter is, perhaps somewhat surprisingly, to develop the analytic skill needed to utilize it. As an example, what if, in the study of United States history, a student were asked to assume the role of a Confederate official in early 1861 and consider what options, if any, were available in addition to war and what outcomes may have occurred. Next, the student might be asked to consider the options from the point of view of President Lincoln. Considerable knowledge of the conditions that existed prior to the Civil War would be needed, and use of appropriate interpretive and decision-making processes would provide experience in informal reasoning. It would make the line of questioning even more interesting perhaps, to ask "Do the issues considered before the Civil War seem, in any way, similar to or different from the issues that the United States faced prior to World War II?".

Consider a similar question about contemporary international affairs, something impacting on the student today: If you were a member of Congress, would you vote for or against Contra aid, and why? To answer such a question, it would be important that the student follow a procedure such that the rationale for the response precluded superficial answers. Of course, once again, the student would need to know the conditions leading to the current state of affairs, that is, the history of United States' interaction with Central American countries. If economics were taught, or even anthropology, similar instructional strategies for building knowledge and informal reasoning skills could be used.

The examples just given lead to two conclusions about the role of and teaching of informal reasoning in the social sciences. First, informal reasoning is a basic component of learning in social sciences, as is solving problems. Second, to develop skill in informal reasoning would require that students purposively accumulate and use more social science subject matter than they currently know. In this writer's opinion, students of elementary and secondary schools are required—or perhaps actually asked—to learn much less about social science subject matter than they are about mathematics and science. On the one hand, this is surprising, because most of the problems facing people today are in the realm of social sciences, not mathematics and natural sciences. On the other hand, however, it is not surprising, because knowledge of mathematics and sciences in today's technological society is regarded, on the basis of pragmatics, to be more useful.

Constraints in Social Studies/Science Instruction.   There are at least four readily identifiable constraints that act to prohibit the development of better social science instruction, which, in turn, prohibits students from having increased experience in informal reasoning. First, as suggested, expectations regarding what is to be learned in social sciences are lower than the expectations for mathematics and sciences. The issue of mathematics' and the natural sciences' utility raises the question of whether the social sciences could not be made more useful by more appropriate instruction. It certainly would seem useful for a graduating high school senior to know the pros and cons of protectionism when political candidates are debating the issue and when the student may be going on the job market. One would think that knowledge of Central America and the Middle East would be useful if a person is contemplating joining a military service or processing a career involving international business. Most important, of course, behind the idea of an educated citizenry lies the hope that those in a democratic society will be equipped to evaluate the reasoning behind the political stances taken by various leaders.

Another constraint on social science instruction, which has much to do with the relatively low amount of learning that is now required, is the education of the teachers. Teachers of social sciences may have had courses in United States History, but their general social science background is usually not strong. One can hardly expect improved student learning when the teachers have relatively limited command of the subject matter. A related constraint is that of the textbooks. Teachers tend to be highly textbook-oriented; until texts are written and adopted that treat social science subject matter in depth, there is little hope that students will receive the kind and level of instruction that the subject matter warrants.

Finally, this social studies curriculum is constrained because social science issues are often controversial. Teachers may avoid controversial issues because it is "safer" to do so, and curricular and textbook adoption decisions are susceptible to political pressures. Controversiality is, admittedly, a difficult problem, but it is not insurmountable. A focus on informal reasoning skills should engender an inquiring, rather than doctrinaire, approach. Conflict can be used to produce learning, and for a student to learn that there are various viewpoints about issues could be highly instructive in the long run.

The topic of international relations is especially controversial. Yet, it is difficult to think of another social science topic currently not taught that should become an important part of the curriculum. Indeed, with respect to international relations instruction, we seem to be decades behind. Although there is, of course, the need for good instruction in United States history, there is an increasing need for people to become more aware of our cultural, political, geographical, and economic ties with the countries in the rest of the world. The world is getting smaller, and contact among the inhabitants of various countries is increasing, as is media exposure. Moreover, it is an assumption of a democracy that the public is informed and, one may add, informed accurately. With the foreign policy issues of this country becoming increasingly important, as they have over this century, high school graduates should have an idea of the problems of Third World nations, the nature of the Middle East controversies, and other matters. However, as noted, unless teachers become informed about such matters, primarily by taking an appropriate set of courses in college, there is little likelihood of our strengthening and improving social science offerings in elementary and secondary schools.

Actions Needed to Improve Instruction in Informal Reasoning.   From the perspective of the field of international relations itself, as well as fields of cognitive science and instructional psychology, analyses of the interpretive and decision-making processes that are characteristic of reasoning in the social sciences are of increasing interest and value. Participants in the study of international relations are becoming aware that cognitive science provides insight into both individual decision makers' modes of thought and the complexities of group decision making. Further research in the social sciences would be particularly valuable to analyses of the way international policy is shaped. In the attempts to bring now-classic models of the decision process to bear in domains in which problems are ill structured, cognitive scientists are expanding and refining their accounts of human reasoning. As investigations proceed, we stand to gain a) scientifically, b) in enhanced understanding of the dynamics of international relations, and c) in providing grounds for improving social studies instruction in topics of historical and current significance.

ACKNOWLEDGMENTS

Preparation of this chapter was supported by a grant from the Office of Educational Research and Improvement of the Department of Education to the Center for the Study of Learning of the Learning Research and Development Center. The opinions expressed are not necessarily those of any of these organizations.

REFERENCES

Abelson, R. P. (1963). Computer simulation of "hot cognitions." In S. Tomkins & S. Messick (Eds.), *Computer simulation of personality* (pp. 277–298). New York: Wiley.

Allison, G. T. (1971). *Essence of decision: Explaining the Cuban Missile Crisis.* Boston: Little, Brown.

Angell, R. B. (1964). *Reasoning and logic.* New York: Appleton-Century-Crofts.

Axelrod, R. (1977). Argumentation in foreign policy settings. *Journal of Conflict Resolution, 21,* 727–744.

Barth, J. L., & Shermis, S. S. (1970). Defining the social studies: An exploration of three traditions. *Social Education, 34,* 743–751.

Bonham, G. M., & Shapiro, M. J. (1977). Foreign policy decision-making in Finland and Austria: The application of a cognitive process model. In G. M. Bonham & M. J. Shapiro (Eds.), *Thought and action in foreign policy* (pp. 306–355). Basel: Birkhäuser.

Chan, S., & Sylvan, D. A. (1984). Foreign policy decision making: An overview. In D. A. Sylvan & S. Chan (Eds.), *Foreign policy decision making* (pp. 1–19). New York: Praeger.

Einhorn, H. J., & Hogarth, R. M. (1978). Confidence in judgment: Persistence of the illusion of validity. *Psychological Review, 85,* 395–416.

Einhorn, H. J., & Hogarth, R. M. (1981). Behavioral decision theory: Processes of judgment and choice. *Annual Review of Psychology, 32,* 53–88.

Etheredge, L. S. (1985). *Can governments learn? American foreign policy and central American revolutions.* Elmsford, NY: Pergamon Press.

Gentner, D. (1983). Structure-mapping: A theoretical framework for analogy. *Cognitive Science, 7,* 155–170.

George, A. (1980). *Presidential decision making in foreign policy: The effective use of information and advice.* Boulder, CO: Westview Press.

Gilovich, T. (1981). Seeing the past in the present: The effect of associations to familiar events on judgments and decisions. *Journal of Personality and Social Psychology, 40,* 797–808.

Harman, G. (1986). *Change in view: Principles of reasoning.* Cambridge, MA: MIT Press.

Hogarth, R. M. (1980). *Judgment and choice: The psychology of decision.* Chichester, England: Wiley.

Holsti, K. J. (1977). *International politics: A framework for analysis* (3rd ed.). Englewood Cliffs, NJ: Prentice-Hall.

Holsti, O. R. (1967). Cognitive dynamics and images of the enemy. *Journal of International Affairs, 21,* 16–39.

Holsti, O. R. (1976). Foreign policy decision viewed cognitively. In R. Axelrod (Ed.), *The structure of decision* (pp. 18–54). Princeton, NJ: Princeton University Press.

Holsti, O. R., & Rosenau, J. N. (1977). The meaning of Vietnam: Belief systems of American leaders. *International Journal, 32,* 452–474.

Jervis, R. (1976). *Perception and misperception in international politics.* Princeton, NJ: Princeton University Press.

Jervis, R. (1986). Representativeness in foreign policy judgments. *Political Psychology, 7,* 483–506.

Klayman, J., & Ha, Y. W. (1987). Conformation, disconfirmation, and information in hypothesis testing. *Psychological Review, 94,* 211–228.

Lee, W. (1971). *Decision theory and human behavior.* New York: Wiley.

Levi, A., & Tetlock, P. E. (1980). A cognitive analysis of Japan's 1941 decision for war. *Journal of Conflict Resolution, 24,* 195–211.

Machiavelli, N. (1980). *The prince.* New York: Signet. (Original work published 1532)

Mandel, R. (1986). Psychological approaches to international relations. In M. G. Hermann (Ed.), *Political psychology* (pp. 251–278). San Francisco, CA: Jossey-Bass.

Morgenthau, H. (1966). *Politics among nations* (4th ed.). New York: Knopf.

Neustadt, R. E., & May, E. R. (1986). *Thinking in time.* New York: Free Press.

Newell, A. (1980). One final word. In D. T. Tuma & F. Reif (Eds.), *Problem solving education: Issues in teaching and research* (pp. 175–189). Hillsdale, NJ: Lawrence Erlbaum Associates.

Newell, A., & Simon, H. A. (1972). *Human problem solving.* Englewood Cliffs, NJ: Prentice-Hall.

Paige, G. D. (1968). *The Korean decision.* New York: The Free Press.

Paige, G. D. (1970). *1950: Truman's decision.* New York: Chelsea House.

Pruitt, D. G. (1965). Definition of the situation as a determinant of interactional action. In H. C. Kelman (Ed.), *International behavior: A social-psychological analysis* (pp. 393–432). New York: Holt, Rinehart, and Winston.

Ravitch, D., & Finn, C. E., Jr. (1987). *What do our 17-year-olds know?* New York, NY: Harper & Row.

Read, S. J. (1983). Once is enough: Causal reasoning from a single instance. *Journal of Personality and Social Psychology, 45,* 323–334.

Read, S. J. (1984). Analogical reasoning in social judgment: The importance of causal theories. *Journal of Personality and Social Psychology, 46,* 14–25.

Reitman, W. (1965). *Cognition and thought.* New York: Wiley.

Salmon, M. H. (1984). *Logic and critical thinking.* Orlando, FL: Harcourt Brace Jovanovich.

Simon, H. A. (1973). The structure of ill-structured problems. *Artificial Intelligence, 4,* 181–201.

Simon, H. A. (1983). *Reasons in human affairs.* Stanford, CA: Stanford University Press.

Simon, H. (1985). Human nature in politics: The dialogue of psychology with political science. *American Political Science Review, 79,* 293–304.

Snyder, G., & Diesing, P. (1977). *Conflict among nations.* Princeton, NJ: Princeton University Press.

Tversky, A., & Kahneman, D. (1974). Judgment under uncertainty: Heuristics and biases. *Science, 185,* 1124–1131.

Tversky, A., & Kahneman, D. (1982). Evidential impact of base rates. In D. Kahneman, P. Slovic, & A. Tversky (Eds.), *Judgment under uncertainty: Heuristics and biases* (pp. 153–160). Cambridge, England: Cambridge University Press.

Tweney, R. D., & Doherty, M. E. (1983). Rationality and the psychology of inference. *Syntheses, 57,* 139–161.

Voss, J. F., Greene, T. R., Post, T. A., & Penner, B. C. (1983). Problem solving skill in the social sciences. In G. H. Bower (Ed.), *The psychology of learning and motivation: Advances in research theory* (Vol. 17, pp. 165–213). New York: Academic.

Voss, J. F., & Post, T. A. (1988). On the solving of ill-structured problems. In M. T. H. Chi, R. Glaser, & M. Farr (Eds.), *The nature of expertise*. Hillsdale, NJ: Lawrence Erlbaum Associates.

Voss, J. F., Tyler, S. W., & Yengo, L. A. (1983). Individual differences in the solving of social science problems. In R. F. Dillon & R. R. Schmeck (Eds.), *Individual differences in cognition* (pp. 205–232). New York: Academic.

Zajonc, R. B., Pietromonaco, P., & Bargh, J. (1982). Independence and interaction of affect and cognition. In M. S. Clark & S. T. Fiske (Eds.), *Affect and cognition* (pp. 211–227). Hillsdale, NJ: Lawrence Erlbaum Associates.

4 Informal Reasoning in the Judicial System

Jeanette A. Lawrence
The University of Melbourne, Australia

The courtroom is an arena where reasoning has a tremendous impact on people's lives. Defendants may walk away with charges against them dismissed, or they may lose their freedom—and in some instances their lives—on the basis of judges' and jurors' reasoning. What happens in court depends on the judgments that some people make about others and their alleged activities, yet courtroom conditions are less than optimal for processing information. Each judgment must be made from incomplete information in a climate of uncertainty and ambiguity and must lead to a verdict whose veracity cannot be put to an incontrovertible test. This takes place in a public arena of adversarial persuasion governed by rules of procedure about how material may be gathered and tested, while evidence is processed with the expectation that all participants will attempt to influence the judgmentmaker.

Reasoning processes used in courtrooms are ill structured, because transformation rules must derive from heuristics rather than from formal logic; consequently, outcomes cannot be tested against absolute truth. Under these conditions, professional and nonprofessional judicial reasoners are forced to rely on their own cognitive resources for making the best possible judgments. Thus, the courtroom is an excellent environment in which to study the processes of informal reasoning in a formal setting.

This chapter focuses on those who make judgments in court, the constraints within which they work, and the legal and procedural rules that dictate how they are to reach a verdict. Once these constraints on judicial reasoning are specified, some recent analyses of juries' and magistrates' decisions are presented to illustrate how courtroom judgmentmakers rely on individualized stories and schemata to think about conflicting evidence.

JUDICIAL REASONERS AND THEIR TASKS

There are two classes of judicial reasoners: professional judges and magistrates, whose role is to make reasoned and legally valid judgments, and nonprofessional citizen jurors, who are expected to be naive. In Australia, stipendiary magistrates are legal professionals who preside alone over hearings in the lower courts of a two-tier system. Professional judges and magistrates are trained and selected for their expertise. They are invested with the responsibility of representing society in testing the soundness of cases against defendants and expressing the community's displeasure towards the guilty (Lawrence & Homel, 1987).

The importance of the processes of courtroom reasoning has become prominent in recent revelations of problems in the judicial system. Professional judges have enjoyed considerable discretion, especially to define and weigh material when sentencing offenders, and there has been strong evidence that sentencers impose different penalties for similar crimes (Diamond, 1981). As a consequence, sentencing guidelines are being introduced that severely curtail the discretionary license of judicial officers (Knapp, 1987).

Jurors are at an even greater disadvantage when making judgments on guilt or innocence, because they reason in alien domains with minimal instruction and under more stringent constraints than professionals. Jury members are selected by ballot or other random methods, and are screened for vested interests in the law or aspects of individual cases. Their very role is defined by their lack of legal expertise and their status as representatives of the community. They must sit passively through the long process of addresses, testimonies, and cross-examination, and, unlike the judge or magistrate, they may not take notes or ask for clarification during the trial. Traditional confidence in the decisions of "12 good men (and women)" has been eroded by evidence that jurors persist in attending to inadmissible evidence and that they are susceptible to pretrial publicity (Monahan & Loftus, 1982). Under circumstances that are anything but optimal, jurors are expected to come to reasonable conclusions.

Each judge, magistrate, and juror's essential task is to listen to conflicting claims and evidence, to consider information, and then to transform them into dispositions of people's lives. Assessing the soundness of claims and cases is a common function of each professional and nonprofessional judge. ("Judge" here is meant in the broadest sense: one who assesses the reasonableness of the arguments and evidence presented for the prosecution's or defense's case.) The professional on the bench has the added task of preserving the judicial properties and rules of information exchange in the courtroom (Atkinson & Drew, 1979; Penman, 1985).

CONTEXTUAL CONSTRAINTS
AND EXPECTATIONS

Assessing evidence and making judgments are constrained by rules about the information that may be used in a decision, rituals about how the information may be obtained and evaluated, and the intentions and abilities of participants. Formal rules and rituals for obtaining information abound in the legal system, such as the laws of evidence that prevent defendants from prejudicing their cases and rules for turn taking and cross-examination. But there are no guidelines for the cognitive mediation and processes by which information is given meaning or by which a sequence of premises can be transformed into a reasonable judgment. Judge and juror alike depend on their own reasoning structures.

The one universal criterion for testing information and decisions is reasonable doubt, a criterion that is itself ill defined and open to various interpretations. Kerr, Atkin, Strasser, Meek, Holt, and Davis (1976) argued that reasonable doubt works like the scientist's null hypothesis. But their analogy breaks down, because reasonable doubt is more loosely defined than statistical probabilities. Trial judges' definitions of reasonable doubt for juries varied considerably, ranging from a doubt "for which any reasons can be given" to doubt that is "not trivial or imaginary." Having excluded hung juries from their analysis, the researchers found that, in six mock juries' deliberations in an actual rape trial, "lax" definitions of reasonable doubt were associated more often than stringent definitions with verdicts of guilt. Although their subjects were able to discriminate between personal views and legal criteria, the data suggest that the court's most significant decision rule, reasonable doubt, may act like an informal heuristic (Tikhomirov, 1983), which can vary in meaning and application, at least for juries. Thus, judicial reasoning is an informal, individualized process of approximating truth and reasonableness. In addition to the parameter of its own uncertain processes, judicial reasoning is limited by the availability of information and the demands of the courtroom.

Before judges or jurors even begin to test arguments or interpret evidence, prosecution and defense attorneys will have already shaped and reconstructed the body of information that they will hear. The attorneys compile, edit, and present their own pictures of events and intentions, and they instruct their witnesses accordingly. The original material is restructured and clothed with valences designed to lead inferences along specified pathways. Formal addresses, tactics, and innuendos are used in complex arguments that are intended to convince the court that one claim is more plausible than another (Linz, Penrod, & McDonald, 1986). Everyone in court has a stake in the outcome, and everyone possesses some information that is not available to the judge. The pressures exerted on the individual judgment-maker to follow one line of reasoning do not usually operate with such urgency and significance in other domains. Because their decisions are so important to people's lives and because their verdicts bear the weight of law, judicial reasoners are obliged to avoid flights of imagination, produce their best approximation of truth, and resist persuasive arguments that contravene rationality.

When analyzing 70 hours of conversation in an Australian supreme court, Penman (1985) identified 19 communication difficulties that were potential barriers to encoding useful information. Barristers were the source of some difficulties, such as when they asked ambiguous or speculative questions; other problems arose from the quality of information, such as when witnesses drew their own conclusions or reported second-hand evidence. As Penman's analysis demonstrates, the rules for obtaining courtroom evidence actually violate the principles of cooperative communication that Grice (1975) perceived in all human verbal exchanges. According to Penman, courtrooms are not places of natural cooperation, but places where presiding judges need to coerce participants to follow rules designed for the efficient exchange of information. At the same time, the task of ensuring the flow of information derives its significance from the assumption that judicial reasoners must have adequate information if justice is to be served.

Although the prosecution and the defense each presents its own case, the information compiled in a trial acquires a life of its own beyond the boundaries of either line of argument. As a case develops, new information and evidence emerges. Even more significantly, the judge creates fresh links and new meanings as he or she sorts and integrates what previously appeared to be disassociated pieces of information. By imposing the rules of evidence and by assessing the new gestalt against legal issues, the presiding judge constructs his or her own view of the events and their implications.

Then, in a trial, as opposed to a hearing, the judge interprets the rules and issues for the juror, imposing further interpretations and valences on the body of information. Holstein (1983) found that jurors used judges' instructions as conversational resources to make or support arguments in the jury room. The judge also conveys to jurors the categories and rules for classifying possible verdicts in relation to the charge. Jurors construct individual representations as they listen and then again on reflection. Armed with their own interpretations, jurors enter the jury room with the mandate to justify or surrender their views of the case. Because they must reach a consensus, jurors must argue and deliberate further to arrive at a verdict. Thus, at no time is the environment in which judge and juror reason benign or neutral.

All judges and jurors reason within broader ranges than the prosecution and defense. Judgments may be conceived as based on possible proofs that range over a continuum, with proven guilt at one end and proven innocence at the other. Of course, absolute proof is not possible, but there are numerous approximations of truth between these two poles, and judges must test more possibilities than either committed party.

The prosecutor seeks to keep the judge's and jurors' thinking at the proof-of-guilt pole, with the specific goal of establishing that the guilt of the defendant is clear. The prosecutor maintains that there can be little, if any, doubt about the defendant's guilt and that those assessing the facts should test evidence at the guilty pole of the continuum.

In contrast, the defense seeks to create doubt and ambiguity and thus to widen the judge's set of possible interpretations of the events. He or she tries to force the question of whether it is reasonable to conclude that the defendant is guilty. It is not necessary for the defense to lead the judge to infer that innocence is proven; rather, the defense attempts to induce doubts that any reasonable person might have about the prosecution's proof. Judges and jurors, for their part, must consider the prosecution's narrow set of possibilities in conjunction with the defense's ambiguities. They must then test each possibility, not against absolute truth or proof, but against a model of possibilities with varying degrees of plausibility.

How, then, do professional and nonprofessional reasoners process evidence under conditions of a heavy load of information, conflicting perspectives, and ritualized decision rules? Mental representations of the events help the judge to decide what took place, interpret the legal significance of overt behavior, and infer the intentions of the defendant. Jurors impose sense on and find coherence in unfamiliar material by using rules and categories provided by others. Magistrates search for information, maintain its flow, and give meaning to details that are familiar and can be routinized.

In the sections that follow, I discuss the nature of jurors' reasoning processes and report on magistrates' information use during judging and sentencing.

JURORS' SENSE MAKING

Pennington and Hastie's (1981) analysis of the series of subtasks in which jurors participate indicates that jurors are passive recipients of information. Yet they must also establish the categories of judgments they will make, select admissible evidence, and construct plausible sequences of events from the testimonies they hear. Pennington and Hastie culminated their sequence of subtasks with jurors' evaluation of the credibility of events and evidence and establishment of a verdict through the application of reasonable doubt. Unfortunately, their critique fails to address the second phase of the juror's work, which takes place in the jury room. There, each juror must test his or her initial conclusions afresh against the arguments of 11 other people and the group's deliberations. A juror's sequence of tasks can overwhelm a naive juror, especially given the memory requirements of the tasks, their multifaceted processing demands, and the requirement of a unanimous verdict. In addition, the information that is the grist of the reasoning mill for a juror comprises biased and conflicting reports.

Bennett and Feldman (1981) and Holstein (1985) have described how jurors impose structure and sense on conflicting information under less-than-ideal conditions. Essentially, jurors constructed stories or sequences of events to make information cohere, reduce uncertainty about the value of certain pieces, and make connections between event sequences and plausible verdicts. Between their story constructions and the judge's specification of verdict categories, jurors' assess the intentions and motives that they can reasonably attribute to the defendant. Of course, all this happens in individual jurors' minds, without overt check or challenge, until the group is required to reach consensus. Initial representations are vital precursors and supports of negotiation. In fact, initial, tentative verdicts have been shown to remain quite firm and to be strongly related to final decisions (Lawson, 1968). According to Holstein, organization and structure are the outcomes of "interpretive schemata," which are like the scripts that enable people to follow a sequence of actions while reviewing common events (Schank & Abelson, 1977). Unlike the person using a familiar script, however, jurors apply their own constructions of reality (Schultz, 1970) to feel their way around unfamiliar events.

Thus, nonprofessional listeners use the informal heuristic (Tikhomirov, 1983) of telling themselves stories in which they commit significant details to memory by weaving them into coherent wholes. In other areas of psychology, stories have been shown to work as powerful devices for organizing disjointed material (Mandler & Johnson, 1977). Holstein (1985) has also provided some useful insights on how jurors use stories to impose sense on evidence.

In a careful simulation experiment using only people who had served 2 months on jury panels, Holstein formed 48 six-member simulated juries and showed them a videotape of the trial of a theft case. The defendant was accused of taking a truckload of bricks that had lain unused on a vacant lot for 2 months. The mock jurors watched the trial and then deliberated under jury conditions. Transcripts of their deliberations revealed how the jurors gave shape and meaning to the original crime events and how their interpretations related to the verdicts expected of them.

Two examples illustrate how differently jurors reconstructed the unseen events recounted in the videotaped trial. Their inferences about intent reveal their interpretations and assessments of the actor. Juror 2 judged the truck driver not guilty and gave this account of the events, adding his own causal attributions: "Sure, he went on the property and took them when he saw them just laying there. . . . But see, in his mind, he says, you know, he didn't feel that they belonged to anyone, even though he saw the sign. Apparently he didn't feel that they belonged, so he took them" (Holstein, 1985, p. 94).

In contrast, using the same courtroom data, Juror 4 put a different cast to the crime events to reach the opposite verdict: "Harris knew what he was doing when he went onto the property and drove away with those bricks. . . . He knew he was taking those bricks from someone. He knew they weren't his bricks, that he didn't own them, so he intended to take them" (p. 89).

These accounts show how each of these jurors wove together reported details with the views they had formed: Juror 4 observed Harris' criminal intent, whereas Juror 2 attributed innocent motives to Harris, noting his reading of a sign at a specific point. Each juror built premises for inducing judgments and reducing some of the uncertainty of the task. There was a wide variation in accounts of the same events (15 for 48 groups) and interpretations of the defendant's intentions. The greater the number of interpretations, the longer, more complex, and more difficult to resolve mock juries' deliberations became. When jurors argued on the basis of different interpretations but reached the same verdict (guilty or not guilty), there was more confusion, and the likelihood of a hung jury increased.

In addition to stories for event sequences, jurors used other data in their deliberations and discussions. The judge's instructions and other jurors' arguments became additional pieces of information and persuasion, which each juror used to recreate and assess the case. Thus, a juror may be regarded as a type of naive judge who imposes his or her interpretations on evidence in spite of the assumptions of attorneys that they establish jurors' interpretive frames in their addresses (Linz et al., 1986).

MAGISTRATES' REASONING STRUCTURES

The judicial system permits judges and magistrates to actively search for information in a fashion that is not possible for jurors. They are at liberty to use notes and other aids to memory and organization, and they may ask questions, as long as they do not place witnesses in jeopardy of self-incrimination. The magistrate may decide which relevant information might be needed and may seek missing material. For example, one magistrate, whose courtroom use of information was studied intensively, had to supplement poor verbal testimony with his own careful scrutiny of maps and photographs to reconstruct the scene of a fatal accident (Lawrence, 1988). A magistrate must define issues and categories of offenses and claims to generate the conclusions that must be weighed in relation to the data.

In civil cases, the investigative process involves identifying the issues to be addressed by opposing parties and the approximations of truth that a good decision demands in the absence of absolute truth. Given that plaintiffs must convince the court with more than an even probability that their claims against a defendant are valid, the burden of proof rests on them.

A qualitative study of one magistrate's activities in a civil claims case demonstrates how this active pursuit of detail enters the judge's inferential equation. Examination of data from the full hearing also shows how the professional's information selection and inferences are used with "what-really-happened" schemata. I gathered the data on this very senior magistrate's courtroom information processing by interviewing him before and after court and by sitting beside him on the bench for the half-day hearing. In an earlier study (Lawrence, 1984), this magistrate had demonstrated an understanding of his own courtroom deliberations that made him a suitable subject for studying a magistrate's reasoning processes during court proceedings, and his or her predictions and reflections before and after a hearing. He articulated the information sources he used to test possible outcomes for a hearing as well as his inferencing processes.

The magistrate described the personalized strategies he used to guide his processing of cases. He typically prepared for a case by extracting major issues from the files and focusing and hypothesizing on these issues. He always held the two antagonistic positions in mind together until he could reach a decision. In a style that he had created for himself, he took two types of notes to obtain an information base for his decisions. Like many of his colleagues, he wrote an almost verbatim account of testimony; then he outlined issues, points, and questions on a diagonal alongside his notes. He used both sets of notes to raise issues, review points, and test hypotheses. By sitting beside him on the bench, I was able to read his notes and develop an independent account of courtroom events. I then used these data to question the magistrate about his system of deciding in favor of the plaintiff or defendant.

A claim for damage to a motor vehicle required the magistrate to frame and test two issues and search for pertinent information in the opposing cases to construct his own argument for a verdict. The magistrate selected, assembled, and tested information from the general body of evidence to decide in favor of the defendant's claim rather than the plaintiff's.

The case involved a business man, the plaintiff, who accused the defendant, a pregnant housewife without an attorney, of backing her vehicle into his more expensive vehicle. He was claiming over $400 costs for damage to his vehicle. The defendant claimed, first, that she had not backed up but that he had driven into her vehicle and, second, that his red Jaguar had not been damaged in the collision. There were no independent observers of the events.

The structure of the magistrate's reasoning is shown in Fig. 4.1, depicting a series of knowledge states and inferences that move from his prehearing identification of the two issues to a verdict. The information the magistrate selected as the premises for his reasoning and the inferences he drew from this information are shown as knowledge states. The inferences that the magistrate made are shown as diagonal lines moving toward the verdict as conclusion; solid horizontal lines depict connecting premises, and possible inferences are shown as dotted horizontal lines.

The magistrate identified two issues in the conflicting evidence about which he had to be satisfied: the primary issue of culpability (Which vehicle moved and therefore caused the damage?) and the secondary issue of amount of damage to the plaintiff's car (What was the quantum of the damages at issue?). Settling the second issue depended on the magistrate satisfying himself about the prior matter of culpability. The figure shows the reasoning leading to his interim conclusions about the two issues and the inconclusiveness of the evidence.

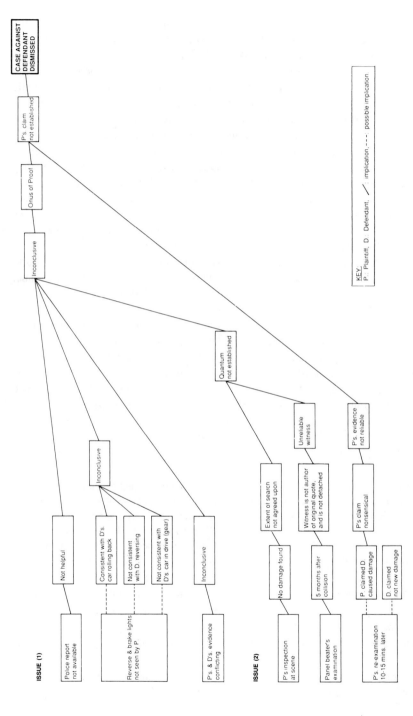

FIG. 4.1. Structure of a magistrate's argument for resolving a civil claims case.

67

Concerning the primary issue of who was responsible for the damage, the magistrate accumulated inconclusive evidence. There was no police report. The plaintiff saw no reverse lights or brake lights, and this information was consistent with his claim that the defendant's car rolled back, but it was inconsistent with his claim that she had put her car in reverse and with her claim that her automatic car was in drive. The plaintiff's and defendant's testimonies about the collision disagreed, and there was no evidential basis for resolving their claims.

Concerning the secondary quantum issue, the magistrate decided that the estimate of damage was unreliable on three grounds: (a) the two parties disagreed about the extent of the plaintiff's on-the-spot search of the damage, (b) they disagreed about the damage the plaintiff later showed the defendant, and (c) the panel beater's (body shop worker's) assessment of the damage was unreliable. The panel beater had made a superficial examination of the damage 5 months after the collision and only a week before the hearing, by following an original quote that another panel beater had given soon after the collision. According to the magistrate, this witness's evidence was not useful because he "didn't really inspect the vehicle himself. He was quite happy to adopt what L [the other panel beater] had written into his quote several months ago." In addition, his evidence was "not detached."

The plaintiff's evidence about his initial inspection and reexamination of the alleged damage 10 to 15 minutes later was not reliable because he reported very different observations. Applying the criteria of reasonable doubt and onus of proof to the argument the plaintiff had presented, the magistrate concluded that, because the plaintiff's claim about the damage was unreliable and clear evidence about the collision was lacking, the plaintiff had not established his claim satisfactorily. The magistrate decided in favor of the defendant. His courtroom summary of the case clearly demonstrates the structure of reasoning behind his verdict on the first issue:

> A contest of credibility. Shall I believe the defendant, or shall I believe the plaintiff? The onus is on the plaintiff. If he wants her money, he must show a preponderance of probability. He hasn't shown it. I can't see why I should believe the plaintiff's evidence over the defendant's. Perhaps if I asked I would believe the defendant over the plaintiff. I don't have to ask that. The plaintiff hasn't shown it was the defendant's fault. No proof of quantum. Plaintiff's case is dismissed.

The magistrate exhibited some story schemata and, in addition, demonstrated rule-keeping tactics. Following the plaintiff's description of the incident, he positioned himself at the scene by a series of questions that permitted him to take upon himself the perspective of the witness (plaintiff):

| Magistrate: | I was in Crimea [Street] was I? |
| Plaintiff: | Yes. |

Magistrate:	Heading?
Plaintiff:	Heading north.
Magistrate:	Towards the shopping center?
Plaintiff:	Yes.

When questioned after court, he articulated, "I am in the mind of the witness there. Not the parties', but the witness'." Perspective taking like this probably serves as a perceptual precursor of interpretive schemata giving the listener a way of using a story to organize information.

The magistrate's responsibility for enforcing courtroom protocol and conversational rules was heightened by the presence of an unrepresented defendant and by this particular magistrate's concern about the advanced state of her pregnancy. He restrained the plaintiff's counsel at several points when he felt that the defendant could not use legal conventions of rebuttal, remarking at one point, "I'd prefer you don't lead while the woman is unrepresented." He instructed the defendant on how to object at one occasion, and he refused to lengthen the proceedings so that the plaintiff could recall a witness who had been allowed to leave. The following example illustrates his direct intervention to correct the plaintiff's testimony:

Prosecuting Counsel:	Can you identify [. . . other driver]?
Plaintiff:	I feel it is the lady in court.
Magistrate:	I don't want your feelings.
Plaintiff:	I am nearly sure.

    Magistrate (wrote down and read out his correction of his notes of the testimony) "I can't identify . . ."

In his reasoning, this experienced judge in a civil case relied on story schemata similar to those that Holstein (1985) had seen jurors use to give crime events a perspective, the kind of conversational rule keeping mentioned by Penman (1985), and the development of a coherent argument structure, applying information to address the two issues.

This account of one senior magistrate's processing provides an example of the strategies that can be employed to organize the nuances of individual cases. While the generalizability of his search and inference structures is an empirical question, qualitative analyses of another magistrate's search strategies indicate that professionals can gather information to draw conclusions and test their initial premises (Lawrence, 1988). When two opposing cases are involved and when the arguments take several hours or even days to present, the magistrate obviously must accrue pieces of information and make causal or consequential links to move from selected premises to judgments. This process requires reasoning structures that have something of an if–then form, and tested inferences, no matter how informal the connections may be.

In contrast, when sentencing on the basis of minimal information, as so often happens when the defendant pleads guilty, magistrates must find coherence quickly, and the full inferencing structure may not be used. A holistic and integrative perspective has to be adopted in criminal cases to pull together information on two factors that influence the choice of an appropriate sentence: the criminality of the defendant's acts and intentions and the circumstances of his or her life. Of course, a magistrate's own judicial views and sentencing goals will be pertinent, as the criminological literature indicates (Hogarth, 1971). But abstract commitments and attitudes need to be translated into working rules that help magistrates identify and analyze the critical features of cases and that reduce their processing effort. A current analysis of simulated sentencing behaviors reveals the strength of using immediately available categorizing schemata to integrate case details into cohesive pictures and match these pictures with patterns in magistrates' knowledge structures (Lawrence, 1987).

MAGISTRATES' SENTENCING SCHEMATA

Nine experienced magistrates from a large Australian city were asked to process court files in a realistic simulation task and to categorize and give sentences to the same six shoplifters. Four "tough" and five "lenient" magistrates were differentiated by the sentences they had given to shoplifters over a 12-month period. Heavy sentences included fines or jail, and lighter sentences comprised dismissal or deferred sentences and bonds for good behavior. Tougher magistrates gave more heavy fines to shoplifters over a large number of cases.

The study focused on the way magistrates used information in sentencing that can be routine for the court but that nevertheless has special significance to each offender. In an earlier study (Lawrence, 1988), expert and novice magistrates presented different sentencing goals and definitions of shoplifting, drunk driving, and cannabis offenses, and their respective views affected their inferences about a defendant's offense, criminal history, or personal characteristics. Given the vast individual differences in sentencing that have plagued the judicial world, and given Holstein's evidence of nonprofessionals' strategies, it was fitting to ask how magistrates process routine cases. Would they apply patterns of common cases to structure case details, or would they use a more formalized sentencing system, in which each legal and extralegal detail was weighed systematically and serially?

Magistrates sorted six shoplifting cases into groups according to their own criteria in a task that was similar to that used by Chi, Feltovich, and Glaser (1981) for well-structured physics problems. The difference was that magistrates worked in their natural environment, used cases similar to those they solved daily, and were asked to choose their own categories of shoplifting offenders and note the number of categories they discerned in the six cases. Magistrates are used to working with file data and verbalizing their reactions, so the processing aspect of the study was fairly familiar. Although the sorting task was less familiar, it had the potential of offering another view of the representations they used in their decision processes. All cases had been taken from courtroom archives of actual shoplifting cases, and all involved pleas of guilty. The facts of the offense were not in dispute, and plea bargaining is not a practice in Australia's lower criminal courts.

The magistrates did not view the cases in a uniform way. Nine of them produced eight different grouping patterns for the six cases, with a mean of 3.2 groups, 2.75 among the tough magistrates and 4.8 among the lenient ones. Only two lenient magistrates' groupings were the same; that was because both had used multiple criteria and insisted that there were no meaningful groups and that each case had to be treated individually and holistically. The groupings were made from different sorting criteria, and the trends in the groups and criteria of tough and lenient magistrates indicate that the magistrates represented the cases differently. The criteria covered the seriousness of the case (used by all tough magistrates and one lenient); shoplifters' intentions (used by one tough and one lenient); a psychologically troubled state (used by no tough but three lenient); and some holistic and undifferentiated criteria (used by one tough and four lenient).

With these differences in initial representations, magistrates' processing of individual cases was analyzed for evidence of consistent impositions of meaning and structure and consistent connections between magistrates' demonstrated style, case features, and tough or lenient sentences. These common schemata for categorizing offenders and organizing information were revealed in the verbal protocols, although tough and lenient magistrates used them in different patterns. These schemata provided clues about, and criteria for selecting salient details, interpreting their significance against known patterns, and supplementing incomplete data. Using these schemata is an economical process for handling familiar profiles of offenders.

At this stage, current data and numerous courtroom observations indicate three recurring and distinguishable classes of shoplifters: (a) people who steal from stores for the sake of acquiring goods without paying for them, whom several magistrates called "the greedy"; (b) those who steal because of financial deprivation and poverty, whom they labelled "the needy"; and (c) those whose acts of theft some interpret as evidence of underlying psychological or social troubles or disturbances and whom I called "the troubled." The greed category is also the default category for routine theft from stores. Each schema enables a gestalt to be perceived in the data that conforms to known patterns of criminal behavior and provides its own set of supplementary inferences.

Table 4.1 depicts the common features of shoplifting cases, together with the different cues for activating each of the three schemata. The function of schemata can be seen by reading through the sections of a typical case, although different

TABLE 4.1
Three Schemata and Critical Cues for Categorizing Shoplifters

	Greed	Need	"Troubled"
		Critical Cues	
Case Features			
Events			
Type of goods	Luxuries	Necessities	Luxuries
Value of goods	High	Low	Low
Manner of stealing	Purposeful	Spur of moment	Purposeless
History			
Prior offence	Serious	Serious or not	Indicative of long-term trouble
Prior penalty	Guide to current penalty	Guide to current penalty	Guide to trouble
Life Circumstances			
Situation	Indicators or non-indicators of sta-	Indicators of eco-nomic difficul-	Indicators of per-sonal or social
Relation	bility or ignore	ties	trouble or dis-
Job			turbance
Income	Indicator of capac-ity to pay checked against events	Indicator of need checked against events	Indicator of trou-ble or distur-bance
Explanation	Confirmation or rejection of events and/or interpretations	Confirmation or rejection of eco-nomic state or need	Confirmation or rejection of in-consistencies, troubles and/or disturbance
Further Informa-tion Required	to determine ca-pacity to pay fine or alterna-tive penalty	to determine need for assistance, suitability for bond, and/or su-pervision	to determine na-ture and extent of trouble, need for assistance, treatment, and/or supervi-sion
Penalty (Outcome)	Fine (as tariff), prison or bond, according to se-riousness, means	Fine or bond, ac-cording to means or need for assistance	Fine or bond ac-cording to trou-bles, need for assistance, and/or treat-ment

Note: From Lawrence, J. A. (1988). Making just decisions in magistrates' courts. *Social Justice Research, 2*(2), 155–176.

interpretations of categorical features are possible. Thus, any feature of a case may not be as significant to one magistrate as it is to another. For example, activating the greed schema leads a magistrate to focus on the events of the crime and to determine its seriousness, whereas activating the troubled schema will focus attention on the life circumstances that point to personal and social problems. The critical cues of the three categorizing schemata can be extracted from sections of evidence taken in court: crime events, the defendant's criminal history, life circumstances and income, explanations offered in court or inferred by the magistrate, and requests for further information.

The three schemata were associated with penalties of differing severity for 49 clear cases of the 54 examined. The greed schema was associated with heavier penalties than the troubled and needy schemata (X^2 (6) = 29.81, $p < .001$). Heavier penalties, involving fines, community service, or weekend jail terms were the outcomes of 79% of cases categorized as following the greed schema, but they were given in only 10.5% of cases categorized as following the troubled schema and in none following the need schema (X^2 (2) = 25.53, $p < .001$). The lighter penalty of bonds with or without conviction were imposed in only 13% (3) of greed schema cases compared with 47% (9) of troubled and 83% (5) of need (X^2 (2) = 12.83, $p < .01$).

Not only were the outcomes different, but tough and lenient magistrates activated the three schemata differently. Tough magistrates followed the greed schema more frequently than lenient magistrates (75% vs. 20%) (X^2 (1) = 14.18, $p < .001$). Lenient magistrates used the troubled schema more frequently than tough magistrates (50% vs. 17%) (X^2 (1) = 5.12, $p < .05$), and tough magistrates did not follow the need schema at all.

The information selection and inferences related to each schema can be seen in the three magistrates' sentencing of one shoplifter. Maria, an unemployed domestic worker whose husband was also unemployed through illness, stole goods worth $47.50 from different parts of a city store while accompanied by her two children. The security staff stopped her and recovered the stolen items. She had no previous convictions.

A tough magistrate (T1) applied the greed schema to Maria's case, whereas two lenient magistrates (L1 and L3) used the need and troubled schemas. Their verbal protocols are presented in diagrammatic form in Figs. 4.2, 4.3, and 4.4. The figures depict the information that a magistrate mentioned, the inferences he made from each piece of information, the judgments and verdicts he reached, and the sequence of this information-to-inference-to-judgment structure.

Following the greed schema (Fig. 4.2), a consistently tough magistrate (T1) used features of Maria's life circumstances (1) and his own knowledge and view of an appropriate penalty for her offence (2) to infer her inability to pay (3). He regarded the goods (4) as luxuries of substantial value (5). Because she had no prior convictions (6) and was unable to pay, the magistrate did not fine her (7) but deferred her sentence with a bond (8). Noticing that she had a husband (1), he

74

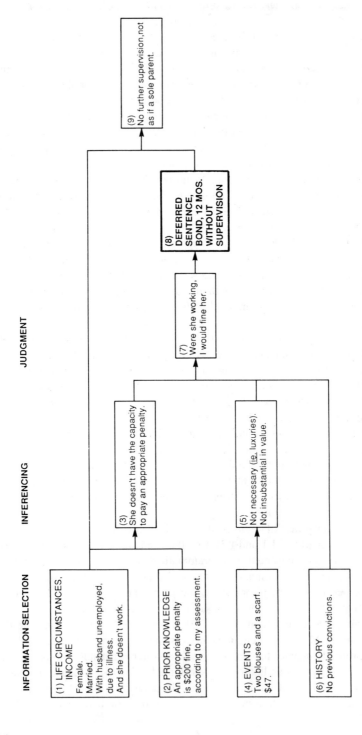

INFORMATION SELECTION **INFERENCING** **JUDGMENT**

(1) LIFE CIRCUMSTANCES, INCOME
Female.
Married.
With husband unemployed, due to illness.
And she doesn't work.

(2) PRIOR KNOWLEDGE
An appropriate penalty is $200 fine, according to my assessment.

(3) She doesn't have the capacity to pay an appropriate penalty.

(4) EVENTS
Two blouses and a scarf.
$47.

(5) Not necessary (ie. luxuries).
Not insubstantial in value.

(6) HISTORY
No previous convictions.

(7) Were she working, I would fine her.

(8) DEFERRED SENTENCE, BOND, 12 MOS. WITHOUT SUPERVISION

(9) No further supervision, not as if a sole parent.

FIG. 4.2. Sentencing a shoplifter using a greed schema (magistrate T1). From Lawrence, J. A. (1988). Making just decisions in magistrates' courts. *Social Justice Research, 2*(2), 155–176.

INFORMATION SELECTION   INFERENCING   JUDGMENT

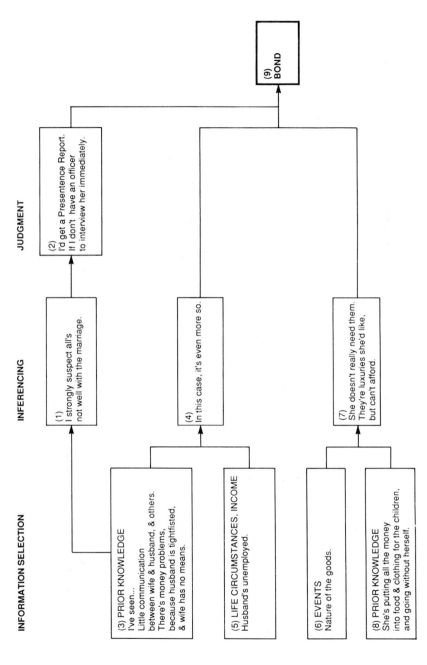

FIG. 4.3. Sentencing a shoplifter using a need schema (magistrate L1). From Lawrence, J. A. (1988). Making just decisions in magistrates' courts. *Social Justice Research*, 2(2), 155–176.

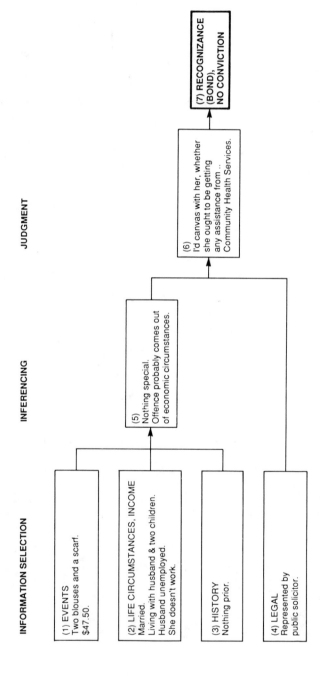

FIG. 4.4. Sentencing a shoplifter using a troubled schema (magistrate L3). From Lawrence, J. A. (1988). Making just decisions in magistrates' courts. *Social Justice Research, 2*(2), 155–176.

INFORMATION SELECTION

INFERENCING

JUDGMENT

(1) EVENTS
Two blouses and a scarf.
$47.50.

(2) LIFE CIRCUMSTANCES, INCOME
Married.
Living with husband & two children.
Husband unemployed.
She doesn't work.

(3) HISTORY
Nothing prior.

(4) LEGAL
Represented by
public solicitor.

(5)
Nothing special.
Offence probably comes out
of economic circumstances.

(6)
I'd canvas with her, whether
she ought to be getting
any assistance from . . .
Community Health Services.

(7) RECOGNIZANCE
(BOND),
NO CONVICTION

also inferred that she did not need supervision (9). By implication, her husband could supervise her because she was "not like a single parent," that is, someone who presumably needed management or assistance. The magistrate did not specify what he meant by supervision in such a case.

A consistently lenient magistrate (L1) processed the same information under the need schema, and his reasoning is shown in Fig. 4.3. The events (1), Maria's life circumstances (2), and the absence of prior convictions (3) led him to an inference contrary to T1's: that there was nothing special about her case and that Maria's offense probably arose from her economic need (5). Because Maria was represented by the public solicitor (4), the magistrate could obtain information from the solicitor about her suitability for community assistance (6). The sentence was recognizance, that is, a bond without conviction (7).

Another lenient magistrate (L3) activated the troubled schema, as shown in Fig. 4.4 and, immediately after reading the case, gave his initial impression of marriage problems (1). This inference led him to want further information in a Presentence Report (2); he also drew on his previous knowledge about common patterns of marriage problems (3 and 5) to consider Maria's case (4). Her circumstances exacerbated the normal troubled pattern (4) because Maria's husband was unemployed (5). He, like T1, inferred from the nature of the goods (6) that they were luxury items that she could not afford (7) and mitigated the offense with the inference that Maria was "putting all her money into food and clothing for the children and going without herself" (8). A report was not on file, so he gave the tentative judgment of a bond, most likely without conviction (9).

The three diagrammed protocols demonstrate how these magistrates placed features in coherent configurations to interpret and classify a defendant according to their own stereotypes. This schematizing then led them to penalties that satisfied their sense of appropriateness. For example, T1 focused on Maria's economic problem to decide that she could not pay the fine he thought appropriate for her crime (1, 7–9), whereas L1 used the same life circumstances to infer that her financial problems probably caused her offense (2–5). One centered on the event in the store, the other on the background characteristics of the defendant. L1's inferences had a slot-filling quality, which T1 exhibited when he decided that Maria did not need supervision because she had a husband. Supplementary inferences and story construction were prominent in L3's protocol, inasmuch as he generated a scenario of Maria's life that he wittingly linked to common patterns he had seen before (1 with 3 and 7 with 8). Coherence achieved by filling in gaps was found in the other protocols, and similar trends appeared in the magistrates' processing of the six cases. There were only a few instances in which magistrates activated conflicting schemata, two among tough and four among lenient magistrates. For the most part, these ambiguous instances were left unresolved pending further information.

In summary, these sentencing activities not only revealed the different criteria by which the same cases were categorized but also gave some consistent indications of the reasoning used to devise penalties. In terms of the disparity found between courts, these data strengthen the argument that explanations of courtroom judgments must include the cognitive dimension of sentencers' organization of information. The tough and lenient styles that Homel (1983) found in his data to be part of the explanation of courtroom statistics are also associated with different interpretations and penalties.

The data support Holstein's (1985) concept of jurors' processing from coherent schemata. In these undefended and routine cases, remembering and sequencing events were not the primary concern. The issue, rather, was the imposition of meaning on selected material, specifically magistrates' matching of details to patterns of shoplifters. In the civil case, the magistrate had the additional task of searching for the information and constructing his own equivalent of an argument structure.

CONCLUSION

The concept of informal reasoning ranges from reasoning in everyday settings to inference structures that cannot be described in terms of formal logic. In this chapter, I have examined reasoning processes not in the laboratory but in the courtroom, noting the messiness with which judgments are made in the context of conflicting claims and persuasive cómmunications. I have interpreted the processes involved in making judicial judgments as the use of information in forming ill-defined conclusions.

Judgments depend on the ways in which information is organized and interpreted. It appears that judges and jurors create meaning and coherence by constructing their own impressions of events and people. To interpret details in a context of conflicting influences, each judge of evidence constructs a story or working model. It is only by putting together a personal view of what actually happened and what the details mean that judges can distinguish the vital features of a case from the elements of courtroom polemic. If conclusions are indeterminate and conditions are ambiguous, there is little alternative to relying on one's experience and the powers of inference to select premises and make the inferences pertinent links to satisfying conclusions.

When unfamiliar material is received under unfamiliar conditions constrained by ritual, as for jurors, meanings are found by constructing story schemata that facilitate the organization and retention of details so that their plausibility can be evaluated. The professional magistrates' categorizing schemata involved small story-like connections between the given case information and the magistrates' prior knowledge. Magistrates also accumulated and combined information to form the premises of their penalty decisions. In the civil case, the experienced magistrate selected significant premises, rejected others that were offered, and constructed a series of inferences to test opposing accounts of events. Yet he also located himself at the scene in his imagination to gain a perspective on the critical events and peripheral details that made each witness' account more or less plausible. In each of these analyses, we are impressed with the importance of judges' re-creation of event sequences and their development of inferencing structures.

Reasoning in the judicial system, then, depends on mental stories and pictures and on the nature of the details that are selected for attention and given significance by inferences and implications. This analysis suggests that judicial reformers must take account of cognitive processes as well as legal procedures. The demands made on juries who are asked to reach conclusions under poor processing conditions, for instance, seem to exceed those placed on reasoners in laboratories. Courtroom reasoners respond to their tasks by using heuristics. Sentencing guidelines that can reduce a judge's inferencing operations are popular with policymakers as ways of eliminating personal styles of handling cases (Knapp, 1987), but inference cannot be entirely eliminated, and it is a moot point whether it should be. Rather, it should be characterized at the appropriate level of explanation. Then, supports for better reasoning can be devised on the basis of analyses of expert reasoning and reasoning during domain-specific procedures, such as medical diagnostics and legal argumentation (Christensen's and Rissland's chapters, this volume).

The effectiveness of story and categorizing schemata and inferencing structures can be evaluated when professional and nonprofessional judges meet the legal criteria of fair hearings. The question of fairness, however, is a legal one and must be tested in courts of appeal. These schemata and inferencing structures can also be assessed according to cognitive criteria. Reduction of uncertainty, efficiency, personal satisfaction with decisions, and jury consensus can be used as markers of the usefulness of processors' reasoning structures. In terms of the social significance of the courtroom, reasonableness enters into the discussion. Is it reasonable and, by implication, fair for a magistrate or judge to rely on his or her stored patterns of common offenders? Reasonable or not, several studies of expertise indicate that experienced professionals reason in this way (see Chi, Glaser, & Farr, 1988). If personal styles are adaptive strategies for dealing with routine, then it may be useful to help experienced practitioners identify and reflect on their categorizing tendencies. The question then arises of how cognitive schemata may serve higher judicial objectives. The civil case magistrate's careful inferences and issue testing may not be universal processes, but they suggest processes that can be identified in other courtrooms or, indeed, in other situations in which judgments are made under ambiguous and complex circumstances. Critics of judicial decision processes will miss the mark if they fail to pursue at least some of their investigations at the level of each individual's reasoning processes. The results of analyses such as those reported here could well form the basis of reflection on the reasoning structures that support judicial decisions.

ACKNOWLEDGMENTS

This chapter was prepared while the author was at the Learning Research and Development Center, University of Pittsburgh, on a grant of support from the Australian Research Council.

REFERENCES

Atkinson, J. M., & Drew, P. (1979). *Order in court: The organization of verbal interaction in judicial settings.* London: Macmillan.

Bennett, W., & Feldman, M. (1981). *Reconstructing reality in the courtroom.* New Brunswick, NJ: Rutgers University Press.

Chi, M. T. H., Feltovich, P. J., & Glaser, R. (1981). Categorization and representation of physics problems by experts and novices. *Cognitive Science, 5,* 121–152.

Chi, M. T. H., Glaser, R., & Farr, M. (Eds.). (1988). *The nature of expertise.* Hillsdale, NJ: Lawrence Erlbaum Associates.

Diamond, S. S. (1981). Exploring sources of sentence disparity. In B. D. Sales (Ed.), *Perspectives in law & psychology: Vol. 2. The trial process.* (pp. 387–412). New York: Plenum.

Grice, H. P. (1975). Logic and conversation. In P. Cole & J. Morgan (Eds.), *Syntax and semantics: Volume 3. Speech Acts* (pp. 41–58). New York: Academic Press.

Hogarth, J. (1971). *Sentencing as a human process.* Toronto, Ontario: University of Toronto Press.

Holstein, J. A. (1983). Jurors' use of judges' instructions: Conceptual and methodological issues for simulated jury studies. *Sociological Methods and Research, 11,* 501–518.

Holstein, J. A. (1985). Jurors' interpretations and jury decision making. *Law and Human Behaviour, 9,* 83–99.

Homel, R. J. (1983). Sentencing in magistrates' courts: Some lessons from a study of drinking drivers. In M. Findlay, S. Egger, & J. Sutton (Eds.), *Issues in criminal justice administration,* pp. 109–125. Sydney, Australia: Allen & Unwin.

Kerr, N., Atkin, R., Strasser, G., Meek, D., Holt, R., & Davis, J. (1976). Guilt beyond a reasonable doubt: Effects of concept definition and assigned decision rules on judgments of mock jurors. *Journal of Personality and Social Psychology, 34,* 282–294.

Knapp, K. A. (1987). Discretion in sentencing. In I. Potas (Ed.), *Sentencing in Australia: Policies, issues and reform* (pp. 89–107). Canberra, Australia: Australian Institute of Criminology.

Lawrence, J. A. (1984). Magisterial decision-making: Cognitive perspectives and processes used in courtroom information processing. In D. J. Muller, D. E. Blackman, & A. M. Chapman (Eds.), *Psychology and Law,* pp. 319–331. New York: Wiley & Sons.

Lawrence, J. A. (1987, April). *Making just decisions in magistrates' courts.* Paper presented at the Biennial Meeting of the Society for Research in Child Development, Baltimore, MD.

Lawrence, J. A. (1988). Expertise in judicial decision making. In M. T. H. Chi, R. Glaser, & M. Farr (Eds.), *The nature of expertise* (pp. 229–259). Hillsdale, NJ: Lawrence Erlbaum Associates.

Lawrence, J., & Homel, R. (1987). Sentencing in magistrates' courts: The magistrate as professional decision-maker. In I. Potas (Ed.), *Sentencing in Australia: Policies, issues and reform* (pp. 151–191). Canberra, Australia: Australian Institute of Criminology.

Lawson, R. (1968). Order of presentation as a factor in jury persuasion. *Kentucky Law Journal, 56,* 523–555.

Linz, D., Penrod, S., & McDonald, E. (1986). Attorney communication and impression making in the courtroom. *Law and Human Behaviour, 10,* 281–302.

Mandler, J. M., & Johnson, N. S. (1977). Remembrance of things parsed: Story structure and recall. *Cognitive Psychology, 9,* 111–151.

Monahan, J., & Loftus, E. (1982). Psychology of law. *Annual Review of Psychology, 33,* 441–475.

Penman, R. (1985, July). *Discourse in courts: Practical reasoning & institutional constraints.* Paper presented at the Australian Communications Association Annual Conference, Canberra, Australia.

Pennington, N., & Hastie, R. (1981). Juror decision making models: The generalization gap. *Psychological Bulletin, 89,* 246–287.

Schank, R. C., & Abelson, R. P. (1977). *Scripts, plans, and knowledge.* Hillsdale, NJ: Lawrence Erlbaum Associates.

Schultz, A. (1970). *On phenomenology and social relations.* Chicago, IL: University of Chicago Press.

Tikhomirov, O. K. (1983). Informal heuristic principles of motivation and emotion in human problem solving. In R. Groner, M. Groner, & W. F. Bischof (Eds.), *Methods of heuristics* (pp. 153–170). Hillsdale, NJ: Lawrence Erlbaum Associates.

5 Everyday Reasoning and the Roots of Intelligence

D. N. Perkins
Michael Farady
Barbara Bushey
Harvard Graduate School of Education

Be reasonable! That familiar imperative serves as just one reminder of the value we vest in people's rational conduct of their own lives and their dealings with others. We want ourselves and those with whom we interact to make sound decisions that reflect thoughtful exploration of the alternatives and the factors that recommend one over another. We want to eschew silly, hasty, and misguided beliefs in favor of a sound picture of the world. Although we may, on occasion, want to take a little fling and do something unreasonable, on the whole we all want to be reasonable.

But how well do we succeed? And, if we do not always succeed so well, on what causal factors does success, failure, or a shade in between depend? Such questions provide an opportunity to engage the issue of the nature of intelligence in its broadest sense. Apart from the technical senses that psychologists have attached to the notion (cf. Baron, 1978; Cattell, 1963; Gardner, 1983; Guilford & Hoepfner, 1971; Jensen, 1984; Sternberg, 1985), intelligence preserves a natural language meaning of great scope. Roughly speaking, intelligence is whatever a person has that empowers the person in some crosscutting way to perform intellectual tasks well. (*Crosscutting* is somewhat negotiable and, in fact, variable from theorist to theorist, but great skill in only a very narrow domain does not normally count as a sign of intelligence.) Accordingly, being reasonable, as an intellectual endeavor, plainly calls on quite different resources that might count as parts of intelligence broadly construed.

WHAT IS IT TO BE INTELLIGENT?

Consider what rival roots of intelligence might contribute to being reasonable. Perhaps good reasoning in everyday life reflects principally general intelligence (*g*) or notions closely akin to it, such as some combination of crystallized and fluid intelligence (Cattell, 1963). Fluid intelligence, particularly, may reflect some kind of largely innate neurological efficiency (Jensen, 1983, 1984); in contrast, some would argue that intelligence depends, in substantial part, on knowing how to handle one's mind well, a matter of metacognitive know-how (e.g., Baron, 1978, 1985; Perkins, 1986a, 1986b; Sternberg, 1985). For yet another contrast, contemporary research on expertise urges that good intellectual performance reflects a rich knowledge base in the domain in question (e.g., Glaser, 1984; Rabinowitz & Glaser, 1985). Arguing in that spirit, one can say that good everyday reasoning might vary principally with an individual's knowledge base relative to the everyday matters in question.

Finally, we must not neglect the affective and attitudinal side of intellectual performance. Contemporary philosophers, particularly, have emphasized that sound reasoning depends partly on strong positive attitudes toward fairness, examining the evidence, objectivity, and so on (Ennis, 1986; Paul, 1986). Moreover, obviously, a person is more likely to reason carefully about something that will have important repercussions for him- or herself or for the world in general. Although it may seem odd to include such attitudinal and affective factors in the roots of intelligence, we do well to cast a wide net rather than a narrow one because we do not want to miss the crucial causes of being more or less reasonable just because they do not fit the typical image of what constitutes intelligence.

In summary, in examining the causes of better or worse everyday reasoning, one inevitably engages fundamental issues about accounting for good intellectual performance, intelligence in its broadest sense. Do we find that everyday reasoning depends principally on *g*, (general intelligence), a knowledge base, metacognitive know-how, attitudinal and motivational factors, an even mix of the four, or what? These questions not only are central to understanding the character of human intellect, but they are also particularly appropriately pursued in this context, because of the face validity of everyday reasoning. Although one may doubt whether IQ tests or even good course grades reflect the kind of intellectual ability that "really counts," everyday reasoning has as strong a claim as one might want that it really counts. This chapter, therefore, addresses everyday reasoning and the aspects of intelligence that contribute most to its good practice.

WHAT SORT OF AN ENDEAVOR IS EVERYDAY REASONING?

When we think of reasoning, we tend to think of logic and its pitfalls: affirming the consequent, denying the antecedent, and so forth. However, to take formal logic as an adequate window on the potential and pitfalls of everyday reasoning would be hasty, indeed. At least in principle, it is possible that difficulties of quite a different character from those found in formal logic do the most mischief in everyday reasoning. Why? Because everyday reasoning demands rather different holistic argument structures.

Consider the following contrasts (Perkins, 1985b). In formal reasoning, the premises are given, and nothing is added to or subtracted from them. In informal reasoning, one may add to or subtract from the premises as one delves into one's knowledge or the newspaper for more information and as one assesses critically what was initially accepted as given. In formal reasoning, a well-formed argument on one side of the case obviates the need to look at the other, because only if the premises are outright inconsistent can there be deductive arguments yielding opposite conclusions. In informal reasoning, however, it is commonplace to find numerous arguments on both sides of the case, each one probabilistic, of course, so that no outright inconsistency results. In formal reasoning, because the steps are deductive, arguments often have a "long chain" character, as in many mathematical proofs. This long chain structure does not serve the needs of informal argument well, because a single long chain of probabilistic steps accumulates uncertainty to the point of bearing negligible weight. Consequently, in good informal reasoning, arguments have a structure that is more like a bush with many short branches.

Of course, none of this proves that informal reasoning, in fact, causes people trouble in quite different ways from formal reasoning. The contrasts show that informal reasoning *might* do so but not that it *does* do so. Equally, informal reasoning might challenge people principally through the classic pitfalls of logic. After all, formal and informal arguments alike tend to consist of principled steps from which some general warrant justifies a particular inference (Toulmin, 1958). The question needs data to resolve it, a point that is revisited later in this chapter.

However, this question, at least, has to be asked now: If we are not necessarily centering on logical lapses, how else can we clarify what we mean casually by the soundness of informal reasoning? And how can we appraise the soundness of samples of informal reasoning? A certain perspective on the nature of informal reasoning offers an approach. We have argued elsewhere (Perkins, 1985b, in press) that everyday reasoning can be characterized as a process of *situation modeling*. That is, the reasoner builds a model of a situation as it is and might be, articulating the dimensions and factors involved in an issue. Such a situation model typically involves one or more imagined scenarios and invokes a variety of common sense, causal, and intentional principles both to construct and to weigh the plausibility of alternative scenarios.

Consider, for example, a question used in some of our research: Would a nuclear freeze reduce the possibility of world war? To construct a situation model that would address this question well, one would have to reach judgments on a number of subordinate causal questions. Would a freeze lead the United States and the Soviet Union to become more peaceful nations? Would they encourage other countries to join the freeze? Would the freeze boost development of alternative armaments? A good model of this situation would also have to include other countries. Would a nuclear freeze between the United States and the Soviet Union make much of a difference in the probability of world war, considering that several other countries, such as China, Iran, and India, also have nuclear weapons? Further, is it possible that a world war could be carried on without nuclear weapons? In this fashion, an agile reasoner would proceed to develop a thorough map of all facets of the issue.

Of course, a situation model can be faulty. For instance, a simplistic response to the nuclear freeze issue just mentioned might be: "A nuclear freeze wouldn't reduce the possibility of world war, because everyone knows that the Russians would cheat. The freeze wouldn't last, because we couldn't trust them." Terse though this may seem, subjects in the line of experimentation discussed here often say little more. Typically, faulty situation modeling quickly affirms one's snap judgment in response to a vexed issue. As this example shows, two basic criteria for evaluating situation models are bias and completeness. As to bias, the example argument is entirely one-sided. As to completeness, the argument does not even elaborate thoroughly the position it adopts; there are many other ways, besides devious Russians, by which a nuclear freeze could fail to reduce the risk of war.

How does this notion of situation modeling contrast with a formal view of reasoning and its pitfalls? Simply in that the problems of bias and completeness do not arise in a formal context. If you have a one-sided, well-formed argument in a formal context, it does not reveal bias; it is a *proof.* If you have a well-formed argument in a formal context, you do not need five other strands of argument to strengthen the case; a proof is a proof. To put it another way, bias and incompleteness in the situation modeling sense are not *formal weaknesses.* Formal weaknesses—and indeed most *informal fallacies* (cf. Engel, 1976: Fearnside & Holther, 1959)—represent inferential gaps: For instance, A does not imply B if there is some shortfall of entailment in A. But problems of bias and completeness are "sins of omission." A may well constitute evidence for B, but what about all the other strands of argument? And what about additional information, rather than a logical weakness, that may impugn the A–B relation?

As these points show, thinking of informal reasoning as a process of situation modeling reveals weaknesses of reasoning with a different character from those that are prominent in formal logic. Whether this distinction plays out in an illuminating way depends on what data say about the reasoning difficulties that people do, in fact, encounter.

A TURN TO METHODOLOGY

If you want to examine people's informal reasoning, what do you do? What do the data consist in? How are they collected? How are they evaluated? Although these questions inevitably allow many answers, more than a decade of work in our laboratory has led to a fairly refined methodology for probing informal reasoning. The answers to the broad questions raised at the outset derive principally from the data this methodology has yielded. Although individual studies differ in their details, most share the broad characteristics outlined in this section.

Issues Employed

The general methodology for assessing informal reasoning involves administering a procedure that asks subjects to think about everyday social and political issues. The issues employed in the research are current and genuinely vexed, allowing several substantial arguments on both sides of the case. Pilot testing has confirmed the vexed nature of the issues for the subject populations, demonstrating that a variety of arguments on both sides appears with no strong consensus. In addition, the issues have been chosen not to depend on subjects' background knowledge, which varies greatly across the subject population; they prove accessible to junior high school students as well as adults. To give the flavor of the issues, we offer the following two questions:

1. Would providing more money for public schools significantly improve the quality of teaching and learning?
2. Would a nuclear freeze agreement signed between the United States and the Soviet Union significantly reduce the possibility of world war?

Outline of the General Procedure

The three-part experimental procedure was designed to probe subjects' reasoning performance and capacity. We first presented an issue and asked for the subject's snap judgment on the question, confidence in the snap judgment, degree of interest in the issue, and amount of time previously spent thinking about the issue.

Second, subjects were asked to think about the issue, reach a position if they felt comfortable doing so, and write down their reasons. Guidance was minimal: Subjects were urged to take their time and to try to be complete in thinking about the issue and recording their thoughts, regardless of whether they seemed important. The wording of instructions was carefully chosen to avoid triggering an argumentative stance and to favor complete, evenhanded reflection. For example, the use of the word "argument" was avoided altogether. This unstructured phase of the procedure provided a naturalistic measure of informal reasoning performance with a nudge toward completeness, which served as a baseline for assessing gains from scaffolding.

The third phase of the procedure provided subjects with generic scaffolding to help them fully and systematically deploy their capacities to reason. *Scaffolding* is a term commonly used to describe how a skilled individual can help a less skilled one to manage a performance by supporting the learner's efforts when the learner is at a loss and hanging back whenever the learner proves able (Greenfield, 1984b; Rogoff & Gardner, 1984). In the research, the questions and instructions used for scaffolding were metacognitive principles that anyone could employ to guide his or her own thinking. The scaffolding emphasized countering the difficulties of bias and completeness salient in the situation modeling perspective on informal reasoning. The scaffolding consisted of prompts to be complete, seek reasons on both sides of the case, and impartially assess their importance.

The point was to see how much further subjects could develop their initial arguments with the help of scaffolding. On the one hand, perhaps their initial arguments would turn out to rise close to some sort of capacity ceiling, with scaffolding having little impact. On the other hand, subjects might prove able to develop their arguments much more extensively in response to the scaffolding. This result would, in turn, suggest that, with a better metacognitive repertoire, subjects could construct much richer arguments on their own.

Over the course of several studies, this procedure was administered in oral as well as in written form, depending on the particular experimental context or question. When reasoning was assessed in a classroom, protocols were written. Written protocols allowed for group administration and self-pacing. When the procedure was administered to individuals in the laboratory, formats were either written or oral. Administration of an oral procedure involved an experimenter's reading instructions and prompts to a single subject and either taping the subject thinking aloud or having the subject write out his or her thoughts. A direct comparison of oral and written reporting of arguments indicated no decisive quantitative or qualitative advantage of either mode.

In addition to the reasoning procedure, each subject completed a short-form IQ measure, either the Quick Word Test (Borgatta & Corsini, 1964) or the Slossen Intelligence Test (Slossen, 1981). The measure of IQ made it possible to investigate the relation of verbal IQ to everyday reasoning.

Scoring Methodology

Two kinds of scoring were employed. Numerical quality measures, consisting of both counts and scales, gauged the extent to which arguments were well developed or subject to bias and incompleteness. Second, error analyses examined the subjects' arguments for qualitative weaknesses in reasoning and classified these lapses. The quality measure scoring was performed by two judges working independently; they coscored a random subsample of the data on which interjudge agreement was based. Judges were blind as to which were solo and which were scaffolded performances. In general, interjudge agreement was high and statistically highly significant.

Analysis of the quality measures focused on comparing the original unstructured reasoning performance to the scaffolded performance. One kind of analysis centered on certain counts. Each unstructured and scaffolded argument was scored for completeness based on the number of "my-side" and "other-side" arguments. My-side arguments are those that support subjects' initial snap judgments, whereas other-side arguments are those that oppose *them*. *Argument* is used here to denote a line of argument, which might be more or less elaborated. For instance, an argument that more money would abet student learning because schools could buy better books would count as one line of argument, regardless of whether the subject elaborated about what kind of books they might be. My-side and other-side arguments were summed to give a "both-sides" count. Separate counts were taken of the initial arguments and the scaffolded performance.

In addition to the various counts, each performance was given two ratings for overall quality, one reflecting the treatment of the subject's side and a second reflecting the treatment of the other side of the case. This holistic rating used a five-point scale ranging from 0 to 4. On this scale, 0 stood for no response at all, and 4 was assigned when most major arguments on the topic were given with good elaboration and connection to other issues. By using this scale, the scoring could incorporate considerations of soundness of the arguments not captured by mere counts. In fact, however, in the statistical treatment of the results the holistic ratings and the counts proved highly intercorrelated and disclosed essentially the same patterns.

The error analysis was conducted on one large sample of arguments gathered from subjects ranging from the first year of high school to the fourth year of graduate school and beyond. Two judges critiqued in natural language one argument from each of more than 300 subjects. The judges were familiar with argumentation in general, including formal and informal argument. They were encouraged to describe the weaknesses they saw in any terms that seemed appropriate to them. Concurrently, a classification system for categorizing weaknesses in everyday argument was developed; the judges were not familiar with this system when they critiqued the subjects' arguments. Subsequently, their criticisms were categorized according to the classification system to yield a picture of what sort of lapses, as naturalistically identified, occurred with most frequency in the sample. This categorizing was accomplished by multiple judges, again with a satisfactory degree of accord.

IS EVERYDAY REASONING GENERALLY SOUND?

Common sense may be as common as its name avers. Many have urged that although people may falter in studies of formal logic, they manage the reasoning demands of everyday life with élan. To be sure, one-sided and underdeveloped arguments seem commonplace in, for example, political speeches, newspaper editorials, and everyday conversations. But possibly they stand out because of their weaknesses; the larger part of everyday reasoning is, perhaps, entirely satisfactory. If everyday reasoning is generally sound, the factors that account for variations in it become a much less interesting issue. What, then, does our decade of research disclose?

Our findings suggest strongly that situation modeling marred by incompleteness and bias is the norm rather than the exception. When asked to reason about vexed political issues of some currency, subjects consistently produce sparse and one-sided situation models. In one study (Perkins, 1985a), first-year high schoolers generated a scant 1.8 lines of argument on their preferred side of the case and 0.6 lines of argument on the other side of the case in response to controversial questions. One might attribute this lackluster performance to the youth of the subjects. However, in the same study, first-year college students and first-year graduate students performed similarly. The college students produced 2.9 arguments and 1.1 objections, and the graduate students produced 3.3 arguments and 1.3 objections.

At least, the graduate students' performance might appear reasonably rich in my-side arguments. But how many lines of arguments are needed to explore an issue? From piloting, we know that at least six lines of argument for each side of the case were presumably within easy access for these subjects. Later scaffolding research bears this out. Therefore, one can conclude that the performances, in general, evinced faulty situation modeling in terms of both bias and depth.

These points emphasize problems of biased and incomplete reasoning. What about the error analysis, which focused on naturalistic critiques of the subjects' arguments? The categorization of critiques revealed that at least three fourths of the identified weaknesses had to do with bias and incompleteness. They were, in the phrase employed earlier, sins of omission, in which the reasoner's line of argument was all right so far as it went but in which the reasoner should have and could have considered other causal chains that would have challenged the line of argument or provided arguments on the opposite side. Thus, the results offer broad support for the notion that everyday reasoning is troubled principally by the bias and incompleteness problems of situation modeling (Perkins, in press).

If informal reasoning is not well done in general, at least the results seem to suggest that it is done better with maturation and education. Older, more educated subjects showed better performance on most of the numerical quality measures. However, this contrast does not mean as much as one might, at first, hope. The effects of education and maturation were examined by comparing the scores of first-year students with those of fourth-year students at the high school, college, and graduate school levels (Perkins, 1985b). At only the high school level did a gain in lines of argument reach statistical significance, and here the gain was still small: 0.4 lines of my-side argument in 3 years. Figures for the whole sample disclose a mean rate of gain in lines of argument of 0.1 per year of education. Other measures demonstrated similarly slow growth rates.

The minimal difference between first- and fourth-year scores *within* high school, college, and graduate school argues that the contrasts *across* high school, college, and graduate school are principally selection effects. In other words, admission processes successively filtered out those with lesser ability, so that, by graduate school, the students as a whole performed much better than students in high school. However, the same graduate students would have performed nearly as well when in high school as they did in graduate school.

Perhaps, of course, formal education is the wrong context in which to seek growth in informal reasoning. People might learn everyday reasoning in the "school of life." To test this hypothesis, the performance of people who had been out of school for a number of years was examined (Perkins, 1985b). Correlations between reasoning measures and years of life experience were negligble. As a broad generalization, the adult, out-of-school subjects performed at about the same level as the school subjects of similar educational achievement.

In summary, the overall pattern of results from several studies argues that everyday reasoning is neither very good nor likely to improve much with maturation, education, or experience of life, at least not beyond the first year of high school, the earliest period sampled. Of course, this conclusion calls for clarification on several points. If maturation, education, and experience of life do not make much difference, what does? Could motivation be the key factor? If so, perhaps people reason well enough when it matters, although in desultory fashion in our experiments. What about the role of the knowledge base? What about the impact of general intelligence? We now turn to these questions.

DOES UNDERMOTIVATION ACCOUNT FOR FAULTY SITUATION MODELING?

Motivation deriving from interest and personal investment in the issues at hand might contribute substantially to good reasoning performance. Indeed, if the results outlined earlier simply reflect low motivation on the part of the subjects, then they present nothing to worry about: People might reason well enough when given good reason to reason. But is motivation the key variable, as one might suppose? The issue of motivation has been part of the series of studies outlined here since the beginning, and at various points along the way the issue of motivation has been specifically addressed.

Subjects in the studies found the issues presented to them moderately interesting. On a rating scale in which 4 was "very interested" and 1 was "not at all interested," across studies most subjects rated their interest at 3, "somewhat interested." Of course, subjects may not have wanted to disappoint the experimenters with their disinterest. But even presuming inflated ratings by subjects, if interest were an influence on reasoning, interest should still correlate with performance. On the contrary, interest consistently failed to correlate significantly with measures of performance. How thoroughly and with what balance a person explored an issue bore little relation to the interest level the person reported.

Subjects' ratings of interest aside, in the one-on-one oral interviews it was possible to gauge directly how hard the subjects were trying, a difficult matter to judge in the strictly paper-and-pencil procedure utilized for many of the studies. We found little evidence of shyness or inhibition on the part of the subjects; they seemed interested and motivated. During the oral interviews general prompts, such as, "Can you say more?" were given. Subjects appeared willing to try to say more but often found that they had simply "run dry" on an issue. (However, with generic metacognitive prompts subjects produced balanced, quite complete situation models, as we discuss later.)

Of course, these indices of interest do not treat true personal involvement. One might expect better situation modeling in cases in which people are deeply personally invested in an issue. To investigate this question, a sample of 39 adults was enlisted. Subjects were recruited by posters soliciting people in the midst of a major decision concerning such issues as employment, health, education, family, or marital status. The subjects were interviewed about their reasoning on their personal issues as well as on one of the usual social issues. As one might expect, these subjects did, in fact, produce significantly more my-side (total of 4.7) and other-side (total of 4.4) arguments about their own decisions than when asked to reason about a social question ($p < .001$, two-tail t-test) (Perkins, in press).

These results show both a more thorough and a more balanced situation modeling of personal issues. So, when it really counts, do people reason perfectly well, making the measures reported earlier not as discouraging as they might seem? Unfortunately, the picture is more complex than that, for several reasons.

First of all, the good pro–con balance of the subjects' personal arguments can be discounted as artifactual, a limitation of the sampling design we were aware of from the outset: These subjects were located for having vexed personal issues to reason about. *Vexed* means that one finds compelling reasons for both sides. Thus, the present study gives no information on whether people tend to develop more balanced situation models for very important personal decisions. It is perfectly possible that, in everyday life, people approach many important decisions with bias, never see their genuine vexedness, and take hasty action on the basis of simplistic situation models.

The data do suggest that when people perceive a personal issue as both important and vexed, they develop a better elaborated situation model than they evolve for the social issues used in most of our studies. A key factor in this seems to be time commitment. Subjects reported spending an enormous amount of time thinking about their personal issues and talking about them with others—an average of 125 hours. They reported that the average amount of time they had spent thinking about the social issue before the investigators raised it with them was 10.5 hours. What do we make of this? On the one hand, it is encouraging to find that people do develop better situation models in such circumstances. On the other hand, one cannot be too impressed that a greater time investment by a factor of 10 yielded situation models that were richer only by about a factor of 2.

It should be added that, although the personal situation models were better elaborated, the situation models for the social issue were predictive of variations in elaboration. Performance on the personal issue correlated significantly with performance on the social issue ($r = .36$, $p < .01$). This is not a very high correlation, but it is about the same as the test–retest correlation between different social issues. Accordingly, the figures suggest that reasoning about the personal and the social issues tapped the same underlying competency, with enormous differences in preparation time accounting for more elaborated personal situation models.

A final point to bear in mind is that many circumstances in life that call for careful, responsible reasoning are not major life decisions. What political candidate to vote for, what position to take on a referendum, what attitude to take toward a troublesome employee or a demanding boss, what car to buy, and what course of action to recommend to a troubled friend are all situations that invite careful thought but that are not likely to secure 125 hours of painstaking attention or even the 10.5 hours reported for the current social issues. So, the motivation of deep personal involvement, insofar as it promotes better situation modeling, cannot be counted on in many situations in which such modeling is needed.

In summary, what can be said about undermotivation as an explanation for sparse and biased situation modeling? First of all, given an occasion that maintains thinking about an issue for a moderate period (a school board meeting, a family discussion about whom to vote for, our experimental setting), variations in topic interest may not account for variations in modeling. At least, across a variety of studies, no such influence emerged. Second, personal involvement in an issue perceived as vexed does yield a gain of about a factor of two in completeness of situation modeling albeit at a cost of enormous time investment. There is no evidence one way or another as to whether people are more likely to take a balanced view of issues that are very important to them, personally. Finally, many occasions that call for careful reasoning are not crucial life decisions. With all these considerations in mind, it seems that motivation, although plainly important, probably does not fully account for sparse and biased situation modeling or allow us to be sanguine about the quality of reasoning in everyday life.

DOES LACK OF KNOWLEDGE ACCOUNT FOR FAULTY SITUATION MODELING?

Recent research on expertise has emphasized the role of context-specific schemata in performances that might be taken to involve mostly general reasoning abilities (cf. Chase & Simon, 1973; Glaser, 1984; Rabinowitz & Glaser, 1985). With this in mind, it is natural to wonder whether the variations in subjects' reasoning as gauged in the experiments described heretofore might simply reflect their knowledge of the issue. To be sure, an effort was made to choose issues that students would not actually study as part of formal education. Nonetheless, older and more educated persons would be more likely to know more about the matter by chance, and individuals would, of course, vary in their degree of chance knowledge.

In investigating the role of knowledge, we presumed that the knowledge most directly relevant would be prior experience in thinking about the issue. One might object to this on the grounds that more prior thinking might mean a more settled position on the issue. However, more prior thinking on a controversial issue, much of which would likely be in conversational contexts with more than one side represented, ought to produce more familiarity with the structure of arguments on both sides and thus a better situation model, however settled one's position. Consequently, subjects were asked whether they had thought about the issue at all before. If they responded positively, they were asked to indicate how much total time they had spent thinking about it in terms of number of minutes up to an hour or number of hours.

In general, the studies did not show significant correlations between this "prior-thought" variable and everyday reasoning performance, as measured by the counts of lines of argument, degree of one-sidedness, and quality ratings. In one study, a significant correlation ($r = -.34, p < .001$) appeared between prior thought and the number of prompts given by the experimenter to keep the subject on the topic under consideration. But this relationship did not correspond to the quality of argument per se. However, it is understandable that a person who has thought extensively about an issue is likely to be able to zero in on it better than a person who is exploring it for the first time.

In sum, no evidence emerged for a relation between the quality of situation modeling and prior familiarity with the issues. But how could it be that prior knowledge does not make a difference? The results suggest that knowledge of the issues did not vary extremely widely in the subject population; had it done so, surely situation modeling would have been affected.

DO VARIATIONS IN GENERAL INTELLIGENCE AFFECT SITUATION MODELING?

As mentioned earlier, the studies reviewed here have found little improvement in everyday reasoning ability in relation to either age or education. Such findings suggest that skill in everyday reasoning may be primarily a function of innate intellectual competence. The relation of IQ to everyday reasoning skills speaks to this issue.

Regression analyses of pooled student and pooled nonstudent data from the major study reported by Perkins (1985a) provided estimates of the role of IQ. For the student sample, sizable correlations emerged between IQ and total number of arguments ($r = .47, p < .001$) and between IQ and other-side arguments ($r =$

.32, $p < .001$), the latter considerably smaller than the former. The nonstudent sample yielded a correlation between IQ and total number of arguments of a somewhat lesser magnitude ($r = .29, p < .06$) and a nonsignificant relationship between IQ and other-side arguments ($r = .10$, n.s.). Subsequent studies revealed similar correlations ($r =$ approximately .3) between my-side arguments and IQ.

The performance-versus-competence study, in which subjects were provided with generic cues to stimulate performance, revealed a curious relationship between IQ and argument production. Although IQ correlated significantly with my-side arguments produced without prompting ($r = .53, p < .02, n = 20$), its correlation with other-side arguments was nonsignificant and negative ($r = -.18, n = 20$). This study was relatively small, but it points up an intriguing pattern of correlations with IQ that is corroborated by data from other studies. To pursue the issue, we pooled the performances of 99 students ranging from first-year liberal arts undergraduates to first-year law school students and graduate students. Analysis of the pooled data disclosed significant correlations between IQ and my-side arguments ($r = .37, p < .001$) but virtually no correlation between IQ and other-side arguments ($r = .08$, n.s.).

In sum, certainly IQ makes a contribution to well-elaborated situation models, but there is an important caveat. It appears that people selectively tap their IQ when reasoning. The pattern that emerged shows weak to moderate positive correlation between intelligence as measured by IQ and my-side arguments, and virtually no correlation between IQ and other-side arguments. Only in one sample of the large Perkins (1985a) study do we find significant correlations between IQ and other-side arguments, and these are considerably lower than the correlations between IQ and my-side arguments. In effect, people invest their IQ in buttressing their own case rather than in exploring the entire issue more fully and evenhandedly.

DOES KNOW-HOW ABOUT REASONING IMPROVE SITUATION MODELING?

Both the problem of one-sidedness and the fact that IQ measures account for only a modest part of the variance in situation modeling demonstrate room for a major role for know-how about reasoning. On the one hand, if people knew better how to handle situation modeling, perhaps they would do a better job of it. On the other hand, it is also possible that people typically reason close to some kind of performance ceiling. They are doing as well as they can, at least when not afforded the luxury of many weeks to think out a problem, as with the subjects who were making major life decisions.

This question was examined by a number of studies in which the authors sought to modify the momentary or long-term know-how of subjects by giving directions or teaching strategies (Perkins, Bushey, & Farady, 1986). For example, a study was designed in which an experimenter presented high school subjects with an issue and instructed them outright to give as many reasons as possible, even if they seemed insignificant, and to give reasons on both sides of the case. The subjects' performance following these instructions was then compared to their previous, unaided performance. In light of the initial performance, subjects' simply being told to generate many reasons and to attend to the other side of the case evoked little change in number of my-side arguments but a substantial increase (from 0.8 to 2.0, or a gain of 150%) in other-side arguments. This study demonstrates that some know-how about reasoning can be transmitted and improve situation modeling simply by changing the broad demand characteristics of the task. It is interesting to note, however, that just asking for more my-side reasons did not yield gains.

If explicit directions can improve momentary performance so easily, at least on the other side of the case, what about longer term instructional programs that support and encourage this sort of reasoning more than conventional instruction? With this and related questions in mind, we examined the impact on students' reasoning of a term in a high school debate class; the first year of a liberal arts program noteworthy for its efforts to develop general reasoning skills; a semester at a graduate school of education, focusing on students taking a course that encouraged exploratory reasoning; and the first year of law school.

The preinstruction levels of performance were lackluster and resembled those discussed earlier (Perkins, 1985a) of conventional education at the high school, college, and graduate school levels. On the posttests, only the debate class and the liberal arts program showed significant gains. These gains were modest: one line of my-side argument for the debate class and 0.6 lines of my-side argument for the liberal arts program. Nonetheless, such figures are substantially greater than the average rate of 0.1 lines of argument per year of education from the earlier studies. Interestingly, the gains appear only on the my-side part of the performance, even though, at least in the debate class, emphasis constantly fell on preparation for arguing either side of the case.

Another study (Perkins et al., 1986) specifically examined gains in situation modeling in response to metacognitive prompts. Subjects reasoned about an issue until they had no more to say. They were pressed on this point, to be sure that they were not holding back reasons that they did not think worth mentioning. Then the investigator offered generic advice. For instance, when subjects mentioned no reasons on the side of the case opposite their own, the investigator said, "You've mentioned some reasons why . . . [the conclusion]. Can you think of any reasons, even though you might disagree with them, why someone might say . . . [opposite conclusion]?". This and other prompts not specific to the issue served as scaffolding to support subjects' continued exploration of the issue. The scaffolds consisted of questions or instructions that, in principle, a person could ask himself or herself.

When the investigator provided the generic know-how after subjects thought they had run dry, they were able to improve on their initial performances dramatically in terms of both bias and completeness. In response to scaffolding, my-side arguments increased by 109% (3.8 new lines of argument), and other-side arguments increased by 700% (4.9 new lines of argument). Because people can balance and elaborate their situation models with generic prompts from an investigator, it follows that, in principle, they can likewise scaffold themselves to perform better. Their premature running dry, despite the experimenter's general urging to say more if they could and their apparent willingness to comply, suggests that they did not know how to scaffold themselves to be more generative.

But can people learn to scaffold themselves to reason more fully? To address this question, a short, high-school-level course in situation modeling was devised. The course consisted of 16 class sessions given at the rate of four 1-hour lessons per week. This was viewed as quite a short intervention, considering that we hoped to affect well-entrenched habits of mental organization. Class content consisted of a variety of exercises, designed to facilitate generativity and attention to both sides of the case. For instance, subjects analyzed the arguments contained in brief essays, wrote short arguments, and learned several strategies to facilitate skilled situation modeling. In essence, this intervention sought to provide basic know-how about generating arguments that are both evenhanded and thorough.

The intervention had its principal impact on bias in situation modeling. Along with a small, nonsignificant increase in my-side arguments, subjects showed a significant increase in other-side arguments, producing one other-side argument before instruction but two afterwards ($p < .001$, one-tailed t test). This is not all that much, but it is more than an order of magnitude greater than the growth rate of reasoning performances without any special intervention. We also believe, in retrospect, that much stronger interventions are possible through even more direct attention to strategies and task demands than these teaching experiments offered. It should be added that there is no presumption of lasting effects or transfer beyond the instructional context. The principal aim of the experiment was to demonstrate simply that change in solo performance is possible. Given evidence that it is, we argue that lasting, transferable change is possible with sufficient effort.

These results join with a larger corpus of findings that suggests that cognitive abilities of various sorts can be enhanced by instruction that emphasizes metacognitive awareness and the use of strategies. For example, in the area of reading, Palincsar and Brown (1984) have demonstrated striking gains by students of low reading ability in their retention and transfer of ability to a variety of settings of reading. Schoenfeld (1982; Schoenfeld & Herrmann, 1982) has reported substantial improvement in college students' mathematical problem solving through an intervention that emphasizes heuristics and metacognitive self-monitoring. Further results of this sort may be found in, for instance, Nickerson, Perkins, and Smith (1985).

In summary, a variety of experiments argue that situation modeling can be improved by direct or even semidirect instruction. Educational intervention can improve the completeness of situation modeling and biased situation modeling as well. The scaffolding study, in particular, forecasts that quite dramatic improvements are possible if subjects learn to scaffold themselves fairly fully in reasoning about an issue. Good situation modeling is, in substantial part, a matter of know-how.

WHY PEOPLE REASON AS THEY DO: A MAKES-SENSE EPISTEMOLOGY

This survey of several factors that impinge on situation modeling has turned up a couple of puzzles that call for resolution. First of all, it appears that people could easily develop situation models much better than they do. Why the shortfall? Second, intelligence in the psychometric sense—IQ—appears not to contribute as straightforwardly to good situation modeling as one might suppose. Why not?

The previous section suggests a broad answer to both of these questions. Good situation modeling involves a certain amount of know-how. You need to know about the traps of one-sided thinking, ways to provoke yourself to think more thoroughly when you seem to be running dry, and so on. The shortfall in situation modeling reflects a lack of this metacognitive know-how. The vexed relation to IQ also is explained: More raw brain power, of the sort that IQ supposedly measures, does not necessarily yield better situation modeling unless it is wisely deployed. The know-how to do so is needed, too.

Okay as far as it goes, this explanation in terms of know-how nonetheless seems fundamentally dissatisfying. The know-how in question is not that esoteric. Why do people not figure it out for themselves? Why are they not taught it in schools? Why do they not pick it up from parents and friends? When nearly every person almost effortlessly learns to speak a native language and navigate in the complex environment of his or her town or city, why does some relatively simple know-how about good situation modeling come so hard? It is almost as though there were something in the way.

Perhaps what is in the way is a competing standard for good situation modeling. When people treat vexed issues like nonvexed issues and generate the barest of situation models, presumably they have satisfied their criterion for "true" or adequate situation modeling. The criterion appears to be that the model "makes sense": It hangs together well and displays high congruence with one's most prominent prior beliefs. Notice how little of a situation model this standard requires. A bald assertion of a claim without reasons can hang together well and display high congruence with prominent prior beliefs. In such a case, the claim seems self-evident. Even if a person has to work a little harder to build a model, the person only has to get to the point of telling one story about the situation that weaves together the facts in one way, from one point of view, congruent with the person's prior beliefs. Then the model "makes sense." When sense is achieved, there is no need to continue. Indeed, because further examination of an issue might produce contrary evidence and diminish or cloud the sense of one's first pass, there is probably reinforcement for early closure to reduce the possibility of cognitive dissonance. Such a makes-sense approach is quick, easy, and, for many purposes, perfectly adequate.

To put a name to this syndrome, we have written before of people having a *makes-sense epistemology* (Perkins, Allen, & Hafner, 1983). A person's epistemology refers to the person's tacit or explicit grounds for belief. A makes-sense epistemology is one in which the primary criterion of truth is making sense in the sense just described. This is, of course, not an epistemology that a person harbors explicitly as an overt philosophy. It is a default epistemology, a pattern that the mind falls into as the simplest, more-or-less functional thing to do.

What makes this makes-sense epistemology so robust? A number of factors can be suggested. First of all, it is quick, easy, and, for many purposes, perfectly adequate. The criteria of hanging together and matching prominent prior beliefs provide a fairly strong filter against bad models, particularly if one has had considerable experience in the domain in question. Second, the makes-sense epistemology suits well the character of the human organism as an information processor of significantly limited capacity (cf. Newell & Simon, 1972): People can stop thinking about something after achieving superficial sense rather than pressing on to more complications. Third, the makes-sense epistemology provides a line of ego defense. If one thinks beyond what makes superficial sense, one may find oneself pressed to question cherished beliefs about who one is or what the world is like (cf. Paul, 1986, 1987).

Two puzzles were introduced earlier: why people do not build better situation models when they easily can do so and why intelligence in the sense of IQ does not contribute more straightforwardly to good situation modeling. A first answer points out that metacognitive know-how is crucial to good situation modeling but is apparently lacking. But, why? The notion of a makes-sense epistemology helps us to explain why. The need for this metacognitive know-how is not very salient, because a makes-sense epistemology keeps people pretty happy with their beliefs and adequately functional most of the time.

HOW PEOPLE COULD REASON BETTER: A CRITICAL EPISTEMOLOGY

It is useful to have a contrasting notion to the makes-sense epistemology just outlined. One might speak of a *critical epistemology* (cf. Perkins et al., 1983). A critical epistemology incorporates higher standards for good situation models. It is not enough for a particular story about a situation to hang together: One must consider what other, rather different stories might also hang together. It is not enough for a particular story to match one's prominent prior beliefs: One should check one's data base of information and experience more thoroughly for inconsistencies. Often, one should seek further information. As we construe it, a critical epistemology includes not only this broad know-how about which criteria to use for a good situation model but also heuristic know-how about how to build a better model, for instance, how to think of more reasons, construct counterexamples, and so on. In addition, a critical epistemology incorporates epistemic feelings and values about objectivity, fair play, the importance of taking multiple perspectives, and so on. In similar spirit, Scheffler (1982) wrote of the importance of "cognitive emotions" in guiding cognition, and Paul (1986, 1987) wrote of the importance of "strong sense" critical thinking, in which the thinker willingly and objectively engages controversies between competing value and belief systems.

Of course, by describing this critical epistemology we do not mean to create an either-you-have-it-or-you-don't dichotomy between a makes-sense and a critical epistemology but rather to define a direction of development. An epistemological continuum exists, reflecting the soundness of the justifications offered for the adequacy of situation models. These justifications range from bald, intuitive assertions on the extreme makes-sense side to more complex, critical models in which an issue may be looked at from a variety of perspectives and may be adjusted for inclinations in the direction of overgeneralization, bias, and other common pitfalls of reasoning. Obviously, one can have a critical epistemology in various respects and to various degrees. Also, everyday experience teaches that we, as individuals, vary from occasion to occasion in the care we take as practicing epistemologists. Sometimes, harried and hurried, the wisest person falls into the pattern of a makes-sense epistemologist. Likewise, not very agile thinkers, in circumstances that neither arouse their prejudices nor provoke indifference, may display much more of a critical epistemology than they usually do.

As noted earlier, a makes-sense epistemology works pretty well most of the time. Perhaps it is worth a moment to stand back from our enterprise of trying to explain why people reason as they do and contemplate how people should reason and why. Critical epistemologists clearly work harder than makes-sense epistemologists. Why should they bother? A makes-sense model is often adequate. Or is it? Makes-sense epistemology is obviously adequate for making the plethora of little decisions that arise during the course of a life. But people do not simply adjust or fit in to a life. The more vigorous and compelling strands of modern psychology and philosophy hold that reasoning is, in fact, constitutive of what we take our lives to be. We do not just stub our toes on reality; we also constitute or generate it. So, a makes-sense epistemology is constitutive of a makes-sense sort of reality, in which a makes-sense sort of life is perfectly at home.

A makes-sense epistemology becomes inadequate, though, when an unusual situation arises in which there is little obvious congruence with one's current beliefs. To make sense of such dilemmas, a hard-core makes-sense epistemologist must work to avoid seeing incongruities even when they virtually abound. Makes-sense epistemologists must conceive a life course that is relatively simple and straightforward, and they struggle inefficiently when messy problems arise. Unfortunately, into each life a few messy problems do fall, be they puberty, divorce, obstreperous children, car repairs, or death. Moreover, modern times are fraught with complex decisions about environmental, economic, and other issues that affect everyone. Because it tends to gloss over incongruities, a makes-sense epistemology leaves people ill-equipped for decisions they have to make in such serious contexts. Because it is inadequate for dealing with problems that afford no solutions that feel right, a makes-sense epistemology constrains people from effectively helping either themselves or others when the needs are greatest.

And what of critical epistemologists? Critical epistemologists must also make sense. To fail to do so is to become incoherent to oneself and to one's fellow travelers, which is no help to anyone. But sense that is critically made is generally richer in its implications, in the constraints that it recognizes, and in the options that it suggests than the sense to which people usually aspire. The endeavor of critical thought approaches a situation not with the goal of avoiding options and possibilities but with an inclination to create them through a deep understanding of the situation.

The habits of the critical epistemologist equip him or her for even the most difficult of decisions. These decisions cannot, of course, be made easily, but by being able to generate several alternatives and consider more than one point of view, a person can feel satisfied that he or she has made a reasonable decision. A well-reasoned decision is less likely to produce surprise or impotence in the face of its consequences. Further, if we grant that people do really make the meaning that is experienced as one's life, then it is clear that critical epistemologists, individually and collectively, generate qualitatively different kinds of lives than makes-sense epistemologists. Critical epistemology leads to the construction of experience that is richer in possibilities and more manageable. Whether critical epistemologists are *happier* we do not venture to say. But it seems plain that their better models of the world afford more perspective, variety, and control over fate and fortune.

THE ROOTS OF INTELLIGENCE

What are the roots of intelligence, broadly construed? This question has been the leitmotif for the present review. Everyday reasoning is plainly an important manifestation of intelligence. To examine what factors in the psychological makeup of the individual make everyday reasoning more or less effective is to examine the roots of intelligence.

This review of research has sought to disentangle several likely contributing factors: interest in issues, knowledge of specific issues, IQ, and metacognitive know-how. In embarking on such an enterprise, one can imagine a worst-case scenario in which the findings indicate that everything contributes moderately in a thoroughly entangled way, and no clear discriminations can be made. Indeed, as a point of logic, such an outcome might seem almost inevitable. How could interest, knowledge, IQ, and metacognitive know-how *not* each count enormously? Even to ask the question is to evoke analogies like asking whether motors or wheels or gasoline are more important to a car: All seem transparently part of the system that gets the result. However, despite these discouraging signs, fairly clear answers have emerged about the relative contributions of these components to everyday reasoning. What are these answers, and why do they come out the way they do?

Prior Knowledge

The findings indicate a relatively minor role of prior knowledge about particular issues to account for differences in good situation modeling. But how can this be, particularly considering the contemporary research on expertise that has emphasized the importance of domain-specific schematic repertoires? In part, the result is an artifact of experimental design: Issues were sought in which no subject group was likely to have high expertise. However, there is a broader reason as well. By its very nature, everyday reasoning constantly engages people in reasoning about problems in which they lack expertise. We have to vote for candidates, consider referenda, advise friends, deal with squabbles in the work place, make major purchase decisions, and so on. We cannot possibly accumulate real expertise in all these things. In other words, everyday reasoning, because of its eclectic reach, intrinsically involves reasoning as best one can with one's general knowledge and experience about issues in which one probably does not have a great deal of specific expertise. Moreover, the teaching and scaffolding experiments show that the same general knowledge base can be brought to bear much more or less fully on an issue, depending on how vigorously and evenhandedly a reasoner probes.

Interest

The results suggest that interest plays a moderate role in building situation models but not nearly as important a role as one might suppose. How can this be? First of all, interest does not necessarily imply good situation modeling: A person may have strong interest yet bring a strong initial bias to a situation, or a person may have strong interest and no great initial bias yet fail to perceive how a situation is vexed and hence not engage in a serious effort to build a careful situation model. Moreover, even if interest straightforwardly promoted good situation modeling, life presents an abundance of situations in which we ought to reason well yet do not have strong interest—or, at least, not self-interest. The motivation, thus, has to come from a sense of responsibility.

IQ

The results show a definite influence of IQ on situation modeling, but a somewhat oblique influence. Higher IQ correlates with more generativity on one's preferred side of a case. However, situation models produced by individuals with higher IQs tend to be more biased, not less, and still fall well short of thorough elaboration even on the preferred side of the case. How can this be? As discussed earlier, the sort of potency measured by IQ can be deployed more or less wisely. Having a high IQ gives no guarantee of one's using it well any more than having alot of horsepower under the hood of your car guarantees your driving the car well.

Metacognitive Know-How

The results argue that metacognitive know-how about the demands, opportunities, and pitfalls of situation modeling has a very substantial influence. Attitudes of objectivity, fair play, and so on, together with this know-how, comprise a critical epistemology that fosters good situation modeling. Moreover, such know-how can be taught, and such attitudes can be fostered.

How is it, then, that we do not see as much of this critical epistemology as we would like in everyday reasoning? Our suggestion is that a makes-sense epistemology, with its tacit criteria that models hang together and match prominent prior beliefs, dominates much of everyday reasoning and, indeed, serves tolerably well in many situations. This makes-sense epistemology stands in the way of people feeling a strong press for and trying to develop a more sophisticated critical epistemology.

Here, of course, is where education can help. In normal educational practice, there is very little direct teaching of a critical epistemology—in fact, there probably is some undermining of it. Yet the opportunity to do better is clear. As noted earlier, not only the present line of investigation but a number of others have produced results suggesting that cognitive skills in general can be improved. Moreover, in many ways, the know-how and attitudes of a critical epistemology are fairly accessible—much simpler in outline than trigonometry. Finally, an effort to teach something for which many people feel no great need is hardly out of place in educational practice: A good deal of education seeks to teach people things they feel no great need to know, such as trigonometry. Indeed, the people may often be right. In the case of a critical epistemology, however, we urge that they are wrong. Because a makes-sense epistemology means that people are not likely to seek out a critical epistemology for themselves, it becomes the responsibility of education to add the critical edge to everyday reasoning.

REFERENCES

Baron, J. (1978). Intelligence and general strategies. In G. Underwood (Ed.), *Strategies in informa-tion processing* (pp. 403–450). London: Academic Press.

Baron, J. (1985). *Rationality and intelligence*. New York: Cambridge University Press.

Borgatta, E. F., & Corsini, R. J. (1964). *Quick Word Test*. New York: Harcourt, Brace & World.

Cattell, R. B. (1963). Theory of fluid and crystallized intelligence: A critical experiment. *Journal of Educational Psychology, 54,* 1–22.

Chase, W. C., & Simon, H. A. (1973). Perception in chess. *Cognitive Psychology, 4,* 55–81.

Engel, S. M. (1976). *With good reason: An introduction to informal fallacies*. New York: St. Martin's Press.

Ennis, R. H. (1986). A taxonomy of critical thinking dispositions and abilities. In J. B. Baron & R. S. Sternberg (Eds.). *Teaching thinking skills: Theory and practice* (pp. 9–26). New York: W. H. Freeman.

Fearnside, W. W., & Holther, W. B. (1959). *Fallacy: The counterfeit of argument*. Englewood Cliffs, NJ: Prentice-Hall.

Gardner, H. (1983). *Frames of mind*. New York: Basic Books.

Glaser, R. (1984). Education and thinking: The role of knowledge. *American Psychologist, 39,* 93–104.

Greenfield, P. M. (1984). A theory of the teacher in the learning activities of everyday life. In B. Rogoff & J. Lave (Eds.), *Everyday cognition: Its development in social context* (pp. 117–138). Cambridge, MA: Harvard University Press.

Guilford, J. P., & Hoepfner, R. (1971). *The analysis of intelligence*. New York: McGraw-Hill.

Jensen, A. R. (1983). The nonmanipulable and effectively manipulable variables of education. *Education and Society, 1*(1), 51–62.

Jensen, A. R. (1984). Test validity: *g* versus the specificity doctrine. *Journal of Social and Biolog-ical Structures, 7,* 93–118.

Newell, A., & Simon, H. (1972). *Human problem solving*. Englewood Cliffs, NJ: Prentice-Hall.

Nickerson, R., Perkins, D. N., & Smith, E. (1985). *The teaching of thinking*. Hillsdale, NJ: Lawrence Erlbaum Associates.

Palincsar, A. S., & Brown, A. L. (1984). Reciprocal teaching of comprehension-fostering and comprehension-monitoring activities. *Cognition and Instruction, 1,* 117–175.

Paul, R. (1986). Dialogical thinking: Critical thought essential to the acquisition of rational knowl-edge and passions. In J. Baron & R. Sternberg (Eds.), *Teaching thinking skills: Theory and practice* (pp. 127–148). New York: W. H. Freeman.

Paul, R. (1987). Critical thinking and the critical person. In D. Perkins, J. Lochhead, & J. Bishop (Eds.), *Thinking: The second international conference* (pp. 373–403). Hillsdale, NJ: Lawrence Erlbaum Associates.

Perkins D. N. (1985a). Postprimary education has little impact on informal reasoning. *Journal of Educational Psychology, 77,* 562–571.

Perkins, D. N. (1985b). Reasoning as imagination. *Interchange, 16*(1), 14–26.

Perkins, D. N. (1986a). Thinking frames. *Educational Leadership, 43*(8), 4–10.

Perkins, D. N. (1986b). Thinking frames: An integrative perspective on teaching cognitive skills. In J. B. Baron & R. S. Sternberg (Eds.), *Teaching thinking skills: Theory and practice* (pp. 41–61). New York: W. H. Freeman.

Perkins, D. N. (in press). Reasoning as it is and could be. In D. Topping, D. Crowell, & V. Kobayashi (Eds.), *Thinking: The third international conference*. Hillsdale, NJ: Lawrence Erlbaum Associates.

Perkins, D. N., Allen, R., & Hafner, J. (1983). Difficulties in everyday reasoning. In W. Maxwell (Ed.), *Thinking: The frontier expands* (pp. 177–189). Hillsdale, NJ: Lawrence Erlbaum Associates.

Perkins, D. N., Bushey, B., & Farady, M. (1986). *Learning to reason* (Final report for grant no. NIE-G-83-0028). Cambridge, MA: Harvard Graduate School of Education.

Rabinowitz, M., & Glaser, R. (1985). Cognitive structure and process in highly competent performance. In F. D. Horowitz & M. O'Brien (Eds.), *The gifted and talented: Developmental perspectives* (pp. 75–98). Washington, DC: American Psychological Association.

Rogoff, B., & Gardner, W. (1984). Adult guidance of cognitive development. In B. Rogoff & J. Lave (Eds.), *Everyday cognition: Its development in social context* (pp. 95–116). Cambridge, MA: Harvard University Press.

Scheffler, I. (1982). In praise of the cognitive emotions. In I. Scheffler (Ed.), *Science and subjectivity* (2nd ed.) (pp. 139–157). Indianapolis, IN: Hackett.

Schoenfeld, A. H. (1982). Measures of problem-solving performance and of problem-solving instruction. *Journal for Research in Mathematics Education, 13*(1), 31–49.

Schoenfeld, A. H., & Herrmann, D. J. (1982). Problem perception and knowledge structure in expert and novice mathematical problem solvers. *Journal of Experimental Psychology: Learning, Memory, and Cognition, 8,* 484–494.

Slossen, R. L. (1981). *Slossen Intelligence Test.* New York: Slossen Educational Publications.

Sternberg, R. J. (1985). *Beyond IQ: A triarchic theory of human intelligence.* New York: Cambridge University Press.

Toulmin, S. E. (1958). *The uses of argument.* Cambridge, England: Cambridge University Press.

6 Informal Reasoning in Inner-City Children

Dalton Miller-Jones
City University of New York Graduate School

This chapter examines the relationship between culture and informal reasoning processes. In the analyses that follow, it is argued that: (a) among the important distinctions between informal and formal reasoning is that of the contextual or situational quality of informal reasoning, and (b) some forms of informal reasoning may be viewed as a function of culture or, more specifically, of particular features of children's social-cognitive ecologies. It is proposed that for some members of a cultural community, reasoning processes become independent of the specific context in which they are developed, whereas for others, reasoning remains situationally contingent.

Before proceeding, it is important to first establish what, in my view, are the critical features of the formal—informal reasoning distinction. A brief review of cross-cultural research on cognitive processes is then provided to locate our work within this larger framework.

INFORMAL REASONING

The definition offered in the introduction to this volume considers informal reasoning as reasoning carried on outside the formal contexts of mathematics and symbolic logic. In involves reasoning about causes and consequences of events or the pros and cons of particular decision alternatives. The individual's task is to use his or her knowledge to identify premises that are relevant to a particular proposition and build plausible lines of argumentation. It should be noted that informal reasoning, according to this definition and others like it, refers both to qualities of the reasoning itself (e.g., determining causes, making inferences) and to the content of the reasoning, or what is reasoned about (e.g., which political candidate to vote for or what model car to buy). At least implied is a third factor: the context or situation. For example, one can reason about voting for a candidate or buying a car either in a school problem-solving context or in the context of the actual event in daily life.

The distinction between formal and informal reasoning that informs the approach taken here attempts to take all of these aspects into account. The inclusion of the problem's content and context, its "situational contingency," as part of the definition of informal reasoning implies that something other than the nature of the reasoning alone determines the distinction—something having to do with the specifics of a situation.

From my perspective, formal reasoning seeks to reduce this "situational contingency" of thinking by relying instead on the underlying logical relations (determined by the imposition of a closed deductive system) whereas informal reasoning seeks utilization of resources that are specific to a situation. In this view, informal reasoning is characterized by the way in which particular factors of the situation enter into the reasoning. Whereas formal reasoning is closed with respect to the deductive system that is employed, informal reasoning may be considered closed with respect to the situation in which it is applied.

Informal reasoning has been conceptualized partly in reaction to judgments about people's reasoning abilities that derive from a conception of "good" reasoning, against which criteria many people's reasoning has been found deficient. This conception of good reasoning is based on a formal system of well-defined concepts allowing logically necessary deductions independent of the particulars of a given situation.

In my view, we need an appreciation of informal reasoning on its own terms that is appropriate under a wide range of conditions in which: (a) judgments are supported by a variety of social and cultural meanings, and (b) the cost of logical deductive certainty taxes resources too much. Under such conditions, an important aspect of situated informal reasoning is its emergent quality, that is, how the solution of a problem is constructed during the encounter with the problem. I am referring here to a distinction between (a) conceptualizing the reasoning in terms of accessing a rule or procedure for solving the problem (a kind of disembodied logic located in the person) that is imposed on the task, and (b) conceptualizing the reasoning as emerging from the dynamic way in which the problem is experienced, the way in which the person enters the problem, and the movement of attention between available information and the question to be answered. Many forms of everyday reasoning seem to have the quality of emergence over time, from the specifics of the current situation.

This emergent quality of situated thinking has most often led to a view of informal reasoning as heuristics, or mental shortcuts that are reasonably effective in most everyday situations. However, heuristics can also foster the kinds of errors in reasoning that Kahneman and Tversky (1972, 1973) have referred to as the representativeness and availability heuristics. Situated informal reasoning, however, need not be fallacious. Indeed, there are ethnographic accounts that show how the deductive qualities of thought can be found in examples of informally situated reasoning (Heath, 1983). For example, Labov (1969) portrayed such well-formed reasoning by a Black adolescent male, Larry, a gang member, interviewed by a Black male adult, JL:

> JL: What happens to you after you die? Do you know?
> Larry: Yeah, I know. (What?) After they put you in the ground, your body turns into-ah-bones, an'shit.
> JL: What happens to your spirit?
> Larry: Your spirit—soon as you die, your spirit leaves you. (And where does the spirit go?) Well, it all depends . . . (On what?) You know, like some people say if you're good an shit, your spirit going' t'heaven . . .'n'if you bad your spirit goin' to hell. Well, bullshit! Your spirit goin' to hell anyway, good or bad.
> JL: Why?
> Larry: Why? I'll tell you why. 'cause, you see, doesn't nobody really know that it's a God, y'know, 'cause I mean I have seen Black gods, pink gods, white gods, all color gods, and don't nobody know it's really a God. An' when they be sayin' if you good, you goin' t'heaven, tha's bullshit, 'cause you ain't going' to no heaven, 'cause it ain't no heaven for you to go to. (pp. 164–165)

Labov outlined the logical form of Larry's argument, which might be obscured by other qualities of the narrative. The basic argument is to deny the interdependent propositions:

(A) If you are good, (B) then your spirit will go to heaven.
(-A) If you are bad, (C) then your spirit will go to hell.

Larry denies (B) and asserts that if (A) or (-A), then (C). His argument may be outlined as follows:

1. Everyone has a different idea of what God is like.
2. Therefore, nobody really knows that God exists.
3. If there is a heaven, it was made by God.
4. If God doesn't exist, he couldn't have made heaven.
5. Therefore, heaven does not exist.
6. You can't go somewhere that doesn't exist.
   (-B) Therefore, you can't go to heaven.
   (C) Therefore, you are going to hell.

Part of the argument is implicit; the connection if (2), then (-B) leaves unstated the connecting links (3) and (4). Otherwise, the case is made explicitly and economically. Labov (1969) observed that:

> This hypothetical argument is not carried on at a high level of seriousness. . . .
> There is no personal commitment to any of these propositions, and no reluctance to

strengthen one's argument by bending the rules of logic as in the (2)–(5) sequence. But if the opponent invokes the rules of logic, they hold. . . . In this case, he (the interviewer JL) pointed out the fallacy that the argument (2)–(6) leads to (-C) [not going to hell] as well as (-B), so it cannot be used to support Larry's assertion (C):

JL: Well, if there's no heaven, how could there be a hell?

Larry: I mean-ye-eah. Well let me tell you, it ain't no hell, 'cause this is hell right here, y'know! (This is hell?) Yeah, this is hell right here! (pp. 165–166)

Larry's move is to deny his original (3)–(4)–(5) argument, and to assert that, because hell is here, conclusion (C) stands. The emergent qualities of the reasoning in this interview can be seen in the speaker's initial reticence to commit himself to anything until the situation is better defined. The opening bid, "Do you know what happens to you after you die?" is met with a simple, "Yes, I know," which returns the onus to define and specify the context to the initiator. This same device is used in response to the question, "Where does the spirit go?" which is followed by the answer, "Well, it all depends," and reveals the gradual and highly contingent process by which the topic of the conversation gets established. Labov noted that, in addition to being quick, ingenious, and decisive, these responses are not "ready-made or preconceived arguments, but new propositions devised to win the logical argument in the game being played" (1969, p. 166).

Although most readers are impressed, as I am, by such ethnographic accounts, there are problems in any attempt to determine systematic cultural influences on reasoning on the basis of collections of these anecdotal accounts. First, it is frequently difficult to locate these performances within the overall structure of culturally organized activities. Second, the extent to which one can extrapolate from the performance of an individual to a characterization of the cultural group as a whole is questionable. At best, it can only be argued that such exemplary performances as the one just represented provide measures of a culture's potential for particular kinds of reasoning. These measures may be referred to, respectively, as task or *context typicality* and *performance representativeness,* and they present difficulties to researchers in any analysis of reasoning performance for "cultural effects."

I consider the reasoning that a person uses to be related to the sociocultural meanings afforded by the task content and context. The research I discuss later was originally designed to describe how the differences of social ecologies may influence the cognitive organizations children bring to problem-solving tasks. It assumed that culture produces relatively enduring reasoning strategies as trait-like characteristics of individuals. Because it was not initially conceived to investigate situated and emergent qualities of reasoning, these qualities of the performance were only observed after the fact. This project represents one tradition in cross-cultural research on cognitive processes; before discussing it, I place our approach to the informal–formal reasoning distinction in the context of cross-cultural research on cognition. I do this because this research has become very concerned with what I have referred to as the situated quality of reasoning.

CULTURE AND REASONING

Investigations of reasoning in different cultural ecologies have contributed significantly to our understanding of factors giving rise to variations in *cognitive processes* and to the formulation of the informal–formal reasoning distinction. A detailed review of research relating to the cultural determinants of cognitive processes is beyond the scope of this chapter. What is offered is a conceptual organization of cross-cultural research that draws heavily on the work of the Laboratory for Comparative Human Cognition (LCHC; 1982, 1983). Two general approaches emerge from cross-cultural research in cognition: one is *universalism,* and the other is *contextualism.*

Universalism

Universalism appears in two forms. One form holds that there are universal structures of knowledge, such as those described by Piaget, invariantly attained across a wide variety of experiences (Piaget, 1974). The other, more functional form claims that the same basic cognitive competencies or capacities (e.g., memory organization, classification schema, etc.) can be found in all human communities (Cole & Scribner, 1974). Both these forms of universalism posit some type of basic central cognitive capacity, progressively more symbolic representational structures on the one hand and basic information organizing processes on the other. The forms differ in their accounts of the nature of the central processor and the variability in reasoning performances, both within and between cultures.

Structural Universal Accounts.   One tradition in cross-cultural research derives from a structuralist approach that argues that people have general cognitive structures to which particular systems of logic adhere (Piaget, 1974). It is important to keep in mind that Piaget's theory is inherently an acultural one. As Glick (1985) has reminded us, the conceptual object of Piaget's theory is to provide a characterization of the development of a logically constrained system of knowing, in which "logical forms can be built in experience by the mind operating on (reflecting on) actions done in the real world" (p. 106). These logical forms are built by systems of inferences that lead to conclusions that have *necessity* and may be constrained by experience but not "fully determined by it" (p. 106). Glick argued that cultural constraints on forms of reasoning are more arbitrary than physical constraints: They are not universal but vary from culture to culture; they apply differentially to different members (e.g., according to social status);

and they may be *less coherent than physical constraints* due to the changing nature of cultures over time.

The evidence from cross-cultural research in the Piagetian tradition is not definitive as to whether formal operation, Piaget's final stage, are universally attained. Although the majority of studies indicate that few individuals (including those in our own culture) evidence formal logic, some studies have reported evidence of attainment of formal logical operations. For example, Saxe (1982), using an indigenous number system for birth order, found evidence of the ability to formally generate hypothetical combinations of birth order among the Papua of New Guinea. Za'rour and Khuri (1977), studying Jordanian children's performances on Piagetian time–distance problems, reported a shift to formal operations by 13-year-olds.

The majority of studies assessing concrete operational thinking provide evidence that these earlier structures of logico-mathematical reasoning may sometimes be attained but that there is substantial variability in the rate of their achievement between cultures (Dasen, 1974, 1977; LCHC, 1983). As it happens, these findings of variations in levels and rates of attainment are in keeping with Piaget's (1974) early formulations regarding the role of social-cultural factors in cognitive development. In addition to biological (epigenetic) and equilibration factors, Piaget claimed that some forms of social interaction are constant and universal whereas other social factors are divergent and culturally relative. He argued, on the one hand, that one can expect a general form of interpersonal coordination arising, for example, from the fact that people interact in all cultures. On the other hand, he acknowledged that differential cultural pressures and educational transmissions can produce variation in cognitive processes from one culture to another.

Cross-cultural research in this tradition suggests either that the postulate of the universality of the specified stage of logical thought is invalid or that the postulate cannot be tested through traditional tasks developed in one specific culture and applied to another. Researchers have dealt with these results by supplementing the contention of universal cognitive structures with the competence–performance distinction. While preserving the basic tenet of universal structures of knowledge, they have acknowledged that variation in performance results from the particulars of a task. The functional universal perspective deals with this distinction in a more basic way.

Functional Universal Accounts.   This approach considers cognition not in terms of universal logical systems but in terms of processes for dealing with information. The optional deployment of particular processes is considered a function of the content and context of the task, that "cultural differences in cognition reside more in the situations to which particular cognitive processes are applied than in the existence of a process in one cultural group, and its absence in another" (Cole, Gay, Glick, & Sharp, 1971, p. 233). However, this approach remains universalistic in the sense that those processes are considered to be capabilities that are available to people in all cultures. Understanding the role of the task is seen as critical for eliciting or deploying these existing capabilities.

Scribner (1977) reviewed cross-cultural studies of reasoning on syllogisms. In this analysis, a distinction was made between reasoning based on empirical grounds (i.e., on the basis of one's own experiences) and theoretical grounds (i.e., on the basis of evidence contained in the premises of the syllogism). Scribner concluded from this review that ". . . the significant comparative conclusion is that, in those instances where they deal with the problem as a formal 'theoretical' one, nonschooled nonliterate men and women display exactly the same logicality as adults and children exposed to Western-type schooling. In the sample at hand, when they are 'theoretical,' they are virtually never wrong" (p. 494). The apparent difficulty is in getting individuals to suspend references to their actual experiences and to focus on the premises instead, which is clearly an extralogical consideration.

Similarly, Hutchins (1980) provided an analysis of Trobriand Islanders' reasoning in land litigations, a common cultural activity. Simulations of decisions in new cases, based on a given set of propositions and inferences derived from them, led Hutchins to conclude that the Trobriands have the same capacity for logical reasoning as do Westerners.

Researchers within the functional universalistic perspective argue that variability across cultures in performance, reflecting particular cognitive processes, is produced by subjects' lack of familiarity with or saliency of the task materials and [or] procedures. Critical to such cross-cultural comparisons is the need to (a) identify tasks in the culturally organized activities of people that embody features of the cognitive processes of interest; and (b) make requests for performances in an appropriate social-communicative mode (e.g., by considering special discourse rules for asking questions). When these adjustments are made and tasks are rendered more appropriate to the cultural registers of persons, performances between cultures are found to be essentially equivalent (Cole et al., 1971; Scribner, 1977). For example, Gay and Cole (1967) found that unschooled Liberians were as skilled in using conceptual systems to classify and reclassify rice as American subjects were with geometric shapes. One criticism of this line of investigation questions whether such modifications of stimuli and changes in procedures have substantially changed the tasks by providing greater contextual support for the reasoning in question.

Cross-cultural research within both the Piagetian structural and the functional perspectives has consistently found a significant positive effect of Western-type schooling on thinking and reasoning skills. In these analyses, schooling is considered *formal,* whereas out-of-school contexts (e.g., apprenticeships) are considered *nonformal,* or *informal.* It has been argued that one of the effects of schooling is that of elevating some reasoning processes to a level of generality such that they can be deployed without the support of particular contexts; that is, they become decontextualized general processing abilities (Sharp, Cole, & Lave, 1979).

Both forms of analysis—reasoning in terms of logical structures and in terms of functions of cognitive processes for organizing information—posit universal capacities. The approaches differ in their treatment of the role of the task in determining the reasoning one engages in: For the structural universalist, task-based variability is viewed as a peripheral concern relative to the primary goal of determining the status of logical structures in various cultures; for the functional universalist, understanding the role of the features of a task in eliciting forms of reasoning has become increasingly the central concern. Two fundamental problems face the functional universal approach. If context is a crucial determiner of performance, then one needs a means of specifying and defining tasks and contexts—in effect, a theory of tasks or contexts (LCHC, 1982; Cole & Means, 1981). Further, the assumption in these earlier studies is that culture acts in a uniform way in influencing all its members. That is, there is an assumption of within-culture homogeneity. Out of these concerns, a context-specific cultural practice theory emerged as an extension and modification of the functional universalist position. In our view, both of these points are concerned with the contexual aspects of thinking.

Contextualism

More recently, there has been a shift to a position in which reasoning is viewed as situated to the extent that there is a deemphasis of the notion that either structures or processes exist outside a specific reasoning context. This form of con-textualism rejects the notions of a universal general cognitive processor and of context as merely an influence on the deployment of commonly held cognitive structures and processes. The position held by LCHC (1982) assumes that learning is context specific. Culturally organized activities determine the task contexts within which specific skills are developed.

Several lines of research are cited to support this interpretive stance. For example, Super (1976) argued that African infants are not generally more precocious in their development, as has been frequently claimed, but are only more advanced in those domains in which they are provided opportunities to practice. Serpell (1979) reported Zambian children performing better on perceptual processing in a wire-modeling task for which there is a cultural practice (children use wire to construct a variety of toys), whereas European children were better in drawing tasks. These findings contradict the functional universalists position because of the failure of competencies to generalize across situations even when attempts are made to make tasks familiar (e.g., by adjusting the content).

Scribner and Cole (1981) reported evidence of context-specific practices' influencing the particular cognitive processes of four groups of literates (schooled in English, Vai, Arabic, and Koranic literacies). Using a variety of classification, memory, and logical reasoning tasks, researchers found few generalized differences between the groups; their results "discouraged the notion that literacy per se produces the general cognitive changes previously associated with schooling" (LCHC, 1982, p. 690). However, analyzing the performances from a cultural practice approach produced clear-cut evidence of function-specific cognitive differences between the literacy groups. Subjects with skills in letter writing (Vai and English), which frequently involves formulating descriptions of places and events for a reader who does not share one's knowledge, showed better performance of metalinguistic communication tasks than their cohorts. Koranic recitation (sometimes without one's comprehending what was being recited) was associated with better serial recall in memory. All literacies for which the understanding of text was important led to better performances on a rebus-like task, which required the coding of symbols in the form of propositions. These results support a cultural practice theory interpretation that emphasizes the relationship between cognition and specific properties of culturally organized activities.

Although a context-specific cultural practice perspective handles the problem of accounting for variability, both between and within cultures, a basic problem remains: Assuming a means for defining and specifying tasks and contexts, how does one account for transfer or intercontextual generalization? The argument advanced by LCHC (1982) is that learning in one context controls performance in another, depending on (a) what is learned in the activity of the first context, and (b) the similarity between the two contexts. That is, transfer depends on the features shared by the current task and prior tasks, not only as objectively defined but as perceived by the subject.

We have tried to show that some accounts of reasoning in different cultures stress cognitive universals, whereas others emphasize the role of context in determining such performances and deny universally held capacities. In the latter accounts, the focus of attention has become the relation of reasoning to its situation. Cognitive analysis thus proceeds in the context of a specific cultural practice. Thus, there is a clear affinity between the evolution of research on the relationship of culture and cognition and our perspective on informal reasoning.

A STUDY OF CULTURAL-ECOLOGICAL
INFLUENCES ON REASONING

It is a well-established fact that a disproportionate number of children from low-income and from culturally and linguistically distinct backgrounds demonstrate inadequate levels of academic achievement. What insight might we gain into the problem of academic failure of "minority" students in our school system from the formal–informal reasoning distinction and the emphasis in cross-cultural research on the influence of contextual factors on reasoning? We have suggested that informal reasoning is related to the specifics of the situation being reasoned about and to an attitude that is antithetical to the explicit use of formal rules of logic to systematically regulate one's thinking. If the poor academic performance of some minority children is related to this distinction, then we might find evidence that low achievers have fewer experiences where rules are used to represent selected features of a problem, exacted and divorced from the particulars of the problem's context. High achievers may have experiences that lead to such "decontextualized" rules having greater priority in their reasoning.

The research to be discussed focuses on the nature and sources of the cognitive processes of low- and high-achieving African-American kindergarten children (Miller-Jones, 1981). The decision to study kindergartners was based on the idea that particular cognitive processes that are developed in the context of cultural and parental practices would still be predominant and that there was less opportunity for the cognitive orientations of these children to be influenced by school experiences than for those of older children. Children from four classrooms were identified by teachers' ratings, the Stanford Binet IQ test scores, and Metropolitan Reading Readiness scores as either high or low achievers. The children's socioeconomic status (SES) was determined by rating the occupation of the family head, income, education, and residence according to Hollingshead and Redlich's (1958) system. The distribution of SES was approximately the same for both high and low achievement.

To assess the kinds of social cognitive organizations children develop at home and in neighborhood settings and use in school, three kinds of data were collected: (a) observations of social interactions, (b) home observations and parent interviews, and (c) individual problem-solving performances.

TABLE 6.1
Social Class, Mean IQ, and Achievement of High-
and Low-Achievement Groups

Social Class	High Achievers	Low Achievers
Lower-Lower	3	4
Lower	6	6
Lower-Middle	3	2
Middle	0	1
High-Middle	1	0
Stanford-Binet IQ	125	88.2
	(s.d. = 10.5)	(s.d. = 4.2)
Reading Achievement	90.3	38.5
	99th percentile	21st percentile
	(s.d. = 5.1)	(s.d. = 8.4)

Social Interactions

First, the children (13 high- and 13 low-achievers) were videotaped for 30 minutes in dyadic social interaction as they participated in a science activity, Batteries and Bulbs. Pairs of children were brought to a science area that included batteries, bulbs, plain and insulated copper wire, miniature sockets, battery holders, wire cutters, screwdrivers, magnets, a compass, and a small, battery-operated motor. They were introduced to the activity as follows:

1. Adult introduction to the task:
"Here are some things you can play with. One of the things you can do is to try to get a bulb to light. Why don't you try working with these batteries, wires, and bulbs, and I'll be back in a few minutes." (2–5 minutes)

2. Peer–peer initial exploration: Students explore materials, no adult present. (10 minutes)

3. Adult introduces diagrams: Adult returns and asks, "How are you doing? Did anyone get a bulb to light?" Each student is shown a drawing of a battery, bulb, and connecting wire, and the adult assists each student until he or she is successful in lighting a bulb. The adult then leaves the room. (8 minutes)

4. Peer–peer post diagrams: Students continue to interact after each has been successful in lighting a bulb. The adult then enters and terminates the activities. (10 minutes)

To assess differences in the patterns of social interactions between high- and low-achieving children, the videotapes were coded for the kinds of consequences children received as well as the behavior patterns antecedent to getting these consequences or payoffs. Three major categories of adaptive consequences were established: (a) *getting information,* (b) *getting services,* and (c) *getting recognition.*

Getting information included: school-related information (identifying numbers, amounts, reading words, etc.); physical environment information (labeling or naming objects and stimulus features, etc.); process information (e.g., indicating how things work); information about rules of social interactions (e.g., taking turns, insuring social justice and equity, etc.); and evaluative information (e.g., assessing peers' and adults' abilities, lack of ability, etc.). *Getting services and resources* included: physical help or assistance, instructions, or advice that helps the student perform the task. Getting recognition included: positive recognitions, which acknowledge an accomplishment or ability, and negative recognitions, such as verbal reprimands and warnings, which result from resistive or noncooperative and nonconforming behaviors.

Low-achieving children, surprisingly, received significantly more total consequences than did high achievers (61 vs. 46.7, respectively, $p < .02$) (see Table

TABLE 6.2
Mean Number of Consequences Received From Peers and Adults By Achievement

Consequence Received	From	Hi Ach. x	Low Ach. x	x Difference	Sign.
Information	peers	15.2	16.8	1.6	ns
	adults	8.3	15.1	6.8	.01
Services	peers	5.0	3.5	1.5	ns
	adults	6.0	7.3	1.3	ns
Recognitions	peers	7.5	12.4	4.9	ns
	adults	4.8	5.8	1.0	ns
Total	peer	27.7	32.7	5.0	ns
	adults	19.1	28.2	9.1	.05
Total Consequences		46.7	61.0	14.3	.02

6.2). Low achievers received relatively more information (.47 vs. .35) and services (.67 vs. .54) from adults than did high achievers, who got relatively more recognition (.39 vs. .32) from adults (see Table 6.3). High achievers were recognized for their abilities and accomplishments whereas low achievers distinguished themselves by violating social rules or misbehaving and by having the accuracy of information they gave denied or questioned, especially by peers. Low-achieving Black children were also found to use a wider variety of behavior antecedent to receiving these consequences.

In the dyads that contained high and low achievers (students were randomly paired, yielding six such mixed dyads), low achievers more actively explored materials, such as attaching wires to sockets using the screwdrivers, screwing bulbs into these sockets, attempting to connect the batteries to wires and to the small motor, noticing that the magnets deflected the compass needle, and so on, leading one low achiever to comment, "I know what we need! We need a fuse to light it up. I hope we don't blow the whole place up!" Low-achieving students

TABLE 6.3
Relative Proportions of Consequences Received by High and Low
Achievers From Peers and Adults

Consequences Received	From	Hi Ach. x	Low Ach. x	% Difference
Information	peers	.65	.53	.12 = Hi Ach.
	adults	.35	.47	= Lo Ach.
Services	peers	.46	.33	.13 = Hi Ach.
	adults	.54	.67	= Lo Ach.
Recognitions	peers	.61	.68	.07 = Lo Ach.
	adults	.39	.32	= Hi Ach.

clearly initiated and determined the direction of the activity in more cases than did high achievers, who more often closely watched and modeled or followed their lead.

High achievers were more selective in the pattern of consequences they elicited, posturing themselves to appear competent to adults by soliciting recognition from adults for their abilities and accomplishments even when these had been borrowed from low achievers' activities and discoveries.

Examination of patterns of social interaction over the 30-minute observation period also revealed differences between the two achievement groups. During the initial exploration period following the adult introduction to the task, low achievers were very active. During this time of greatest ambiguity and uncertainty about the situation, in which the children were attempting to define and structure their activity, low achievers evidenced what might be considered an inductive or implicit approach to the task by gathering lots of particular bits of information. They made many attempts to determine the functional properties of various materials. When the adult returned and provided instructions for lighting the bulbs, low achievers drew on this rich context of exploration to ask adults task-related questions (information and service consequences). High achievers were busy displaying what they knew and getting recognition from the adult for their accomplishments, demonstrating more selectivity in how they interacted. They showed considerable skill at balancing the need to be perceived as competent with their very real needs for information and services.

The adaptive significance of low achievers' strategic social orientation may be understood in terms of its value in situated learning. When faced with new situations or those that are less predictable than usual, these children may typically seek wider stimulus inputs from which patterns, regularities, and rule-governed principles can be extracted or induced.

Home Observation

Is there any evidence that the social strategies observed in social interactions have determinants in a child's home-based ecology? Data obtained from home interviews and observations in neighborhood settings suggest that there is. The data show that high achievers from various social backgrounds experience a more systematic exposure to rule-governed or structured social systems. There are typically more regular times for meals, television viewing, and bedtime routines than there are for low achievers, and interviews suggest that these routines are monitored and enforced. These conditions afford the possibility for rule-regulated principles to be divorced from their specific situational contexts.

Low achievers experience more varied, flexible, or contingent patterns. Observations of neighborhood play show that low achievers more often engage in large group games in which rules are frequently violated. They experience many situations in which the structural parameters are implicit or highly changeable.

Under these conditions, an inductive approach to determining structure seems reasonable.

Problem-Solving Task

Our definition of informal reasoning, coupled with the cross-cultural emphasis on situated reasoning, suggests that the poor performance of low achievers on problems may be due to a lack of an orientation toward expecting situations to be regulated by simple rules. The absence of this belief and the orientation, instead, that things are more situationally determined may account for their failure. They do not start from the orientation that things are determined in simple isolation, because their salient experiences have been in social situations whose regulations are highly contingent. If their experience is with high situational contingency, then they may require more time in novel situations to induce some underlying regularity. They cannot be expected to guess this regularity or to use a hypothetical-deductive approach; rather, they need to amass a significant body of evidence from which the underlying regularities can be detected and rules induced.

To assess our characterization of high achievers as having a greater expectation of rule-regulated structure and low achievers as having a greater reliance on more situated, inductive acquisition processes, we administered several classification tasks. The data from one of these tasks will be presented for the purposes of illustration.

Venn Diagram Problem

All children were introduced to the Venn diagram problem by showing them two string loops in the form of nonoverlapping areas (see Fig. 6.1). Using a set of 32 blocks consisting of four shapes (circles, squares, triangles, and diamonds), four colors (red, blue, green, and yellow), and two sizes (large and small), they were told:

> The rule for the kind of blocks that go inside this string is squares. All the square blocks go in here (E points). The rule for this string is red (E points to second string area). All the red blocks go in here. Can you do that? Put all the square blocks in this string and all the red ones in this one.

All of the children needed help to create the overlapping intersection that permitted red squares to be in both areas. The string loops were left overlapping for a second training problem using the rules for blue and circular blocks for the two string areas respectively (see Fig. 6.2). All children were successful on this second problem.

Children were then asked to select a third string, which was added to the other

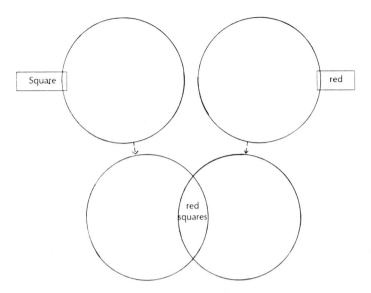

FIG. 6.1.   Attribute Blocks Venn Diagrams. Pretraining I

two to form three overlapping areas. Instead of explicitly stating the rules for each string area, we placed blocks in the appropriate areas to demonstrate the rule (see Fig. 6.3): A large red diamond exemplified the rule "Red Blocks" for one area; a large yellow circle exemplified the rule "Circle-shaped Blocks" for the second area; and a small yellow diamond and small green triangle represented the rule "Small Blocks" for the third area. These exemplars were selected because it was possible to deduce the rules from them without any further evidence. The children were told that this time they had to figure out what the rules were for placing blocks in the various areas. Children were instructed to try placing the blocks, one at a time, where they thought they ought to go and that they would be told if they were correct or not according to the rule for each string

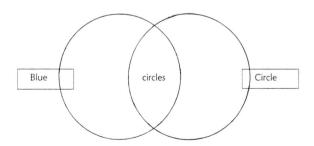

FIG. 6.2.   Attribute Blocks Venn Diagrams. Pretraining II

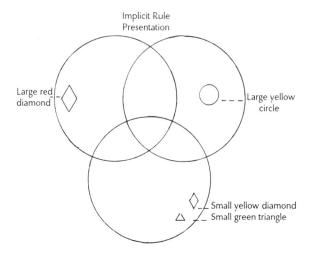

FIG. 6.3.   Attribute Blocks Venn Diagrams. Implicit Rule Presentation

area. Each attempted placement was counted as a trial. All sessions were videotaped.

This problem was intentionally designed to surpass the expected developmental competencies of the children to reveal the underlying organization of their reasoning strategies. Because the majority of high achievers experience the kind of rule structure that enables the dissociation of logic from situations, they were expected to evidence hypothesis testing qualities in their performance, showing greater selectivity and systematicity in their attempts to place blocks. Low achievers, for whom reasoning is more situated and who have no a priori anticipation of a particular form or structure, were expected to evidence an emergent organization as the problem was encountered, initially showing less systematicity and selectivity in attempts to place blocks, using blocks that did not fit the rules and repeating attempted placements for which they had been given error feedback. As they progressed through the problem, generating information about the task from which underlying regularities could be induced, they were expected to show greater systematicity and rule-regulated reasoning.

RESULTS

There were several interesting findings (see Table 6.4), but we focus on a description of children's strategic approaches to the task.

1. High achievers, at least initially, were more selective about the blocks they chose. They examined the information more frequently and searched among the

alternative blocks for placement. Low achievers more often picked a block, apparently at random, and placed it immediately.

2. High achievers showed a more systematic pattern of attempted placements. They typically would pick a block and try it in an area that had at least one attribute in common with it (e.g., a blue diamond in the area with the red diamond where the intended rule was red). Alternatively, they would pick an area and systematically try different blocks in that one area. These qualitative aspects of their performance are reflected in significantly fewer trials to reach a criterion of four consecutively correct placements in at least two different areas (Hi = 21.7; Lo = 31.7; $p < .05$), as well as in the mean number of consecutively correct placements (Hi = 6.6; Lo = 4.2; $p < .05$).

3. Low achievers showed a more random pattern of placements, rapidly moving from one to another or switching blocks frequently. This led to many repeated attempts with the same block. High achievers showed many fewer repeated placements, indicating greater attention to feedback about errors (The mean number of blocks that did not fit the rules for any of the string areas: Hi = 9.5; Lo = 18.7).

4. Low achievers did show increasing organization in their attempts to solve this problem. To correct for the large number of attempted placements of blocks that did not go on the Venn diagram, we divided each student's total number of attempted block placements into thirds (first third-early, second third-middle, and last third-late). Of the 18 blocks that could be placed, high achievers averaged 7.5 in their early placements versus 3.9 for low achievers. Conversely, low achievers correctly placed an average of 8.4 late in their performance (i.e., the last third of their placements), compared to 5.3 for high achievers. Further, more of low achievers' consecutively correct placements occurred late in the tasks, whereas high achievers' occurred early.

In sum, high achievers showed a pattern of performance that could be tentatively called *hypothesis testing*. Their performance suggested to us that they may have had some a priori organization of the task or a greater expectation of rule

TABLE 6.4
Venn Diagram Performance for High and Low Achievers

	Hi Ach.	Lo Ach.	Sign
Trials to Completion	52.8	58.8	ns
Trials to Criterion (3 consecutive correct in at least 2 areas)	21.7	31.7	.05
Areas correctly placed at criterion (of 7)	3	4.1	ns
Consecutive Correct	6.6	4.2	.05

structure. For example, high achievers were more successful early in the task, when they typically worked systematically on the simpler rule areas. But their performance began to deteriorate over the final third of their placements, looking more similar to that of low achievers early in the task. The coordinations required for the intersecting areas may have exceeded their abilities, and their performance, which seemed based on the application of rules, deteriorated. Perhaps this is a case in which using a systematic logic taxed cognitive resources too much.

Low achievers, by contrast, seemed to adopt a strategy that led them to get as many "hits" (i.e., correct placements) as possible through a kind of trial-and-error procedure. Once a critical number of blocks were placed, these students may more readily have observed or detected the patterned regularities among the blocks in the various areas. We believe that this possibility shows the emergent quality of their reasoning, because later in their performance low achievers manifested the same kinds of coordinated operations to make their placements as did high achievers. It cannot be concluded, however, that they induced in explicit form the rule from this data base. For example, many high achievers could state the rules for one or two of the string areas with one attribute (e.g., shape, color, or size), when periodically asked during the task. Few low achievers were able to do so. Whatever rule representation low achievers did use was implicitly held. However, this form of tacit knowledge organization also appears to be the case for high achievers as well since both low and high achievers were unable to explicitly state the rules for the intersecting areas (e.g., size and color or color and shape), even when the task was successfully completed.

The original premise of the research was that the social-cognitive ecologies of many Black, low-income, and other culturally distinct communities determine children's information processing strategies. This position assumes that environments pose problems and provide structures that organize children's thinking and that children call on these social and cognitive organizations when they encounter tasks; that is to say that culture influences the way various universally available strategies are located in an individual's organized repertoire of problem-solving heuristics. This position is representative of the functional-universalistic perspective and differs from cultural practice-contextualist theory because it assumes that both what people know and their ways of finding out are carried around inside their heads and imposed on situations.

These analyses point out that our initial hypothesis and characterization of differences in reasoning between the groups is only partially supported. In fact, both high and low achievers at various times seem to be using what might be called *structure-using* (explicit) and *structure-seeking* (implicit) procedures. From our point of view, the critical data for understanding performances such as these are how the subjects move through the problem and how their reasoning emerges over time in the problem context. The cultural practice variety of contextualism seems to better account for the kinds of performances we have observed.

Discussion

The analyses presented here of the situated and emergent qualities of reasoning among young, low-achieving students depart from both the deficit and difference (cultural relativism) hypotheses typically invoked to account for academic failure. Are the observed differences in reasoning due to fundamental differences in ability? The deficit explanation, that differences in performance are the result of either a biologically or environmentally determined absence of ability, is clearly not supported by these and other data (Ginsburg, 1972; United States Department of Health, Education, & Welfare, 1968). Low achievers do display the capacity for two-dimensional coordinations and an understanding of superordinate-subordinate relations in classifications. The groups are defined in terms of traditional achievement or ability criteria as high- and low-achieving, and we have attempted to characterize the features of reasoning that constitute such designations and that lead to the reported differences in performance.

The cultural difference explanation has two forms: (a) that individuals may acquire different but no less inferior or superior cognitive abilities as a result of specific cultural experiences; and (b) that individuals all possess the same cognitive capacities but that culture influences how they are organized in an individual's repertoire (i.e., that culture produces differences in cognitive styles or in the organization of optional cognitive processes). This cultural difference or cultural relativism point of view is reflected in the original conception of the research reported here. The distinction may be a subtle one, but what is suggested by the difference hypothesis is that individuals have reasoning styles as trait-like qualities that are imposed on tasks relatively independent of the features of a problem's content or context. This hypothesis is represented, for example, by Witkin's field dependent–field independent distinction in personality theory as it has been applied to cross-cultural research (Witkin & Berry, 1975). The evidence, however, best supports a more contextual interpretation of reasoning, that there may be culturally conditioned predispositions to engage in one form of reasoning or another but that experience in a problem space exerts significant influence on the reasoning that one ultimately manifests.

Although we are encouraged by these attempts to systematically account for the problem-solving approaches children use in terms of their experiences in particular social cognitive ecologies, two basic problems remain. We assumed, initially, that performances in formal or even informal reasoning situations can be understood by positing specific reasoning structures or strategies as being characteristic of individuals. Although the performances on the Venn diagram problem show that low and high achievers have a characteristic stance initially, these are modified as the problem is encountered. High achievers' rule-regulated reasoning frequently deteriorates as the problem's complexity (i.e., the demand to systematically coordinate several dimensions within an overall conceptual organization of the problem) is experienced. To us, this represents a developmental limitation and not a cultural one. On the other hand, low achievers show increasing systematicity as aspects of the problem's rule structure become apparent. Therefore, we are not convinced that low achievers are inductively oriented and high achievers are deductively oriented in all task contexts.

Moreover, if individuals cannot be characterized by such trait-like reasoning qualities and instead have organized repertoires of reasoning structures and strategies, how are we to understand what motivates the selective use of any of these thinking procedures at a particular point in time? From my point of view, what is needed are studies that examine the deployment of reasoning processes as a function of the structure of the task.

CONCLUSION

What we have learned regarding cultural influences on reasoning is that there is no basis for assuming that some populations lack the capacity for formal logical reasoning. The analyses of informal reasoning presented here argue that a critical feature of reasoning is its emergence from the particulars of the situation at hand.

The analyses of informal reasoning and cultural influences on such reasoning processes presented here have several implications for educational practices. First, they suggest that an awareness of differences among students is needed for a supportive learning context. The approach advocated here calls for problems to be posed in as rich and fully contexted a manner as possible. The analysis argues that instructors should first seek to determine the organization of a student's prevalent or preferred reasoning strategy and then design curricular activities that help the student himself or herself become explicitly aware of the organization of his or her thinking. Such metacognitive awareness may be facilitated by demonstrating that the student's reasoning, although legitimate in its own right, is but one among many other possible approaches to the problem. This objective might be accomplished by having students share their approaches with one another and to discuss the relative adequacy of their alternative approaches, perhaps reaching a consensus as to the most complete account.

For example, to answer the question, "How big is X?", consider the contrast between an approach that takes advantage of context and the situated and emergent qualities of informal reasoning and a more traditional whole-class lesson on measuring the size of an object. A more traditional approach might typically start with an explicit statement of the lesson's objectives, the metric and the measuring tool that should be used, an outline and demonstration of good reasoning, and an illustration of the typical errors or fallacies of less complete and well-thought-out thinking.

Imagine the question posed to third- or fourth-grade students, "How big is this desk?". One of the first things a teacher might want to know is whether a student understands the ambiguity inherent in the question; that is, what does one mean by *big:* height, length, weight, and so forth? Some students may explicitly ask, "What do you mean by big?", a sophisticated question. The choice at this point is to either tell them or ask what they think, the latter being the more informative. Others may be disposed to a particular dimension, say length or width: "I think how long it is is how big it is." One could accept this response and have the student select a unit to measure its length and note the appropriateness of the unit, such as centimeters, meters, inches, feet, or even yards. (Miles or angstroms are possible and even appropriate units under some circumstances.) This means that a variety of measuring tools needs to be available that would permit selection of appropriate as well as inappropriate units of measure. One can observe in this process whether students can approximate the measure by estimating, how they deal with parts of a unit (i.e., fractions), which computational procedures (addition, division, etc., and combinations of these) students select, and how they apply them given the dimension selected (e.g., volume or area). When they have completed their measurements, it is critical to see if they perceive other ways to determine how big the desk is and go on through the cycle of procedures again. If students have difficulty generating alternative dimensions, one could put the question in a different context: "How would you measure how big it is if you had to get it through the door?", "How would you measure its bigness if you wanted to know how many children would be needed to carry it if each child could safely carry or lift 20 lbs.?", "Will it fit under a window in the room or in a space available along a wall?"

This approach does not penalize either those students with an expectation for rule-governed structure or those who are more contingently dependent on context. The instructional approach just outlined permits observation of students' reasoning and fosters some degree of autonomous self-regulation whereas little is revealed by starting the instructional activity by defining everything for the learners.

The task of instruction is to show the utility of students' own reasoning and aspects of others' approaches and to locate both in a more fully articulated, complete, and systematic account of formal reasoning. It is a matter for further research to determine exactly at what point in the learning process such explicitly stated formal reasoning might most profitably be modeled to produce reorganization of student's thinking. The literature reviewed here suggests that, even when successful, such changes in the organization of reasoning might not be generalizable to other task situations but remain specific to the experienced problem context. We need to know how much practice in various forms of reasoning is necessary and in which problem structures it can function to develop effective and appropriate optional use of informal and formal reasoning processes.

The social-cognitive ecologies of some children may lead to a greater reliance when reasoning on the structure of the information in a given situation. Because the determinants of such reasoning appear to reside in the patterns of everyday experiences, schooling may not be effective in changing these reasoning strategies unless it can achieve comparable meaning in the lives of children. We have to pay attention to the details of the environments that produce the problems in which children do invest cognitive effort. This point underscores our remarks on the indeterminate and highly contingent nature of low achievers' experiences.

Unless we take into account the details of how people construct an understanding of a particular problem, the inner coherence of their reasoning will elude us. We will be left only with a fragmentary view of their reasoning when contrasted with some more complete, ideal system of coordinations. We do not quarrel with the idea that the development of reasoning can enable the application of particular logical systems to a variety of contexts so that the logical form becomes an entity that is independent of particular content or context. But to reach this stage, the logical form must first gain meaning within particular situations. Only later do logical forms emerge as meaningful structures in their own right, significant enough to achieve generality across specific task contexts.

We acknowledge that there is a privileged position for formal reasoning. Any degree of knowing involves, of necessity, a knowing through concepts, and formal reasoning comprises reasoning in which the particular characteristics of concepts are most fully used to generate logically necessary deductions. Our acknowledgement of the resources of time and effort and, often, the freedom from consequences needed for this type of reasoning, as well as the appropriateness of informal reasoning in many situations, should leave intact the recognition that, as the constraints and supports of daily life and familiarity are removed, the special position of formal reasoning becomes increasingly apparent. Whereas informal reasoning is not concerned with the explicit articulation of the underlying system of formal relations, formal reasoning is concerned to do just that in its search for autonomy from the particulars of the situation being dealt with. Its privileged position may also be seen in that it conceptually clarifies the usefulness of the methods of informal reasoning.

ACKNOWLEDGMENT

I am indebted to Dr. Joseph Becker for this formulation and for his many other helpful suggestions on the chapter.

REFERENCES

Cole, M., Gay, J., Glick, J., & Sharp, D. W. (1971). *The cultural context of learning and thinking.* New York: Basic Books.

Cole, M., & Means, B. (1981). *Comparative studies of how people think.* Cambridge, MA: Harvard University Press.

Cole, M., & Scribner, S. (1974). *Culture and thought.* New York: Wiley.

Dasen, P. R. (1974). The influence of ecology, culture and European contact on cognitive development in Australian aborigines. In W. Berry & P. R. Dasen (Eds.), *Culture and cognition* (pp. 381–408). London: Methuen.

Dasen, P. R. (1977). Are cognitive processes universal? A contribution to cross-cultural Piagetian psychology. In N. Warren (Ed.), *Studies in cross-cultural psychology* (Vol. 1). London: Academic Press.

Gay, J., & Cole, M. (1967). *The new mathematics and an old culture.* New York: Holt, Rinehart and Winston.

Ginsburg, H. (1972). *The myth of the deprived child.* Englewood Cliffs, NJ: Prentice-Hall.

Glick, J. (1985). Culture and cognition revisited. In E. Neimark, R. DeLisi, & J. Newman (Eds.), *Moderators of competence* (pp. 99–115). Hillsdale, NJ: Lawrence Erlbaum Associates.

Heath, S. B. (1983). *Ways with words.* New York: Cambridge University Press.

Hollingshead, A. D., & Redlich, F. C. (1958). *Social class and mental illness: A community study.* New York: Wiley.

Hutchins, E. (1980). *Culture and inference: A Trobriand case study.* Cambridge, MA: Harvard University Press.

Kahneman, D., & Tversky, A. (1972). Subjective probability: A judgment of representativeness. *Cognitive Psychology, 3,* 430–454.

Kahneman, D., & Tversky, A. (1973). On the psychology of prediction. *Psychological Review, 80,* 237–251.

Laboratory of Comparative Human Cognition. (1982). Culture and intelligence. In R. J. Sternberg (Ed.), *Handbook of human intelligence* (pp. 642–719). New York: Cambridge University Press.

Laboratory of Comparative Human Cognition. (1983). Culture and cognitive development. In W. Kessen (Ed.), *Mussen handbook of child development* (Vol. 1, pp. 295–356). New York: Wiley.

Labov, W. (1969). The logic of nonstandard English. *Georgetown Round Table on Languages and Linguistics.* Washington, DC: Georgetown University Press. Reprinted in F. Williams (Ed.). (1970). *Language and poverty* (pp. 153–189). Chicago: Markham.

Miller-Jones, D. (1981). Differences in social and cognitive information processing between high and low achieving five year old Black children. In J. McAdoo & W. Cross (Eds.), *Proceedings of the Fifth Conference on Empirical Research in Black Psychology* (pp. 76–107). Ithaca, NY: Cornell University, Africana Studies & Research Center.

Nurss, J. R., & McGauvran, M. E. (1976). *The Metropolitan Readiness Tests.* New York: Harcourt, Brace, Janovitch.

Piaget, J. (1974). Need and significance of cross-cultural studies in genetic psychology. In J. W. Berry & P. R. Dasen (Eds.), *Culture and cognition: Readings in cross-cultural psychology* (pp. 299–309). London: Methuen.

Saxe, G. B. (1982). Developing forms of arithmetic thought among the Oksapmin of Papua New Guinea. *Developmental Psychology, 9,* 151–166.

Scribner, S. (1977). Modes of thinking and ways of speaking: Culture and logic reconsidered. In P. N. Johnson-Laird & P. C. Wason (Eds.), *Thinking: Readings in cognitive science* (pp. 483–500). Cambridge, England: Cambridge University Press.

Scribner, S., & Cole, M. (1981). *The psychology of literacy.* Cambridge, MA: Harvard University Press.

Serpell, R. (1979). How specific are perceptual skills? A cross-cultural study of pattern reproduction. *British Journal of Psychology, 70,* 365–380.

Sharp, D. W., Cole, M., & Lave, C. (1979). Education and cognitive development: The evidence from experimental research. *Monographs of the Society for Research in Child Development, 44* (1–2, Serial No. 178).

Super, C. M. (1976). Environmental effects on motor development: The case of African infant precocity. *Developmental Medicine and Child Neurology, 18* (5), 561–567.

Terman, L. M., & Merrill, M. A. (1973). *Stanford-Binet Intelligence Scale.* Chicago: Riverside Publishing.

United States Department of Health, Education, and Welfare. National Institute of Child Health and Human Development. (1968). *Perspectives on human deprivation: Biological, psychological and sociological.* Washington, DC: Author.

Witkin, H. A., & Berry, J. W. (1975). Psychological differentiation in cross-cultural perspective. *Journal of Cross-Cultural Psychology, 6,* 4–87.

Za'rour, G. I., & Khuri, G. A. (1977). The development of the concept of speed by Jordanian school children in Amman. In P. R. Dasen (Ed.), *Piagetian psychology: Cross-cultural contributions* (pp. 216–226). New York: Gardner Press.

7 Contexts of Informal Reasoning: Commentary

Ralph H. Johnson
J. Anthony Blair
University of Windsor

When one considers the vast, little-explored territory that the term *informal reasoning* may be taken to designate, however it eventually is defined, one is naturally puzzled by the sparse extant research in this area. How can such a broad region have gone largely uncharted and unexplored? We find the most obvious answer to be the best one: Explorers have been too busy in other areas to have noticed this fascinating territory so close to home. What are those other domains that have for so long captivated the affection of the company of inquirers?

Perhaps our own experience in logic is germane (cf. Johnson & Blair, 1985). The history of our discipline in the 20th century has, for the most part, been the history of formal logic. We can only suspect that the same drive at work behind research in formal logic has had its measure of influence in this volume as well, with the result that the study of reasoning has been thought largely to be the study of formal mechanisms and procedures. This drive, in turn, must be seen in the context of the positivist research program in the natural and formal sciences: its zeal for systematic or, preferably, axiomatic knowledge, displayed in terms of formal relationships among concepts wherever possible and supplemented by reference to the world of experience (sense data) whenever necessary.

This penchant for formal systems has had an immense impact on how reasoning has been both understood and studied. According to the thinking of this influential—though now waning—research program, the highest form of reasoning is that which yields the best form of knowledge: mathematical knowledge. Why is mathematical knowledge thus revered? Because it is certain, necessary, and immutable. If one then asks why this form of knowledge is held to be superior, the answer is quite involved but ultimately takes us back to Plato, for the very terms we have just used to characterize this highest form of knowledge embody precisely those values apotheosized in the Platonic concept of form.

So, when inquirers have sallied forth to explore the territory of reasoning, they have not uncommonly been guided by formalist prejudices in two ways. First, the reasoning they have sought to capture has been, by and large, formal. Thus, studies of reasoning tend to focus on syllogistic logic (Piaget & Inhelder, 1958) or, to a lesser extent, propositional logic (Revlin & Meyer, 1978; Wason & Johnson-Laird, 1972). A second manifestation of the formalist tendency is the idea that the study of reasoning should not merely focus on formal reasoning but should itself, when possible, be formalized. The project undertaken by Montague and his followers (Thomason, 1974) is perhaps the most striking exemplar of this urge.

It seems, then, that it is not anything inherent in the various contexts of reasoning that has caused the situation just described so much as the influence of a certain ideal. To return to the metaphor we used at the start: It is not areas of knowledge per se but rather the way they have traditionally been charted that has caused the study of informal reasoning to remain so long in the background.

However, at least in logic and philosophy in the last 30 years, the paradigm that guided investigation for the first half of the 20th century has lost ground. Although Carnap (1928) and his followers are still important forces, they no longer enjoy a monopoly. It became apparent to us some years ago that important changes were occurring in logic. Logicians were no longer content to assume that formal logic and logic were identical. Instead of targeting logistic systems, they began to focus with increasing interest on the sort of reasoning and argumentation found in the context of everyday life. Something known as *informal logic* began to make it presence felt.

Before we offer some general comments from our perspective, we want to pass along a conclusion drawn from our own experience that may benefit those working on informal reasoning. If we had it to do over again, we would avoid the term *informal* for two reasons. First, there is the problem of negative definition: stating what you are not rather than what you are. Part of the failure (which we discuss hereafter) to arrive at a clear picture of informal reasoning may stem from researchers' having conceived of it negatively in this volume, that is, as reasoning that is not formal, not mathematical. Second, the term *informal* suggests a casual approach: We recall a cartoon in which the frame, labelled "informal logic," shows a man casually dressed with a sweater and open collar. It also suggests a lack of rigor in subject matter (Massey, 1981). Perhaps *deliberative reasoning* would be a better term: It serves to distinguish the reasoning of problem solving and decision making from that of calculating or of working out entailments. Still, both the recent history of informal logic and this volume convince us that, in other areas no less than logic, the study of informal reasoning is emerging as a vital research interest. Without wishing to denigrate the value of formal methods in their place, we believe this new focus is a healthy and stimulating one.

In the next section, we offer some general observations on informal reasoning, stimulated by our own experience as informal logicians and built around a medley of points. In the third section, we offer our own perspective on the five chapters in Section I of this book. We seek to indicate the contribution of each chapter to informal reasoning and also to raise certain questions. In the last section, we provide some concluding reflections.

GENERAL OBSERVATIONS

In this section, we make five observations about informal reasoning.

Observation 1: Informal Reasoning is Not a Separate Subject Matter.   This point may seem painfully obvious, but we make it nonetheless. There is, at present, no recognized branch of knowledge called informal reasoning; none even called reasoning. Logic is often thought to be the science of reasoning or the art of reasoning, but it is clear that the concerns expressed in the chapters in this section go well beyond the boundaries of logic as it is conventionally understood. Indeed, the study of informal reasoning as represented in this volume is noticeably interdisciplinary, even though the disciplines are not equally represented. By our reckoning, the following disciplines are represented: psychology, philosophy, education, and cognitive science. Such a multidisciplinary undertaking is certainly praiseworthy. Our only note of caution is that the study of informal reasoning may gain much from disciplines not represented at this ground-breaking conference, such as speech communication.

Researchers may also discover that this point has ramifications down the road as they confront the question of which norms and standards should be employed and what rationale can be furnished for these choices.

Observation 2: There is No Agreement Yet as to What is Meant by Informal Reasoning.   As informal logicians and philosophers who are concerned with conceptual clarity, we cannot help but be struck by the many different senses in which the terms *formal* and, by extension, *informal* have been used. The editors did propose an explicit conception of informal reasoning in the letter announcing the conference from which this volume is drawn. Because many of the authors appear to have relied heavily on this letter for their understanding of informal logic, it is worth quoting here:

> Informal reasoning is the reasoning carried on outside the formal contexts of mathematics and symbolic logic. It involves reasoning about causes and consequences and about the advantages and disadvantages or pros and cons of particular propositions or decision alternatives.

We note, with approval, the broad scope of this conception of informal reasoning. Still, this gloss is not entirely satisfactory because some reasoning about the pros and cons of a particular decision is mathematical; for example, one uses Bayseian calculus to estimate the utility of a particular course of action.

The editors then contrasted formal and informal reasoning:

> Informal reasoning differs from formal reasoning in important ways. For example, in the latter, the individual's task is to draw logically necessary conclusions from given premises; in informal reasoning, the individual's task is to use his or her knowledge to identify premises relevant to a particular proposition and build plausible lines of argumentation.

We believe that this way of contrasting the two terms needs some revision. Clearly, some mathematical reasoning, such as applications of statistics and probability calculus, yields conclusions that follow necessarily from the premises, yet the conclusions are probabilistic, not logically necessary, propositions. It is the inference from premises to conclusion that is necessary in formal reasoning, not the conclusion itself. The contrary point is also valid: There are instances in which reasoning is informal but not argumentative. For instance, we distinguish problem solving or decision making from argumentation, although we grant that arguments can be, and typically are, used in both. In problem solving, the problem is in some sense set, and the task is to discover the best solution. Reasons (i.e., arguments) are offered for and against alternative solutions, but the process of finding alternatives in the first place is not argumentation, although it can be more or less rational. Similarly, in decision making there are more and less rational ways to make a decision, and assuredly alternative approaches and options can be subject to argumentation, but the overall process is not argumentation.

It seems to us that the crucial feature that makes informal reasoning what it is is the way in which it is conducted; that is, in natural language and without recourse to formal procedures or other formal mechanisms. Informal reasoning is open-ended rather than algorithmic. Better still, it is reasoning for which the ideal of an algorithm would be out of place, an intruder.

Yet, even when thus revised, this definition of informal reasoning goes just so far and no further, for it omits recognition of the fact that the term *formal* is far from having a univocal sense. It is used in quite different ways. In fact, as we reviewed the chapters in this section, we were able to detect no fewer than seven senses of the term. We list them here:

1. Sometimes *formal* is used as a rough equivalent to *mathematical,* and hence informal reasoning would mean nonmathematical or nonquantitative approaches to reasoning. (In chapter 2, Christensen and Elstein adopt this view

although it should be noted that they never suggest that medical reasoning should always be informal in this sense.)

2. Sometimes *formal* is used to mean conceptual, as opposed to empirical. Thus, logic and mathematics are formal sciences; that is, their truths are conceptual in nature, not empirical.

3. Sometimes *formal* is used to mean a priori or necessary, in which case it contrasts with *contingent*.

4. Sometimes *formal* is used as a synonym for *deductive*, in which case informal means nondeductive. (Dalton Miller-Jones displays this tendency in chapter 6.)

5. Sometimes *formal* is used as a rough equivalent for *algorithmic;* here, informal means something like nonsystematic; perhaps it is this sense of *formal* and *informal* that accounts for the emergence of the term *heuristic* as a mode of informal reasoning.

6. Sometimes *formal* means having to do with the form of reasoning and/or argument as opposed to the content or premises; it is this sense of *formal* that is rightly associated with formal (symbolic) logic, in which the form of an argument is studied symbolically rather than through natural language. (For some understanding of the many problems associated with this notion of form, see Govier [1986] and Massey [1981].)

7. Sometimes *formal* means rigidly proscribed or circumscribed as opposed to something that is not so, hence the contrast between a person who is quite formal, that is, who stands on protocol and proper procedure, and one who is more informal or casual. It is probably this sense that leads to the idea of informal reasoning as connected with everyday reasoning in contradistinction to more academic or discipline-bound reasoning or as contrasted with tightly structured reasoning.

It seems that this last sense of informal reasoning is somewhat misleading inasmuch as the reasoning done in everyday life or in the pursuit of normal everyday objectives itself varies greatly, depending on many factors, among them the intellectual (and other) resources of the individual. Suppose that one wished to arrive at a good judgment about the quality of meals served at a local restaurant. If one had unlimited funds, time, and resources, one might well attempt to draw a representative sample of cuisine. Such a procedure could be carried out formally, which is to say scientifically, which is to say in accordance with the known procedures for drawing a representative sample. Yet such a procedure would rarely be used, for obvious reasons. Most people would use a less formal strategy. Perhaps they would sample reports from friends and perhaps go once or twice themselves before forming an opinion. They might use the representativeness heuristic (see Kahneman, Slovic, & Tversky, 1982, pp. 4–

11). The use of such a procedure might be thought to be informal when compared to the prior procedure; but even with this approach there would be a range between those who form snap judgments based on a very limited sample and those who, though still using a limited sample, draw tentative conclusions and qualify their judgments.

Our point, then, is that until the term *informal reasoning* receives clearer definition, one should be careful to ascertain its precise meaning in any context in which it is encountered.

Observation 3: Students of Informal Reasoning Ought to Be Cautious About the Concepts They Borrow. In our view, students of informal reasoning should tread warily when using well-established concepts. These might fit in their original contexts, but they cause distortions when applied to informal reasoning. In addition, we should not get carried away by the spirit of interdisciplinary cooperation. Borrow from fields other than your own, by all means, but do so with caution. For example, we note with distress the tendency of authors in this volume to invoke the distinction between deductive and inductive reasoning as though it were nonproblematic. The *Informal Logic Newsletter* published a series of exchanges from 1979 through 1983 that raise serious and still-unanswered questions about how to understand this distinction.

We notice that several authors refer to bias, but not all of them use that term in the same way. In fact, we detect three distinct uses of *bias*. In chapter 2, Christensen and Elstein speak of bias as a blinder or a block to sound reasoning. This is *bias* in a pejorative sense. Perkins, Farady, and Bushey (chapter 5) use *bias* in a pejorative sense too, but they mean a quite specific sort of blinder, namely a lack of balance, seeking to defend an opinion without considering arguments against it—exclusively "my-side" thinking. In contrast, Voss (chapter 3), used the word *bias* to refer to a point of view, so that each of two people might quite legitimately have his or her own point of view or bias. This notion of bias is neutral: It carries no condemnation. Confusion is likely to arise if careful attention is not paid to precisely how key terms are used, and, consequently, they cannot be borrowed willy-nilly from one another's research.

Observation 4: Informal Reasoning Needs to Be Guided by a Clear Conception of Reasoning and a Theory of Its Types. What are the connections between problem solving, decision making, and argumentation, to name three areas in each of which a large literature exists? If one of these is crowned—or even nominated—as the Queen of Informal Reasoning, will this selection not impose on the study of informal reasoning a potentially distorting vantage point? If any one area is studied independently of the others, will this study not be, in important respects, incomplete? Are these the Big Three, or do others belong on a list of major areas of study?

Our worry is that work is proceeding along lines set up some time ago and that, although they obviously are extremely fruitful and important, these lines developed originally as a result of historical accident rather than out of a comprehensive theory of reasoning. Each project goes merrily along its traditional path, trying to assimilate others to itself. We would like to see some effort at creating overviews. Granted, there is a danger at the other extreme of working with a prioristic conceptions; we have just begun to escape the hegemony of formalism, and we do not want to flee into the arms of an equally restrictive general theory of reasoning. Still, we find ourselves asking the questions, "What are we all discussing? Are we all discussing the same thing or are we using the same term to talk about very different things?" These are questions that deserve answers soon.

Observation 5: It Ought Not to Be Assumed That Informal Reasoning is Second Best.   Perhaps we are unduly sensitive because we have been goaded by Big Brother. Informal logic has been sneeringly derided by some logicians and other philosophers as "baby logic," "soft logic," "loose logic," "low-level logic," "introductory logic," and thought of as the logic to be taught to the dull undergraduates who cannot yet master the real thing—formal logic. This attitude is based on ignorance and blind prejudice; it is an attitude that considers the axe an imperfect scalpel. However, such is the influence of intellectual fashions and graduate school indoctrination that we used to feel guilty about developing tools of argument analysis and criticism that are designed to meet the demands of such activity (forging the axe to fell and shape the tree) instead of trying to force the raw material to fit then standard tools (cursing the tree because it was so unyielding to the scalpel).

Informal reasoning is not low-level, imperfect, flawed, second-best reasoning that we make do with for the time being until all of its operations can be taken over by formal tools. If a formal decision procedure is what is needed to do a job, it should be developed. But, one of the major lessons of the chapters in this volume, if we understand them correctly, is that there are certain kinds of reasoning that are, by their nature, informal, and explanations of their operation as well as the norms governing their best exercise will be ineluctably informal. If these assumptions are true, there is no need to apologize for informal reasoning. We should seek robust explanatory and normative theories of informal reasoning. Taken together, the chapters we comment on herein constitute a formidable start in that direction.

COMMENTS ON INDIVIDUAL CHAPTERS

By its applications of ingeniously modified protocol analysis techniques to Michael Faraday's scientific diaries, Tweney's chapter, "Informal Reasoning in Science," is impressive in the power of its explanation of this line of interpretation. It left us, however, scratching our heads about the payoff of the word *informal* in the title. Would not "Reasoning in Science" have done just as well?

To be sure, Tweney makes it clear that Faraday's thinking, as he moved through a series of experiments toward the discovery of electromagnetic induction, was not tied down by deductive entailments. But Tweney is trying to understand and explain Faraday's methods of scientific discovery, and, as far as we know, no one has suggested that the reasoning of scientific discovery is largely formal, that is, in closed systems with procedures available to enable scientists to decide the answers to the questions. What is the gain, then, in alluding to informal reasoning as the framework for Tweney's interesting project? Perhaps there is none, a point that represents no loss so far as Tweney's project goes—it does not stand or fall on this point.

One contrast Tweney has in mind is the one between the problems uncovered by certain protocol analyses and Faraday's problem. The protocols of chess masters, for example, are based on a definite goal (to win) and prescribed limits to the way in which the goal might be achieved (the rules of chess). Hence, one can create computer models of the reasoning of chess masters, or what are termed *expert systems.* Faraday's situation was different. He had no closed problem space, his goals were open-ended, and his work was driven as much by his data and by his religious values as by any rules or methodology. Although methodology assuredly was exhibited in Faraday's work—and Tweney's paper nicely exposes its distinctive features—there is an organic rather than a mechanical relationship between the schemata (organizations of experience), scripts (recurring patterns of activities), and heuristics (strategies for attacking problems), which are the key operators in this methodology.

Although, undoubtedly, there are differences between the protocols analyzed in much of the cognitive psychology literature and Faraday's scientific diaries, these differences do not make the former formal and the latter informal (not that Tweney suggests that they do). Whether a chess master's heuristics consist of a quasimechanical elimination of possibilities or of intuitive leaps is an empirical question, and there is no a priori reason to rule out the latter just because of the nature of the problem space in a chess game. The terms of contrast here should be *circumscribed* and *open-ended,* or *context free* and *context rich,* not *formal* and *informal.*

Tweney points out that Faraday himself did not formalize the relationship between electricity and magnetism; his work set the stage for Maxwell to describe the relationship in mathematical terms. It may be, then, that the distinction between formal and informal reasoning is to be seen as the distinction between the reasoning that leads to discovery and the reasoning that is reflected in a proof or demonstration. (Such a contrast harks back to a much earlier distinction in the philosophy of science between the logic of discovery and the logic of justification.) However, even Maxwell's reasoning, when he was in the process of generating the mathematical formulae, may not have consisted of deriving logical entailments from a set of propositions; whether, in fact, it did is an empirical question.

In sum, what we find interesting about Tweney's analysis is not his point that Faraday's reasoning is not formal or mathematical but the details of the interpretive apparatus Faraday used in his reasoning.

Tweney uses the term *schemata* to refer to the recurring conceptual organizations he found Faraday using to describe and interpret his experiences. These schemata appear very like Lawrence's schemata, the frameworks magistrates use to build plausible representations of the events of cases. (And the predictable nature of the different requests for presentencing information and the variations in the penalties that Lawrence found to be imposed by magistrates operating with different schemata seem analogous to the *scripts,* or action clusters associated with different schemata, that Tweney found in Faraday's discovery procedures.) The presence of these terms reflects the influence of current work in cognitive psychology. Perhaps we are trying to force distinct concepts into the same pigeon hole, but we find the affinities striking.

We believe, too, that informal logicians, who have it as one item on their agendas to understand how people actually do reason, ought to see if this concept of schema and schemata can be used to explain the occurrence of certain logical errors. Are some of the informal fallacies, for example, illuminated by being characterized as argument schemata that have a function for those who employ them? Here is a question that we think bears examination.

Tweney's account of the reasoning of scientific discovery—or at least of Faraday's in the discovery of induction—may well deploy explanatory concepts that can be exported to other domains. It should, in our view, be carefully studied by philosophers of science who want their theories of scientific discovery to be informed by how working scientists actually reason to discoveries. But, even apart from these general applications, Tweney's study of Faraday's reasoning is quite fascinating in its own right.

Medical reasoning, that is to say the reasoning engaged in by physicians as they practice their craft, is the subject of chapter 2, "Informal Reasoning in the Medical Profession," by Christensen and Elstein. Although medical reasoning seems a paradigmatic case of reasoning, it is not entirely clear to us that all medical or clinical reasoning can rightfully be said to be informal in the sense outlined by the authors: "Informal or everyday reasoning has been defined as reasoning carried on outside the formal contexts of mathematics or symbolic logic." For example, a clinician who uses base rate information to calculate a 9% possibility of cancer must use mathematical—hence, by this account, formal— reasoning. Moreover, computer programs, though not themselves formal, must pass through a formal stage.

Yet it is apparent that clinical reasoning is subject to numerous hazards, none of which can plausibly be construed as formal. (Whatever kind of mistakes they may be, anchoring and framing do not seem to be formal mistakes.) Thus, we are inclined to think that if informal reasoning is taken as not employing a calculus or a mechanical decision procedure, then most clinical reasoning is informal. The interesting issues here are: What does the research show? How can clinical reasoning be improved? What lines of future research are suggested?

After describing the constraints within which medical reasoning occurs, chapter 2 contrasts two approaches to the study of clinical reasoning: the information processing approach (IPA) and the behavioral judgment decision-making approach (JDM).

IPA rests on close analysis of protocols obtained from problem solvers, that is, expert clinicians, and comparison with those of novices. The protocol analysis of experts in pediatric cardiology revealed that "the knowledge base of expert . . . [is] highly organized into clusters by deep pathological principles."

Christensen and Elstein make a fairly standard move in seeking to study clinical reasoning by studying the reasoning of expert reasoners (one that is made elsewhere, such as in the study of the reasoning of a creative scientist such as Faraday). Two questions we raise here are: How is it determined that a given clinician is an expert reasoner, and what are the qualities of a clinical decision that make it a good one? There must be some antecedent answer to these questions to allow those engaged in research to select their sample.

Protocol collection, in some cases, requires subjects to recall the reasoning they employed on a task. This point suggests to us a question about the very nature of reasoning proficiency: To what degree and in what ways is proficiency in reasoning a function of memory? It has been stated that expert reasoners appear to have the capacity to store and retrieve knowledge by chunking it. But this seems to mean that reasoning is signally dependent on memory. (Have our students been right all along in thinking that learning consists of memorizing and that a superior student is one with a better memory?)

Another method of investigation, propositional analysis, indicates that "all of the experts . . . used bottom-up forward reasoning whereas the experts with inaccurate diagnoses used at least some top-down backward reasoning." We consider this result intriguing but find ourselves wishing for more explanation of these contrasting terms.

The JDM school is less sanguine than the IPA about the reasoning processes of experts. From the standpoint of the JDM school, "informal decision making, whether undertaken by experts or novices, often appears suboptimal because it is compared with the decisions produced by [a] normative statistical model." JDM leans heavily on the research done in cognitive psychology by Kahneman, Slovic, and Tversky (1982), which reveals a number of cognitive biases in clinical decision making, among them the neglect of base rates; anchoring; hindsight bias; framing; and regret.

We sense a tension between the recognition of the need for and the importance of informal reasoning and the occasionally clear implication that the formal method is superior. Thus, for example, the view of JDM seems more clearly committed to the superiority of formal reasoning. We discuss this issue in greater detail in our comment on Miller-Jones's chapter.

The influence of the work of Kahneman et al. (1982) is evident in chapter 2. The term *heuristic,* a rule of thumb employed in reasoning, is used here, and it is used in such a way as to bring it very close to the term *bias.* As we said in our introduction, we think that some caution is needed with respect to the use of each of these terms.

In chapter 3, "Informal Reasoning and International Relations," Voss takes a wide-ranging look at research on informal reasoning in the broad context of political reasoning and decision making. He discusses research results in the general area of international relations, focusing for the most part on how countries perceive their own situation and those of others. Research shows the influence of interpretation on cognition and understanding. From Voss's perspective, the salient result of the research is the demonstration of the degree to which attitude influences cognition.

Another interesting result that meshes with results in other chapters is the role that the concepts of heuristics and bias play in our understanding reasoning in the international context. For instance, Voss writes:

> A heuristic that has received considerable study . . . is that of analogy. A basic tenet of cognitive processing is that individuals interpret input information in terms of what they already know, and, in so doing, they strive to reduce uncertainty and to reduce ambiguity. When therefore an event requires interpretation, it is not unlikely that the individual may refer to historical situations which seem, at least at face value, to be analogous to the existing situation.

We call attention to Voss's use of the term *heuristic* to describe the use of analogy. Indeed, *heuristic* is used by most of the authors, and a quick look at the index will probably reveal that almost every chapter includes some mention of this term. What is happening here?

First, about the term *heuristic* itself, it is our impression that the term has gained currency as a result of the work of two pairs of psychologists, Richard Nisbett and Lee Ross and Daniel Kahneman and Amos Tversky. In *Human Inference,* Nisbett and Ross (1980) wrote:

> This book contends that the seeds of inferential failure are sown with the same implements that produce the intuitive scientist's [their term for the lay reasoner] more typical successes. These intuitive procedures are of two broad types— "knowledge structures" . . . and "judgmental heuristics" which reduce complex inferential tasks to simple judgemental operations. (pp 6–7)

Here, they have located the term *heuristic* within a framework and have described its effect, but they have not declared its meaning. But they then wrote:

> Besides knowledge structures, people also use a few simple judgmental heuristics. These cognitive strategies, or rules of thumb, are the layperson's tools for solving a variety of inferential tasks. (p. 7)

Thus, as introduced by the psychologists, this term denotes a rule of thumb, or a cognitive strategy, simpler than the normatively appropriate strategy but good enough to yield valid results in a great many cases. The two heuristics on which Kahneman and Tversky have focused are the availability heuristic and the representativeness heuristic. One question that is raised by Voss's use of the term here (and others' use elsewhere) is: Is the term being used in this sense, or has it undergone a modification?

We raise this question because, in the present case, the use of analogy to process information and form judgments has at least two other conceptual frames: In the tradition of rhetoric, analogy is called a *trope,* and in informal and inductive logic, an argument from an analogy can be either cogent or, if improperly used, *fallacious.* One question that future research may need to raise concerns the relationship between these three terms: heuristic, trope, and fallacy.

An interesting result reported by Voss is that, whereas the ordinary reasoner in most contexts tends to ignore base rate information (remember that in chapter 2 this result is also reported in clinical reasoning), in international reasoning just the reverse obtains: Reasoners show a tendency to cling to base rate information and ignore individual cases. Such findings may have some ramifications for research in psychology.

Next, Voss discusses reasoning in the decision-making process, and several interesting results are reported here. Like clinical reasoning, reasoning in this context may be seen as an exercise in *bounded rationality* (see Simon, 1983, 1985), in which the goal of the reasoning process should be seen as "satisficing" rather than optimizing. Research shows that, in dealing with an ill-structured problem, knowledgeable individuals begin by developing a representation of the problem, but just what counts as a representation is not further explained.

The next section deals with the question of justification in decision making. For the most part, the context here is that of policy making in government. One important study holds that the debate model of argumentation is not an appropriate model for these negotiations. Voss also takes up the question of the way in which argumentation is related to belief and reports on the preliminary study he has done that shows that attitudinal components and arguments may conceivably develop independently.

In sum, Voss's chapter shows that the field of international relations and governmental decision making is rife with questions for those interested in the study of informal reasoning.

Lawrence's chapter, "Informal Reasoning in the Judicial System" (chapter 4), does for the world of the courtroom what Christensen's does for medical decision making and Tweney's does for scientific reasoning: It gives a good glimpse of the real world, where the complexities of reasoning are orders of magnitude greater than those envisaged by the reduction of all reasoning to the working out of chains of deductive entailments. Like the other chapters, Lawrence's lends support to the conviction underlying the informal logic reform movement that the real world of argumentation is extremely varied and complex and that many nonformal patterns of argument are quite legitimately at work in reasoning to conclusions.

A major implication of Lawrence's findings is that the large cognitive load that judges and magistrates (expert judges) and jury members (naive judges) must carry and the great variety of "contextual constraints" that influence their thinking make an accurate account of their cognitive processing a far more complex goal than could be achieved through the simple model of drawing conclusions from premises. Lawrence supports this interpretation with evidence from other studies and her own that show that each component of a trial entails numerous tasks, including complicated syntheses of interpretations of facts and of other interpretations.

One concept that strikes us as having interesting connections with some work in informal logic is that of interpretive schemata. We see the interpretive schemata that jurors use (reported in Holstein, 1985) and that magistrates employ (described in Lawrence's studies) as specifications of the general concept of worldview that was popularized by Paul (1982). These are specific ways of thinking, dispositional interpretive frameworks that we use to classify and evaluate the information we receive. Lawrence's constructs of *greed, need,* and *troubled* schemata, employed by magistrates to interpret the data of shoplifting cases and to process decisions leading to sentencing, show that interpretive frameworks can have quite particular elaborations related to particular contexts. Such generalized worldview characterizations as *liberal* and *conservative* fail to capture the rich detail of the interpretive frameworks that Lawrence found operating in magistrates' "information processing."

The results of the studies Lawrence reports strike us as independent corroboration of Perkins et al.'s thesis that people use "makes-sense" epistemologies to organize their interpretive schemata. The schemata employed by magistrates seem to be functions of general epistemologies that they share with others and that operate outside as well as within the courtroom to guide their selections of schemata.

Informal logic, unlike formal logic, has been characterized through empirical as well as normative approaches to reasoning and argumentation. That is, it is crucial that norms for reasoning incorporate an accurate understanding of actual reasoning processes. Still, we remain committed to a normative mission—the improvement of reasoning and the reform of reasoning practices and institutions to improve the prospects for fair judgments and well-grounded beliefs and decisions. Lawrence's account of informal reasoning in the judicial system is the sort of essential contribution to our understanding of actual processes of reasoning that it would be naive—and indeed counterproductive—to ignore when one thinks normatively about legal reasoning. Our view is that this sort of study should be used as a basis for prescriptions. We worry that the mere finding of different reasoning schemata among legal reasoners may hastily be taken as evidence of the relativism of values. Such a conclusion would be not warranted: The mere fact of differences does not mean that there is no way to choose a best or most justified approach. There is, undoubtedly, pressure on players in the judicial system to employ these findings to manipulate the system to their own advantage. A lawyer might even be thought of as under an obligation to take advantage of his or her knowledge that certain magistrates are more lenient than others. We hope these studies would also be used by magistrates, legal educators, and legislators as a basis for designing changes in judicial systems that may increase fairness.

Chapter 5, "Everyday Reasoning and the Roots of Intelligence," by Perkins, Farady, and Bushey works with a conception of informal reasoning that is very close to our own. Our critical comments, therefore, are more than friendly; they are self-interested. The authors of chapter 5 study informal reasoning in terms of one's having or giving reasons for one's opinions—arguing for a point of view—and not in terms of problem solving or decision making. Thus, although such reasoning is an application of intelligence in its broadest sense, it is not the only type of application of intelligence in reasoning. Still, those who might identify informal reasoning exclusively with problem solving or decision making are forced by studies such as those discussed in chapter 5 to make room for the domain of argumentation as well.

Perkins et al.'s concept of informal, or everyday, reasoning is initially drawn in contrast with formal reasoning, which they take to be the reasoning deployed in formal logic, which can be understood as typified by deductive proofs. This is the fourth sense of *formal* that we presented in our introduction. In contrast, they note, informal reasoning is many-sided, or multiperspectival (there are several different, legitimate points of view on questions); open-ended, or nondecidable (different, even incompatible, beliefs can be plausible, well supported by evidence and reasons); probabilistic (no conclusion follows necessarily from even the best reasons); and exfoliating, or branching (there are usually different, independent lines of support for and opposing any interesting position). In contrast, deductive proofs are uniperspectival (there is only one point of view) and have decidable entailments or straight-line chains of entailments (if the reasons are true, then the conclusion must be granted).

The term *everyday reasoning* is used by Perkins et al. to make at least two contrasts. Everyday reasoning is reasoning about everyday social and political issues as opposed to reasoning that requires technical or specialized knowledge.

(The latter is reasoning in the seventh sense of *formal* that we presented in our introduction.) The methodology of the studies reported deliberately addressed reasoning that does not require specialized knowledge or expertise. (One false inference that might be drawn here is that technical, domain-specific, or expert reasoning is formal. Perkins et al. do not claim this, and it is clearly untrue: Most reasoning in law, policy making, literary criticism, business, and philosophy, to cite just a few examples, is decidedly nonformal.) In addition, Perkins et al. contrast everyday reasoning with critical reasoning, characterizing everyday reasoning as typically biased (that is, one sided, intended only to defend the reasoner's point of view) and incomplete (leaving out of consideration many of the reasons that bear on either side of the question). These two contrasts produce a complex conception of everyday reasoning.

The connection Perkins et al. make between habits or styles of reasoning and their related epistemologies is illuminating. However, we find a certain tension in the concept of a makes-sense epistemology. On the one hand, a makes-sense epistemology is characterized as generally adequate. Although it can result in biased and incomplete reasoning, it survives because it works adequately in many situations. On the other hand, a makes-sense epistemology is contrasted with a critical epistemology, one in which a reasoner takes into account a variety of plausible points of view and seeks information not immediately present that may have a bearing on the issue at hand. So, a makes-sense epistemology is not always adequate.

Perkins et al. contrast two pairs of concepts: everyday reasoning and a makes-sense epistemology, on the one hand, and critical reasoning and a critical epistemology, on the other. Is there a parallel between these two sets? They presuppose a makes-sense epistemology as underlying everyday reasoning, which is noncritical reasoning. The concept of a makes-sense epistemology is defined independently of everyday reasoning, which is entirely appropriate given that a makes-sense epistemology functions to explain one-sidedness and incompleteness in everyday reasoning. However, as far as we can see, the idea of a critical epistemology is not defined independently of, or seen as underlying, critical reasoning. Just the reverse: A critical epistemology presupposes, or is constructed on the basis of, critical reasoning; a critical epistemology is what results from the exercise of critical reasoning. We find not entirely clear, then, the connection between these two pairs of constructs.

We suggest that the main explanatory and normative concepts in this theory of everyday reasoning could stand a degree of disentanglement and refinement, but we do not regard the problems just noted as creating insuperable problems for Perkins et al.'s results.

We also have some questions about a couple of details of methodology. One concerns the testing for the influence of lack of prior knowledge on faulty situation modeling. Perkins et al. presume that the knowledge most directly relevant to everyday reasoning is prior experience in thinking about a subject.

But much ill-informed prior thought would not likely improve the quality of a situation model, whereas subject-specific background information or experience could be expected to improve the quality of a situation model, even in the absence of much prior thought. Therefore, we question whether prior thought is the only variable that should be considered in testing for the influence of knowledge on the quality of situation modeling.

Our second comment relates to the procedure used to obtain samples of reasoning: asking subjects for a snap judgment on a vexed question and then asking them to produce their reasons for their judgment. It is important that subjects be and feel free not to have an opinion if they are genuinely undecided. Otherwise, they might feel forced to defend a position they were not comfortable with, and their reasoning might then be more my-sided and incomplete than it would normally be.

The payoff for Perkins et al. in studying informal reasoning is, first, that informal reasoning seems to them—in our view, entirely correctly—to be the sort of reasoning employed for personal and public issues in everyday life and, second, that their approach permits them to study and understand how and why much everyday reasoning is flawed and so build a theoretical basis for devising ways to improve it. Good reasoning—critical reasoning—has, they think, both pragmatic and idealistic benefits. It produces sound (or the best possible) beliefs about complex issues, and it constitutes a style of thought that they regard as inherently satisfying.

From our point of view as informal logicians, Perkins et al.'s series of studies and the theory that is beginning to emerge from them are beneficial in that they help us understand hitherto ill-understood phenomena. We have long noticed, for example, that students give "one-shot" arguments and have difficulty engaging, or even giving a serious hearing to, points of view that are different from theirs, and we have wondered why. An explanation in terms of the construct of a makes-sense epistemology makes sense!

In chapter 6, "Informal Reasoning in Inner-City Children and Adolescents," Miller-Jones reports the findings of his research on the contrasting reasoning styles of high and low achievers among Black inner-city school children. The task he gives is described as an informal one; he has found that high achievers use a *structure-using* (deductive) approach rather than the *structure-seeking* (inductive) approach of low achievers. (There is a further hypothesis about the cognitive ecology of the respective types, but it is not of immediate importance for the purposes of this commentary.)

This article fuses nicely with the others in this section, all of which focus on real reasoning—how people (here, inner-city Black children) actually reason, or appear to. It is difficult to be certain about this point, because the investigators did not have access to the actual reasoning processes of the children but only their behavior.

Miller-Jones's chapter, no less and no more than the others, raises these questions: Why should such a study be termed an investigation of informal reasoning? What is the warrant for so categorizing this type of investigation? To answer these questions, we need to know how Miller-Jones himself understands the nature of informal reasoning. There is no direct answer, but Miller-Jones's concept of informal logic may be deduced from the following text: "Any degree of knowing involves, of necessity, a knowing through concepts, and formal reasoning comprises reasoning in which the particular characteristics of concepts are most fully used to generate logically necessary deductions." The influence of the statement circulated by the organizers of the conference seems apparent in this text. Following it, Miller-Jones adopts the notion that at least part of the essence of formal logic is that it yields necessary deduction. This notion of logic corresponds to the fourth sense of *formal* as elaborated in our introduction. Yet, in an earlier passage, Miller-Jones appears to think of informal reasoning as reasoning that occurs in daily life rather than in a structured, academic situation: "For example, one can reason about voting for a [political] candidate or buying a car either in a school problem-solving context or in the context of the actual event in daily life." This view corresponds to our seventh sense of *formal*. We do not wish to make nuisances of ourselves, but we think it important to point out how the concept of informal reasoning seems, in chapter 6 and in others, to drift about as though it had not yet been anchored. Yet another sense of *informal* emerges when Miller-Jones writes: ". . . in this study both the individual's reasoning and the task structure could be considered informal. On the other hand, children could engage in more formal reasoning if they interpreted the adult's instructions as formal instructions." We find this passage somewhat perplexing. How could the children have engaged in more formal reasoning? How formal was their reasoning? What would it mean to have interpreted the adult's instructions as formal? We find ourselves drawing blanks as we search for answers to these questions, and so we pose them here, not as though they constituted insuperable objections but as queries and worries from interested participants.

Miller-Jones's chapter is a contribution to the study of informal reasoning in that it helps us fill in precious details of the slowly emerging picture of how the novice reasoner goes about one sort of task: problem solving. Perhaps studies of children from different social strata would serve to indicate to what degree these conclusions are based on a particular cognitive ecology and process of socialization underlying it—or on something else. (It looks as if the nature–nurture debate lingers in the background.)

We have other questions about this chapter. We wonder if the terms *inductive* and *deductive* are the best for describing the alternative approaches to the task. In the first place, these terms have proven somewhat thorny for logicians in their own research (see Johnson & Blair, 1985). Second, even if we suppose that a clear demarcation can be drawn between the deductive and the inductive, we wonder if the contrast between *structure-using* and *structure-seeking* is not clear enough by itself.

We now raise a question related to chapter 6 and others that we think is a serious one: Is informal reasoning by nature inferior to formal reasoning? Is informal reasoning by nature a stop-gap or lower-level alternative, to be pressed into service when there is not time to engage in formal reasoning? This question is cued by Miller-Jones: ". . . the special position of formal reasoning becomes increasingly apparent. . . . Its privileged position may also be seen in that it conceptually clarifies the usefulness of the methods of informal reasoning." We are not in a position to answer this question in any detail, but we are suspicious of the tendency—still very much in evidence in the 1980s—to assume that formal strategies are inherently superior and that informal ones, therefore, are always suspect and never anything better than a second-string quarterback who stays on the bench as long as the first-string quarterback performs adequately. Such views echo the philosophical convictions of Plato and later of Descartes. But philosophical developments in the last 25 years in logic, the philosophy of science, epistemology, and indeed even in ethics suggest that these old ideals—one would like to say, following Nietzsche, idols—have entered the twilight of their influence.

Consider, for instance, the most recent work of Harman, a philosopher who has devoted a fair amount of research to classical problems in epistemology. Harman's latest work, *Change in View: Principles of Reasoning* (1986), marks a new direction in his research. Now Harman is much more interested in reasoning than in knowledge, and he explicitly rejects the idea that formal logic can furnish the required principles of reasoning.

Other challenges to the positivist research program in which formal reasoning and necessary deduction are enshrined can be found in the works of MacIntyre (1981) and Rorty (1979). Indeed, the strongest challenge to this ideal may have been the observation made by Aristotle in the *Nicomachean Ethics,* who reminded us that "it is the mark of the educated man not to expect more precision than the subject matter affords" (1094b25).

We mention these developments because we believe that it is important for those who are interested in informal reasoning not to employ in their research projects borrowed conceptualizations, agendas, and ideals that have become problematic in contemporary philosophy.

CONCLUSION

The chapters we have discussed in this commentary share the theme "contexts of informal reasoning." Each chapter focuses on informal reasoning in a different context: scientific inquiry, medical practice, international relations, the courtroom, everyday thinking, and the inner-city schoolroom. If these contexts are not nicely parallel, that is forgivable; any such collection requires the adroit use of a shoehorn to fit the scholars one wants to hear from into each section.

In the cases in which *context* designates a distinct practice or subject matter—scientific inquiry, medicine, foreign policy formulation, and judicial reasoning,—we note that in each case context seems to make a difference to the reasoning practices at work. Michael Faraday's open-ended task of trying to understand the relationship between electricity and magnetism connects with a methodology that—although, as Tweney demonstrates, it was clearly specifiable and functionally efficient—permitted twists and turns, reversals, and changes of direction. It is hard to imagine capturing Faraday's reasoning by using a tight, binary-code information-processing model of the sort that, as Christensen and Elstein show, applies so effectively to medical problem solving. The context of the latter, however, is much more determinate: The goals are clear, and, given the abundant diagnostic and treatment information we possess, the choices are relatively circumscribed.

Although it would be surprising if personal schemata or points of view did not affect physicians' reasoning, there is even more scope for the influence of personal, idiosyncratic attitudes, beliefs, and values in the more open-ended contexts of the courtroom and the state department conference room or Oval Office. We are struck by Lawrence's and Voss's studies, which show to what a significant degree personal outlooks influence the selection and organization of data, even prior to the consideration of alternative choices of actions or policies.

Yet, in spite of the clear context-relativity of some elements of the reasoning methods, there also seem to be general similarities between the reasoning in different contexts. In each case, the reasoner employs patterns of organized information, uses finite sets of strategies to find solutions, and relies on quite circumscribed sets of action responses. If one attends to these general features of reasoning, one will not be lost moving from the hospital to the courtroom to the state department.

There do seem to be differences between the reasoning of experts in their fields and the reasoning of ordinary citizens or children about day-to-day events. (We suspect, however, that the expert who reasons efficiently in his or her field may reason no differently in everyday circumstances from the nonexpert.) This point should hardly be surprising inasmuch as expertise presumably consists of, among other things, well-developed, continuously tested and improved ways of reasoning. The difference, though, is one of degree, not kind. Perkins et al.'s metacognition is available to the man and woman in the street no less than to the scientist or physician.

Finally, we have made a bit of a hubbub about the term *informal*, having found it difficult to pin down exactly. This is not to say that there is no tiger in the forest, for we are quite convinced that there is. It will, we think, turn out to be one with many stripes, and so will be, as this volume is, interdisciplinary. But to get this tiger in clear sight will not be easy.

Most of all, we fear that a perception may have been created that, if not tempered, could prove misleading to future research. This is the notion that informal reasoning is somehow second best. We hope that the chapters in this section and our comments have given any who entertain this idea pause for further reasoning—informal, of course.

REFERENCES

Blair, J. A., & Johnson, R. H. (Eds.) (1980). *Informal logic: the first international symposium.* Inverness, CA: Edgepress.

Carnap, R. (1928). *Der Logische aufbau der welt* [*The logical construction of the world*]. Berlin (now Meiner, Leipzig).

Govier, T. (1986). Logical analogies. *Informal Logic, 7*(1), 27–33.

Harman, G. (1986). *Change in view: Principles of reasoning.* Cambridge, MA: MIT Press.

Johnson, R. H., & Blair, J. A. (1985). Informal logic: The past five years: 1978–83. *American Philosophical Quarterly, 22,* 181–196.

Kahneman, D., Slovic, P., & Tversky, A. (1982). *Judgment under uncertainty: Heuristics and biases.* New York: Cambridge University Press.

MacIntyre, A. (1981). *After virtue.* Notre Dame, IN: University of Notre Dame Press.

Massey, G. (1981). The pedagogy of logic. *Teaching Philosophy, 4,* 303–336.

Nisbett, R., & Ross, L. (1980). *Human inference: Strategies and shortcomings of social judgement.* Englewood Cliffs, NJ: Prentice-Hall.

Paul, R. (1982). Teaching critical thinking in the "strong" sense. *Informal Logic, 4*(2), 2–7.

Piaget, J., & Inhelder, B. (1958). *The growth of logical thinking from childhood to adolescence: An essay on the construction of formal operational structures.* (A. Parsons & S. Milgram, Trans.) New York: Basic Books.

Revlin, R., & Mayer, R. E. (1978). *Human reasoning.* Washington, DC: V. H. Winston.

Rorty, R. (1979). *Philosophy and the mirror of nature.* Princeton, NJ: Princeton University Press.

Simon, H. A. (1983). *Reasons in human affairs.* Stanford, CA: Stanford University Press.

Thomason, R. H. (Ed.). (1974). *Formal philosophy: Selected papers of Richard Montague.* New Haven, CT: Yale University Press.

Wason, P. C., & Johnson-Laird, P. N. (1972). *The psychology of reasoning: Structure and content.* London: Batsford.

II
MODES AND MODELS OF INFORMAL REASONING

8 Informal Reasoning and Informal Logic

Merrilee H. Salmon
University of Pittsburgh

Reasoning consists of many different skills: the abilities to think coherently, to comprehend instructions and advice, to understand the difference between unsupported claims and arguments, to recognize when unsupported claims need support, and to marshall support from general background knowledge or from new investigations. Reasoning also includes formulating problems and figuring out their solutions, drawing conclusions from premises, designing thought experiments or real experiments that can test claims, formulating and using principles to evaluate arguments, seeing the force of counterexamples, making judgments of information's relevance, as well as surveying and assessing possible outcomes of decisions and plans.

Logic, in today's scholarly usage, is more narrowly concerned with investigating and framing general principles concerning the relation between premises and conclusions of correct arguments. Looked at this way, logic is simply one aspect of reasoning, but it has received a disproportionate amount of scholarly attention for reasons that are partly historical. Logic in the sense just described was invented by Aristotle some 2,300 years ago. His invention was reckoned a smashing intellectual success by his contemporaries, and it has stood the test of time as a body of knowledge that has been taught in schools from antiquity to the present day.

In past centuries, the word *logic* referred to more than the evaluation of arguments according to principles. For example, the famous 17th-century work, *The Art of Thinking* (commonly known as the "Port Royal Logic") devotes only about a quarter of the discussion (the section entitled "Reasoning") to the principles of evaluating arguments; the rest of the treatise is concerned with other aspects of the subject that was then called logic but is now called reasoning. The

153

author of the treatise, Arnauld (1964), raised doubts about whether the formal rules of reasoning, which he admitted to be "the only aspect of logic traditionally treated with any care," are "as useful as is generally believed" (p. 175). He said, "If any man is unable to detect by the light of reason alone the invalidity of an argument, then he is probably incapable of understanding the rules by which we judge whether an argument is valid—and still less able to apply those rules" (p. 175). One could hardly offer a more succinct case than Arnauld's for the priority of informal reasoning over formal logic and for the importance of studying informal reasoning.

In this chapter, I adopt the practice of using the word "logic" to refer to the study of the principles of correct reasoning, whether these principles are formal or informal. Formal logic is so called because it focuses on the structural or formal relations in arguments, such as class inclusion, class exclusion, conjunction, negation, and implication while ignoring any specific content or subject matter. Informal logic, by contrast, does not abstract from the content of the arguments, but takes both content and context into account in the framing of its principles. Informal logic recognizes structural aspects of arguments, but these do not form an exclusive basis for evaluation.

The study of the relation "following from" that holds between premises and conclusions in correct arguments is broad, in the sense that arguments suitable for logical analysis and evaluation occur in the physical, social, and biological sciences; the humanities, mathematics, medicine, the arts, business, and everyday life. At the same time, from its inception, logic as a discipline has focused on the structure or form of the arguments, in virtue of which the conclusion follows from the premises, rather than the particular content of arguments. Aristotle's system of logic was a formal system. It was, in fact, the very first axiomatic system, even earlier than Euclid's axiomatic formulation of geometry (Mates, 1972; Ross, 1949). Although, obviously, it was possible to construct correct arguments and to criticize weak arguments before Aristotle developed formal logic (e.g., Plato's criticisms of the Sophists' arguments), the study of the general principles of "following from" began with Aristotle's formal logic.

Although Aristotle specified a formal system for evaluating arguments, his construction of the theory depended on informal reasoning in crucial ways. His logic was motivated by the problem of deciding, in certain cases, whether or not a property could be attributed to (or predicated of) the subject of a sentence. Aristotle was particularly interested in demonstrating scientific truths, but his theory has obvious application in everyday life. In some cases (e.g., "All chickens have feathers"), the predication is obviously true, but in other cases (e.g., "All whales suckle their young"), it is less so. In the harder cases, Aristotle saw that judgment is aided by an intermediate idea or middle term through which the two original terms may be connected. "Mammal," for example, is the middle term connecting whales and things that suckle their young, for whales are mammals, and all mammals suckle their young.

Aristotle's theory defined precisely the sorts of arguments (called *syllogisms*) to which his formal rules applied. Premises and conclusions of these argument's are sentences that relate a subject term and a predicate term in one of four ways: by saying that the subject class is (a) completely included in the predicate, (b) completely excluded from the predicate, (c) partially included, or (d) partially excluded. Thus, each sentence that is a premise or conclusion of a syllogism can be expressed in one of the following forms: "Every A is a B" (universal affirmative); "No A is a B" (universal negative); "Some A is a B" (particular affirmative); "Some A is not a B" (particular negative). Syllogisms have exactly two premises that relate the subject and predicate terms of the conclusion through a term that occurs only in the premises (the middle term). Each syllogism contains only three terms; each premise contains one of the terms of the conclusion as well as the middle term. This framing of the definition of the syllogism, which amounts to the formulation of a problem in a way that allows for its solution, was itself an impressive accomplishment of informal reasoning. Aristotle set out the problem in such a way that there are only a finite number of possible forms of argument to consider. Within this framework, a systematic search for rules governing the correct forms of reasoning is possible.

Given Aristotle's definition of the syllogism, there are 64 formally possible pairs of syllogistic premises (when the order of those premises is ignored). Aristotle showed, by constructing counterexamples, that most of these pairs cannot validly yield a conclusion. In other words, argument forms with these premise pairs are invalid. An argument form is called invalid if it is possible for an argument with that structure to have true premises and a false conclusion. Although invalidity is thus defined as a matter of form or structure, here again, informal reasoning plays a role, for it is necessary to understand the content of what is said in order to see that an actual argument (an instance of an argument form) such as "All animals are substances, and all men are substances; therefore, all animals are men" has true premises and a false conclusion. Aristotle used this example to show that the argument form "Every A is a B, and every C is a B; therefore, every A is a C" is invalid. It is possible (as shown by the example) for an argument in this form to have true premises and a false conclusion. There are no formal rules for generating such counterexamples; informal reasoning and ingenuity are required. Aristotle, not lacking ingenuity, was able to eliminate as many as eight forms at a time by a suitable choice of terms (Mates, 1972, chap. 12).

Aristotle grouped the correct or valid types of syllogisms on the basis of their *figures*. The figure of a syllogism is determined by the position of the middle term in the pair of premises. In Aristotle's first figure, the middle term is the subject of one of the premises and the predicate of the other premise; in the second figure, the middle term is the predicate of both premises; and in the third figure, the middle term is the subject of both premises. He selected as axioms the valid forms in the first figure and then proved forms in other figures valid by reducing them to these axioms. According to Kneale and Kneale (1962), Aristotle's reason for choosing the first figure forms as axioms was that, when the terms are arranged in his usual order, the transitivity of the connection between the terms is obvious. For example, a literal translation of Aristotle's statement of one of the valid first-figure forms reads "For if A is predicated of all B and B of all C, it is necessary for A to be predicated of all C" (Kneale & Kneale, 1962, p. 73). In this arrangement, the middle term, B, drops out, and the connection between A and C is straightforward.

Aristotle's theory incorporated such modern features as the use of variables. He also recognized that his choice of axioms was somewhat arbitrary, for he saw that the system could have been constructed in a different way, using some of his derived theorems as new axioms and then deriving the old axioms as theorems in the new system (Mates, 1972, chap. 12).

Aristotle's insight that the correctness of syllogistic arguments depended on such logical relations as class inclusion and class exclusion, as well as his success in providing general rules for the evaluation of arguments, inspired his followers to restructure arguments to apply his principles to them and to construct further formal techniques to handle arguments that could not be transformed to syllogisms. The practice of those who tried to reinterpret apparently nonsyllogistic arguments as syllogisms (so that they could be evaluated by Aristotle's methods) was guided by the following principle of informal reasoning: If an available method of solution does not fit a problem, try to restructure the problem to make the method work.

Thus, in traditional treatments of the syllogism, we find sections on how to translate various sentences into one of the four standard forms and how to reduce the number of terms in an argument so that a standard syllogism results. Informal reasoning is required to replace expressions with their synonymous equivalents and to replace negated terms with their positive forms, with suitable adjustments to preserve meaning. Consider, for example, the following argument taken from a recent magazine story about home decoration: "[All] rooms look their best if they are used by the people they belong to. Unless a room is arranged in a way that allows it to function comfortably, it will never be used. Therefore no room will look its best until it is comfortably arranged" (Hampton, 1987, p. 28). Using our informal understanding of the meanings of these sentences, we can construct the following standard syllogistic argument: Every room that looks its best is used; no room that is used is uncomfortably arranged; therefore, no room that looks its best is uncomfortably arranged.

Aristotle framed formal rules to guide some of the required transformations (e.g., in a universal negative sentence, meaning is preserved when subject and predicate terms are interchanged). But there are no rules for many other sorts of transformations, and informal reasoning is required to understand the whole process.

Informal reasoning is also employed to reorganize complex arguments involving more than three terms and more than two premises into a series of syllogisms. The following example of such a complex argument is taken from "The Port Royal Logic":

(i)   Stingy men are full of desires.
(ii) Those who are full of desires lack things desired because it is impossible to satisfy all desires.
(iii) Those who lack what they desire are miserable.
      Therefore, stingy men are miserable. (Arnauld, 1964, p. 177)

In this argument, the first two premises can be combined to yield the preliminary conclusion that "Stingy men lack what they desire." This preliminary conclusion is then used as a premise, along with the third premise, to yield the stated conclusion. Of course, not every argument that can be reduced to a series of syllogisms is as straightforward as this one; some require more strenuous use of informal reasoning to sort out the premises in the proper way.

Other writers after Aristotle concentrated on constructing techniques for formally evaluating other types of arguments. In antiquity, for example, the Stoics developed formal methods for analyzing arguments in which correctness depends on the semantics of sentential connectives such as *or, and, not,* and *if . . . then,* methods that were further refined in this century with the introduction of truth tables, natural deduction systems, and axiomatic theories of sentential logic. Further advances in the 19th and 20th centuries provided formal methods for handling arguments in which validity depends on structural relations among individuals rather than among properties of individuals. With the major development of symbolic apparatus and techniques by the giants of modern logic such as Russell, Frege, Tarski, and others, still more complex types of arguments were brought within the scope of formal analysis. In each of these cases, however, the new methods depended for their construction on informal reasoning, just as Aristotle's own work did.

The point of these historical remarks is to show that informal reasoning plays an integral part in the construction of formal systems. Moreover, given the history of logic, it is easy to understand the tendency to regard all logic as formalizable, for the successful construction of ever more powerful formal systems supports a view dear to logicians: any argument that is correct can be shown to be correct in virtue of its logical form. This claim is borne out by the history of logic, insofar as it can be read as the history of increasingly elaborate formal systems devised to exhibit the formal structure of more and more complex arguments and to allow their evaluation by general principles referring only to their form. No logician thinks the work is complete. Indeed, the principle motivates continuing research in such areas as logics that employ modal operators (necessity and possibility), deontic operators (obligation and permissibility), and tense operators, as well as the logics of questions, of commands, and of other specialized topics. Unfortunately, many accounts of the development of these formal systems ignore or fail to emphasize the contributions of informal reasoning to the enterprise.

No one can deny that formal logic has developed an impressive array of techniques designed to further the goal of analyzing arguments. Moreover, although the invention of these tools required the genius of an Aristotle, a Chrysippus, or a Frege, the techniques have been streamlined to the point where many are now accessible to beginning college students. Thus, it seems appropriate to many teachers of logic to introduce students to logic by presenting techniques of formal analysis, such as truth tables and Venn diagrams, and applying these to examples of arguments in ordinary language. As widespread as this practice is, and as plausible as it may seem, I believe that it is a mistake.

In the first place, although most students can master the fundamentals of translating simple arguments in English into the appropriate symbolic forms and then applying the rules to demonstrate that the conclusion follows from the premises, only rarely do the students see the point of the exercise. Whatever fascination such formal exercises may hold for some, logic taught this way is seen as something apart from life, not something important or even useful. The arguments that are dealt with in logic classes are either types not often met in real life, or they are examples so simple that the machinery brought forth to analyze them seems to be more trouble than it is worth. For most students, the subject is seen as a pointless and often painful requirement to get through somehow and forget as quickly as possible.

Furthermore, in these treatments of logic, the students never really get a glimpse of the power and beauty of formal logical systems, for they see nothing of the context of the original problem or the demonstration of skills in informal reasoning that gave rise to these accomplishments. The techniques of logic are seen, at best, as a bag of tricks—and not especially useful tricks at that.

Recent psychological studies of reasoning indicate that formal instruction in logic is strikingly ineffective; the skills allegedly taught do not transfer to situations outside the classroom. When subjects who have had some training in logic are presented with relatively simple logical problems, such Wason's selection problem (Johnson-Laird, 1983, p. 30), they cannot solve it.[1] Nisbett, Fong, Lehman, and Cheng (1987), who are optimistic about the possibility of teaching certain pragmatic inferential rules, such as statistical heuristics, nevertheless

---

[1]In one version of the selection task, the subject is presented with four cards, displaying the following symbols: $E, K, 4, 7$. The subject (who already knows that each card has a number on one side and a letter on the other) is asked to select those cards that need to be turned over to determine whether or not the generalization "If a card has a vowel on one side, then it has an even number on the other side" is true. Most subjects, even after some instruction in the principle of *modus tollens,* fail to see that the card with the 7 must be turned over, in addition to the card with the E.

share Johnson-Laird's skepticism about training students to use formal, deductive logical rules in situations that are different from the context of instruction (p. 625).

Nisbett et al. cited a number of empirical studies that were designed to evaluate students' ability to master abstract rules of logic and to transfer such rules to new situations. However, the data supporting these results are quite limited. Instruction in formal logic is given primarily in philosophy departments—or, at least, classes devoted to formal logic as the primary subject matter are conducted there. Despite the urging of a few pioneers, such as Michael Scriven and Robert Ennis, very little attention is paid to evaluating even such basic features as the improvement of students' logical skills from the beginning to the end of the course, where a simple pretest and posttest might provide valuable information. Evaluating the students' ability to transfer any logical skills acquired in the course by doing follow-up studies poses greater obstacles and is almost never attempted. Greater cooperation between philosophers who are teaching logic and psychologists who are trying to understand how logic is learned would obviously be beneficial for increasing our knowledge of how effective formal training is.

One conclusion that Johnson-Laird (1983) drew from the selection-task experiments, as well as experiments that show that some forms of syllogisms are much more difficult to solve than others, is that none of the traditional theories of inference are adequate as psychological descriptions or explanations. Johnson-Laird (1983) cited seven goals for adequate theories:

1. A descriptively adequate theory must account for the evaluation of conclusions, the relative difficulty of different inferences, and the systematic errors and biases that occur in drawing spontaneous conclusions.
2. The theory should explain the differences in inferential ability from one individual to another.
3. The theory should be extensible in a natural way to related varieties of inference rather than apply to a narrow class of deductions.
4. The theory should explain how children acquire the ability to make inferences.
5. The theory must allow that people are capable of making valid inferences, that is, that they are potentially rational.
6. The theory should shed some light on why formal logic was invented and how it was developed.
7. The theory should ideally have practical application to the teaching of reasoning skills. (pp. 65–66)

Aristotle's own theory of the syllogism, when properly understood in the context of the informal reasoning that guides its construction, I want to argue, fulfills all of these criteria.

It should be clear from what has been said that Aristotle's theory can be extended in a natural way to related varieties of inference, that it allows that people are capable of making valid inferences, and that it sheds some light on why formal logic was invented and how it has developed.

To show that Aristotle's theory accounts for the evaluation of conclusions, the relative difficulty of different inferences, and the systematic errors that occur in drawing spontaneous conclusions, I begin with a point on which Aristotle and Johnson-Laird agreed: Syllogisms of the following form in Aristotle's first figure are intuitively obvious to almost everyone, not only because they are recognized as correct when presented, but because the correct conclusion is drawn spontaneously when just the premises are presented:

1. Every artist is a beekeeper.   Every *A* is a *B*.
   Every beekeeper is a chemist.   Every *B* is a *C*.
   Every artist is a chemist.   Every *A* is a *C*.

Also intuitively obvious is another first figure syllogism:

2. Every spider is an eight-legged creature. Every *A* is a *B*.
   No eight-legged creature is an insect.   No *B* is a *C*.
   No spider is an insect.   No *A* is a *C*.

Only slightly less obvious are the other two valid first figure forms:

3. Some crow is an albino.   Some *A* is a *B*.
   Every albino is white.   Every *B* is *C*.
   Some crow is white.   Some *A* is *C*.

4. Some rich men are fools.   Some *A* are *B*.
   No fools are honored.   No *B* are *C*
   Some rich men are not honored. Some *A* are not *C*.

The contribution of the figural effect (the obviousness of the transition from subject to predicate term of the conclusion, with the middle term dropping out) to the simplicity of these forms has been discussed. In addition, the *atmosphere effect*, whereby a negative premise suggests a negative conclusion and a particular premise suggests a particular conclusion, also noted by some writers (Johnson-Laird, 1983, p. 73), plays a role here.

The psychological suggestiveness of the atmosphere effect is backed up by sound logical principles. The link between the subject and predicate terms in the conclusion occurs as a result of their connection by means of the middle term. If one of the premises is negative, then the connection through the middle term must be one of total or partial *exclusion*, resulting in a negative conclusion. Similarly, if one of the premises is particular, then the connection can only be a *partial* inclusion or exclusion, not a total inclusion or exclusion, and in such a case the conclusion is a particular, rather than a universal sentence.

Aristotle's theory of the syllogism proceeds by showing how any correct syllogism can be reduced to one of the four correct first figure syllogisms. For this, he employed principles of informal reasoning, such as pointing out that the order of premises is irrelevant and that sentences can be replaced with other sentences that are equivalent in meaning but different in form. Displaying his skills at formal manipulation, he showed further that the less obvious first figure forms, 3 and 4, can be reduced to 1 and 2 by first transforming them to second figure syllogisms and then showing that all second figure syllogisms can be reduced to the two most obvious forms, 1 and 2 (Mates, 1972, chap. 12). A *measure,* then, of the difficulty of any syllogism can be based on the number and difficulty of transformations required to reduce it to one of the obvious forms. (This is not to say, of course, that people typically solve syllogisms by performing reductions of this type.)

Johnson-Laird (1983) has said that the following syllogism is very difficult in the sense that most respondents, when presented with the premises, either say that no conclusion follows or draw the wrong conclusion. Because this is not a first figure form, Aristotle would also consider it less obvious than the preceding examples. Here are the premises:

All bankers are athletes.	All *B* are *A*.
None of the councillors are bankers.	No *C* are *B* (p. 67).

Note, first of all, that when this more difficult syllogism is framed using terms that refer to classes that are understood to be related in real life by class inclusion and class exclusion, it is easier to solve.

All first basemen are athletes.	All *B* are *A*.
No catchers are first basemen.	No *C* are *B*.

Very few people who know anything about baseball would draw the incorrect conclusion that some catchers are not athletes, and most would correctly conclude that some athletes are not catchers. The phenomenon of so-called familiarity has been noted in analyzing poor performance in sentential reasoning involving *modus tollens* and the selection task, but is has not been given special attention in the syllogistic case. Even though we may be familiar with all the terms of the syllogism ("athletes," "councillors," and "bankers"), the classes these terms refer to do not have the relationship to one another stated in the premises. Thus, we are familiar with the terms but not with the relationships referred to in the premises.

Another difficulty with this form of syllogism is that although both premises are universal, the correct conclusion is a particular sentence. In fact, on the modern interpretation of syllogisms, which takes a different view of the semantics of universal sentences from the Aristotelian, no conclusion follows validly from an argument form with premises of this type. (Using the modern interpretation, we can never validly derive a particular conclusion from a pair of universal premises, because the universal premises are said to lack "existential import," whereas the particular conclusion claims that something does exist (Kneale & Kneale, p. 65). Nevertheless, using Aristotle's theory, which seems to accord with common sense better than the modern interpretation, in some respects, we can show what conclusion does follow. We can also explain why this form of the syllogism is so difficult. To transform the syllogism into an equivalent first figure syllogism, several steps are required.

Both premises must be converted; that is, the order of the subject and predicate terms must be reversed. In a universal affirmative sentence, such as "Every *B* is an *A*" (or, equivalently, "All *B* are *A*"), the sentence says something about each and every member of the class *B* but not about everything that is an *A*. Therefore, the subject and predicate cannot simply be reversed if meaning is to be preserved. However, if "All *B* are *A*" is true, then it must be the case (given the Aristotelian interpretation of universal sentences) that "Some *A* are *B*," and this type of limited conversion is applied to the original sentence. In the universal negative premise, both *C* and *B* are *distributed,* that is, the sentence says something about each and every member of the classes that *C* and *B* refer to; this sentence converts simply to "No *B* are *C*." Reformulated, the syllogism looks like this correct first figure form:

Some *A* are *B*.
No *B* are *C*.
Some *A* are not *C*.

Aristotle formulated rules governing conversion: Universal negative and particular affirmative sentences convert simply; universal affirmative sentences convert in a limited way; particular negative sentences do not convert. The rules of conversion, however, are grounded in considerations of informal reasoning concerning the meanings of such sentences, and they involve informal understanding of the nature of class exclusion and inclusion. To say "No men are women" is to say that the classes are mutually exclusive. This can be expressed as "No women are men" without change of meaning (insofar as meaning reflects certain features of class relationships, many other nuances obviously may not be captured). Particular affirmative sentences state that two classes share some members; thus, "Some women are executives" means the same as "Some executives are women." Limited conversion of universal affirmative sentences, in which "All *A* are *B*" is converted to "Some *B* are *A*," is harder to understand than simple conversion; thus, syllogisms requiring this are more difficult. Understanding why particular negative sentences, such as "Some animals are not horses," do not convert also poses some difficulty.

In general, the greater the number of transformations—and conversion is just one type—and the more difficult the transformations required to bring a syllogism into the obvious first figure forms, the harder the syllogism will be to solve. It is widely accepted that negative claims and particular claims are more difficult to understand than affirmative and universal claims.

Thus, we see that Aristotle's theory does account for relative difficulty in handling different syllogisms, for systematic errors, and for differences in inferential ability from one person to another. Furthermore, it throws light on how children acquire the ability to make inferences. Children do manage to grasp the concepts of negation and predication or class inclusion and exclusion required for understanding syllogisms without any training in formal rules. Actually, from a very early age, they are presented with syllogistic arguments in answer to their questions, such as: "Why do chickens have feathers?" "Because they're birds, and all birds have feathers." And "Do all birds fly?" "No, ostriches are birds, but ostriches can't fly."

Interestingly, when the second question and answer are put into the form of a standard syllogism, the result is an example of the very form that proved so difficult for Johnson-Laird's subjects:

All ostriches are birds.
No ostriches can fly.
Some birds cannot fly. (1983, p. 67)

It should now be clear that Aristotle's theory of the syllogism, viewed in connection with the motivating considerations of informal reasoning that guide the theory, meets the criteria set by Johnson-Laird. At the same time, it is clear that the power of the theory is disguised when syllogistic logic is taught as a formal exercise. Training in the formal rules can increase understanding, but only if such training is properly motivated and informed by considerations of informal reasoning. (For similar views on instruction, see chapters 16 and 17, this volume.)

Understanding syllogistic arguments is valuable; such understanding not only allows us to construct and evaluate these common arguments; it also shows us how to reason correctly from any syllogistic premises. Mastery of this well-understood type of reasoning provides access to more difficult types. We can agree with Arnauld's remark that the intuitive validity of correct syllogisms is usually easier to grasp than the rules of validity and, at the same time, recognize the benefit of becoming aware of the principles governing the validity of these syllogisms. Ferreting out principles is a considerable task. As noted, it calls on an array of informal reasoning skills, such as recognizing similarities among arguments with widely varying subject matter, focusing on the relevant features of total or partial class inclusion and total or partial class exclusion, understanding how principles are related to everyday causal as well as scientific reasoning, recognizing that the meaning of sentences can be preserved through various grammatical transformations, and honing the ability to produce and recognize counterexamples. If these skills were more strongly emphasized in the teaching of syllogistic logic, I believe that students would be able to transfer them successfully to other domains, even if they were to forget how to construct Venn diagrams or to employ the formal rules to evaluate nonobvious forms of syllogisms.

Moreover, although I have only data from my own teaching experience and conversations with colleagues as support, I believe that when formal techniques are introduced to students in the context of the informal considerations that originally motivated them, the students see formalisms as a way of simplifying reasoning rather than of making the process more obscure. This is true not only for syllogistic reasoning but for propositional logic and the logic of relations as well. For this reason, I believe that some formal methods are appropriate and useful even for students who are taking courses to improve their reasoning ability rather than to prepare for advanced courses in formal logic. Teachers can help students see the broad applicability of the formal techniques by carefully selecting examples and exercises from literature; from the physical, biological, and social sciences; and from business and writings about the arts. Instructors can also encourage students to look for particular forms of reasoning in their own reading, whether that is assigned texts, recreational literature, or newspapers. It is ill-advised to focus on formal methods as exemplified only in artificially constructed, tidy arguments and then to expect students to apply these methods to the messy arguments they meet in the real world. If students are to find any use for formal methods, a considerable amount of instructional time has to be devoted to recognizing and reconstructing arguments in natural discourse that are incompletely stated, ambiguous, or meaningful only when referents in the circumstances from which they arise are fleshed out.

Thus far, I have talked about the interplay of informal reasoning and informal logic in connection with reasoning that lends itself to formal analysis. There is another area, however, in which informal logic and informal reasoning are extremely important: inductive reasoning. I use the term *inductive argument* to refer to a broad class of arguments that, even when they are successful, do not have premises that provide conclusive support for their conclusions. In other words, inductive arguments are those in which it is possible for all the premises to be true and the conclusion to be false, even though no mistake occurs in drawing the conclusion from those premises. Given this characterization, no matter how sophisticated the advances in formal techniques, there is no possibility that arguments of this type could ever be subject to the principle "Any argument that is correct is correct in virtue of its logical form." It is generally recognized that this principle applies only to *deductive* arguments (arguments in which the truth of the premises guarantee the truth of the conclusion).

Inductive arguments include those that draw conclusions about populations on the basis of observed samples, those that hold that things that are similar in certain observed respects will also be similar in some further, unobserved respect (arguments from analogy), those that are statistical syllogisms (e.g., A TV set will be trouble-free because most TV sets from that manufacturer are trouble-free), and arguments that attempt to establish causal relations on the basis of correlations. In general, inductive arguments draw conclusions about what is unobserved on the basis of what is observed. Their conclusions go beyond the information contained in the premises, instead of recombining that information or drawing out connections that are implicit in the premises.

Despite the pervasiveness and the importance of inductive arguments, standard logic textbooks treat them, if at all, in the sections near the end of the book that get cut when time runs out. Furthermore, at the beginning of the texts, arguments are classified as valid or invalid. Valid arguments are defined as those in which the truth of the premises guarantees the truth of the conclusion. The correctness of an argument, the texts repeat again and again, depends on its logical form. If and when the subject of inductive logic is broached, students have to be told that more than formal considerations are required to evaluate inductive arguments and that they are not valid, inasmuch as this special truth-preserving correctness applies only to deductive arguments. Inductive arguments do have their own kind of correctness, the texts admit, but at this point the textbooks have stigmatized them as incapable of preserving truth with certainty: At best, they lead to conclusions that are probably true, if the premises are true. (It is often said, not entirely in jest, that in the first part of logic texts you learn what the fallacies are, and in the latter part you commit them.)

Inductive reasoning plays too vital a role in everyday life to be treated in this second-class way. Most of the arguments that we are called on to construct and evaluate as consumers, citizens, or just persons who make contingency plans and judgments about consequences of our actions are inductive. Whether or not we vote for a particular political candidate is apt to depend more on the candidate's or the party's past performance than on whether the candidate has committed some formal logical error, such as affirming the consequent, in a speech. Many everyday economic decisions (as well as not-so-everyday ones) are based on analogies, on past experience, or on advice of friends and experts. Causal reasoning is pervasive in our everyday lives, but no formal techniques guarantee the correctness of the conclusions of these arguments; formal logic simply cannot offer standards that are adequate for their evaluation.

In assessing inductive arguments, many considerations not required for evaluating deductive arguments demand our attention. Background information, which is not contained in the premises, is necessary to judge whether or not more information should be gathered, whether bias is present, whether the similarities in analogical arguments are relevant, whether samples are large enough, or whether the types of causal forces appealed to are reasonable.

Although the correctness of inductive arguments is not simply a matter of form, some formal considerations can help in their evaluation. In the first place, understanding their form helps, as it does in deductive arguments, to draw attention to gaps or missing premises. For example, if someone argues that a student will do well in graduate school because he or she scored well on the Graduate Record Examination, then the suppressed premise might be "Most students with high GRE scores do well in graduate school," or it might be "Most of *our* students with high GRE scores have done well." Exposing such premises is useful, because only then can their accuracy be assessed. Here again informal reasoning, rather than formal reasoning, is required to make such judgments.

In addition, knowing the form of the argument is important for identifying informal standards to apply to it. Because standards vary for the assessment of different kinds of inductive arguments, it is useful to have ways of distinguishing types, and so the notion of form of an argument is helpful, even though logical correctness does not depend solely on form, as it does in the deductive case.

For example, suppose that a particular work-rehabilitation program, such as the recently reported one in which new prison buildings are being built by crews of prisoners, working for pay, supervised by an inmate-contractor, had been successful in one state prison. Suppose, too, that many of the worker-inmates had learned new skills and, as a result, had jobs waiting for them when they were released. On the basis of this case, someone might argue that the program will work in another prison. To dismiss the argument because the sample size is too small would not be appropriate; the argument is probably best understood as an argument by analogy rather than as an inductive generalization based on a sample of one. The different forms of the two types of arguments can be characterized as follows:

Inductive Generalization

$Z\%$ of observed A's are B's

$Z\%$ of all A's are B's

Argument by Analogy

x has properties $A, B, \ldots Z$.

y has properties $A, B, \ldots$.

y has property Z also.

In an analogical argument, the most appropriate questions to ask before accepting or rejecting the conclusion are questions about relevant similarities and dissimilarities between x and y. We do not know, for example, the exact cause of the success of the building program in the first prison (x), so we cannot investigate directly to see whether that cause (probably a complex system of causes) is present in the other prison as well. But if we can point out some similarities between x and y that are plausible positive causal factors and show no striking dissimilarities that might interfere with y's success, we can argue by analogy for the construction program in case y. For example, does y's inmate population contain a labor pool with the requisite skills, like x's, to get the project started and carry it through? Or was the success of the first project a function of the unique skills and character of the contractor who is serving a life term in x.

In analogical arguments, the issues of sample size, bias, and possible counterinstances are less important than the relevance of similarities mentioned in the premises. When we are concerned with inductive generalizations, sample size and absence of bias are crucial. Where we have the skills, we can employ formal statistical methods, if sufficient information is available. However, correctness of the conclusion is not guaranteed by the formal structure. When we lack either the statistical skills or the information, it is useful to consider such questions in an informal way, if only to recognize that conclusions may have to be tentative. Whether or not we can use any formal methods, some understanding of the form of the argument under consideration is helpful in asking the right informal questions.

Because inductive reasoning is so context-dependent, courses such as the history course described by Kevin O'Reilly (chap. 18, this volume) provide an excellent opportunity for instructors to teach principles of good reasoning so compellingly that students can hardly fail to see their applicability. Other courses in humanities and social studies also can be structured to draw students' attention to the various forms of reasoning involved in the disciplines. Most of us, after all, acquire our skill in reasoning in such contexts rather than in courses that are wholly devoted to reasoning.

The possibility of teaching reasoning skills in various disciplinary courses does not obviate the utility of courses in logic or reasoning. In the first place, the skills are so important that they can hardly be overemphasized, and, in the second place, exposure to training in reasoning in many different contexts is a good way to insure that students will internalize the skills. Courses in reasoning should provide them with an opportunity to organize and reflect on principles that they may have grasped only in a vague, intuitive way.

The considerations raised earlier concerning the connections between informal reasoning and formal logic apply as well to the relations between informal reasoning and informal logic. In the case of informal rules, it is equally important to understand the force of the rules and how to apply them, and such understanding is a matter of informal reasoning.

Informal logic, as the subject is taught today, often focuses on the avoidance of mistakes in drawing conclusions from premises (fallacies). It is certainly useful and important to point out to students typical ways in which arguments go wrong. This chapter has focused on how to judge the correctness of arguments, but, in this context, fallacies can be seen as failures to observe one or more of the formal or informal rules for arguing correctly. For example, basing an argument from analogy on *irrelevant* rather than relevant similarities between the instances mentioned in the premises and the instance mentioned in the conclusion violates a rule and yields a fallacious argument. Basing an inductive generalization on a sample that is too small violates another rule and involves the arguer in the fallacy of hasty generalization. The rules "Base analogies on relevant similarities" and "Base inductive generalizations on samples of adequate size" are informal. A formal rule is "Every valid syllogism must have its middle term distributed at least once." Syllogistic arguments that fail to adhere to this rule cannot establish a proper connection between the subject and predicate terms of their conclusions and are said to commit the fallacy of the undistributed middle.

Philosophers, who are the usual teachers of logic, tend to regard fallacies just as mistakes that arise because of superficial similarities between correct and incorrect forms of argument, such as the similarity between the correct form of *modus tollens* (If P then Q, and not Q; therefore not P) and the fallacious form of denying the consequent (If P then Q, and not P; therefore not Q). Although philosophers are aware that fallacious arguments may be presented and accepted as correct for psychological reasons, the really interesting investigations of this phenomenon have been carried out by psychologists who are concerned with the reasons for systematic bias and error (e.g., Tversky & Kahneman, 1974; Nisbett & Ross, 1980; and Johnson-Laird & Wason, 1977). Incorporation of the results of their work into introductory logic courses would certainly go some way toward improving the student's comprehension and retention of the subject.

The relationships between informal reasoning and formal and informal logic discussed here only sample the many issues at stake but suffice, I hope, to stimulate further work. It is clear, I believe, that a better understanding of this topic would result in more effective teaching of reasoning. The benefits of living in a society whose members are skilled at reasoning hardly needs to be argued.

REFERENCES

Aristotle's Prior and Posterior Analytics, A Revised Text. (1949). (W. D. Ross, Ed.) Oxford: Oxford University Press.

Arnauld, A. (1964). *The art of thinking.* (J. Dickoff & P. James, Trans.). Indianapolis: Bobbs-Merrill. (Original published in 1662).

Hampton, M. (1987, March). The fine points of placement. *House and Garden,* pp. 24–30.

Johnson-Laird, P. N. (1983). *Mental models.* Cambridge, MA: Harvard University Press.

Johnson-Laird, P. N., & Wason, P. C. (Eds.). (1977). *Thinking: Readings in cognitive science.* Cambridge, England: Cambridge University Press.

Kneale, W. & Kneale, M. (1962). *The development of logic.* Oxford, England: Oxford University Press.

Mates, B. (1972). *Elementary logic* (2nd ed.). Oxford, England: Oxford University Press.

Nisbett, R., Fong, G. T., Lehman, D. R., & Cheng, P. W. (1987). Teaching reasoning. *Science, 238,* 625–631.

Nisbett, R., & Ross, L. (1980). *Human inference: Strategies and shortcomings of social judgment.* Englewood Cliffs, NJ: Prentice-Hall.

Tversky, A., & Kahnemann, D. (1974). Judgment under uncertainty: Heuristics and biases. *Science, 185,* 1124–1131.

9 Beliefs About Thinking

Jonathan Baron
Department of Psychology
University of Pennsylvania

Attempts to improve thinking and reasoning assume that people do not think as well as they might. The actual conduct of thinking does not measure up to an ideal standard. For example, I and others have argued that people are often biased toward views they already hold. They often fail to consider alternative views, counterevidence, or goals that their favorite plans will subvert. In making this argument, I hold up (and defend) a standard of *active open-mindedness* as an ideal.

Yet, people have their own standards. They are capable of thinking of themselves as careful, fair-minded, thoughtless, biased, decisive, faithful to their beliefs, or wishy-washy. They also apply these standards to others, as when they judge their friends, co-workers, or political leaders.

I argue here (with some preliminary data) that part of the discrepancy between people's thinking and ideal standards is that people's own standards differ from the ideal. Thus, people who think poorly by ideal standards may reject those standards. They may think they are thinking well when they are actually thinking poorly. This argument implies that the teaching of thinking may involve modification of people's standards. It is not just a matter of prodding people to live up to the standards they already hold.

My argument requires a specification of good thinking. If we are to claim that people are thinking poorly and don't know it, we need a clear standard that we can oppose to theirs. I begin, therefore, with a summary of the theory of good thinking as explained in Baron (1985, 1988a). I then discuss its implications for the formation of standards about thinking. Following this, I present some preliminary evidence concerning judgments of thinking.

WHAT IS THINKING?

Before introducing the sketch of the theory of good thinking, we need a general way of talking about thinking itself. By "thinking," I mean a conscious response to doubt or ignorance. (Baron, 1985, chap. 3, elaborates this account.) It is what we do when we are at a loss, at least for a moment, about what to do, what to believe, or what to adopt as a personal goal. For example, I read in the newspaper the suggestion that surrogate mothering be regulated by law. What do I think about that?

We may analyze all thinking into search and inference. We search for possibilities, evidence, and goals. These are the elements of thinking. They are conscious representations of actions or propositions. *Possibilities* are possible answers to the question that inspired the thinking: prohibition, no law at all, or something in between. Possibilities (like goals and evidence) may be in mind before thinking begins, or they may be added as a result of search or suggestion from outside. In the surrogate mother case, I might think that it should be outlawed or that the law should stay totally out of it except for the enforcement of contracts.

Each possibility may be seen as having a strength, which represents the extent to which it is seen by the thinker as satisfying the criteria that constitute the goal. When the goal of thinking is to assess the appropriateness of a belief (e.g., that surrogate mothers want to keep the babies they bear) as a basis for action (e.g., outlawing the practice), we may speak of the strength of a possibility as the thinker's degree of belief in it, or, in some cases, its probability. In decision making, the strength of a possibility corresponds to its overall desirability of an act, taking into account all relevant goals. In such cases, we might sometimes imagine that a possibility is evaluated on several dimensions, each corresponding to a goal, and the overall strength of the possibility is some sort of combination of these separate evaluations. For example, the possibility that surrogates be outlawed is good for those who might change their mind but bad for those who would not and for those who employ surrogates. These dimensional strengths can be used to guide the search for new possibilities; for example, we might require more stringent consent procedures rather than a total ban.

Evidence is anything that can be used to decide among the possibilities: reports of actual cases (e.g., of surrogate mothers who were happy with their action and those who were not), imagined cases, moral principles and arguments (freedom of contracts, freedom from exploitation), and so on. Evidence may be sought or made available. One possibility can serve as evidence against another, as when we challenge a scientific hypothesis by giving an alternative and incompatible explanation of the data.

Goals are the criteria used to weigh the evidence. How much do I care about the welfare of children, the freedom and sanctity of contracts, the feelings of biological mothers? Goals are not all given. I have to search for them and sometimes discover them just as I search for and discover evidence. The goal determines what evidence is sought and how it is used. For example, the goal of protecting the feelings of surrogate mothers leads to a search for evidence about those feelings. Goals and evidence together affect the strength of possibilities, but we do not speak of a piece of evidence being satisfied or reached, although we may say this of a goal.

One type of goal is a subgoal, a goal whose achievement will help us achieve our main goal. For example, the idea of obtaining informed consent might help to protect surrogate mothers. As Duncker (1945) pointed out in a different context, a subgoal is also a partial possibility. The idea of informed consent is a partial solution, and it also sets up a new goal (how to obtain consent).

The use of evidence, in the light of the goals, to increase or decrease the strengths of the possibilities may be called *inference*. It is useful to think of each piece of evidence as having a weight with respect to a given possibility and goal. The weight determines how much it strengthens or weakens the possibility in the light of the goal. This weight depends on the thinker's knowledge and beliefs. A weight by itself does not determine how much the strength of a possibility is revised; rather, the thinker controls this revision. Thus, a thinker may err by revising the strength of a possibility too much or too little.

Inference is only part of thinking. The rest is search. This is why logic is incomplete (at best) as a normative or prescriptive theory of thinking.[1]

The relationship among the elements of thinking may be illustrated as follows:

$$
\begin{array}{ccc}
\text{G} & \text{G} & \\
& & \text{E} \\
\text{P} & & \text{E} \\
\text{P} & & \text{E} \\
\end{array}
$$

The evidence affects the strengths of the possibilities, but the weight of the evidence is affected by the goals. Different goals can even reverse the weight of a piece of evidence. For example, if I am trying to decide between two cars (possibilities), one of which is heavy (evidence), concern with safety (a goal) might make the size a virtue (positive weight) but concern with mileage (another goal) might make it a detriment (negative weight).

Why just these phases: search for possibilities, evidence, and goals and in-

---

[1]Another problem with logic as a standard is the practical problem of applying it. If we are charitable in granting the right unstated premises to a thinker (as is Henle, 1962), we may find almost any thinking to be logical. If we are not charitable, insisting that premises be stated or, at least, conscious, we might find good thinking to be nonexistent outside of the logic classroom. On the other hand, the fallacies studied by "informal" logicians might be useful heuristics for detecting poor thinking.

ference? The idea is that thinking is a method of choosing among (or otherwise evaluating) potential possibilities—that is, possible beliefs, actions, or personal goals. For any choice, there must be a purpose or goal, and the goal is subject to change. I can search for (or be open to) new goals; hence, search for goals is always possible. There must also be elements that can be brought to bear on the choice among possibilities; hence, there must be evidence, and it can always be sought. Finally, the evidence must be used, or it might as well not have been gathered. These phases are necessary in this sense.

WHAT IS GOOD THINKING?

Baron (1985, chaps. 1–4) has argued that good thinking involves *optimal search* for possibilities, evidence, and goals and *fairness* in the search for evidence and in inference. These criteria are designed to maximize the expected desirability (utility) of the outcome of thinking in terms of the thinker's goals—not just the immediate goals but all the goals that are affected by the thinking in question. In other words, people who conform to these criteria will, on the average, do best at achieving their own goals.

Thinking goes wrong for three reasons. First, our search misses something that it should have discovered. For example, if I argue for surrogate motherhood on the basis of respect for contracts, I may ignore the argument that contracts made under various forms of duress or ignorance are already invalid. For example, we may be unfair to some of the possibilities at hand. I may ignore evidence when it goes against a possibility I initially favor. The same favoritism for a possibility may cause me to cut off my search prematurely for alternatives to my first idea (e.g., regulation) or for reasons why it might be wrong. Third, we may think too much. Like any other activity, thinking has a cost, and after some amount of thinking, its cost exceeds its expected benefits (Baron, Badgio, & Gaskins, 1986).[2]

Poor thinking is usually characterized by too little search and, most importantly, by biases in favor of possibilities that are favored initially. By contrast, good thinking is actively open-minded. It consists of search that is thorough in proportion to the importance of the question and fairness to possibilities other than the one we initially favor. Like thrift, good thinking is a virtue that is best practiced in moderation. We call it a virtue because most people do not have enough of it. There are more spendthrifts then penny-pinchers, and there are more people who

---

[2]There are, of course, other reasons why thinking may go wrong, such as thinking that occurred prior to the episode in question, mental capacities, or opportunities for acquisition of relevant knowledge (Baron, 1985, chap. 5). The three reasons given refer to the conduct of thinking at the time.

are resistant to new possibilities, goals, and evidence than people who are open (as argued by Baron, 1985, chap. 3). This may be particularly true in the domain of citizenship, where the benefits of our thinking for others may have little effect on the amount of thinking we do.

These two principles—optimal search and fairness—are also the standards we apply in academic settings. When I read a student's or colleague's paper, or sometimes even my own, the things I look for are omissions of relevant evidence, omissions of statements about goals or purposes, and omissions of alternative possibilities—that is, other answers to the question at issue. I also look for partiality to the thesis of the paper, partiality that may itself cause the omissions just mentioned. When students take these kinds of criticisms to heart and try to become more thorough and more impartial, they become more intelligent thinkers. They begin to acquire habits and values that will increase their effectiveness just as surely as would an improvement in their memory or their mental speed.

People who follow these standards are those who seek the truth, not those who feel that their first intellectual obligation is to defend a certain belief and make it seem true despite the evidence. Intelligent thinkers are those who try to make the best decisions for themselves and others, not those who want only to say, "I told you so." They are people who want to *be* right, not those who want to *have been* right.

So far, I have not said how to implement these standards. That is part of the *prescriptive* theory that specifies how thinking should actually be conducted. The model sketched so far is *normative;* it specifies standards without saying how to achieve them in the real world.

What Kind of Theory Is This?

I have argued (Baron, 1985, chaps. 1–4) that a normative model of thinking may be justified in terms of expected utility theory, a normative model of decision making. By this theory, the best we could do with the knowledge available to us at the time of a decision is to imagine all possible consequences of each possible action. We should determine the probability of each consequence and its desirability. If we could measure subjective probability and desirability, we could multiply them for each consequence and sum across consequences to arrive at a subjective expected desirability, or expected utility.

We may apply this model to the general description of thinking as a decision process, and thus arrive at a general normative model for thinking. We thus apply expected utility theory to the question of whether we ought to search for an additional possibility, an additional goal, or an additional piece of evidence. We should carry out these searches when the expected utility of doing so is positive, all things considered. Finally, we may apply the same theory to the question of how evidence ought to be weighed. Specifically, we ought to weigh evidence fairly—that is, in a way that is most helpful in achieving our goals.[3]

Note that this is still a normative model.[4] In order to figure out whether looking for an additional possibility is worth the effort, we must step outside of the specific situation and carry out a full analysis. A normative theory like this one is distinct from a prescriptive theory, which tell us actually how we ought to do something, because the former is idealized. (For further discussion of this and related distinctions, see: Baron, 1986, 1988b; Hare, 1981.) When we take normative theories seriously as guides for action, they usually become self-defeating (in the sense of Parfit, 1984). For example, if we attempted to use expected utility theory for deciding whether to continue thinking, we would spend so much time making that decision that we would, on the whole, achieve more of our goals if we followed some simple rule of thumb instead.

Nonetheless, we would want our decisions to conform to normative models if we could make them do so. Thus, the normative model of decision making may provide not only an idealized method of making decisions but also a standard by which to evaluate our actual thinking. If our rules of thumb are questioned, our ultimate standard for evaluating them is the extent to which they help us achieve our goals. Fortunately, expected utility theory provides a measure of closeness to this end.[5] We can, therefore, estimate the expected utility of different methods of decision making, including proposed prescriptive models and descriptive models of what people actually do without our advice, for a certain type of problem (as done by Johnson & Payne, 1985).

To justify a prescriptive model, we must argue that the model in question can bring people closer to this standard than they would be without it. We must argue that people depart from this standard in certain systematic ways and that the prescriptive model in question counteracts these departures or biases. The application of expected utility to the conduct of thinking provides a way of arguing that people do not think as they ought to and that they may be helped by thinking somewhat differently.[6]

More specifically, I have argued that people tend to search too little when thinking is important and to be biased toward possibilities that they already favor.

---

[3]Note that this specification allows some self-deception. For example, if one has decided that knowing the time of one's death will not affect one's decisions and will only cause dread, one should ignore evidence for the possibility that one will die soon.

[4]There may have been a bit of ambiguity on this point in Baron (1985).

[5]This is not necessarily true of any normative model. For example, formal logic provides a right answer but not a measure of degree of departure from the right answer.

[6]It might be possible to apply utility theory to heuristics of thinking directly, rather than applying it first to the general framework of search and inference. However, the search–inference framework captures all the relevant aspects of the conduct of thinking itself, so it provides a reliable guide for evaluation of the effect of heuristics on goal achievement.

(The "too little" and "biased" refer to departures from the normative model of thinking.) Anything that counteracts these departures will be prescriptively advisable.

Even if these particular claims are wrong, the framework I have sketched makes clear a major role of empirical psychology. This role is to determine just how people deviate from the normative model of thinking, and to assess the effectiveness of possible prescriptions to reduce the deviations.

The theory so far does not dictate prescriptions in any sense. Prescriptions are designs or inventions, the purpose of which is to achieve a certain goal, the goal of bringing our thinking more into line with this normative theory. The business of prescriptive theory is a process of invention—invention of our culture and ourselves.

In thinking and decision making, prescriptions may concern three general objects: rules of action (including informal rules of thumb), personal goals, and beliefs. These correspond to the three elements of any decision, with rules of action being analogous to options or possibilities. The decision in this case is how to conduct one's thinking. *Rules of action* include such things as heuristics and more formal methods. Polya's (1945) heuristics are a good example of these. They are things to do when one is stuck. Other heuristics may be generally useful in counteracting natural biases: thinking of alternative possibilities, looking for evidence against an initial idea, asking about goals. Other heuristics may be specified, and conditions may be stated for when each heuristic is most useful (e.g., when the issue is important), but these are not my concern here.

Personal goals (as elements of prescriptions) may be seen as parts of one's life plan (Baron, 1985, chap. 2). They may be adopted by a process of decision making, but they are long-term decisions that constitute the goals for other decisions. Again, some personal goals may be more conducive than others to thinking in conformity with the normative model. For example, the goal of making a certain belief true is not only impossible to achieve but also contrary to good thinking about the belief. "Faith" is a word that defends a self-defeating goal. Similarly, the goal of being a perfect decision maker on the first try will prevent one from revising one's decisions in the light of good argument.

I use the term *beliefs* here in a narrow sense, which refers to beliefs that form the basis of personal goals. Like other choices, personal goals are based on beliefs about how other goals are best achieved. Religious beliefs are a good example of beliefs in this sense. A person who holds these beliefs has adopted personal goals that would not have been adopted if the beliefs were in sufficient question. Many things that we call "values" are beliefs in this sense, although some are more properly thought of as goals. The standards for good thinking that are the main topic of this chapter are also beliefs of this sort. People who believe that a certain way of thinking is good (for something) will then establish (to varying degrees) personal goals of thinking in that way.

PRESCRIPTIONS FOR BELIEFS
ABOUT THINKING

I turn the focus now to prescriptions concerning beliefs. I do not mean to imply that heuristics and goals are unimportant; indeed, I have suggested that these three kinds of objects are closely interrelated (Baron, 1985, ch. 7). The reason for being particularly concerned with beliefs is that efforts to influence them might be quite effective in making people better thinkers. Most of our educational system is set up to impart beliefs, facts, and habits, but not goals. Of these three, beliefs may be the most general in their effect on thinking.

The idea of a prescriptive theory of beliefs about thinking may be more plausible through an analogy with other belief systems. In many other domains, it has been suggested or shown that people hold naive theories, which must yield to more mature theories either through drastic reorganization or gradual change (e.g., Vosniadou & Brewer, 1987).

The closest parallel to the distinction between naive and sophisticated theories in the domain of beliefs is the developmental theory of Kitchener and King (1981; King, Kitchener, Davison, Parker, & Wood, 1983). Their analysis does not concern subjects' beliefs about thinking itself but, rather, about justification of beliefs and the nature of knowledge. They have proposed a developmental sequence (similar to those of Kohlberg, 1971, and Perry, 1971) in subjects' assumptions about reality, knowledge, and justification, as expressed in interviews about belief dilemmas.

There are seven stages. Subjects move through the stages as they get older, very likely in part as a result of education. The first four stages involve a gradual break with the idea that truth is absolute and known to all. The breakdown of this idea is what leads to subjectivism or relativism. At Stage 4, one person's belief about anything is as good as another's. No evaluation is possible. The top three stages involve a gradual recognition of the possibility of general standards of justification such as those advocated here.

The important point about this theory and the evidence supporting it is that it points out the existence of naive beliefs about beliefs themselves. Although the sequence does not concern thinking, decision making, and belief formation themselves, it is clear that the beliefs tapped by Kitchener & King are relevant to thinking. The higher stages provide reasons for the value of thinking, whereas the lower stages do not.

There are many beliefs that make for good thinking in general—that is, those that counteract the biases I have sketched—and many beliefs that tend to encourage these biases. Among the former are the beliefs that thinking often leads to better results, that difficulties can often be overcome through thinking (rather than, say, through luck), that good thinkers are open to new possibilities and to evidence against possibilities they favor, and that there is nothing wrong (per se) with being undecided or uncertain for a while. Among the latter are beliefs that changing one's mind is a sign of weakness, that being open to alternatives leads to confusion and despair, that quick decision making is a sign of wisdom or expertise, that truth is determined by authority, that we cannot influence what happens to us by trying to understand things and weigh them, and that use of intuition alone is the best way to make decisions. The former beliefs act to oppose the natural biases I have described, and the latter act to support them (whatever germ of truth they might otherwise contain).

The importance of beliefs in thinking is consistent with the suggestion of Perkins, Allen, and Hafner (1983) that poor thinking often results from a "makes-sense epistemology," in which the thinker believes that the way to evaluate conclusions is by asking whether they "make sense" at first blush. It is also consistent with the claims of Dweck and Elliott (1983) that children's beliefs about the nature of intelligence influence their response to failure in problem solving. Both the belief that error is due to stupidity and the belief that success is due to effort may become self-fulfilling in the long run. (See also Kreitler & Kreitler, 1976 and elsewhere, concerning the role of beliefs in general.)

If people do not believe that thinking is useful, they will not think. This is perhaps the major argument one hears against thinking about things like nuclear war, religion, or morals: "These matters are beyond me. They are best left to experts who are capable of thinking about them—if anyone is."

HOW PEOPLE JUDGE THINKING

We may study people's beliefs about thinking by giving them examples of think-ing—in the form or thinking-aloud protocols supposedly generated by others, for example—and asking our subjects to evaluate the thinking.

This is not only a useful research tool but also a potential educational tool. One problem in the teaching of thinking has been the measurement of success of such instruction. It is difficult to test thinking directly, because its success or failure depends on so much besides the quality of the thinking. However, the judgment of others' thinking is fairly easy to test; it can even be done objectively, in multiple-choice format. Instruction in thinking ought to improve performance on such a test. Even if students merely learn the standards without internalizing them, this may be sufficient success. Arguably, the goals of instruction in think-ing should not take the form of indoctrination but rather of simply placing before the student a set of standards that the student may accept or reject. A fair test is one that insures that the student has *understood* the standards, so that they may be applied correctly to new instances of thinking. Whether students then go on to apply them to their own thinking may be a matter for them to decide (although, for reasons I discuss herein, we ought to hope that they do this).

As an illustration of the possibility of assessing students' judgment of think-ing, I report next some preliminary results from research conducted in collaboration with John Sabini and Andrea Bloomgarten. Initially, we simply wanted to measure individual differences in students' judgment of the thinking of others and in the beliefs that supported these judgments. We examined the effects of three variables: whether evidence was one- or two-sided, the strength of the conclusion drawn (which may or may not agree with the total evidence presented), and the subjects' own beliefs (which may lead them to evaluate statements more favorably when they agree with the conclusion). We did not, in these studies, address other issues, such as the thoroughness of evidence search in general (aside from its two-sidedness) or the relevance of the evidence to the issue. These remain for future study.

In the first study, to assess subjects' judgment of the thinking of others, we presented the following task to 96 undergraduates at the University of Pennsylvania:

> "*Instructions.* Imagine that each of the following selections is a record of a college student's thinking while answering a questionnaire . . . Give each selection a grade for the *quality of thinking* it represents: A, B, C, D, or F. You may use plusses and minuses. Briefly explain your reasons for giving different grades (if any) to different selections in the same group (1–8).
>
> Item A: Automobile insurance companies should charge more for city dwellers than for suburbanites.
>
> 1. My first thought is that each group of people should pay for its own accidents. City dwellers surely have more accidents, and their cars get broken into and stolen a lot more. I'll say 'strongly agree.'
> 2. My first thought is that each group of people should pay for its own accidents. City dwellers surely have more accidents, and their cars get broken into and stolen a lot more. I'll say 'slightly agree.'
> 3. My first thought is that each group of people should pay for its own accidents. City dwellers surely have more accidents, and their cars get broken into and stolen a lot more. On the other hand, it doesn't seem fair to make people pay for things they can't help, and a lot of people can't help where they live. I'll say 'slightly agree.'
> 4. My first thought is that each group of people should pay for its own accidents. City dwellers surely have more accidents, and their cars get broken into and stolen a lot more. On the other hand, it doesn't seem fair to make people pay for things they can't help, and a lot of people can't help where they live. I'll say 'strongly agree.' "

Selections 5–8 were analogous in form, but on the opposite side of the issue. The other items, each with eight analogous selections, were: "Social Security benefits should be taxed," and "The nations of the world need to make special efforts to reduce the growth of population."

Each group of eight responses was divided into two groups of four, one group on each side of the issue. Within each group of four, the first two considered arguments (evidence) on one side, and the last two considered arguments on both sides. Within each of these pair, the items differed in the strength of the opinion expressed. A more moderate opinion would seem more appropriate when both sides had been considered.

The grades were converted to a numerical scale, from 12 for A+ to 0 for F. For the four responses in each group, the mean graders were 6.89 (s.d. = 1.83), 6.38 (1.85), 8.31 (1.95), and 4.77 (2.56), respectively (i.e., B−, C+, B, and C). The best grade was given to the thinking that considered both sides and reached a moderate conclusion (e.g., selection 3 in the preceding example). The worst grade was given to the thinking that considered both sides and reached a strong conclusion (e.g., selection 4). In general, then, the consistency of the conclusion with the arguments presented was more important to these subjects than whether or not both sides were considered.

However, there were substantial individual differences. We noted seven different types of justifications.

1. *Content* (given by 47% of the 89 subjects whose answers could be scored). These justifications pointed to the substance of the argument presented, often arguing back or pointing out counterarguments, such as "Some people have no choice but to live in the city . . ." The implicit assumption behind these justifications was that the *correctness* of the evidence and conclusions brought forward was a reliable index to the quality of thinking. Correctness, of course, was determined by consistency with the judges' own beliefs. For example, in the item on taxing social security benefits, many subjects said (falsely) that rich people do not collect social security benefits, so this was not an issue. A couple of subjects used nothing but this type of justification. One of them wrote several pages, taking issue with every detail. (In later studies, conclusions were expressed as either "agree" or "disagree," thus removing the chance to assess agreement between the *strength* of the conclusion and the arguments. In those studies, a much higher proportion of subjects gave justifications in terms of content alone.)

2. *Weight* (45%). These were based on the consistency or inconsistency of the conclusion with the arguments that were thought of. The judgment was based on the strength or goodness of the arguments according to the subject's own judgment, as, for example, "Strongly disagreeing isn't fair . . . ," followed by a substantive argument. I take weight judgments to be normatively correct and very likely prescriptively correct as well. Some arguments are indeed better than others, and it would be inappropriate to ignore this fact. However, justifications of this sort are open to bias. A judgment of the consistency of an argument and a conclusion may be affected by the judge's agreement or disagreement with the conclusion.

3. *Logic* (61%). These pointed to the consistency of the conclusion with the arguments presented on *formal* grounds. There were three forms of such arguments. In the most common form, subjects felt that bringing up both sides of an

issue should lead to a weak conclusion. Hence, the strong conclusion in Item 4 (and Item 8) was not justified, simply because the thinker had seen both sides. In another form, subjects felt that one-sided arguments justified strong conclusions, so Item 2 was given a low grade. In a third form, however, judges felt that one-sided arguments were consistent with *weak* conclusions. These subjects suggested that a person who thought of only one side could not know how strong the argument would be on the other side, so they should not be so confident in their own side. Hence, selection 1 was given a low grade. The use of these kinds of justifications may be seen as a prescriptive rule, which serves the function of avoiding the kind of bias that weight judgments are prone to. Rather than attempting to assess the true weight, one avoids the issue by simply counting pros and cons, making judgments on formal grounds alone.

4. *One-sided* (8%). A judgment was positive for one-sided arguments or negative for two-sided arguments on the basis of form. That is, one-sidedness was seen as a virtue. For example, a justification for grades of D and F for two-sided answers was, "These don't even make sense. They can't make up their minds."

5. *Two-sided* (52%). A judgment was positive for two-sided arguments or negative for one-sided arguments on the basis of form. That is, two-sidedness was seen as a virtue.

6. *Strength* (13%). Strength of the conclusion is itself seen as a virtue, as, for example, "conviction."

7. *Moderation* (7%). Moderation is itself seen as a virtue.

Conceptually, it may be reasonable to speak of a continuum here. At one end are purely formal judgments, such as the judgment that moderate conclusions are appropriate to two-sided arguments, and extreme conclusions are appropriate to one-sided arguments, regardless of content. Many subjects adopted this approach, giving identical grades to arguments on both sides throughout. At the other extreme is an attempt to make a judgment of the appropriate weight of each argument. The danger of this approach is that subjects will impose their own beliefs on those they judge, so that inferences are judged as good ones if the conclusions agree with theirs. This may be analogous to a kind of hindsight effect (Fischhoff, 1975), and it is worthy of study in its own right. Normatively, to judge the thinking of another, we must try to put ourselves in that person's position. This may be difficult to do, however, and the formal approach may be a good prescriptive device to avoid the bias of judging thinking by its conclusions.

The results suggest that, although many people believe that consideration of opposing arguments is a manifestation of good thinking, many other people do not notice such two-sidedness, and at least a few others find it bothersome. Many people also evaluate thinking according to its conclusions. This effect is well known in the study of logical reasoning (e.g., Morgan & Morton, 1944), but its effects may be more insidious in everyday reasoning, where the weight of arguments depends on subjective judgment. It may be a major means by which people resist evidence against views they favor. If people think that the criteria of good thinking allow them to judge evidence in this way, they will think in a biased way without knowing that they are being biased.

Aside from content, judgments were based primarily on the consistency of the conclusion and the arguments that were thought of. It seems as if those subjects who do attend to the form of the thinking (as opposed to its content) base their judgments predominantly on the consistency of the conclusion and the evidence *that the thinkers think of.* Roughly, this is the ideology of the logician. What matters is consistency, and less attention is paid to whether or not one is optimally thorough and fair in the search for the evidence one uses.

One difficulty with the present study was that the presence of "strongly agree" versus "slightly agree" (and "disagree") answers may have focused subjects' attention on the consistency of the strength of the answers with the arguments presented. In subsequent studies, we attempted to eliminate this problem by removing degrees from the conclusion drawn.

One study was done on my undergraduate class. They were given the following moral dilemma and were asked to evaluate the thinking exhibited in a series of responses to it on the assumption that each response was given by another student in a thinking-aloud task:

> "Professor Smith teaches a class with 50 students. After final grades are posted and summer vacation has begun, Jones, a student in the class, finds that he has just missed getting the B he needs in order to keep his scholarship, which he needs quite badly. (There are 5 other students in the class who came just as close to getting a B, and they have left.) He asks Smith whether he could rewrite his paper (on which he got a C) so as to raise his grade. Should Smith let Jones rewrite the paper or not? Explain."

Eight of the responses were two-sided; for example:

> "No. On the one hand, it will help Jones, and it will set a precedent for other humane acts by Smith and anyone else who hears about it. However, it would also set a precedent for breaking other rules that people expected would be followed. Also, the number of scholarships is limited, and if Jones gets one, this will deprive someone else who is probably more deserving. These factors outweigh the others.

> Yes. On the one hand, it would set a precedent for breaking other rules that people expected would be followed. Also, the number of scholarships is limited, and if Jones gets one, this will deprive someone who is probably more deserving. However, it will help Jones, and it will also set a precedent for other humane acts by Smith and anyone else who hears about it. These factors outweigh the others."

Nine responses were one-sided. These stated one or two of the arguments used in the two-sided arguments. The students assigned grades on a scale from A to F, as in the last study. To derive an overall score for the value accorded to two-sidedness, the (total, converted) grades assigned to one-sided arguments were subtracted from the grades assigned to the two-sided arguments.

The same class was given the following dilemma in an earlier assignment. They were told to think about it and transcribe their thoughts as literally as possible as they occurred:

> "It is suspected that great mineral wealth will be discovered at the sea bottom in the next few decades and that some countries will be in a technological position to mine it. The oceans are now property of no nation, and their bottoms have never before been contested. Imagine that you are attending a conference to discuss: how this wealth should be allocated among nations; how to motivate people to make the required (major) investment to begin the mining; and how future decisions (such as modifications of the scheme) should be made. What kind of arrangements do you think would be best?"

Some protocols showed actively open-minded thinking; for example:

> Wealth must be divided among nations fairly. What does "fairly" mean? Should allocation be based on the *size* of the country? Some nations are significantly larger than others. But some countries have more people per unit area. Should allocation be based on overall population size? It would be *very* difficult to get all nations concerned to agree their shares were fair. Wait, the United Nations has a certain number of representatives from each country. They would be the ideal group to handle this. Total wealth should be divided by overall number of representatives, then allocated according to the number of representatives per country. *But* some nations would be better able to *use* the mineral wealth. These would be nations with greater technology. Therefore, underdeveloped nations would be unable to benefit as well as nations that are financially more secure. That would be unfair. (This goes on for a couple of pages.)

Others showed no evidence of criticism of an initial idea (other than working out its details) nor of consideration of other possibilities; for example:

> I believe that the most logical way of allocating the mineral wealth beneath the ocean is to allocate the ocean floors by extending national borders outward along the ocean floors. In effect, this plan would treat the ocean floor in the same way as exposed land surfaces. The water above the floor should still remain international territory, except where it is already considered national property. . . . Establishing boundaries in this manner is fairly simple, but it will favor nations with long coastlines along large bodies of water, but is no less fair than the rules for establishing national air space. (This goes on as well.)

Answers were classified into these categories, with questionable answers omitted. (The classification was blind with respect to the other data.) The two groups of subjects differed significantly ($t_{82} = 1.97, p < .02$) in the difference between the grades for two-sided responses and the grades for one-sided responses. The 71 open-minded subjects gave mean grades of 7.3 (B−) and 3.7 (C−) to two-sided and one-sided arguments, respectively. The 13 "close-minded" subjects gave mean grades of 6.3 (C+) and 4.1 (C−), respectively. Thus, there does seem to be a relationship between the standards used to judge the thinking of others and the kind of thinking one does on one's own.

A third study of individual differences examined 40 subjects' responses to each of four moral dilemmas, like (and including) the one about Professor Smith. In addition to answering each dilemma, subjects were asked to "briefly list all the relevant considerations and principles." Their answers were scored (blindly) for whether they mentioned arguments on both sides or not. The proportion of scorable answers that were two-sided correlated with a measure of *belief* in two-sidedness consisting of the difference between grades assigned to two-sided and grades assigned to one-sided answers to the Smith dilemma: $r = 0.26, p < .05$. (This measure was like the one that was used in the last study except that the answers used were matched so that they contained identical arguments. Thus, one-sided arguments contained *two* arguments on the same side, which were recombined for the two-sided arguments. Perhaps because answers were matched in complexity, the mean difference was not significantly different from zero; subjects did not, on the whole, consider two-sided arguments to be better than equally thorough one-sided arguments.)

As an additional measure of subjects' beliefs about thinking, we included three scenarios involving belief formation, such as, "Judy had to decide which of two candidates to vote for in a primary election. She initially favored one of them, but wondered whether this was right. What should she do? Why?" The other two scenarios dealt with a decision about which of two friends to hurt and a decision about which bank to use. Written responses to these scenarios were scored (blindly to other information) with respect to whether further thinking was mentioned or not. For example, some subjects said that Judy should gather more information, whereas others said that she should go with her initial feeling. The number of scenarios in which additional thinking was recommended correlated with use of two-sided thinking in the dilemmas themselves: $r = 0.28, p < .05$. (A third measure of belief in two-sided thinking, based on a questionnaire about the scenarios, did not correlate significantly with anything except the scenario measure just described, although all correlations were in the predicted direction.)

There seem to be competing beliefs about thinking in our culture. Where do these beliefs come from? Why doesn't everyone think that two-sided thinking is better than one-sided thinking? It would be easy to argue that beliefs in one-sided thinking are the result of the evolution of institutions, such as organized religions and nations. To survive—that is, to keep its adherents from one generation to the next—each of these institutions must convince its adherents that its views are correct even though many outsiders will argue otherwise. Those institutions that inculcate an ideology in which defense of one's belief is a virtue and questioning is a vice are the ones that are most likely to overcome challenges from outside. By this argument, enough of these institutions still survive as to have a substantial influence on our culture.

There may be some truth in this, but I think there may be another answer to the question, which will be the subject of future research. It is possible that people are simply confused about two different standards concerning thinking, which we might call the "good thinker" (the standard I have been advocating) and the "expert." In many ways, experts appear to be the opposite of good thinkers. Because they *know* the answer to most questions, they do not have to think very often, compared to novices. Thus, when a news commentator criticizes a political candidate for waffling and being unsure (as might befit a good thinker faced with many of the issues that politicians must face), the implication is that the candidate is not expert enough to have figured out the right answers yet. Similarly, a person who adopts a "know it all" tone of voice—speaking without qualification or doubt—is giving a sign of expertise in the matter at hand. Some parents (perhaps because they *are* experts about the matter under discussion) may talk this way to their children, who come to think of it as a "grown up" way to talk.

This confusion of expertise and good thinking may reinforce the institutional pressures mentioned earlier (if they exist). Those who are considered wise and respected members of the institution may talk like experts, encouraging their followers to know rather than to think. And how are they supposed to know? Without thinking, there is only one way: listen to the experts.

Although expertise and good thinking both contribute to success in achieving goals (Baron, 1985, chap. 5), they are not the same thing. We must not assume (or allow others to assume) that an understanding of expertise will solve the problem of providing standards for thinking.

CONCLUSION

The view of thinking I have presented herein may be seen in an interpersonal, moral context (Baron, 1985, chap. 6). The standards of thinking are analogous to other standards of interpersonal conduct, such as those of business competition (or even international relations). In all these cases, we may adopt an aggressive, uncooperative stance or a cooperative one. In the domain of thinking, the aggressive stance is the belief that one should defend one's own beliefs. The cooperative stance is the belief that one should be open to the arguments of others, evaluating them on the basis of their form rather than their conclusions, and letting them influence one's own beliefs to the extent that they are good arguments.

If most people took the cooperative stance (and if enough people could distinguish good arguments from poor ones), then the best arguments would usually prevail (because they would be fairly considered by all), and we would all benefit (Baron, 1985, chap. 6). The aggressive stance has no comparable justification. One might argue that one must defend one's beliefs, for if one does not, truth might not prevail. However, those who think this way cannot condemn their opponents for thinking the same way. If nobody were open to persuasion, we might as well not talk at all. Those who take advantage of the openness of others without being open themselves are free riders, like those who watch public television without contributing. In sum, good thinking as I have defined it is not just good for those who do it; it is good for us all.

I have argued that the way we carry out our thinking is influenced by our beliefs about how we ought to think. Few of us think we are thinking poorly, especially on matters of morals or public affairs. If I am right, this is an optimistic conclusion. We are in a position to improve our mutual thinking through influence on beliefs about thinking. This is promising, because arguments may be brought to bear—arguments of the sort I have sketched here—to discuss, determine, and persuade people of the right kind of thinking. It is more difficult to change desires. It is also convenient for the practice of education, for it is easy to measure beliefs and easier still to measure the extent to which certain standards are understood. I hope that the line of work sketched here will ultimately lead to the development of methods for assessing beliefs about thinking and, therefore, to the improvement of thinking itself.

ACKNOWLEDGEMENT

This work is supported by a grant from the National Institute of Mental Health. John Sabini is a co-investigator and has been helpful in designing the studies reported herein, as has Andrea Bloomgarten. (Both are in the Psychology department of the University of Pennsylvania.) I also thank John for his comments on the chapter.

REFERENCES

Baron, J. (1985). *Rationality and intelligence.* New York: Cambridge University Press.
Baron, J. (1986). Tradeoffs among reasons for action. *Journal for the Theory of Social Behavior, 16,* 173–195.
Baron, J. (1988a). *Thinking and deciding.* New York: Cambridge University Press.
Baron, J. (1988b). Utility, exchange, and commensurability. *Journal of Thought, 23,* 111–131.
Baron, J., Badgio, P., & Gaskins, I. W. (1986). Cognitive style and its improvement: A normative approach. In R. J. Sternberg (Ed.), *Advances in the psychology of human intelligence, Vol. 3* (pp. 173–220). Hillsdale, NJ: Lawrence Erlbaum Associates.
Duncker, K. (1945). On problem solving. *Psychological Monographs, 58* (Whole No. 270).
Dweck, C. S., & Elliott, E. S. (1983). Achievement motivation. In P. H. Mussen (Ed.), *Carmichael's manual of child psychology,* Vol. 2 (pp.■■–■■). New York: Wiley.

Fischhoff, B. (1975). Hindsight ≠ foresight: The effect of outcome knowledge on judgment under uncertainty. *Journal of Experimental Psychology: Human Perception and Performance, 1,* 288–299.

Hare, R. M. (1981). *Moral thinking: Its levels, methods and point.* Oxford: Clarendon Press.

Henle, M. (1962). On the relation between logic and thinking. *Psychological Review, 69,* 366–378.

Johnson, E. J., & Payne, J. W. (1985). Effort and accuracy in choice. *Management Science, 31,* 395–414.

King, P. M., Kitchener, K. S., Davison, M. L., Parker, C. A., & Wood, P. K. (1983). The justification of beliefs in young adults: A longitudinal study. *Human Development, 26,* 106–116.

Kitchener, K. S., & King, P. M. (1981). Reflective judgment: Concepts of justification and their relationship to age and education. *Journal of Applied Developmental Psychology, 2,* 89–116.

Kohlberg, L. (1971). Stages of moral development as a basis for moral education. In C. Beck & E. Sullivan (Eds.), *Moral education* (pp. 23–92). Toronto: University of Toronto Press.

Kreitler, H., & Kreitler, S. (1976). *Cognitive orientation and behavior.* New York: Springer.

Morgan, J. J. B., & Morton, J. T. (1944). The distortion of syllogistic reasoning produced by personal convictions. *Journal of Social Psychology, 20,* 39–59.

Parfit, D. (1984). *Reasons and persons.* Oxford: Clarendon Press.

Perkins, D. N., Allen, R., & Hafner, J. (1983). Difficulties in everyday reasoning. In W. Maxwell (Ed.), *Thinking: The expanding frontier* (pp. 177–189). Philadelphia: Franklin Institute.

Perry, W. G., Jr. (1971). *Forms of intellectual and ethical development in the college years: A scheme.* New York: Holt, Rinehart & Winston.

Polya, G. (1945). *How to solve it.* Princeton: Princeton University Press.

Vosniadou, S., & Brewer, W. F. (1987). Theories of knowledge restructuring in development. *Review of Educational Research, 57,* 51–67.

10 Example-Based Reasoning

Edwina L. Rissland
University of Massachusetts

One of the most important sources of an expert's knowledge is the corpus of concrete instances or examples. This is certainly true in mathematics, computer science, and law. This chapter explores the process of reasoning with examples and cases, particularly how they are generated, for instance, as counterexamples in mathematics and as hypotheticals in law. One particular type of example-based reasoning that is discussed is case-based reasoning, which is exemplified by the kind of reasoning used in law, in which cases and hypotheticals play a central role.

Even though much of the emphasis of classical mathematics is on the usual trinity of definitions, theorems, and proofs, examples are also very much part of the knowledge of expert mathematicians. Experts in mathematics know heuristics, examples, taxonomic classifications, and rankings of items according to their usefulness and importance to various tasks, such as proving new theorems or generating counterexamples (Rissland, 1978). Teachers of mathematics know these and more because teaching involves not only mathematics itself and one's understanding of it but also a model of students' views and understanding of it; this latter type of pedagogical and student modeling of knowledge involves likely misconceptions, remedial measures, the interdependency of topics for presentation, good problems and exercises, and so forth. Although it is true that some novices also have a rich variety of mathematical knowledge, it tends not to be as deep or as highly organized and interconnected as that of a master teacher or an expert. This is also true in other domains, such as medicine, in which the expert's knowledge is much more tightly organized, dense, and flexible than the beginning physician's. (See chapter 2, on informal medical reasoning, in this volume.)

However, whether one is a research mathematician, mathematics teacher, or mathematics student, a central component of knowledge is the collection of examples. Although it is sometimes overlooked, this corpus can be extensive, well organized, and populated with examples of diverse character and importance, ranging from standard textbook cases to anomalous, weird, or hard-to-understand examples and counterexamples. One difference between the novice and expert seems to be the facility to generate new examples on demand, to reexamine existing ones from new perspectives, and to assess their importance and taxonomic class, which is often only knowable with hindsight.

This diversity of knowledge and the importance of examples are present in other domains, such as law. In fact, law is an interesting discipline to compare and contrast with mathematics. As opposed to mathematics, in law there are no black-and-white concepts or rules; there are competing answers; these are highly dependent on context and point of view and are subject to change; and so forth. (Gardner, 1987; Levi, 1949; Llewellyn, 1960; Rissland, 1988). Furthermore, law is deliberately adversarial and argumentative. Despite such differences, in law and in mathematics proposed solutions and answers are tested with examples, that is, real and hypothetical cases.

In law, some of the obvious types of information are cases, statutes, constitutions, learned treatises, restatements, which distill and discuss various principles of the law and illustrate the discussion with both real and hypothetical cases, and conceptual hierarchies for case classification and information retrieval. In law, these sources are explicit and accessible to all, whereas in mathematics, for the most part, they are less so because some sources, such as examples and heuristics, are more tacit, less well catalogued, and harder to locate. There are, of course, several important exceptions to this point as it applies to mathematics: Polya's (1973) discussions of heuristics, for instance, in *How to Solve It* and the compendia of examples, *Counterexamples in Analysis* (Gelbaum & Olmstead, 1964) and *Counterexamples in Topology* (Steen & Seebach, 1978). Unfortunately, however, examples and heuristics as an important type of knowledge in their own right frequently tend to be overlooked in math. In fact, in mathematics many practitioners and experts convey quite the opposite impression, that is, that what really matters or all that matters are aspects like proving theorems and solving exercises. This message is often conveyed effectively through problem sets in which almost no problem asks students to generate a new example or hypothesis, compare and contrast theorems, methods, or examples, rank items such as theorems according to their importance, or discuss the limitations of certain concepts and results.

In contrast to mathematics, in law, examples—that is, cases—are, as a matter of course, recorded, disseminated, and published. In particular, the opinions of most appellate-level courts are published through numerous commercially published "reporters." (For this discussion, a case is a legal dispute brought to and decided by a court and discussed in a court's opinion.) In law, there is an assumption that a practitioner or student will refer to diverse sources of knowledge, particularly cases, and develop a facility with them.

At any rate, cases in law are analogous to examples in mathematics. What is not similar between these two domains is the exalted and special role played by cases, particularly in Anglo-American law, which is a common law system based on cases and in which the bona fide mechanism to justify an argument is *stare decisis,* or the doctrine of precedent, which roughly says that similar cases should be decided similarly. This mechanism demands careful comparison of cases and detailed consideration of competing, proposed similarities and differences with past cases (Ashley & Rissland, 1987). There is also a distinction between real and hypothetical cases that is not present in mathematics, because any example is as real or hypothetical as another.

A hypothetical case, or *hypo,* is not a real case in the sense of its facts being those of an actual dispute brought before the court, actually litigated, or decided. However, hypos often do bear strong resemblance to real cases although they are often more streamlined, abstract, or focused in the facts and issues they raise (Rissland, 1984). Hypos serve useful and pointed roles in several legal contexts, such as Socratic dialogue in law school classes, oral arguments before various courts like the United States Supreme Court, as testing and reasoning aids in preparation of arguments by practitioners, and in law school examinations. Since there is a very large space of possible hypos, an interesting task to study is how one chooses or generates legally meaningful or plausible hypos. Clearly, law school professors and Supreme Court justices are very good at this and use hypos with impressive skill and to great effect. Investigating the knowledge and processes required to do this is a rich vein of research (Rissland, 1983, 1987; Rissland & Ashley, 1986).

In summary, examples are exceedingly important in a variety of disciplines, and their use and generation are interesting cognitive skills for study. In general, this chapter describes how examples and cases are used in reasoning and how they are generated. More specifically, this chapter presents a preliminary discussion of examples, cases, and case-based reasoning; discusses the problem of generating examples and hypotheticals and presents examples of their usage in the law school classroom and oral argument; and presents a model of precedent-based case-based reasoning.

ON THE NATURE OF EXAMPLES AND CASES

Examples as Distilled Experience

Examples are concrete instances. This means that they are instances of something and, as such, are a distillation of an experience or set of facts seen through the eyes of that something. For instance, when one says that $f(x) = x^2 - 1$ is an example of a *function,* one is attending to aspects of $f(x) = x^2 - 1$ that relate to its "functionhood," such as its well-defined, nonlinear, a mapping of elements from one set to another, that is not one-to-one nor onto, that is continuous, that achieves a minimum value at the origin, that is an "even" function, and so forth. One unconsciously drops or diminishes the importance of features not relevant to this perspective, such as the choice of variables used to write the function or the fact that the function does not perform an affine transformation, such as a rotation. If one said, instead, that $f(x) = x^2 - 1$ is an example of a *quadratic*, one would attend to features that are particular to quadratics, such as the absence of terms whose exponent is greater than 2 and the presence of a term with exponent exactly 2, that its roots can be found using the quadratic formula or by inspection, that it is a conic whose graph is a parabola, that it has the same shape as the "reference" example of x^2 and can be thought of as generated from it by a shifting downwards, and so forth. Thus, one can view an example as a set of facts or features viewed through a certain lens. As such, examples are filtered snapshots of the world that emphasize some aspects and forget others, and all of this is done for some purpose, such as illustrating a concept, making a rhetorical point, or accomplishing some problem-solving goal. Although this might, perhaps seems an obvious point, it is important to note it, especially in situations in which a particular experience can be viewed in many ways, as is almost always the situation in law and, to a lesser degree, in mathematics.

The need for multiple perspectives is present in any example- or case-based reasoning domain. It is inherent in legal cases, in which there are, by definition, two opposing points of view. The facts of a legal case represent a story of what has happened or what is at stake; the plaintiff and defendant can—and usually do—have very different renditions of this story. In appellate cases, the court's opinion explains how it interpreted and understood the stories and reached its decision. Thus, the court's opinion attends to certain facts, principles, and past cases that it believes are relevant, controlling, or persuasive and omits, dismisses, or distinguishes others that are not. In difficult cases, there is always more than one way to approach the legal problem—otherwise, there would be no legal dispute or appeal—and in deciding a case, the court settles on one approach although alternatives are often advanced in dissenting opinions. In fact, the law is extremely different from mathematics in that there is no one right answer to a legal question. Not only can a set of facts be told from different perspectives for a given legal question, but also it can be viewed as supporting questions from different areas of law; for instance, the unlawful use of a computer file could be viewed from a criminal (e.g., trespass) or torts (e.g., misappropriation of trade secrets) or constitutional (e.g., privacy) perspective. Note that the same is true of certain examples in mathematics, which can be viewed for their algebraic, geometric, analytic, or topological content. Even our humble but important example of $f(x) = x^2 - 1$ supports such a variety of perspectives.

The need for multiple perspectives is particularly relevant in the context of representing examples and cases in an artificial intelligence program that models reasoning with cases or examples or that uses them in a tutoring situation. Each representation has a bias: that is, each makes certain features readily apparent and others not; each makes certain lines of reasoning easier to do and others not; and each makes certain things describable and other not. This is true even of a scheme as seemingly neutral as logic, because, there the predicates define the language in which concepts and propositions will be couched. This is, of course, a well-known and inescapable problem of artificial intelligence, philosophy, and psychology. Because no representation is value neutral, the interesting question is how to manipulate or shift a bias to strengthen certain ways of viewing a situation; a standard approach is to add new terms or predicates and thereby make additional concepts describable. In law, choosing a good representation framework or refining an existing one can have significant implications for how a case is viewed or decided. Although in this chapter we do not consider this fundamental and difficult problem, it is wise to be aware of its existence. Manipulating cases—for instance, by focusing analysis on a subset of features—and creating hypotheticals—for instance, by carrying certain aspects to extremes—is one way to deal with this problem while working under the constraint of a given, fixed, representation language. There is a fundamental relation between knowledge representation and learning. However, inventing or revising a representation is more of a problem in learning than in case-based reasoning. (Note, it is interesting to view the law as a learning system that at various times introduces new concepts and rules and to model the law's processes of change [Rissland & Collins, 1986].) Thus, because examples and cases are potent pedagogical tools for teaching a learner, whether machine or person, work on example- and case-based reasoning has direct links to work on learning.

Thus, there are several difficult problems concerning the representation of examples and cases: (a) trying to minimize, circumvent, and otherwise deal with the bias inherent in any representation; (b) allowing for various perspectives and interpretations within a given representation; and (c) reasoning with different senses of similarity and relevancy. We do not tackle the first problem other than to say that, within a given area, one does one's best to engineer a representation to do the job that one is interested in. The second and third problems are central issues explored in research on case-based reasoning.

Ways in Which Examples Aid Reasoning

There are many ways in which examples aid reasoning:

- Examples introduce concepts and issues. Certain examples, *start-up* examples, are particularly good at this because they are relatively simple and require a minimum of background knowledge.
- Examples provide the basis for inductive generalization. A rich enough set can suggest new concepts and lines of attack on a problem.

- Examples can provide standard points of reference. A reasoner can use such a set of *reference* examples as a standard collection of textbook cases.
- Examples are tools to explore the implications. Having created new solutions, rules, concepts, and so forth, a reasoner needs to explore their limitations and implications, particularly how they will bear on future problems.
- Examples bound concepts and issues. In particular, counterexamples help a reasoner determine the boundaries of a concept and the conditions under which certain results will fail.
- Examples provide templates to help organize domain knowledge. Prototypical examples provide a mechanism to help one organize one's knowledge and to judge how (un)remarkable a new case is.
- Examples allow caching of past problem-solving experience. By saving one's problem-solving experience in an example, one can refer to it in the future and obviate the need to produce an analysis or solution from scratch.

Hypotheticals in the legal domain aid in these ways and more. In particular:

- Hypos remake experience. They allow one to redefine a fact situation and reanalyze it, in particular to generate new arguments about it.
- Hypos create experience. When there is a paucity of real cases, hypos can provide *gedanken experiments* to help a reasoner augment the existing case base with meaningful test or training instances.
- Hypos can organize a case base. For instance, by providing stereotypical cases, which because of certain factual differences have not actually occurred, one can generate a case in memory from which to "hang" other case memories. Hypos can provide an intermediate linkage between a real past case and a new fact situation.
- Hypos can refocus cases. By eliminating distracting and irrelevant details, one can give a case, actually a hypo spawned by it, a new focus. In particular, one can factor a complex situation into component parts, for instance, by exaggerating or eliminating certain features.
- Hypos can redirect the course of an argument. By introducing new issues and emphases, one can use hypos to steer the argument to one's strong points or one's adversary's weak ones; one can even introduce rhetorical "red herrings" (Rissland, 1984, 1986).

In summary, examples and hypotheticals can provide a reasoner with a great deal of leverage.

As an example of their power, consider the following sequence taken from an oral argument before the United States Supreme Court. In the case being argued, *Lynch v. Donnelly,* 104 S. Ct. 1355 (1984), the issue is whether a Christmas creche displayed by a city on municipal land violates the constitutional principle forbidding the establishment of religion by the state. The Justices posed the following hypos to the attorney for the city:

Q: Do you think . . . that a city should display a nativity scene alone without other displays such as Santa Claus and Christmas trees. . . ?

Q: [C]ould the city display a cross for the celebration of Easter, under your view?

To the attorney opposing the display, the Justices posed the following hypos:

Q: [S]upposing the creche were just one ornament on the Christmas tree and you could hardly see it unless you looked very closely, would that be illegal?

Q: What if they had three wisemen and a star in one exhibit, say? Would that be enough? . . . What if you had an exhibit that had not the creche itself, but just three camels out in the desert and a star up in the sky?

Q: Well, the city could not display religious paintings or artifacts in its museum under your theory.

Q: There is nothing self-explanatory about a creche to somebody . . . who has never been exposed to the Christian religion.

Q: Would the display up on the frieze in this courtroom of the Ten Commandments be unconstitutional then, in your view?

Q: Several years ago . . . there was a ceremony held on the Mall, which is federal property of course. . . . [T]here were 200,000 or 300,000 people . . . and the ceremony was presided over by Pope John Paul II. Would you say that was a step towards an establishment of religion violative of the religion clauses? . . . Then you think it would be alright to put a creche over on the Mall? . . . How do you distinguish a high mass from a creche? . . . [T]here was a considerable involvement of government in that ceremony, hundreds of extra policeman on duty, streets closed. . . . That was a considerable governmental involvement, was it not?
(*SUP, Lynch v. Donnelly,* Case No. 82-1256, Fiche No. 5.)

In the preceding questions, one can see the justices modifying the fact situation along various dimensions:

- Location, size, and focus of the display.
- Religious content of the display.
- Nature of the viewer.
- Degree of government involvement.

Sometimes the purpose of the modifications (and thus the derivative hypos) is to compare the fact situation to actual cases previously decided by the Court to test whether the current case presents stronger or weaker facts.[1] A hypothetical case, such as the Mall example, may be significant because it did not give rise to litigation.)

Types of Reasoning with Cases and Examples

Before delving into a specific type of example-based reasoning, called precedent-based, case-based reasoning, we briefly explore closely allied reasoning techniques. Example-based reasoning (EBR) is simply reasoning that uses examples. These examples are used to accomplish goals, such as refuting a conjecture (by generating a counterexample) or comparing and contrasting two solutions to a problem (by simulating, or applying them to the examples). By contrast, logic-based reasoning uses deductive mechanisms of mathematical logic, such as certain proof procedures, to accomplish reasoning goals, the primary one of which is to prove a theorem. Rule-based reasoning, a specialized form of logic-based reasoning used in current expert systems and logic programming methodologies, focuses on the aspect of logical reasoning involving chaining if–then rules together and not on other, more complex mechanisms of logic, such as the manipulation of quantifiers or proof techniques themselves. In logic-based reasoning and its specializations, examples hold no particular status. Mathematical reasoning, which involves proving theorems as well as certain example-based tasks, such as refuting with counterexamples, is thus a hybrid of both logic-based reasoning and EBR. (Lakatos,1976)

As remarked earlier, EBR is critical to learning (by person or machine). For instance, inductive learning involves abstracting a new concept from a set of examples or incremental refinement of an existing concept in response to new examples. One type of machine learning, sometimes called *deductive learning* or *explanation-based generalization*, involves the detailed examination of a proof or explanation in a specific instance to abstract from the proof (e.g., changing constants to variables) a general description of a concept. The gist of this technique is that through detailed examination of a specific case, particularly one that is prototypical in some sense, one might be able to form a general description of the concept of which the case is an exemplar. For instance, one could examine how to prove some general proposition about right triangles by focusing on a certain well-known specific case, such as a 3–4–5 or 45–45–right triangle, then try to recouch and generalize the proof steps so that they will still be true for right

---

[1]*Stone v. Graham*, 449 U.S. 39 (1980): posting copies of the Ten Commandments in schools held unconstitutional; *Gilfillan v. City of Philadelphia*, 637 F. 2d 924 (CA3, 1980): city-financed platform and cross used by Pope John Paul II to celebrate public mass held unconstitutional; *McCreary v. Stone*, 575 F.Supp. 1112 (SDNY 1983): not unconstitutional for village not to refuse permit to private group to erect creche in public park.

triangles in general, and finally, from this proof, form a description of the concept of "right triangle."

A markedly different approach to machine learning involves *connectionism* (Rumelhart & McClelland, 1986): Here, one uses a large number of training examples to cause the overall state of a system to change, that is, learn. As opposed to inductive and explanation-based methods, which are symbolic, this approach uses numerical algorithms (e.g., propagation of numerical weights among processing elements) to affect change. Furthermore, such systems are usually highly parallel or composed of many processing elements. In connectionist learning and related methods, such as memory-based reasoning (Stanfill & Waltz, 1986), examples are reasoned with as a group, and the influence of individual examples cannot be examined individually.

A very important subclass of EBR is case-based reasoning (CBR). CBR can be characterized as the generating, analyzing, or interpreting of new situations in light of a collection of past and hypothetical cases and the solving, explaining, or justifying of new solutions or analyses in terms of past ones. CBR techniques are used by experts in many domains, including law, mathematics, design, planning, and policy analysis. As I mentioned earlier, Anglo-American common law, with its doctrine of *stare decisis,* or reasoning by precedent, is a paradigmatic example of a domain where CBR techniques are used for analysis and interpretation of a new case in terms of old cases and where the bona fide way of justifying a decision is with cases.

Architectural design is another excellent example of a domain where reasoning with cases is used for complex problem solving. For instance, in designing a new house or hospital surgical suite, designers examine already existing designs, analyze the match between the strong and weak points of the old designs and the desiderata and constraints of the new one, and, if possible, map over the old design and modify it with suitable adaptations. In this type of problem-solving CBR, new solutions are found through analogical transformations of past ones; cases are indexed both in terms of success and failure and of similarities and differences; and new problem solutions and patches to old ones are remembered in a memory of cases (Carbonell, 1986; Hammond, 1986; Kolodner, Simpson, & Sycara-Cyranski, 1985).

Similar strategies can also be seen in such disciplines as computer programming and linguistics, in which a primary means of generating and testing conjectures is with the use of examples. In programming, for instance, one tries to get as much mileage out of existing and working program designs as possible. Also, in programming one relies heavily on sets of test data, that is, examples, to probe and debug programs because of programming's fundamentally empirical nature. Thus, examples play two roles in computer programming: (a) as sources of new solutions constructed through adaptation and (b) as sources of data to test solutions.

These examples illustrate two basic kinds of CBR:

1. Precedent-based CBR, in which past cases (precedents), are used not only to create a new solution, typically an analysis or interpretation together with its pros, cons, and sensitivity to various factors, but also to justify it and explain its rationale.

2. Problem-solving CBR, in which past cases are used to create a new solution, typically a plan or a detailed problem solution, but in which the new solution is typically offered without justifications in terms of the contributing cases.

Both types of CBR share many elements, such as the need for a significant memory or corpus of cases and ways to index them. Major differences between the existing systems of these two types include (a) the indispensibility of justification in precedent-based CBR and (b) the central role of plans and adaptation in problem-solving CBR. In precedent-based CBR, the relevant precedents, or citations to them, are woven into the solution. In problem-solving CBR, the relevant cases contribute information but are not necessarily cited explicitly, even though parts of them might be incorporated verbatim into the new solution. Precedent-based CBR typically does not delve into the individual steps of the problem solution, whereas problem-solving CBR does.

Figure 10.1 shows taxonomic relationships of these various types of reasoning: EBR, CBR, pb-CBR, ps-CBR, MBR, logic-based and rule-based reasoning. (Yes, logic-based reasoning should *not* be an offspring of EBR but rather a sibling.)

THE EXAMPLE GENERATION PROCESS: SOME ILLUSTRATIVE EPISODES

To give an idea of the richness of the process of generating examples, I present two protocols of example generation, one from mathematics and one from law.

Constrained Example Generation in Mathematics

One point about examples in mathematics is that they are often generated to meet very specific constraints, that is, a list of properties that the example must and must not exhibit (e.g., a function must be continuous but not differentiable). The constraints come from the goals of the reasoner, a few typical ones being: Show that a condition is necessary, show that a condition is not sufficient, show that one concept class is a proper subclass of another, show that the converse of a theorem is not true, and show that a conjecture is false. For these tasks, the examples required are counterexamples, because they are used to limit, refute, force refinement, and so forth. By contrast, positive examples are needed for tasks such as show that there is hope that a conjecture might be true by finding some examples in which it is true or generate instances from which to generalize a new concept or conjecture. (For some beautiful examples, see Polya's *Induction and Analogy* [1968]). Open any math book; take just about any statement or theorem: It suggests an invitation to find or generate an example. In fact, the mature reader of a math book easily sees the invitation (Rissland, 1978). For instance, the statement that "differentiable functions are continuous" naturally suggests finding a function that is continuous but not differentiable to show that converse is not true. Although a little schooling about learning what questions to always ask—like those just indicated—teaches one to see the invitation, it is not nearly as easy to see how to produce the example called for by the invitation. This process of finding suitable examples, which I call *constrained example generation* (CEG), is a rich one (Rissland, 1980, 1981; Rissland & Soloway, 1980).

To get a glimpse of the CEG process, consider the following problem, which I call the 1–1/1000th problem. Note that I am cutting the problem loose from its context, so one might rightly ask, "Why should one care about this CEG problem?". However, for this discussion, let us suspend the desire for a problem-solving context, which might be a discussion of integral calculus, and concentrate on what the episode shows by way of problem-solving behavior:

> Give an example of a nonnegative, continuous function defined on the entire real line with the value 1000 at 1, and with area under its curve less than 1/1000. (Rissland, 1981).

In examining approximately two dozen protocols, approximately half of which were those of undergraduate students at a leading technology institute in Massachusetts, a quarter of which were those of graduate students in computer science, and a quarter of which were those of professors or researchers, we found that most subjects, regardless of background, began by selecting a standard, concrete example of a function that was well known or the subject's favorite— that is, a reference example, according to my taxonomy—and then manipulated and modified it to create a new example that satisfied the constraints set forth in the problem. One cluster of solutions all began with a unimodal distribution function, as exemplified in the following protocol of an expert mathematician:

> Start with the function for a normal distribution. Move it to the right so that it is centered over it x = 1. Now make it "skinny" by squeezing in the sides and stretching the top so that it hits the point (1,1000).
>
> I can make the area as small as I please by squeezing in the sides and feathering off the sides. But to demonstrate that the area is indeed less than 1/1000, I'll have to do an integration, which is going to be a bother.
>
> Hmmm. My candidate function is smoother than it need be: The problem asked

only for continuity and not differentiability. So let me relax my example to be a "hat" function because I know how to find the areas of triangles. That is, make my function be a function with apex at (1,1000) and with steeply sloping sides down to the x-axis a little bit on either side of $x - 1$, and 0 outside to the right and left. (This is OK because you only asked for nonnegative.) Again by squeezing, I can make the area under the function (i.e., the triangle's area) be as small as I please. And I'm done. (Rissland, 1981, pp. 33–34)

There are a number of observations about this protocol:

1. Two crucial kinds of knowledge for the CEG task are a corpus of examples (e.g., normal distribution, hat function) and a library of modification techniques (e.g., squeezing, translating).
2. Subjects make many implicit assumptions, such as the symmetry of the solution (about $x = 1$) and maximum of the solution (1000); neither was necessary, although both are "natural."
3. This solution followed an overall strategy of retrieval plus modification.

These observations of human problem solving were used to motivate a computational model of CEG (Rissland & Soloway, 1980). Our work led us to ask whether such a computational model of working with examples might be useful in other domains. Ultimately, our work led us to the legal domain. It is interesting to note that a similar approach, called prototypes plus deformations, was introduced by McCarty and Sridharan (1980) at about the same time to address certain aspects of legal reasoning.

Hypotheticals in Law

In law, the problem that is analogous to generating examples is that of generating hypothetical cases. As in mathematics, hypotheticals are used to fulfill a variety of reasoning goals, such as showing the undesirability of a proposition, interpretation, doctrine, or outcome. One difference between the use of examples in law and mathematics, especially in teaching, is the use of a set or sequence of examples and their close tie to argumentation and rhetorical goals.

A set of examples, the order of which is not particularly important, is often used to test the sensitivity of a legal proposition to a variety of factors. Such a probing set is used by all types of legal reasoners: law school professors, litigators, and judges. It is usually formed by perturbing a seed case to form a heuristic constellation of cases. Thus, it fits into the general retrieve-then-modify framework, and its use is similar to a mathematician's testing of the scope, necessity, and sufficiency of conditions of a mathematical proposition. However, in law there is the added complexity that the predicates used in legal propositions are "open-textured".

Open texture refers to the fact that certain kinds of concepts cannot be defined in terms of necessary and sufficient conditions. For instance, most people have two legs, two arms, ten fingers, and so forth, but none of these conditions is either necessary or sufficient for being a person. In fact, it is exceedingly difficult, if not impossible, to give a definition of being a person in the mathematical senses of necessary and sufficient conditions. The concept of personhood is not an artificial one but a natural one. (Compare this concept with a mathematical one, such as "quadrilateral.") Furthermore, there is no hope of ever grounding the definition of such a "natural kind" concept, to use the philosophical term (Wittgenstein, 1958, 1978), in primitive concepts that themselves need no further definition. (Again, compare this with mathematics, in which one can agree as to the primitiveness of concepts like "point" that thus require no further definitional scaffolding.) In the legal domain, attempts at backchaining to fulfill preconditions of definitions usually "run out" before the judgment has been made as to whether a given instance is "in" or "out" (Gardner, 1987).

The preponderence of legal concepts share such definitional problems. For instance, even the concept of *income,* as it pertains to the internal revenue code, cannot be so tightly defined as to eliminate interpretation problems. Obvious sources of definitional problems are terms like *reasonable* or *good faith.* No matter how hard one tries, for instance, in statutes, one cannot purge such concepts of their blurry definitional boundaries. The best one can do is examine closely related cases to ascertain whether a new situation is or is not similar enough to other instances or noninstances of a concept, to resolve the question or, at least, fashion arguments and analogies to that effect. Case examples, both real and hypothetical, are the legal reasoner's tools for working with such concepts and for testing the ramifications of various interpretations of them.

Following is an example of generating legal hypotheticals to test and probe a legal concept (Rissland, 1982, 1984, 1986). It concerns the concept of consideration in contract law—that is, what the promiser received from the promisee in return for his promise—and the doctrinal principle that the law does not enforce donative promises. The doctrine of consideration reflects the equity idea that one does not, or should not, get something for nothing. This fragment of the sequence explores the idea of what constitutes consideration; it occurred in one of the first lectures in a first-year law school course on contracts. The point of this sequence is to help the students explore the concept of consideration—in particular, the penumbra where things are not so clear cut, and to expose their own prejudices and default assumptions. In general, the Socratic method in law school, as well as in mathematics, is used to unmask assumptions, some seemingly harmless and reasonable but perhaps not really so, which can come back to haunt the reasoner and invalidate the chain of reasoning or even the conclusions themselves.

Hypothetical 1 (seed): I promise to give you $10,000.

Hypothetical 2: Hypo-1 with the addition that you offer, in return, to give me your third-grade painting.

Hypothetical 3: Same as Hypo-2, except that you offer to mow my lawn, which we both know is quite large.

Hypothetical 4: Same as Hypo-2, except that your last name is Picasso.

In this sequence, the seed hypothetical is recognized by everyone to be an example of a donative promise, without consideration. Hypothetical 2 is a "fix" added by the promisee so that there is an appearance of consideration; it mostly inspires derision. Hypothetical 3 is a revision of Hypothetical 2 so that the consideration is worth something. Hypothetical 4 is offered to show that things are not always what they seem.

Having discussed this sequence, the class is now well aware of its own, perhaps erroneous, assumptions about the worth of certain objects from the point of view of the consideration doctrine. In fact, one principle in this area of contracts is that the law should not look into the value of the consideration (although it sometimes does), because worth is such a chimera. Rather, one should let the parties decide if they agree on their bargain as long as something has been exchanged. The metalessons of such a sequence of hypotheticals are: (a) that legal concepts like consideration are typically open-textured, (b) that as a practical matter this means that one cannot define away interpretation problems, and (c) that one can almost always form arguments for and against an interpretation.

With regard to how the sequence is structured, one hypothetical is derived from others by perturbing a key feature. Also, the seed case, Hypothetical 1, is a reference case of the course (known as the Mr. Cramer case, because it was to Mr. Cramer that the professor initially addressed the promise). It, in fact, is an abbreviated version of the very first case assigned to the class. Thus, the idea that one retrieves a known example (reference) and then modifies it seems to fit here as well as in mathematics.

A second type of situation in which a number of hypotheticals is used is the "slippery slope" sequence. In this situation, one starts off with a seed case—real or hypothetical —and in a gradual, incrementally ordered fashion, perturbs one aspect of it to end up with an extreme or *reductio* example that typically refutes or discredits the approach that had seemed reasonable enough in the seed. In mathematics, one does not usually use such an incremental sequence; rather, one simply jumps to the extreme case, because in mathematics there is not rhetorical need to make one's opponent unwittingly take the bait and get hooked.

The following is an example of a slippery slope (Rissland, 1986). The issue being tested here is what constitutes *mutuality* in a contract situation. In particular, if only one party has the right to cancel an agreement (e.g., a rental agreement on an apartment or a retail store) or to specify the amount of time needed to cancel the agreement, even a "reasonable" amount of time, is there anything mutual about the bargain? The sequence is:

Hypothetical 1 (seed): I give you 90-days written notice. This seems OK.

Hypothetical 2: Above with 30 days. Still OK.

Hypothetical 3: Above with 1 week. Uncomfortably brief.

Hypothetical 4: Above with 30 seconds. Clearly too little.

Hypothetical 5: (the *reductio* case): any time I feel like it.

This is a classic example of "haggling about the price." That is, there really is no principled way to argue that 30 days is OK and that 10 days is not; the argument depends on circumstances and one's view of what is fair or reasonable. In fact, it is very hard to defend an arbitrary cutoff or threshold in such situations against such slippery slope arguments. Any parent of a 5-year-old can provide numerous examples of completely isomorphic arguments, for instance, about bedtime's being at 8:00 p.m. when there is an interesting TV program on later. (One classic ploy is "can't I see a *little* bit. . . ?")

The point about such sequences in the law school classroom is that if one is not careful, one can be forced into a corner when an argument is based on a quantifiable cutoff. This has implications both defensively and offensively in argument. Even more disturbing than the fact that the *reductio* case is a counterexample to one's position is the fact that it might call into question the validity of one's position on the seed case. So, for instance, having admitted that "anytime I feel like it" is hardly an instance of a mutual situation, why should one regard 90 days' notice as any better? For one thing, the slippery slope has established that there is no one hallowed cutoff, and, for another, what looks OK in one situation might not be so in another.

Other examples of hypotheticals in law can be found in (Ashley, 1988; Rissland, 1982, 1983, 1987; Rissland & Ashley, 1986).

A COMPUTATIONAL MODEL OF REASONING WITH CASES AND EXAMPLES

On the basis of observations about examples, such as those presented in the previous sections, one can enumerate a number of features and desiderata needed in a computer program which reasons with examples or cases:

1. There must be an examples-knowledge-base (EKB).
2. There must be a way to index, search, and retireve from the EKB.
3. There must be a library of modification techniques.
4. There must be a way to judge if a retrieved or modified example satisfies constraints or to select the most "promising" candidate for doing so.
5. There must be a way to assess progress toward the overall satisfaction of constraints and production of solutions.
6. There must be a control mechanism enabling me to know when to give up on an example and its derivative modifications.
7. There should be a mechanism to save past solutions in the EKB—both the

actual examples and the methods to generate them—for future CEG problem solving.

For precedent-based CBR, the requirements are very similar:

1. There must be a case-knowledge-base (CKB).
2. There must be a collection of indices into the CKB.
3. There must be mechanisms to determine relevance and similarity.
4. There must be mechanisms to alter existing cases.
5. There must be mechanisms to explain and exploit similarities and differences among cases.
6. There must be mechanisms to generate and assess arguments.
7. There must be mechanisms to save past solutions in the CKB and change the indexing scheme so that it can track the case law.

Such desiderata have been used to build systems to generate examples given a set of constraints, such as the CEG System (Rissland, 1981; Rissland & Soloway, 1980), and systems to generate legal arguments given a new fact situation, such as the HYPO system (Ashley & Rissland, 1988). We discuss the HYPO system in the next section.

The HYPO Model of Precedent-Based, Case-Based Reasoning

HYPO is a case-based reasoning program that operates in the area of trade secret law (Ashley, 1988; Ashley & Rissland, 1987, 1988). In moving from an input fact situation to arguments about it, HYPO follows a basic sequence, consisting of:

1. Statement of the current fact situation (cfs).
2. Analysis of the cfs.
3. Retrieval of relevant existing cases from a CKB.
4. Positioning of the cfs with respect to retrieved cases.
5. Heuristic (hypothetical) variation of the cfs and attendant analyses.
6. Manipulations of the cfs together with the retrieved and hypothesized cases.
7. Argument formulation, experimentation, evaluation, and revision.
8. Explanation/justification of analysis and argument in terms of cases.

One of the primary mechanisms used by HYPO is a *dimension*. It summarizes ways of arguing or approaching an issue and relates clusters of legally relevant facts to particular conclusions. In particular, a dimension indicates what variations of the facts, especially those focal aspects that are at the crux of an issue, make the case weaker or stronger for one side or the other. Although HYPO operates in the area of trade secrets law, the idea of a dimension is quite general.

As an illustration of a HYPO dimension, consider the typical trade secrets case, in which the plaintiff and the defendant produce competing products and the plaintiff alleges that the defendant misappropriated secret production information. Additional facts might be that the plaintiff disclosed secret information to the defendant, perhaps in connection with an attempt to enter into a sales or other agreement with the defendant, or that a former employee of the plaintiff with knowledge of the trade secret enters the employ of the defendant and brings with him or her trade secret information that he or she learned or developed while working for the plaintiff.

There are several standard ways of approaching such a trade secrets case; for instance, one can emphasize either the employee who switched or the disclosures made. These standard approaches are the basis of HYPO's dimensions. If one emphasizes the disclosures made by the plaintiff—that is, the dimension in HYPO called *knowledge-voluntarily-disclosed*—the more people to whom such disclosures were made, the worse off the plaintiff is, at one extreme, there may have been so many disclosures that there is essentially no one left to have a secret from. (At the other extreme, there would have been no disclosures.)

Dimensions encode the legal knowledge of which clusters of facts, according to a particular point of view summarizing lines of cases, have legal relevance for a particular claim, are prerequisite for dealing with a claim, and contribute to weaknesses and strengths. A key aspect of dimensions is that they organize prerequisite facts in such a way that the most important ones—the focal slots—can be analyzed and manipulated in a legally meaningful way, for instance, to strengthen or weaken a case. The HYPO trade secrets dimension knowledge-voluntarily-disclosed captures the knowledge that the more people who have been told about the secret, the worse off the teller is, and its focal slot is the number of disclosures. For this dimension to be applicable, several prerequisite conditions must be fulfilled: There must be two competing corporations, they must market a similar product, and so forth, and of course, there must have been voluntary disclosures. This last aspect is the focal facet or slot and is really at the heart of the issue, inasmuch as without disclosures there is not much sense in arguing along this dimension, furthermore, the number of disclosees (the focal slot's value) is critical and determines how strong or weak the parties' positions are. Another HYPO dimension is *telltale-signs-of-misappropriation;* according to this dimension, the plaintiff's argument is strengthened if there are certain telltale signs that the defendants sought to misappropriate the plaintiff's alleged trade secret information, such as that the corporate defendant paid a very high bonus to get the employee to bring with him or her a copy of the code he or she worked on for the plaintiff.

Dimensions are used by HYPO in several ways. They are used as indices to the CKB, and they are used by various submodules in HYPO's case-based reasoning. The library of dimensions and CKB are two primary repositories of HYPO's legal knowledge; others include normative information, such as how to assess the on-pointness or importance of a case.

HYPO starts with a statement of facts, proceeds through a dimension-based legal analysis, and concludes with presentation of an argument outline complete with case citations. Given a statement of *the current fact situation, cfs,* HYPO begins its legal analysis. A *case analysis* module runs through the library of dimensions and produces a *case analysis record,* which, among other things, records which dimensions apply to the cfs and which nearby apply (i.e., which are near misses). On the basis of this analysis, the *fact gatherer* may request additional information from the user. Given a "complete" set of facts, the *case-positioner* module uses the case analysis record to create a *claim lattice,* which organizes cases from the CKB according to a measure of applicable and near-miss dimensions shared between cases and the cfs and allows HYPO to determine which cases are most on-point, least on-point, or in between. This module also allows HYPO to spot conflict dimensions—that is, dimensions that point to conflicting conclusions—and gaps in the case base. The *best case selector* and 3-ply argument modules then select cases offering support for the user's case and those cutting against it, which must be distinguished, and suggest the skeleton of an argument, complete with case citations.

The dimensions, case analysis record, and claim lattice also enable the *hypo-generator* module to spawn legally interesting hypotheticals: for instance, a *conflict hybrid* case, which brings together two competing lines of cases that conflict, or a hypothetical that fills in a sparse area of the CKB. With its use of dimension-based heuristics, such as "Make a case extreme (with respect to a given dimension)," "Enable a near-miss dimension," "Disable a near-get dimension," "Make a hybrid," "Pose a conflict," the hypo-generator, in effect, does a heuristic search of the space of all possible cases.

Heuristic Generation of Hypotheticals

Given the knowledge and processes of the HYPO model, one is in an excellent position to describe some heuristics that can be used to generate hypotheticals by modifications of a seed case. Some heuristics using the dimension idea are:

1. Pick a near-miss dimension—that is, a dimension that but for nonsatisfaction of a prerequisite condition would apply to the seed—and modify the facts so that it does apply.

2. Pick an applicable dimension, and make the case weaker or stronger with respect to this dimension.

3. Pick an applicable dimension, and make the case extreme with respect to this dimension.

4. Pick an applicable dimension and a target case to which it is also applicable, and modify the seed to make it identical to or weaker or stronger than the target case along that dimension.

5. Pick a near-win dimension—that is, a dimension for which the case just barely meets the prerequisites—and make it a near miss or a solid win.

As an illustration of how these heuristics work, consider the hypothetical *Widget-King* case (Rissland & Ashley, 1986):

> Plaintiff Widget-King and defendant Cupcake are corporations that make competing products. Widget-King has confidential information concerning its own product. Cupcake gained access to Widget-King's confidential information. Cupcake saved expense in developing its competing product. (p. 293)

In this case, Widget-King would like to argue that Cupcake misappropriated its secret; Cupcake would like to defend itself against this claim. The only applicable dimension (which would be determined in the case analysis phase) is *competitive-advantage-gained,* and there is a near-miss dimension, *knowledge-voluntarily-disclosed.*

One can create many hypotheticals by using Widget-King as the seed:

1. Apply the near-miss heuristic with regard to the knowledge-voluntarily-disclosed dimension by positing some number of voluntary disclosures. One could do this by randomly choosing a number or by referring to the CKB, where there exist several cases with explicit numbers of disclosees.

2. Make the seed stronger from the plaintiff's point of view along the competitive-advantage-gained dimension by increasing the ratio of plaintiff's-to-defendant's expenditures. For instance, make the ratio 2:1, which is what was found in a real case, the *Telex v. IBM* case (1973), in which the plaintiff, IBM, won.

3. Make the seed extreme. For instance, take the result of the application of the near-miss heuristic in 1, and make the number of disclosees extreme. There are several extremes here: (a) zero, which is the best possible value from the plaintiff's point of view; (b) some arbitrarily large number, like 10,000,000, which is the worst value for the plaintiff (who's left to have a secret from?); or (c) an extreme actually existing in the CKB, such as 6,000 from the *Data General* case (1975).

By applying such heuristics, one is exploring in a legally meaningful way the space of all hypotheticals. One can think of this as moving a case around through this space or as generating a constellation of derivative hypotheticals from it.

For instance, in *Lynch v. Donnelly* (1984) one can describe what the Justices were doing as just that. They could be said to be perturbing the actual fact situation along various dimensions, such as the location, size, and focus of the creche display; the religious content of the display; the nature of the viewer; the degree of government involvement; and so forth.

For instance, the Justices made the fact situation weaker and stronger along the focus-of-attention dimension by: (a) removing all secular images and leaving only the religious one; (b) physically shrinking the symbol to an extreme and relegating it to a trivial position; (c) removing the religious symbols and leaving only the secular ones.

They weakened the case for unconstitutionality along the dimension of civic-content-of-message by changing it to a municipal art museum and a courtroom frieze. They compared the case along the dimension of government involvement to an extreme example, the noncase of the Pope's mass on the Washington Mall.

Note that such a post hoc or descriptive analysis of a sequence of real hypotheticals involves two kinds of knowledge: (a) Domain-independent heuristics, such as the five we have listed; and (b) Domain-specific information about cases and dimensions, such as that found in HYPO. The need for the second kind of knowledge makes such an analysis a knowledge-intensive effort; that is, one cannot perform it without knowing something of the law.

Evaluation of the HYPO Model

There are two primary ways in which we have tested the HYPO model of legal reasoning:

1. Running HYPO on cases and evaluating its output. For instance, we have run HYPO on real cases and compared its analysis to that given by the courts in their opinions (Ashley, 1988; Ashley & Rissland, 1987, 1988).
2. Using HYPO's framework to analyze "real" hypotheticals, that is, those produced in actual oral argument before the United States Supreme Court (Rissland, 1989; Rissland & Ashley, 1986).

Work is currently under way to compare HYPO's performance on a selection of cases with that of second- and third-year law students and practicing attorneys.

CONCLUSIONS

In this chapter, I have examined various aspects of example-based reasoning, such as the generation of constrained examples and hypothetical cases; the examples have been taken from mathematics and law. I have also presented a model of a particular kind of EBR called precedent-based, case-based reasoning, in which one reasons with cases and hypotheticals in a precedent-based manner.

There are several lessons to be gained about EBR:

1. For teaching in general: Examples play an important role in reasoning; their potency should not be overlooked. By teaching students how to generate and use them, one should enable them to become better, more active students.

2. For mathematics teaching: There is no reason why generating examples, particularly counterexamples, should remain an arcane skill. At the very least, one could tell students about models such as CEG. In particular, one could convey ideas about an EKB and modification procedures, especially ideas of the "folksier" kind, and give students practice with them. For instance, one could assign CEG exercises in the context of refuting a proposition known or suspected to be false.

3. For law school teaching: Similarly, there is no reasoning why proposing hypotheticals—particularly, nettlesome ones—should remain a mystery. At the very least, one could tell students about models such as HYPO and then give them the opportunity to use it. For instance, one could set up argument contexts in which they are the ones to pose the "nasty" hypotheticals.

Of course, there is no reason why the preceding suggestions should be limited to teaching. There are many situations—doing research mathematics, preparing for litigation—in which one could profitably employ such reasoning skills. There is, of course, also no reason why such analyses of EBR should be confined to mathematics or law.

Although we are not so naive as to posit that CEG and HYPO are the only models, we are confident that they are good first steps. If more researchers, teachers, and practitioners seriously examine EBR, there will be many second and third steps diverse and robust enough to cover a variety of disciplines and tasks involving examples.

REFERENCES

Ashley, K. D. (1988). *Modelling legal argument: Reasoning with cases and hypotheticals.* (COINS Tech. Rep. No. 88-01). Amherst: University of Massachusetts, Department of Computer and Information Science.

Ashley, K. D., & Rissland, E. L. (1987). Compare and contrast. A test of expertise. *Proceedings of the Sixth National Conference on Artificial Intelligence, 1,* 273–278.

Ashley, K. D., & Rissland, E. L. (1988). *A case-based approach to modelling legal expertise. IEEE Expert, 3*(3), 70–77.

Carbonell, J. G. (1986). Derivational analogy: A theory of reconstructive problem solving and expertise acquisition. In R. S.Michalski, J. G. Carbonell, & T. M. Mitchell, (Eds.), *Machine Learning: An Artificial Intelligence Approach* (Vol. 2, pp. 371–392). Calif: Morgan Kaufman.

Gardner, A. L. (1987). *An artificial intelligence approach to legal reasoning.* Cambridge, MA: MIT Press.

Gelbaum, B. R., & Olmstead, J. M. H. *Counterexamples in analysis.* San Francisco, CA: Holden-Day.

Gilfillan v. City of Philadelphia, 637 F.2nd 924 (CA3 1980).

Hammond, K. (1986). CHEF: A model of case-based planning. *Proceedings of the Fifth National Conference on Artificial Intelligence, 1,* 267–271.

Kolodner, J. L., Simpson, R. L., & Sycara-Cyranski, K. (1985). A process model of case-based reasoning in problem solving. *Proceedings of the Ninth International Joint Conference on Artificial Intelligence, 1,* 284–290.

Lakatos, I. (1976). *Proofs and refutations.* New York: Cambridge University Press.

Levi, E. H. (1949). *An introduction to legal reasoning.* Chicago: University of Chicago Press.

Llewellyn, K. N. (1960). *The bramble bush (rev. ed.).* Dobbs Ferry, NY: Oceana Publications.

Lynch v. Donnelly, 104 S. Ct. 1355 (1984).

McCarty, L. T., & Sridharan, N. S. (1980). The representation of an evolving system of legal concepts: II. Prototypes and deformations". *Proceedings of the Third National Conference of the Canadian Society for Computational Studies of Intelligence, 1,* 304–311.

McCreary v. Stone, 575 F.Supp. 1112 (SDNY 1983).

Polya, G. (1973). *How to solve it* (2nd ed.). Princeton, NJ: Princeton University Press.

Polya, G. (1968). *Mathematics and plausible reasoning: Vol. 1. Introduction and Analogy in Mathematics.* Princeton, NJ: Princeton University Press.

Rissland, E. L. (1978). Understanding Understanding Mathematics. *Cognitive Science, 2*(4), 361–383.

Rissland, E. L. (1980). Example Generation. *Proceedings of the Third National Conference of the Canadian Society for Computational Studies of Intelligence.*

Rissland, E. L. (1981). *Constrained example generation.* (COINS Tech. Report 81-24). Amherst: University of Massachusetts, Department of Computer and Information Science.

Rissland, E. L. (1982). Examples in the legal domain: Hypotheticals in contract law. *Proceedings of the Fourth Annual Cognitive Science Conference 1,* 96–99.

Rissland, E. L. (1983). Examples in legal reasoning: Legal hypotheticals. In Alan Bundy (Ed.), *Proceedings of the Eighth International Joint Conference on Artificial Intelligence* (Vol. I, pp. 90–93). Karlsruhe, West Germany: William Kaufmann, Inc.

Rissland, E. L. (1984). Argument Moves and Hypotheticals. In C. Walter (Ed.), *Computer power and legal reasoning* (pp. 129–143). St. Paul, MN: West Publishing Co.

Rissland, E. L. (1986). Learning to argue: Using hypotheticals. In J. L. Kolodner & C. K. Riesbeck (Eds.), *Experience and reasoning* (pp. 115–127). Hillsdale, NJ: Erlbaum.

Rissland, E. L. (1989). Dimension-based analysis of hypotheticals from Supreme Court oral argument. *Proceedings of the Second International Conference on AI and Law, 1,* 111–120.

Rissland, E. L. (1988). Artificial intelligence and legal reasoning: A review. *AI Magazine, 9*(3), 44–45.

Rissland, E. L., & Ashley, K. D. (1986). Hypotheticals as heuristic device. *Proceedings of the Fifth National Conference on Artificial Intelligence, 1,* 289–297.

Rissland, E. L., & Collins, R. C. (1986). The law as a learning system. *Proceedings of the Eighth Annual Cognitive Science Society Conference, 1,* 500–513.

Rissland, E. L., & Soloway, E. M. (1980). Overview of an example generation system. *Proceedings of the First National Conference on Artificial Intelligence, 1,* 256–262.

Rumelhart, D. E., & McClelland, J. L. (1986). *Parallel Distributed Processing.* Cambridge, MA: MIT Press.

Stanfill, C., & Waltz, D. (1986). Toward memory-based reasoning. *Communications of the ACM, 29,* 1213–1228.

Steen, L. A., & Seebach, J. A. (1978). *Counterexamples in topology* (2nd ed.). New York: Springer-Verlag.

Stone v. Graham, 449 U.S. 39 (1980).

Wittgenstein, L. (1958). *Philosophical Investigations.* New York: Macmillan.

Wittgenstein, L. (1978). *Remarks on the Foundations of Mathematics* (rev. ed.). Cambridge, MA: MIT Press.

11 Informal Reasoning in Decision Theory

Jonathan W. Leland
Carnegie Mellon University

A great deal of research has been conducted on informal reasoning in a specific context, namely in reasoning about choices. Thus, it seems expedient to examine recent evidence on how well people reason in this context to see what implications can be gleaned concerning our prospects for developing a curriculum in informal reasoning. My purpose in this chapter is to discuss two lessons implied by this research. The first reflects positively regarding the possibility of teaching people to reason better, whereas implications drawn from the second are far less promising. Specifically, I demonstrate that, for one class of situations in which people reason poorly, in the sense that their choices imply contradictions, they can, at least in principle, be taught to reason better. Conversely, there is a second class of situations with respect to which it is not clear that we can either assist individuals or instruct them in resolving the contradictions reflected by their choices.

With these objectives in mind, the following section proposes and defends a set of criteria commonly accepted as rules that individuals should require their choices to obey in all circumstances. These are the axioms and metapostulates of the normative *theory of individual choice* found in economics and decision theory. To the extent that individuals' choices contradict any of these criteria, they have reasoned poorly.

The second section of the chapter reviews evidence that people's choices systematically violate each of the axioms of choice. The third section of the chapter considers the extent to which individuals can be helped to resolve the contradictions between their choices and the axioms. The types of violations for which remediation is possible are examined first. For these violations, remediation seems appropriate, and the problem that remediation should assist the individual in overcoming is identifiable. I then consider situations in which remediation is not clearly appropriate and discuss why this is so.

Before proceeding, it should be pointed out that, although this paper focuses almost exclusively on reasoning vis-à-vis choice, there are good reasons to believe that the implications drawn apply to a much broader domain. First, from a practical standpoint, we might expect that because people engage in reasoning about choice frequently and because the penalties for poor reasoning in such situations may be substantial, they should reason relatively well in this context. To the extent that they do not, we may suspect that they will not reason well in other contexts with which they have less experience and/or in which there are fewer incentives. Second, although all of the axioms of choice theory may not be appropriate requirements to impose on reasoning in other contexts, many have very general applicability. To the extent that people violate these axioms when reasoning about choice, we might anticipate that they will violate them in other contexts as well.

SOME FUNDAMENTAL REQUIREMENTS
FOR NORMATIVELY APPEALING CHOICE

The theory of individual choice, as espoused in economics and decision theory, can be interpreted normatively or prescriptively as providing the set of rules that we should require our choices to obey in all cases. Choices that violate these rules are normatively unacceptable in that they are inconsistent with criteria believed to be fundamental to the conduct of rational choice. Five such rules are presented herein, along with (I hope) what are compelling explanations for why we should wish to obey them.

As an introduction, it is useful to define precisely what our discussion of individual choice assumes. For individual choice to be meaningful, we assume that individuals have preferences for goods such that quantities of some are preferred to quantities of others, and more of any is preferred to less. Goods are defined, circularly, as those things for which individuals have preferences. The problem of choice arises due to scarcity. The individual faces a finite set (the opportunity set) of commodity bundles (combinations of goods) that are available and affordable. The individual's objective is assumed to be to select the most preferred bundle from the opportunity set. If there is a most preferred subset of bundles in the opportunity set, we assume that the selected bundle comes from this subset.

Although this description of choice seems very general, it does impose an important restriction on choices namely, that they should depend only on the individual's preferences and the opportunity set from which the selection is to be made. Any aspect of the choice situation not represented in these is irrelevant. To make the requirement more concrete, we need to ask what identifiable aspects of choice situations we feel should be irrelevant either because we do not have or think we should not have preferences for them or because they are not in the opportunity set. Starting with the latter possibility, we note that decisions made in the past, although they may have a profound effect on the nature of the opportunity set, are not elements of the opportunity set. Therefore, past decisions should not influence current choices. In other words, given one's preferences and a specific opportunity set, the best choice out of this set should be the same independently of how one has arrived at the current situation.

To illustrate this, consider the following scenario. Suppose that, just prior to boarding a plane for a business trip, you realize that you have a raffle ticket offering a free dinner at an expensive restaurant. Unfortunately, you must personally attend the drawing to receive the prize, something you cannot do because you will be on the plane. You mention this problem to a couple sitting next to you in the airport lounge, and one of them offers to buy the ticket for one dollar because they will be able to attend the drawing. Your opportunity set in this case consists of two options: to sell the ticket for a dollar or to refuse. Selling the ticket is clearly the superior option, and it is the superior option whether you originally paid $.50 or $5 for the ticket. The decision to buy the ticket was made in the past and cannot be unmade.

A second aspect of choice situations that should not influence our choice, insofar as it is not represented in our preferences, concerns labels, or the way in which the commodity bundles are described. One would not, for example, want to be anything but indifferent between 1 pound of chocolates and 16 ounces of identical chocolates. Nor would one wish to prefer an offer of $4 to five greenbacks. This is not to say that all labels or descriptions should be irrelevant, just those for which one has no preference. It is, for example, acceptable to prefer a Brooks Brothers suit to an identical suit without the label if one has a preference for being known as someone who wears Brooks Brothers suits. Likewise, one might prefer to receive $5 in bills than $5 in pennies because one has a preference for the convenience of bills. It is only those labels for which, upon reflection, we believe we do not or should not have a preference that must be ignored. This requirement, the second rule, is sometimes referred to as preference *invariance*.

A third restriction on choice given preferences and opportunity set concerns the assumed objective of the individual: to select the most preferred bundle from the opportunity set. For this objective to be meaningful, our choices or more specifically, our preferences must be transitive. *Transitivity*, the third rule, requires that if an individual prefers some commodity bundle A to another B, and B to another denoted C, then he or she must also prefer A to C. If an individual's preferences are intransitive, such that he or she prefers A to B and B to C and C to A, then he or she will be unable to determine which of the three bundles is most preferred, but he or she will not be indifferent among them.

Another compelling reason for requiring that one's choices always reflect *transitive preferences* is that an individual whose preferences are intransitive can be turned into a *money pump*. Consider an individual whose preferences for commodity bundles A, B, and C are as last described and assume that the individual initially has bundle A. I could then offer to trade him or her a C for that A and perhaps a trivially small but positive amount of money, say, a penny. Because he or she prefers C to A, the offer is accepted. Now I offer to trade him or her a B for that C and a penny, an offer that is again accepted, because he or she prefers B to C. Now I offer to exchange that B for an A and a penny, an offer that is again accepted, because he or she prefers A to B. But, in this sequence of exchanges, he or she has paid a positive amount of money (in this case 3¢) only to end up where he or she started, with A.

The preceding discussion of the problem of choice concerns choices made under certainty. Individuals are certain of receiving the commodity bundles they choose. To extend the description to situations of uncertainty, we must think of individuals as having preferences not only for commodity bundles but for lottery tickets, in which the commodity bundles serve as the prizes. The opportunity set now consists of the available and affordable set of lottery tickets. Although it may seem somewhat contrived to represent actual choices as choices among lottery tickets, this is, in fact, a useful representation. An individual's decision about whether to insure his or her home against fire can, for example, be viewed as a choice between (a) suffering a relatively small sure loss (the insurance premium) and (b) holding a lottery ticket that offers a large probability of no loss (the house not burning down) and a small probability of a large loss (the house burning down).

In the case of *choice under uncertainty,* two additional restrictions on choice seem fundamental from a normative perspective. First, we require that lotteries be evaluated according to the rules of probability. This requirement serves several purposes. First, it implies that probabilities are meaningful to the individual, a necessary restriction in any discussion of individual's having preferences over lotteries. It also prohibits certain preferences among lotteries that would violate other requirements necessary for choices to be normatively appropriate. One might, for example, make choices among lottery tickets implying in a probabilistic context a preference for fewer goods to more. Lotteries that offer probabilistically more than others are said to stochastically dominate the others. To illustrate what this means, consider the pair of lotteries shown below. (Here and throughout the remainder of the paper each letter refers to a lottery ticket of the form $X_1,p_1;\$X_2,p_2; \ldots ;\$X_n,p_n$ in which $\$X_1$ will be received with probability p_1, $\$X_2$ will be received with probability p_2, and so forth. If a lottery ticket offers a prize to be received with certainty, the p notation is suppressed.)

$$A:(\$X,p;\$Y,1\text{-}p) \qquad B:(\$Z,p;\$W,1\text{-}p)$$

If X is greater than Z, and Y is greater than or equal to W, one should always prefer the first ticket, because for identical probabilities it offers a better outcome in one state of the world and at least as good an outcome in the other(s). Alternatively, suppose that the choice is between ($\$X,p;\$Y,1-p$) and ($\$X,q;\$Y,1-q$) and that X is greater than Y. If p equals q, one should be indifferent between the two lotteries. If probability mass is now subtracted from $1-p$ term and added to p term so that p is now greater than q, *stochastic dominance* requires that one prefer the first lottery to the second because it offers a higher probability of winning the more desirable prize and a lower probability of winning the less desirable one.

To see how violations of the rules of probability might lead to violations of dominance, imagine that I offer to bet you either $1 that the Denver Nuggets will play in the National Basketball Association championship finals next year or $1 that the Denver Nuggets and the Detroit Pistons will play in the finals. If you choose to bet at all, you should bet on the former because, for identical payoffs, the probability of Denver's reaching the finals must, by the rules of probability, be at least as great as the probability that both Denver and Detroit will reach the finals.

The second restriction on choices made under uncertainty is that they must be consistent with the fifth and last rule, which is commonly referred to as the *independence axiom*. Independence requires that if one prefers some prize A to another B, then one must also prefer a ticket to a lottery that offers A with probability p and some other prize C with probability $1-p$ to a lottery that offers B with probability p and C with probability $1-p$. Stated differently, independence requires that choices among lottery tickets depend only on those components of the tickets that differ. To illustrate this point, notice that independence is neither a necessary nor appealing restriction to impose in the case of choice under certainty. Under certainty, one might quite rationally express a preference for a soft drink to black coffee but prefer black coffee and an ounce of cream to a soft drink and an ounce of cream. In this case, coffee and cream are complementary goods, so their utility in combination is greater than the sum of their utilities when consumed separately. Under uncertainty, there is no opportunity for complementarity. For example, if a person prefers a 50:50 chance of a soft drink or nothing to a 50:50 chance of a cup of black coffee or nothing, then this preference should not change if we replace the "nothing" in both lotteries with an ounce of cream because one will either get coffee or cream but not both.

To summarize, an individual's choices under certainty should depend only on the available options, should be invariant to irrelevant restatements of the choice situation, and should reflect transitive preferences. In cases of uncertainty, we also require that options be evaluated in accordance with the tenets of probability theory and that the individual's choices be consistent with the requirements of the independence axiom.

EVIDENCE ON PEOPLE'S COMPLIANCE
WITH THE RULES OF CHOICE

We are now in a position to review the evidence concerning whether people's choices actually obey the axioms of choice theory. This question has been addressed primarily by behavioral decision theorists. However, it should be noted that the following discussion is not an exhaustive survey of the types of biases and errors in reasoning that have been identified by researchers in this field. (Readers interested in a broader coverage of this research should also see Chapter 2 in this volume, which discusses a complementary set of biases and errors in reasoning.) We now consider situations in which each of the five proposed rules is violated by a significant number of people.

People's inability to adhere consistently to the independence axiom has probably been recognized longer and studied more extensively than any other type of violation. Two of the most common ways in which independence is violated have been proposed by Allais (1953): the *common ratio effect* and the *common consequence effect*. As discussed earlier, the independence axiom requires that one's choice among prospects depend only on the components of the prospects that differ. What Allais and others have found is that, in certain circumstances, common components are not ignored. Consider a choice between the following prospects.

A:($2500,.33;$2400,.66;$0,.01)   B:($2400)

Now consider a choice between these prospects:

A':($2500,.33;$0,.67)   B':($2400,.34;$0,.66)

Kahneman and Tversky (1979) have found that of the first pair of prospects most people prefer B, whereas of the second pair of prospects, most people prefer A'. Both of these choices appear quite reasonable. In the choice between prospects A and B, the additional $100 offered in A does not appear to be sufficient compensation for the possibility of receiving nothing. In the choice between A' and B', the trivially higher probability of winning a prize in B' does not sufficiently compensate for the additional $100 offered in A'. Although these justifications may seem reasonable, an individual preferring B to A and A' to B' is violating the independence axiom. The prospects A and B can be rewritten in the following equivalent forms:

A:($2500,.33;$2400,.66;$0,.01)   B:($2400,.66;$2400,.34)

Although this restatement of the problem seems trivial, it does make clear that the component (2400,.66) is common to both A and B. As such, it should not influence the individual's choice between the two prospects. A' and B' are simply prospects A and B with the common consequence (2400,.66) subtracted from each. Thus, independence requires that an individual prefer either A and A' or B and B'.

To illustrate the second common violation of the independence axiom, imagine choosing between these two lottery tickets.

$$A:(\$6000,.5;\$0,.5) \qquad B:(\$3000,.9;\$0,.1)$$

Now suppose, instead, that the choice is between A' and B':

$$A':(\$6000,.01;\$0,.99) \qquad B':(\$3000,.018;\$0,.982)$$

People tend to prefer B in the first situation and A' in the second. Again, there is a "reasonable" explanation for both of these preferences. B is preferred to A because the additional $3000 offered in A does not compensate for the substantially higher probability of receiving nothing in A. In the second choice, A' is preferred to B' because the difference between the probabilities of winning the prizes appears trivial relative to the difference in the payoffs offered. Although both are compelling, an individual who chooses A and B', or B and A', for that matter, is violating the independence axiom. The choice in the second case is equivalent to playing a preliminary lottery in which there is a 2-in-100 chance that one will get to choose between lottery tickets A and B and a 98-in-100 chance that one will not get to choose between tickets, in which case one receives nothing. Thus, the 98% chance of receiving nothing is common to both lottery A' and lottery B' and should be irrelevant according to the independence axiom. This is shown as follows:

$$A':(A,.02;0,.98) \qquad B':(B,.02;0,.98)$$

Another large body of evidence suggests that people are not better at conforming to the rules of probability than to the independence axiom. From a practical standpoint, certain types of violation, such as the failure to correctly reduce a very intricate compound lottery to its fundamental form might be expected in the same way that arithmetic errors might be expected in complex calculations. Unfortunately, many of the observed violations are not attributable to errors in computation. Rather, they are violations of fundamental tenets of probability theory, and they occur in fairly simple contexts. Two such examples are provided hereafter. In the first, people choose, in a manner that is inconsistent with the requirement of probability theory, that the sum of the probabilities of mutually exclusive and exhaustive events must equal one. In the second, their evaluations and choices violate the extension rule of probability theory, which requires that the probability of the conjunction of two events occurring cannot be greater than the probability of either one of the events occurring.

To illustrate the first example, imagine two urns, denoted 1 and 2. Urn 1 contains 50 red and 50 black chips; urn 2 contains 100 chips, an unknown proportion of which are red and the rest of which are black. One has the choice of betting on drawing red or on drawing black; if the chip one draws is of the wagered color, one receives $20, and if it is of the other color, one receives nothing. Now suppose one is asked whether one prefers to bet on drawing a red chip from urn 1 or drawing a black chip from urn 1. People are generally and quite reasonably indifferent between these alternatives because the chances are 50:50 in either case. Likewise, people tend to be indifferent between betting on drawing a red chip or drawing a black chip from urn 2, because they know nothing about the proportions of red and black chips in the urn other than that their sum is 100%.

But suppose one is asked whether one prefers to bet on drawing a red chip from urn 1 or urn 2. People in this situation generally prefer urn 1. The common and apparently reasonable justification for this choice is that at least one knows that one has a 50:50 chance with urn 1. Likewise, if asked to choose between betting on drawing a black chip from urn 1 or urn 2, the same people tend to prefer urn 1 again because the proportion of black to red chips in urn 1 is known. Preferring to bet on red from urn 1 to red from urn 2 implies that one believes that the proportion of red chips in urn 2 is less than 50%. Yet preferring to bet on drawing a black chip from urn 1 rather than a black chip from urn 2 implies that one believes that the likelihood of drawing a black chip from urn 2 is likewise less than 50%. Taken together this pair of beliefs is inconsistent with the more general principle that the sum of mutually exclusive and exhaustive events must equal 1.

This is one of several examples typifying the *Ellsburg Paradox* (Ellsburg, 1961). In more complicated variations of the problem, individuals who by almost any criteria would be considered experts in probability and expected utility theory, failed to respond in a coherent manner.

Tversky and Kahneman (1983) have found numerous situations in which people make probability estimates violating the extension rule. Consider, for example, the following description of Linda:

> Linda is 31 years old, outspoken and very bright. She majored in philosophy in college. As a student she was concerned with issues of discrimination and social justice, and also participated in antinuclear demonstrations. Which of the following is more probable:
> A: Linda is a bank teller.
> B: Linda is a bank teller and is active in the feminist movement.
>
> (p. 229)

Eighty-five percent of Kahneman and Tversky's 142 Berkeley undergraduates succumbed to what is called the *conjunction fallacy* because they regarded Linda's being both a bank teller and a feminist as more likely than her being a bank teller. This response violates extension, because the set of all bank tellers includes that subset who are also feminists. Violations of extension occur when people evaluate likelihoods using the *representativeness heuristic:* basing their probability estimates on how representative a specific category or event is of a stereotype. In the preceding example, the probability that Linda is a feminist is evaluated as very high because the description of Linda fits (is representative of) the stereotype (model) of a feminist. The description of her does not, on the other hand, fit the stereotype of a bank teller, and as a result, her being a bank teller is judged unlikely. The representativeness heuristic leads people to judge the probability of an individual's possessing a likely characteristic (feminist) and an unlikely one (bank teller) as some weighted average of their probability assessments of the two.

As with the Ellsburg Paradox, having expertise in probability or in the subject matter does not necessarily prevent errors. In fact, familiarity with a subject may make violations of extension more likely because it offers the opportunity to develop stereotypes.

Violations of transitivity can be classified either as direct or indirect. The former are attributable to the preferences themselves being intransitive, whereas the latter may be attributed to violations of other normative rules of choice. Direct violations appear to arise because people sometimes tend to ignore small differences between components of commodity bundles or lotteries. A simple if contrived example occurs when we chain together a person's claims of indifference between pairs of options. For example, a person might reasonably state that he or she is indifferent between a 1-week vacation in the Bahamas or a 1-week vacation in Jamaica and $1, the latter or a week's vacation in the Bahamas and $2, and so forth up to some point at which he or she states indifference between, say, a week in the Bahamas and $999 versus a week in Jamaica and $1000. However, if the entire chain of indifference statements is taken literally, it implies that the person is indifferent between a week in the Bahamas, a week in Jamaica and $1; and a week in Jamaica and $1000, yet the last option clearly dominates either of the others. Thus, by chaining indifference statements, one can produce violations of transitivity.

A subtler and more disturbing violation of transitivity, operating on a similar principle, has been identified by Tversky (1969). He found that people's preferences for certain sets of gambles were frequently intransitive. Suppose, for example, that of the following set of gambles, *a* through *e* you are to state whether you prefer *a* or *b*, then *b* or *c*, then *c* or *d*, and finally *d* or *e*.

$$a = (\$5.00, 7/24)$$
$$b = (\$4.75, 8/24)$$
$$c = (\$4.50, 9/24)$$
$$d = (\$4.25, 10/24)$$
$$e = (\$4.00, 11/24)$$

Most people prefer *a* to *b*, *b* to *c*, *c* to *d*, and *d* to *e*, when the gambles are presented in this sequential manner. However, when asked to choose between gambles *a* and *e*, the same individuals tend to prefer *e*, thus violating transitivity. As with violations of independence and the rules of probability, there is a seemingly reasonable justification for each choice. When the pairs of gambles are presented sequentially, the difference in the probability of winning the prize, 1/24, seems trivial relative to the difference in the payoffs. In the choice between *a* and *e*, however, the difference between the probabilities of winning is no longer negligible relative to the difference in the payoffs.

In addition to having difficulty making choices in accordance with independence, probability theory, and transitivity, people appear to have a great deal of trouble ignoring irrelevant aspects of choice situations. Specifically, they fail to ignore past decisions and inconsequential changes in the description of the opportunity set. Individuals who let past decisions influence current choices succumb to what is called the *sunk cost fallacy*. In the previous section, we argued that if one has a lottery ticket and the option of either selling it for $1 or keeping it, in which case it is worthless, one should always take the dollar. If one refuses because one has paid $5 for the ticket and to sell it for $1 would mean losing money, one would be honoring a sunk cost.

When cast in this manner, the nature of the sunk cost fallacy is obvious. However, in a wide variety of circumstances it appears that sunk costs are not ignored. Consider the following example suggested by Thaler (1980).

> A family pays $40 for tickets to a basketball game to be played 60 miles from their home. On the day of the game there is a snowstorm. They decide to go anyway, but note in passing that had the tickets been given to them, they would have stayed home.
>
> (p. 47)

Many people see nothing inconsistent or irrational in the family's decision to go to the game even though, if the tickets had been free, they would have preferred to stay home. After all, if they do not go to the game, they will be wasting the $40. But this conclusion is not true. The decision to buy the tickets was made, and the $40 is gone regardless of whether the family goes to the game or not. The $40 is not an element in the opportunity set. The opportunity set consists of two options: (a) going to the game and (b) staying home.

How frequently and in what situations people tend to honor sunk costs is not clear, although several researchers have suggested that sunk costs may influence choices in a wide variety of contexts from business decisions concerning abandoning unprofitable projects (Arkes & Blumer, 1985) to overcoming substance addiction (Dawes, 1988). Casual observations also support this conjecture. Popular proverbs such as "waste not, want not" and "in for a penny, in for a pound," far from being maxims to live by, are prescriptions for making bad choices. Once one has ordered dinner at a restaurant, one should eat the entire meal only if that amount of food or a greater amount is most satisfying; otherwise, one should leave some on the plate. Likewise, if one finds oneself in for a penny, one should forget about the penny. The only relevant issue concerning whether to continue with an endeavor is whether the additional pound yields greater benefits spent on this project than it would if it were spent on any other option.

A final type of violation concerns the failure of choices to be invariant to objectively irrelevant changes in the way the choices are presented. Contrary to the rule of invariance, inconsequential changes in the description of choices frequently affect the choice made. These effects are referred to as *framing effect*. Consider, for example, the following pairs of gambles from Tversky and Kahneman (1986):

A: A sure gain of $240
B: A 25% change to gain $1000 and a 75% chance to gain nothing.
C: A sure loss of $750
D: A 75% chance to lose $1000 and a 25% chance to lose nothing.
If you were allowed to choose either A or B and either C or D, which combination would you most prefer?
A and C   A and D   B and C   B and D

(p. 255)

When faced with these two pairs of choices, people tend to prefer the combination of A and D. As usual, there is an apparently reasonable explanation or defense for this pair of choices. A is preferred to B because A offers $240 with certainty, whereas with B there is a large probability of gaining nothing. As for the second pair, one is sure to lose $750 if C is selected, whereas with D there is at least some chance of losing nothing. As reasonable as these justifications seem, the pair of choices A and D implies a violation of stochastic dominance. To see why the choice pair A and D is dominated by B and C, consider what the pairs imply when combined:

A&D: 25% chance of gaining $240 and a 75% chance of losing $760.
B&C: 25% chance of gaining $250 and a 75% chance of losing $750

When the pairs are rewritten in this format, the superiority of B and C is apparent.

As a final example of violations of invariance, consider another problem posed by Kahneman and Tversky (1982).

Imagine that the U.S. is preparing for the outbreak of a rare Asian disease which is expected to kill 600 people. Two alternative programs to combat the disease have been proposed.
If program A is adopted, 200 people will be saved.
If program B is adopted, there is a ⅓ probability that 600 will be saved and a ⅔ probability that none will be saved.
Which of the two programs do you prefer, A or B?

(p. 166)

Now suppose the two programs are as follows:

If program C is adopted 400 people will die.
If program D is adopted there is a ⅓ probability that nobody will die and a ⅔ probability that 600 will die.
Which of the programs do you prefer, C or D?

(p. 166)

It is clear when the problems are presented together in succession that they are identical, the only difference being that one is stated in terms of lives lost whereas the other is stated in terms of lives saved. Nevertheless, this inconsequential rewording dramatically influences the choice of program. In the lives saved frame, the majority of people prefer to save 200 people for certain. This is called a *risk averse response* because the individual prefers a sure amount to a lottery with an expected value equal to that amount. The justification for this choice is that if option A is chosen, 200 people will surely be saved, whereas with option B there is some probability that all will be saved, but it is more likely that none will. Conversely, in the lives lost frame, the majority of people prefer option D. This response implies risk seeking; people prefer to take a gamble rather than receive the expected value of the gamble with certainty. The justification for preferring D is that if C is chosen, 400 will certainly die, whereas with D there is some hope that none will be lost. Either justification seems reasonable, but to subscribe to both by preferring A when the problem is described one way and D when it is described another implies a contradiction that one both prefers and does not prefer one option to another.

PROSPECTS FOR INSTRUCTING PEOPLE TO REASON BETTER

The evidence reviewed in the previous section clearly indicates that people do not necessarily reason well, at least regarding choice. Moreover, these violations occur in situations that are extremely simple relative to many situations that we encounter on a daily basis. It thus seems advisable not to place too much faith in people's ability to reason well regarding tasks or problems involving any degree of complexity. The evidence reviewed also warns us not to assume that the apparent reasonableness of choices or evaluations necessarily reflects their acceptability or validity. As every example shows, there are "reasonable" justifications for contradictory choices.

Regarding instruction, it seems that, because errors in reasoning occur with respect to each of the axioms of choice and occur in relatively simple contexts, we have prima facie evidence in favor of remediation. However, as mentioned in the introduction, the evidence reviewed suggests that this conclusion must be qualified. Specifically, there is a class of situations in which this is the case and another class in which it is not obvious how remediation might help. Violations falling into the first class are those in which, during the process of discovering the incompatibility of a choice or choices with an axiom, it becomes clear to the individual that the choice or one of the choices is a mistake. Once this is recognized, the decision maker willingly recants. Consider the violation of stochastic dominance presented earlier. In this example, the tendency to choose the dominated pair of alternatives stems from the specific way in which the problem is presented. When told to choose an alternative from the first pair of lotteries and an alternative from the second pair, people tend to approach the problem by treating each of the choices in isolation. The presentation obscures the fact that if one is to choose an alternative from the first and an alternative from the second, then these alternatives should be integrated when one makes a decision. When the choices are integrated for the decision maker, the original pair of choices is obviously inferior to others, and the individual willingly revises his or her decision.

Other examples in the previous section are similar in this respect. People are prone to honor sunk costs because the statement of the problem or the way it is formulated by the individual suggests that the alternatives are different from what they really are. Once the nature of each alternative is unambiguously and clearly defined, the appropriate choice becomes clear, and people willingly refuse to honor sunk costs. Similarly, the tendency to evaluate likelihoods through the representativeness heuristic is another instance in which, when the true implications of people's likelihood assessments are clearly revealed to them, they realize that their assessments are illogical and willingly revise them to accord with the extension rule of probability theory.

In all these situations, through a demonstration that a choice or choices contradict one of the axioms, the choice or one of the choices is revealed to be an error resulting from the way the problem is stated or perceived by the decision maker. The implication regarding the appropriate form of remediation is obvious if not very profound: Teach people how to restructure decision problems in ways that reveal their fundamental structure. This is the same strategy employed to instruct people in formal logic. To evaluate the validity of a syllogistic argument, for example, students are taught to restate the argument symbolically and to represent it in a manner that makes its validity or invalidity transparent, such as by using a Venn diagram. In this process, irrelevant aspects of the problem are stripped away, and ambiguities are identified and resolved. Once this is accomplished, ascertaining the validity of the argument is trivial.

Concerning the remaining examples presented in the previous section, not only is the appropriate type of remediation far from obvious, but it is not even clear that remediation is possible. In these situations, identifying choices as inconsistent with an axiom does not reveal one of the choices to be an error. Nor does one formulation or presentation of the problem seem clearer and more parsimonious than the other. Instead the decision maker is left on the horns of a dilemma. The axiom appears to be one that all choices should follow, yet each of the contradictory choices seems to be the preferred one, given the specific context in which it is made.

The violation of invariance obtained by stating choices in terms of either losses or gains is, perhaps, the best example of this situation. Invariance seems fundamental to good decision making and good reasoning in general. Restatements of the problem that are inconsequential should not have any impact. However, although it is easy to demonstrate to people that their choices when the alternatives are stated in terms of gains contradict their choices when the alternatives are stated in terms of losses, this contradiction does not reveal to people that one of the two choices is an error. Each choice appears to be the preferred one, given the frame in which the problem is posed. Nor does either way of framing the alternatives seem simpler or more natural. As such, people's choices seem to reflect a fundamental ambivalence that cannot be resolved in a nonarbitrary way.

Common ratio and common consequence effects, the Ellsburg paradox, and the direct violations of transitivity are also instances in which revealing the contradictory nature of choices does not indicate that an error has been made. Nor can we help individuals identify which of a pair of mutually inconsistent choices reflects their true preferences.

CONCLUSIONS

Our ability to teach people to reason better in other contexts may be subject to the same qualifications proposed here with respect to reasoning about choices. Although not all of the axioms of choice theory are applicable in other contexts, some, such as adherence to the laws of probability theory and invariance, seem fundamental in a wide variety of circumstances. Suppose, for example, that we are considering how people evaluate the degree to which a given set of premises or evidence supports a proposed conclusion. If we find that people's estimates reflect evaluations of likelihood based on the representativeness heuristic, we may be in a position to offer assistance and tutelage. Conversely, when what they see as inconsequential changes in the statement of the premises produce disagreement among reasoners' conclusions, we may be unable to provide assistance until we better understand why such contradictions arise. This is clearly an area in which future research is required.

REFERENCES

Allais, M. (1953). Le Comportement de l'homme rationel devant le risque, Critique des postulates et axiomes de l'ecole Americaine. *Econometrica, 21,* 503–546.

Arkes, H., & Blumer, C. (1985). The psychology of sunk cost. *Organizational Behavior and Human Performance, 35,* 129–140.

Dawes, R. (1988). *Rational choice in an uncertain world*. San Diego, CA: Harcourt Brace Jovanovich.

Ellsburg, D. (1961). Risk, ambiguity and the Savage axioms. *Quarterly Journal of Economics, 64*, 528–556.

Kahneman, D., & Tversky, A. (1979). Prospect theory: An analysis of decisions under uncertainty. *Econometrica, 47*, 263–291.

Kahneman, D., & Tversky, A. (1982). The psychology of preferences. *Scientific American, 246*, 160–173.

Thaler, R. (1980). Toward a positive theory of consumer choice. *Journal of Economic Behavior and Organization, 1*, 39–60.

Tversky, A. (1969). The intransitivity of preferences. *Psychological Review, 76*, 31–48.

Tversky, A., & Kahneman, D. (1983). Extensional versus intuitive reasoning: The conjunction fallacy in probability judgment. *Psychological Review, 90*, 293–315.

Tversky, A., & Kahneman, D. (1986). Rational choice and the framing of decisions. *Journal of Business, 59*, S251–S278.

12 Rhetoric and Informal Reasoning: Disentangling Some Confounded Effects in Good Reasoning and Good Writing

Joseph M. Williams
University of Chicago

Perhaps a more accurate title for this chapter would be "Informal Reasoning about Informal Reasoning about Informal Reasoning." I am not concerned here with the ways that rhetorical theory relates to informal reasoning or to the increasingly complex kit of heuristics that teachers of composition have been assembling to help students think about what they are writing. I want, instead, to examine—informally—some of the considerations that are apparently used by those who informally judge the quality of a writer's informal reasoning on the basis of the way that writer evidences reasoning in continuous written discourse.

RHETORIC AND PERCEIVED REASONING

In ordinary circumstances, we judge the quality of reasoning on the basis of the evidence that reasoners provide. In many ecologically valid contexts, this evidence consists of the content we find in continuous discourse, often written discourse that offers the thinking behind the solution to the problem. My question is this: To what degree do matters of perceived discourse form and rhetorical convention influence our judgments of the informal reasoning reflected by that discourse?

This is not a trivial matter, for when we have only writing as evidence of reasoning, we cannot avoid folding the issue of what counts as competent or incompetent discourse into the question of what counts as good or bad reasoning, a problem made more complicated if we confuse naive or otherwise inappropriate rhetorical strategies with less-than-competent thinking or writing. For example, Voss, Green, Post & Penner (1983) proposed a number of characteristics of how experts solve ill-formed problems in the social sciences. The experts typically devoted a substantial portion of their out-loud protocols (their discourse) to decomposing and defining the problem to be solved and to setting constraints, much more than did the novices. Voss and his colleagues did consider the issue of evaluating problem-solving protocols in the context of how the question was put and its tacit rhetorical frame:

> . . . the observations indicate how the surroundings in which the problem is presented may provide constraints and influence what the individual states. Indeed, there apparently are "audience effects" in social science problem solving just as in writing and speaking. We might add that the bulk of our research has been conducted in a relatively "open" atmosphere and the solver is aware that anonymity will be preserved. In this respect constraints were hopefully reduced. (p. 209)

It is just this problem, the role of audience effects, that may, however, result in our confounding appropriate rhetorical moves with higher level informal reasoning, for it is impossible to imagine a situation where the production of discourse for any audience in any context has no rhetorical constraints. In the case of the social science experts explaining how to improve agricultural output in the Soviet Union, the experts knew they were talking to an audience of nonexperts who, at the same time, were highly educated and experts in their own right. Under those circumstances, do experts speaking to those whom they consider highly educated nonexperts conventionally—as a predictable rhetorical move—devote a substantial portion of their discourse to formulating the problem? If so, then we have to be cautious before we assume that expert reasoning is typically characterized by a rich decomposition and description of the problem space. It might be more appropriate to say that experts are capable of it and that they often do it. But the overt production of that rich description may also characterize the way experts typically talk to educated experts, the way they rhetorically solve two problems simultaneously—what I call the *problem-proper*—and the academic expert's rhetorical problem of talking to academic experts in other fields.

In contrast to this rhetorical situation is Voss's report (chap. 3, this volume) of the minutes of meetings among Japanese military planners prior to the attack on Pearl Harbor in 1941. Voss showed that when those planners—experts, we might assume—were speaking to one another, they spent substantially less time providing reasons for their positions than when they were presenting much the same arguments to Emperor Hirohito. In a rhetorical situation where the planners constituted a small interpretive community, a small discourse community, they apparently did not feel rhetorically constrained to provide explicit reasons for their positions, presumably because they shared so much background information in the first place. But when they were speaking to their Emperor, they were required to be more explicit in delineating their reasoning because he was not an expert peer but a nonexpert superior.

On the basis of this evidence, do we conclude that in the peer group the planners were reasoning less complexly than when they were speaking to someone outside their group, to their Emperor, because they did not explicitly delineate the patterns of their reasoning? That hardly seems plausible. Almost certainly, in their peer group, they were behaving in ways expert peers behave with one another: They were leaving a substantial amount unsaid, because they could take it for granted. Taking shared knowledge for granted is the first sign of an expert talking to an expert in the same field.

Now the nice question: Do readers judge the quality of a writer's reasoning on anything like a similar basis? Do readers expect certain rhetorical patterns, gestures, and devices as evidence of complex reasoning? Or, more interesting, perhaps, do readers expect not to see certain rhetorical patterns, gestures, devices, and information when those readers expect to be addressed as peers in a community of discourse defined by them and the writer?

In the world of everyday problem solving, it is never the case that there are no rhetorical constraints. Problems usually get solved because (a) someone poses a problem and then requires that someone else solve it, or (b) someone poses a problem and then solves it because he or she believes that there are potential consumers of the solution. Either way, one cannot escape how audience/solution-consumers influence the problem solver in shaping the rhetorical form of the discourse in which the solution is couched.

When we consider the relationship between a writer's reasoning through to the solution to a problem and the discourse form that evidences that process and solution, we have to disentangle four substantially different kinds of behavior: (a) incompetent writing in some fundamental sense of rhetorical incompetence, (b) incompetent writing as defined by a writer's failing to meet the particular rhetorical expectations of a discourse community, (c) incompetent reasoning in some fundamental generic sense, and (d) incompetent reasoning as defined by the local standards of some discourse community. (I assume here that a discourse community defines a reasoning community. [Bazerman, 1981; Toulmin, 1958; Toulmin, Rieke, & Janik, 1979]. Without discourse about the object of reasoning, and without metadiscourse about the quality of reasoning and the quality of discourse, there would be slim evidence that reasoning was taking place at all.)

Now, when I refer to bad writing, I do not mean the way that problems of spelling, punctuation, grammar, usage, or nonstandard dialects influence the way we judge the quality of reasoning (although judgments about the quality of reasoning are, in fact, influenced by those matters). I refer instead to the way a problem solver successfully or unsuccessfully goes about finding solutions to four distinct but intertwined problems:

1. The primary problem posed, or what I call the problem proper (i.e., what should we do about AIDS?).

But when asked to solve the problem proper, not in conversation but *in writing*, the problem solver must solve at least three other problems as well. The first problem among these three is, obviously enough, the problem of producing the text:

2. The writer must solve the problem of controlling and producing text that meets general rhetorical demands of competent writing, principles of discourse that transcend individual discourse communities. This is partly the stuff of freshman composition courses—competent spelling, punctuation, grammar but also coherent organization, relevance, and so on.

But this basic problem is confounded by at least two constituent problems:

3. The writer must simultaneously meet the usually tacit demands that particular discourse communities set for their writers. What is the acceptable form of a brief, of a research paper in educational psychology, of a grant proposal, or of an internal memorandum? (And of course, each of these problems comprise nested sets of subproblems [Flower & Hayes, 1981].)
4. The writer must solve one of the most common problems found in the nonacademic world: the problem of defining (a) the nature of the problem and then (b) making that clear to the reader by means of the rhetorical conventions of a field.

To put this last issue in crude but familiar terms, does the problem poser define the problem as ill structured or well structured, and has the writer perceived that problem in the same way (Newell & Simon, 1972)? How the problem solver/writer resolves this question will significantly influence his or her rhetorical choices. I want to consider here how the writer seems to address (a) the problem proper, (b) the general demands of competent writing, and (c) the tacit demands of a particular discourse community in the context of (d) how that writer defines and articulates the problem structure.

JUDGMENTS OF GOODNESS AND LOCAL CONVENTIONS

So far as I know, none of those who has inquired into what counts as good informal reasoning has addressed how particular discourse communities simultaneously judge not only the quality of the problem solving but also the quality of the discourse in which the solution is expressed and how the effects interact. I am addressing here the way in which the consumer interprets the solution to the problem proper in light of how that consumer perceives the solution to the rhetorical problem.

I raise the issue because as someone who has worked with writers ranging from ninth graders to state supreme court judges—and in recent years substantially more with adults—I have regularly found myself disagreeing with "experts" in a field over the problem of distinguishing "bad" reasoning from "bad" writing. Quite regularly, those who feel at home in a field seem to confound the quality of reasoning and the rhetoric of the writing that evidences the reasoning. I am regularly puzzled by a judgment that a piece of discourse is "terribly written" when it has seemed to me to be perfectly clear—wrong perhaps, perhaps too clearly wrong, but well formed; or that the discourse was well written when, in fact, it seemed to me to be less than entirely competent discourse.

Students' Approaches to Problem Definition

A number of my colleagues who teach the first-year social science courses at the University of Chicago have complained that we who teach first-year humanities courses do not teach freshmen how to write or think in a coherent, organized way. My colleagues perceive the papers of many first-year students as wandering through issues without establishing any coherent point of view, unable to come to grips with what those colleagues believe is a straightforward problem. In fact, they appeared most often to have provided as examples of badly written papers those that worked toward a conclusion and did not, in a sentence or two at the end of the introduction, put forward a statement that would count as the major claim of the paper, but rather that made that claim as a kind of discovery at the end of the paper (Colomb & Williams, 1985; Flower, 1979). The inductively organized papers seemed to be judged badly written more often than the deductively organized papers.

In an informal survey, 10 social science faculty members were asked to evaluate, on a scale of 1–5, the holistic quality of reasoning in 20 three-page papers, 10 organized inductively and 10 organized deductively. The same papers were given to 10 humanities teachers. The gross scores, without any statistical analysis are shown in Table 12.1.

On the basis of this informal survey, it appears that social science faculty are more likely to respond unfavorably to an inductively organized paper than are humanities faculty.

TABLE 12.1
Informal Faculty Assessment of Freshman Papers

	Deductively Organized Papers	Inductively Organized Papers
Total of Ratings by Social Sciences Faculty	320	210
Total of Ratings by Humanities Faculty	350	330

In fact, a number of my humanities colleagues said they specifically look for students who, in their papers, demonstrate their ability to work through or think through a problem in the act of writing about it, that is, students who can raise a question and then, in writing, wrestle with it, inductively seeming to arrive at a conclusion only after they have demonstrated the quality of their inquiring minds and their ability to consider different sides of a question. In fact, some thought that those students who provided a flat answer to a question in the first few sentences of a paper "obviously had not thought through the problem" or "were oversimplifying."

Clearly, whatever the effect of the choice between these two kinds of rhetorical organizations, the organizations themselves are not necessarily a matter per se of better or worse writing or better or worse reasoning. The perceived difference in quality of reasoning may be a matter of whether a writer has met usually unexpressed but wholly conventionalized rhetorical expectations that are, perhaps, peculiar to different discourse communities (although I suspect more peculiar to individuals in those communities). As I try to explain more fully hereafter, those rhetorical conventions may reflect the way a writer perceives a problem—as a well-formed problem requiring a well-formed written solution or as an ill-formed problem but still requiring a well-formed written solution.

To put it simply at this point, some of my social sciences colleagues appear to be putting to their students what they may believe are well-structured problems that invite them to state a solution at the beginning of a paper, but the students mistakenly perceive the problems to be ill-structured for at least two reasons: First, from their novice point of view, the problems are, in fact, ill structured, and a typical response of a novice student working through a problem is to demonstrate that working through on paper (Flower, 1979).

Second, some students may have been successfully trained by some of their humanities faculty to respond rhetorically to what appear to be complex problems (effectively, all problems that require extended discourse) as ill structured, to demonstrate their appreciation of complexity. (And, of course, regardless of the expectations of faculty of whatever discipline, not every first-year student has the rhetorical competence to write inductive papers that seem to hang together, that is, that seem to demonstrate simultaneous control over not only the text but over the student's intellectual progress in reasoning about the problem.)

Experts' Problem Definitions

Rhetorical posture toward a problem is an issue not unrelated to a kind of responses to ill-structured problems in the social sciences that Voss et al. (1983) found in their work with experts and novices in Soviet affairs. The experts in Soviet affairs—social scientists, interestingly enough—assumed a rhetorical stance that, at first glance, looks more like what many of my humanities colleagues seem to look for in the writing of their students than what my social science colleagues do. As described earlier, in their out-loud protocols, the experts in Soviet affairs devoted a substantial amount of time to defining the problem space of an ill-structured problem, decomposing it into its parts, emphasizing its complexity, the constraints on its solutions, before they articulated their specific solutions. The social science novices spent less time defining the problem (at least partly, of course, because they simply did not thoroughly control the amount of factual information that went into the expert's formulation of the problem) and concentrated on lower level, more concrete elements of the problem.

How would we account for the apparent difference between the practice of the social science experts in Voss's group's research and the seeming preferences of social science faculty in reading student papers? Bazerman (1981) has pointed out one significant difference in the practice of humanists and social scientists as they initially construct the problem space *in their writing*. The social scientist (but even more predictably the physical scientist) typically engages a problem that is already "in the air." The writer typically is able to cite other writers who have previously addressed the problem before, offering a new solution or new point of view. The humanist, by contrast, particularly the literary critic, perhaps, regularly has to create a problem where no problem has been suspected. In order to do that, the humanist must spend a substantial amount of time persuading the reader that, in fact, a problem exists. As a logical consequence, the writer has to postpone offering a solution to a problem that not everyone is even aware of. To this extent, typical problems in certain areas of the humanities have to be treated as ill structured because they are previously unperceived problems.

It may also be that, as Voss has suggested (personal communication), social scientists are more interested in the solutions to known problems that in the creation of hitherto unknown ones and not in the activity of the mind in creating and solving a problem but in results. I think that that is probably true and that the rhetorical patterns that have come to characterize the humanities and social sciences reflect those different epistemologies. One of the standard arguments we in the humanities give for having students read broadly in the canon of Western texts is that we teach our students how to read and how to think critically. The only evidence we have of that critical thinking is the thinking we infer from the essays we read. It is at least possible that, in their introductory courses, social scientists value the sheer content of their teaching more prominently than do humanists. (My experience as sometime chairman of a core program suggests that humanists are more willing than social scientists to give up content for the sake of close reading and careful writing. In no sense does this indicate that my social science colleagues are uninterested in close reading and careful writing.)

Whatever the sources of these similarities and differences, they have consequences for the way judgments get made. On the one hand, we can take as a given the fact that complex, ill-structured problems are best perceived as such by those who control the data that define the problem and that when the experts are asked about the problem they will be able to describe it in complex and therefore relatively detailed ways. On the other hand, there is that other legitimate question here: Does that extended problem formulation characterize what we take to be a conventional rhetorical sign of expertise in a field—or one sign to be deployed by experts speaking to novices, experts who are expected to appreciate and encode signs of complexity in their discourse? In other words, is this rhetorical situation defined by experts asking other experts a question in the others' field and then responding by introducing their answer with a complex statement of the problem that they think those not in their field would find useful?

Voss et al., (1983) noted the significance of one expert who behaved rather differently. An expert on Latin America, he was asked what he thought American policy should be toward El Salvador. He appeared to spend little time defining the problem and substantially more time laying out a solution. He had, in fact, had prior experience talking on the same matter. To that extent, this particular subject may have perceived the problem not as an ill-formed problem, as hoped but, because of his experience answering the problem in public, as at least a better formed problem, not only substantively but also rhetorically. He thus may have solved the discourse problem in a way that differed from the other experts: If the other experts had not rehearsed answering the problem, then to them the rhetorical problem of the discourse may itself have been a less-than-well-formed problem. To the expert experienced in answering the question out-loud, not only was the problem proper well formed, but so was the formal problem of the discourse. One might speculate how expert problem solving would be have been described if all the experts in Soviet affairs had had substantial experience answering exactly the same question posed to them on many panel discussions.

Rhetorical Strategies and Judgments about Reasoning

Here are two more examples—one formal, the other stylistic—of the way rhetorical strategies and judgments may intersect. In the last ten years, about two out of three articles in what some still believe is the major journal of scholarship in literary criticism, *Publication of the Modern Language Association,* have opened with some version of "You might think X to be the case. But in fact, X is not the case. Y is the case." The first example was written by Reeves (1986):

> Of the many ways of speaking about social convention, one of the most productive and philosophically perspicuous is David Lewis's *Convention: A Philosophical Study* (1969). Taking as his point of departure a game-theoretic analysis of human agreement and cooperation Lewis defines fully and forcefully the kind of behavioral regularity that might reasonably be designated a convention. The terms of his definition may initially seem inappropriate for the purposes of literary inquiry—for an effort such as this one, which seeks to clarify the phrase "literary convention."

But [italics added] what appears a disadvantage is precisely the definition's crucial heuristic advantage, a source of disanalogy by which to force a certain conceptual clarity in poetics. (p. 798)

There is no doubt that this is a conventionalized rhetorical move, one that characterizes some fields and not others. This opening move is deployed very rarely by writers of articles appearing in journals in pure mathematics. Essays from the last 5 years in five pure mathematics journals virtually never begin by stipulating an area of agreement and then continue by contradicting it (3%; 3 of 100). The most common overt opening move in those journals is simply to join the historical conversation in progress, moving it in roughly the direction it appears to be going. Consider this, for example, by Scharlemann (1987):

Following Thurston [**Th**], define the complexity $_{x-}$(S) of an oriented surface S to be $_{-x}$(C), where C is the union of all nonsimply connected components of S and $_x$(C) is its Euler characteristic. Hence $_{x-}$(S) $\geq$ 0. For M a compact oriented 3-manifold and N a (possibly empty) surface . . . . (p. 362)

The text goes on to play out the mathematical consequences of these postulates, without contradicting anything.

The rhetorical moves that we in the humanities appear to value—at least to the degree that value is reflected in their frequency of use—are moves that our colleagues in mathematics appear either to avoid or, more likely, simply do not consider as rhetorically plausible. These different strategies very likely arise from the different ways problems are formulated in literary criticism and mathematics: In literary criticism, the problem is one that often does not even exist for the discourse community before the writer formulates it. As suggested, the writer must convince the audience that a problem, in fact, exists. In mathematics, on the other hand, it appears that a problem is more often already in the domain of the community, waiting to be solved. (This difference is reflected in the struggle that graduate students in English departments have in finding a dissertation topic. I assume that graduate students in different parts of the social sciences less frequently engage in that kind of search.)

This particular "We-believe-*X*-but-*Y*-is the case" opening move, however, is rarely used in the papers by first-year college students (18 of 100 papers among first-year students writing humanities papers at the end of their first quarter) but is more frequently found in senior theses written by English majors (46 of 100). Do those 46 seniors think better than the 82 first-year students, or, as is more likely, have they simply acquired the conventional rhetorical move? Did the 18 freshman who used the move think better than the 82 who did not, because they more closely modeled the standard rhetorical move of "expert" literary critics, or, merely by displaying it, did they only appear to think better? Or is learning the move, in fact, evidence of their beginning to think better? Is this characteristic of more advanced informal reasoning, or is it only a conventional rhetorical move that characterizes literary studies?

A striking example of a discrepancy between judgments of quality, on the one hand, and a widely condemned but widely practiced rhetorical move, on the other, might be found in some work on perceptions of style (Hake & Williams, 1981, 1985). Several groups of teachers of composition at institutions ranging from high school through junior college to 4-year university were asked to evaluate a series of paired essays, supposedly written for freshman composition placement purposes. They assigned a holistic numerical score (1–5) and then wrote a short comment explaining their evaluation. The members of these pairs of essays were presented separately, over 2 weeks, interspersed among many other papers, so that the evaluators did not know they were responding to pairs of papers. These pairs differed *only in their styles*. Where one paper consistently expressed its ideas in a manner that relied on verb usage—in a *verbal* style—the other expressed its ideas in a *nominal* style.

The differences can be captured in this pair of sentences:

A: I would prefer to live in a big city because there I would be free to behave as I chose.

B: My preference is for life in a big city because there I would have freedom of choice as to my behavior.

In some sense, (A) is more direct, more concise, and more readable; (B) is turgid, wordier, more diffuse, and unnecessarily complex. Our alleged preference for a verbal style is one of the features of discourse that arguably qualifies as a universal principle of style (Lanham, 1976; Williams, 1988). Everything else was held constant in these pairs of essays: built-in grammatical and spelling errors, paragraphing, logical consistency, and even handwriting and strikeovers. Among the pairs of papers were also included pairs that had been independently judged to be intrinsically well organized and well argued and pairs that were judged to be poorly organized and poorly argued.

High school teachers systematically judged the papers written in the nominal style—regardless of whether the paper was designed to be intrinsically good or bad—as significantly better than the matching member written in the more direct verbal style. Representative comments written on the same pair of papers by the same evaluator illuminated the quantitative evaluations:

Pair 1: (Nominal version) Score of 4; "Intelligent understanding of problem."
(Verbal version) Score of 2; "Flippant and without purpose other than criticism. Lacking in sentence/paragraph structure."

Pair 2: (Nominal version) Score of 5; "Good introduction. Followed a logical organization. Used excellent vocabulary. Used good figures of speech. Developed a good conclusion."
(Verbal version) Score of 3; "Not well organized."

College teachers responded in a more complex way. They tended to evaluate the reasoning reflected in the intrinsically well-organized paper written in a nominal style more highly than the reasoning in the paired paper, which was equally well organized but written in a verbal style. Conversely, they tended to evaluate the reasoning reflected in the intrinsically badly organized paper written in a nominal style lower than the reasoning in the same disorganized paper written in a verbal style. We believe that the results turn on the apparent fit between an abstract, nominal, so-called educated style and good organization and argument and the apparent lack of "fit" between the same abstract, nominal, educated style and bad organization and argument. The rhetorically abstract language benefits an apparently well-organized paper. It does not fit an apparently disorganized, naively reasoned paper.

Let me, at this point, be clear about what I am *not* asserting. I am *not* asserting that seeming to think well—or write well—is merely equivalent to reasoning well or writing well or that the job of teaching reasoning or writing entails merely identifying and teaching the signs of good reasoning. I am asserting that judgments about reasoning well seem often to depend on whether a writer has deployed those conventional rhetorical signals—in this case, inflated language— that make him or her seem to be reasoning and writing well.

My point in rehearsing this research is to lay the groundwork for a more detailed account for a possible relationship between judgments about good reasoning and good writing and the way these judgments are deeply embedded in a larger context defined by (a) the nature of the problems addressed by the writer, (b) the stage of socialization of the writer into a community of discourse, and (c) the nature of the problem as mutually perceived—or misperceived—by problem poser and problem solver. In particular, I want to explore the implications of the rhetorical frame in which the problem is posed and understood: Is the problem posed and understood as well or ill formed on both sides?

PROBLEM TYPES: A PRELIMINARY TAXONOMY

I start with a simple taxonomy of problem types and then complicate it. I began with the perhaps overly simple distinction between content and rhetorical form. I slightly complicated that by cross-cutting between well- and ill-structured problems. That gives us a simple 2 x 2 matrix as shown in Fig. 12.1.

	Well Structured	Ill Structured
Problem Proper		
Form Problem		

FIG. 12.1. Problem Matrix

I draw most of my discussion here from the two discourse types that I am most familiar with: academic essays and the discourse of the law.

1.   Well-Formed Problem Proper/Well-Formed Problem of Form.   A well-formed problem proper would be one that the writer has addressed and solved many times, all in essentially the same way; a well-formed problem in rhetorical form would be a familiar form that the discourse community predictably and unselfconsciously uses. An example from the law would be a kind of decision drafted by administrative law judges in the state of Minnesota regarding unemployment benefits. Virtually all such decisions are single paragraphs, all of them identical in form and virtually identical in general content. It is a case where the court could put the rather limited variety of decisions on a computer and drop in different names and dates as necessary. The problem of rhetorical form is certainly well formed, and the content gives every appearance of being well formed as well.

A similar example from academic writing is the familiar five-paragraph essay on, say, dormitory food. The skilled high school graduate taking a placement text can turn out this kind of essay on demand. But in contrast to approving, or at least not judging bad, the cut-and-dried quality of a legal decision, such cut-and-dried paragraphs are regularly condemned as insubstantial, lacking genuine voice, and lacking commitment. Indeed, freshman composition textbooks are regularly advertised as teaching students how *not* to write such five-paragraph essays.

2.   Ill-Formed Problem Proper/Ill-Formed Problem of Form.   An ill-formed problem proper and an ill-formed problem of form is illustrated by the well-known supreme court decision on abortion, *Roe v. Wade.* The problem of abortion had no obviously authoritative legal precedent; its justification required the use of sociological, biological, medical, and other forms of evidence. And the decision obviously has not settled the matter; it was and is a classic ill-formed problem. Moreover, although most supreme court decisions do have a relatively predictable outer structure, *Roe v. Wade* reflects, according even to many of those who support the decision, serious rhetorical difficulties in justifying the decision. The drafter of the decision had to solve a complex rhetorical problem that did not yield to any conventional rhetorical structure.

The comparable example in an academic setting is any attempt to write an academic essay in the humanities about any particularly complex issue. I specify humanities papers because, unlike the conventional pattern observed in many social science papers, they follow no formal pattern of introduction, problem, methods and materials, results, discussion, and conclusion. The writer must invent the appropriate form to match the problem.

3.   Ill-Formed Problem Proper/Well-Formed Problem of Form.   An example of an ill-formed problem proper and a well-formed problem of form would be a contract involving a particularly complex financial relationship of a new kind. Contracts have predictable parts, particularly contracts that originate in the so-called "boiler plate" where they are used so often that they simply become standard forms. But frequently, situations arise where attorneys will use a standard contract and then shoehorn in clauses anticipating ill-formed problems not covered by standard boiler-plate—problems whose consequences cannot always be anticipated. In cases of this kind, the lack of fit between problem proper and problem of form results in a tension that may defeat the intention of the drafters. Some contracts become what are called "Christmas trees," on which hang clauses and conditions that make the contract seem to be a very badly thought-out document. By contrast, there are legal forms, such as the one-page decision of the Minnesota administrative judges, that do not require new forms even when the rare new problem arises, because there is no need to reflect in the decision the process by which the problem proper was solved. In this case, the mismatch between problem proper and form problem does not ordinarily create tension.

4.   Well-Formed Problem Proper/Ill-Formed Problem of Form.   An example of a well-formed problem proper that has no corresponding well-formed problem of form is a client letter that gives a mix of complex but perfectly clear-cut and well-understood (to the attorney) good and bad news, news that requires substantial background information to be understood and appreciated, but that cannot be given separate from the particulars of the good and bad news. What does one address first, bad news or good? Does one organize the letter as a narrative or as a series of categories? It is a common kind of problem that attorneys of all sorts fail to solve well. When they fail, they typically allow the structure of the problem, however that might be understood, to provide the formal structure of the text.

A Complicating Factor: Different Perceptions About the Nature of the "Same" Problem

It is exactly this issue of problem structure that, I think, substantially complicates this simple-minded taxonomy. As problem posers, we judge the writings of those who write for us (or whose writing we consume as interested readers) based, in no small part, on our perception of whether those writers have matched their perception of the problems they had to solve against our perception of those problems. Do writers and audiences share the same rhetorical frame? The singular example is that of the expert in Latin American affairs producing an apparently cut-and-dried, that is, a rhetorically well-formed, protocol. This example suggests that the same problem put to experts with different understandings of the rhetorical context of the problem may elicit different solutions.

A striking example of this was provided by Simon and Simon (1979) in their study of problem solving in a problem about surviving on the moon. Simon and Simon gave the same "Tom Swift" problem to a professor of engineering and a professor of physics: *Imagine you have crash landed on the moon. You have an indefinite supply of oxygen, a certain amount of pipe, and an energy source. You have located water in one area and arable land in another.* But the Simons varied the formulation of the problem. The professor of engineering was interested in textbook problems and their solutions. To this subject, they put the problem as a textbook problem. The professor promptly began to work through the formula for flow of fluids through pipes, computing friction, gravity, and so forth. This expert produced a standard textbook solution to what appeared to him to be a standard, well-formed, textbook problem.

To the other subject, a professor of physics, they put the problem as a genuine problem, not in the well-formed textbook engineering, but as an ill-formed problem of survival. This expert, in a very early statement, indicated that he saw the problem not as one that would yield to formulae about flow and resistance, but as a problem about surviving on the moon. His out-loud protocols indicated a more flexible, more imaginative attack on the problem. He hit on novel problems and novel solutions unanticipated by the problem posers.

In this case, the kind of reasoning demonstrated depended on how the problem was put and what the problem solver was looking for. But as tempted as we might be to assert that the more imaginative solution demonstrated better reasoning, we cannot, for the solutions were in accord with the perception of the problem, and we cannot criticize one perception as better than another independent of the rhetorical context of the problem.

So, compounding the varying perceptions of a problem as ill or well formed is the issue of the perceived context of the problem. Problems in and of themselves may be correctly treated as either well or ill formed, depending not on the nature of the problem but on the circumstances in which the problem, the problem poser, and the problem solver reside.

When we extend this matter to the problems raised by conflating distinctions between rhetorical well-formedness and richness of problem solving, we ought to recognize how complex is the interplay of rhetorical expectations and performances that result in differing judgments about the quality of informal reasoning.

In the legal world, there is a document called a *reply brief,* a brief that answers a prior brief submitted by the other side. A typical (although by no means inevitable) way that inexperienced attorneys approach this issue is to address the problem proper as either a well-structured or an ill-structured problem, but the formal problem as a well-structured problem. An inexperienced attorney typically maps his discourse, his reply brief, directly onto the form of the opposing brief, responding point-by-point to what the opposing attorney has written, while trying to make his own case. In short, although the problem proper may seem to be ill- or well-formed, the problem of form appears to the novice attorney to be well-structured, defined by the rhetorical structure of the opposing brief.

But the more expert attorney may treat the problem of form differently. Rather than responding to the structure of the other side's argument, he or she finds a form that encompasses the other side's argument but reflects what the attorney thinks is the underlying theory of his or her own case. The experienced attorney has to discover a form that solves two problems simultaneously: replies to every salient point and yet, does not necessarily let the other side set the form of the argument. Thus, the inexperienced attorney mistakes an ill-formed problem of form for a well-formed problem. A common response when the senior attorney evaluates a junior attorney's reply briefs that simply follow the form of the original brief is that "he does not write well," or "he does not think well," or both.

The reverse also often holds true. New attorneys hired by large firms are ordinarily set to work writing memoranda researching legal questions assigned to them by senior associates or partners. Because the best law firms seek out those law students who were most successful in their academic careers, they will be predictably chosen from among those who worked on the school law review. A typical, although again not invariable, way a new attorney approaches the problem of writing his or her first memo is to address the problem of form as if the memorandum were a journal article. And the organization of a journal article is regularly perceived by law students as an ill-formed problem of form. There is no perceived formulaic, well-structured solution to the structural problem of an academic essay. (Again, the problem proper may or may not be well formed, but that is irrelevant to the question.)

In most large firms, however, legal memos do have a very explicit structure: question presented, short answer, facts, discussion, and conclusion, a structure that reduces at least the outer rhetorical frame of a legal memo to a well-structured problem. The discussion section also has an equally predictable structure: opening paragraph summary, short statement of facts, legal history, application of history to the issue in point, description of possible complications or reservations, then a restatement of conclusion. The problem of form in a legal memorandum is, at least in its outer shell, a well-formed problem.

If the inexperienced attorney casts the problem proper into the rhetorical form of an academic essay, however, and if we assume that the appropriate form of such an essay is, at least to some degree, a problem that is more ill formed than a legal memo, then the new attorney has mistaken a well-formed formal problem for an ill-formed formal problem and may offer a journal account of the problem, often an even-handed exploration of alternatives, before arriving at a conclusion. (I do not suggest that only the novices make mistakes about problem definition; many experienced attorneys mistake ill-structured problems for well-structured problems, too.) In this case, the perception of bad writing or bad thinking is a function of the rhetorical community for which the writer is writing. What may have been an appropriate form in law school is predictably an inappropriate form in a law office.

It should be increasingly clear that judgments about the quality of informal reasoning in these matters is deeply entrenched in the particular community of discourse that defines not only the forms of reasoning and the forms of discourse but the appropriate perception of when either involves a problem that is well or ill formed.

One More Complication: The Socialized State of the Problem Poser Against the Socialized State of the Problem Solver/Writer.

This discussion of illustrations from the professional world reflects an aspect of the academic world where most of these same problems obtain: Many—perhaps most—of our students do not have enough experience to know what counts as a well-formed problem, much less to deal with an interestingly ill-formed problem. In fact, this issue of experience, of the relatively socialized state of the problem solver and of the problem poser, substantially complicates what is already complex.

The characteristics that distinguish novices and experts are well known (Chi, Feltovich, & Glaser, 1981; Larkin, McDermott, Simon, & Simon, 1980). Novices solving well-formed problems frequently seize on surface features of the problem, particularly features that are relatively more concrete, or more visible than the more abstract nature of the problem. Novices are unable to quickly and accurately categorize the problem into more abstract categories of problem types. They follow ends–means routines in solving a problem. Experts, on the other hand, are not distracted by concrete features of problems but rather recognize their categories, are able to access these and assign a category of solutions, and then work straight toward the solution.

Experts' and novices' performances in solving ill-formed problems reflect some of these features. According to Voss and his colleagues (1983), novices tend to concentrate on low-level concrete features of a problem and do not recognize the more abstract, more general problem that the concrete features instantiate. They seem to move from point to point without a well-formed plan. Experts begin at a higher, more abstract level, and go more deeply into fewer features. Experts also spend more time decomposing the problem, setting constraints, categorizing, describing, and creating the problem space than do novices. (As mentioned, Voss et al. did have one expert on Latin America who behaved somewhat differently: The person who had spoken on the problem of relations with El Salvador before and who seemed to have turned what was originally conceived of as an ill-structured problem into a well-structured rhetorical problem.)

The point that I open up here is that the point at which a writer/problem solver is, in regard to membership in a community of discourse, strongly determines how that problem solver formulates the problem. Novices and experts differ not only in how they go about solving a problem and not only in how they define the problem space of the problem; in many cases, they will also differ in whether they see the problem as well-formed or ill-formed.

My original taxonomy of ill- and well-structured problems was first complicated by the suggestion that there were two kinds of problems, the problem proper and the problem of rhetorical form and then by the suggestion that the problem of form is not only a matter of some set of transcendentally defined qualities of good discourse, but embedded in rhetorical conventions local to particular communities of discourse. I complicated the problem once again when I suggested including in the account a distinction between the perception of the problem solver and the perception of the problem poser or consumer of the solution. When the problem is complicated yet one more time by addressing the particular stage of the problem solver in regard to fully socialized membership in a community of discourse, we face issues that, in some ways, English teachers have had to face for decades.

Complaints directed to English teachers about the writing that students produce typically occur at those points in our system of education and employment where the writer is moving from outside a community into that community: Freshman English teachers complain about the quality of preparation in writing of high school graduates; faculty in advanced courses complain about the quality of preparation in writing of their upperclass students; faculty in professional schools complain about the quality of writing of college graduates. And, at least in the world of the law, it is standard to complain about the quality of writing of new attorneys. Compounding this judgment is another, not uncommon judgment: Few of these student have been trained to think well. Hence, the current interest in courses in critical reasoning and problem solving, often combined with courses in writing. At writing conferences everywhere, increasing numbers of papers address the connection between good writing and good reasoning.

The crudest model for connecting good reasoning and good writing, and improving both, rests on the assumption that, with early good instruction in reasoning and writing, our students will, once they master the basic skills of reasoning and writing, build on them and gradually improve in a more or less smooth upward curve, in about the way they grow taller and heavier.

That model, at least in its crudest form, has been rejected by those who have spent much time working with writers-cum-thinkers at different academic and professional levels. Just as it is now widely recognized that generic training in critical reasoning and problem solving has provided little or no empirical evidence that such training carries over into specific fields, so is it increasingly clear to many that generic training in writing at the freshman level, at least as that training is widely practiced, does not mean that junior or senior students will automatically pick up at the level of writing they may seem to have achieved in May of their freshman year and then improve steadily from there.

Although there are students who seem to do that, there are at least as many more—I suspect a great many more—who seem to have forgotten what they learned in some previous writing course, who seem to be writing in ways that are substantially below the level that they might have achieved earlier, and who reflect a good deal of the intellectual incompetence associated with novices in both problem solving and writing. Let me offer what I now take to be a touch-stone anecdote that specifically applies to writing.

In law schools, writing courses are typically first-year courses, so faculty are obliged to make judgments about the quality of first-year law students very quickly, students who presumably are, if not proficient, at least competent, writers: They have graduated from college, passed LSAT tests, and so forth. They are by no means in need of the kind of remediation that is directed toward basic first-year college writers.

At the end of one seminar in which I said some of these same things about progress in writing not typically being a smooth upward curve, a law faculty member who teaches legal writing recounted that she had received a doctorate in anthropology, was a publishing anthropologist—with tenure—and was generally regarded as a proficient writer. She became bored with anthropology and decided to go to law school. For the first few months of law school, she said, she was half-afraid she was suffering from a degenerative mental disease of some sort, because she could no longer write. Her prose was tangled and turgid—substantially weaker than what she thought she had been writing in anthropology. After a few more months, she said, she seemed to recover and began to write coherently again.

The point of this anecdote is that competence in writing is not necessarily a global skill that can be deployed independent of its context. When a novice labors under the cognitive burden of mastering new concepts, new habits of thought, particularly new conventions of discourse, the performance of that novice will predictably degrade (Hake & Williams, 1985; Jacobs, 1982; Nielson, 1979).

A typical assignment in a first-year legal writing course, which is called a case synthesis, sheds light on a further issue. It requires a law student to read three or four cases that address some common issue in the law and then write a paper that extracts what those cases have in common in order to make a point about the law. One such an assignment might involve three or four cases in which young children injure someone. From the point of view of the teacher of legal writing, this is a well-formed problem that can be solved in a well-formed manner: What is common to the cases is the question of requisite intent and of the ability to foresee consequences: Can a 5-year-old be said to form a legal intent to injure; can a 5-year-old foresee that his or her actions will result in injury? The discourse should be organized around those abstract components of the law. Instead, a frequently (indeed, typical) first-year response is to organize the essay around the names of the cases and to identify the issue in common as "defendants who are between the ages of 4 and 9."

In this case, the instructors have a straightforward understanding of the nature of the two problems of form and content, but from the point of view of many of the problem solvers, the students, the problem seems to be very ill formed: Having never seen anything like a case synthesis before, they do not know what counts as a good solution to the problem. As a consequence, I think, they behave the way novices tend to behave in such situations. They seize on the most concrete aspects of the problem, the names of the cases and the ages of the children, as their principle of organization. The least competent among them do not recognize the more abstract legal issues behind the cases—intent, foreseeability, and so on.

In short, they appear to have solved the problem in a deficient way—they seem not to be able to think abstractly or to organize their material in a way that reflects the problem. It is the typical behavior of a novice not only responding to the concrete surface features of the problem but at the same time trying to socialize himself or herself into a new community of discourse. And the problem posers, the law faculty, typically evaluate the first-year students as writing badly, because they choose the wrong topics, the more concrete elements of the problem, around which to organize their answers.

But the problem is even more complex than this. Some of the instructors do not understand that, from many of the students' points of view, the problem was perceived as an ill-structured problem. For the instructors, the problem is quite clearly structured, and they do not understand why their students do not see the problem in the same way. In fact, many of these instructors are themselves novices in teaching legal writing (legal writing courses are often assigned to the least senior faculty, or, more typically, to adjunct instructors who are not part of a regular law faculty). For many of them, the problem of teaching legal writing is a well-structured problem, when, in fact, they should be viewing it as an ill-structured problem. As a consequence the mismatch between perceptions of the problems by faculty and students often confound any useful judgments at all.

In this particular situation, we have a complex mix of judgments: novice teachers teaching novice students, expert (i.e., a few experienced) teachers teaching novice students, expert teachers teaching expert students (students who have been paralegals in law firms and so are at least familiar with issues of the law), novice teachers teaching expert students, all their judgments turning at least partly on their relative perception of what is and is not a well-formed problem proper and a well-formed formal problem.

This matter of the novice problem solver experiencing a degradation of performance in solving rhetorical problems in the face of difficulty in understanding the problem proper now wholly confuses the difference between competent informal reasoning in solving either of the problems. In short, the novice may write badly while thinking clearly, or may write clearly (though too simply) while thinking badly.

LEAVING UNSAID WHAT SHOULD NOT BE SAID

There are many more problems involving the confusion between novice thinking and generically incompetent thinking, but one last problem deserves a small bit of attention—the matter of not saying what need not be said. As Voss (chapter 3, this volume) suggested in his discussion of the Japanese military leaders planning the attack on Pearl Harbor, experts speaking to experts leave a good deal unsaid. The following paper was the first paper written by a first-year law student at a very selective school of law. This student graduated in the upper 10% of his class from a prestigious private university in the midwest, scored in the top 10% on the LSAT, and wrote an application essay that was impeccable. This paper was judged "inadequately thought out" by the student's instructor of legal writing. The paper was to be written in the voice of a judge sustaining or reversing a lower court decision. (I explain the italics and the boldfacing, after.)

> *It is my opinion that* *the ruling of the lower court concerning the case of* Haslem v. Lockwood *should be* **upheld,** *thereby denying* *the appeal of the plaintiff.* ***The main point supporting my point of view*** *on this case* **concerns** *the tenet of our court system which holds that in order to win his case, the plaintiff must prove that he was somehow wronged by the defendant. The burden of proof rests on the plaintiff. He must show enough evidence to convince the court that he is in the right.*
>
> ***However, in this case, I do not believe that*** *the plaintiff has satisfied this requirement.* In order to prove that the defendant owes him recompense for the six loads of manure, he must first show that he was the legal owner of those loads, and then show that the defendant removed the manure for his own use. ***Certainly, there is little doubt as to*** *the second portion of the evidence;* the defendant admits that he did remove the manure to his own land. **Therefore,** the plaintiff must prove *the first part of the requirement*—***that is,*** *that* he had legal ownership of the manure.
>
> *The manure was left by horses hitched to a post in a public park owned by the borough of Stamford. Had the owners of each horse desired to remove the manure of his own horse, there would certainly be no objection.* **However,** the manure to which the plaintiff lays claim was not left by his own horse, but rather, by several horses of presumably different owners. **Therefore,** the manure became the property of the owner of the park, the borough. If the plaintiff had received authorization from the borough, or any officer thereof, he might have been able to state a case for ownership. **But this is not the case. Furthermore,** the plaintiff left no notice by the manure to stake his claim to it when he left it for over twelve hours. *When the defendant came upon the manure, he had no way of knowing to whom it belonged, and it is alleged that he went out of his way to discover if anyone owned the manure.* ***Thus, on the basis that*** *the* plaintiff did not prove his legal ownership of the manure, ***I agree*** *with the lower courts ruling for the defendant.*

I have boldfaced what I call *metadiscourse* (Williams, 1988), that is discourse about discourse, or discourse that describes the acts of thinking and writing rather than the primary matter of the discourse. The amount of metadiscourse is substantially above that which characterized papers on the same subject that received a far higher evaluation. Here is the first paragraph of such a paper, with the discourse boldfaced:

> The plaintiff gathered manure from along a public highway one evening, intending to take it to his own property the following day. The next morning the defendant discovered the piles, attempted unsuccessfully to determine who had gathered the piles, and removed them to his property. Neither the plaintiff nor the defendant had obtained permission from the proper public officials to remove the manure. The plaintiff brought an action for trover against the defendant in the amount of six dollars, the value of the manure. The trial court found for the defendant. **The issue presented here** is whether the plaintiff has proven a sufficient interest in or right to possession of the manure to warrant recovery of damages. The manure was public property, produced by horses tied at a public park, and deposited on a public road. The plaintiff failed to obtain authority from public officials to remove the manure, and made no reasonable effort to identify himself as the gatherer of the manure. The plaintiff's claim for damages **must** rest on a theory that his labor, "calculated to improve the appearance and health of the borough," justifies a rule of "earned" possession.

The amount of metadiscourse is substantially less than in the first passage, suggesting that this writer was not compelled to encode his thinking about the problem, not compelled, in other words, to say that which did not need to be said. Furthermore, the second passage does not say anything that someone familiar with the law would find wholly self-evident and so unnecessary to state. That is, it is self-evident in the world of the law that, **"The main point supporting my point of view** on this case **concerns** the tenet of our court system which holds that in order to win his case, the plaintiff must prove that he was somehow wronged by the defendant. The burden of proof rests on the plaintiff. He must show enough evidence to convince the court that he is in the right."

To an expert, knowing what to leave unsaid may be at least as important as knowing what to say.

CONCLUSION

In a sense, I have come full circle to the matter I opened with: the distinction between experts and novices and the characteristics of their informal reasoning in solving ill- and well-structured problems. The distinctions traditionally made will serve to sharpen our understanding of how different reasoners informally reason, but it may be at least as important to understand that the perceived quality of appropriateness of the reasoning itself does not exist in a pure form, independent of a rhetorical context—certainly never in any ecologically valid, real-world setting. We regularly make judgments about the quality of reasoning based, at least partly, on the appropriateness of a reasoner's solution to the rhetorical problem that must be solved either after or simultaneously with solving the problem proper. Unless general rhetorical competence and control over local conventions are distinguished from informal judgments about informal reasoning, we risk conflating competence in thinking and in controlling local rhetorical conventions. And unless we distinguish novice thinking about solutions to rhetorical problems from novice thinking about solutions to problems proper, we risk conflating inexperience in one mode—discourse form—with incompetency in the other.

REFERENCES

Bazerman, C. (1981). What written knowledge does: Three examples of academic discourse. *Philosophy of the Social Sciences, 11,* 361–387.

Chi, M., Feltovitch, P., & Glaser, R. (1981). Categorization and representation of physics problems by experts and novices. *Cognitive Science, 5,* 121–152.

Colomb, G., & Williams, J. (1985). Perceiving structure in professional prose. In L. Odell & D. Goswami (Eds.), see p. 5 *Writing in nonacademic settings* (pp. 87–128). New York: Guilford Press.

Flower, L. (1979). Writer-based prose: A cognitive basis for problems in writing. *College English, 41,* 19–37.

Flower, L., & Hayes, J. (1981). A cognitive process theory of writing. *College Composition and Communication, 32,* 365–387.

Hake, R., & Williams, J. (1981). Style and its consequences. *College English, 43,* 433–451.

Hake, R., & Williams, J. (1985). Some cognitive issues in sentence combining: On the theory that smaller is better. In D. Daiker, A. Kerek, & M. Morenberg (Eds.), *Sentence combining: A rhetorical perspective* (pp. 86–106). Carbondale, IL: University of Southern Illinois Press.

Jacobs, S. (1982). *Composing and coherence: The writing of eleven pre-medical students.* Washington, DC: Center for Applied Linguistics.

Lanham, R. (1976). *Style: An anti-textbook.* New Haven, CT: Yale University Press.

Larkin, J., McDermott, J., Simon, D., & Simon, H. (1980). Expert and novice performance in solving physics problems. *Science, 208,* 1335–1342.

Newell, A., & Simon, H. (1972). *Human problem solving.* Englewood Cliffs, NJ: Prentice-Hall.

Nielson, B. (1979). Writing as a second language: Psycholinguistic processes in composing. (Doctoral Dissertation, University of California at San Diego). *Dissertation Abstracts International,* AAD80–02941.

Reeves, E. (1986). "Conveniency to nature": Literary art and arbitrariness. *Publication of the Modern Language Association, 101,* 798–810.

Scharlemann, M. (1987). The thurston norm and 2-handle addition. *Proceedings of the American Mathematical Society, 100,* 362–375.

Simon, D., & Simon, H. (1979). A tale of two protocols. In J. Lochhead & J. Clements (Eds.), *Cognitive process instruction* (pp. 119–132). Philadelphia: Franklin Institute.

Toulmin, S. (1958). *The uses of argument.* Cambridge, England: Cambridge University Press.

Toulmin, S., Rieke, R., & Janik, A. (1979). *An introduction to reasoning.* New York: Macmillan.

Voss, J., Green, T., Post, T., & Penner, B. (1983). Problem-solving skill in the social sciences. *The Psychology of Learning and Motivation, 17,* 165–213.

Williams, J. (1988). *Style* (3rd ed.). Glenview, IL: Scott Foresman.

13

Intuitive Belief Systems and Informal Reasoning in Cognitive Development

Frank C. Keil
Cornell University

What makes informal reasoning work, and what makes it work better (or at least seem to work better) for older children and adults? In this chapter, I suggest that some patterns of semantic and conceptual development are closely related to the development of successful reasoning, especially of the more informal sort. More broadly, I claim that the study of concepts and conceptual change really cannot be divorced from the study of reasoning.

Certainly, part of what makes informal reasoning work, and possibly improve with age, is an understanding of how patterns of reasoning are constrained, that is, an awareness of which are cognitively natural and easy to engage in and which are nonnatural and to be avoided because they are engaged in only with great difficulty. Three general sorts of cognitive constraints help shape the possible types of reasoning into those that are cognitively easy and natural and those that are not:

1. Some constraints reflect the most general properties of humans as information processors; they govern any case of information processing, whether it be reasoning, pattern recognition, or talking. Such constraints could include on-line processing capacity restrictions, associative laws that relate classes of mental structures, and requirements for parallel processing, such as the delta rule (McClelland, Rumelhart, & the PDP Research Group, 1986).

2. Some constraints apply specifically to what we normally think of as patterns of reasoning and not more broadly to all forms of information processing. These could include difficulties with disjunctions, mistakes made with counterfactuals, and more complex biases, both on deductive paths and on induction. If there are universal patterns of constraint on a causal operator, as there seem to be

247

on a disjunctive operator, they would also work at this level. Other causal relations are more and more knowledge-dependent with development.

3. Finally, some constraints have less to do with the process of reasoning than with the structure of the knowledge that is being reasoned about. Such constraints are minimized when people reason about abstract artificial constructs or arbitrary symbol concatenations, tasks that reveal the first two types of constraints in their purest forms; local knowledge constraints, however, may be the predominant influence on informal reasoning about most everyday phenomena.[1]

In this chapter, the developmental implications of constraints of this third type are examined, initially from the viewpoint of novice-to-expert knowledge changes. This account is then challenged, however, by the proposal that, throughout all periods of development, essentially the same sorts of cognitive structures and procedures are responsible for easy and successful reasoning. The discussion focuses not on reasoning studies directly, but on studies of categories and concepts that are fundamentally related to issues of induction and, with just a little extrapolation, to issues of analogy and transfer.

On the Relevance of Concepts and Conceptual Change

An initial look at patterns of conceptual change seems to reveal a coherent developmental account along the following lines: Early on, children figure out categories and word meanings, by using the most general principles of learning and information processing possible: procedures like exemplar abstraction, prototype generation, feature correlation detection, and the like. These are relatively content-independent modes of reasoning that simply monitor frequencies of instances and frequencies of properties within those instances, as well as the correlations between those properties; and, presumably, they work in pretty much the same way in any domain of knowledge, be it learning about random visual dot patterns or learning about new mammals.

As children learn more about a domain, however, their knowledge appears to become structured so that future learning in that domain changes from being governed mostly by domain-general principles to being heavily governed also by structural principles that are specific to the type of knowledge. Thus, the child's *hypothesis space* becomes narrowed more and more by local, knowledge-specific constraints as opposed to general ones. No longer do general principles of prototype abstraction, for example, primarily account for details of new conceptual structures; instead, conceptual growth is increasingly a function of how prior

---

[1]There is another important class of constraints that have to do with the formal properties of the problem itself. Formal analyses of the task domain reveal logical possibilities available to the problem solver or the formal equivalance of large subsets of these possibilities. I do not address this important class of noncognitive constraints here.

knowledge in the domain has been organized. Considerable evidence supports this view. For example, children's sense of kinship concepts, such as "uncle," are apparently first formed by general probabilistic operations on the salient features of the most typical instances but are later structured primarily according to the critical blood line relations that organize all kinship terms. I have called this the *characteristic-to-defining shift* (hereafter, C/D shift), that is, a shift from a general summation over all the features that are characteristic of typical instances to concepts that are organized around a few critical defining features or dimensions (Keil & Batterman, 1984).

The usual technique for assessing the C/D shift is to present two types of story to children: a story that describes many of the most characteristic features of an entity but also describes anti-defining features (the $+c/-d$ story) and a story that indicates the critical defining features and many highly atypical properties as well (the $-c/+d$ story). Thus, with the kinship term as "uncle," the characteristic features might include typical behavioral, dispositional, and physical properties of uncles, such as their tending to socialize with one's parents, their often visiting on holidays and perhaps bringing gifts, their often talking with parents about childhood and their being roughly the same age as one's parents. The defining features would simply be the uncle's being the brother of one's mother or father.[2] A $+c/-d$ story for uncle would, therefore, describe a man of roughly one's parents age, who is friendly, visits, gives gifts, and the like but who is not related to one's father or mother. A $-c/+d$ story might describe a 2-year-old who drools over one's clothes, breaks one's toys, and cries a lot, but who is also one's father's brother.

The C/D shift can be thought of as a close relative to other, more venerable shifts such as the holistic-to-analytic shift (Werner, 1948), the concrete-to-abstract shift (Vygotsky, 1934/1986) and more recently, the integral-to-separable shift (e.g., Kemler & Smith, 1978). For over 50 years a wide range of theoretical perspectives have generated surprisingly similar descriptions of change in concept structure as abandonment of relatively atheoretical, global tabulations of all frequently co-occurring features for more principled highly specific sets of relations that seem to organize concepts in a domain.

These shifts in conceptual structure dovetail smoothly with accounts of developmental changes in reasoning that argue for younger children's reasoning according to principles that refer to clusters of characteristic properties. They cling to appearances in setting up categories and in seeing new relationships, they reason more concretely, and they prefer to think in a more global and diffuse than focused or concentrated way. By contrast, older children seem to attend to the critical dimensions or factors in the task, ignoring other typically associated but

---

[2]There is a social sense of the term *uncle* that adults will use that corresponds to the typical behavioral and dispositional features; but the biological definition is strongly preferred in the adult and older children populations that we have studied.

irrelevant variables. The shift from use of domain-general principles to domain-specific structural principles, therefore, seems to apply to changes in both conceptual structure and in at least some types of reasoning.

In reasoning with analogies, younger children are often said to think in holistic and perceptually bound terms. This, too, suggests close links to developmental changes in conceptual structure. Young children can evidently only formulate analogies on the basis of surface similarities or another form of general summation across all available features and not on the basis of deeper principles. In studies of many analogical reasoning tasks, younger children have appeared to be trapped at this surface level, whereas older children easily transcended it (see Brown, 1990, for a review).

One might try to account for such changes by focusing on constraints on the reasoning process itself (those of the first two sorts) and arguing that there are developmental differences in their influence. That is, younger children may be unable to reason beyond a certain level on virtually all reasoning tasks. Such accounts almost inevitably support global, stage-like theories of development. Recent work, however, construes the younger children's modes of reasoning as reflecting the absence of expertise in the domains relevant to the tasks, rather than a global deficit. Brown (1990) has shown that even 3-year-olds can engage in sophisticated analogical transfer if they have well-structured knowledge in the relevant domains. That is, they can think in ways that are perceptually liberated and not holistic if they have access to the appropriate knowledge structures. To quote Brown (1990):

> If there is (1) similarity at the level of causal structure and (2) the type of causality has been differentiated within the child's emergent theories of the world, then rapid transfer would be expected. . . . Young children do show rapid insightful transfer, if they are familiar with the mechanism of causality that underlies the deep structure similarity. If we are dealing with such privileged domains, transfer is not an issue, it can be assumed. Even two-year-olds can override surface features of physical similarity and respond in terms of causal relations, in terms of function.

Brown has shown that young preschoolers easily override perceptual similarity in tasks requiring transfer of their knowledge about certain tools, such as those that enable pulling. Thus, shifts in analogical reasoning skill may be largely a function of sophistication about familiar causal relations. We may learn little about how reasoning develops and changes if we focus on constraints of the first two sorts, for they may change very little in contrast to the potentially enormous changes in constraints on reasoning imposed by increasing expertise.

The claim that the C/D shift is also domain-specific and not global is, of course, compatible with much of the novice–expert work that shows how dramatic shifts in knowledge in one domain often has no impact on performance in other domains. Perhaps the most dramatic example of this specificity is seen in individuals who can be trained to recall rapidly presented sequences of more than 90 digits but who perform no better than untrained adults when also asked to recall sequences of letters (e.g., Ericsson, Chase, & Falcon, 1980). Two follow-up studies in the C/D paradigm are also particularly relevant. One demonstrated that the shift occurs on a domain-by-domain basis (Keil, 1986b; 1989). For related sets of terms, such as the social transgression terms *lie, cheat,* and *steal,* the kinship terms *uncle, grandfather,* and *cousin,* or the cooking terms *boil, bake,* and *fry,* the shift occurs at roughly the same time for terms in a domain but at markedly different times across domains (in this case, terms for transgressions are followed by those for kinship, which are followed by those for cooking). A second follow-up study explored the consequences of teaching defining and characteristic features for new concepts to children who either had or had not already shifted to using defining features for familiar concepts in the same domain (Keil, 1989). If the children had well-developed knowledge in the domain and were thus conceptually ready to learn a new concept, they would focus on the defining features from the start; if not, they would rely on characteristic-based representations. For example, if a child had already shifted for the more familiar cooking terms, he or she tended to understand the central role of defining features for a new, unfamiliar, cooking term, even if those features were completely intermixed with a large set of highly characteristic features. By contrast, a child who had not yet shifted was far more prone to treat defining and characteristic features similarly.

Redescribing the C/D Shift for Natural Kinds

Young children who lack sufficiently structured local knowledge appear to reason according to weak general principles. Without the support of structured local knowledge, they fall back on all-purpose, but not very efficient, procedures such as prototype abstraction. Poor performance may also reflect less efficient use of content-free, domain general principles as well; even on totally novel, artificial reasoning tasks, younger children are apt to do worse than older ones. Local expertise, however, appears to be the major factor behind developmental differences on more natural tasks.

The account becomes more complicated if, instead of looking at concepts that have simple definitions (like uncle, island, and news), one examines concepts for natural kinds, such as animals. Natural kinds cannot be described by anything like simple definitions or short lists of necessary and sufficient features (Kripke, 1972; Putnam, 1975). Thus, there may be no C/D shift for such terms. Alternatively, there might be a shift, not to definitions, but to interconnected sets of beliefs that facilitate induction. One clear theme in the philosophy of science is that inductions are powerful only to the extent that they rely on rich sets of interrelationships governing the properties of the kinds being thought about. Thus, younger children, who have only cruder probabilistic representations to rely on are weaker in their inductive reasoning skills and tend to induce along simple probabilistic continua. This has been one of the main findings in Carey's work (1985) on children's concepts of animals.

Examining induction is only one way of attempting to learn about the child's conceptual structures for natural kinds. I have relied heavily on two techniques that are very different from Carey's but that seem to yield converging evidence of closely related developmental patterns. The techniques are known as *discoveries studies* and *operations studies*. They are described extensively in Keil (1986a), and Keil (1989).

Discoveries Studies

Children were asked to make judgments about an object's kind, given certain discovered properties, and then to justify their responses. For example, they were told that a group of animals looks and acts just like raccoons, but that scientists have discovered that their insides (skeleton, blood, organs, etc.) are the same as those of skunks and that their parents and babies are skunks. The children were then asked what the animals are.

An analogous story was presented for artifacts. For example, the children were told of the discovery that something that looks and functions just like a coffeepot is really made out of a metal used for bird feeders and comes from melted-down bird feeders and that the apparent coffeepot will be melted down in the future to make new bird feeders. Contrasting children's judgments about artifacts with those about natural kinds allows us to assess whether developmental changes are knowledge-driven or reflect a changing response bias, such that, as children get older, they tend to defer more to authority figures and, therefore, agree with scientists. Several studies have found that younger children treat discoveries about artifacts and natural kinds in essentially the same way, judging in both cases that the discovery does *not* require that their judgment of kind change. Older children and adults treat the two differently; they judge discovery critical to deciding for natural kinds but irrelevant for artifacts. (Incidentally, younger children distinguish between artifacts and natural kinds on other grounds, as other studies by our group and others have shown.)

Operations Studies

The discoveries studies make strong presuppositions about the child's idea of underlying essences. The child is supplied with a theory that biological essence is revealed in blood, cells, organs, and genetic stock, and this knowledge is pitted against the characteristic features. But the child might have a very different theory of essence from that which is typical of Western biological science, and this theory could also override characteristic features. A different technique, operation studies, addressed this concern by presenting descriptions of animals in which virtually all the salient characteristic features that people normally mention were replaced with agreed on characteristic features of another animal. The underlying biological principles were never mentioned. Thus, raccoons were made to look just like skunks and to act just like skunks, and a coffeepot was made to look and function just like a bird feeder. Across several studies, a pattern closely related to that for the discoveries studies was found. For younger children, operations changed attributions of membership of both animals and artifacts; for older children, operations only changed those for artifacts and not for natural kinds. When the same sort of studies were conducted with the Yoruba of Nigeria (see Jeyifous, 1986), equally strong shifts were observed from characteristic features to underlying theory for natural kinds, even though conceptions of biological essences in that culture are quite different from those of Western science.

One Possible Account of Conceptual Change and the Development of Reasoning

The studies on natural kinds suggest that early concepts can be dissociated from theories and that, with development—or, more accurately, with increasing expertise—theory gradually infiltrates more associatively organized concepts. Children seem to cease being spineless phenomenolists and become staunch essentialists. Thus, any reasoning by young children of an inductive or an analogical kind will be of a fundamentally different sort from that engaged in when they have rich domain knowledge. The only constraints on early reasoning will be the content-independent, process-oriented ones discussed earlier, and the nature of the reasoning will be necessarily shallow, brute force probability matching, and so forth. Developmental change is thus primarily a consequence of change in the third type of constraint on reasoning. These natural kind studies suggest that the C/D shift may be an inaccurate way of characterizing the supposedly well-defined terms. These terms turn out to be notoriously difficult to define fully by simple rules or necessary and sufficient feature lists and are better thought of as having their meanings structured by somewhat oversimplified theories (see Keil, 1989).

Perhaps the most explicit analysis specifically relating conceptual change and changes in the nature of reasoning is available in Gentner's structure-mapping theory (Gentner, 1983). Gentner has suggested that we map relations from one domain (the base) to another (the target) on the basis of three rules (a) the properties or attributes of the objects in the base are removed from consideration; (b) the relations among objects in the base are preserved, subject to the condition that (c) higher order relations (relations among relations) are preserved at the expense of lower order relations. This last rule known as the principle of "systematicity," is especially important; it is at this level that causal structures are especially emphasized, and, in consequence, connected sets of relations rather than isolated predicates are likely to be transported across domains.

Gentner often uses the examples of analogy or transfer between Rutherford's model of the atom and the solar system. Transfer across these two domains is said to be predicted in a "syntactic" objective manner that makes little or no reference to content. In the case of the solar system analogy, the first step is simply to ignore one-place predicates, such as "is yellow" and "is gaseous," and focuses on two or more place predicates. The second, more interesting step is to focus on relations that are more systematic, where systematicity is defined according to several related criteria and results in "higher order relations that connect the lower-order relations . . . . into a mutually constraining structure" (Gentner, 1983, p. 164). These criteria include a deep hierarchical embedding of relations within other relations and strong interconnections among relations.

An analogy that focuses on systematicity maps little or no object attributes and emphasizes the highest order relational ones possible. Systematicity is crucial for knowing why some two-place relations, such as "more massive than" (sun, planet), are likely to be mapped, whereas "hotter than" (sun, planet) are not. Gentner (1983) has argued that "to the extent that people recognize (however vaguely) that the system of predicates connected with central forces is the deepest most interconnected mappable system for an analogy, they will favor relations that belong to that system in their interpretations" (p. 164). Gentner's model suggests several different sorts of similarity:

1. There is mere-appearance based similarity, in which only object attributes are used to compare kinds.
2. There is literal similarity, in which both attributes and relations are used.
3. There is relational similarity, in which only relations are matched.
4. There is a kind of abstract similarity, in which more systematic structured relations are considered.

Forbus and Gentner (1986) have speculated on how these different kinds of relations are differentially involved over the course of learning and development. They have argued that mere appearance and literal similarity methods of construal are highly accessible and therefore appear very early in children and in adults who are novices. They have cited some of the C/D studies described earlier as supporting this sort of argument. They have suggested specifically that prototype-like representations of the sort that Rosch (Rosch & Mervis, 1975) proposed are primarily consequences of literal similarity comparisons among similar experiences. Moreover, they have pointed out that prototype, and other mere appearance or literal similarity, based representations "are of limited use in deriving causal principles" (p. 17). There is a continuum of similarity relations moving away from these easily accessible representations to the abstract ones, which are the least accessible but also the most theoretically informative. DiSessa (1983) also has noted a similar transition from phenomenological primitives to richer intuitive theories.

Do Content-Dependent Constraints Emerge Only Later On?

The relations between recent work on analogy and transfer and the studies described earlier are evident. Other, more relevant studies, however, suggest important ways in which the account may be incorrect. The problems are best seen by considering further studies with natural kinds that suggest that even the youngest children may be subject to strong domain-specific, content-dependent constraints.

Based on prior work (Keil, 1979), I suspected that young children might make use of distinctions among such fundamental categories as plants, animals, and artifacts, which are sometimes called *ontological categories,* and, in so doing, be theory-driven essentialists. In a study of both across-ontological-category operations (with such transformations as turning a porcupine into a cactus or a toy mouse into a real mouse) and within-ontological-catagory operations (a horse into a zebra or a lion into a tiger), we found the same 5-year-olds agreeing to kind membership shifts for within-ontological-category changes but denying that kind could shift for across-ontological changes. Thus, a real horse could be changed into a real zebra, but a real porcupine remained a porcupine even when it looked and "acted" exactly like a cactus. What appeared, at first blush, to be children with completely characteristically based concepts were, in fact, children with more principled beliefs as well.

This sort of study alone does not unequivocally show that the ontological level is special. Perhaps to the extent that categories are more dissimilar, there is more resistance to kind changes. Note that the preceding animal–animal transformations were between closely related animals, such as zebras and horses. One way to check on this is to do studies of transformations between closely related and distantly related animals, as well as cross-ontological studies, and see if there is something special about the cross-ontological boundary or whether it is merely a part of gradual continuum of intercategory distance.

In a follow-up study, we had the children judge not only horse–zebra and porcupine–cactus kinds of examples but also mouse–spider (tarantula), fish–butterfly, and lizard–grasshopper operations, among others. The most relevant finding was simply that kindergartners judged highly dissimilar animal–animal pairs as just as likely to change kind membership as the highly similar pairs. (Incidentally, these children had no problem telling us that a zebra is more like a horse than, say, a spider is like a mouse, illustrating that a different metric of surface similarity was not driving their judgment of operations outcomes.)

Going Further Beyond Appearance

Perhaps the kindergartner's emerging theories of biology are considerably more complex than simple ontological distinctions between animals and other kinds. To further probe the subtleties of their knowledge of animals, a closer look at what sorts of property transformations are and are not relevant to changes of identity is needed. In another series of studies (Keil, 1989), three new types of transformations that varied along a continuum of what one might call superficiality and permanence were used. The most superficial and potentially impermanent transformation involved simply putting animals into costumes of related animals, such as a horse into a zebra costume. The second transformation involved exactly the same story as was used in the operations studies, except that we told the children that the changes would wear off unless they were reapplied. Thus, for example, the paint for the stripes of a tigerized lion would wear off and the lion's fur would grow back, unless it was repainted periodically. We also said that these changes were done surreptitiously and so often that the lion always looked and acted exactly like a tiger. We assumed that, if the children knew more about animals than merely their characteristic features, perhaps they would be more prone to resist accepting changes in kind in these conditions as well. The final transformation tied more deeply into adult versions of biological principles and, consequently, was hypothesized to delay the age at which the children might judge type of animal to be preserved. For this transformation, we explained that an animal had received an injection, pill, or some other form of chemical administration right after birth and then had gradually grown into the other kind of animal. Thus, a zebra received an injection at birth that made it grow up to look and act like a horse. We postulated that this manipulation is related to more subtle and deeper biological knowledge and thus might cause even older children to think that the animals' kind had changed.

The results clearly supported these predictions, with approximately 80% of kindergartners saying that the costumes did not change the identity, 70% saying so for the temporary changes, and roughly 30% saying so for both the permanent and internal developmental changes. Moreover, fourth graders were more than twice as likely to say that internal developmental changes transformed an animal than they had been in the prior operations studies, illustrating that internal developmental changes are closer to adult biological theories of what constitutes an animal kind.

The same animal photographs were used in all three types of transformations; transformations were merely described in different terms. Because the pictorial stimuli were the same in all cases, this manipulation ruled out explanations of the developmental change as simply children's learning to override the perceptual with the conceptual. More importantly, it showed that the vast majority of kindergartners must have some subtle beliefs about biological kinds that make it impossible for them to accept a change in kind because of a mere costume. They evidently have some beliefs about what are and are not likely to be biologically relevant properties, regardless of salient characteristic features. More recent data (Keil, 1989) suggest that, even by age 3, children may know that costumes do not change natural kinds. In contrast to kindergartners, however, they may see the temporary surface part transformations as more relevant.

These studies reveal that even very young children may not be the pure phenomenalists they appear to be. Preschoolers may not be sorting natural categories based solely on literal similarity or mere appearance. Even if the notion of appearance is construed more broadly to include any tabulation of characteristic features, including event-related ones, such as Forbus and Gentner's (1986) "protohistories," there are strong reasons for suspecting that more principle-based relations also structure their conceptual spaces.

Causal Relations, Mechanisms, and Concept Structure

These studies also strongly suggest a special importance for causal relations. Structure-mapping theory, by contrast, sees the core of conceptual structure as the higher order relations that are extracted by various principles of systematicity. Although causal relations tend to be common at these most systematic levels, in structure mapping theory they have no special status in organizing conceptual relations. By that account, any other sort of conceptual relations that are heavily intertwined, such as sets of logical or spatial relations, could be equally important for organizing that conceptual space and for promoting transfer to other domains. For concepts concerning most naturally occurring phenomena, however, causal relations may play a particularly important role above and beyond that of other sorts of tightly compacted relations. The most critical aspects of meaning may involve notions of cause and explanation, not just interrelation.

The general point here is that natural concepts may always need to be embedded in causal theories to have meaning or inductive "oomph." Those causal relations provide the power to make inductions and see analogies, and they also provide coherence to the elements that make up concepts. They form a kind of conceptual glue that binds together the features that co-occur (cf. Murphy & Medin, 1985). Contrary to prior accounts, the younger children do not try to avoid thinking in terms of abstract relations or rich causal theories; on the contrary, if those theories are meaningful and have real explanatory power for them, they will use them wherever they can, for they provide meaning and power in their thinking. I am suggesting here that "having a concept" should not be construed as knowing a static set of properties, features, and frequencies. Instead, for most real-world categories, it fundamentally and centrally involves knowing a set of dynamic causal relations that help us understand why a cluster of properties have become grouped as an interactive unit and what processes maintain that interactive unit and thereby lend continuity to the kind. Our concept of an inanimate object, such as a cactus, is much more dynamic than the cactus itself because it involves an understanding of the ecological forces at work that make the cactus's cluster of features a superb adaptation for its environment.

The idea of static objects being represented in dynamic terms has been examined in the realm of perception as well. Freyd (1987) for example, has conducted a series of experiments demonstrating that the perception of static forms such as handwriting and photographs often involves an encoding of the dynamic movements of either creating the perceived form or predicting likely future movements. Although the relations of perception of objects to concepts of kinds are quite indirect, both lines of work do serve to illustrate how mental representations of non-events might nonetheless entail an event-like component as part of understanding.

There are now increasingly powerful demonstrations that young children are capable of sophisticated causal reasoning and that they use this reasoning to make distinctions between fundamentally different sets of kinds. Some of the most elegant demonstrations come from Gelman's work on preschooler's understanding of the distinction between animates and inanimates   (e.g., Gelman, 1990). It is clear that, in distinguishing between the two, even 3-year-olds rely heavily on strong beliefs about what sorts of mechanisms are responsible for the motions of animates and inanimates. Animates move by what Gelman has called "the innards principle," wherein movement is a consequence of internal forces operating in strong conjunction with psychological goals and states. By contrast, inanimates move because of the movements of other external objects that apply forces to them. Thus, much of the understanding of these two kinds rests on a set of rich causal beliefs about the different sorts of mechanisms responsible for what may be superficially very similar classes of motions.

The argument that young children can strongly benefit from knowledge of well-elaborated causal links is also reinforced by research on story comprehension. Stein and Glenn (1979), for example, have shown that young children are much better at recalling a story if the elements in the story are causally rather than just temporally linked to each other. I am arguing here that the same holds for concepts: Children will have a much better time remembering all of a concept's details to the extent that they have causal theories that tend to unify the details and explain how they interact as lawlike units with the other things in the world. In a sense, concepts provide theoretical "stories" about the clusters of properties associated with members of a kind.

To push the argument to the extreme, even the young infant's concepts may be meaningful only to the extent that they are embedded in meaningful theories. Consider, for example, the so-called object concept. Much of Spelke's work (e.g., Spelke, 1988) can be interpreted as demonstrating that infants do not just have a concept of an object, but rather an intuitive theory of physical mechanics that, in essence, yields the object concept. Thus, Spelke has argued that infants adhere to such principled beliefs about objects as that they are substantial (they cannot move through each other), spatiotemporally continuous (no object is distributed over different places in time and space), and bounded (they are not amorphous). These principles lead to strong causal expectations about how physical objects can and cannot interact with each other—expectations that can be construed as part of the object concept itself.

Patterns of reasoning may be just as weak and impoverished without causal theories as concepts are. It is clear how this must be true in analogical reasoning, if we assume anything like the Gentner (1983) model. Even the youngest child may attempt to embed analogical reasoning in such theories wherever possible. If reasoning depends critically on expertise, which, in turn, requires concepts embedded in tightly compacted causal belief systems or theories, then it will be weak or ineffective to the extent that those concepts do not connect to theories. This is often the case for reasoning about laboratory-created concepts, but I have suggested that, for informal reasoning, even the youngest child has some domain-specific causal belief structures that give their reasoning power beyond that granted by weak domain-general procedures. Put differently, for informal reasoning about real-world phenomena, the child may never be working purely at the level of surface similarity or summations on characteristic features.

The same relation may be involved in inductive reasoning. Carey (1985) has argued that the young child's concepts of animals are so atheoretical that they only make inductive generalizations about new features by crude probabilistic algorithms. And yet, the studies discussed here suggest that they may have more principled beliefs for biological kinds. Alonso Vera and I have recently shown that preschoolers make more powerful and systematic inductions when they are presented not just with new features but also with certain causal functional roles for those features that clarify how such features fit into their available theories. (Vera & Keil, 1988). Thus, the findings suggest that degree of success at inductive reasoning is largely a function of having a well-elaborated causal belief system within which to interpret the properties under question. Moreover, we may underestimate the sophistication of children's available theories because we assume that the observed pattern of induction when new features are introduced alone is the only one available. In at least some cases, simple causal statements about sets of properties can radically alter childrens' patterns of induction by making the properties more relevant to a different, more elaborated, inductive base.

HOW SHOULD THEORIES BE REPRESENTED?

All of this talk about theories skirts an important point. There is a powerful need for a better theory of theories. How should theories be structurally described? How are they constrained? Such intricate causal belief systems may be at the heart of our understanding of both concepts and categories and most instances of everyday reasoning in the real world, and yet we know much too little about them. My argument here is that a better account of such beliefs will be fundamental to understanding not only concepts but also reasoning, especially of the informal sort. Our current work suggests that, sometimes, these beliefs do not have the structure of explicit belief clusters, or theories, at all. In our work, we have asked preschoolers how one catches a cold or how food makes one grow, or how properties are passed on from parent to offspring; the vast majority have indicated that they have no idea, and many certainly seemed to have never considered such problems before. The same children, however, showed strong preferences for some classes of hypothetical mechanisms over others, when those mechanisms were presented in a forced-choice paradigm. Apparently, although they have nothing like an explicit theory represented, they nonetheless do have strong biases represented at a sufficiently abstract level to rule out whole classes of explanations despite their never having specifically considered those explanations before. Clearly, a major challenge is to develop a model of representation that can accommodate this kind of phenomenon.

THEORIES, INFORMAL REASONING, AND INSTRUCTION

The general arguments made in this chapter about the importance of causal theories in understanding informal reasoning are relevant to instruction, but in subtle and often indirect ways. Nonetheless, they suggest a few general themes:

1. If children do, in fact, possess well-elaborated sets of theories or, at least, implicit biases to prefer some classes of explanations over others, it is obviously important to understand what these theories and biases are and which ones are most relevant to instruction in various domains of knowledge. As has been argued now for several years in the misconception research (e.g., Novak & Gowin, 1984), it is essential to know what sorts of biases the child brings to the learning situation and to design the curriculum and methods of teaching with those biases in mind. We should attempt to work with the biases and exploit the tremendous cognitive economies they are capable of providing rather than trying to remove, level, or avoid them. Similarly, our assumptions about children's typical patterns of reasoning in a given task should reflect close attention to the clusters of beliefs on which that reasoning is operating.

2. When trying to teach new concepts, we should focus not just on feature frequencies and correlations but also on the causal relations that explain those phenomena. The C/D studies and the natural kind studies suggest that, although it is obviously helpful to give instances that have all typical features, it is clearly not enough; we also must teach the underlying causal relations. (Even at this point, however, there are unresolved issues, such as whether instruction should start by first presenting typical properties and instances and then offering appropriate principles or reverse the order. Although leading with principles becomes a

more frequent practice with older students, it is not yet clear that this so-called "scientific mode" (Vygotsky, 1934/1986) is more effective—although some speculations seem warranted.) Instruction should also provide information on the difference between the merely characteristic and the principled, perhaps by presenting atypical but correct instances and incorrect instances with many of the most typical features. The pattern of input to select in any circumstance is still an empirical open question, but it is clear that the learner should come to understand the difference between typical features and causes from the start and that a concept is not complete without both.

3. Not all sets of causal relations may be equally effective instructionally. In particular, those that form rich homeostatic clusters may be the most cognitively effective at unifying a set of properties in a learner's mind.

4. Optimal strategies of instruction may vary dramatically with domain. At the most extreme, consider the differences between teaching a new body of highly conventionalized, arbitrary knowledge and teaching a body of knowledge corresponding to a natural class of phenomena. Much of schooling consists of learning arbitrary conventionalized patterns, such as the alphabet, large parts of reading, and some rules of writing. In these areas, there is little or no causal structure, and the child must memorize correlations, frequencies, and various temporal patterns. Even here, however, causal structure may be helpful; instruction might map such sets of arbitrary relations onto a familiar causal sets as a mnemonic device. With natural phenomena, the instruction should heavily emphasize the causal relations, explaining the typical properties and correlations. It is often assumed that such instruction should only come later, after instruction on surface similarities has been drilled in. Instead, the two should go hand in hand from the start. Mathematics is an intriguing middle-ground domain, because it does consist of an intricate set of highly interconnected links, much like those of the causal homeostasis for a natural kind, but those links are not causal. Mathematics instruction may well be much more effective when taught in a way that allows the young learner to apprehend these systematic interrelations (see chapter 16, this volume), and it may be that learners tend to make some of these links quasicausal to give even more coherence to the system. Certainly, some children seem to use what are, at least, causal metaphors in discussing their knowledge of mathematical interrelations. Such a focus on differences in strategies across domains may be the best way of resolving the issue raised in point number 2 concerning whether to use principles or instances first in instruction.

5. Informal reasoning in children does not occur in isolation, as some sort of content-independent process module. It is intimately linked to the nature of conceptual structure and, in particular, to connected sets of causal beliefs in local domains. Instruction should not be based on assumptions about changes in domain-general patterns of reasoning at various points of development. Such characterizations may be of little help in understanding the what a child brings to a

particular learning situation and where the teacher can "hook" into already well-developed knowledge.

Most broadly, I am suggesting that recent views of concepts and how they are related to theories and informal reasoning suggest that we should look at young children as coming to most learning situations with powerful sets of tools in terms of their systematic domain-specific beliefs and that our teaching will be effective to the extent that we can capitalize on those structures rather than fall back on analyses of relatively weak domain-general learning procedures.

ACKNOWLEDGMENTS

Preparation of this chapter and much of the research described was supported by NSF Grant BNS 83-18076 and by NIH grant 1-R01-HDZ23922-01. Many thanks to Karen Guskin, Jim Voss, Judy Segal, and Michelle von Koch for comments.

REFERENCES

Brown, A. L. (1990). Domain-specific principles affect learning and transfer in children. *Cognitive Science, 14,* 107–134.

Carey, S. (1985). *Conceptual change in childhood.* Cambridge, MA: MIT Press.

DiSessa, A. (1983). Phenomenology and the evolution of intuition. In D. Gentner & A. Stevens (Eds.), *Mental models* (pp. 128–159). Hillsdale, NJ. Lawrence Erlbaum Associates.

Ericsson, K. A., Chase, W. G., & Falcon, S. (1980). Acquisition of memory skill. *Science, 208,* 1181–82.

Forbus, K. D., & Gentner, D. (1986). *Learning physical domains: Towards a theoretical framework.* (Tech. Rep. No. VIV CDCS-R-86-1316). Urbana: University of Illinois, Department of Computer Science.

Freyd, J. J. (1987). Dynamic mental representations. *Psychological Review, 94,* 427–438.

Gelman, R. (1990). First principles organize attention to and learning about relevant data. *Cognitive Science, 14,* 79–106.

Gentner, D. (1983). Structure-mapping: A theoretical framework for analogy. *Cognitive Science, 1*(2), 155–170.

Jeyifous, S. (1986). *Atimodemo: Semantic conceptual development among the Yoruba.* Unpublished doctoral dissertation, Cornell University, Ithaca, NY.

Keil, F. C. (1979). *Semantic and conceptual development: An ontological perspective.* Cambridge, MA: Harvard University Press.

Keil, F. C. (1986a). The acquisition of natural kind and artifact terms. In W. Demopoulos & A. Marras (Ed.), *Language learning and concept acquisition* (pp. 133–153). Norwood, NJ: Ablex.

Keil, F. C. (1986b). On the structure dependent nature of stages of cognitive development. In I. Levin (Ed.), *Stage and structure* (pp. 144–163). Norwood, NJ: Ablex.

Keil, F. C. (1989). *Concepts, kinds and cognitive development.* Cambridge, MA: Bradford Books.

Keil, F. C., & Batterman, N. (1984). A characteristic-to-defining shift in the development of word meaning. *Journal of Verbal Learning and Verbal Behavior, 23,* 221–236.

Kemler, D. G., & Smith, L. B. (1978). Is there a developmental trend from integrality to separability in perception? *Journal of Experimental Child Psychology, 26,* 498–507.

Kripke, S. (1972). Naming and necessity. In D. Davidson & G. Harman (Eds.), *Semantics of natural language* (pp. 253–355). Doedrecht, Holland: Reidel.

McClelland, J. C., Rumelhart, D. E., & the PDP Research Group. (1986). *Parallel distributed processing: Explorations in the micro-structure of cognition* (Vol. 2). Cambridge, MA: MIT Press.

Murphy, G., & Medin, D. (1985). The role of theories in conceptual coherence. *Psychological Review, 92*, 289–316.

Novak, J. D., & Gowin, D. B. (1984). *Learning how to learn.* Cambridge, England: Cambridge University Press.

Putnam, H. (1975). The meaning of "meaning." In K. Gunderson (Ed.), *Language, mind and knowledge. Minnesota studies in the philosophy of science, VII* (pp. 131–193). Minneapolis, MN: University of Minnesota Press.

Rosch, E., & Mervis, C. B. (1975). Family resemblances: Studies in the internal structure of categories. *Cognitive Psychology, 8*, 382–439.

Spelke, E. S. (1988). The origins of physical knowledge. In L. Weiskrantz (Ed.), *Thought without language* (pp. 168–184). Oxford: Oxford University Press.

Stein, N., & Glenn, C. (1979). An analysis of story comprehension in elementary school children. In R. Freedle (Ed.), *New directions in discourse processing* (Vol. 2). Norwood, NJ: Ablex.

Vera, A., & Keil, F. C. (1988, November). *The development of inductions about biological kinds: The nature of the inductive base.* Paper presented at the annual meeting of the Psychonomics Society, Chicago.

Vygotsky, L. S. (1986). *Thought and language* (A. Kozolin, Trans.) Cambridge, MA: MIT Press. (Original work published 1934).

Werner, H. (1948). *Comparative psychology of mental development* (2nd ed.). New York: International Universities Press.

14 I Win—You Lose: The Development of Argumentative Thinking

Nancy L. Stein
Christopher A. Miller
University of Chicago

Argument, by nature and definition, covers a wide range of behaviors and carries multiple meanings. In one sense of the term, argument refers to a verbal dispute in which two or more people maintain what they construe to be incompatible positions regarding an assertion or belief. Moreover, participants mutually attribute argumentative intentions to each other. That is, the parties assume that their assertions are incompatible and that the main goals for each arguer is to win—that is, to arrive at an end state where his or her viewpoint prevails. Thus, *winning* here means being able to proceed unencumbered in an attempt to maintain a position or to pursue a course of action.

The primary plan of attack in this type of argument is to remove any obstacle that stands in the way of one's success. If physical force and coercion are necessary, then these serve as appropriate means of goal attainment. If persuasion, either by appeal or by threat, works, then this will be perceived as legitimate. The important point in a disputative argument is that almost any plan that facilitates and supports the desired position will be used. All other goals are subservient to the primary one of winning.

A second definition of argument emerges from the study of philosophy, logic, and rhetoric. Here, argument is defined as a form of verbal discourse in which a position, claim, or belief is asserted, and then reasons are given to substantiate this assertion. By substantiation, we mean that an arguer uses reasons as evidence for supporting an assertion and persuading others to accept it. Reasons may be evaluated according to certain criteria, including logical coherence. Reasons are assessed by raising objections to them. Objections must be considered seriously, because they contain information that challenges the validity of a reason. In essence, objections are reasons for not believing a particular assertion.

In arguments fitting this second definition, an explicit conflict between two positions need not exist, and the primary purpose of the argument can no longer be characterized by a simple win strategy. Rather, the overriding goal is one of evaluation: to consider the logical consistency and validity of the evidence presented in support of the position. If valid objections can be raised to the evidence offered, then new evidence must be introduced that either counters or avoids these objections. If the objections cannot be countered, then the claim being advanced must be abandoned. Thus, thinking and reasoning employed in this type of argument must conform to strictures imposed by both logical and social criteria as laid out in philosophical (Plato, 1949; Toulmin, 1958), rhetorical (Rottenberg, 1985), and cognitive (Nickerson, 1986) approaches to argument.

In real-world interactions, however, pure examples of verbal disputes and rhetorical arguments rarely occur. In verbal disputes, some effort is generally made to pursue a reasoned course of argument, especially in the initial phases of the interchange. In evaluative (rhetorical) arguments, viewpoints are rarely assessed in a purely objective fashion without personal commitment to their maintenance. Instead, the more common form of argument lies at the intersection of these two categories, partaking in aspects of both of them. We have labelled this the *interactive* form of argument.[1]

As in a dispute or quarrel, interactive arguments are based on a clear disagreement between two (or more) individuals who hold (or believe they hold) mutually exclusive positions. The goal of each party is to win, that is, to be permitted to pursue a desired course of action or to maintain a particular set of beliefs. The methods of winning, however, are normally limited to a particular type of verbal discourse in which evidence must be offered to substantiate the claim being asserted. In this sense, the interactive argument is similar to the philosophical form of argument.

Objections are a normal part of an interactive argument. Unlike rhetorical argument, however, they are provided almost exclusively by one's opponent. Assertions are evaluated but only because the opposition forces the arguer to defend his or her position. The opposition also forces the consideration of an alternative position, including the evidence that might substantiate it. Thus, all the parts of the philosophical form of argument are present in an interactive argument (i.e., a claim, evidence to support the claim, objections to the evidence, counters to the objections, etc.); the unfolding of the discourse, however, is driven primarily by an overt conflict between the goals and beliefs of two or

---

[1]Our concentration on the interactive form of argument is not meant to imply that the rhetorical form of argument is ill conceived or that it plays no role in the real world. Indeed, this form of argument is the one most frequently taught in school settings and, according to Toulmin (1958), the most valued. Our contention, however, is that understanding and using the rhetorical form of argument is preceded by an understanding of the interactive form and may, in fact, be dependent on it.

more persons. Any desire to evaluate positions and evidence serves only this primary goal.

In considering the significance of the interactive argument, we contend that this type of communication serves two basic functions. First, it facilitates social interaction, inasmuch as arguing allows individuals to negotiate, to resolve differences, and to generate codes that regulate the conditions under which actions and beliefs can be maintained. Thus, argument is a primary mechanism in the resolution of social conflict and in the construction of socially appropriate norms. In this sense, the results of an argument can set precedents for the way in which future interactions are structured. Second, arguing facilitates learning, in that it almost always forces the two parties to acquire new information about the specific conflict under consideration. By using each other as sources of knowledge, arguers learn about objections to their own point of view. They also learn about the evidence that supports an alternative position, and they develop an awareness that only certain kinds of evidence are deemed valid, logically consistent, and socially acceptable. Finally, they learn how to counter objections to their own positions by using information provided by their opponents during the course of the argument. In fact, trial lawyers who are renowned for winning difficult cases readily admit that their success depends on their on-line use of information from their opponents, in addition to their own preconceived representation of the evidence. That is, the type of evidence that wins a case is often constructed on line through a full consideration of the context established by an opponent rather than before the trial proceedings begin.

In developing our theoretical framework for studying argumentative skill, both social and learning functions play a critical role. The social function of interactive argument provides a basis for constructing a theory of the relative importance of various kinds of evidence. In particular, we are interested in discovering: (a) the types of information considered to be appropriate evidence in different contexts: (b) the reasons why certain types of evidence appear to be more important than other types; and (c) the basis on which a judge weighs evidence and chooses one position over another. Clearly, specific beliefs and norms about appropriate social interaction regulate the value and appropriateness of evidence. The way in which these beliefs are used to make decisions and the relative importance of two pieces of evidence remain to be described.

With respect to the learning function of the interactive argument, we are particularly interested in the relationships among the amount of prior knowledge people have about an argument domain, the positions they choose to support, and the following: (a) the evidence people use to support one point of view over another; (b) the estimates they make about how likely they are to win an argument given that they have taken a particular position; (c) their raising or lowering this estimate as they proceed through an argument; and (d) the accuracy of these estimates. Furthermore, we are interested in discovering just what is learned as a function of arguing with another individual in various contexts. Finally, we would like to better understand the cumulative effects of participating in repeated arguments. If we were to ask people to participate in repeated debates on the same topic but with new opponents for each new argument, how would this experience affect all of the dimensions just discussed?

A MODEL OF THE DEVELOPMENT OF ARGUMENTATIVE SKILL

To address the issues previously discussed, we first present an abbreviated analysis of the development of argumentative skill. Specifically, we focus on the goals people have when they argue, the types of evidence they use to substantiate claims, and the ways in which these two aspects of argumentation change with age. According to our theoretical framework, the earliest forms of argument arise out of a need to satisfy both personal and social goals (Stein, 1986, 1988). Thus, the child's first notion of argument is bound up with the concepts of conflict and dispute. From as young as 5 years of age, children understand that an opponent in an argument holds a viewpoint that conflicts with their own and that this viewpoint impedes their achievement of a goal. Children at this age also understand that their goal in the argument is to get what they want by some means of action or interaction. That is, they believe that their objective is to win, that is, to ensure that their goal prevails and that their antagonist's goal fails. Thus, the basic structure of argument here is a form of conflict resolution, in which one side wins and the other side loses.

The basis upon which disputes are settled, however, changes as a function of development and learning. It is also influenced by the social context in which the argument occurs. Initially, many disputes are settled by physical intimidation and coercion. Young children may use physical force on an antagonist, or they may use verbal strategies that retain elements of physical threat. For example, young children often resolve disputes through name calling, verbal threats, and appeals to higher authorities, who may also use physical force (Shantz & Shantz, 1985; Stein, 1988). Likewise, young children are often the victims of physical coercion and readily give in during an argument when they sense that physical harm will result from their continued objections. Thus, the resolution of a dispute is often based on physical strength, verbal abuse, and the ability to inflict harm.

This type of resolution is not only used by young children; it also remains an acceptable solution in many social contexts. The duel and the structure of warfare rely on physical threat and harm to personal well-being. Moreover, resolution of conflict by death is the prototypic way some cultures and societies resolve disputes. A good example of this type of conflict resolution occurred recently in the film *The Untouchables,* in which Sean Connery stars as a cop. In one scene, Connery instructs a colleague in the proper means of resolving a dispute: "He pulls a knife, you pull a gun. He puts one of ours in the hospital, you put one of theirs in the morgue." Depending on the importance of the goal and the context in which the dispute occurs, resolution by physical force and harm is a viable and even socially acceptable course of action.

In most cultures, however, the normal mode of dispute resolution does not include physical violence. In fact, punishment for a physical act of violence is often severe. Furthermore, coercive tactics often prove to be unsuccessful in that they result in counteraggression and a continuation of the dispute. Even a shift to verbal tactics does not ensure a socially acceptable resolution. Threats, lies, slander, and shouting contests may be no more successful than physical coercion, and they incur only slightly less societal disapproval. Necessity or the willingness to abide by social rules changes the nature of argumentation and brings reasoning and explaining to the center of focus.

Disputes, although varied, have a regularity to them. They most often involve conflicts over possessions and appropriate social behavior (Shantz & Shantz, 1985; Stein, 1988). Through repeated experience with conflicts, social groups generally construct and evolve a set of agreed-upon rules that are used to resolve such disputes. The type of dispute and the appropriate method of resolution vary across cultures, and it is the task of all participants in a particular culture to learn the appropriate rules for conflict resolution. Although many solutions can be generated to resolve a conflict, only certain ones are socially acceptable. The successful solutions are those that conform to the prevailing belief systems of a society in terms of the costs and benefits to the people involved in the dispute and to the society at large. Thus, the nature of socially acceptable conflict resolution implies an adherence to rule-guided behavior both in selecting an appropriate position and in offering socially acceptable reasons to support that position.

As we begin to understand, value, and accept social and cultural modes of appropriate interaction, we begin to make the shift from disputative to reasoned interaction. The very act of arguing by reason implies some awareness and acceptance of the viability of a social-moral code. The choice of a position and the specific reasons used to support it are critical to constructing a viable argument. It is here that the learning and social functions of argumentation intersect. Because an interactive argument can be won or lost only on the basis of the reasons given, the participant with the superior knowledge of the rules and belief systems underlying socially appropriate behavior will be in the better position to argue effectively.

In our model of interactive arguing, different types and levels of reasoning can be used to defend a position. These levels can be organized hierarchically such that each successive level has a greater sphere of complexity and relevance. At the first and most primitive level of argumentation, assertions are justified solely on the basis of personal preference. Thus, when one arguer says to another, "I think we should see the movie *Chariots of Fire* because I like it and I want to see it," personal preferences and goals are being given as reasons for accepting a particular position. The rule appealed to seems to be something in the form of "If

I want something and I like it enough, I should get it." Indeed, in our society, reasoning by appeal to personal preference is omnipresent. Although this type of reason can be qualified in thousands of ways, it retains some force. Our belief in the strength of the individual and the legitimacy of the unique contributions individuals can make to society fosters this deeply held belief.

Nevertheless, exclusive use of this type of reasoning would result in frequent losses and in the prolongation of the conflict. All an opponent would need to do is resort to a similar strategy: "Yeah, but I want to do Y because I like it," or "I don't want to see *Chariots of Fire* because I don't like it." In fact, this is the type of conversation children (and some adults) often have with each other, and the most frequent outcome is a resort to more disputative forms of argument, such as name calling, shouting, or physical force.

Through explicit intervention, usually from an adult, or because of a need to accommodate the desires of the opponent, a second level of argumentative reasoning is learned. Here, evidence is based on knowledge of social consequences and rules that take both parties' needs into account. At this level, the two parties are not only aware that they have opposing points of view, but they also know that they must address the legitimacy of their opponent's claims as well as their own. Moreover, they understand that convincing arguments rest on reference to shared beliefs about the social benefits and costs to each individual. And finally, increasing experience with the interactive argument form teaches them that virtually any claim, including their own, can be challenged and shown wanting under certain circumstances.

We present the following scenario as an example of argumentation at this level. Suppose that a husband and wife have decided to go out together one evening, but they disagree on what they should spend their time doing. He wants to see *Chariots of Fire,* but she would rather go to the ballet. One of the first steps in an argument at this level is for each party to learn why the other holds the viewpoint that he or she does. On questioning his wife, the man learns that she wants to go to the ballet because Barishnikov is dancing this evening and she has always wanted to see him. Furthermore, she doesn't want to see *Chariots of Fire* because she has heard that it is a boring film.

The husband's attempts at persuasion will then take the form of presentation of counterevidence to his wife's reasons. These can be classified into two broad categories: He may attempt to undermine his wife's objections to his goal, or he may attempt to offer objections to the reasons she has given for her goal. For example, he may attempt to convince her that the film is not boring by describing it in terms of themes that he knows will appeal to her. Thus, he makes the mutual attractiveness of the film explicit. If she rejects these claims, he may continue to generate other reasons that bear on the mutual attractiveness of his goal in a continued effort to achieve this goal.

Alternatively, he may attempt to undermine her goal by offering counterevidence to her reasons (e.g., he's read a review that says that Barishnikov is dancing very poorly in this production) or by showing negative outcomes to her plan (e.g., they can't really afford the cost of ballet tickets), and so on. Meanwhile, of course, the wife may attempt to convince the husband of the superiority of her goals by using the same types of strategies.

If one party agrees with the reasons or objections offered by the other, then the argument may be resolved in that direction: the second party wins, and his or her goal prevails.[2] Winning, however, is based on the number and strength of agreed-upon benefits and advantages that each party can muster in favor of his or her goal as opposed to the number and strength of agreed-upon disadvantages and negative outcomes raised against that goal by the opponent.

At this second level of argumentation, then, the use of evidence is determined by an evaluation and comparison of the costs and benefits of pursuing each course of action. During the evaluation process, an importance hierarchy is constructed by each party such that certain outcomes become more valued than other outcomes. Value can be determined by a consideration of the type and number of other goals that will be affected by supporting one arguer's claim over the other's. The value hierarchies of the arguers may range from very similar to very different, and this factor plays a large role in determining the likelihood of the parties' reaching a mutually agreeable resolution to their argument.

It is possible to discuss a third level of interactive argument, at which participants cease to be concerned solely with their own goals and needs and choose to broaden their scope to include the needs of others or society as a whole. This concern covers not only other people in general but also the rules or codes of society that have been formalized and taught in different social contexts. These codes are frequently embodied in maxims or catch phrases and represent the cultural ideal of what a person should do or think, such as, "If you make a promise, you should keep it," and "If you start something, you should finish it."

These reasons are given to invoke cultural norms of appropriate behavior. They imply that if the code is violated, negative consequences will ensue. However, it is not always clear what the consequences of violation might be. Many times, these social codes are invoked because children have been told that under certain conditions, specific behaviors should follow. They gradually begin to understand that standard, normal expectations exist as to how behavior should be governed.

Reference to social or moral codes does not necessarily entail more complex thinking or a greater understanding of the consequences of an argumentative position. However, invoking these codes does show some awareness that people, in general, have specific beliefs and expectations about appropriate behavior and that adhering to the maxims that reflect these beliefs provides acceptable justifi-

---

[2]Other outcomes are, of course, possible, including compromise (perhaps they could go to a movie starring Barishnikov) and "agreeing to disagree" (perhaps they could go to dinner together and then to their separate activities afterwards).

cation for a behavior. Furthermore, knowledge of societal codes provides access to evidence that should carry shared value within the society. Unlike personal preference or even potentially shared benefits, these codes may be expected to be shared by any opponent who is a part of one's society. Moreover, evidence that relies on definite social codes or contracts cannot be easily countered by participants in that society. (It is difficult, for instance, for an opponent to argue that a true, applicable promise, once made, should not be kept.)

In spite of the emphasis on the interests of others at the second and third levels of interactive argumentation, it should be remembered that in an interactive argument the primary goal is still to win. Thus, when one party attempts to assess and evaluate an opponent's claim to legitimacy, the aim may not be to understand the evidence from the opponent's perspective. Rather, the main goal of the arguer may be to understand the opponent's evidence in terms of how it undermines his or her position and how it can, in turn, be used against the opponent. For this reason, we predict that, in many instances, arguers have difficulty giving a fully accurate account of their opponent's position.

The degree of investment in maintaining a particular position should influence accurate comprehension of an alternative position. For those who enter into an argument or debate with little knowledge and/or investment in a particular viewpoint, the initial goal may be to understand each position in terms of its potential force. This is one instance in which an evaluative attitude is taken toward each position. In these cases, taking an evaluative stance implies either that the arguer does not yet have enough knowledge to make a judgment about the validity of one position versus another or that the arguer can see validity in both points of view.

In our experience, however, most individuals clearly prefer one viewpoint to another. Individuals come to an argument predisposed to accept the validity of certain assertions but not that of others. In fact, it has been well documented that certain beliefs and attitudes are quite resistant to change. For this reason, models of the argumentation process must be able to describe and explain those situations in which a detailed evaluative stance is never taken as well as those cases in which a major effort is made to ascertain the strengths and weaknesses of all positions in the argument.

It may be that a truly evaluative stance towards an argumentative situation requires the arguer to understand that valid reasons can be given for mutually exclusive viewpoints and that, depending on the values and beliefs of the culture as well as the individual, either viewpoint could be considered legitimate. Thus, winning an argument depends in the end on which values and preferences are considered most important. If an individual understands that the argument is continually affected by deeply held beliefs about appropriate social norms and that different beliefs can be brought to bear on the validity of any assertion, then a more detailed evaluation, which takes these beliefs into account, may be given to each position. In these situations, the individuals must evaluate each position as it impacts on their own assertions and with regard to the logical structure of its supporting reasons. Moreover, the values that underlie each participant's assertions must be considered.

When true evaluation is the goal of argumentation, a different type of conflict resolution may emerge. Compromise positions, wherein a different set of assertions is made that incorporates some of the beliefs and values of each of the formerly conflicting positions, are easier to obtain. During the process of evaluating possible solutions, the deeply held beliefs of each of the arguers are brought out, examined, and shown to be in conflict with each other. If a compromise is to be reached, each arguer must realize that although some cherished beliefs may be maintained, others may need to be revised to formulate a new and evaluatively better position. Thus, true evaluation may lead to a position that neither of the arguers supported at the outset of the interaction. However, the emphasis on thoroughly understanding an opponent's position, combined with the overall motive of finding the best possible position, insures that the final position reached, whether it is a compromise or not, will be seen as the best one possible under the circumstances by both argument participants.

Although the traditional, philosophical approach to argumentation focuses on the rational evaluation of reasons, the role of compromise as a solution is rarely considered. In fact, the legalistic nature of the argumentation favored by philosophers and rhetoricians often forces a win/loss strategy. Yet from our perspective compromise frequently forces the most extensive evaluation of each position. In the context of real-world interactions, in the arena of political debate, and in the field of international relations, the best solution frequently is a compromise that is, an accord by which each side recognizes and adheres to the belief that the other side has a legitimate course of action worth pursuing. In these contexts, the quality of the evidence brought to bear on each position is as much a function of preference as it is a function of the logical consistency of the supporting reasons.

DATA ON THE DEVELOPMENT OF ARGUMENT SKILL

To explore argumentative reasoning and decision making, we focus first on the development of these skills. From our review of previous research, it became immediately clear that by the age of 5 children understand the basic structure and nature of an interactive argument. By observing the social interaction of children from 4 years of age onward, several investigators (Chittenden, 1942; Eckerman & Stein, 1982; Eisenberg & Garvey, 1981; Shantz & Shantz, 1985) have noted that the majority of children's social interaction is spent in assertion, defense, and negotiation—activities designed to enable children to achieve important personal goals.

In our descriptions of children's disputes or quarrels, several dimensions are worth noting. First, most quarrels arise out of goal conflict situations, in which two children want something and the attainment of one child's goal is mutually exclusive of the attainment of the other child's goal. Second, children understand that a dispute or argument involves asserting beliefs about a particular claim and that each claim asserted is not necessarily true. Moreover, children understand that they, as well as others, can hold false beliefs and that these beliefs can be challenged. After hearing evidence to support a claim, even young children can think of qualifications that negate the initial claim (Stein & Trabasso, 1982; Wellman, 1988; Wimmer, Hogrefe, & Sodian, in press). Third, a child's idea of an argument is that of an interleaved discourse in which participants alternate in their presentation of assertions, reasons, and counterclaims rather than one in which a single person advances a claim and defends it by the presentation of reasons and responses to hypothetical objections.

Thus, the evidence seems to support the claim that young children know that an argument consists of asserting and defending a point of view and that all points of view in an argument can be both substantiated and challenged (Shantz & Shantz, 1985; Stein & Trabasso, 1982). Furthermore, children also understand that, under normal conditions, the goal of each participant is to win. Thus, the purpose of engaging in an argument is not merely to assert and defend a particular position but ultimately to be able to act on a set of beliefs without interference. In other words, the goal of arguing is to be able to carry on in a desired fashion.

The development of knowledge about the argument form may emerge quite early, because it corresponds roughly to the structure of goal conflict episodes, in which children learn to communicate about and defend goals that are important to them (Chittenden, 1942; Eisenberg & Garvey, 1981; Shantz & Shantz, 1985). The empirical data on children's social interaction suggest that the bulk of children's time is spent in negotiation or argument, in which they attempt to persuade or coerce others to their way of thinking about a particular goal. The nature of these quarrels seems to be captured nicely by our disputative argument form and by the first level of interactive argument: coercion and appeals to personal preference (see also Shantz & Shantz, 1985; Stein, 1988).

Yet, when children are asked to evaluate a moral dilemma posed by a story protagonist faced with a choice between accomplishing a valued goal (e.g., making a medicine to help a sick person) but having to do it at the expense of hurting another (e.g., pulling whiskers from a tiger to make the medicine, harming the tiger in the process), Stein and Trabasso (1982) found that children as young as 5 years of age can easily take a position for or against this action and defend it. Moreover, reasons pertaining to moral or social codes were offered as support for the children's assertions, falling primarily at the second and third levels of interactive argumentation (consideration of others' concerns and generalized rules with social impact).

The age of the children in the Stein and Trabasso (1982) study did not determine the level of reasoning used to defend a position. Rather, developmental differences pertained more to whether or not children condoned the protagonist's actions. Five-year-old children almost always opposed the protagonist's decision to take the whisker, stating that the tiger would suffer too much harm if the medicine were to be made. This assertion was made even when 5-year-old children acknowledged that negative consequences would result if the sick person were to be denied his or her medicine. Older children, however, always supported the protagonist, asserting that it was more important to help a sick friend than to worry about harm to a tiger.

Given that age determined which position children supported, the basic difference between the older and younger children's reasons centered on the amount of harm inflicted by the protagonist's action. Younger children opposed any action that would result in harm to an innocent individual. Older children compared the degree of harm each party would suffer under conditions of acting in the service of the sick person versus acting in the service of the tiger.

These data suggest that knowledge about the consequences of actions in conjunction with knowledge about moral and social codes underlies the decision-making process for 5-year-old children as well as older children and adults. However, the type and degree of knowledge about the consequences of an action, plus the tendency to engage in a comparison of the negative effects of various actions, directly affect which position an arguer chooses to support. Furthermore, a comparison of the consequences of action choices is also directly related to the type of explanations children give for classifying arguments as better or worse.

The results of the Stein and Trabasso (1982) study, as well as the findings from several of our ongoing studies of children arguing and negotiating, raise important questions about the nature and development of argumentative skills. First, are there developmental differences in understanding and reasoning about interactive arguments? If so, how can we characterize these differences? Do young children understand arguments in the same detail and with the same causal connectedness that an adult does? If developmental differences do occur, is there a significant relationship between the way an argument has been represented and the type of decision-making and reasoning strategies that are used to support it? And, if differences do exist in argumentative skill in general, exactly what is the nature of these differences?

Classically, developmental differences in argument and/or reasoning skill have been attributed to a lack of ability to carry out advanced types of logical reasoning. Indeed, an examination of this claim has occupied much of the developmental literature for the past 15 years (Gelman & Baillargeon, 1983). Intensive examination across many domains, however, has resulted in the growing consensus that young children are not disadvantaged logically as much as they lack relevant knowledge with which to make decisions.

Several studies (see Stein, 1986 for a review) have shown that when the amount and organization of knowledge are equated across age groups, few developmental differences are observed. Indeed, some studies have shown that when children have more knowledge of a domain than adults, they outperform the adults along several dimensions. Thus exploring what children know about the content, structure, and functions of argument, in general, and about the domains relevant to a given argument, in particular, becomes an important concern. If knowledge differences are the basis of representational differences, and if both lead to differences in decision-making strategies, instructional programs in argument skills must be sensitive to what children know if they are to be at all productive.

Providing an accurate account of what children know is also critical to evaluating the current literature on the development of argument skills. To date, most attempts to explore children's argumentative reasoning have been carried out in the context of moral dilemma studies (Berkowitz & Gibbs, 1986; Shweder & Much, in press; Stein & Trabasso, 1982; see Rest, 1983 for a general review). The results of these studies are inconsistent. Some investigators (e.g., Berkowitz & Gibbs, 1986) contend that children lack many logical skills and have yet to develop certain argumentative competencies, whereas other researchers (e.g., Shweder & Much, in press; Stein & Trabasso, 1982) stress the substantial amount of knowledge that children have acquired and show extensive similarities between children and adults in the reasoning strategies employed in arguments.

The methodology used to examine argument skills varies widely across the studies. In general, when investigators report a developmental sequence in children's ability to use some types of argumentative logic, a production paradigm has been used (Berkowitz & Gibbs, 1986; Berkowitz, Oser, & Althoff, in press; Damon & Killen, 1982). Thus, the burden of producing the entire form and content of the argument was placed on the child. Investigators (Stein & Trabasso, 1982) who claiming that young children have already acquired much knowledge about the function and structure of argumentation use recall and recognition procedures along with production procedures.

In some studies (Shweder & Much, in press), naturally occurring arguments have been analyzed. These episodes tend to reveal substantially advanced argumentative skill in comparatively young children, though perhaps not as advanced as that in children in the more recognition-oriented studies just cited. In these natural arguments, an interleaved dialogue occurs spontaneously in the course of interaction. Here, children can more easily use the assertions of the other parties involved in the argument to develop and elaborate their own positions. This interleaving continually presents new information that helps structure the child's responses, as in a recognition or probed-recall study. Furthermore, because these arguments are naturally occurring, we can assume that they concern topics about which children have both interest and knowledge, a condition that may be violated frequently in studies using production paradigms, especially those that assess moral development.

In our argument studies, elements of all three techniques have been used to fully measure and control subjects' initial knowledge about argument in general and about the topic at hand in particular. Furthermore, we have used both recognition and recall procedures to assess how different types of argumentative knowledge are understood and remembered. In this way, we hope to discover whether developmental differences are due to different types of knowledge and beliefs, to encoding difficulties, or to some general logical skill that young children lack.

In addition to questions about children's argumentative abilities, a second set of questions needs to be raised concerning adults' argumentative understanding and reasoning skills. Earlier, we attempted to show that the definition of argument has several meanings. Given that most everyday arguments occur in social contexts in which the primary objective is to win, how is it that adults combine the desire to pursue their goals unhindered with the desire to evaluate courses of action in terms of valid justifications?

Although we may like to think that adult reasoning is systematic and corresponds to formal and symbolic logic, this is clearly not the case. We know from a variety of sources (Cosmides, in press; Gelman & Baillargeon, 1983; Wason & Johnson-Laird, 1972) that even skilled logicians sometimes have difficulty with the formalisms of logic. Subjects who are naive to mathematics and probability theory exhibit systematic biases in making estimates about the occurrence of probabilistic events (Kahneman, Slovic, & Tversky, 1982; Tversky & Kahneman, 1983). Most instructional texts concerning the nature of argument skill caution students to be careful about inappropriate conclusions and errors in logic when constructing arguments (Nickerson, 1986; Rottenberg, 1985). In fact, both Nickerson (1986) and Meiland (1981) have given numerous examples of errors in reasoning during argumentation, such as failure to include all the relevant parts of an argument and failure to evaluate the logical nature of connections between the components of an argument. Thus, even adults may have difficulty sustaining a systematic line of argumentation, especially on the first pass through a topic (see chapter 3, by Voss, in this volume).

If adults cannot be shown to be strictly or formally logical, then we need to explain just what they are doing when they attempt to understand an argument or the logical structure of a problem. There are instances of argumentation in which adults thoroughly understand and agree that one position in an argument may be better than others because of the logical nature of the reasons supporting it, yet they choose not to accept that position. Arguments about topics that evoke intense personal feelings, such as war, crime, divorce, and so forth, tend to fall into this category simply because personal preference—even survival—is more important than adhering to logic or the rules prescribed by society at large. Further examination is necessary to determine why adults choose certain positions over others, whether they are aware of the logical difficulty of maintaining certain positions, and whether they sense uncertainty in their ability to maintain these positions.

A COMPARATIVE STUDY OF ARGUMENTATION

To investigate these questions, we completed a series of studies on understanding and reasoning about interactive arguments. Our subject population consisted of students from the University of Chicago and children from two grade levels (second and sixth).

To insure that the argument stimuli we used were familiar and interesting to children as well as adults, materials were constructed in the following fashion. First, children at each of the two grade levels were interviewed and asked to generate arguments in which they had been involved. Then they were asked to recall and enact parts of these arguments. Examples from the arguments thus generated were shown to a second group of children and to a group of adults, and each group was asked to reason about and judge each case. From the data thus collected, one argument topic was chosen on the basis of the frequency of its occurrence, the interest it generated in participants of all ages, the judgment of normalcy that children gave it, and the fact that resolutions to it differed consistently between adults an children. The topic of this argument was a conditional promise.

Two narratives were then constructed, each conveying the context in which an argument about such a promise took place. In these narratives, the two participants in the argument (always one male and one female) made a promise to help each other achieve an individual personal goal (e.g., completing chores) to enable the achievement of a common goal (e.g., going to a baseball game together). Through events beyond their control, the common goal became unobtainable before either had started to help the other. Then one participant claimed that they no longer had to help each other attain their individual goals, but the other participant asserted that they did have to continue helping each other. At this point, no evidence had been presented for or against either of the positions. Table 14.1 contains the basic outline of this argument narrative as it was presented to children and adults in two different experimental conditions.

Both versions of the narrative included the conditions that led to the promise. The narratives specifically stated that the promise was made because each protagonist realized and agreed that without the other's help, neither could finish his or her chores in time for the game. Failure to finish the chores in time would prevent them from going to the game. Thus, the conditions that led to the promise were three hypothetical events that were causally related to each other in an "if not–then not" fashion.

Using Mackie's (1980) criteria for necessity and sufficiency conditions, we can conclude the following about the logical structure of this promise.[3] Helping

---

[3]Using Mackie's (1980) counterfactual criterion for establishing necessity in the circumstances, we see that if the two had not helped each other, they would not get their chores done in time for the game. If they did not get their chores done in time, then they could not go to the game.

TABLE 14.1
Content of Argument Context Story for Implicit
and Explicit Conditions

Story Events:	Implicit	Explicit
If Sarah and Dan worked separately	X	X
they would not finish their chores in time;	X	X
if they did not finish their chores in time,	X	X
they could not go to the baseball game.	X	X
If they helped each other,	X	X
then they would be done in time,	X	X
and they could go to the game.	X	X
So they promised	X	X
to help each other with their chores	X	X
so that they could go to the game.	X	X
If the game was cancelled,		X
then the promise would be off,		X
and they would not have to help each other.		X
Saturday morning, it rains,	X	X
and the game is cancelled.	X	X

Dan's claim: They do not have to help each other.
Sarah's claim: They still have to help each other.

each other is necessary for getting the chores done in time, and getting the chores done is necessary for going to the baseball game. However, neither helping each other nor getting the chores done is sufficient for going to the game. Many conditions, including the weather, also have a direct bearing on whether or not the two parties will get to go to the game. Indeed, in our argument narrative it rains, and the baseball game is called off.

Promises are frequently stated in such a way that they do not explicitly cover all of the events that may occur in relation to the promise. When an event occurs that is not explicitly anticipated in the wording of the promise, people must make inferences about how the promise should be applied to the circumstances that obtain. In our pilot studies, the protagonists in the argument story promised "to help each other so that they could go to the baseball game." When told that the game had been cancelled, subjects asserted that helping either was or was not still required. The choice of which position to support was based primarily on the inferences a subject made about the requirements of the promise. Some subjects said that the ability to achieve the goal (e.g., to go to the game) was a necessary condition for keeping the promise. Thus, the parties needed to help each other *if and only if* they had an opportunity to go to the game. Other subjects said that the opportunity to attend the game was not necessary for keeping the promise: The parties should help each other independent of whether or not they could go to the game. In our initial studies, the choice of position was highly correlated with age. Children interpreted the promise as all-encompassing, admitting no exceptions, whereas adults saw the promise as conditional.

We interpreted this difference as the result of appeal to different normative codes by the different age groups. For adults, the normal code of social behavior permits the assumption that when the goal of a conditional promise is no longer achievable, neither party may want to pursue the promise. For children, the social code does not permit this inference; instead, the ambiguity is resolved by appeal to the general rule that promises, once made, must be kept.

We postulated, however, that, for either group, if the wording of the promise had been extended so that it explicitly covered the events that occurred in the world, then the ambiguity would disappear. In such circumstances we expected both children and adults to make similar decisions. To test this hypothesis we varied the statement of the promise so that it either did or did not explicitly state a relationship between the game cancellation and the necessity of helping each other with the chores.

In our first experimental condition, which we labelled the *implicit condition,* the promise was related without any mention of conditions that might limit helping behavior. The two story participants simply promised "to help so that we can go to the game together," apparently without thought to conditions that should operate if, for example, the game were cancelled. Thus, if conditions were thought to limit the operation of the promise, this fact was implicit and had to be inferred by the subject. In the *explicit condition,* however, the promise made between the protagonists was more elaborate. The promise was explicitly extended to cover conditions that would operate if the game were cancelled. Subjects were told that the protagonists had foreseen the possibility of a game cancellation and had included a clause in their promise agreeing that if the game were cancelled, the promise was not binding and the two did not have help each other any longer (see Table 14.1).

After hearing the story with either the implicit or explicit statement of the promise, all subjects participated in the following tasks. First, they had to decide which side of the argument they would support: helping or not helping. Second, they had to recall as much of the argument narrative as they could. Third, they had to give reasons for supporting the position that they chose. And fourth, they were asked a series of probe questions that sought to verify: (a) how they had encoded the argument text, (b) whether or not certain inferences had been made about the nature of the promise, and (c) whether or not they were sure that a particular position should prevail. Moreover, all subjects were asked to generate arguments from the perspective of each of the story's protagonists, that is, both for the side of the argument they had chosen and for the opposing side.

After this set of data was collected, a second set of tasks was administered. Here, each subject was read the text of an argument in which each protagonist asserted that his or her position should be accepted and gave evidence in the form of a specific line of reasoning to support this claim. Thus, one participant's statement represented a pro position towards helping, and the other a con position. The two statements, presented to all subjects across both conditions, are presented in Table 14.2.

To select the content of the evidence used to support each position in this argument, we selected those reasons that had been given most frequently during the pilot testing of our materials. Both the pro and the con statements focused on an interpretation of the requirements set forth in the promise that had been made. The pro or Help argument maintained that making the promise was a sufficient condition for helping, whereas the con or "No Help" argument claimed that, because the game had been cancelled, the two parties no longer had to help each other.

Subjects were asked to make two types of judgments about these arguments. First, each argument was presented individually, and subjects were asked to assign a scalar rank to the argument text on the basis of how good the argument was. *Goodness* here was defined in terms of how convincing the reason was for the claim it supported. A scale of 1 to 7 was used, 1 denoting a very poor argument and 7 denoting a very good one. Second, the two arguments were presented together, and subjects were asked to compare the pair and make a forced-choice decision evaluating one argument as better than the other in terms of its power to convince. After this paired comparison, subjects were asked to elaborate on why they made the selection they did.

Table 14.3 contains data from all three judgment tasks. Statistical analyses revealed differences due to age and experimental condition. In the implicit condition, both groups of children consistently supported the position of continuing to help each other despite the cancellation of the game. Adults consistently supported the position of not helping. The type of decision task did not significantly affect the judgments of any of the subjects.

The data indicated that when necessary conditions for helping were not made

TABLE 14.2
Arguments Constructed for Goodness Ratings and Paired Comparison Procedure

---

Dan, who does not think he and Sarah have to help each other, gave this argument:

The whole reason that we made our promise was so that we could go to the baseball game. We agreed that we would help each other only so that we could go to the game. That means that if we can't go to the game, we don't have to help each other anymore. Well, there's not going to be any game, so I'm not going to help anymore.

Sarah, who thinks they still have to help each other, gave this argument:

We made a promise to help each other with our chores and when you promise to do something, you're supposed to do it. It doesn't make any difference that the game has been called off. You still promised to help me. If you don't help me, then you're breaking you're promise and that's wrong.

TABLE 14.3
Scores on Three Different Decision Making Tasks

Implicit Condition:	Second	Sixth	Adult
A. Initial Decision:			
Proportion of ~H choices	.00	.30	.90
B. Scale rating scores:			
Help Argument	5.90	5.10	3.10
~Help Argument	2.40	4.40	5.80
C. Paired Comparison			
Proportion favoring ~H argument	.00	.30	.90

Explicit Condition:	Second	Sixth	Adult
A. Initial Decision:			
Proportion of ~H choices	.30	.60	1.00
B. Scale rating scores:			
Help Argument	5.10	3.80	2.80
~Help Argument	3.00	5.80	5.20
C. Paired Comparison:			
Proportion favoring ~H argument	.50	.80	.80

explicit, children from both age groups believed that the promise always served as sufficient cause for requiring help. In other words, the fact that the promise was made was, in and of itself, sufficient to demand that it be kept. No other conditions (e.g., the existence of the game) were required or important. The children were rejecting the possibility that the two protagonists agreed to help each other if and only if they could go to the game. Children understood helping as a necessary condition for being able to go to the game. Unlike the adults, however, the children thought the two parties should help each other without regard to whether or not they were able to go to the game. Being able to go to the baseball game was not seen as a constraining condition for helping each other.

For children, making a promise was unconditional, in that the contract was sufficient to require the fulfillment of the obligation (helping, in this case) independent of further conditional constraints. Thus, children rejected the following counterfactual reasoning, which adults were willing to accept: "Given that we agreed to help each other in order to go to the game, we also agreed that if the game is cancelled, we don't have to help each other." That is, children rejected an "If not B, then not A" argument.

The data from the explicit condition told a different story. Here, developmental differences emerged between the two groups of children. Sixth graders' decisions paralleled the adults', in that the majority of both groups supported the position of not helping. This shift in the position of the sixth graders was reflected in all three types of decision-making tasks. When the promise explicitly stated that helping was contingent on the game, sixth graders were willing to accept the game as a necessary condition, even though they did not spontaneously make this inference in the implicit condition.

Second graders, however, still rejected (or ignored) this piece of information. Only 30% of them consistently supported the position that the promise implied that helping was necessary. Thus, for the majority of second-grade children, the Help argument was still rated higher than the No Help argument. Even in the paired comparison task only half of the second graders accepted the No Help argument as better than the Help argument.

To understand the nature of the difference between the age groups, we analyzed the probe questions. The results pertaining to how the promise was understood are presented in Table 14.4. The data revealed that, in the explicit condition, 70% of the second graders had difficulty either encoding or retrieving information about the conditional nature of the promise. These children understood that the protagonists had promised to help each other in order to go to the game; they understood that if the protagonists did not help each other, they could

Table 14.4

Proportion of Subjects Giving Specific Responses to Probe Questions about the Nature of the Promise

| Probe Question: | Implicit Conditions | | | Explicit Condition | | |
| | Group | | | Group | | |
	2	6	A	2	6	A
Why did they agree to help each other?						
1. To get their chores done in time	.20	.60	.40	.30	.70	.50
2. To go to the game	.80	1.00	1.00	.80	.90	.80
What would happen if they did not help each other?						
1. The chores would not get done	.70	.30	.80	.30	.50	.70
2. They could not go to game	.60	.70	.80	.60	.80	1.00
Did they get to go to the game?						
No	1.00	1.00	1.00	1.00	1.00	1.00
Did they make a promise about what they would do if the game was cancelled?						
Yes	.00	.00	.00	.60	.50	1.00
What did they promise they would do if the game was cancelled (Asked only in explicit condition)?						
Not have to help each other	—	—	—	.30	.50	1.00
Does the fact that the game was rained out mean that they don't have to help each other anymore?						
Yes	.00	.30	.89	.30	.70	1.00

not go to the game; and they understood that when the game was cancelled, the protagonists did not get to go.

Most of the second graders, however, were incapable of stating the conditional part of the promise even when they correctly recalled that the protagonists had included specifications as to what they would do if the game were rained out. Moreover, when asked to generate reasons for the No Help position (the position that most of them opposed), only 20% referred to the nature of the conditions under which the promise would operate, as explicitly stated in the narrative. In fact, most of the probe question data supported the hypothesis that the majority of second graders in the explicit condition did not encode the conditional part of the promise accurately even though their recall of the rest of the story does not differ substantially from that of the other age groups.

From an analysis of the protocols of each second grader in the explicit condition, the following can be ascertained. On the one hand, of those children who supported the No Help position when the game was cancelled (30%), *all* maintained total consistency over the three decision-making tasks. Moreover, their answers to probe questions regarding the conditional nature of the promise revealed an accurate account of the conditions as specified in the explicit argument story. Finally, given that they supported the decision to discontinue helping, they invariably supplied the same type of reason that adults did for having done so.

On the other hand, those second graders (70%) who supported the position of helping despite the conditional nature of the promise, showed little evidence of having remembered exactly what the conditions of the promise were. Information about the conditions never appeared in their free recalls, nor were they able to retrieve any relevant information when probed directly for it. Moreover, when asked whether the protagonists had to help in spite of the game's being rained out, all of the second-grade children who had supported the helping position said "yes."

Thus, both responses to probe questions and recall data suggest that the second-grade children had difficulty encoding the conditional nature of the promise in the explicit condition. Two explanations may account for these findings. The first postulates a failure to understand the logic of a conditional promise. To recall the promise correctly, subjects needed to understand that a specific condition was necessary to help to be required. Thus, subjects needed first to determine whether or not the game was to be played, and then they had to understand that helping was directly contingent on that fact.

When we explicitly asked the second-grade children if help had to be given even when the game was cancelled, 70% in the explicit condition said, "Yes, helping had to occur." When we rephrased the question and asked, "Does the fact that the game was rained out mean that the two do not have to help each other anymore?", only 30% of the second-grade subjects in the explicit condition agreed that the protagonists no longer had to help each other. Even during our paired comparison judgment, in which children were explicitly reminded of the conditional clause in the promise, only half of them agreed that the No Help argument was the better one.

Given children's resistance to accepting the conditional nature of the promise, our second explanation for the observed developmental differences lies more in the realm of understanding the concept of a *promise*. All of the data supported the hypothesis that second graders believe a promise to be unconditional. The act of promising to do something was seen as independent of the reason for promising to do it, and the fact that the promise was made was sufficient reason for keeping it. If children really believe that promises are unconditional (or that they should be unconditional), then the presence of an explicit agreement to the contrary may not be seen as important in their choosing a position and citing evidence in favor of it. Astington's recent work (1988) offers some support for the notion of differences between the promise concepts of young children and adults along these dimensions.

All subjects were asked to provide an explanation or defense for the decision that they made. Analysis of these explanations showed that second graders ignored the use of the promise in their reasons and greatly favored explanations that dwelled on the costs and benefits (both social and physical) to both protagonists. This was true even in the implicit condition, in which the statement of the promise could be used to support a Help position quite directly. Adults, on the other hand, favored evidence based on the contractual nature of the promise. Sixth graders, although performing much like adults, showed more variability in their choice of strategies and a greater tendency to use both types of strategies to defend their positions. (See Table 14.5.)

Defining a promise in an unconditional manner may serve to highlight the negative social consequences of failing to fulfill a contract. The uniformity of the decisions made by second graders and adults gives weight to the idea that subjects in each age group can be relatively certain that their peers will see this issue the same way they do. Thus, a second grader's failure to help a fellow second grader, even in our explicit condition, would be a serious social offense, because both parties would see it as "breaking the promise." An adult's failure to help a fellow adult, perhaps even in the implicit condition, would not be nearly as serious because, statistically, most adults expect a promise to be called off when all of its goals can no longer be achieved.

Thus, it may be that this developmental difference in decision making is the result of reference to different social norms. The code of behavior that is understood and used by children, emphasizing consequences to the individuals involved, admits no possibility of breaching a promise. The code used by adults, emphasizing strict adherence to an informal contract law, specifies voiding the promise under certain circumstances. If a difference in the value of each of these codes is regulating support for a particular position, then children may have fully understood the conditional aspects of the promise. For them, however, taking a position in favor of helping would ensure that their goals of maintaining fairness

TABLE 14.5
Proportion of Subjects Using Three Different Types
of Explanation Strategies to Support a Given Position

Subjects Supporting a HELP Position:

	Implicit			Explicit		
Explanation Strategy	*2* *n = 10*	*6* *n = 7*	*A* *n = 1*	*2* *n = 7*	*6* *n = 4*	*A* *n = 0*
Promise obligates them to Help	.20	.29	1.00	.14	.25	—
Consequences of Helping or ~Helping given in support of a Help position	.60	.14	.00	.86	.75	—
Both of the above strategies	.20	.57	.00	.00	.00	—

Subjects Supporting a NO HELP Position:

	Implicit			Explicit		
Explanation Strategy:	*2* *n = 0*	*6* *n = 3*	*A* *n = 9*	*2* *n = 3*	*6* *n = 6*	*A* *n = 10*
Promise was conditional (not obligated)	—	.67	.78	.00	.83	.80
Consequences of Helping or ~Helping given in support of a ~Help position	—	.33	.00	.33	.00	.00
Both of the above strategies	—	.00	.22	.67	.17	.20

to all parties and avoiding negative social consequences would be more fully met.

Finally, there is a sense in which adults understand that making a contractual agreement involves a series of trade-offs. In a premarital agreement, for example, an individual gives up certain rights and benefits to acquire other benefits. Given that the decision to enter the contract was freely made, it may be assumed that the individuals who agreed to the contract decided, through some sort of comparative analysis, that the benefits obtained through the contract were worth the risk of losing other benefits. Thus, when strict adherence to a contract results in some unfairness to one or the other of the parties involved, adults feel justified in setting aside the interests of the individuals in favor of supporting the letter of the law.

Young children may not carry out these comparisons or make these assumptions as automatically as adults do. The reason for this is unclear. It is not the case that they lack the ability to carry out a comparative analysis (Stein & Trabasso, 1982); rather, they may lack situational and conditional knowledge that allows them to know when such assumptions are justified. Insofar as the assumption is justified by the majority of people in our society, then this strategy is one that would have to be learned by young children. We maintain, however, that such learning is perhaps best accomplished through interactive arguments and that children's approaches to this and similar dilemmas will change only as they use strategies that are confronted and overpowered by the strategies of older children and adults. Our future studies must investigate this learning process more thoroughly.

IMPLICATIONS FOR THE STUDY OF ARGUMENTATIVE REASONING

The data presented thus far indicate that taking a stand in an argument and bringing evidence to bear on that position is a function of knowledge and beliefs about the domain of the argument (in this case, about promises). Almost all the data showed that adults believed in and supported a notion of promises as conditional even when the nature of the conditions had to be inferred. That is, adults believed that parties entering into a contract should be able to foresee and implicitly consider conditions that might void the contract. If these conditions become operative, they serve as reasons to nullify the contract. Children, especially those at the second grade level, discounted the foreseeability issue. Rather, they believed that promising to help someone meant an obligation to carry out those actions whether or not other goals of the promise could be fulfilled.

These results have two important implications for argumentative reasoning. They indicate that beliefs about appropriate social norms vary significantly and that these beliefs directly influence the position chosen in an argument and the types of evidence used to support this position. Because these differences are developmental in nature, it becomes quite easy to use a knowledge-based explanation to account for variations in beliefs about appropriate social norms. Younger children have neither experienced nor been exposed to as many contract or promise negotiations as adults. Therefore, their knowledge about contractual arrangements is comparatively limited. Given this limitation, they fail to realize that important personal goals may be threatened as a result of treating all promises as unconditional. Adults and older children, however, have broader and more detailed knowledge of the impact of unforeseen circumstances on promises and therefore expect contracts to be conditional. In this sense, for older children and adults, emphasis on the explicit and implicit conditions of a contract permits as great a concern for self-protection as for mutual benefits.

Future studies may again show that choice in argumentative contexts, although regulated by belief in the propriety of certain social codes, is also regulated by the amount of knowledge one has about how social norms serve to regulate interaction. In fact, we argue that the value imputed to a set of social norms is often a direct function of the goals that are served by the code. Knowing which goals are involved should be critical to determining the value that is placed on one social code versus another.

The importance of acquiring evidence to support either position must also be examined. The ability to make accurate predictions about whether an argument will be won or lost depends on an astute prediction of the evidence that each party will present. A lack of knowledge about an opponent's position or a lack of knowledge about objections to one's own position could easily lead to overconfidence in predicting the outcome of an argument. Failure to understand the fundamental assumptions of an opponent's viewpoint might well prove disastrous, especially if these assumptions are shared by a judging third party. For example, if we asked the second graders in our study to make judgments about their confidence in winning an argument, we would expect their confidence ratings to be quite high. However, these children also have very little knowledge about the evidence that older opponents would use and even less knowledge about the objections that could be raised against their own position. If older children and adults served as judges in an argument over this topic, these children would surely lose, given the data from our present study.[4]

Knowing the evidential basis for reasoning in argumentative contexts, however, is only part of the knowledge needed to win an argument. Knowing how to use evidence to raise objections and knowing how to bring counterevidence to bear on an opponent's objections are also essential. Moreover, the element of timing is critical. Knowing when to introduce evidence can be just as important as knowing that certain types must be presented. We could easily envision a group of adults being overconfident about winning an argument because of access to critical evidence that should be persuasive. However, a poor presentation of this evidence might well lose the argument for them. Ultimately, an implicit notion of how judges construct an understanding of an argument is just as important as an understanding of the critical evidence necessary to support each position.

Losing an argument can be due to a clear lack of knowledge about how to present evidence or to a failure to correctly predict how an opponent will use evidence to support his or her position. As we have previously mentioned, winning or losing an argument is contingent on a number of factors. The misrepresentation of unexpected evidence or incorrect inferences made by a judge due to a defendant's failure to raise objections at the critically appropriate mo-

---

[4]It is worth pointing out here that, were young children to judge this debate, adults would probably not fair much better. Our data indicate that adults have no significantly better insight into alternatives to their own position (that conditions on a promise should be inferred in all cases) than do young children for theirs. Indeed, it is possible that the sixth graders, who seem to lie at a midpoint between the extremes with some insight into both, might perform best with judges from either of the other groups.

ment all serve as factors that regulate judicial decision making. Thus, winning an argument involves a fair amount of risk. Understanding how arguments are won or lost requires knowledge about both the process of constructing an argument and content that may serve as adequate evidence to defend a position.

Although our study of argumentative reasoning is in its initial phase of formulation, certain issues with respect to learning about arguments can be discussed. One that is especially appropriate concerns the ability to compose arguments that are coherent and meet certain standards of rhetoric. From an analysis of the rhetorical (Rottenberg, 1985) and psychological (Nickerson, 1986) literatures, we find one factor continually overlooked in approaches to argumentation: whether or not arguers have acquired an adequate knowledge base to defend successfully one position over another. Most instructors assume that the nature of a conflict is well understood and that evidence can easily be brought to bear in supporting one position versus another.

In our analysis of argumentation skill, we find that, in many conflicts— especially those involving domains that are explicitly taught in school (e.g., history, economics, and biology)—most people don't have enough knowledge about either position in an argument to take a stand that they can support. Thus, asking people how strongly they support a position and asking them how much knowledge they have about a position appear to be essential. Collecting confidence ratings on people's assessment of whether they have enough knowledge to construct a coherent representation of a position is as important as discovering how accurate people are in predicting whether they will win or lose an argument. Given our emphasis on the relationships between confidence judgments, knowledge, and accuracy in producing successful arguments, an assessment of what people know seems to be the first step in formulating a more detailed theory of argumentative reasoning.

REFERENCES

Astington, J. (1988). Children's understanding of the speech act of promising. *Journal of Child Language, 15*, 157–173.

Berkowitz, M. W., & Gibbs, J. (1986). The process of moral conflict resolution and moral development. In W. Damon & M. Berkowitz (Eds.), *New directions in child development: Vol. 29. Peer conflict and psychological growth* (pp. 71–84). San Francisco: Jossey-Bass.

Berkowitz, M. W., Oser, F., & Althof, W. (in press). The development of sociomoral discourse. In W. N. Kurtiness & J. L. Gewirtz (Eds.), *Moral development through social interaction* (pp. 322–352). New York: Wiley.

Chittenden, G. F. (1942). An experimental study in measuring and modifying assertive behavior in young children. *Monographs of the Society for Research in Child Development, 7* (1, Serial No. 31).

Cosmides, L. (1989). The logic of social exchange: Has natural selection shaped how humans reason? *Cognition, 31*, 187–276.

Damon, W., & Killen, M. (1982). Peer interaction and the process of change in children's moral reasoning. *Merrill-Palmer Quarterly, 28*, 347–367.

Eckerman, C., & Stein, M. (1982). The toddler's emerging interactive skills. In K Rubin & W. Ross (Eds.), *Peer relations and social skills* (pp. 41–72). New York: Springer-Verlag, Inc.

Eisenberg, N. R., & Garvey, C. (1981). Children's use of verbal strategies in resolving conflicts. *Discourse Processes, 4,* 149–170.

Gelman, R., & Baillargeon, R. (1983). A review of some recent Piagetian concepts. In P. H. Mussen, J. H. Flavell, & E. M. Markman (Eds.), *Handbook of child psychology: Vol. 3. Cognitive development* (pp. 167–230). New York: John Wiley and Sons.

Kahneman, D., Slovic, P., & Tversky, A. (1982). *Judgment under uncertainty: Heuristics and biases.* New York: Cambridge University Press.

Mackie, J. L. (1980). *The cement of the universe.* Oxford: Clarendon Press.

Meiland, J. W. (1981). *College thinking: How to get the best out of college.* New York: New American Library.

Nickerson, R. (1986). *Reflections on reasoning.* Hillsdale, NJ: Lawrence Erlbaum Associates.

Plato. (1949). Meno. (p. 58). Indianapolis: Bobbs-Merrill.

Rest, J. (1983). Morality. In P. Mussen (Ed.), *Carmichael's manual of child psychology* (4th ed.) (pp. 556–629). New York: John Wiley and Sons.

Rottenberg, A. T. (1985). *Elements of argument.* New York: St. Martin's Press.

Shantz, C., & Shantz, D. (1985). Conflict between children: Social-cognitive and sociometric correlates. In W. Damon & M. Berkowitz (Eds.), *New directions in child development: Vol. 29. Peer conflict and pscyhological growth* (pp. 3–22). San Francisco: Jossey-Bass.

Shweder, R., & Much, N. C. (1987). Determinations of meaning: Discourse and moral socialization. In W. M. Kurtiness & J. Gewirtz (Eds.), *Moral development through social interaction* (pp. 197–244). New York: Wiley.

Stein, N. L. (1986). Knowledge and process in the acquisition of writing skills. In E. Z. Rothkopf (Ed.), *Review of research in education* (vol. 13, pp. 225–258). Washington, DC: American Educational Research Association.

Stein, N. L. (1988). The development of children's storytelling skill. In M. B. Franklin & S. Barten (Eds.), *Child language: A reader* (pp. 282–298). New York: Oxford University Press.

Stein, N. L., & Trabasso, T. (1982). Children's understanding of stories: A basis for moral judgment and dilemma resolution. In C. Brainerd & M. Pressley (Eds.), *Verbal processes in children: Progress in cognitive development research* (pp. 161–188). New York: Springer-Verlag.

Toulmin, S. E. (1958). *The uses of argument.* Cambridge, England: Cambridge University Press.

Tversky, A., & Kahneman, D. (1983). Probability, representativeness, and the conjunction fallacy. *Psychological Review, 90*(4), 293–315.

Wason, P., & Johnson-Laird, P. (1972). *Psychology of reasoning: Structure and content.* London: Bastford.

Wellman, H. (1988). *Young children's reasoning about beliefs.* Unpublished manuscript, University of Michigan, Ann Arbor.

Wimmer, H., Hogrefe, J., & Sodian, B. (1988). A second stage in children's conceptions of mental life: Understanding informational accesses as origins of knowledge and belief. In J. Astington, D. Olson, & P. Harris (Eds.), *Developing theories of mind* (pp. 193–206). New York: Cambridge University Press.

15 Modes and Models of Informal Reasoning: A Commentary

Raymond S. Nickerson
Bolt Beranek & Newman Inc.

FORM IN FORMAL REASONING

Informal reasoning is sometimes defined, if only by default, as reasoning other than formal reasoning. One way to launch a discussion of informal reasoning, therefore, is to begin by considering what formal reasoning is and, thereby, establish, at least, what informal reasoning is not.*

Formal reasoning, as the term suggests, involves reasoning in accordance with certain canonical forms. Logicians find it useful to express the rules of logic in an abstract symbology, in order to preclude confusing form with substance; if an argument has semantic content, that content may complicate the task of judging the validity of the argument's form. Consider, for example, the following syllogism:

No squirrels are pachyderms.
No pachyderms are reptiles.
Therefore, no squirrels are reptiles.

This argument might be judged valid because both of its premises and its conclusion are true. In fact, it is not valid; the conclusion does not follow from the premises. Moreover, it is easy to construct arguments of the same form that have true premises and a false conclusion.

No cats are spiders.
No spiders are mammals.
Therefore, no cats are mammals.

---

*Citations without dates refer to chapters in this volume.

Constructing an argument that has true premises and a false conclusion always suffices to demonstrate the invalidity of the argument's form. Unfortunately, as the first example illustrates, the fact that an argument contains true premises and a true conclusion does not assure that its form is valid. To be sure that a form is valid, we have to convince ourselves that it is not possible to construct an argument with that form that has true premises and a false conclusion, and that makes the task difficult; an inability to produce such an example may, for most of us, be less than compelling evidence that none exists.

The form of both of the arguments just used can be symbolically represented as:

No *A* are *B*.
No *B* are *C*.
Therefore, no *A* are *C*.

This representation makes it somewhat easier to focus on the form of the argument. Because the argument now has no content, we cannot judge (or misjudge) its validity or invalidity by reference to the truth or falsity of its premises and conclusion. But there are other ways to assess the validity or invalidity of argument forms that do not involve deciding the truth or falsity of assertions about the world. One of the best known methods is the one invented by Euler, which makes use of diagrammatic representations of the relationships expressed in the statements comprising the argument. For example, by representing the classes *A, B,* and *C* by circles, we can show various ways in which they might be related that would be consistent with both premises, but inconsistent with the conclusion.

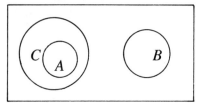

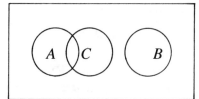

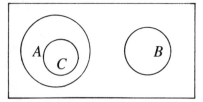

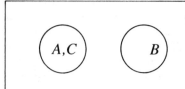

Again, this is enough to determine that a form is invalid. To be sure of the validity of a form, we must be convinced that there is *no* legitimate representation that is simultaneously consistent with the premises and inconsistent with the conclusion. This is likely to be harder to do. So, even with abstract formal arguments, demonstrating the validity of valid forms typically is somewhat more difficult than demonstrating the invalidity of invalid ones.

Although the use of abstract argument forms does permit one to focus more on form than on content, it does not permit one to escape from semantics completely. Consider, for example, the assertion *All A are B*. One can hardly imagine a simpler or less ambiguous assertion. But is it really so crystal clear? Is this statement to be considered true if *A* is a class with no members? What if both *A* and *B* are classes with no members? Or consider the expression *Some A are B*. Suppose *A* and *B* are the same class, like people and human beings, or that *A* is a subclass of *B;* should the assertion be considered true in these cases? Similar questions can be raised with respect to other, equally simple assertions. Logicians answer such questions by agreeing on how these expressions will be interpreted when used within formal arguments. But the need for agreement illustrates the ambiguity of the expressions, and the conventions on which logicians have agreed are sometimes at odds with the prevailing connotations of expressions in everyday language.

For example, the word *and,* as used in logic, has a special meaning that is considerably more precise than its meaning in everyday speech. In logic, *A and B* is understood to denote all entities that are members *both* of the class *A* and of the class *B;* it does not mean all members of class *A* plus all members of class *B*. Logicians represent the latter concept by the term *A or B*. Thus, for example, if the class of all dentists were represented by *A* and the class of all golfers by *B*, the combined class that included all dentists as well as all golfers would be *A or B*. To the logician, *A and B* would represent all dentists who play golf, or, if one prefers, all golfers who practice dentistry. In short, although the emphasis in formal logic is definitely on form, issues of meaning are not avoided entirely.

The study of logical forms dates back at least to the early Greek philosophers, and especially to Aristotle, who invented the categorical syllogism and developed a taxonomy of the various forms that it can take. As Salmon notes, the form, as opposed to the content, of argument has remained the focus of logic as a discipline from Aristotle to the present time. Salmon also points out, however, that although we remember Aristotle for building an axiomatic system of formal logic, that feat, like the building of any formal system, depended in crucial ways on informal reasoning. The syllogism itself is the product of informal reasoning. And the primary method used by Aristotle himself to test the validity of a specific syllogistic form was to attempt to fit the form with premises known to be true and a conclusion known to be false. As noted earlier, success in this endeavor shows a form to be invalid; inability to find such a fit, in spite of concerted effort, is taken as some evidence of the validity of the form.

SUBSTANCE IN REASONING

Equipped with the rules of formal logic, we are in a position to distinguish between valid and invalid argument forms, and this, in my view, is an asset, if not a necessity, for effective critical thinking. The idea of logical implication should be understood by anyone who aspires to reason well. But reasoning that matters to us in life has substance as well as form. Usually we are interested not only—or even primarily—in whether the form of an argument is valid, but also in whether the conclusion should be believed. The rules of formal logic, by themselves, do not tell us that. If we can cast an argument in a syllogistic form, then formal logic can tell us whether the conclusion follows from the premises. If it does, and if we believe the premises to be true, logic tells us that we must also believe the conclusion to be true. If we believe one or more of the premises to be false, it tells us that we are not compelled, by virtue of the premises, to believe the conclusion to be true. But it does not tell us that we are obliged to believe it to be false. Moreover, it gives us no help in deciding whether the premises are true or false. Without an opinion on this matter, knowledge of the validity or invalidity of an argument's form gives no clue to the truth or falsity of the conclusion. What logic provides is not inconsequential: Knowing if a conclusion follows from the premises that are advanced in its support is an essential aspect of argument evaluation. But logic alone is not sufficient.

The deductive arguments that we encounter in everyday life are not, for the most part, expressed in a canonical form, and recasting them may take some doing. Often they are incomplete, so missing elements have to be supplied, and, at the same time, they are encumbered with irrelevancies that must be stripped away. After they have been made whole and tidied up, there is the problem of deciding whether to believe the premises. In many real-life arguments, one can neither accept nor reject the premises with complete certainty. Assertions in natural language, as well as the words that comprise them, are often ambiguous and open to interpretation. *Dogs are larger than cats.* Is this true or false? *All birds lay eggs.* True or false? The answer in both cases, of course, depends on what the assertions are taken to mean. It is true, as a general rule, that dogs are larger than cats (that is, if "cat" is taken to connote the typical housecat), that the average-size dog is larger than the average-size cat, and that most dogs are larger than most cats. It is not true that all dogs are larger than all cats. It is true that all species of birds lay eggs. It is not true that every individual bird lays eggs. Male birds do not lay eggs, nor do baby birds, dead birds, or even every single adult, living, female bird.

Even when the meaning of an assertion is clear, one may accept it with reservations or reject it with some lingering doubt as to whether it really is false. Commonly, one neither completely accepts nor completely rejects claims but attaches to them greater or less degrees of certitude or plausibility. In short, the truth-preserving quality of formal deductive arguments is somewhat less straightforward than is usually acknowledged. A valid form preserves no more truth than is resident in the premises to begin with, and the syllogism itself gives one no help in determining how much truth there is to preserve. So, a knowledge of formal logic, though valuable, is not enough to ensure effective reasoning about substantive matters, even when one limits attention to reasoning that is deductive and canonical in form.

FORM IN INFORMAL REASONING

A second reason that knowledge of formal logic does not suffice to ensure effective reasoning in everyday life is, as Salmon notes, that much of the reasoning that is required is not readily cast in a standard deductive form. This is not to suggest that such reasoning has *no* form. Given the emphasis on form in formal reasoning, there is a tendency to think of informal reasoning as lacking in form; from that perspective, the rubric under which this and several preceding chapters were prepared, "Modes and models of informal reasoning," might be viewed as a contradiction in terms, inasmuch as one of the dictionary definitions of *mode* is *form*. Although informal reasoning is not constrained to fit precise forms to the same degree as is syllogistic reasoning, it should not be thought of as entirely devoid of form. Among the forms or modes of informal reasoning that might be identified, the following are emphasized in this volume:

- *Induction.* Induction is the form of reasoning that is most often contrasted with deduction. In its most common meaning, induction involves generalizing and extrapolating, that is, going beyond the information in hand. It means reasoning from particular statements to general statements, from observations to principles, or from data to laws. Many of the scientific laws that play such important roles in our understanding of the world are products of induction. Induction also plays a critical role in everyday thinking. Without it, we could not learn, and we could not form concepts; we would be mentally impoverished indeed.
- *Analogical reasoning.* Analogies, metaphors, models, and similies pervade reasoning in technical or professional contexts (e.g., scientific theorizing, legal debate) and in everyday life. The role that analogies have played in the development of theories in various knowledge domains has been of interest to several investigators (Boden, 1977; Gentner & Grudin, 1985; Hadamard, 1945). Bronowski (1965) has argued that the ability to see analogies is basic to both science and the arts: "In the act of creation, a man brings together two facets of reality and, by discovering a likeness between them, suddenly makes them one. This act is the same in Leonardo, in Keats, and in Einstein" (p. 51). Analogies are often used as vehicles for explanations. Some-

thing that needs explaining is likened to something with which one is assumed to be familiar. They are sometimes employed as existence proofs. If, for example, one argues that a certain claim cannot be true of X because X has properties A, B, C, a compelling refutation is the observation that the claim in question is true of Y, which is analogous to X in that it also has properties A, B, C. Analogies are misused when they are pressed beyond their limits. As Salmon points out, from the fact that X and Y are analogous with respect to properties A, B, and C, it does not follow that they are analogous also with respect to any other properties. This form of argument can be useful in the generation of hypotheses: X has properties A, B, . . . Z, and Y has properties A, B, . . . ; therefore, it is reasonable to consider whether Y may also have property Z. Unfortunately, it is often misused to support the assertion that Y must have Z.

- *Disputative argument.* This form of argument is prototypical of what one sees in a debate or a courtroom trial. The point is to determine the credibility—or lack thereof—of some assertion (charge or allegation). Evidence is presented, some favoring the judgment that the assertion is true and some favoring the judgment that it is false. The process is recursive in that assertions that are offered as evidence can, themselves, become the objects of scrutiny whose credibility must be ascertained. What makes a disputative argument different from what Stein and Miller refer to as a philosophical argument is that, in the former case, the two sides of the argument are developed by different individuals, each of whom has a vested interest in a particular outcome. A philosophical argument is a debate with oneself, so to speak, in which one tries to develop both sides of the argument and is indifferent to where it leads.

- *Dialectical reasoning.* The term suggests a process of confrontation, of opposing ideas, or, at least, of alternative ways of viewing or explaining things. It suggests a process of juxtaposing conflicting views in the hope that something new and better will emerge. The form comes from the conception of history as a dialectical process of thesis, antithesis, and synthesis that was put forth originally by the 18th/19th century German philosopher, Georg Hegel. Dialectical reasoning is more philosophical than disputative argumentation, in that the point is not to win but to resolve differences; it goes somewhat beyond other notions of philosophical argumentation, however, in that the resolution, or synthesis, is expected to be a new perspective on the situation, not just an endorsement of one of the original views.

These forms of informal reasoning are not mutually exclusive. An extended dialectical reasoning process may include inductive and deductive inferences, as well as argument by analogy. Nor are they exhaustive; they are mentioned simply for the purpose of illustrating that such forms can be distinguished.

It is important to emphasize that these identifiable forms are somewhat less precise and less well understood than those of deductive logic and that, especially when the observable aspects of a complicated reasoning episode are imbedded in a noisy context, these forms may be difficult to discern. Moreover, they do not provide a systematic basis for evaluating arguments. The evaluation of complex informal arguments can be a difficult undertaking. Intelligent people of good will, after struggling to understand all sides of a controversial issue, often do come to different conclusions. In particular, when two people with initially conflicting views examine the same evidence, they sometimes each find reasons for increasing the strength of their existing views (Lord, Ross, & Lepper, 1979). To account for this tenacity, it is not necessary to assume, although it could be the case, that people adhere to different standards in their uses of evidence. The same evidence may appear quite different because of differences in the background knowledge people bring to its interpretation.

Formal deductive reasoning rests on the fundamental cognitive act of inferring—making explicit what is contained implicitly in the information in hand. Informal reasoning draws on a variety of cognitive skills or abilities and requires judgments of various sorts, including judgments of relevance (e.g., how central some fact is to a decision that must be made), judgments of plausibility (e.g., how much credibility to attach to an assertion), judgments of value (e.g., whether a particular goal is worth pursuing), and judgments of probability (e.g., the likelihood of some future event).

EXAMPLES IN REASONING

An aspect of reasoning, both formal and informal, that has not received as much attention as it perhaps deserves is the use of examples for a variety of purposes. Rissland points out that example-based reasoning is important in many contexts and suggests that the ability to generate and use examples, therefore, is an interesting cognitive skill to study. To illustrate the usefulness of examples across disciplines, she points to mathematics and law. Law differs from mathematics in that it is not characterized by black-and-white concepts or rules but by competing and changing answers that are dependent on context and point of view. Law and mathematics are alike, however, in their heavy reliance on reasoning based on examples, which, in law, are cases.

Examples aid reasoning in several ways, Rissland suggests; they provide the basis for inductive generalization, serve as points of reference, and facilitate the exploration of implications. Prototypical examples can serve as templates and thus help organize domain knowledge, and counterexamples can help delimit conceptual boundaries. Counterexamples play an important role in assessing the truth value of universal assertions. We need find only one example of an A that is not B to conclude that the statement "All A are B" is false. Unfortunately, although the observation of many As that are B does not suffice to prove the truth of the assertion "All *A* are *B,*" we often ignore this constraint in our everyday thinking and happily proceed to the conclusion that all *A* are indeed *B* after seeing a few that are. We sometimes also invoke examples to demonstrate the truth of generalizations: "Dobermans are vicious dogs; my neighbor has two of them. . . ." But the fact that we misuse examples in such ways does not gainsay their value when used appropriately.

Example-based reasoning is strongly dependent on domain-specific knowledge. One can reason from examples only if one has a cache of examples in the appropriate domain from which to draw. But having appropriate examples in memory does not ensure that they will be accessed and used effectively. Rissland emphasizes the need to teach students to generate and use examples and gives two protocols of example generation, one from mathematics and one from law, to illustrate how the process may work. How to improve individuals' ability to retrieve examples when they are needed is a fundamental question for memory research.

MODELS OF INFORMAL REASONING

Commonly, a distinction is made in the literature on thinking, and especially decision making, between normative or prescriptive models, on the one hand, and descriptive models, on the other. *Normative* and *prescriptive* are typically used as synonymous terms to connote representations of correct or ideal performance; a normative or prescriptive model indicates how something should be done. A descriptive model, in contrast, shows how something is done, in fact.

Baron makes a distinction between normative and prescriptive models, reserving the term *normative* for models of what an ideal thinker (decision maker, problem solver)—one not subject to human constraints and limitations—would do, which is to say the best that can be done, theoretically, in a given situation. A *prescriptive* model, as he uses the term, indicates the best that can be done when human limitations and constraints are taken into account. According to this view, a prescriptive model is a reasonable standard for human behavior, but a normative model is not. This distinction is similar, in spirit, to Good's (1983) distinction between *Type 1* and *Type 2 Rationality,* and to Simon's (1957) distinction between *optimizing* and *satisficing.* Cherniak (1986) also distinguishes between ideal and feasible reasoning requirements. Not only is it impossible, in his view, for finite agents to realize the ideal requirements, but they do not use them when attributing beliefs to other people. In his words, we distinguish "good enough" from "perfect." It would be irrational, Cherniak holds, for a nonsuicidal creature in the "finitary predicament" even to try to satisfy the ideal conditions. It would be wasting time and resources that could be put to more productive use.

What are the human limitations and constraints that any prescriptive model of informal reasoning should take into account? Keil identifies three types: (a) limitations of human beings as information processors (e.g., capacity or memory limitations), (b) limitations of humans as reasoners (e.g., difficulties with disjunctions or mistakes with counterfactuals), and (c) knowledge limitations. The lack of domain-specific knowledge is an especially important limitation in young children's reasoning, in his view, and is evident in the course of conceptual development. Early on, children rely primarily on typical characteristic features to determine instances of natural-kind conceptual categories (e.g., lions, skunks). At some point, however, they begin to think of concepts in terms of a few critical defining features. The use of defining features presupposes a deeper knowledge than does the use of characteristic features. For this reason, Keil argues, inductive or analogical reasoning by young children is likely to differ fundamentally from the reasoning that they can engage in after they have acquired a rich knowledge of the domain.

Among the limits that characterize the human being as a reasoner, those imposed by memory have probably received the greatest emphasis. Both the limited capacity of working memory and the imperfect accessibility of the information in long-term memory are seen as significant constraints. Cherniak (1986) has noted, for example, that human beings are not aware at any given moment of all they know or believe and, therefore, may entertain conflicting beliefs without being conscious of doing so. If one never has two conflicting beliefs in working memory at the same time, one may never discover their incompatibility. To use Cherniak's language, "Part of the human condition is, in fact, to fail to 'make the connections' sometimes in a web of interconnected beliefs, to fall short of a synoptic view of one's belief system" (p. 50).

If one accepts the distinction between normative and prescriptive models, a way to arrive at a prescriptive model of informal reasoning is to start with a normative model and modify it to take account of whatever human limitations are identified. However, although there are normative models that are applicable to certain limited domains (e.g., Bayesian models of decision making under uncertainty), there is no model of what constitutes normative informal reasoning in a general sense. Moreover, experts may disagree on what is normative even in a narrow context; Good (1983) once estimated that there are more possible types of Bayesians than there are members of the American Statistical Association. (For compelling evidence of the lack of agreement as to what constitutes rational behavior, see Cohen, 1981, Kyburg, 1983, and associated commentaries.)

IDENTIFYING FALLACIES OF INFORMAL REASONING

In formal logic, a fallacy is committed when the structure of an argument violates one or more of the rules of deductive inference. The argument, "If p, then q; not p; therefore, not q," is said to be invalid because the conclusion does not follow from the premises. This is straightforward and unambiguous. In informal reasoning, things are not nearly as clear. One may search in vain for an explicit normative or prescriptive model of informal reasoning of very broad scope. Nevertheless, a sizeable literature attests to the prevalence of the belief among philosophers and psychologists that informal reasoning commonly falls short of any ideal, and lengthy lists of ways in which reasoning goes astray suggest the existence of standards, even if incomplete and only implicit, in investigators' heads. Kahane (1984) has defined fallacious reasoning as failing to satisfy one or more of three criteria: "To reason cogently, or correctly, we must: (1) reason from justified premises, (2) include all relevant information at our disposal, and (3) reason validly" (p. 47). But what does it mean for a premise to be justified; what determines the relevance of information to a problem; and what are the criteria for validity outside the domain of formal logic?

Fallaciousness in informal reasoning is sometimes a matter of opinion. Consider, for example, the "sunk-cost fallacy" described by Leland. The fallacy is illustrated with the hypothetical case of a person's having paid $40.00 for tickets to a basketball game that is to be played 60 miles from home. On the day of the game, there is a snow storm, but the ticket holder decides to go anyway, although he admits that had he been given the tickets he would have stayed home. From one point of view, this certainly can be perceived as irrational behavior. The $40.00 has been spent whether or not the ticket holder goes to the game; it is a "sunk cost." The decision of whether to go to the game or to stay at home should be made on the basis of the costs and benefits that are still within the individual's control. But is it clear that the individual's decision to attend the game because he paid for the tickets rather than obtained them free of charge must be seen as irrational? Suppose his reason for deciding to go stems from a sense of obligation to follow through on decisions that have cost money. Perhaps this is a consistently applied discipline that he intentionally uses to force himself to think twice before spending money, and he wishes not to relax it. Such a reason is more psychological than logical, but, if rationality consists in maximizing subjective expected utility, as some theorists hold, psychological costs and benefits must be part of the equation.

An analogous example is that of a person who develops tennis elbow soon after joining a tennis club but continues to play, in agony, to avoid wasting the cost of membership (Thaler, 1980). As in Leland's example, this looks like irrational behavior. But is it necessary to view it as such? Kahneman and Tversky (1984) suggest that payments are more acceptable to people than are dead losses of the same amount. By continuing to play, the individual is able to perceive the cost of membership as a payment, whereas if he were to stop playing he would see it as a loss. Given his view, perhaps his behavior makes sense; in his personal system of utilities, being able to think of an expenditure as a payment has greater value than an elbow that does not hurt.

Consider another illustration that Leland uses. In this case, an urn, A, contains 50 red chips and 50 black ones, and another urn, B, contains 100 chips in an unknown proportion of red and black. As Leland notes, when given a choice of betting either on drawing a red or on drawing a black chip, people tend to be indifferent about which color they bet on, regardless of which urn is involved. However, when they are asked whether they would rather bet on red from urn *A* or from urn *B*, they generally prefer urn *A*. Similarly, when asked whether they would prefer to bet on black from *A* or *B*, they again typically prefer *A*. Here, the claim is that having these two preferences simultaneously is irrational. The argument is that if, when betting on red, they prefer urn *A* over urn *B*, they are implying that they believe the probability of drawing a red from urn B is less than .5. Similarly, if, when betting on black, they also prefer urn *A* over urn *B*, they imply the belief that the likelihood of drawing a black from urn *B* is also less than .5. These two beliefs are inconsistent with the general principle that the sum of the probabilities of mutually exclusive and exhaustive events must be 1.

But is it necessary to view the preference for urn *A* as irrational? In the better's mind, a difference between urns *A* and *B* lies in the fact that he knows something about *A* that he does not know about *B*, namely, the proportion of the red to black chips. When given the option, he may prefer to go with *A* because he knows the likelihood of drawing the named color is .5 rather than to go with *B* because the likelihood is unknown and could be anything from 0 to 1. In the absence of any information to the contrary, the default assumption regarding the contents of urn *B* should be the maximum-uncertainty assumption of equal proportions of red and black chips, but this would be an assumption. In the case of urn *A*, it is a given. The difference between these two situations is recognized by some decision theorists, but its implications for decision theory are a matter of debate (Einhorn & Hogarth, 1985; Ellsberg, 1961; Frisch & Baron, 1988).

The point is that determining what constitutes a fallacy of informal reasoning may be somewhat less straightforward than if often appears. Many of the forms of informal reasoning that have been described as fallacious are fallacious only in specific contexts or from specific points of view. In other contexts, or from other perspectives, they may be quite functional. This is not to suggest that there is no such thing as fallacious or improper informal reasoning; my point is simply that determining whether a given instance of informal reasoning is faulty may be more difficult than is sometimes assumed.

IDENTIFYING PRINCIPLES OF
GOOD REASONING

Confusion or controversy about what constitutes faulty informal reasoning suggests the need for a prescriptive model that can serve as a standard against which instances of reasoning can be judged. But it also points up the fact that, to date, no generally acceptable model that meets this need has been developed. Perhaps the most one can hope to do, at the present, is to identify principles of good reasoning that one is willing to defend, on whatever grounds, as standards worthy of use for the purposes of setting educational objectives and evaluating instructional results. Are there certain principles that, if stated, would be acknowledged more or less universally to be appropriate to govern informal reasoning?

Nisbett, Krantz, Jepson, and Kunda (1983) see inductive reasoning as involving concept formation, generalization from instances, and prediction and argue that induction should satisfy certain statistical principles:

> Concepts should be discerned and applied with more confidence when they apply to a narrow range of clearly defined objects than when they apply to a broad range of diverse and loosely defined objects that can be confused with objects to which the concept does not apply. Generalizations should be more confident when they are based on a larger number of instances, when the instances are an unbiased sample, and when the instances in question concern events of low variability rather than high variability. Predictions should be more confident when there is high correlation between the dimensions for which information is available and the dimensions about which the prediction is made, and, failing such a correlation, prediction should rely on a base rate or prior distribution for the events to be predicted. (p. 339)

Note that, unlike the case with deductive inference, in which one tends to think in terms of arguments being either valid or invalid, these criteria are all matters of degree. One should, according to his view, have more or less confidence in one's classifications, generalizations, or predictions, depending on specified considerations.

If there are universally recognized principles of good thinking, consistency seems like a prime candidate. Children are quick to detect contradictions in arguments that their parents make on issues that matter to them and may protest bitterly about unfairness, with phrases like "But yesterday you said . . . ," without referring explicitly to inconsistency or contradiction. Among people who have acquired these concepts, I suspect most would agree that one should not knowingly hold mutually contradictory beliefs at the same time and that one should not apply one standard of truth to assertions one wishes to believe and another to assertions one prefers not to believe. Most would view the tendency to contradict oneself as justification for not taking one's statements very seriously. It is generally considered unfair to demand a standard of conduct of others that one is not willing to apply to oneself. Similarly, we tend not to hold in high esteem individuals who adjust their standards of conduct from time to time for purposes of convenience.

But the consistency principle, intuitively compelling as it is, is not as straightforward as it may seem. First, it must be recognized that consistency can have many referents: internal consistency among beliefs, consistency of beliefs with evidence, consistency between beliefs and actions, and consistency in the application of standards. This detail aside, the distinction between normative and prescriptive models prompts the question, "How consistent is it reasonable to strive to be?". Harman (1986) discusses this question at length. In particular, he considers how beliefs should be revised in the interest of consistency. According to one of the views he considers (the foundations theory), reasoned revision of beliefs requires either subtracting from one's beliefs any that are not justified (except certain foundational beliefs, from which all other beliefs are derived) or adding new beliefs that are justified by other beliefs or are themselves foundational. According to another view (the coherence theory), an existing belief does not require justification unless one has a special reason to doubt it; the fact that one may not be able to remember the reasons for appropriating a certain belief in the first place is not justifiable grounds for discarding that belief. Revising beliefs, in this case, means changing them minimally, in the interest of resolving conflicts that have come to light, or increasing overall coherence. Harman subscribes to the coherence theory as the normatively correct one (prescriptively correct, in Baron's sense) and dismisses the foundations theory on the grounds that it requires one to keep track of the original reasons for one's beliefs, which is more than mere mortals can do. The foundations theory places a considerably greater cognitive burden on the individual than does the coherence theory: The former requires that one be prepared to justify any of one's beliefs at any time; the latter requires only that one be prepared to justify changes in existing beliefs, not the beliefs themselves.

Assuming that consistency, on some interpretation, is a necessary condition for good thinking, is it a sufficient one? Baron defends an activist view of good thinking, according to which impartiality or fairness in the treatment of evidence on any particular issue, which is a form of consistency, is only one term in the equation. The other is active and thorough search for evidence. I like this characterization and have encoded it as *active fair-mindedness*. This means actively seeking evidence that runs counter to a claim before accepting that claim as true; it means being careful to give special attention to evidence that weighs against conclusions one would especially like to draw; it means trying hard to see situations from other people's points of view; it means actively putting hypotheses, particularly favored hypotheses, to the falsifiability test. In short, it means going out of one's way to guard against the development and maintenance of biased views.

REASONING PRODUCTS AND
REASONING PROCESS

Williams notes that there may be a difference between thinking well and seeming to think well, but that this difference can be obscured because the quality of one's thinking is often judged by its observable effects. Focusing, in particular, on written discourse, he rejects the conventional wisdom that the ability to write well and the ability to think well are one and the same, and he argues that we have to learn to tell the difference if we are to use instruction in writing as a means of enhancing reasoning. When students show improvement in their writing after training, it is difficult to tell whether they are actually thinking better or only expressing their thinking more effectively. The problem of distinguishing between competence in thinking and competence in the use of language is compounded, in Williams's view, because one's written representation of an argument is likely to depend on what one assumes about the intended audience and its familiarity with the issue and knows of the rhetorical conventions of the community of discourse that is involved.

The importance of the distinction between process and product pertains not only to writing but also to other vehicles for representing the results of thinking, such as mathematical theorems, works of art, and scientific laws. The final product of the mathematician, the artist, or the scientist may reveal very little of the thinking that went into its development and refinement. Moreover, especially when the product is a highly formal structure such as a theorem or a theory, its polished form provides few clues to the complex, messy, undescribable thinking process that produced it. The product shows us only where one arrived; it does not give us a map of the path one took to get there.

Polya (1965) called attention to the fact that mathematics textbooks obscure the psychology of mathematics because they typically present only finished proofs and seldom reveal the mathematician at work trying to develop them for the first time. Historians of science and students of scientific thinking (e.g. Holton, 1973; Kuhn, 1970; Tweney, 1985) have documented the essential role of informal reasoning in science, including analogical reasoning, the following of hunches, and trial-and-error exploration. Its role is not usually documented very usefully in textbook presentations of scientific theories.

More generally, a major difficulty associated with the study of reasoning processes is that of determining the bases on which conclusions are drawn. It has been claimed that what appears to be illogical reasoning often can be attributed to misinterpretation or transformation of one or more of the premises of an argument (Henle, 1962). If the conclusion follows from the premises, as interpreted or as transformed by the reasoner, the reasoning should be considered sound, according to this view, and the problem viewed as one of language usage. The complementary position has also been taken that what appears to be sound deductive reasoning may, in fact, be the result of appeal to knowledge derived from experience, rather than a consequence of drawing an inference from premises. Or, it could be the consequence of consultation of a mental model, schema, or other means of representing a situation (Cheng & Holyoak, 1985; Evans, 1982; Johnson-Laird, 1983). The idea that what may pass as effective use of rules of inference to arrive at correct answers to reasoning problems really results from use of memory of problem-related experiences has also been gaining some support (Griggs & Cox, 1982; Manktelow & Evans, 1979; Reich & Ruth, 1982). In short, it has been claimed, on the one hand, that people sometimes draw the wrong conclusions in spite of reasoning logically, and, on the other, that they sometimes draw the right conclusions without reasoning, in the conventional sense, at all. Of course, these are not mutually exclusive possibilities; both claims could be true.

EVIDENCE WEIGHING VERSUS CASE BUILDING

The word *argument* has an interesting ambiguity. In logic, it means reasoned justification of some claim, a sequence of assertions that leads, by implication, to a conclusion. In common parlance, it means a verbal dispute, a fight. As noted earlier, in the former case the goal is to make sure the conclusion that is drawn is really implied by the assertions that are given in its support; in the latter case, the goal is to win.

Stein and Miller see the philosophical and disputative forms of argument as conceptual abstractions that are not adequately descriptive of the kinds of arguments that commonly occur in the real world. The more typical form of argument, which they refer to as the interactive form, has aspects of both categories, in their view. An interactive argument, like a dispute, is based on a disagreement, and the goal of each party is to win. However, admissable methods for winning are constrained by certain rhetorical conventions and rules of evidence. As in the case of philosophical arguments, evidence is offered in support of claims, and counterevidence is advanced in opposition to them; but the unfolding of an interactive argument is driven by the conflict between the arguers, who are motivated to arrive at different conclusions. Stein and Miller see interactive argument as serving the two basic functions of facilitating social interaction by allowing people "to negotiate, to resolve differences, and to generate codes that regulate the conditions under which actions and beliefs can be maintained" and of facilitating learning by forcing the participants to acquire new information about the topic of the conflict.

I think Stein and Miller's point, that the interactive arguments that one typically encounters or engages in in the day-to-day world have some aspects in common both with arguments in the philosophical sense and with disputes, is well taken. My own impression, however, is that the correspondence with disputes is the greater and that the motivation to win tends to be considerably stronger than any sense of obligation to abide by the rhetorical rules. This is not to deny a desire to maintain the appearance of logicality and fair-mindedness, and perhaps even a preference for winning on the basis of sound reasoning, when that is possible, but it is to suggest that winning is paramount, and other considerations are, usually, given less importance.

Stein and Miller remind us that children as young as 4 or 5 years of age understand what an argument is in the disputative sense. They know, in particular, that it consists of asserting and defending a point of view and that the goal is to get the best of one's opponent. Methods for realizing this goal may include name-calling, verbal threats, appeals to higher authorities, and physical force. One suspects that children are not greatly different from adults in this regard. The 19th-century German philosopher, Arthur Schopenhauer, wrote an essay called *The Art of Controversy* in which he identified numerous strategems for winning arguments without necessarily speaking to the point. These include pretending one's opponent has made a more general assertion that he really has and attacking that assertion (putting words in one's opponent's mouth); claiming that a conclusion one wishes to draw follows from assertions to which one's opponent has already agreed; and diverting attention from the main point of the dispute when one's opponent is getting the upper hand. The individual who has an extensive repertoire of such strategems and is able to use them cleverly will undoubtedly "win" many arguments in the sense of putting his opponent down. The skill of winning arguments by devious means is presumably not what proponents of the teaching of thinking have in mind as an objective, which is not to suggest that the effective use of dispute-winning strategems requires no thinking.

In my view, few distinctions related to reasoning are more important than the distinction between engaging in disputes with the goal of winning and engaging in constructive dialogue with the hope of converging on a consensus supported by evidence and sound reasoning. It is a distinction that should be taught explicitly to children, and one that all of us need to be reminded of frequently. Closely related is the distinction between figuring out what to believe and defending an existing belief. This is essentially the distinction between evaluating evidence and building a case. The goal in evaluating evidence is to arrive at conclusions that are supported by the weight of the evidence, in its entirety. When one builds a case, one begins with a conclusion and looks for evidence to support it. Case building involves the selective use of evidence and, in particular, the discounting of evidence that counts against the conclusion one wishes to draw. In a court of law, attorneys are expected to build cases. The lawyer for the prosecution tries to build a case for a guilty verdict; the defense attorney tries to justify acquittal. It is up to the judge or jury to weigh the evidence presented and to bring a verdict that takes all of it into account.

It is important to understand the difference between weighing evidence impartially and building a case. It is not that one of these activities is intellectually demanding, whereas the other is not. Case building requires thinking, as does evidence weighing; the more knowledgeable and clever the case builder, the more persuasive the resulting case is likely to be. The critical difference between these activities is the objective. Evidence weighing is aimed at getting at the truth; case building is done to make some claim plausible, whether it is true or not. Unlike evidence weighing, case building requires that information be used in biased ways. Perhaps the greatest challenge to teachers of reasoning is to give students the ability to distinguish between evidence weighing and case building in their own behavior. I suspect that all of us find it very easy to believe that we are doing the former, when, in fact, we are doing the latter, and this form of self-deception is more than a little responsible for a great many interpersonal and international difficulties, both petty and profound.

BELIEFS, GOALS, ATTITUDES AND AFFECTIVE FACTORS IN REASONING

Baron emphasizes the importance of beliefs and, in particular, beliefs *about* thinking as determinants of the quality of thinking. He gives examples of beliefs about thinking that would, in his view, work against some of the natural biases that occur (e.g., that thinking often leads to better results; that good thinkers are open to evidence against favored hypotheses) and examples of others that would tend to support them (e.g. that changing one's mind is a sign of weakness; that being open leads to confusion). Stein and Miller note that beliefs about social norms can influence the positions people take in arguments and how they support them, and they illustrate the point in a developmental context by showing that young children (2nd graders) are more likely than adults to consider promises to be unconditional and binding, independently of the continuing tenability of the assumptions that motivated them.

Like beliefs, goals, in Baron's (1985) view, have a lot to do with the quality of one's thinking; good thinking may be fostered by:

> . . . the goal of thinking well (as something one can take pride in); the goal of knowing the truth, of getting to the bottom of things; the goal of making good decisions; the goal of being reasonable in the sense of being likable for one's openmindedness and receptivity to the suggestions of others; and the goal of being moral or doing the right thing (since it often requires good thinking to decide what the right thing is); the goal of being a good citizen; or the goal of thinking for its own sake, as something that is enjoyable as an activity (socially or alone) (p. 256).

On the other side of the coin are goals that work against good thinking, such as "the goal of being steadfast (in sticking to one's conclusions despite counter evidence); the goal of reaching conclusions quickly; the goal of being authoritative (powerful in some sense) and the goal of honoring authority (despite counterevidence)" (p. 256). These seem to me to be points that deserve considerable emphasis. In general, I believe that volitional, attitudinal, and affective variables play more significant roles in determining the quality of thinking than is usually realized. Some types of thinking are very effortful—hard work, one might say; some are rough on the ego. In neither case are they pursued in the absence of relatively strong motivation. Although wanting to think well surely does not guarantee that one will do so, having no desire to do so probably does guarantee that one will not.

Many of the reasoning fallacies that have been identified in descriptive accounts of informal reasoning (Kahane, 1984; Nickerson, 1986; Ruggiero, 1984) can be seen to have attitudinal or volitional bases. Several common reasoning difficulties, for example, involve partiality in the use of evidence (one form of inconsistency). Most of us find it easy to give more weight to evidence that agrees with a favored opinion than we give to evidence that tells against it, easier to seek information that will support existing views than to seek information that will oppose them, and easier to build cases than to weigh evidence fairly. We seek and use information in biased ways because we are vested in existing views and wish to defend and strengthen them, not to put them to hard tests. When engaged in a verbal dispute, our goal is not to converge with our opponent on a conclusion we can both accept because it is supported by the weight of evidence when viewed objectively, but to put our own position in the most favorable light.

Applying such a principle as active fair-mindedness is surely, in part, a cognitive affair. One must know what it means and be aware of the many ways—some quite subtle—of violating it. But applying it is just as surely a matter of attitudes and intent. As the title of this book indicates, a primary impetus to its production was an interest in the possibility of improving informal reasoning through education. A major challenge facing educators and anyone else concerned with the issue is not only to teach young people how to reason well but to cultivate the desire and intention to do so.

REFERENCES

Baron, J. (1985). *Rationality and intelligence.* New York: Cambridge University Press.

Boden, M. (1977). *Artificial intelligence and natural man.* New York: Basic Books.

Bronowski, J. (1965). *Science and human values.* New York: Harper & Row.

Cheng, P. W., & Holyoak, K. J. (1985). Pragmatic reasoning schemas. *Cognitive Psychology, 17,* 391–416.

Cherniak, C. (1986). *Minimal rationality.* Cambridge, MA: MIT Press.

Cohen, L. J. (1981). Can human rationality be experimentally demonstrated? *Behavioral and Brain Sciences, 4,* 319–370.

Einhorn, H. J., & Hogarth, R. M. (1985). Ambiguity and uncertainty in probabilistic inference. *Psychological Review, 92,* 433–461.

Ellsberg, D. (1961). Risk, ambiguity, and the Savage axioms. *Quarterly Journal of Economics, 75,* 643–669.

Evans, J. St. B. T. (1982). *The psychology of deductive reasoning.* London: Routledge & Kegan Paul.

Frisch, D., & Baron, J. (1988). Ambiguity and uncertainty. *Journal of Behavioral Decision Making, 1,* 149–157.

Gentner, D., & Grudin, J. (1985). The evolution of mental metaphors in psychology: A ninety-year retrospective. *American Psychologist, 40,* 181–192.

Good, I. J. (1983). *Good thinking.* Minneapolis, MN: University of Minnesota Press.

Griggs, R. A., & Cox, J. R. (1982). The elusive thematic-materials effect in Wason's selection task. *British Journal of Psychology, 73,* 407–420.

Hadamard, J. (1945). *The psychology of invention in the mathematical field*. Princeton, NJ: Princeton University Press.

Harman, G. (1986). *Change in view: Principles of reasoning*. Cambridge, MA: MIT Press.

Henle, M. (1962). On the relation between logic and thinking. *Psychological Review, 69*, 366–378.

Holton, G. (1973). *Thematic origins of scientific thought*. Cambridge, MA: Harvard University Press.

Johnson-Laird, P. N. (1983). *Mental models*. Cambridge, MA: Harvard University Press.

Kahane, H. (1984). *Logic and contemporary rhetoric: The use of reason in everyday life* (4th ed.). Belmont, CA: Woodsworth.

Kahneman, D., & Tversky, A. (1984). Choices, values, and frames. *American Psychologist, 394*, 341–350.

Kuhn, T. S. (1970). *The structure of scientific revolutions* (2nd ed.). Chicago, IL: University of Chicago Press.

Kyburg, H. E., Jr. (1983). Rational belief. *The Behavioral and Brain Sciences, 6*, 231–273.

Manktelow, K. I., & Evans, J. St. B. T. (1979). Facilitation of reasoning by realism: Effect or non-effect? *British Journal of Psychology, 70*, 477–488.

Nickerson, R. S. (1986). *Reflections on reasoning*. Hillsdale, NJ: Lawrence Erlbaum Associates.

Nisbett, R. E., Krantz, D. H., Jepson, C., & Kunda, Z. (1983). The use of statistical heuristics in everyday inductive reasoning. *Psychological Review, 90*(4), 339–363.

Polya, G. (1965). *Mathematical discovery: On understanding, learning and teaching problem solving. Vol. II*. New York: Wiley.

Reich, S. S., & Ruth, P. (1982). Wason's selection task: Verification, falsification and matching. *British Journal of Psychology, 73*, 407–420.

Ruggiero, V. R. (1984). *The art of thinking: A guide to critical and creative thought*. New York: Harper & Row.

Schopenhauer, A. (undated). The art of controversy. In *The essays of Arthur Schopenhauer* (J. B. Saunders, trans.). New York: Wiley.

Simon, H. A. (1957). *Models of man: Social and rational*. New York: Wiley.

Thaler, R. (1980). Toward a positive theory of consumer choice. *Journal of Economic Behavior and Organization, 1*, 39–60.

Tweney, R. D. (1985). Faraday's discovery of induction: A cognitive approach. In D. Gooding & F. A. J. L. James (Eds.), *Faraday rediscovered: Essays on the life and work of Michael Faraday, 1791–1867*. New York: Stockton Press.

III INFORMAL REASONING AND INSTRUCTION

16

On Mathematics as Sense-Making: An Informal Attack On the Unfortunate Divorce of Formal and Informal Mathematics

Alan H. Schoenfeld
The University of California—Berkeley

This chapter explores the ways that mathematics is understood and used in our culture and the role that schooling plays in shaping those mathematical understandings. One of its goals is to blur the boundaries between formal and informal mathematics: to indicate that, in real mathematical thinking, formal and informal reasoning are deeply intertwined. I begin, however, by briefly putting on the formalist's hat and defining formal reasoning. As any formalist will tell you, it helps to know what the boundaries are before you try to blur them.

PROLOGUE: ON THE LIMITS AND PURITY OF FORMAL REASONING QUA FORMAL REASONING

To get to the heart of the matter, formal systems do not denote; that is, formal systems in mathematics are not *about* anything. Formal systems consist of sets of symbols and rules for manipulating them. As long as you play by the rules, the results are valid *within the system*. But if you try to apply these systems to something from the real world (or something else), you no longer engage in formal reasoning. You are applying the mathematics at that point. Caveat emptor: the end result is only as good as the application process.

Perhaps the clearest example is geometry. Insofar as most people are concerned, the plane or solid (Euclidean) geometry studied in secondary school provides a mathematical description of the world they live in and of the way the world must be. For example, it appears patently clear that there is always one and only one line through any given point that is parallel to a given line, that parallels never intersect, and that the sum of the angles of a triangle is always 180 degrees. It appears so clear, in fact, that for 2,000 years the world's finest mathematicians tried to prove these results. The most intensively explored problem in the history of mathematics was the attempt to show that Euclid's parallel postulate was a logical consequence of the other Euclidean axioms. Yet, as we know, that is not the only possibility. There are other perfectly consistent geometries in which there are either infinitely many parallel lines to a given line through a given point or none at all. And in these geometries, the measures of the angles of a triangle do not add up to 180 degrees. Such non-Euclidean geometries are not simply mathematical curiosities, bearing no relation to reality. The various geometries are, in fact, differentially useful for characterizing different aspects of our physical world. Euclidean geometry serves perfectly well for building bookshelves or laying out a garden on a flat piece of land, but it does not work, for example, for astrophysics; on a celestial scale, space is curved, and non-Euclidean geometries are more useful. That is, neither Euclidean nor non-Euclidean geometry is right or wrong. Both are logically consistent, and it just happens that each seems to fit certain circumstances better than the other.

In the use of any formal mathematical system, the mathematics is valid if it is internally consistent; its applications to the real world, however, are something else altogether. In a statistical model, for example, if the conditions of an experiment fail to match the assumptions of the statistical tests that are used to analyze the data, then, regardless of the correctness of the statistical manipulations used to analyze the data, the statistical analysis is invalid. Or in formal logic, consider the following syllogism, offered by Ray Nickerson (chapter 15, this volume):

> Nothing is better than eternal happiness.
> *A ham sandwich is better than nothing.*
> ∴. A ham sandwich is better than eternal happiness.

This reductio ad absurdum shows that the mere use of formally correct syllogistic reasoning is no guarantee of the validity of the conclusion. The whole of the reasoning process is no better than any of its parts, which include the appropriateness of the syllogistic form in the first place and the accurateness of the translation of the argument into syllogistic form.

In general, the quality of reasoning using formal systems depends on the quality of the maps from the situation being explored to the formal system, on the correctness of the reasoning within the formal system, and on the interpretation of results in the formal system that is transferred to the situation being analyzed (see Fig. 16.1). All of these must be valid for the reasoning using formal systems to be valid. The mere use (or abuse) of formal systems as one component of the reasoning process guarantees nothing about correctness, just as the mere trappings of the scientific method (i.e., scientism rather than science) guarantee nothing about the scientific correctness of a piece of research.

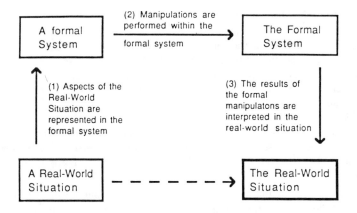

Steps 1, 2, and 3 combined yield an analysis of the real-world situation.
Note that the quality of the analysis depends on the mappings to and from
the formal system. If either one of those mappings is flawed, the
analysis is not valid.

FIG. 16.1. Using formal systems to interpret real-world situations.

Following are a series of vignettes that illustrate our culture's general (mis)understanding of the role and uses of mathematics. I then speculate, in Essay 1, on why these misconceptions are fostered by certain common teaching practices in the typical classroom setting. In a second set of vignettes, I describe some cases of successful classroom instruction, and, in concluding Essay 2, surmise why these approaches work and how they suggest lines of investigation in developing more effective mathematics learning.

FOUR VIGNETTES ON THE MAKINGS OF
MATHEMATICAL NONSENSE

Vignette 1: On the Authoritarian/Totalitarian Nature
and Uses of Mathematical Formalism, or Formalismus
Uber Alles

Like many rulers of great nations, Catherine the Great amused herself by inviting people of intellectual stature to visit her court. Among those who visited Catherine's court was Denis Diderot, French philosopher and author of the famed *Encyclopedia*. E. T. Bell (1937) described the visit:

> Much to her dismay, Diderot earned his keep by trying to convert the courtiers to atheism. Fed up, Catherine commissioned [the great mathematician Leonhard] Euler to muzzle the windy philosopher. This was easy because all mathematics was Chinese [!] to Diderot. (p. 146)

Quoting from De Morgan's *Budget of Paradoxes,* Bell continued:

> Diderot was informed that a learned mathematician was in possession of an al-
> gebraical demonstration of the existence of God, and would give it before all the
> Court, if he desired to hear it. Diderot gladly consented . . .
>   Euler advanced toward Diderot, and said gravely, and in a tone of perfect
> conviction:
>   "Sir, $(a + b^n)/n = x$, hence God exists; reply!"
>   It sounded like sense to Diderot. Humiliated by the unrestrained laughter which
> greeted his embarrassed silence, the poor man asked Catherine's permission to
> return at once to France. She graciously gave it. (pp. 146–147)

Commentary.   Mathematics is a weapon of great potential power. For those who
understand the mathematics, of course, Euler's assertion is laughable. For those
who believe that mathematics is coherent and bound by logic, Euler's pronounce-
ment is an assertion to be questioned (and probably to be found laughable). But
for those who believe mathematics to be a mystical domain—a source of incontrovertible wisdom that is accessible only to a few geniuses—mathematics
can be a battering ram that knocks them senseless.

Vignette 2: Euler Comes to Madison Avenue, or With Mathematics You Can Fool Most of the People Most of the Time

Picture a typical American woman seated at an interview table. She has a miserable headache, her head is pounding, and she is in desperate need of relief.
(During the 1960s and 1970s, this woman appeared thousands of times on
millions of TV screens.) In front of her are three boxes, each of which contains a
pain-killing medicine. Her interlocutor, an authoritative man, asks which medicine will be best. She lifts the first box, reads the label, and says "650 milligrams." She lifts the second box, reads the label, and says "650 milligrams."
She lifts the third box, reads the label, and says "800 milligrams. Wow, that's
strong. I'll take that one." Minutes later her headache is gone, and we have all
learned that Extra Strength Brandname is the powerful powerful medicine you
should take when you have a *real* headache.

    What's wrong with this commercial? Nothing, until you look at the price of
Extra Strength Brandname: The 800 milligrams of extra strength tablets (two 400
mg tablets) cost more than double the 650 milligrams of ordinary tablets (two
325 mg. tablets of the same medicine). Instead of taking the 800 milligrams of
extra strength painkiller, any thinking person could take three of the ordinary
tablets (975 milligrams) and get more painkiller for less money.

Commentary.   Here, as in Vignette 1, mathematics is used as a weapon with the
presumption that, simple as they are, the mathematical assertions in the adver-

tisement are sufficiently intimidating that people will question no further. The ad campaign for Extra Strength Brandname was one of the longest running and most successful in American television history. It could only be successful if people abdicated responsibility for thinking, took the ad's assertions at face value, and did not try to make sense of the situation being described.

I must add that such abuse of mathematics is hardly limited to the packaging of objects. It is used, with comparable effectiveness, for the packaging of political candidates. Overspending and the budget deficit were major issues in the 1980 presidential race. Facts and figures were thrown around in "white papers," but the whole matter came to a head in the debates themselves. The Republican candidate, communicating at his best, responded to a budget question with something like this: Now the economists tell me it works like this. There's a line that goes like this (moves his arm in an upward direction, from left to right) and another line that goes like this (moves his arm in a downward direction, from left to right). When those two lines cross, we'll have a balanced budget.

That put the matter to rest. This completely meaningless assertion was not followed up with probing questions, either during the debate or in the media after the debate. Unmitigated mathematical gobbledygook went unquestioned, and America bought the product. (I bought pain reliever.)

Here, as in Euler's humiliation of Diderot, is another example of the totalitarian power of mathematics. Throw enough formalism or appeal to mathematical authority in front of people, and they will back down. For some reason, people do not expect heavily mathematical statements to make sense to them. They assume that they make sense to somebody (the experts), abdicate responsibility for understanding, and usually accept the statements at face value.

Vignette 3: On the Stultifying Nature of Formal Instruction qua Formal Instruction, or Formal Operations versus Common Sense

In his dissertation research, Kurt Reusser (1986) asked 97 first- and second-grade students the following question: *"There are 26 sheep and 10 goats on a ship. How old is the captain?"* (p. 36). Seventy-six of the 97 students "solved" the problem, providing a numerical answer obtained by adding 26 and 10.

He obtained similar results with the following problem: *"There are 125 sheep and 5 dogs in a flock. How old is the shepherd?"* (p. 38). Reusser made recordings of students working this problem out loud. One of his recordings, which he claimed was typical, was transcribed as follows: "125 + 5 = 130, this is too big . . . and 125 − 5 = 120, this is still too big . . . while 125/5 = 25, that works. I think the shepherd is 25 years old" (p. 38).

Reusser gave a more complicated problem to 101 fourth and fifth graders: *"Yesterday 33 boats sailed into port and 54 boats left it. Yesterday at noon there were 40 boats still in the port. How many boats were still in the port yesterday evening?*" (p. 42). Of those 101 students, 100 produced a numerical solution to the problem; only one complained that the task was ill-defined and unsolvable. The students were prompted to reconsider their answers. After the prompting, only 28 of the students said they doubted the correctness of their solution, and only 5 called the problem formulation into question in any way (e.g., said, "this problem is difficult" or "strange").

Commentary.   If you insist that problem statements make sense—that is, that the situations described in word problems must be reasonable and that the answers you obtain must be derivable from the given information—then you must reject Reusser's problems out of hand. The students he interviewed not only failed to note the meaninglessness of the problem statements but went ahead blithely to combine the numbers in the problem statements and produce answers. They could only do so by engaging in what might be called *suspension of sense-making*—suspending the requirement that the problem statements make sense.

It is important to realize that the suspension of sense-making documented by Reusser is anything but anomalous. It is, rather, an all-too-frequent occurrence. The best documented case in point comes from the third National Assessment of Educational Progress (NAEP). The NAEP bussing problem (see Carpenter, Lindquist, Matthews & Silver, 1983) has already achieved folklore status. It reads as follows: "An army bus holds 36 soldiers. If 1128 soldiers are being bussed to their training site, how many buses are needed?" (p. 656).

Roughly 70% of the stratified nationwide sample of students who worked the problem on the exam successfully performed the appropriate arithmetical operation. They divided 36 into 1,128, obtaining a quotient of 31 and a remainder of 12. However, fewer than a third of those students (23% of the total) went on to deduce that the number of buses required is 32. More than a third (29% of the total) said that the number of buses needed is "31 remainder 12," with the rest of those performing the division correctly (18% of the total) saying that the answer is 31. Here, as in Reusser's examples, the students gave an answer that simply does not make sense if you take the problem statement seriously. (If the students were ordering buses to take their school on a picnic, they certainly would not ask for 31 remainder 12 buses.)

Kilpatrick (1987) reported similar phenomena:

> Recently, some [German] children from kindergarten to grade 6 were confronted with "problems" in which no question was posed:
> Mr. Lorenz and 3 colleagues started at Bielefeld at 9am and drove the 360 km to Frankfurt, with a rest stop of 30 minutes.
> These stories were inserted into a set of ordinary word problems. The higher the grade level, the more likely the children were to attempt a calculation to solve the problems. (p. 140)

There is reason to believe that such suspension of sense-making develops in school, as a result of schooling. The origins of such behavior is explored at length in Essay 1.

Vignette 4: When Proof Means Nothing or Less, or Deductio ad Absurdum

A few years ago, I gave a talk at the Undergraduate Cognitive Science Society at the University of Rochester. Fifteen upper-division students, among the best and brightest at the university, were in attendance. Each had put together his or her own interdisciplinary major, most frequently including extensive coursework in computer science and psychology. All of the students had strong science and mathematics backgrounds.

To generate the context for a discussion of high school students' understanding of geometry, I gave the students a proof problem to solve. The problem, present-ed in Fig. 16.2, was written on the chalkboard. Without hesitation, the students produced a complete and correct solution to the problem. They dictated the answer, and I wrote the proof on the board. The whole process took less than 3 minutes from start to finish.

I then posed the construction problem that appears in Fig. 16.3. Of course, the proof problem the students had just solved provides the solution to the construc-tion problem.[1] I expected the students to be amused. Then I would show these students how high school students failed to see the connection between the proof and construction problems.

After writing the problem on the board, I turned to the group and asked, "All right, how do we do the construction?" Almost immediately one student said, "The bottom point of tangency—call it Q—is obviously the same distance from V as the point P. I bet that PQ is the diameter of the circle. So bisect PQ and use the midpoint as the center" (Fig. 16.4a). A second student objected. "No," he said, "if you sketch the circle in, it looks like the center of the circle should be further to the left. I bet you should use the arc through P and then get its midpoint by using the angle bisector" (Fig. 16.4b). A third student demurred. "You've forgotten that the radius has to be perpendicular at P. I bet that the part of the perpendicular between the two lines is the diameter of the circle. Bisect that and you'll get the center" (Fig. 16.4c). A fourth student, who graduated at the top of the class and was to go on to graduate school with a full fellowship, suggested the

---

[1]The proof applies to *all* diagrams like the one in Fig. 16.2, where a circle is tangent to two lines at points denoted P and Q, respectively. In any such diagram, the center of the circle lies on the perpendiculars to P and Q, and the line segment CV bisects angle PVQ. Hence, in the construction problem, the center of the circle lies at the point of intersection of the perpendicular to P and the bisector of angle PVQ.

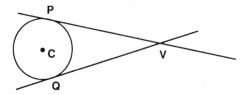

The circle in the figure above is tangent to the two given lines at the point P and Q. Prove the following:

1. The line segments PV and QV are the same length.

2. The line segment CV bisects angle PVQ.

FIG. 16.2.   A proof problem.

correct solution (Fig. 16.4d). Somewhat amused at his fellow students, he did not take part in the following discussion. The remaining students argued for more than 10 minutes, on purely empirical grounds and without reaching a consensus, about which of the four suggested constructions might be right. During their whole discussion, the proof they had generated (which rules out the first three conjectures and provides the solution) was on the blackboard in front of them.

Commentary.   There are two strong parallels to the work described in Vignette 3. First, we see a similar suspension of sense-making. The proof problem applies to all diagrams like the one in Fig. 16.2. How could the students fail to see that it applies to the construction problem? Second, the phenomenon just described is every bit as robust as the phenomena reported in Vignette 3. I was surprised to see it emerge with such talented and advanced students, but there is ample

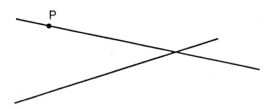

You are given two intersecting straight lines and a point P marked on one of them. Show how to construct, using straightedge and compass, a circle that is tangent to both lines and that has the point P as the point of tangency to the top line.

FIG. 16.3.   A construction problem.

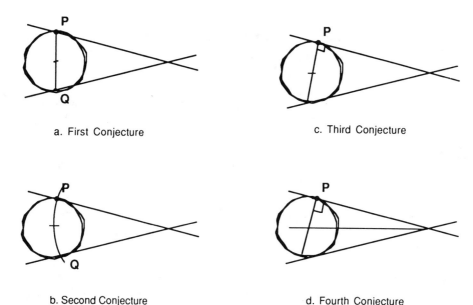

a. First Conjecture

c. Third Conjecture

b. Second Conjecture

d. Fourth Conjecture

FIG. 16.4.   The students' conjectures.

documentation (Schoenfeld, 1985 [esp. chapters 5 and 10], 1986, 1988) that high school and college students see very little connection between the world of deductive Euclidean geometry and closely related construction problems that they are asked to solve. More than 200 students (all of whom completed a year's study of Euclidean geometry) have been interviewed working problems like those in Figs. 16.2 and 16.3. When given the construction problem before the proof problem, roughly 67% made the conjecture shown in Fig. 16.4a. They performed the construction and accepted or rejected it based on how good it looked; if they rejected it, they made other conjectures and tested them empirically, until they either gave up or found a construction that worked. For the vast majority of students (all but three, in fact), the standard for acceptance or rejection was purely empirical: A construction was correct if, when performed, it met suitable empirical standards. When given the proof problem before the construction problem, most students saw the connection between the two. They made their conjecture based on the solution suggested by the proof problem but were not always confident that it would work and usually relied on empirical testing to confirm its correctness. Even so, about 30% of the students who provided a correct solution to the proof problem went on, like the students described earlier, to make a conjecture that contradicted what they had just proven.

ESSAY 1: SPECULATIONS ON THE SCHOLASTIC/CULTURAL ORIGINS OF NONSENSE IN PEOPLE'S MATHEMATICAL BEHAVIOR

Although there are significant differences among the scenes sketched in Vignettes 1 through 4, there is also an extraordinary homogeneity among them. Mathematics is accorded high status in our culture, and those who master it, or use it as a weapon, are accorded status and power. That mathematics is seen as the apotheosis of reason is the source of its power and the justification for the huge amount of mathematics instruction in the schools. Yet, at the same time, the result of schooling in mathematics seems to defy the intended goals. In Vignettes 3 and 4, there is evidence of significant nonreason in students' school mathematics behavior, of a divorce between the tools of reason and situations to which that reason can be applied. Vignettes 1 and 2 illustrate this nonreason in extremis: Those who have come to believe that mathematical sense making is not to be theirs can be the victims of mathematical puffery and nonsense.

This essay offers some speculations regarding the origins of such mathematical nonsense. Of course, there are multiple explanations for all of the behavior illustrated in Vignettes 1 through 4. From the time of the Greeks, mathematics (in particular, a Platonic conception of mathematics) has had privileged status in western culture. Advertising relies on many things, of which nonmathematical (more broadly, nonrational) thinking is only one. And a wide range of factors drive students' classroom behavior: They trust their teachers; the scholastic setting of the problems coerces them into school-like behavior; they expect problems to be reasonable, to have answers derivable from the data given in them, and so on. Even so, I propose that there is a coherent cultural explanation at the core of all these behaviors. I suggest that, despite the best of intentions to the contrary, much of the mathematical nonreason I have described has its origins in our schools. The underlying idea, borrowed from anthropologists, is that students learn what mathematics is all about from the practices of their mathematics classrooms.

What follows is an attempt to sketch out how mathematical nonreason might result from typical classroom instruction. The case is hardly well documented. Rather, I offer a plausibility argument that has more holes in it than a mountain of Swiss cheese. If the argument seems plausible, then it might be appropriate to launch a serious program of research into the issue.

The basic thrust of the argument is that classrooms (and more broadly, schools) are cultural milieux in which everyday activities and practices define and give meaning to the subject matter taught within them; culturally transmitted meaning—what students come to understand about mathematics as a result of their experiences with it—may or may not correspond to the intended meaning. A first illustration of how such definition takes place comes from a story told by

320

Paul Cobb at the 1984 National Council of Teachers of Mathematics research pre-sessions. Cobb asked students from four different schools to complete work-sheets containing elementary addition and subtraction problems. A typical work-sheet started like this:

$$9 - \Box = 6$$
$$\Box - 5 = 7$$
$$8 = \Box - 3$$
.
.
.

Most of the students did pretty well. However, Cobb noted some rather odd answers from the students who came from one particular classroom. Many of their answers were unreasonable, and consistently so. For example, these stu-dents would have produced answers of 3, 2, and 5, respectively, for the three problems listed. Frequently, they answered the first problem right but gave the wrong answer for a disproportionate percentage of the other problems.

Cobb's classroom observations pointed to the source of difficulty. It is typical classroom practice for students to do extensive amounts of seatwork. The teacher hands out dittoed worksheets, and the students sit at their desks working the exercises on the sheets. This took place in all of the classrooms Cobb visited. But in this particular classroom, the teacher's worksheets had a property absent in the others. All of the problems on each worksheet were of the same type, for example:

$$9 - \Box = 6$$
$$7 - \Box = 5$$
$$8 - \Box = 3$$
.
.
.

Such problem sets have an interesting and unintended property: Once you figure out how to solve the first problem (in this case, subtract the smaller number from the larger), that method works on all the problems. Suppose you are a student in this particular class. If you start doing the worksheets the way I have suggested, using the procedure that worked on the first problem for all the rest, you get both faster and better. It takes you less time to work the problems, and you get them all right! As far as you know, you are doing the right thing. Of course, it is not what the teacher intended, but you do not know that, and the teacher does not see it. The teacher just sees the end product (the worksheets) and, on the basis of those, commends you for your work. In short, you have been trained by your experience. You now have the following (not necessarily explicit or conscious) strategy: Solve all of the problems by using the procedure you developed for the first one. That procedure, applied to the first problem set, yields the answers 3, 2, and 5, respectively.

At one level, the misconception that arose in this example is of little importance. One can assume (one hopes!) that, in their next course, the students will receive corrective feedback that sets them on the right track arithmetically and results in their (quite possibly unconsciously) abandoning the strategy they have developed. At another level, however, the example is worth taking seriously. It illustrates how the students' behavior emerged as a perfectly natural response to their classroom experiences. Those experiences, the hours of plowing through exercises on worksheets, which occupied the vast majority of class time, had a much more profound impact on the students' behavior and their implicit understanding of the mathematics than did the formal classroom presentations in which the correct procedures were explained.

One can also note that the requirement that mathematics make sense has already been suspended in this classroom. The students have learned to solve problems by applying a certain procedure to them. In a sense, that procedure is applied blindly: Given a new problem, the students use a predetermined algorithm, without checking to see if the algorithm is really suited for the problem.

Lest I be accused of reading too much into one example, I shall move to a second. Problem solving has been a major theme in mathematics education in the 1980s. In the elementary grades, one major effect of this curricular shift has been that word problems occupy a large part of the curriculum. The following word problem is typical: *John had 7 apples. He gave 4 apples to Mary. How many apples does John have left?* There is good reason to have such problems in the curriculum. Working them, the student can learn, at a very elementary level, of course, what mathematical modeling is all about. The student might represent John's collection of apples with a set of seven counters. Because John is giving some of them away, the student can act out the removal, which suggests that the appropriate arithmetic operation is subtraction. In this context, the act of transforming the story into the arithmetic operation $7 - 4 = x$ is an act of sense making, an act of imparting meaning to mathematical symbols. In this way, word problems can be used to foster mathematical reasoning.

The goal of enabling students to solve such problems is important. As teachers and curriculum developers have discovered, however, it is not an easy goal to achieve. One of the reasons is that solving word problems, unlike solving drill-and-practice arithmetic problems, depends on other skills, particularly, the ability to read. You can't fail a kid in math because he has difficulty reading, can you? Instead, you find ways to help. You limit the vocabulary in the problem statements, but that doesn't help enough. You present all the problems in the same formal, stilted syntax (*A* has *B* *X*s. *A* gives *C* *X*s to *D*. How many *X*s does *A* have left?), but that doesn't quite do it either. So you decide to give the students some help in decoding. Enter the *key word method,* perhaps the most frequently used method for solving word problems.

The basic idea behind the method is that certain key words are the ones that really tell the student what's happening in a word problem. For example, the word *left* is a cue to a subtraction problem: Whenever the word *left* appears in a problem statement, the student subtracts. Even if the student cannot understand the story being told in a word problem, he or she now can solve it. Consider the word problem given previously. Looked at through the filter of the key word method, it appears as

. . . . . 7 . . . . 4 . . . . left?

That is all you need to see; because *left* is the cue in subtraction, all the student needs to do is compute 7 − 4 and he or she has solved the problem.

Although the people who invented and promoted the key word algorithm did not intend to subvert the intention behind the inclusion of word problems in the curriculum, that was the result. As in the classroom that Cobb visited, using the wrong procedure frequently results in getting the right answer. That is, you can solve the word problems in some of the major textbook series without reading them. Circle the numbers, locate the key word, and perform the appropriate operation, and there is a good chance you will obtain the right answer. (Estimates are that in some textbook series you will be correct 95% of the time.)

As the previous example illustrates, students soon learn what works. Interviews with students revealed their solution methods. Describing the way that he solved word problems, one student said, "I look through the problem and circle the numbers. Then I start reading from the back, because the key word is usually at the end." This student and many others have learned—again, through their experience with the mathematics in their classrooms—that word problems do not have to make sense. Of course they are supposed to; that is the rhetoric and that was the reason for teaching them in the first place. But the reality of the classroom, as reflected in classroom practice, is as follows: Teachers give you rules for solving problems, which you memorize and use. Those rules don't have to make sense, and they may not, but if you do what you're told you will get the right answer, and then everybody will be happy. The result, in the short term, is that some students manage to solve word problems that they might not otherwise be able to solve. In the long term, the result is that students come to understand that school mathematics is arbitrary, that the situations described in so-called real problems are not real at all, and that they do not have to understand them to solve them.[2]

---

[2]Part of the folklore surrounding word problems includes the assertion that a significant fraction of the students asked to solve the problem *John had 7 apples. Then Mary left John 4 apples. Now, how many apples does John have?"* circled the word *left* and wrote "7 − 4 = 3." Indeed, the follow-up assertion is that many of the students given the problem *Mr. Left had 7 apples* also circled the word *Left* and wrote "7 − 4 = 3."

Thus far, I have focused on the ways that learning to play by the rules in math class may, despite the best of intentions, teach students that math problems (and their solutions) do not make sense. If this seems too large a pill to swallow, let me offer a smaller one. Let us make the generous assumption that a student has learned to convert a word problem like the apples problem into mathematical symbols, using the following procedure: (a) read the problem; (b) model the problem to pick the right operation; (c) translate the problem into mathematical symbolism; (d) perform the indicated operations; and (d) write down the answer. This procedure will produce the right answer 99% of the time. However, it will also, to return to an example from Vignette 3, result in producing "31 remainder 12" as the solution to the NAEP bussing problem.

Recalling Fig. 16.1 in the prologue, the proper use of formal systems in mathematics for solving word problems requires more than translating verbal descriptions of (ostensible) real-world situations into formal mathematical systems and then performing manipulations within the formal system. It also calls for checking that the result of the formal manipulations is reasonable. If you fail to do that, the result, though the procedure suffices for most of the school math problems you are called on to solve, may well turn out to be nonsense. In a deep sense, then, the five-step procedure represents a serious violation of mathematical sense-making. Even the small pill is a bitter one to swallow.

The first two examples I discussed came from the elementary school curriculum; the third comes from secondary school. The description is telegraphic, but details may be found in Schoenfeld (1988).

One of the main points of Vignette 4 was that students see little or no connection between mathematical proofs and the objects to which the proofs should apply. Having proved that all circles in a certain configuration must have certain properties, they will then conjecture, while working a construction problem, that a particular circle in that same configuration will have different (indeed, contradictory) properties. I argue that this disjunction between the world of proof and the world of construction develops as an unintended consequence of the geometry instruction the students receive.

In the academic year 1983–1984 a high school teacher gave me carte blanche to observe and videotape his geometry classes. The teacher was not a superstar, but his teaching was considered to be quite solid. He taught in a very well regarded suburban school, the vast majority of whose students went on to college. It was clear that he liked and respected his students and that, in turn, they liked and respected him. He was careful and conscientious, and it showed. His students did quite well on the end-of-year performance measure, the New York State Regents' Examination. By all of the standard criteria, he was a good teacher.

For many years, including the year during which the classroom observations were made, New York State had a statewide Regents' geometry curriculum. All of the Regents' geometry students in the state took a uniform end-of-year examination that had a standardized form and was, in no uncertain terms, the goal of instruction. Students, teachers, and school districts were judged by student performance on the exam. Proof was a major component of both the course and the exam. The test contained one required proof, worth 10 out of 100 total points. The proof problem was chosen from a list of a dozen specially designated theorems. Students were expected to memorize all of the required proofs, with the expectation that they would reproduce one of them on the exam. Constructions were a less important part of the curriculum. The exam contained one required construction, also selected from a list of about a dozen required constructions. This construction was only worth two points. No explanation was required for the construction. Students would receive full credit if the right set of arcs and lines appeared on the page and the construction looked good (that is, any angle bisector appeared to divide the angle into two equal parts). Deviations from the prescribed standards of accuracy caused students to lose points.

As in the case with word problems, there is a solid rationale for focusing on proofs and for having a unit on constructions in a course on geometry. In addition, this teacher believed that proofs are important, and he told his students so. He made the point both in general ("The reason we study proofs is so that we learn to think more precisely.") and in particular, with regard to constructions ("The proofs tell you why the constructions are right."). Yet his classroom practice, which was largely shaped by the New York State Regents' curriculum and mirrored in classrooms around the state, if not the nation, delivered quite a different message.

The major focus of the course was on proof, but on a certain specialized, ritualized kind of proof, a written argument in two-column form. At first, students resisted this arcane convention, but they slowly succumbed under the weight of classroom (and grading) pressure. An unfortunate consequence of the emphasis on form, however, was that the substance of proof as a logical and coherent chain of reasoning that guarantees that something must be true became obscured. Writing a proof became a ritual procedure.

From the students' point of view, the course was almost completely ritualistic. As a case in point, consider a standard required theorem, *base angles of an isosceles triangle are equal.* Long before they take a geometry course, students know that base angles of an isosceles triangle are equal; they will claim that it is obvious if you look at any such triangle. From their perspective, this proof and most of the others they are compelled to memorize merely serve as formal confirmations of facts that are patently obvious. Moreover, they know that millions of students before them have memorized and reproduced the same proof. Day after day, hour after hour, students work on proofs. But the focus is on detail, on mechanics. The things being proven are of little interest to them. More important, the proofs they write serve only to confirm results that are already known. The very form of a proof assignment, "Prove that X is true," is interpreted as "It is known that X is true. Your task is to write the formal argument confirming this result."

Constructions were a different matter altogether. As noted before, the grading standard was purely empirical. Although theory was important in some grand background sense ("The proofs tell you why the constructions are right."), the real bottom line was empirical accuracy. The students' job was to get the arcs and lines down on the page so that the end product looked good. Classroom behavior reinforced this message over and over, in a variety of ways. The students spent more than 90% of the class time during the unit on constructions with straight-edge and compass in hand. In their seats, students laboriously and meticulously copied the constructions that the teacher or other students demonstrated at the blackboard. Unintentionally, the teacher's classroom comments reinforced the notion that accuracy alone is what counts. During the very first day of the unit, he said, "Mainly, with constructions, it's going home and practicing." In discussing a test, he made it clear that "What I will not take is a lot of trial and error." When students practiced constructions in class, he had them check to see if they were accurate: "Then, just to check yourself, you measure . . . . " And students learned their lessons well.

That last sentence is meant to be interpreted in two different ways. When one judges by the standard performance measures, the students did learn what they were supposed to. They mastered the mechanics of proof and the empirical skills required for constructions and did well on the Regents' exam. But then, the students also learned some very unmathematical lessons in their course, not from the rhetoric but from their understanding of what they did on a day-by-day basis. They learned that proof is a ritual activity in which they confirm results that are already known to be true and that were intuitively obvious to begin with. They learned that proof has nothing to do with discovery or invention. They learned that when they work a construction problem, what really counts is whether the construction looks right. If the sequence of arcs and lines they put down produces the desired result, then it must be right.

Combine these two perspectives, and the result is the behavior of the students at my cognitive science talk described in Vignette 4. There, students were confronted with a construction problem, which had as its goal the construction of a particular circle. The problem was a discovery problem, in which they had to find the center of the circle. As noted previously, the lesson learned from class-room practice is that proof has nothing to do with discovery or invention; hence, the result of the previous proof problem was irrelevant and was not considered in the context of working the next one. The students did what came naturally, using their intuition to guess where the center of the circle should be. Having made the guess, how did they test it? By doing the construction and seeing if it worked.

The students in the cognitive science talk, without straightedge and compass available, were up in the air and debated for 10 minutes without arriving at a consensus. Other students, who had the tools of the trade accessible to them, let those tools make the decision for them. One of the more dramatic examples of *proof by accurate construction* is given in Schoenfeld, 1985. A pair of students working together on the construction problem considered a number of constructions as possible solutions to the problem. They focused on two of them and managed to make each of those constructions look pretty good. It happens that the two constructions were contradictory, for they resulted in different points being called the center of the circle. However, the students failed to notice this contradiction. Satisfied with the accuracy of their work, they handed me the two contradictory solutions and asserted, "We can prove it two different ways."

There is a long history in western culture of perceiving mathematics as a powerful tool with magical properties. Its application, even to the most commonplace situations, frequently is accepted without question. As indicated, this suspension of sense making appears to be promoted by widespread practices of mathematics teachers in our schools. Although the isolated examples I offer hardly combine to make a compelling case, they suggest a line of inquiry into explaining what students really learn in classroom instruction by focusing on the lessons they extract from classroom practice that should be pursued with vigor. Now, lest it seem that formal mathematics and good thinking are not only separated, but that the chasm between them is nearly unbridgeable, I turn to some examples that try to show that students can learn, in mathematics classes, that mathematics is a vehicle for sense making.

FOUR VIGNETTES ON MAKING MATHEMATICS MAKE SENSE

Vignette 5: Mathematicians Do and Discuss Mathematics or It's Not Formal All the Time

Peggy Strait, my instructor in a probability course some 20 years ago, walked to the blackboard to write the statement of a theorem. She paused, because she had forgotten the precise statement. "I never remember this result," she said, "but that's no problem; it's so easy to derive." Then she derived the result, explaining how things fit together. Having done so, she wrote the result, the statement of the theorem, at the top of the board.

Persi Diaconis, magician and world class mathematician, discussed collaboration in Albers and Alexanderson's (1985) *Mathematical People*. He wrote the following:

> There is a great advantage in working with a great co-author. There is excitement and fun, and it's something I notice happening more and more in mathematics. Mathematical people enjoy talking to each other . . . . Collaboration forces you to work beyond your normal level. Ron Graham has a nice way to put it. He says that when you've done a joint paper, both co-authors do 75% of the work, and that's about right . . . . Collaboration for me means enjoying talking and explaining, false starts, and the interaction of personalities. It's a great, great joy to me. (pp. 74–75)

Commentary.   The episode in the probability class has stayed with me for more than two decades, because it crystallized an important realization: If you understand how things fit together in mathematics, there is very little to memorize. That is, the important thing in mathematics is seeing the connections, seeing what makes things tick and how they fit together. Doing the mathematics is putting together the connections and making sense of the structure. Writing down the results—the formal statements that codify your understanding—is the end product, rather than the starting place.

Diaconis was talking about research mathematics, pushing back the frontiers of our understanding, when he extolled collaboration. He is a superb formalist, but one sees little that is formal in his description of what it is to *do* mathematics. One often thinks of the stereotype, the isolated mathematician alone in his office, struggling to prove a new theorem. This is certainly a part of mathematics, but there is a social aspect to it as well, an aspect that Diaconis captured perfectly. Coming to grips with mathematics involves "talking and explaining, false starts, and the interaction of personalities." All of it, not the least of which is the challenge of the false starts, is indeed a great joy.

Vignette 6: To Know and Love a Symbol, or What Is Formal to You May Be a Living, Breathing Object to Me

Two scientists are hard at work solving elementary physics problems. The first, a psychologist, is a good problem solver who is new to the domain of kinematics. The second, an economist and computer scientist, is thoroughly familiar with the domain. Both work the following problem: *An object is dropped from a balloon that is descending at a rate of 4 meters per sec. If it takes 10 sec for the object to reach the ground, how high was the balloon at the moment the object was dropped?*

The newcomer does what one would expect. She identifies the relevant formula, $s = v_0 t + \frac{1}{2} g t^2$, from the text. She identifies the terms in the problem statement that correspond to values of variables in the formula ($v_0 = 4$ m/sec., $g = -9.8$ m/sec^2, $t = 10$) and performs the appropriate (formal) symbol manipulations. She gets a negative answer for distance. Unlike the students in the bussing problem, she checks to see that the result makes sense. Her checking causes her to (correctly) use the absolute value of g and arrive at the right answer.

The expert approaches the problem quite differently. He does not look up any formulas, though he obviously knows many of them. He starts by noting that the object starts out at 4 m/sec. Over the 10 seconds it falls, at an acceleration of 9.8 m/sec^2, it develops a "total additional velocity" of 98 m/sec. Its final velocity is thus 102 m/sec., so its average velocity for the 10 second fall is 53 m/sec.; hence it travels a total of 530 feet.

Commentary. The newcomer did what she was supposed to, following the procedures outlined in Fig. 16.1. No surprises there; she used a formal system according to the rules. The expert, however, went outside the formal system. Greeno (1983) has noted that, for the expert, the symbols are much more than formal objects manipulated according to formally acceptable rules. The symbols have entailments and meanings, to the point where two concepts represented by standard symbols, initial and final velocity (v_0 and v_f respectively), are conceptually linked by a term for which there is no standard symbol, the *total additional velocity* of the object. According to Greeno, v_0, v_f, and the total additional velocity are *conceptual entities,* or terms that have come to have a status of their own as objects in the expert's *mental model* of the laws of kinematics.

The point is that, if you work with a symbol system long enough, the symbols take on a life of their own. Consider the following description of function composition: "*g* carries *X* to *Y*, and *f* carries *Y* to *Z*, so (*f* o *g*) takes *X* to *Z*." Or, for a more extended example, consider the following theorem: "Let $f(x)$ and $g(x)$ be differentiable functions with the property that for all x, $f'(x) - g'(x) \geq C > 0$. Then there exists a point, x_0, with the property that for all $x > x_0$, $f(x) > g(x)$." This is the way a colleague explained the theorem to a student: "*f* is moving faster than *g*, so if there's ever a point where *f* gets ahead of *g*, it will stay ahead. Now suppose there's a point where *f* is behind *g*. Since f' is at least C larger than g', on each interval of length 1, *f* cuts the distance between them by C or more. So even if *f* starts way behind *g*, it'll eventually pass *g*—and once it does, *g* will never catch up.

In both of these examples, the mathematicians' language is anything but an anthropomorphic slip of the tongue. For the mathematician, these abstract objects are very, very real.

Vignette 7: Trivial Is in the Mind of the Beholder, Good Thinking Is Good Thinking, Formal or Not

This vignette illustrates some aspects of good informal reasoning in mathematics. It presents a very distilled version of a classroom discussion of the problem given in Fig. 16.5.

On its surface, the problem is trivial. Indeed, most people can solve it by trial and error in 10 or 15 minutes. My intention is to indicate that the problem, trivial as it seems, can be used both to illustrate important aspects of mathematical thinking and to generate some substantive mathematics. The schematic outline of a classroom discussion of this problem follows. Valuable heuristic approaches to the problems are noted in italics.

To begin, what additional information would make the problem easier to solve? Clearly, the problem would be easier to approach if we knew the precise sum of each row, column, and diagonal. *Establishing subgoals—trying to obtain*

Can you place the digits 1,2,3,4,5,6,7,8,9 in the box to the right, so that the sum of the digits along each row, each column, and each diagonal is the same? The completed box is called a "magic square."

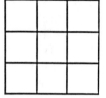

FIG. 16.5. The magic square problem.

a partial result, and use that as a springboard for the rest of the solution—is a consistently valuable problem-solving strategy.

How can we find that sum? Often, it helps to imagine you have a solution, and then derive the properties that the solution must have. Suppose we had filled in the magic square correctly. Then each of the three columns would have the same sum, say S. Add up the three columns, and the sum is $3S$. But (see Fig. 16.6) that also yields a sum of 45; hence, $S = 15$. *Working backwards, in particular, assuming you have a solution and determining the properties it must have, is a useful problem-solving technique.*

Now, what's the most important square to fill in? The center, of course. Focus on key points that give you leverage. Can 9 go in the center? Of course not; with 9 in the center, it would be impossible to place 8: They would be in some sum together, and the triple that contained both of them would add up to more than 15. For that matter, none of 8, 7, and 6 can go in the center; where would 9 go in that case? Similarly, 1 cannot go in the center: 2 would go somewhere, and 12 would be required to complete the triple. And 2, 3, or 4 cannot go in the center; where would 1 go? That leaves 5 as the only possibility. This reasoning, incidentally, is another example of a general strategy: *Exploit extreme cases.*

With 5 established in the center position, where might 1 go? As indicated in Fig. 16.7, there are only two places to consider. This reasoning illustrates another powerful idea: *Exploit symmetry.*

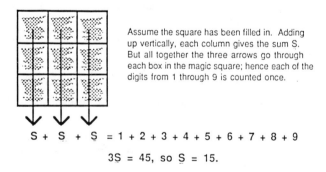

Assume the square has been filled in. Adding up vertically, each column gives the sum S. But all together the three arrows go through each box in the magic square; hence each of the digits from 1 through 9 is counted once.

$$S + S + S = 1 + 2 + 3 + 4 + 5 + 6 + 7 + 8 + 9$$

$$3S = 45, \text{ so } S = 15.$$

FIG. 16.6. Determining the sum of each column of the magic square.

Suppose you had a solution to the magic square with the number 1 in the upper right hand corner. By rotating 90 degrees counterclockwise, you'd get a solution with a 1 in the upper left. Each one exists only if the other does, so you only have to check for one of them. Similarly, you only have to check one "side slot."

FIG. 16.7. A symmetry argument reduces the number of cases you have to consider.

From this point on, the solution is easy. Suppose you place 1 in the upper left-hand corner. The digit 9 then goes in the lower left-hand corner. Again, by symmetry, there is only one place for 2, the middle right box. This choice forces a 4 in the top right box, and then you are stuck: You need a 10 in the top center. Hence, there is no solution with a 1 in the top left corner (or any corner, for that matter). That leaves 1 in the top center as a possibility. Start again, with our last hope including the digits 1, 5, and 9 placed vertically in the middle column. There are (again, by symmetry) two possible places for the 2: the middle right side or the bottom right side square. If you try the former, you discover that the digit 3 cannot be successfully placed. With the latter, you obtain the solution shown in Fig. 16.8.

Are we done? In most mathematics classes, the answer is yes. Early in the semester, my students all say yes, expecting me to go on to another problem. My answer, however, is a resounding no. In most classes, so-called problems are exercises; you are done when you show that you have mastered the relevant technique by getting the answer. Here, however, the goal is to understand the magic square. If we can solve the problem another way, so much the better. How about another approach?

Because the problem calls for finding triples (sets of three digits) that add up to 15, it might be a good idea to list them. Then we know what tools we have to work with. *Work forwards—see how far you can get with combinations of the objects at your disposal.*

I ask for suggestions, and the class calls out triples that add up to 15. Typically, the list the students generate looks like this: 3 5 7, 8 1 6, 4 5 6, 1 5 9, 7 6

FIG. 16.8. The completed magic square.

2, 6 8 1, 2 4 9, at which point things slow down. Someone notices that (8 1 6) and (6 8 1) are redundant; the second triple is crossed off the list. I ask if we have all the triples that add up to 15. Nobody can say. After all, they were generated randomly, so how can you know when you are done? *It helps to be systematic.* The class decides to generate the triples in increasing order. In just a minute or two, the students produce the following list: 1 5 9, 1 6 8, 2 4 9, 2 5 8, 2 6 7, 3 4 8, 3 5 7, 4 5 6.

As we noted earlier, the center square is the most important one; it is involved in four sums (two diagonal, one horizontal, and one vertical). Looking at the list we just generated, only one of the digits appears in four different sums: the 5. Hence, if there is a solution, 5 must go in the center. (Note that this is a completely different proof from the one we arrived at before.) Now, what about the corner squares? Each corner square is involved in three sums, and the middle squares are involved in two each. If you look at our list, the digits 2, 4, 6, and 8 each appear three times, whereas 1, 3, 7, and 9 each appear only twice. So, if there is a solution, the even numbers must go in the corners. And you quickly find out where they go. *There's more than one way to skin a mathematical cat.*

Now we have solved it two ways. Are we done yet? No. What about extensions? Generalizations? Up to this point, we have only answered someone else's problem. We make it our own by playing with the ideas it raises. For example:

1. Our magic square uses the digits 1 through 9. Is there a magic square with the digits 2 through 10? 87 through 95?
2. Same question, but with the numbers, 3, 6, 9, 12, 15, 18, 21, 24, and 27—or any multiples of 1 through 9.
3. Same question, but with the numbers 5, 8, 11, 14, 17, 20, 23, 26, and 29—or any arithmetic sequence.

These are easy. If M is any magic square, than aM (the square you get when you multiply each element of M by the constant a) and $M + b$ (the square you get when you add the constant b to each element of M) are magic squares. Hence, any grid of the form $aM + b$ is a magic square. But tougher questions lurk around the corner:

4. In this magic square, the magic number—the sum of each row, column, and diagonal—is 15. Can you find a magic square with a magic number of 84? How about 85? (The answers are yes and no, respectively.)
5. We saw, in the preceding paragraph, that there are infinitely many magic squares of the form $aM + b$. Are there others? That is, suppose you have a 3×3 grid G, where the sum of each row, column, and diagonal of G is the same. Do there exist constants a and b, such that $G = aM + b$?
6. Why stick to 3×3 grids? What can you discover about 4×4's? $n \times n$'s?
7. And lots more.

Commentary. I deliberately chose a trivial problem for this vignette to indicate how much substance can be mined from such problems. As any mathematician will tell you, I have barely indicated the tip of the mathematical iceberg: One can develop some very solid mathematics with magic squares. Be that as it may, I am far less interested in the problem's mathematical potential than I am in the way the problem can be used as a springboard for explorations of mathematical thinking. Even this cursory and superficial discussion of the problem illustrated the use of the following powerful mathematical ideas: (a) establishing subgoals, (b) working backwards, (c) focusing on key points for leverage, (d) exploiting extreme cases, (e) exploiting symmetry, (f) working forwards, (g) using systematic generating procedures, and (h) having more than one way to solve a problem. Each of these ideas is central to good mathematical thinking. Although they were illustrated in this discussion, they can and should be developed in a problem solving class. Problems like the magic square, and, of course, many other problems with much more substantive (and clearly recognizable) mathematical content, can be used to introduce students to these fundamental aspects of mathematical thinking. Similar explorations of more standard subject matter—for example, the Pythagorean theorem (e.g., Brown & Walter, 1983)—can result both in the mastery of solid, standard mathematics and in the development of mathematical thinking skills.

There is another, more important aspect of the problem-solving instruction from which Vignette 7 was abstracted. Unfortunately, that aspect of the instruction—the classroom dynamics or, in the language of extended Essay 1, the mathematical microculture of the problem solving classroom—is difficult to convey in this small amount of space. Suffice it to say that the classroom style did not reflect the revealed truth exposition of this vignette. Instead, the classroom dynamics reflected the dynamics of real mathematical exploration—in Diaconis's words, enjoying talking and explaining, false starts, and the interaction of personalities. I have more to say about this issue in Essay 2.

Vignette 8: Formal Schmormal, or Who Says You Can't Get Transfer If You Do It Right?

For this last vignette, we travel back in time 50 years to Harold Fawcett's geometry classes at the Ohio State University laboratory school. The details of Fawcett's 2-year (68-week) course, found in his 1938 NCTM Yearbook, *The Nature of Proof,* are well worth examining.

Simply put, Fawcett believed that mathematics can help you think—in particular, that a course in geometric proof can help students learn to reason clearly about a wide range of situations. Following Dewey, Fawcett (1938) hoped to help his students develop *reflective thinking*—"active, persistent and careful consideration of any belief or supposed form of knowledge in the light of the grounds that support it and the further conclusions to which it tends" (p. 6). Following Christofferson, Fawcett sought to develop in his students "an attitude of mind which tends always to analyze situations, to understand their interrelationships, to question hasty conclusions, to express clearly, precisely, and accurately non-geometric as well as geometric ideas" (p. 5). Among his goals for students were that, in situations sufficiently important to them, they would (a) ask that important terms be defined; (b) require evidence in support of conclusions that they are pressed to accept; (c) analyze the evidence and distinguish fact from assumption; (d) recognize stated and unstated assumptions; (e) evaluate the assumptions; and (f) evaluate the argument, accepting or rejecting the conclusion. Moreover, they would do so reflectively, constantly re-examining the assumptions that lay behind their beliefs and guided their actions.

Fawcett realized that transfer from the mathematics to other situations was unlikely if the formal mathematics was studied purely on its own terms. He claimed that such an approach "tends to stifle the very outcomes claimed for the subject," and that "If the kind of thinking which is to result from an understanding of the nature of proof is to be used in non-mathematical situations such situations must be considered during the learning process" (1938, p. 13). Hence, his examples came from the world of mathematics and the world in which the students lived. Definition is important in mathematics, for example, and his students examined definitions both in and outside mathematics. Regarding an award the school had established for teachers who made outstanding contributions to the school, they discussed such issues as: Was the librarian a teacher? What counts as a contribution? Turning to another matter, the class debated: What does it mean to be tardy? "One pupil made the point that he was considered tardy for one class and not for another, although the circumstances were not the same" (p. 33). They also discussed: What is 100% Americanism? What is an obscene book? Or, returning to mathematics, what are adjacent angles?

In all these cases, Fawcett's students proposed definitions and argued over them. To pursue the mathematical example, one student suggested defining adjacent angles as "angles that share a common side." That was ruled out by Fig. 16.9a. Another student suggested that the definition be "angles that share a common vertex." That was ruled out by Fig. 16.9b. The proposal "angles that share a common side and a common vertex" had a good deal of support, until it was ruled out by Fig. 16.9c. Finally, the class settled on "angles that share a common vertex and have a common side between them" (pp. 43–45).

In comparable fashion, Fawcett's students debated current issues. They read newspaper editorials, looking for (and finding without difficulty) flaws and inconsistencies in the arguments made by the authors. They examined advertisements, looking for implicit assumptions in the advertising copy. Most importantly, they did mathematics.

Fawcett changed the rules of the game. In Essay 1, I noted that the standard statement of a mathematical theorem, "prove that X is true," gives the game away. It means: "We know X is true, and we are telling you so; your job is to confirm it by formal means." Fawcett never used this form. Instead, he asked

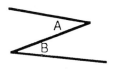 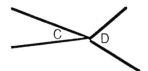 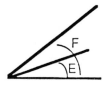

a. "Two angles that share   b. "Two angles that share   c. "Two angles that share
a common side."   a common vertex."   a common vertex and a
                                                                     common side."

FIG. 16.9. Students' examples rule out possible definitions.

students what they thought was true and asked them to defend it. Consider, for example, the following two standard theorems: The diagonals of a parallelogram bisect each other (but are not necessarily perpendicular to each other), and the diagonals of a rhombus are perpendicular to each other. Fawcett's assignment might have looked like this:

1. Consider the parallelogram ABCD in Fig. 16.10a, with diagonals *AC* and *BD*. State all the properties of the figure that you are willing to accept.
2. Suppose you assume, in addition, that $AB = BC$, so that the quadrilateral ABCD is a rhombus (Fig. 16.10b). State all the additional properties of the figure that you are willing to accept.

Of course, some students were willing to accept things that others were not. Fawcett had them battle it out; if a student claimed something was true, he or she had to present an argument that justified it. The class (subtly guided by Fawcett, I imagine) served as jury. It was an active and reflective jury, one should note. The class debated about what it found convincing and why—not only the specific arguments, but their general nature was fair game for discussion (e.g., Can you always trust an inductive proof? Is the converse of a true statement always true? The inverse? The contrapositive?).

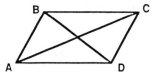 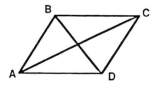

a. ABCD is a parallelogram. What do   b. ABCD is a rhombus. What else do
you think must be true?   you think must be true?

FIG. 16.10. The kinds of questions Fawcett asked.

Commentary.   According to Fawcett, the course was tremendously successful. I am predisposed to believe him. Just why the course worked as well as it did is the subject of my second essay.

ESSAY 2: ON CLASSROOM CULTURES OF MATHEMATICAL SENSE-MAKING

In his summary discussion, Fawcett (1938) characterized the aspects of the course that made it successful. The course was individualized, and, although there were numerous class discussions, each student proved his or her own theorems at his or her own pace. In consequence, the theorems were obviously meaningful to the students. Much of the mathematics was arrived at by consensus. Terms for definition were selected by the class, and the definitions were negotiated. The class was not given results to prove, but instead was invited to look at interesting situations and to make conjectures ("properties you are willing to accept"). Those conjectures had to be defended, and the arguments over their validity were matters of public debate. Whether the topic of debate was mathematical or from the real world, students were encouraged to look for underlying assumptions and question their validity. Transfer to nonmathematical domains was emphasized, and parallel reasoning within and without mathematics was made explicit. Finally, the class periodically took stock, reflecting both on their work and on the methods they used.

Although the subject matter covered in the two courses is different, there are very strong parallels between Fawcett's geometry course and my problem solving courses. Fawcett aimed for a certain broad kind of transfer, the use of logical reasoning outside the mathematics classroom. He took a correspondingly broad-gauge approach to the reasoning procedures he taught. One of my major goals was to enable students to use a variety of problem-solving strategies, which are more narrowly defined and which need a more precise training to achieve a similar transfer. Hence, there were differences in detail, corresponding to differences in the reasoning processes we wished students to learn; however, there were far more similarities than differences in the ways our classes ran. (For details, see Schoenfeld, 1985, 1987; for an analysis of aspects of my course and related apprentice-like instruction in writing and reading, see Collins, Brown, & Newman, 1989.)

My course, like Fawcett's, had a minimum of presentation from the instructor. Like Fawcett, I structured and shaped the classroom interactions, but that shaping consisted of working with the ideas generated by the students and serving as moderator for classroom discussions. The vast majority of our class time was spent in collaborative efforts, either in small groups or as a committee of the whole. And that time was spent doing mathematics.

I need to illustrate that last phrase, which is central to this essay, with another classroom vignette. One of the problems the class explored was the following: We all know the Pythagorean theorem, which says that, if A and B are the legs and C is the hypotenuse of a right triangle, then $A^2 + B^2 = C^2$. A triple of whole numbers (A,B,C) that satisfies the equation $A^2 + B^2 = C^2$ is called a Pythagorean triple. For example, since $3^2 + 4^2 = 5^2$, $(3,4,5)$ is a Pythagorean triple. Are there others? Are there infinitely more? Can we find all of them?

There is a straightforward solution to this problem, which is presented in most courses on number theory. If M and N are any two integers, the triple $(M^2 - N^2, 2MN, M^2 + N^2)$ is a Pythagorean triple. Moreover, all Pythagorean triples are of this form. In a standard lecture class, I could have presented a complete proof of this result in 10 to 15 minutes.

Our class discussion of this and related problems, interspersed with discussions of other problems, took place over 3 class days. The students began by noting that there are infinitely many solutions, namely multiples of the $(3,4,5)$ solution (e.g., 6,8,10, and so forth). They quickly decided that those were boring, as were all multiples of any known solution. Hence, we would look for triples (A,B,C) where A, B, and C were relatively prime. The balance of our discussion assumed that no two of A, B, and C have common factors.

The discussion began empirically: What Pythagorean triples do we know? The students generated a list: $(3,4,5)$; $(5,12,13)$; $(7,24,25)$; $(8,15,17)$; $(12,35,37)$. They noticed that the hypotenuse is always odd, a fact that they then proved; also, that if the first term is odd, then the middle term is even. On the basis of the first three triples, they conjectured that there are infinitely many triples, one beginning with each odd number. They also noted that in each of the triples they knew, the second and third term differed by either 1 or 2; they conjectured that this too must be the case. Hence, they set out (a) to find all triples of the form $(X,Y,Y + 1)$, where X is odd and Y is even; (b) to find triples of the form $(X,Y,Y + 2)$, where X is even and Y is odd; and (c) to prove that there are no other triples. After some algebra, they proved the following results:

1. For each integer Z, the triple $(2Z + 1, 2Z^2 + 2Z, 2Z^2 + 2Z + 1)$ is a Pythagorean triple. Hence, as they had conjectured, for each odd number X there is one triple of the type $(X, \text{even}, \text{even} + 1)$.

2. For each integer Z, the triple $(4Z, 4Z^2 - 1, 4Z^2 + 1)$ is a Pythagorean triple. These are the only triples of the form (even, odd, odd + 2).

3. There are no triples of the form $(X, Y, Y + 3)$.

At this point, the students were confident that the pattern in Result 3 would hold. That is, they believed that no other (relatively prime) Pythagorean triples would be found and that they had discovered all of the ones that did exist. A student asked me, assuming, of course, that we could finish off the argument, if their result was publishable.

Of course, it was not; their conjecture was wrong, and the results they had obtained were a subset of the complete answer, which is well known. But that is not the point. Although I knew the standard solution to this problem, I did not know the results that the class generated; what they did was new to me and quite nice on its own terms. In the course of working the problem, the students made some interesting conjectures. In the give and take of the mathematics, including false starts and much interaction, they managed to prove some of them. Following up their own ideas, the students made discoveries that were new to them, that were new to me, and that they hoped were new to the mathematical community. In short, the students were doing mathematics. At their own level, they were engaged in the discipline—conjecturing, debating, proving—in precisely the way that professionals are engaged in the discipline.

To state things differently, what Fawcett's course and mine shared was that they were both microcosms of (certain aspects of) mathematical culture. The day-to-day practices in the classroom reflected the day-to-day practice of mathematics. The name of the game in both environments (and in mathematics, of course) was understanding; the coin of the realm was argumentation. In each course, the daily classroom activities—the rituals and practices that really shape behavior and understanding—made it natural to think mathematically. What I have called the mathematical aesthetic, the predilection to analyze and understand, was simply part of the atmosphere. And, in the same way that the practices described in Essay 1 had a negative effect in terms of students' deep understanding of mathematics, the practices in these two courses had a corresponding positive effect.

I can point to three other courses that, although substantially different in detail, seem to have the same underlying characteristics. The first is Magdalene Lampert's work at the elementary school level, which she described in her 1987 article "Knowing, doing, and teaching multiplication." For Lampert and her students, learning multiplication is a collaborative enterprise. Rather than present the material that the students are to master, Lampert works with the students to figure out what multiplication is really all about. Her classroom discussions might be characterized as meaning negotiations in which she and her students come to shared understandings of what the mathematics means. It requires subtlety, sensitivity, and flexibility on her part to model the students' conceptualizations and to work with the students, from that base, toward the appropriate mathematical understandings (which include the underlying cognitive models that the students have for the process of multiplication and for the ways it works).

The second example is Nicolas Balacheff's (1987) highly structured middle school lesson sequence, which develops the proof that the sum of the angles of a triangle is 180 degrees. On the surface, Balacheff's lesson structure differs significantly from Lampert's. The sequence of activities, laid out in advance of instruction, includes: (a) have each student draw a triangle, measure its angles, and report the sum; (b) collect the data, make a histogram, and have the class discuss the results; (c) repeat the process with a particular triangle (copies of which are distributed by the teacher), but have the students predict the result before they compute, and discuss the difference afterwards; (d) have teams of students do the same task (predict, measure, resolve) on a handout sheet containing three specially chosen triangles designed to elicit misconceptions; and (e) have a classroom discussion to resolve the issue in a committee of the whole. Yet, at its core, Balacheff's approach is entirely compatible with Lampert's. The teacher refrains from imposing results or suggesting the answers in advance; various methods are employed to bring out students' understandings and compare and contrast them; and the final result (conjecture and proof) is arrived at by social consensus in a way that is meaningful to the students because it sprang from them.

The third example is at the college level, in John Mason's course on thinking mathematically (Mason, Burton, & Stacey, 1982). Mason, too, is concerned with the negotiation of understanding, first among individuals (students and teacher, and students themselves), and ultimately by each individual himself or herself. Like the others, he does not present problem solutions. Rather, he discusses problem resolutions, processes by which one comes to grips with mathematical situations. What is a proof? In some sense it is an airtight, formal argument, but in a deeper sense it is a means of communicating mathematical understanding. So, how do you develop one? First you convince yourself, marshalling enough evidence so that, at a gut level, you believe the result. Then you convince a friend, laying out your reasons in such a way that the case is plausible and coherent. Then you convince an enemy, buttressing your friendly argument to the point where it is incontrovertible and stands against attack. Who are this friend and this enemy? Initially they are your peers, engaging in a mathematical dialectic in which all of you, together, endeavor to make sense of the mathematics. Ultimately, the friend and the enemy are internalized: Your own approach to the mathematics is that you understand when you can defend your intuitions carefully against the most pointed opposition proposed by yourself.

Although there are substantial differences among the five programs of instruction discussed herein, there is also an extraordinary homogeneity among them. Although none slights mastery (all are concerned with students' ability to know the appropriate mathematical facts and to perform the appropriate mathematical procedures), all have as their underlying goal that students develop a deep, rather than superficial, understanding of mathematical objects and processes. All five programs are predicated on the notion that the development of meaningfulness and understanding comes from interaction and negotiation and that that process is inherently social. And whether by conscious design or not, all five resulted in the creation of social environments in which the daily practices and rituals in which students engage make it natural for them to internalize the mathematics in this way.

As in Essay 1, the conclusions I draw at this point are highly speculative. If the statements in the previous paragraph seem to have some face validity, they should be taken as a research hypothesis. My hunch is that mathematically positive classroom cultures can serve as the antidote to the mathematically negative classroom cultures. If that is the case, some serious research into (a) the mechanisms of those classroom cultures, based on case studies of ones that seem to work, and (b) the design of such classroom cultures would seem to be in order.

CONCLUDING DISCUSSION

In this highly speculative chapter, I have tried to make the case for a particular kind of research agenda on the culture of schooling, on seeking a way to develop classrooms that are microcosms of mathematical sense making. Underlying the call for that agenda is the belief, documented as best I can, that the practices of schooling determine its outcomes. And, of course, implicit in that agenda is the idea that such research will help change our schools for the better. In this concluding discussion, I trim my speculative sails and offer the prognosis for such an approach. I begin with two preliminary comments.

First, in invoking the notions of culture and sense making, I have blundered clumsily onto anthropological turf. The largely vernacular way in which I have used the terms here does serve to get the fundamental ideas across. However, it also does violence to the technical sense of the terms and deprives me of their power. Consider sense making, for example. Taking the stance of the western rationalist trained in mathematics, I characterized student behavior on the NAEP bussing problem, a violation of my particular epistemology, as a violation of sense making. As I have been admonished, however, such behavior is sense making of the deepest kind. In the context of schooling, such behavior represents the construction of a set of behaviors that results in praise for good performance, minimal conflict, fitting in socially, and so forth. What could be more sensible than that? The problem, then, is that the same behavior that is sensible in one context (schooling as an institution) may violate the protocols of sense making in another (the culture of mathematics and mathematicians). There is much work to be done in sorting all this out, and I look forward with pleasure to doing so.

Second, a clear consequence of my underlying assumption is that many of the quick fixes suggested at the informal reasoning conference (e.g., "Just show kids how to do X, and then they will deal with Y in the way we would like.") will not work. Patterns of behavior are deeply embedded, the result of sense making in the anthropologist's sense. The quick fixes are almost guaranteed to be contextually bound and not to transfer to other, deeply engrained (and equally contextually bound) behavior. Real change is hard.

Having now claimed that real change is difficult to achieve, let me turn to the prospects of this approach. Assuming that some progress can be made, what likelihood is there that it can make a difference (besides adding to our understanding, which I do not consider a trivial achievement)? In particular, I have characterized Fawcett's course as a formidable success. Larry Cuban has pointed out that it could also be characterized as a significant failure. Its impact has been so small that 50 years after he taught it, I had to exhume it to use it as a case in point—an existence proof, and only one of five at that! That observation is certainly chastening.

The explanation, again, must be cultural in nature. Classrooms are not autonomous entities, but parts of a much larger system. Joe Crosswhite (1987), who served as Fawcett's graduate assistant at Ohio State, told a story that makes the point all too well:

> I remember well one student teacher who tried valiantly to capture Fawcett's philosophy. She taught geometry in a suburban high school at a time when our student teachers had only a half-day teaching responsibility. She believed deeply in the Fawcett philosophy and had captured it very well—so well, in fact, that I had to make an emergency trip to the school for a conference with the student teacher, her cooperating teacher, and the principal. The cooperating teacher had complained to the principal that our student teacher was doing subversive things in mathematics, like letting the students debate about whether they would accept the text definition. She had even permitted—no, encouraged—students to go in different directions about their thinking in geometry! I had to try to explain why one of our students would do such unorthodox things.
>
> In spite of that confrontation, the student teacher was hired in that same school the next fall. She was given a six-class assignment with four different preparations, was responsible for the school yearbook, and supervised the cheerleaders—all in her first year of teaching. She no longer found time to do many of the thoughtful, creative things she had done as a student teacher. She could no longer individualize her instruction, allowing students to go in different directions in their thinking. She taught one year and quit. She told me that if she could not teach the way she was capable of teaching, she would not teach at all. (p. 271)

Crosswhite attributed the student's difficulty to Fawcett's not creating a ready-to-wear version of his course, one that could reasonably be used by a teacher working under the conditions that existed in the schools. That is certainly one explanation of the failure, and the approach that Crosswhite suggested should be pursued. To the degree that one can package bits of curricula that achieve the desired intent while not challenging school structures, one should do so. At the same time, however, one does not have to accept the idea that schools must be the way they are. One can work toward the goal of creating schools that support the kind of learning activities that took place in Fawcett's classroom, a goal that, in turn, is only attainable if the communities in which those schools are embedded will tolerate the change in their goals and practices.

The problem is recursive, a problem of negotiated meaning up and down the line. The mutual definition of reason that must take place in the mathematics class (of the type I have championed here) must take place between teachers and administrators in the schools and between the schools and society at large. In my opinion, there is reason to be more optimistic now than in 1938. We understand more about the processes we wish to engender, we have more and better technological tools at our disposal, and the political climate may allow for some change. At minimum, we should be able to document and better understand some existence proofs at the school, not just at the classroom level. Of course, we cannot be terribly sanguine about the likelihood of success on a large scale. However, the small probability of revolutionary success should not stop us. The insights to be gained in the effort are likely to be tremendously rewarding, and we never know how and where such insights might pay off.

ACKNOWLEDGMENT

The work described in this chapter was partially supported by the National Science Foundation through NSF grant MDR-8550332. That support does not necessarily imply NSF endorsement of ideas or opinions expressed in this chapter.

REFERENCES

Albers, D. J., & Alexanderson, G. L. (1985). *Mathematical people: Profiles and interviews*. Chicago: Contemporary Books.

Brown, S. I., & Walter, M. I. (1983). *The art of problem posing*. Philadelphia: Franklin Institute Press.

Balacheff, N. (1987). Devolution d'un probleme et construction d'une conjecture: Le cas de "la somme des angles d'un triangle." [The evolution of a problem of construction and of a conjecture: The case of the "sum of the angles of a triangle."] Cahier de didactique des mathematiques No. 39, IREM Universite Paris VII.

Bell, E. T. (1937). *Men of mathematics*. New York: Simon and Schuster.

Carpenter, T. P., Lindquist, M. M., Matthews, W., & Silver, E. A. (1983). Results of the third NAEP mathematics assessment: Secondary school. *Mathematics Teacher, 76*(9), 652–659.

Collins, A., Brown, J. S., & Newman, S. (1989). Cognitive apprenticeship: Teaching the craft of reading, writing, and mathematics. In L. B. Resnick (Ed.), *Knowing, Learning, and instruction: Essays in Honor of Robert Glaser*. Hillsdale, NJ: Lawrence Erlbaum Associates.

Crosswhite, F. J. (1987). Cognitive science and mathematics education: A mathematics educator's perspective. In A. Schoenfeld (Ed.), *Cognitive science and mathematics education* (pp. 265–277). Hillsdale, NJ: Lawrence Erlbaum Associates.

Fawcett, H. P. (1938). *The nature of proof (1938 Yearbook of the National Council of Teachers of Mathematics)*. New York: Columbia University Teachers College, Bureau of Publications.

Greeno, J. G. (1983). Conceptual entities. In D. Gentner & A. Stevens (Eds.), *Mental models* (pp. 227–252). Hillsdale, NJ: Lawrence Erlbaum Associates.

Kilpatrick, J. (1987). Problem formulating: Where do good problems come from? In A. Schoenfeld (Ed.), *Cognitive science and mathematics education* (pp. 123–148). Hillsdale, NJ: Lawrence Erlbaum Associates.

Lampert, M. (1987). Knowing, doing, and teaching multiplication. *Cognition and instruction, 3*(4), 305–342.

Mason, J., Burton, L., & Stacey, K. (1982). *Thinking mathematically.* London: Addison-Wesley.

Reusser, K. (1986). *Problem solving beyond the logic of things.* Manuscript submitted for publication.

Schoenfeld, A. H. (1985). *Mathematical problem solving.* New York: Academic Press.

Schoenfeld, A. H. (1986). On having and using geometric knowledge. In J. Hiebert (Ed.), *Conceptual and procedural knowledge: The case of mathematics* (pp. 225–264). Hillsdale, NJ: Lawrence Erlbaum Associates.

Schoenfeld, A. H. (1987). What's all the fuss about metacognition? In A. Schoenfeld (Ed.), *Cognitive science and mathematics education* (pp. 189–215). Hillsdale, NJ: Lawrence Erlbaum Associates.

Schoenfeld, A. H. (1988). When good teaching leads to bad results: The disasters of "well taught" mathematics classes. *Educational Psychologist, 23*(2), 145–166.

17

Nonformal Reasoning in Experts and in Science Students: The Use of Analogies, Extreme Cases, and Physical Intuition

John Clement
University of Massachusetts—Amherst

This chapter discusses evidence from problem-solving case studies that indicates that analogies and extreme cases can play important roles as forms of nonformal reasoning in scientific thinking. Examples of experts spontaneously reporting the use of imagery while making predictions are also discussed, motivating the hypothesis that experts sometimes use elemental concepts at a perceptual-motor level; these are commonly referred to as physical intuitions. Although some people may consider these methods more "casual" than deductive reasoning, one of my purposes is to describe how expert problem solvers can rely on them in a rather formal context, the context of doing their best to think about a physics problem. In a second section, I discuss attempts to utilize nonformal reasoning in science instruction and describe a study that shows significant differences in students' performances that favor experimental high school physics classes using these methods.

There are a number of accounts of the role of different types of nonformal thinking in scientific discovery (e.g., Koestler, 1964). These reports are often based on scientists' retrospective recountings of a discovery. Although they are certainly of value, one of their limitations stems from the difficulties of exactly recalling a train of thought. Especially when the train of thought leads to a significant conceptual change, it can be difficult to recover a previous state of mind. Often, multiple sources contribute to a synthesis, and it can be difficult to recall their exact sequence in the train of ideas. Therefore, it is desirable to gather more direct evidence for the role of nonformal thinking in science. The evidence collected for this study consists of videotaped interviews in which scientifically trained subjects were asked to think aloud as they solved problems.

One of the most significant types of nonformal reasoning is analogical reasoning. Of the few existing psychological studies of analogy, most have focused on provoked analogies, where at least part of the analogy is presented to the subject. This chapter describes research, instead, on spontaneous analogies, where the subject initiates and forms the entire analogy. These occur when the subject, in thinking about problem situation *A*, shifts, without being prompted, to consider situation *B*, which differs in some significant way from *A*, and intends to apply findings from *B* to *A*. In successful solutions by analogy, the two contexts being compared are often perceptually different but are seen to be functionally or structurally similar in some way. Such solutions can sometimes radically restructure the subject's understanding of the problem situation and are most useful for unfamiliar problems where the subject is not able to apply a familiar principle in a direct manner.

In describing the activities of scientists, philosophers of science have tended to separate the *context of discovery*, or hypothesis generation, from the *context of demonstration*, or hypothesis testing. The process of hypothesis generation remains much less well understood than the process of hypothesis testing. However, it is now widely acknowledged that reasoning by analogy may play an important role in hypothesis generation (Black, 1979; Campbell, 1957; Darden, 1983; Hesse, 1966; Knorr, 1980; Nagel, 1961; and Oppenheimer, 1956). Although the problem used in this study is not a problem on the frontier of science, in most cases the subjects were giving a scientific explanation of a phenomenon they were unfamiliar with; that is, the problem was on the frontier of the subject's own personal knowledge base. Thus, it is plausible that the thought processes analyzed in the study share important characteristics with those used in scientific research.

NONFORMAL REASONING IN EXPERTS

Source of Data

In the study, 10 subjects were asked to solve the spring problem shown in Fig. 17.1. The correct answer to the problem is that the wide spring will stretch farther. This seems to correspond to most people's initial intuition about the problem, but giving a careful justification for this answer is a difficult task.

Subjects were told that the purpose of the interview was to study problem-solving methods and were asked to think aloud as much as possible during their solution attempt. All were advanced doctoral students or professors in technical fields and, thus, expert problem solvers in the sense that they had high levels of experience in solving technical problems.

Subjects were told to solve the problem "in any way that you can," and they were asked to give rough estimates of confidence in their answers. Probing by the interviewer was kept to a minimum; it was usually a reminder to keep talking.

A WEIGHT IS HUNG ON A SPRING. THE ORIGINAL SPRING IS
REPLACED WITH A SPRING:
        --MADE OF THE SAME KIND OF WIRE,
        --WITH THE SAME NUMBER OF COILS
        --BUT WITH COILS THAT ARE TWICE AS WIDE IN DIAMETER.

WILL THE SPRING STRETCH FROM ITS NATURAL LENGTH, MORE, LESS, OR
THE SAME AMOUNT UNDER THE SAME WEIGHT? (ASSUME THE MASS OF THE
SPRING IS NEGLIGIBLE COMPARED TO THE MASS OF THE WEIGHT.)

WHY DO YOU THINK SO?

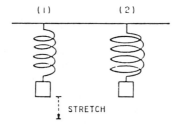

FIG. 17.1. Spring problem.

Occasionally the interviewer would ask for clarification of an ambiguous report. All sessions discussed here were videotaped.

Observations from Transcripts

The solutions collected were up to 90 minutes long, and there were a number of different types of nonformal reasoning used. The main purpose of my account here is to document a set of revealing examples of the phenomena of analogical reasoning and use of extreme cases and to develop initial constructs for describing and classifying the underlying processes. I attempt to provide a close-up view of nonformal thinking in science by concentrating on examples from the protocols of two subjects solving the spring problem.

Analogy Generation. First, consider a short excerpt that provides an initial example of an analogy from the solution of a research physicist, S1. To dispel doubt that analogies are used only by those who lack more formal reasoning methods, it should be noted that this subject was a Nobel laureate in physics. He had actually wound springs in the lab, and, after stating with confidence, on the basis of experience, that the wider spring would stretch more, he proceeded to consider the harder quantitative question of how much more.

S1: . . . The equivalent problem that might have the same answer is—suppose I gave you the problem in a way instead of being a coiled spring, it's a long U spring like that, just like a hairpin [draws Fig. 17.2]. And now I hang a weight on the hairpin, and see how far it bends down. Now I make the hairpin twice as long with the same wire and see how far it bends down. Now that goes with the cube. That's the deflection in the length of the cantilever beam. Heh, heh—and maybe it comes out that way with the spring. So my—I would bet about, about 2 to 1, I would bet that the answer to this is that it [the wider spring] goes down 8 times as far.

Here, the subject generated an analogous case in the form of a U-shaped wire or hairpin. He was able to make a confident quantitative prediction about the behavior of this analogous case and proposed that he might be able to transfer this prediction to the original problem concerning the spring. Note, however, that his confidence in the conclusion was not 100%—in his words, warranting a bet with only "2 to 1" odds. Unlike the process of deductive reasoning from assumed principles, reasoning by analogy from assumptions cannot be done with certainty. Apparently, it can be done with relatively high or low confidence, however (as is discussed later in this study). This subject also used more formal methods in his solution, but his starting point in attacking this problem was the hairpin analogy.

Other subjects had less experience with springs, and, for them, the qualitative question of why the wide spring stretches more was more challenging. In the remainder of this chapter, I discuss only the qualitative aspects of the problem. The 10 subjects generated 38 analogies altogether. An analogy was classified as significant if it appeared to be part of a serious attempt to generate or evaluate a solution and as nonsignificant if it was simply mentioned as an aside or commentary. Thirty-one of the analogies were significant according to this criterion. Eight of the 10 subjects generated at least one analogy, and 7 of the 10 generated at least one significant analogy. Thus, a large number of analogies were observed.

It is useful to distinguish between two parts of an analogy: the *analogous case* and the *analogy relation*. The analogous case in the preceding example was the hairpin experiment itself, and the analogy relation was the relationship proposed, by the subject, of a partial equivalence between the spring and the hairpin. The subject appeared to have high confidence in his understanding of the analogous

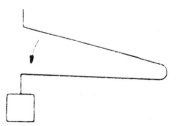

FIG. 17.2.   S1's hairpin analogy.

TABLE 17.1
Fundamental Subprocesses Involved in Reasoning by Analogy

(P1)   *Generating the Analogy.*   A conception of a situation *B* that is potentially analogous to *A* is accessed in memory or constructed. A tentative analogy relation is set up between *A* and *B*.

(P2)   *Establishing Confidence in the Analogy Relation.* The validity of the analogy relation between *A* and *B* is examined critically and is confirmed at a high level of confidence.

(P3)   *Understanding the Analogous Case.* The subject examines and, if necessary, develops his or her understanding of the analogous case *B,* and the behavior of *B* becomes well understood, or at least predictable.

(P4)   *Applying Findings.* The subject applies conclusions or methods gained from *B* back to *A.*

---

case, but only moderate confidence in the validity of the analogy relation. In other cases, subjects have been observed to reject the validity of an analogy relation; that is, they would decide that the analogous case was not similar enough to the original problem to draw any conclusions from it.

Subprocesses Used in Analogical Reasoning.   From observations of this kind, the general hypothesis was formulated that the subprocesses listed in Table 17.1 are fundamental in making an inference by analogy (Clement, 1982, 1988). This hypothesis is consistent with the further observation that many solutions by analogy are proposed tentatively, and processes P2 and P3, especially, can be quite time-consuming. (When it is not clear from the context, the word *analogy* alone refers to the analogous case and the analogy relation taken together.) Observations also indicate that the last three processes can be initiated in any order and that subjects can go back and forth between them several times while gradually completing each subprocess. This suggests that the subjects do not use a simple, well-ordered procedure for controlling their solution processes at this level.

Analogies and Extreme Cases from a Second Subject

I next examine the initial approach to the problem by subject S3, an advanced PhD candidate in computer science who had worked as an electrical engineer. The actual protocols for these problems are quite long; therefore, I present only relevant verbatim segments here. Immediately after reading the problem, S3 proceeded as follows:

008 S3:   . . . Umm, well right off the bat I have no idea. Umm, and my first
          thought is that the length . . . of the coil spring being greater (traces
          circles in air with finger spiraling downward) and the strength of the metal

being the same means that there's going to be kind of more leverage for bending [in the wider spring].

009 S3:   And that therefore it's going to hang farther down. And that's pretty much strictly an intuition based on my familiarity with metal and with working with metal. . . . Let me just think through that. . . . .

010 S3:   (Draws horizontal rods in Fig. 17.3) . . . And my intuition about that is that if you took the same wire that was fastened on the left here [short horizontal rod] and doubled the length and hung some weight on it, that the same material uh, with some weight on it, would bend considerably further. . . .

019 S3:   It would seem that that means that um, that back in the original problem, the spring in picture 2 [the wider spring] is going to hang father; it's going to be stretched more.

021 S3:   . . . and I have a confidence of about 75%. . . .

022 S3:   . . . I have a great deal of confidence that *Da* [the displacement of the long rod] is greater than *Db* [the displacement of the short rod] in any case. I would say 100% confidence.

Further Evidence for Subprocesses in Analogical Reasoning.   The major episodes appearing in this first section were the following:

1. S3 first described thinking about an intuition that predicted that the larger spring will stretch farther (line 009).

2. Line 010 indicates that he spontaneously generated an analogy when he drew the picture of an analogous problem involving bending rods. He decided, again on the basis of intuition, that the long rod would bend more than the short rod and was able to state a 100% level of confidence in this prediction. This indicates that he had completed processes P1 and P3 in Table 17.1 (generating and comprehending the analogous case).

3. He gave evidence for completing step P4 (applying findings) in line 019, where he said that his analogy indicates that the larger spring in the original problem will stretch further. However, he was still not 100% certain about his answer to the original problem. A plausible explanation for this lack of confidence is that he was not fully satisfied with requirement P2 (evaluating the analogy relation between *A* and *B*).

This transcript and others indicate that processes P1 through P4 can indeed take place separately. S3 had apparently, by this point, completed processes P1,

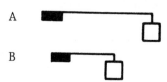

FIG. 17.3.   S3's bar analogy.

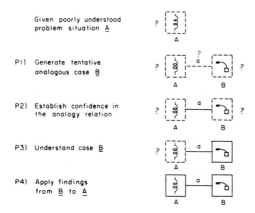

Given poorly understood
problem situation <u>A</u>

P1) Generate tentative
analogous case <u>B</u>

P2) Establish confidence in
the analogy relation

P3) Understand case <u>B</u>

P4) Apply findings
from <u>B</u> to <u>A</u>

FIG. 17.4. Major steps in successful use of a spontaneous analogy.

P3, and P4. Note that, as described here, process P4, applying findings, can take place before steps P2 and P3 are completed. In other words, a tentative prediction about the original case *A* can be made before the analogy relation has been confirmed or before the analogous case is fully understood. This is another sense in which analogical reasoning can involve a conjecture.

In order to begin the task of modeling the internal cognitive processes responsible for this type of analogical reasoning, it is useful to use the notation in Fig. 17.4 showing the four major subprocesses. In this notation, dotted squares and solid squares represent poorly understood and well understood conceptions, respectively. Dotted and solid lines between squares represent unconfirmed and confirmed analogy relations between conceptions, respectively. Again, the order in which steps P2, P3, and P4 are initiated may vary.

A diagram showing the status of the analogy at the end of this first protocol section is shown in Fig. 17.5. A poorly understood conception of the spring is linked by analogy to a well-understood conception of the rod. The dotted line indicates that the analogy relation has not yet been confirmed. That is, even though the subject was sure that he understood how the bending-rod situation works, he was still unsure that that situation was a good analogy for a spring, that is, that the rod can be considered equivalent to a spring and can be used to predict its behavior. Thus, I refer to a *tentative or unconfirmed analogy relation* at this point.

Extreme Cases.   S3 was among the subjects who spent less than a half-hour on this problem without reaching a complete answer or 100% confidence level. These subjects were asked to spend more time considering the problem in order to push their confidence level up higher. In S3's case, this led the subject to take a new approach that involved use of an extreme case:

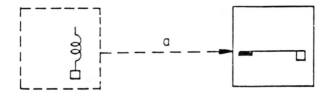

FIG. 17.5.   Status of S3's analogy in the first section of his protocol.

030 I: Ok, let me push you a little. . . . Is there any way you can increase your confidence in your prediction?

049 S3:   Ok. Good. Um, well the way to increase my confidence would be to examine the contrary hypothesis that the notion that um . . . the stretch is the same or possibly even less.

050 S3:   Here's the thought experiment that I can perform.

051 S3:   The way to really eke out my intuitions, given [that] the behavior of the material is at all linear, would be to take the coiled spring in 1 down to . . . . Make this [the narrow spring] extremely tightly coiled [even narrower] . . . . It'd still only be 5 turns.

052 S3:   It's very clearly in the limit . . . . It's almost . . . no distance from side to side of the spring. And obviously, in that case, it can't stretch very far . . . . There isn't material to come from to contribute to a stretch. So um, my intuition that my answer's correct has just jumped up to 85 or 90% as I examined that in the one extreme . . . . As you make that smaller (brings palms of hands close together), it's going to stretch less.

This excerpt provides an example of *extreme case generation* where the subject minimizes or maximizes an aspect of the problem to create a special case that may be easier to solve. In this case, considering an extremely narrow spring allowed the subject to make a more confident prediction that drew on his physical intuition and was based on what he called a "thought experiment":

056 S3:   . . . My confidence is now much higher mm, er, 85–95% (stares at drawing). Even more. Even more. 95.

057 I: Did anything new happen to get the "even more," or . . . ?

058 S3:   Just I was thinking about, I was just running—let my intuition about that really taking the diameter of the spring to zero and the limit. In which case the stretch goes to zero.

059 I: How do you feel when you're "running that intuition"?

062 S3:   Um, it's just I have a—I mean the picture of taking the diameter of the spring to zero is a straight wire, which wouldn't stretch. . . .

066 S3:   So it's good . . . pushing the parameters of the problem to extremes as a way of, uh, getting clearer intuitions about the behavior of a system.

067 I: Is there any way you could increase your confidence even more?

085 S3:   . . . I guess, er, my tendency is to think about a big spring. Push the . . . diameter up and picture in my mind a really big spring with that

weight hanging from it. And uh, it's just really obvious that it's gonna hang further . . .

086 I: What are you thinking about there?

087 S3:   I have a picture in mind.

In lines 058 through 066, S3 mentioned thinking again about his first thought experiment. This time, he took it even further by letting the width actually go to zero, in which case the spring becomes a straight wire. The extreme case here seems to increase his confidence even more. He is also able to support his conclusion, in line 085, by considering the second extreme case of a very wide coil.

Physical Intuition and Imagery Reports.   In line 010, S3 referred to his prediction that a long wire will bend more than a short wire as an "intuition." I term this kind of statement an *intuition report.* It suggests that he was using some type of direct knowledge about manipulating metal. I use the term *physical intuition schema* in a manner similar to diSessa (1983), who has described primitive physical intuitions as knowledge about common physical phenomena without explanatory substructure or justification. In addition, I assume that the strength of belief in a physical intuition is determined by the subject rather than being dependent only on the evaluation of an authority. In everyday terms, an intuition "makes sense" to the subject to a certain degree.

Because this is relatively undeveloped psychological territory, a number of definitions of terms will be proposed here to allow an initial discussion. In what follows, I attempt to separate the terms for external behaviors (such as an intuition report) that are observable relatively directly in the transcript from the terms for internal unobservable mental processes (such as the use of a physical intuition schema) that are hypothesized to exist in the subject.

Subject S3 also reported thinking about a "picture" in line 062. This is an example of an observable, external *imagery report,* where the subject refers to imagining, picturing, hearing, or feeling what it's like to manipulate a situation. (The interviewer was careful not to be the first to introduce suggestive terms such as *image, picture,* or *analogy* in the interviews.) Of course, subjects may actually experience imaging more often than they make imagery reports. In line 062, the subject also made a prediction. I also call such a case an *imagistic prediction report,* in which the subject produces an imagery report accompanied by a prediction or conclusion. These predictions do not appear to follow from prior conclusions; they appear to be evidence for primitive beliefs for which the subject seeks no further justification. (DiSessa, 1983, has referred to such beliefs as *phenomenological primitives.*)

I have already put forward the hypothesis that the subject was using a physical intuition that is based on personal experience with the physical world, rather than academic knowledge or hearsay alone. I can now state several further hypotheses about these observations taken together. These hypotheses are somewhat speculative, and I include them here in the hope that they will stimulate further research. They represent an early stage in what should be a continuing process of hypothesis generation, criticism, and revision in the development of a theory of physical intuition.

First, the observations suggest that this *physical intuition schema* possessed the following additional characteristics:

1. It was more general than an episodic memory of a single event and should, therefore, apply to a range of situations. (S3 does not refer to a memory of any particular "extremely narrow spring" in his experience.)

2. The co-occurrence of imagistic prediction reports and intuition reports (in lines 058–066 and 085–087) suggests that the process of using physical intuition schemata here involved imagery.

3. This is consistent with the hypothesis that these physical intuition schemata exist at a perceptual-motor level, rather than at a more formal level. In this view, imagistic prediction reports derive from a type of mental simulation in which a perceptual-motor schema is used to imagine what will happen at a perceptual level fairly directly, rather than inferring it from a more formal assumption. Such an image can then be described verbally.

Second, it appears that a major function of the extreme cases used by S3 was to enable him to apply a physical intuition schema with high confidence. For example, it is reasonable to hypothesize that the extreme case of the very wide spring coil, once generated, was assimilated by an existing physical intuition schema that embodied knowledge about long, thin pieces of metal, and a confident prediction for it was made in line 085. The present problem concerns a direction-of-change relationship between the two variables of width and deformation. Making the assumption of a monotonic relationship between these variables, the subject was then able to transfer predictions from the extreme case back to the original problem.

Multiple Approaches.   S3 used multiple approaches to increase his confidence level. He made use of an *analogy* to a simpler situation involving bending rods of different lengths. He used *physical intuition* beliefs to make predictions about such simpler situations. Finally, he used two different *extreme cases,* a very narrow spring and a very wide spring, to further support his initial answer. S1, the first subject, also went beyond the use of an analogy in his first approach to the problem by using more analytic methods in order to confirm his predictions generated by the hairpin analogy.

A more subtle understanding of exactly how the spring deforms arose from a third subject's generation of an analogy to a square-shaped spring coil. This led him to formulate the hypothesis of a new causal mechanism operating in the spring—that the spring wire is *twisting* as it stretches. With the square-shaped coil model, one can envision one of the sides of the square acting like a wrench to twist the next side—and so on down the spring. The square-shaped coil model can also be used to predict the result that the stretch of the spring depends on the cube of the coil's diameter. (See Clement, 1981, 1989, for a discussion of this insight episode and further examples of analogies, extreme cases, and physical intuition schemas.) Thus, a variety of nonformal approaches were observed for this problem.

Discussion

Nonformal Knowledge Versus Nonformal Reasoning.   In addition to nonformal reasoning processes, examples have also been presented of intuition reports and imagistic prediction reports that indicate the use of physical intuition knowledge. This suggests a distinction between nonformal reasoning and nonformal knowledge. In the case of S3, his arguments seemed to be grounded at the most basic level on physical intuition schemas constructed from prior experiences with physical objects (e.g., the intuition that long objects are easier to bend than short objects) rather than on formal knowledge. In this sense, he used a kind of nonformal knowledge. On the other hand, analogical reasoning and extreme case reasoning appear to have allowed him to transfer this knowledge, with some degree of confidence, to the given problem situation. These two types of nonformal reasoning, then, allowed him to apply his nonformal knowledge in the form of physical intuition schemas to the problem with confidence. Thus, nonformal knowledge and nonformal reasoning can work together in tandem.

Flexibility and Uncertainty.   The flexibility exhibited in scientific thinking that involves extreme cases and analogies is impressive. As discussed in the first part of this chapter, such flexible methods may play an important role in the hypothesis generation process in science. Analogy generation is a creative and divergent process in which the subject must somehow break away from the normal assumptions implied by the problem and shift his or her attention over to a significantly different but related problem. This is difficult for some people to do, probably because of the shifting involved in breaking out of the assumptions or psychological set built up in considering the original problem. It is also somewhat chancy, because there is no guarantee that the results will pay off; one does not have the security of perceived certainty that is experienced in deductive reasoning. When such flexible and unguaranteed processes do pay off, they are often admired and described as insight. In spite of the inherent uncertainty of the methods he used, however, at the end of his protocol, subject S3 was "95% confident" in his (correct) prediction about the behavior of the spring. He achieved this level without using formal methods. Presumably, the fact that he arrived at the same prediction in three different ways played an important role in boosting his confidence. Even though individual nonformal reasoning methods involve a degree of uncertainty, the convergence of several methods on the same result can raise the subject's confidence to a high level. Collins (1978) described specifications for a program that simulates reasoning under uncertainty of this kind. A discussion of a number of methods experts can use to increase their confidence in the validity of an analogy is given in Clement (1986).

Summary: Nonformal Reasoning Processes

Examples have been presented that illustrate the following types of spontaneous nonformal reasoning: the use of analogous cases; the presence of various levels of confidence in different beliefs and reasoning steps; the use of extreme cases; and the presence of imagistic prediction reports. These processes have also been described in the context of mathematical thinking (Polya, 1954; Clement, 1983). The fact that we can now collect and describe such examples suggests that it will be possible to develop and evaluate cognitive models and theories for certain patterns of nonformal scientific reasoning. In addition, the following hypotheses were proposed:

1. There are four subprocesses involved in using analogical reasoning: generating the analogy; establishing confidence in the analogy relation; understanding the analogous case; and applying findings.

2. Multiple agreeing arguments with moderate certainty levels lead to a higher overall certainty level

3. An expert can use nonformal knowledge in the form of perceptual-motor physical intuition schemas.

4. One major function of analogous and extreme cases is to enable the subject to activate and/or apply with high confidence a physical intuition schema that can be used to make a prediction. In successful cases, such a prediction can be transferred back to the original problem.

NONFORMAL REASONING IN SCIENCE INSTRUCTION

Difficulties in Learning Physics

In this section, I turn to studies of physics teaching that attempt to utilize many of the nonformal reasoning processes observed in the study of experts. Larkin (1982) and Simon and Simon (1978) have found that expert problem solvers use qualitative methods in the early stages of solving textbook problems in mechanics, whereas novices who have received good grades in introductory physics do so far less often, preferring to use formulas immediately. Why? It is possible that the novices have had difficulty in learning both an adequate knowledge base of qualitative physical conceptions and models and the nonformal analogical skills needed to apply them. The teaching studies discussed in this section begin to address these issues.

There is now a rather large literature documenting the presence in science students of misconceptions that lead to nonrandom error patterns on tests of qualitative concepts (see McDermott, 1984, Helm & Novak, 1983, and Novak, 1987). Furthermore, many of these misconceptions have been shown to be persistent, in that they are not only present at the beginning or middle of a course but also after instruction. In Newtonian mechanics, persistent misconceptions have even been observed in third-year engineering majors after 2 years of college physics and calculus courses (Clement, 1982). These studies have shown that students can learn to use fairly meaningless algorithms for manipulating formulas with little understanding of the principles underlying the formulas. It is as if the teachers (and the students) are in a hurry to use the most compact formalisms available for expressing the content of the subject. Perhaps instructors believe that this is the efficient or sophisticated approach, and perhaps students believe that it reduces the amount they have to learn. However, the studies of misconception suggest that, in addition to emphasizing mathematical formalisms, instruction should give more emphasis to conceptual understanding at a qualitative level by making sure that the symbol system of mathematical expressions is grounded in concrete examples and qualitative generalizations.

Teaching Studies

I describe first some recent efforts to design teaching experiments that deal with these difficulties in physics by utilizing nonformal reasoning or nonformal knowledge statements, and I then report one such study of our own. Champagne Klopfer, and Gunstone (1982) described an early attempt to: (a) draw out students' preconceptions in a laboratory setting; (b) focus on observations that conflict with these preconceptions; and (c) revise or replace them through class discussions. Similar techniques are described by Rosenquist and McDermott (1985). This type of careful attention to students' nonformal knowledge and developing conceptions seems to be required in any discipline where there are intuitive misconceptions or where there is need for feedback and correction in the learning of new concepts. A number of other studies have focused on particular nonformal reasoning strategies. Zietsman and Hewson (1986) investigated students' misconceptions about velocity comparisons. They found that the use of extreme case examples plus didactic description in a computer simulation was significantly more effective than pre- and posttesting alone. Minstrell (1983) reported large gains in his own physics classes in different years when he shifted to an emphasis on constructing qualitative concepts in teaching Newton's laws. His methods included drawing out nonformal preconceptions in discussions, designing a lab that provided data that conflicted with these preconceptions, encouraging students to generate and criticize alternative hypotheses that might explain the data, and having students search for and discuss examples from their own experience that were seemingly in conflict with newly formed principles. In addition, several successful approaches to teaching basic concepts in electricity have been reported. All depend on the use of one or more analogue models, such as fluid or particle models (Gentner & Gentner, 1983; Steinberg, 1987; Johsua & Dupin, 1987; the latter two studies attempt to start from a primitive model and then build up more refined versions of the model via criticism and modification).

Use of Bridging Analogies and Anchoring Intuitions

Clement et al. (1987) described a teaching study that made an explicit attempt to use analogies and tap physical intuition schemas in instruction. One simple but fundamental misconception it addressed was students' inability to believe that static objects can exert forces. A table cannot push up on a book, they would say; it's only in the book's way, a barrier that keeps the book from falling. The physicist, in contrast, views the table as elastic, as deforming a tiny amount in response to the force from the book and providing an equal and opposite force upward to keep the book from falling.

In the study, the following techniques were used in high school physics classes. First, an *anchoring example* of a hand pushing down on a spring was used to draw out a physical intuition (in the sense defined previously) in the students that was in basic agreement with accepted physical theory. Once students agreed that the spring pushes up on the hand a chain of *bridging analogies* was introduced, as shown in Fig. 17.6. Here, an attempt was made to gradually transfer the students' intuition from the anchoring example of the hand on the spring, first, to a near case of the book on a foam pad, then to the book on a thin flexible board and, finally, to the book on the seemingly rigid table. The analogy relations linking each pair of examples in this chain are each easier to understand than the original, more distant analogy between the hand on the spring and the book on the table. The teachers taught Socratically during this 30-minute section, posing questions, summarizing and paraphrasing student comments, and keeping the discussion from wandering off track but not revealing their own views. In many classes, this led to some unusually animated discussions.

Toward the end of the lesson, the teacher provided a microscopic model of solids as made up of atoms with spring-like bonds between them. (In some cases, this model had already been introduced by a student during the discussion.) Following a technique used by Minstrell (1982), the teacher then performed a demonstration in which a laser beam or arc light was bounced off a mirror lying on a table onto the wall. When the teacher stood on the table, students could see the deflection of the beam on the wall, indicating that the table was bending.

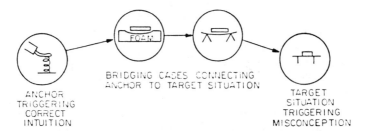

FIG. 17.6.   Bridging analogies.

Thus, there were multiple approaches used to raise the plausibility level of the ideas in the lesson: a chain of bridging analogies grounding the concept in an anchoring example, a visualizable microscopic model that was also grounded in the anchoring example, and an empirical demonstration supporting the deformation idea.

Seven one-period lessons of this general design were taught to experimental classes over 5 months, while control classes used their normal curriculum. The experimental groups achieved significantly greater gains on identical pre- and posttests than the control groups. This was true in each of the three areas studied: normal forces, frictional forces, and Newton's third law of action and reaction.

This result provides reason to be encouraged that one can obtain a measurable effect using nonformal reasoning methods in lessons designed to deal with qualitative misconceptions. In essence, the approach attempts to anchor the students' learning in the useable portion of their physical intuitions; analogies and extreme cases are used to do this convincingly. Thus, the approach uses both nonformal knowledge and nonformal reasoning.

The teaching experiments discussed herein have provided some encouraging initial findings. Studies of instruction that is sensitive to nonformal knowledge, and especially instruction that uses nonformal reasoning are still relatively rare, however, and more work is badly needed. For example, the approaches cited herein strive for deeper levels of understanding on the part of the student but may require extra time to achieve it. This depth-versus-breadth trade-off continues to be an important focus of debate in science instruction. Schools are likely to put added emphasis on depth without research results that support their importance.

CONCLUSION

In conclusion, I list the most important parallels between the nonformal reasoning strategies observed in expert protocols and the instructional strategies I have described.

1. Use of visualizable examples and thought experiments. In addition to abstract statements and principles, experts can focus on more specific, visualizable examples. They report their imagining what would happen in doing experiments with these examples. Some use of examples in physics instruction is standard practice, but more intensive discussions of key examples, as was done in the study using anchoring and bridging examples, appear to be desirable.

2. Anchoring in physical intuitions. Experts were observed to ground arguments in familiar physical intuitions in which they had high confidence. This highlights the importance of helping students ground new knowledge in anchoring intuitions.

3. Analogical reasoning. This is a powerful type of reasoning; it allows experts to modify problem representations and sometimes leads to the development of a new mental model that is found to be generally useful. Students, as well as experts, can benefit from using analogical reasoning as a tool to help them change their view of certain physical situations and to help them eventually build more powerful mental models.

4. Extreme case reasoning. As was observed in the experts' protocols, extreme cases appear to be potentially very useful in promoting conceptual change. The instructional example from the classroom study of a book on a very flexible board can be seen as the extreme case of a very thin table.

5. Need for criticism and evaluation. The creation of new cognitive structures in experts, as well as novices, involves nonformal criticism and evaluation processes prior to the stage of formal justification. These are less formal than checks for logical validity and they involve strategies such as mental simulation, use of multiple methods leading to the same result, and checks for conflicts with other beliefs. These strategies were encouraged in the classroom by the use of thought experiments, multiple levels of instruction, and conflict-generating discussions.

6. Levels of certainty in beliefs. Such confirmation strategies serve to increase the expert's confidence in a belief, rather than to prove the truth of an assertion. Raising the degree to which a concept makes sense and thereby raising the degree of certainty attached to it appears to be an underemphasized and important educational goal.

7. Model construction. Perhaps the most ubiquitous and significant type of nonformal reasoning documented in experts is the construction of a qualtitative structural model that provides an explanation for a phenomenon (Clement, 1989). All of the educational researchers cited herein appear to recognize, at least implicitly, that students must actively contribute to the construction of the new explanatory models they are learning, and Minstrell (1983) has explicitly focused classroom discussions on generating hypotheses. In the present view, model development is a constructive process, much of which is not a deductive, formal reasoning process.

It is important to bear in mind the distinction between the nonformal reasoning processes used in the construction and initial evaluation of a qualitative scientific model and the formal reasoning processes used to justify arguments for them formally. The goal during construction is to have the new model make sense of the phenomena, to connect it to familiar experiences, and to see it as a plausible hypothesis that provides a satisfying explanation. While the goal during formal justification is to provide the tightest possible logical argument and the most accurate and compelling measurements providing empirical support. The studies discussed here provide evidence that achieving the former goals via nonformal reasoning is of central importance in scientific thinking and in science instruction.

ACKNOWLEDGMENT

Research reported in this chapter was supported by NSF Awards No. MDR-8470579 & MDR-8751398.

REFERENCES

Black, M. (1979). More about metaphor. In A. Ortony (Ed.), *Metaphor and thought* (pp. 19–43). Cambridge, England: Cambridge University Press.

Campbell, N. R. (1957). *Foundations of science.* New York: Dover.

Champagne, A., Klopfer, L., & Gunstone, R. (1982). Cognitive research and the design of science instruction. *Educational Psychologist, 17*(1), 31–53.

Clement, J. (1981). Analogy generation in scientific problem solving. *Proceedings of the Third Annual Conference of the Cognitive Science Society, 3,* 137–140.

Clement, J. (1982). Analogical reasoning patterns in expert problem solving. *Proceedings of the Fourth Annual Meeting of the Cognitive Science Society* (pp. 79–81). Hillsdale, NJ: Lawrence Erlbaum Associates.

Clement, J. (1983). Use of analogies and spatial transformations by experts in solving mathematics problems. *Proceedings of the Fifth Annual Meeting of the International Group for the Psychology of Mathematics Education, North American Chapter* (Vol. 2), *5,* 102–111.

Clement, J. (1986). Methods for evaluating the validity of hypothesized analogies. *Proceedings of the Eighth Annual Conference of the Cognitive Science Society* (pp. 223–234). Hillsdale, NJ: Lawrence Erlbaum Associates.

Clement, J., Brown, D., Camp, C., Kudukey, J., Minstrell, J., Palmer, D., Schultz, K., Shimabukuro, J., Steinberg, M., & Veneman, V. (1987). Overcoming students' misconceptions in physics: The role of anchoring intuitions and analogical validity. In J. D. Novak (Ed.), *Proceedings of the Second International Seminar on Misconceptions and Educational Strategies in Science and Mathematics* (pp. 84–97). Ithaca, NY: Cornell University.

Clement, J. (1989). Learning via model construction and criticism: Sources of creativity in science. In J. Glover, R. Ronning, & C. Reynolds (Eds.), *Handbook of creativity* (pp. 341–381). New York: Plenum.

Clement, J. (1988). Observed methods for generating analogies in scientific problem solving. *Cognitive Science 12*, 563–586.

Collins, A. (1978). *Studies of plausible reasoning: Final report*. Report #3810. Cambridge, MA: Bolt Beranek and Newman.

Darden, L. (1983). Artificial intelligence and philosophy of science: Reasoning by analogy in theory construction. *Philosophy of Science Association, 2*, 147–165.

diSessa, A. A. (1983). Phenomenology and the evolution of intuition. In D. Gentner & A. Stevens (Eds.), *Mental models* (pp. 95–34). Hillsdale, NJ: Lawrence Erlbaum Associates.

Gentner, D., & Gentner, D. (1983). Flowing waters or teaming crowds: Mental models of electricity. In A. Stevens & D. Gentner (Eds.), *Mental models* (pp. 99–130). Hillsdale, NJ: Lawrence Erlbaum Associates.

Helm, H., & Novak, J. D. (Eds.). (1983). *Proceedings of the First International Seminar on Misconceptions in Science and Mathematics*. Ithaca, NY: Cornell University Press.

Hesse, M. (1966). *Models and analogies in science*. South Bend, IN: University of Notre Dame Press.

Johsua, S., & Dupin, J. (1987). Taking into account student conceptions in an instructional strategy: An example in physics. *Cognition and Instruction, 42*, 117–135.

Knorr, K. (1980). *The manufacture of knowledge*. Cambridge, England: Oxford University Press.

Koestler, A. (1964). *The act of creation*. New York: MacMillan.

Larkin, J. H. (1982). The role of problem representation in physics. In D. Gentner & A. Stevens (Eds.), *Mental models* (pp. 75–98). Hillsdale, NJ: Lawrence Erlbaum Associates.

McDermott, L. (1984). Research on conceptual understanding in mechanics. *Physics Today, 37*, 24–32.

Minstrell, J. (1982). Explaining the "at rest" condition of an object. *The Physics Teacher, 20*, 10–14.

Minstrell, J. (1983). Teaching for the development of understanding of ideas: Forces on moving objects. A.E.T.S. yearbook XI, *Observing classrooms: Perspectives from research and practice*.

Nagel, E. (1961). *The structure of science: Problems in the logic of scientific explanation*. New York: Harcourt, Brace & World.

Novak, J. (Ed.). (1987). *Proceedings of the Second International Seminar on Misconceptions and Educational Strategies in Science and Mathematics*. Ithaca, NY: Cornell University.

Oppenheimer, R. (1956). Analogy in science. *The American Psychologist, 11*(3), 127–135.

Polya, G. C. (1954). *Mathematics and plausible reasoning, Vol. 1: Introduction and analogy in mathematics*. Trenton, NJ: Princeton University Press.

Rosenquist, M. L., & McDermott, L. C. (1985). *A conceptual approach to teaching kinematics*. (Tech. Rep.). Seattle, WA: University of Washington, Physics Dept.

Simon, D. P., & Simon, H. A. (1978). Individual differences in solving physics problems. In R. Siegler (Ed.), *Children's thinking: What develops?* (pp. 325–348). Hillsdale, NJ: Lawrence Erlbaum Associates.

Steinberg, M. (1987). Transient electrical processes as resources for causal reasoning. In J. Novak (Ed.), *Proceedings of the Second International Seminar on Misconceptions and Educational Strategies in Science and Mathematics* (pp. 480–490). Ithaca, NY: Cornell University.

Zietsman, A., & Hewson, P. (1986). Effect of instruction using microcomputer simulations and conceptual change strategies on science learning. *Journal of Research in Science Teaching, 23*, 27–39.

18 Informal Reasoning in High School History

Kevin O'Reilly
Hamilton-Wenham Regional High School
South Hamilton, MA

In a nationwide poll of public school teachers (*USA Today,* 1986) regarding the main purposes of education, the alternative picked most often was teaching reasoning and analytical skills. Yet, as an article in a recent special issue of the *American Psychologist* has pointed out, "assessments of student achievement suggest that today's students may be failing to develop effective thinking and problem-solving skills" (Bransford, Sherwood, Vye, & Rieser, 1986, p. 1078). There is a gap between our goals and student performance.

This chapter focuses on a project that has improved student thinking skills in the discipline of history, "Critical Thinking in American History" (CTAH, hereafter). It first examines some of the problems involved in teaching reasoning in history and recommends an approach to instruction. The major part of the chapter then describes the author's instructional methods and materials.

The definition of *informal reasoning* used here is providing good reasons for beliefs. This definition is derived from a conceptualization of rational thinking offered by Robert Ennis (1980). It encompasses many different skills, such as evaluating evidence and recognizing assumptions, as well as many different attitudes, such as the willingness to suspend judgment and to go beyond simple solutions.

FOSTERING INFORMAL REASONING IN HISTORY

The Current State of Instruction

Which of the following questions and tasks are likely to elicit from the responder reasoning, as opposed to the rote recall of previously acquired information?

1. What was Theodore Roosevelt's policy in Latin America called?
2. Describe the changing role of the Roman Catholic Church in Europe from 300 A.D. to 1100 A.D.
3. Was the United States justified in dropping the atomic bombs on Hiroshima and Nagasaki in August, 1945?
4. List four causes for World War I, and explain how one of the causes led to the war.
5. What is the background of the company for which I've just been hired to work?
6. Who wrote the Declaration of Independence?

It is clear that questions 2, 3, and 5 generally demand reasoning, whereas questions 1, 4, and 6, as typically used in secondary school classrooms, mainly or exclusively demand memory work. Yet, sadly, it is the latter type that occupies most of the students' time in many high school history courses, where the three *T*'s dominate—*t*eachers and *t*extbooks impart information to students, who passively memorize it to be regurgitated on *t*ests. May "heaven" help those with poor memories.

Questions 1 and 6 are representative of single fact questions requiring no thinking at all beyond memory. Question 4 involves remembering several facts and also calls for an explanation. However, in many classes this question would not be asked unless the textbook or teacher had already explained how each cause had led to the war. Thus, the students again must simply recall information.

Question 2 involves weaving diverse pieces of information into a coherent theme, even if the teacher has already lectured on most of the key points. If the students have read only documentary evidence, answering this question will, indeed, require extensive reasoning. Question 3 involves reasoning no matter how it is taught. Because ethical considerations are raised, students may well disagree with the teacher. Question 5 is interesting because it is typical of the historical problems we encounter in daily life. No secondary sources are generally available for these types of questions, so we are forced to use informal reasoning to answer them.

Barriers to Improving Instruction

Good reasoning is at the heart of serious history. Historians make inferences, test hypotheses, and evaluate sources of information. Similarly, in graduate seminars, students are constantly taking tentative positions and then revising them as they encounter different perspectives, new information, and thoughtful questions. In contrast, in many high school history courses, students are not challenged to think more clearly. In these courses, the most likely questions are: "Will this be on the next test?" (revealing the student's understanding of the rules of the game) and "Why are we learning this?" (showing the student's recognition that memorizing information may not be of any use).

The lack of thoughtfulness in high school history instruction is not necessarily the fault of the teachers, however. First, given the factory model of high school education in which a teacher may have 150 to 180 students in five classes, it is logical that many will eventually resort to multiple-choice testing. Only a small number of thinking skills can be tested using multiple-choice items and, even for these skills, the questions are difficult to construct (Karras, 1978); hence, the focus on facts.

Another factor that detracts from an emphasis on reasoning in history classrooms is the lack of time that teachers have to design their own instructional materials. In some states, many of the key curriculum decisions are made at the state level. In others, curriculum decisions and revisions are done by administrators and curriculum specialists (curriculum coordinators and department heads). This model puts teachers in the position of implementing someone else's ideas about thinking skills. As Robert Sternberg (1987) has pointed out, teachers have to be good reasoners if they are to succeed in helping students learn to reason. We are fooling ourselves if we think we can improve instruction by putting commercially developed materials into the hands of teachers who lack the time and training to determine how best to adapt these materials to meet the needs of their students.

Some thinking skills leaders, most notably Robert Swartz of the "Critical and Creative Thinking Program" at the University of Massachusetts at Boston, advocate an infusion model for critical thinking. Teachers are trained at the University to restructure their teaching to infuse thinking skills into their lesson plans. This approach goes a long way toward making teachers curriculum innovators.

A third problem for instruction in reasoning in social studies is the gap between theory and practice. Theoretical models of thinking skills, such as Bloom, Engelhart, Furst, Hill, and Krathwohl's (1956) taxonomy or Guilford's Structure of Intellect (Meeker, 1985), may have great conceptual power in explaining how students think. These models, however, fail to offer clearcut implications for subject-specific instruction; teachers do not know how to modify their lessons to make them consistent with the model.

In addition, teachers have a different perspective from theorists. As practitioners, teachers must create their lessons by trial and error in the classroom. They stick with strategies that work and discard ones that "bomb." As Sergiovanni (1985) put it, teachers view professional knowledge in a clinical rather than a theoretical manner. Unlike the theoretician, whose goal is to enhance long-term understanding, the teacher's goal is to identify ideas from the theoretical literature that promise to be immediately useful in the classroom. This clinical perspective is why teachers who attend conferences and seminars sometimes ask, "That theory sounds fine, but what does it have to do with what I'll be teaching next Monday?"

Nevertheless, although well-designed curriculum materials alone are not enough to improve informal reasoning in history, they are an important ingredient in the process. When teachers see an actual lesson plan focusing on informal reasoning, they can more easily write similar lessons and adapt them to their own classes and teaching styles.

Arguments for a Direct Approach to Instruction

There are a number of different approaches to the teaching of informal reasoning. Some of these, such as Paul's (1984) dialectical approach and Lipman, Sharp, and Oscanyan's (1980) Philosophy for Children program, attempt to teach reasoning by involving students in classroom discussions that offer both opportunities to formulate criteria for effective reasoning and opportunities to come to value such reasoning. Other theorists, such as Barry Beyer, have endorsed similar goals but have recommended a more direct approach to instruction. Beyer (1985) conceived of reasoning as a set of skills that can be improved with both knowledge and practice. He advocated teaching these skills by breaking them into small steps, explaining the nature of each step, and providing repeated practice to promote fluency.

Much of the CTAH project focuses on the direct teaching of specific skills, as proposed by Professor Beyer. It is based on the assumption that thinking skills are like athletic skills and should be taught in a similar way. For example, a golf pro giving a lesson to a beginner breaks the swing down into its component parts, such as grip, stance, backswing, and so forth. He or she also explains each component. Then, the learner takes a few practice swings, with the pro offering corrections. Next, a ball is introduced, and the pro suggests still additional changes to remedy new problems that arise. Finally, the student is told to practice and return for another lesson at a later date.

On one hand, if thinking skills really are like athletic skills, then we should teach them in a similar fashion—instruction on the component parts of the skills, guided practice or coaching, repetition, and further coaching. No golf pro is going to say "You're hooking the ball—don't do that," without giving any instruction in how to correct this habit. Yet, that is what we sometimes do with thinking skills. We say, "No, that's not the effect—it's the cause," without going through the steps of the skill with students to find out where he or she went wrong.

On the other hand, thinking skills are not exactly like athletic skills. Too much instruction on which skills to use and how to use them may unnecessarily limit student creativity and insights. The CTAH project recognizes and seeks to foster the creative, affective aspects of thinking skills, also.

THE PROJECT DEFINED

The CTAH project uses four books, along with associated teachers' guides (O'Reilly, 1983–1985). These materials are designed as supplementary resources for high school American History courses. The books are made up of historical problems and interpretations as well as skills worksheets that identify a broad range of informal reasoning skills. As noted previously, both a step-by-step and a less structured, more philosophical approach to instruction are utilized. Skills are first demonstrated in the context of familiar everyday problems. Following the demonstrations, students are gradually guided in applying the skills in working with historical content. Initially, they are given interpretations of historical events written by others, and they are asked to evaluate the adequacy of the reasoning involved. Subsequently, they are asked to construct their own interpretations from original source materials, using the skills taught to evaluate their own reasoning.

This section describes the project. The first subsection discusses its rationale. The second subsection describes the skills taught and offers examples of typical instructional materials. Section 2 highlights changes in student attitudes that result from using these materials.

Rationale for the CTAH Project

Suppose some high school students were asked to evaluate the following brief excerpt from an interpretation by historian Sternberg (1935) of President James K. Polk's role in causing the Mexican War:

> The strength of Polk's policy of expansion by covert aggression lay in the popular support he could count upon in bringing on war if Mexico should plausibly be presented as the aggressor. Confining his secret plans of conquest to the discreet circle of his immediate agents and advisors, and leaving the public to learn them only through events, Polk soon after the war began hypocritically assured the New York Democratic leaders—and doubtless others—that he "had no schemes of conquest in view in respect to Mexico, no intention to take possession of any portion of her territory with a view to hold it!" If he openly avowed his intention of taking a large territorial indemnity (which he was determined upon long before the actual coming of the war), the world would perhaps be even less credulous of his inconsistent assertions that he was waging a war "commenced by Mexico" to "redress American grievances." Even by magnifying the private claims—which could not be taken seriously as *cause* for a large and costly war—the apologists have not been able to make a very plausible case for "peaceable Polk," for vain is their endeavor to ignore or read away Polk's aggressive view and belligerent handling of the Texas boundary question, a matter in which contemporaries perceived the most significant key to the Mexican War and its instrumental cause. (pp. 67–68)

There are at least three significant obstacles, for most high school students, in evaluating this interpretation. First, the vocabulary is too difficult. After all, historians write for adults, not for high school students. Second, no footnotes are included, so the students have no idea what evidence was used to build the interpretation. Third, even if the interpretation were written in a comprehensible vocabulary and all the evidence were included, most students would have no idea how to evaluate it.

The CTAH materials were designed specifically to overcome these problems. As is shown in Figure 18.3, these interpretations are written at a high school vocabulary level, and many include footnotes. Most importantly, the booklets specifically teach many of the skills necessary for evaluating the kinds of arguments offered by historians.

As noted, each skill is taught through a sequence of lessons. The initial one involves a concrete demonstration because, according to research, almost all high school students think at a concrete rather than a formal operational level according to Piaget's cognitive stages, as applied to proficiency in historical reasoning (Hallam, 1970; Day, 1981). That is, they find it difficult to reason about abstract historical events unless they are helped to relate these events to more familiar everyday experiences (Rosenzweig & Laville, 1982).

Skills Emphasized in the Critical Thinking Program

Identifying and Evaluating Evidence.   I introduce this skill by having five students role-play a robbery in the hallway outside my classroom. Upon their return, the other students are instructed to ask questions to determine who the robber was. The initial questions are not very good, but eventually some relevant information is elicited. The class learns that three people say that Alice committed the crime. They also see a letter indicating that Alice needs money quickly, and they find out that Alice's fingerprints are on the stolen wallet.

After the role-playing and questioning, I write the word *evidence* on the chalkboard and ask, "What is evidence?". After some discussion, I tell the class that evidence can consist of a verbal statement, a written document, or an object. At this point, I make a distinction between evidence and information (Bloch, 1953; Carr, 1961; Norris, 1979). I point out that the information contained in documents, statements, and so forth achieves the status of evidence only when the source of the information is also indicated. This distinction is an important one. When students know the source for an item of information, they can begin immediately to evaluate the information, without having to go to the library to locate its source. Without a source, students can neither ask questions nor make evaluations.

The role-playing example is used as the basis for helping students formulate criteria for evaluating evidence. The following criteria are introduced and discussed:

1. Is the source offered a primary or a secondary one?
2. Does the source have a reason to distort information?
3. Is there other evidence supporting this evidence?
4. Is the evidence public or private?
5. Is the person reporting the event an expert on the event observed?
6. How long after the event occurred was the report given?

Although I have certain criteria in mind for evaluating evidence, I feel it is important for students to develop their own criteria (within limits) and to establish their own acronyms for remembering these criteria. This way, they feel that even the criteria for informal reasoning are open to question and debate. They also find them easier to remember.

Criteria for identifying and evaluating evidence, along with other skills involved in the analysis and evaluation of arguments, are contained in the front of each student's book, in a 20-page section called "A Guide to Critical Thinking" (O'Reilly, Vol. I). Students can refer to the guide and to associated classroom posters for help in remembering these criteria.

Examples of some of the exercises used to provide practice in evaluating evidence appear in Fig. 18.1. The first set is used early in instruction to offer students experience in applying the criteria to different types of evidence.

Give the strengths and weaknesses (at least a total of 4) for each piece of evidence below:

Evidence	Strengths	Weaknesses
1. Helen tells the teacher that she did not copy the homework from Rick.		

Evidence	Strengths	Weaknesses
2. A newspaper article in 1860 report that, according to a mill owner, the conditions in the Lowell mills in the 1840s were good.		

FIG. 18.1. Evaluating evidence.

Through a gradual progression of exercises, students become proficient at applying the criteria to their own oral and written arguments and to longer historical interpretations, such as the one that follows (from O'Reilly, 1983a):

Salem Witch Trials

Girls in Salem Village started acting strangely in 1692 mainly because they ate rye bread, which caused pain and made them hallucinate. The rye bread was infected with a fungus that caused ergot poisoning, and the symptoms of ergot poisoning are the same as those the girls say they had: choking; painful, itchy skin; visions or hallucinations; and so forth. Most of the girls ate rye produced on land that was perfect for ergot growth (several of the girls ate bread from the Putnam farm, which was reported in records to be swampy lowlands).

Several diaries from the village report that the weather in 1691 was warm and rainy, which is ideal for ergot growth. Also, women and children have been more susceptible to ergot poisoning in some epidemics, and it was female teenagers who were afflicted by the symptoms in 1692.

[After reading this passage, they are asked:] 1. *What evidence is offered by this historian to back up his argument?* (a) *The girls hallucinated.* (b) *Diaries from the village reported warm, rainy weather in 1691.* (c) *Women and children have been more susceptible to ergot poisoning.* (d) *The rye bread was infected with a fungus.* 2. *Evaluate the evidence according to the four questions you have learned.* (p. 55)

With all these bits of evidence, students are encouraged to examine the source for each assertion and why they should believe it.

Distinguishing Conclusions from Premises.   The task of assessing the evidence in the witch trial passage also requires another skill—that of finding the main idea or thesis of an interpretation. All of the other critical thinking skills are of little use if the student does not know what the historian is arguing. I teach students the following strategies for identifying the main point of a passage of text:

1. Look for cue words, such as "therefore," "thus," and "so."
2. Ask yourself, "Therefore, what? . . . What is this person driving at?".
3. For longer readings, write down the main idea of each paragraph, then check your proposed main idea to see if it contains all the other ideas.

I teach students also how to analyze arguments into premises (statements that support the argument) and conclusions (the point of the argument—which follows from the premises). Again, I alert them to cue words that may be helpful. As with the other skills, I introduce this skill through a familiar example and provide worksheets that offer practice in analyzing both everyday and historical arguments into premises and conclusions.

Identifying Unstated Assumptions.   Students who have worked with premises and conclusions can more easily identify unstated assumptions in arguments. These are arguments in which the major premise (the second premise in a classical syllogism—that is, the one stated in general terms) has been omitted.

The following is an example: I knew that Fred was not a football player, because he weighs only 130 pounds. I teach a specific strategy for identifying unstated assumptions.

1. Find the conclusion.
2. Rewrite the first premise in your own words.

3. Combine the unique part of the premise with the unique part of the conclusion in a new statement.

4. Phrase the new statement in *general* terms (i.e., people who weigh only 130 pounds are not football players).

Students are given worksheets on this skill also, but I have had difficulty in getting most students to employ the skill successfully on longer interpretations. They tend to focus on unsupported but stated premises in the arguments, which reveals that they have not mastered the technique of finding the unstated assumptions.

Identifying Imprecise Words.   Precision in terminology is important to the expression of arguments. Students need to become conscious of imprecise words that can allow assertions to blur troublesome questions. Words such as *rich* and *lazy* are likely to be used imprecisely. People have different ideas of how much wealth it takes to be rich and how much leisure it takes to be lazy. These words reveal attempts to draw lines where none may exist. How slowly does one have to work before one is justifiably considered lazy? The word alone offers no precise measurement. The argument, "Medicare pays for many unnecessary operations, so we should cut down on Medicare payments" requires definition of the word unnecessary. We should not accept this argument without a definition of that word and of the number involved in *many,* and we should ask what evidence there is to support the claim.

Language can also sway us. Words with positive emotional connotations, such as *liberty* and *democracy,* can dispose us to be more accepting of an argument and arguer. This is why politicians use these terms so frequently. Adjectives and adverbs can also tip us off to the point of view or bias of the author of an argument.

Identifying Connections Among Parts of an Argument.   Reasoning is the way a person gets from a premise (which is established by evidence) to a conclusion. To put it another way, we might say, "Suppose there is enough evidence to show, beyond doubt, that the premise is true. Does that make the conclusion reasonable?" For example, suppose you want to know if Rita borrowed your car, and suppose I bring in 10 witnesses who swear that Rita knows how to drive standard shift cars and argue that she, therefore, borrowed the car. The evidence reasonably establishes a premise, but you probably will not be convinced by my argument, because there is something lacking in my reasoning—namely, that I failed to establish a connection between the cause and the effect.

In the CTAH project, students are taught five basic types of reasoning used in history: cause and effect, comparison, generalizing, proof, and debating. The first two are the most important, both because they are central to more arguments in history and because competency in evaluating these types of reasoning seems to empower students more fully in distinguishing weak from strong arguments. Thus, these two types of reasoning receive emphasis in the program.

Students are encouraged to keep two questions in mind in analyzing cause-and-effect situations. These are: (a) Did the historian show the connection between the proposed cause and the effect, and (b) have other possible causes been eliminated?

Students are given the visual model shown in Fig. 18.2 to help them understand the steps involved in evaluating cause-and-effect reasoning. In using this model, they are encouraged first to identify the effect (oftentimes an action or event) and the cause alleged by the arguer and then to consider whether a strong connection has been established between the cause and the effect. Thereafter, they are instructed to cover the cause and attempt to identify other possible explanations for the effect. Several worksheets offer practice in evaluating cause–effect relationships.

After students have become comfortable using this model to analyze simple cause–effect arguments, more complex ones are introduced. The set of passages in Fig. 18.3 shows an example designed to help students determine when a clear connection has been established between a cause and an effect. In this exercise, students are offered three explanations for the Spanish–American War, all of which propose the same cause—the yellow press. By keeping cause and effect constant, the lesson highlights the way historians explain the connections between them. Students are instructed to read these explanations and determine which is the strongest. We then discuss their assessments as a class.

Most students feel that Historian B offers the strongest reasoning. My own analysis runs this way: These historians are obligated to show a connection between the yellow press and the U.S. declaration of war. Historian A shows how the press influenced popular opinion, but does not show how public sympathy for Cuba translated into Congressional votes for war. Historian C doesn't even show the connection of the newspapers to public opinion. Historian B relates the yellow press to public opinion and public opinion to the decision to declare war. In short, Historian B offers the clearest demonstration of how the cause produced the effect.

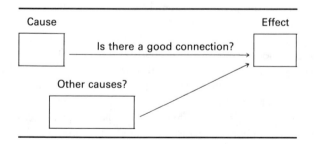

FIG. 18.2.   Cause-and-effect diagram.

The Causes of the Spanish–American War

In April, 1898, the United States declared war on Spain. Several theories have been advanced by historians as to what the main cause was of the U.S. declaration of war. One theory is that the yellow press was the primary reason. Below are three historical arguments, all of which say that the yellow press was the main cause. Write down which of the three arguments is the strongest and explain why.

HISTORIAN A

The main cause of the Spanish–American War was the yellow press. The penny newspapers competed for readership in cities so they could sell more advertising. This was especially true in New York City where the papers owned by William Randolph Hearst and Joseph Pulitzer were in fierce competition. In order to compete, each paper printed the gruesome details of the revolution in Cuba. As a result, the American public became sympathetic with the rebels, and the U.S. declared war to help the Cubans against the Spanish.

HISTORIAN B

The main cause of the Spanish–American War was the yellow press. These newspaper, which competed for readers, often exaggerated and distorted the situation in Cuba. As William Randolph Hearst said to an artist in 1898, "You furnish the pictures, I'll furnish the war."

Millions of Americans were influenced by the newspapers. With elections coming up in the fall of 1898, the politicians in Congress and President McKinley were quite aware of the sentiment to protect the Cubans through war with Spain.

HISTORIAN C

The main cause of the Spanish–American War was the yellow press. These newspapers exaggerated the situation in Cuba. For example, the *New York Times* declared, "The horrors of the barbarous struggle (by the Spanish) for the extermination (wiping out) of the native population (the Cubans) are witnessed in all parts of the country." The papers also printed graphic drawings of the Cuban revolution. With such distortions in the papers, the country could not help but be pushed into war.

FIG. 18.3. Connections between cause and effect (Source: O'Reilly, 1985, Vol. IV, pp. 26–27).

Once students have an understanding of the basic elements of cause-and-effect reasoning, they can be led to think about causation in a more complex way. Causes and effects often exist in chains in which there are many causes for a given effect, and effects can become causes for still other effects. Diagrams are provided as visual aids to help students trace out these more complex cause–effect relationships.

Historical analogies (or comparisons), like issues of causality, are at the very heart of historical reasoning. Decision makers often call upon historical analogies to help shed light on present situations. But comparisons should not be accepted at face value—a false analogy is probably more dangerous to us as decision makers than no analogy at all.

Analogical reasoning is introduced by this everyday example: "You drove your 1985 Dodge Aries in an autocross race at one of the shopping center parking lots last week, and your best time on the course was 31.5 seconds. Suppose that Harry told you that he drove in an autocross race 2 weeks ago, and his best time was 28.2 seconds, so he's a better driver than you. What would you ask him?"

(What kind of car did he drive? Was it the same course? Were the weather conditions the same?)

Almost every student with whom I have used this example has been able to ask one of these three questions. This result indicates that, on familiar material, high school students already know how to examine comparisons. That is, they intuitively know that they should explore the extent to which the two cases are really similar. The problem is that students cannot always recognize analogies when they are used in history. Thus, they are instructed to look for words and phrases such as *like, as, similar to,* and greater than. These cue words often help students find the analogies.

Generalizing is another issue to which the project teaches students to be alert. A generalization is, of course, a conclusion about a whole group (of people, wars, countries, depressions, Republicans, college students, etc.) that is based on information about a sample of the group's members. Students are taught to ask about the size and representativeness of the sample. They are also questioned about how far they can generalize from given information.

They also become aware of the convention of proof. Historians' methods for proving points include evidence, examples, authority, and/or eliminating alternatives. Students are taught to ask if evidence or examples actually prove a point in question, if the expert is really an expert on this particular point, and if all of the alternatives have really been eliminated.

When a historian debates an argument made by another historian, students are taught to ask whether the historian is being fair in his or her attack. That is, they are taught to ask whether the attack is directed at the argument or the person (the *ad hominem* fallacy) and whether the attack distorts the argument (the straw man fallacy).

One topic that is not emphasized in the CTAH program is fallacies. I find that learning the above types of reasoning represents a more powerful conceptual tool for students than memorizing fallacies. Encouraging students to ask questions that apply widely in evaluating evidence also has the advantage of helping them recognize gradations in the strength of arguments (including some fallacies), and it promotes thinking over memorizing.

Evaluating Ethical Claims.   Argument evaluation also often entails assessing ethical claims. The first hurdle that students must surmount is identifying these claims. The process is initially like finding unstated assumptions. For example, what is the ethical claim in the following argument: "The U.S. was justified in taking a strong stand against the Soviets in the late 1940s, because the Soviets had broken their promise to hold free elections in Eastern Europe."? There are several ethical claims involved, and questioning any one of them would provide the basis for an interesting discussion: Is it ever right to break a promise? Is one always justified in taking strong action when someone breaks a promise?

Students learn to identify the conditions associated with various ethical principles. If they can think of exceptions to a principle, they are taught that the principle must be modified to take these exceptions into account, as in the following example:

John—You are always justified in taking strong action when another person breaks a promise.

Felicia—Oh no. You can't kill someone who promised to save your candy bar for you but didn't.

John—Well, O.K. Then, you are justified in taking strong action in proportion to the significance of the promise broken.

John has qualified his ethical position, and he might have to qualify it further.

If on the other hand, they cannot think of exceptions, students are taught that they may have identified a strong principle.

OTHER KEY INSTRUCTIONAL FEATURES OF THE CTAH PROJECT

Providing Students with Relevant Background Information

A look at review articles in history journals shows that the main method for evaluation of historical works by scholars is by comparing the arguments presented with information that the scholar already knows. Unfortunately, high school students have very little information from which to draw to evaluate historical arguments. (I suspect that this is one reason why they have more difficulty in evaluating historical analogies than everyday ones.) Even when students do know some potentially useful information, they may not realize that it is relevant.

To overcome this problem, students are frequently given handouts called *relevant information sheets*. These sheets contain many different types of information (including some statements that are irrelevant to the interpretations in question) that provide background for a more complete analysis of the viewpoints.

Establishing a Framework for Argument Analysis

By this point, students have learned the major informal reasoning skills involved in evaluating arguments. To help them remember these skills, I introduce an acronym, such as the following:

M – Main point
A – Assumptions
R – Reasoning

L – Language
E – Evidence
R – Relevant information

I then engage them in exercises that require that they use all of these skills in an integrated fashion. More lengthy and complex historical interpretations and notes on the primary and secondary sources that support the argument are introduced, as in Fig. 18.4. This exercise was adapted from arguments presented by the historian Stanley Elkins (1959) in a volume entitled *Slavery*. Students in all of my classes have been able to point out the weakness of footnote 1 (the publisher is an anti-slavery society, and the author may have exaggerated) and the weakness in footnote 3 (it is a secondary source). They have also been able to point out the analogy of slavery to concentration camps and have asked how they might be different. Some students have not known enough about concentration camps to assess the analogy, so I have given them a relevant information sheet on slavery and concentration camps. Using it, students have said that slavery was a system of labor, whereas the purpose of concentration camps was death. Thus, inmates in concentration camps were probably treated much more harshly than slaves. On these grounds, students argue that the historian's comparison is a poor one.

Some students also notice the cause-and-effect reasoning in the argument—namely, the historian's claim that the total dependence of slaves on owners (the cause) was responsible for their passive Sambo behavior (the effect). After questioning, the students become aware that there may be other possible explanations for the slaves' passive behavior, such as passive resistance. Some students also comment that the existence of the Sambo personality may itself be questioned because of the weaknesses noted earlier in the evidence for this argument.

Extending Skills to New Contexts

As noted earlier, the CTAH program utilizes a step-by-step approach to instruction. The final step involves students' learning how to construct and evaluate their own arguments. After students become adept at analyzing arguments written by others, they are asked to participate in classroom debates and prepare essays presenting their own views on controversial issues in American history. They are then given worksheets guiding them in applying the criteria taught in the program to the evaluation of their own arguments.

Changes in Student Attitudes

One of the most rewarding parts of teaching the CTAH project is to watch students change their view of the nature of knowledge. They begin to see it as fragmentary, tentative, selective, and open to interpretation. They begin to see knowledge as something to be sought after rather than something served them as

The topic of slavery in the United States has been studied for many years by historians. One of the central questions they have dealt with is: How bad was slavery? Some historians have said that slavery in the United States wasn't that bad, but they are wrong. Actually, slavery in the United States was like a concentration camp in Nazi Germany in many ways.

Unlike slaveowners in other countries, slave owners in the United States had almost complete power over their slaves. Owners could beat their slaves with little worry of government interference.

Slaves in the United States had no civil rights, no right to own property, no right to marry, or any other rights.[1] American slaves could not leave the plantation without the owner's (or overseer's) permission, so they were under the absolute control of their owners.[2]

The result of this total dependence of the slave on the owner was the "Sambo" personality. Slaves acted like Sambos—that is, they passively did whatever they were told. They didn't work hard or do anything with a lot of energy; they just shuffled around and didn't cause any trouble for the slaveowners. There is a lot of evidence to show that many slaves acted like Sambos.[3]

This passive Sambo personality is just what people exhibited (acted like) in concentration camps in Hitler's Germany.[4]

Like the slaveowners, the guards in the concentration camps (called S.S.) had almost complete control over the prisoners. The prisoners passively accepted the cruelties and tortures and offered no resistance. There were few revolts—even when the prisoners were being herded into gas chambers.[5]

It is obvious that slaves acted, in many respects, like people in concentration camps. Slavery destroyed the personality of slaves in addition to denying them freedom. Slavery in the United States was incredibly bad.

---

[1]William Goodell (1953). *The American slave code in theory and practice.* New York: American and Foreign Anti-Slavery Society: "A slave is in absolute bondage (in the United States): he has no civil rights, and can hold no property, except at the will and pleasure of his master" (p. 92).

[2]John Codman Hurd (1958). *The law of freedom and bondage in the United States.* Boston: Little, Brown: "Should a white man be attacked by a slave and be injured or maimed, the punishment was automatically death. A 1669 Virginia law declared it not a serious crime if a master or overseer killed a slave who resisted punishment" (p. 232).

[3]Samuel Eliot Morison and Henry Steele Commager (1942). *The Growth of the American Public* (a textbook used in high school and college history courses). New York: Oxford University Press.

[4]Bruno Bettelheim (1943, October). Individual and Mass Behavior in Extreme Situations. *Journal of Abnormal Psychology, 38,* 141: "The prisoners developed types of behavior which are characteristic of infancy or early youth."

[5]Eugene Kogan (1946). *The Theory and Practice of Hell* (New York: Farrar, Straus: "With a few altogether insignificant exceptions, the prisoners, no matter in what form they were led to execution, whether singly, in groups, or in masses, never fought back!" (p. 284).

FIG. 18.4. Slavery—A summary Interpretation for Student Analysis (Source: O'Reilly, Vol. II.)

so many facts to be memorized. One student asked, "Do you mean everything in this textbook isn't true?". Another student, at the end of the course, commented on a newspaper article, "This article sounds convincing, but I'll bet there is a Historian B out there somewhere with another view." Students also begin to make judgments for themselves, based on evidence and inferences. They start asking, "What is your source for that information?". This kind of questioning and independent thinking help make students more thoughtful citizens, less open to the emotional manipulation that is the hallmark of demagoguery.

At yet another level, some students have demonstrated a willingness to be more self-reflective. Journal entries on a decision-making simulation on the Vietnam War showed a great deal of empathy for historical decision makers. In journal entries on the Civil Rights Movement, several students commented on and analyzed their own prejudices, assumptions, and stereotypes. Dealing with assumptions, overgeneralizations, frames of reference, and so forth seems to have raised student consciousness and given them time to examine their own thinking. This philosophical self-reflection—what Richard Paul (1982) termed *critical thinking in the strong sense*—is a key component of informal reasoning.

CONCLUSION

The CTAH project has developed over the past 10 years as a result of trials and errors in teaching informal reasoning in the context of history. Teachers in other schools have purchased and used the materials, but I have had little feedback from them. My own experience indicates that high school students can learn a number of the skills in evaluating a historical interpretation and apply them to new arguments. Further, as indicated in the last section, they have changed their view of knowledge. They are more actively involved in learning. They become more skeptical and more confident in forming their own judgments. Based on these observations, I believe that the project has been successful in improving students reasoning about the world and about themselves.

REFERENCES

Beyer, B. (1985). Teaching critical thinking: A direct approach. *Social Education, 49*, 297–303.

Bloch, M. (1953). *The historian's craft.* New York: Random House.

Bloom, B., Engelhart, M., Furst, E., Hill, W., & Krathwohl, D. (1956). *Taxonomy of educational objectives, Handbook I: Cognitive domain.* New York: McKay.

Bransford, J., Sherwood, R., Vye, N., & Rieser, J. (1986). Teaching thinking and problem solving. *American Psychologist: Special Issue: Psychological Science and Education, 41*, 1078–1089.

Carr, E. H. (1961). *What is history?* New York: Random House.

Day, M. C. (1981). Thinking at Piaget's stage of formal operations. *Educational Leadership, 39*, 44–47.

Elkins, S. (1959). *Slavery.* Chicago: University of Chicago Press.

Ennis, R. (1980). A conception of rational thinking. In J. Coombs (Ed.), *Philosophy of education, 1979*. Bloomington, IL: Philosophy of Education Society.

Hallam, R. (1970). Piaget and thinking in history. In M. Ballard (Ed.), *New movements in the study and teaching of history* (pp. 162–178). Bloomington, IN: Indiana University Press.

Karras, R. (1978). Writing multiple-choice questions: The problem and a proposed solution. *The History Teacher, 11*, 211–218.

Lipman, M., Sharp, A. M., & Oscanyan, F. S. (1980). *Philosophy in the classroom*. Philadelphia: Temple University Press.

Meeker, M. (1985). Structure of intellect (SOI). In A. Costa, (Ed.), *Developing minds: A resource book for teaching thinking*. Alexandria, VA: Association for Supervision and Curriculum Development.

Norris, S. (1979). The reliability of observation statements. *Rational Thinking Report* (No. 4). University of Illinois, Urbana.

O'Reilly, K. (1983–1985). *Critical thinking in American history* (Vols. 1–4). Pacific Grove, CA: Midwest Publications.

Paul R. (1984). Critical thinking: Fundamental to education for a free society. *Educational Leadership, 42*, 4–14.

Paul, R. (1982). Teaching critical thinking in the "Strong Sense." *Informal Logic Newsletter*, May, 1982.

Rosenzweig, L., & Laville, C. (1982). Teaching and learning history: Developmental dimensions. In L. Rosenzweig, (Ed.), *Developmental perspectives in the social studies* (pp. 54–66; Bulletin number 66). Washington, DC: National Council for the Social Studies.

Sergiovanni, T. (1985). Landscapes, mindscapes, and reflective practice in supervision. *Journal of Curriculum and Supervision, 1*, 15.

Sternberg, R. (1935). The failure of Polk's Mexican War intrigue of 1845. *The Pacific Historical Review, 4*, 39–68.

Sternberg, R. (1987, February 24). Thinking critically [Interview with Fred Hechinger]. *The New York Times*, p. 9.

USA Today (1986, April 30). [National Center for Education Information poll of 1,144 teachers], p. 1.

19

Higher Order Thinking in the Teaching of Social Studies: Connections Between Theory and Practice

Fred M. Newmann
University of Wisconsin, Madison

This chapter interprets, for the field of social studies, the recent general literature on the teaching of thinking. Two questions are addressed: (a) What is the nature of higher order thinking in social studies, and (b) how can such thinking be fostered in classrooms? The intent is to encourage dialogue between researchers and practitioners that will advance knowledge on instruction for thinking. Toward this end, the chapter explores the implications of current scholarship for practice, and it highlights special practitioner concerns that need to be taken into account if the findings from future research are to speak more directly to social studies teachers.

The chapter is organized into four sections. The first section identifies various bodies of knowledge that can enhance our understanding of the nature of higher order thinking in social studies and argues for the development of a new conceptual framework, drawing on these sources, to guide instruction. The second section presents the framework. It is grounded in views of thinking that enjoy considerable support in the research literature and among teachers, but it also delineates new dimensions to take into account the particular challenges posed by social studies content. The third section explores the implications of this framework for instruction, mainly by identifying barriers that teachers confront as they try to foster thinking in actual high school classrooms. The fourth section discusses implications for research, advocating studies of the degree of thoughtfulness characteristic of different instructional environments and describing ways in which this variable can be translated into a set of empirical measures.

THE NEED FOR A GENERAL FRAMEWORK

For decades, educators have proposed a variety of specific approaches to the teaching of thinking in social studies. The more thorough formulations have been conceptualized as critical thinking (Beyer, 1985; Ennis, 1962; Feeley, 1976; Giroux, 1978), reflective thinking (Hunt & Metcalf, 1968), social scientific inquiry (Barr, Barth, & Shermis, 1977; Morrissett, 1967), and jurisprudential reasoning (Oliver & Shaver, 1966). Because each approach (and others) can be justified through persuasive rationales, and they often incorporate common elements, it is not productive to try to choose the best. It makes more sense to search for a common conception that embraces diverse emphases but attracts professional consensus. To date, however, no such framework has been developed.

Within the last 10 years, an avalanche of literature has emerged on the nature of thinking and how to teach it. Much of this scholarship is oriented toward general thinking strategies rather than the teaching of thinking in particular school subjects. The literature, too vast to summarize here (for summaries, see Chipman, Segal, & Glaser, 1985; Mayer, 1983; Kohlberg, 1981; Sternberg & Wagner, 1986; and Voss, 1989), identifies the nature of problems (e.g., well-structured, ill-structured; descriptive, analytic, prescriptive; academic, practical), describes the processes or approaches we use to think about problems (e.g., deductive and inductive reasoning; formal and informal reasoning; stages of moral reasoning; analytic and creative thinking; concrete and abstract thinking; expert and novice thinking; metacognitive strategies), and offers general models of intelligence or the workings of the mind (e.g., associationist, gestalt, developmental, and information-processing theories). Descriptions of instructional programs and research on their effects can be found in Chance (1986); Costa (1985); Nickerson, Perkins, and Smith (1985); Segal, Chipman, and Glaser (1985); and Sternberg and Bhana (1986). But this diverse work has not been synthesized into a general framework that might address more specific concerns within social studies.

Missing in the social studies literature is a base of empirical research base that documents the effects of various approaches. Evidence exists that many forms of thinking have been successfully taught. Research on the teaching of public issues (Levin, Newmann, & Oliver, 1969; Oliver and Shaver, 1966) indicates that students can be taught to develop well-reasoned positions on ill-structured descriptive, analytic, and prescriptive problems dealing with public controversy. Studies of school effects and of more specialized instruction in specific disciplines show that students learn to solve academic problems (Voss, 1989). Research shows some success in teaching deductive and inductive reasoning (Herrnstein, Nickerson, De Sanchez, & Swets, 1986; Lipman, 1985), in moving students from preconventional to conventional moral reasoning (Rest, 1986), and in teaching informal reasoning (Perkins, 1986). Similarly, studies can be found that show success in teaching creative thinking (Perkins, 1984), as well as metacognitive strategies and information processing activities (Covington, 1987; Palincsar & Brown, 1984).

This may lead to the optimistic conclusion that just about any kind of thinking can be taught to some degree. On the other hand, research within social studies is so fragmented that we know very little about the extent to which different types of thinking can be taught by specific curricula and teaching techniques (reviews on the topic are offered by Metcalf, 1963, and Cornbleth, 1985). A lack of replication and proper experimental design, along with a failure to use common dependent variables and common treatment variables, have prevented the accumulation of knowledge (Armento, 1986; Shaver & Larkins, 1973). A possible exception is in moral development, where a more coherent research tradition has evolved (Mosher, 1980; Rest & Barnett, 1986), but elsewhere there is little replication and almost no information on effect sizes.

In short, the literature within social studies lacks a general framework that incorporates the diverse approaches within the field and the more general, recently developed knowledge on the nature of thinking and informal reasoning. The empirical research offers little guidance on the effectiveness of particular approaches for specific purposes in social studies or on the conditions required to implement them.

To build a cumulative knowledge base on the teaching of thinking in social studies, a general conceptual framework is needed, and the mission of this chapter is to offer one. To be helpful, the framework should include a conception of higher order thinking that is responsive both to the general literature on thinking and to the particular content of social studies, and it should suggest an agenda for empirical research to which a variety of approaches within social studies can contribute. In developing the framework, I have reviewed the philosophical and empirical literature on higher order thinking and research that is more specific to social studies.

To insure that the framework incorporates views of social studies teachers, I have also relied on preliminary findings from an on-going empirical study of the promotion of higher order thinking by high school social studies teachers. This project began by observing classes and interviewing teachers (Newmann, 1990), department chairs, and students in five high school departments that try to emphasize higher order thinking on a department wide basis. The study developed an observational instrument for describing the kinds of thoughtfulness promoted in classes. Interviews explored teachers' conceptions of thinking and their perceptions of the conditions in school that facilitate and inhibit their efforts to promote it. Students were asked to describe the kinds of lessons that challenged them to use their minds and their reactions to these lessons. The five departments studied in this phase of the project were, presumably, unusual in their emphasis on higher order thinking, but instruction in these schools was organized according to the typical high school structure (e.g., about 120 students per teacher, five classes of 50-minute periods per day). In subsequent phases, the project will make similar inquiries in two additional contrasting sets of schools: those that claim no special departmental focus on higher order thinking and those that emphasize thinking but have also made major changes in the structure of instruction and teachers' work.

Research to date cannot settle all of the conceptual issues related to higher order thinking in social studies, nor can it identify the most effective instructional techniques. A framework based on more recent scholarship can, nevertheless, be helpful to teachers by proposing criteria to guide their teaching. It can help school administrators by suggesting issues in the organization of instruction and staff development that must be confronted. And, for researchers, the framework can suggest an agenda for empirical work that avoids the fragmentation of previous efforts while speaking to specific concerns of social studies teachers.

THE FRAMEWORK

The framework consists of three parts: a general definition of higher order thinking grounded in tasks that present nonroutine challenges; the cultivation in students of knowledge, skills, and dispositions to succeed in the challenges; and the recognition of four specific challenges in social studies.

Higher Order Thinking and Nonroutine Challenges

Rather than concentrating on a specific conception, such as critical thinking, informal reasoning, moral reasoning, or divergent thinking, at this time it is prudent to work toward a broad conception. Our research with history and social studies teachers indicates that calls for specific types of thinking (e.g., critical, inductive, moral) are unlikely to generate widespread consensus for any particular type. Instead, social studies teachers are likely to perpetuate their previous emphases on a plurality of types of thinking, but even these will be grounded primarily in the teaching of their *subjects*. Thus, a broad conception of thinking, adaptable to a variety of content and skill objectives, is more likely to attract wide support from high school teachers.

Second, a broad conception can strike at the heart of an underlying malady identified by many studies. At best, much classroom activity fails to challenge students to use their minds in *any* valuable way; at worst, much classroom activity is nonsensical or mindless. The more serious problem, therefore, is not the failure to teach some specific aspect of thinking; it is the profound absence of thoughtfulness in classrooms (Cuban, 1984; Goodlad, 1984; Morrissett, 1982; Perrone & Associates, 1985; Powell, Farrar, & Cohen, 1985; Stake & Easley, 1978). Even programs designed to teach thinking skills can fail to promote thoughtfulness. A general conception of thinking can address this basic issue.

Any human mind that receives stimuli from the environment engages in thought, in the sense that the brain functions to code, store, and process information. Further, almost all cognitive processes, from watching television commercials to reading road signs, are complex in a neurological sense. What, then, distinguishes higher order thinking from other forms of thought?

The difference is suggested in the familiar critique of classrooms as dull places and in the plea that they become more challenging. Lower order thinking demands only routine, mechanistic application of previously acquired knowledge, for example, repetitive exercises, such as listing information previously memorized, inserting numbers into previously learned formulae, or applying the rules for footnote format in a research paper. In contrast, higher order thinking challenges the student to interpret, analyze, or manipulate information, because a question to be answered or a problem to be solved cannot be resolved through the routine application of previously learned knowledge.

The importance of a novel problem that requires use of prior knowledge but cannot be solved through routine application of algorithms has been emphasized in previous reviews of literature in psychology and cognitive science (e.g., Patterson & Smith, 1986; Resnick, 1987). It is also useful in philosophical analyses of thinking, as Schrag (1988) has shown with the analogy of the explorer trying to travel successfully over unknown terrain. To reach the destination successfully, the explorer needs substantial knowledge and skills (e.g., map and compass use, knowledge of weather or survival techniques), but the novelty of the task poses a significant mental challenge: how to apply the knowledge.

This definition emphasizes using or going beyond the information that one has previously acquired in order to solve a problem. Tasks of this sort appear in many forms: in well- or ill-structured problems (within social studies, the latter often seem more challenging), in academic or practical problems. They may involve descriptive issues (How did the economy of the South depend on slavery?) or ethical and prescriptive issues (Under what conditions, if any, can violence against a government be morally justified?). Proposed solutions can involve deductive reasoning, inductive reasoning, formal and informal reasoning, analytic thinking, creative thinking, and metacognition. The definition embraces a number of the criteria suggested by Resnick (1987). That is, when students use information to solve a novel, challenging problem, this is likely to entail uncertainty, nonalgorithmic solutions, self-regulation, the imposition of meaning, and measured judgment. All higher order challenges, however, need not manifest all of Resnick's criteria.

This definition stipulates what an individual should do with information (interpret, analyze, manipulate), and the occasion necessary to provoke such use (a challenging problem). Individuals differ, of course, in the kinds of problems they find challenging. For one person, trying to understand how to read and follow a bus schedule may require higher order thought; for another, the same task will be routine. In this sense, higher order thinking is relative: to determine the extent to which an individual is involved in higher order thinking, one presumably needs to know something about the person's intellectual history. Furthermore, to assess the extent to which an individual actually participates in the analysis, interpretation, and manipulation of information, one needs to "get inside" the person's head or experience his or her subjective state of thought. This, of course, poses an operational problem. It may be difficult to determine reliably the extent to which a person is involved in higher order thinking.

Teachers interacting with several students at once have little opportunity to assess students' individual mental states. Instead, they must make assumptions about the prior knowledge of groups of students and about the kinds of mental work that certain tasks are likely to stimulate. The teaching of thinking, therefore, is an imprecise enterprise, but, to the extent that our assumptions about students' prior experience are correct, we can pose appropriately challenging problems. The goal is to engage students in what we predict will be challenging problems, guide their manipulation of information to solve them, and support their efforts.

Knowledge, Skills and Dispositions to Meet the Challenges

Research on the nature of thinking (summarized for teachers by Walsh & Paul, 1987) indicates that for students to cope successfully with cognitive challenge, both within and beyond social studies, they need a combination of in-depth knowledge of subject matter, skills in processing information, and attitudes or dispositions of reflectiveness. These three components are the core of a curriculum implied by the conception of higher order thinking just presented.

Knowledge.   Experienced teachers insist, and scholars have shown, that previously acquired knowledge is critical to solving problems that require going beyond the information given. In social studies, solutions to such problems depend on extensive knowledge of social life beyond the student's immediate experience. In a broad review, Nickerson (1988) distinguished several types of knowledge identified in studies of thinking: domain-specific knowledge, knowledge of normative principles of reasoning, knowledge of informal principles and tools of thought, and metacognitive knowledge. Social studies teachers tend to give much attention to communicating knowledge of their subjects, that is, domain-specific knowledge (e.g., historical facts, social science concepts, principles of government); but they have been criticized for merely transmitting the knowledge to students, rather than helping students to use the knowledge to master higher order challenges. If domain-specific knowledge is properly taught, however, a strong case can be made that this will inevitably entail higher order thinking, because adequate mastery of most subjects requires the use, manipulation, and interpretation of knowledge in the subject area (Glaser, 1984; McPeck, 1981).

A serious problem in social studies is the tendency to transmit knowledge largely through surveys of diverse topics covering a broad range of human experience. Because of the superficiality of content and the difficulty in drawing connections between topics, the material offers little substance for dealing with critical issues (e.g., Was violence against England adequately justified by colonial patriots?). It is also easily forgotten. To be more useful in meeting higher order challenges, social studies knowledge should be organized more toward depth on a smaller number of related topics.

Skills.   Good thinkers are often described as having special skills, such as the ability to identify problems, state alternative solutions, offer evidence, judge logical consistency, detect bias, and find new sources of information. In addition to general skills, high-quality thinking in specific subjects is said to depend on domain-specific skills, such as solving quadratic equations in mathematics, use of laboratory equipment in science, or jurisprudential reasoning in social studies. Those who stress a curriculum of skills maintain that content alone is insufficient, that students must be taught specific techniques, including metacognitive strategies, for analyzing, interpreting, and manipulating content (e.g., Beyer, 1987; Brown, Bransford, Ferrara, & Campione, 1983; de Bono, 1983; Herrnstein et al., 1986).

The effort to enumerate the skills that constitute higher order thinking can usefully focus attention on educational goals other than the didactic transmission of information. But whether thinking itself can be adequately conceptualized as a particular set of skills and whether those skills can be taught to be transferred beyond a highly specific application is questionable. Critics argue that skills are, in essence, really only manifestations of knowledge or of dispositions, that the transferability of skill mastery is hard to demonstrate, and that skills may be taught and practiced in ways that undermine as well as enhance thinking (Cornbleth, 1985; Paul, 1982; Schrag, 1988; Siegel, 1985).

In spite of these difficulties, a skills perspective can contribute to a curriculum for higher order thinking, because it provides a common language that helps to generate activities beyond gathering of information that must be conducted in order to participate in disciplined inquiry. These activities include scrutinizing arguments for logical consistency; distinguishing between relevant and irrelevant information and between factual claims and value judgments; using metaphor and analogy to represent problems and solutions; using rhetorical strategies such as stipulation of disputable claims to let an argument proceed; and implementing discussion strategies such as asking for clarification, pressing people to stay with an issue, and summarizing the progress of the conversation. Such activities can help students to think when these activities are applied to organizing the knowledge needed to solve a particular problem.

Dispositions.   Higher order thinking requires something even more fundamental than knowledge or skills, namely, a number of dispositions that together constitute thoughtfulness. Those who emphasize dispositions (e.g., Cornbleth,

1985; Norris, 1985; Passmore, 1967; Schrag, 1988; Walsh & Paul, 1987; Wiggins, 1988) suggest several traits: a persistent desire that claims be supported by reasons (and that the reasons themselves be scrutinized); a tendency to be reflective—to take time to think problems through for oneself, rather than acting impulsively or automatically accepting the views of others; a curiosity to explore new questions; and the flexibility to entertain alternative and original solutions to problems. Thoughtfulness thereby involves attitudes, personality or character traits, and general values and beliefs, or worldviews, about the nature of knowledge (e.g., that rationality is desirable; that knowledge itself is socially constructed, subject to revision, and often indeterminate; and that thinking can lead to the understanding and solution of problems). Knowledge and skills will be important for the mastery of particular challenges, but without dispositions of thoughtfulness, content and skills can be taught and applied mechanistically and nonsensically. Thus, thoughtfulness must be reinforced in the curriculum as a necessary, though not sufficient, condition for higher order thinking. Programs that are consistent with this emphasis include those described by Adler (1982); Feurstein, Rand, Hoffman, and Miller, (1980); Lipman, Sharp, and Iscanyan (1980); and Sizer (1986).

To summarize, in order to help students successfully master the solution of nonroutine problems, teachers must provide the opportunity to gain in-depth knowledge; activities that help them practice skills in the analysis, interpretation, and manipulation of knowledge; and support for developing dispositions of thoughtfulness. These elements have been separated and distinguished for the purpose of presenting a framework, but to be applied effectively, they must be integrated in practice.

Special Challenges in Social Studies

The framework thus far is relevant well beyond social studies, for it has been grounded largely in research on thinking in general. What more precisely characterizes the intellectual terrain that challenges explorers within the social studies territory? Hundreds of concepts, explanations, and issues have already been articulated by numerous curriculum projects and committees. Here, however, we suggest that the countless specific social studies problems that challenge students to think can be construed as a smaller set of generic higher order expeditions. Actual student work on particular tasks may involve more than one of the expeditions, for they are not mutually exclusive. These challenges may not be unique to social studies, but they seem to lie at the core of its higher order dimension.

Empathy. Social studies seeks to expand students' social experience across time, space, and culture to develop a more complex perspective on their own lives. To find meaning in the life of classical Athens, the tragedy of the Holocaust, or the teachings of Buddha involves extending the mind and spirit beyond the tangible, the concrete, and the familiar. The challenge here is not simply to learn new vocabulary, but to see and to feel the world from another's point of view. To reason about moral problems, to explain the puzzles of cultural variation, or to hypothesize about historical causation, student must incorporate into their own thinking the experience of others. The task of reorganizing one's understanding of human affairs to assimilate and accommodate foreign information is a formidable cognitive task, especially because it is not possible for students to encounter these experiences directly. Human lives and institutions must be represented by authors, film producers, and teachers, who try to move students to incorporate, identify with, and ponder circumstances beyond the familiar.

Abstraction.   Much of the knowledge we use to solve nonroutine problems consists of factual claims, concepts, and theories that describe concrete activity in more general language. Such knowledge can be particularly powerful when it permits the perception of relationships not previously noticed. The disciplines of history and social science introduce abstractions that are not likely to be encountered elsewhere (e.g., Plato's discussion of virtue, Marx's analysis of class, King's observations on nonviolent protest), and social studies teachers consistently worry about whether students can really use these abstractions to make sense of social events. Will they transfer their knowledge of the United States Constitution to understand issues in the contemporary criminal justice system? Can they use economic principles to explain a rise or decline in employment? Can they see the influence of colonialism on current issues in foreign policy or of racism on social stratification? Unfortunately, abstractions are often taught only didactically, as vocabulary, and students are asked only to reproduce what has been said by the teacher or text. But when teachers help students to use abstractions to go beyond the information given to solve new problems, they promote higher order thinking.

Inference.   Drawing inferences from limited data is central to historical and social scientific inquiry, and social studies teachers want students to struggle with comparable inferential challenges. To determine who provoked the violence that launched the American patriots' rebellion against England, for example, teachers may ask students to scrutinize historical evidence and possible biases of the observers at Lexington and Concord. They may ask students to draw conclusions on the general causes of war or to predict the effects of increased interest rates on employment. As teachers encourage students to ask why,—to develop explanations of the past or predictions of the future—they invite the formulation and substantiation of inferences. Because, by definition, inference entails going beyond the information given to draw conclusions, it is an important type of higher order challenge.

Evaluation and Advocacy.   Social studies teachers want students to make and to intelligently defend value judgments about what is good or bad, right or wrong, just or unjust in public life. Was the South justified in seceding from the Union?

In what ways, if any, should the state promote cultural traditions of minority groups? What economic-political system is most likely to meet human needs equitably? What limits on national sovereignty are warranted in order to assure world peace? Evaluative judgments on such issues are the lifeblood of democratic citizenship, and citizens' decisions presumably influence the quality of public life. To the extent that citizens refrain from this sort of problem solving, or if they do so unintelligently, consent of the governed becomes a farce.

Working toward a defensible position on controversial social issues may entail challenges of empathy, abstraction, and inference, but, in addition, one must arrive at evaluative criteria. These may be introduced formally in the study of history and the disciplines (e.g., economic equality, social harmony, technological progress, individual liberty, fairness, national security, short-term versus long-term benefit), but the criteria are usually problematic. Deciding which evaluative criteria to apply lies at the root of the inquiry in social studies, but strategies for resolving such issues have received little attention in the research on thinking.

Critical Discourse—An Overriding Issue.   Social studies teachers committed to higher order thinking stress the importance of students thinking independently and critically. They applaud students who ask the unconventional question or who dare to defend a dissenting point of view. They value students who generate their own solutions to problems in their own language and who participate actively in dialogue and argument—written or oral. In short, they characterize good thinkers as those who generate critical discourse as they cope with the challenges of empathy, abstraction, inference, and evaluation.

A *critical* posture is equated with the tendency to question the facts, concepts, conclusions, assumptions, or logic of an argument and cast the information in a new light. *Discourse* refers to language produced with the intention of providing a narrative, argument, explanation, or analysis. The generation of critical discourse represents a higher order challenge, because it requires students to develop original questions, reactions, and language, rather than simply to reproduce the knowledge of others.

Having offered a general definition of higher order thinking, described the importance of knowledge, skills, and dispositions in mastering higher order challenges, and identified five types of challenges inherent in social studies instruction, it is time to consider implications of the framework for instructional change.

IMPLICATIONS FOR INSTRUCTIONAL CHANGE

As mentioned earlier, except for a few specific curriculum projects, empirical research in social studies offers little guidance on effective instructional techniques for promoting higher order thinking. Research beyond social studies has shown important differences in information processing between expert and novice problem solvers (Chi & Glaser, 1986; Voss, 1989), but this work (which has not focused on social studies challenges) has not been able to attribute the differences to specific instructional procedures. It is, therefore, reasonable to conclude that expertise is gained largely through extensive experience, practice, or opportunities to learn (Denham & Lieberman, 1980; Heyns, 1978; Sorenson & Hallinan, 1977). Because students have had little practice in facing higher order challenges in the social studies, we ought to increase student practice with diverse, wide-ranging forms of problem solving.

Our current research project suggests that, in addition to lack of knowledge on the effectiveness of specific techniques, critical barriers stand in the way of substantially increasing student practice with higher order challenges. These barriers include lack of informed commitment to the goal of higher order thinking by teachers and the society at large, the dilemma of how to balance depth and breadth in the curriculum, the dilemma of how to teach so that students both acquire knowledge and use it, organizational constraints on the conduct of instruction, and lack of opportunities for staff development. If student experience with higher order thinking is to be substantially expanded, attention to these issues is more critical, at the present time, than prescription of specific instructional strategies.

Cultural Resistance

Compared to other objectives for schooling, and in spite of rhetoric on thinking skills, the promotion of thinking and reasoning has consistently received little attention from parents and policymakers (Cuban, 1984). Critical inquiry in social studies can be disquieting. It asks us to demystify what has been taken for granted, to search for exploitation or contradiction in relationships that on the surface may appear voluntary and harmonious, and to continue to work for a better world rather than accepting what we have. Even in the most supportive settings, humans have great difficulty subjecting their beliefs to continuous scrutiny, exercising independent judgment, seriously considering ideas that may challenge conventional wisdom, resolving ambiguity and contradiction, and sustaining interest in abstract issues of justice. In short, for many people, critical inquiry is likely to involve a painful struggle, not an immediate sense of joy, growth, or positive accomplishment. It involves hard mental work, and because it may also threaten existing personal or group interests, the results may not always be rewarding for the student. For many students, it is more satisfying simply to take in the information dispensed and to reproduce it for teachers, employers, and test-makers with minimal effort—why think if you don't have to?

There may be a cultural press to avoid thoughtfulness, but, at the same time, we have seen social studies classes where it is rewarded and celebrated and where students have become intensely engaged in and excited about problem solving in social studies. Through their personal commitments and expectations, teachers of these classes seem to overcome dominant cultural resistance, and they use a variety of instructional strategies in doing so.

Depth and Coverage of Knowledge

As indicated earlier, to meet higher order challenges successfully requires in-depth understanding, but, due to the effort to expose students to a wide variety of topics, the knowledge transmitted in social studies is often superficial. A strong case can be made that the point of education is, in a sense, to cover material—that is, to expose students to and make them familiar with new information. To become educated involves learning the meanings of thousands of words and mastering hundreds of conventions for manipulating information and communicating effectively. If teachers want students to be familiar with major events, institutions, ideas, and people in history, there is simply not enough time to study everything in depth. Thus, depth versus coverage presents a dilemma that cannot be resolved simply by choosing one over the other (Newmann, 1988). Instead, teachers need to work toward a balance that permits, on the one hand, significant inquiry into higher order challenges and, on the other, adequate coverage of that knowledge required for literacy in the subject (Hirsch, 1987). According to our initial findings, teachers who excel in the promotion of higher order thinking recognize the dilemma, but they make deliberate and reasoned choices to reduce coverage in favor of in-depth study.

Teaching for Acquisition and Exploration

The conception of thinking and curriculum advanced here suggests that students must be afforded opportunities to solve problems by analyzing, interpreting, and manipulating information, rather than given superficial exposure to it. That is, pedagogy should engage students in active exploration. At the same time, they must acquire knowledge that maximizes the possibility of success on the expedition. Ideally, the stages of acquisition and exploration should be integrated through problem-solving activities that themselves provoke students to acquire new information and that displace the often-tedious routine of receiving information first and then solving a problem. This is a complicated pedagogical task, but the work of Wiggington (1985) and others indicates that it can be accomplished with much success.

Both acquisition and exploration can benefit from a more active pedagogy than is commonly used. This calls for individual quiet study, to be sure, but also for students to manipulate information orally, in writing, and by making and interpreting physical artifacts (pictures, models). As the student becomes more of a *worker* (Sizer, 1984; Wiggins, 1988), so does the teacher. Because right answers are not often apparent or conclusive in social studies, to gain a sense of success, students must rely more on teachers' responses to their work. That is, teachers need to give students more elaborate feedback about criteria for success, procedures, and improving the oral and written discourse through which they demonstrate success.

Teachers and researchers have suggested that students will resist an active pedagogy oriented toward higher order challenges. Many seem to prefer a passive role and well-defined algorithmic tasks, simple answers, and the absence of conflict (McNeil, 1986; Powell et al., 1985; Willis, 1977). The validity of this claim and its remedies depend, in part, on how we understand the sources of student resistance.

Resistance could be explained as information deficit: Students find it unrewarding to concentrate on problem solving, because they lack information on most topics presented in history and social studies. It could be attributed to either an innate psychological condition or a developmental deficit: Humans naturally resist ambiguity and conflict in favor of certitude and harmony; young people have not developed sufficient powers of abstract cognitive thought. It could be the result of social conditioning that has reinforced a self-fulfilling lower order mindset about knowledge and inquiry in school. The mindset may include several beliefs: (a) Most knowledge is certain, rather than problematic, (b) knowledge is created primarily by outside authorities, not within oneself, (c) knowledge is to be comprehended and expressed in small, fragmented chunks (d) knowledge is to be learned as quickly as possible, rather than pondered (e) knowledge may seem counterintuitive or mysterious with respect to one's experience, but it should be believed anyway, and (f) arguments and conflict about the nature of knowledge are personally risky, because winners are favored over losers.

To generate more student engagement in thinking, these sources of resistance must be considered and addressed explicitly by teachers and researchers. Some of them may be difficult to overcome, but our current research indicates that both individual teachers and whole departments can minimize their impact and thereby engage students in active inquiry.

Organizational Constraints

Our research suggests that many teachers can conceive of effective curriculum and pedagogy to promote higher order thinking in social studies. The mystery arises when this must be accomplished with 30 students of vastly diverse motivation and knowledge, meeting in one room, for a 50-minute period each day, with curriculum guidelines for content coverage that prevent in-depth reflection, and the teacher must also respond daily to 100 additional students in similar circumstances. Rather than inventing pedagogical miracles to manage this teaching environment, it might be wiser to create environments that allow existing pedagogical knowledge to be used.

What kind of an environment is needed to help students manipulate information in response to the challenges of empathy, abstraction, inference, evaluation, and critical discourse? As indicated before, there must be opportunity for extensive interaction between students and teachers. Success in these tasks could also be enhanced by cooperative work in which students help one another through criticism, division of labor, and comparison of perspectives. Because the problems to be explored vary substantially, they are most productively studied in flexible time periods, rather than in identical routine blocks. Finally, developing empathy, perceiving the concrete meaning of abstractions, and constructing more defensible evaluative judgments of the social world often require study beyond the classroom—more contact with the outside community should be encouraged.

To build such conditions, changes in school organization such as the following should be pursued: (a) reduced teacher load and class size to provide more opportunity for teacher feedback on individual work; (b) flexible scheduling of classwork to allow more sustained, continuous investigation of problems than is possible in the 50-minute period, 5 days a week; (c) reduction in the number of separate courses that students take simultaneously (to further support in-depth study); and (d) increased opportunity for community study. Organizational change is a necessary, though not sufficient, condition for the promotion of higher order thinking, because organizational change alone is unlikely to alter curriculum and pedagogy without appropriate changes in teachers' conceptions of their work.

Staff Development

The thrust of this analysis is that our failure to promote higher order thinking in social studies is due not primarily to a lack of knowledge of technique, but rather to a lack of an informed, reflective commitment to the goal. Teachers are the key, and, although many agree with the general goal, they face substantial obstacles. Some barriers arise from organizational constraints and external pressures, but others are rooted in philosophical confusion, persisting dilemmas of teaching, and pedagogical traditions that teachers have had few opportunities to examine. Teachers need more opportunity to build self-conscious conceptions of thinking that resolve some of these matters. Our clarification of challenges central to social studies and our discussion of content, skills, and dispositions offer a foundation on which to build. But even this analysis leaves much unfinished business. Teachers will need to interrogate their own priorities as they face such persisting dilemmas as how much breadth must be sacrificed for depth of understanding and how much knowledge students must master before they can be considered ready to solve problems. They must determine how to keep students actively involved in both acquisition and exploration.

IMPLICATIONS FOR RESEARCH

Because of the many types of problems toward which thinking in social studies might be directed and because of the vast amount of knowledge and skills that might be taught, extensive research on specific pedagogy could well lead to further balkanization of knowledge on teaching, an endless effort to discover all the different ways of teaching the skills required to solve specific problem types. Such specialization would make it ever more difficult to synthesize findings usefully for practitioners. To minimize such problems, we have proposed a general framework for conceptualizing higher order thinking in social studies. It would be useful for future research to address higher order thinking in a similarly broad fashion so that findings would be applicable to a wide array of teaching situations. Ideally, such a research agenda would (a) develop a set of reliable indicators by which to assess the degree of higher order thinking or thoughtfulness promoted in social studies lessons, (b) establish a positive relationship between classroom thoughtfulness and individual student success in meeting higher order challenges, and (c) explain the variation in thoughtfulness between classes by addressing how teachers, departments, and schools cope with the barriers or obstacles identified here or those modified by future inquiries.

Our research has begun this agenda (Newmann, 1990), and, as mentioned, an instrument has been developed to assess classroom thoughtfulness. Using five-point scales, lessons were rated on 17 dimensions, some of which are:

1. In this class, there was sustained examination of a few topics, rather than superficial coverage of many.
2. In this class, the teacher asked challenging questions and/or structured challenging tasks (given the ability level and preparation of the students).
3. In this class, students offered explanations and reasons for their conclusions.
4. In this class, the teacher carefully considered explanations and reasons for conclusions.
5. In this class, students assumed the roles of questioner and critic.
6. In this class, students generated original and unconventional ideas, explanations, hypotheses, or solutions to problems.

The initial sample was limited to five schools that were presumably unusual in their emphasis on higher order thinking, but results show that these indicators of classroom thoughtfulness can be reliably coded and that the more thoughtful classes distinguished themselves by careful consideration of reasons; extensive

Socratic questioning; students often generating original ideas and articulate, relevant comments; and greater reliance on class discussion and the use of sources other than textbooks.

Students considered their most challenging classes also to be the most engaging ones, and the main challenges they identified in social studies were forming opinions, making inferences, and other tasks that are consistent with our definition of higher order challenge.

Teachers cited the large numbers of students taught as the most significant organizational barrier, and there was wide agreement that the pressure to cover content, whether external or self-imposed, often inhibits thinking. Teachers occasionally complained about mandated tests and lack of appropriate instructional materials, but these were less formidable barriers.

Student ability or background did not appear to be a barrier to classroom thoughtfulness in these schools. Teachers rarely attributed problems in promoting thinking to student characteristics. Quantitative analysis of lesson scores showed only minor effects of student background, and the teachers who scored the highest taught more low-achieving students than did their colleagues who scored lower.

As this research proceeds, we will be able to elaborate on these issues, especially on the extent to which institutional program variables—in contrast to individual teacher characteristics and various student characteristics—influence the level of thoughtfulness in classes. In this sample, for instance, over 25% of the variation in thoughtfulness occurred between schools, rather than between teachers. The three highest performing departments differed from the two lowest in having a departmentally based program, strong instructional leadership from the department chair and principal, and a strong collegial culture within the department.

Comparisons between the high- and low-scoring teachers suggested that important barriers may reside in teachers' goals and conceptions of their work. Perhaps not surprisingly, teachers with the most thoughtful classes placed higher priority on thinking as an educational goal, articulated more elaborate conceptions of thinking, and placed more value on depth than breadth of coverage. This raises, but cannot answer, the question of the extent to which teacher beliefs must be considered the central target for reform in this area, in contrast, for example, to materials and organizational conditions.

Such research should contribute to the improvement of practice. In-service work with teachers suggests that these observational categories can help teachers to conceptualize and to plan more effectively for the promotion of higher order thinking in social studies. Information on how some departments have overcome obstacles, whereas others have failed to address them effectively, should provide guidance for implementation of future programs.

SUMMARY

Approaches to the study of thinking are so diverse that the field has been characterized as a "conceptual swamp" (Cuban, 1984, p. 676). Nevertheless, the framework offered here attempts to incorporate major theoretical orientations as well as the views of teachers. The conception emphasizes interpretation, analysis, and manipulation of information to solve problems that cannot be solved by routine application of previously acquired knowledge. To solve such problems successfully requires a combination of in-depth knowledge, skill-directed activities, and the reinforcement of thoughtful dispositions. Social studies teachers who emphasize thinking want students to confront a variety of challenges that can be summarized as empathy, abstraction, inference, evaluation advocacy, and critical discourse.

This framework and emerging findings from an on-going research project suggest that, if instruction is to change productively along these lines, special attention must be devoted not primarily to elucidation of specific instructional techniques, but to five more fundamental issues: cultural resistance to higher order thinking as an educational priority; the balance between depth and coverage of knowledge; creating an active pedagogy that helps students to at once acquire and explore knowledge; organizational constraints on higher order thinking; and staff development opportunities for dealing with these issues.

The framework recommends a research agenda that concentrates on the assessment of specific dimensions of thoughtfulness in classrooms, that investigates the ways in which teachers and schools promote these dimensions and overcome persisting obstacles, and that attempts to establish a connection between dimensions of classroom thoughtfulness and individual student success in facing higher order challenges.

ACKNOWLEDGMENT

This paper was prepared at the National Center on Effective Secondary Schools, School of Education, University of Wisconsin, Madison, which is supported in part by a grant from the Office of Educational Research and Improvement (Grant No. G-008690007). Any opinions, findings, conclusions, or recommendations expressed in this publication are those of the author and do not necessarily reflect the views of this agency or the U.S. Department of Education. Thanks to Catherine Cornbleth, Larry Cuban, Michael Hartoonian, Alan Lockwood, Cameron McCarthy, Joseph Onosko, Francis Schrag, and Robert Stevenson for reactions to the manuscript, to 40 high school social studies teachers nationwide who shared their views on the problem, and especially to Judith Segal for creative and painstaking editorial help.

REFERENCES

Adler, M. (1982). *The paideia proposal: An educational manifesto.* New York: Macmillan.
Armento, B. J. (1986). Research on teaching social studies. In M. C. Wittrock (Ed.), *Handbook of research on teaching* (3rd ed.) (pp. 942–951). New York: Macmillan.
Barr, R., Barth, J. L., & Shermis, S. S. (1977). *Defining the social studies* (Bulletin 51). Arlington, VA: National Council for the Social Studies.
Beyer, B. (1985). Critical thinking: What is it? *Social Education, 49,*(4), 270–276.
Beyer, B. (1987). *Practical strategies for the teaching of thinking.* Boston: Allyn & Bacon.
Brown, A. L., Bransford, J. D., Ferrara, R. A., & Campione, J. C. (1983). Learning, remembering, and understanding. In J. H. Flavell & E. M. Markman (Eds.), *Cognitive development* (Vol. III of P. H. Mussen (Ed.), *Handbook of child psychology,* pp. 77–166). New York: Wiley.
Chance, P. (1986). *Thinking in the classroom: A survey of programs.* New York: Teachers College Press.
Chi, M. T. H., & Glaser, R. (1986). Problem-solving ability. In R. J. Sternberg (Ed.), *Human abilities: An information processing approach* (pp. 237–250). New York: W. H. Freeman.
Chipman, S. F., Segal, J. W., & Glaser, R. (Eds.). (1985). *Thinking and learning skills: Vol. 2. Research and open questions.* Hillsdale, NJ: Lawrence Erlbaum Associates.
Cornbleth, C. (1985). Critical thinking and cognitive processes. In W. B. Stanley (Ed.), *Review of research in social studies education: 1976–1983* (pp. 11–63). Boulder, CO: ERIC Clearinghouse for Social Studies/Social Science Education.
Costa, A. (Ed.). (1985). *Developing minds: A resource book for teaching thinking.* Alexandria, VA: Association for Supervision and Curriculum Development.
Covington, M. V. (1987). Instruction in problem-solving planning. In S. L. Friedman, E. K. Scholnick, & R. R. Cocking (Eds.), *Blueprints for thinking: The role of planning in cognitive development* (pp. 469–511). New York: Cambridge University Press.
Cuban, L. (1984). Policy and research dilemmas in the teaching of reasoning: Unplanned designs. *Review of Educational Research, 54*(4), 655–681.
de Bono, E. (1983). The direct teaching of thinking as a skill. *Phi Delta Kappan, 64*(10), 703–708.
Denham, C., & Lieberman, A. (Eds.). (1980). *Time to learn.* Washington, DC: National Institute of Education.
Ennis, R. H. (1962). A concept of critical thinking. *Harvard Educational Review, 32*(1), 81–111.
Feeley, T., Jr. (1976). Critical thinking: toward a definition, paradigm and research agenda. *Theory and Research in Social Education, 4*(1), 1–19.
Feuerstein, R., Rand, Y., Hoffman, M. B., & Miller, R. (1980). *Instrumental enrichment: An intervention program for cognitive modifiability.* Baltimore, MD: University Park Press.
Giroux, H. (1978). Writing and critical thinking in the social studies. *Curriculum Inquiry, 8*(4), 291–310.
Glaser, R. (1984). Education and thinking: The role of knowledge. *American Psychologist, 39,* 93–104.
Goodlad, J. I. (1984). *A place called school: Prospects for the future.* New York: McGraw-Hill.
Herrnstein, R. J., Nickerson, R. S., De Sanchez, M., & Swets, J. A. (1986). Teaching thinking skills. *American Psychologist, 41*(11), 1279–1289.
Heyns, B. (1978). *Summer learning and the effects of schooling.* New York: Academic.

Hirsch, E. D. (1987). *Cultural literacy: What every American needs to know.* Boston: Houghton Mifflin.

Hunt, M. P., & Metcalf, L. (1968). *Teaching high school social studies.* New York: Harper & Row.

Kohlberg, L. (1981). *The philosophy of moral development: Moral stages and the idea of justice.* New York: Harper & Row.

Levin, M., Newmann, F. M., & Oliver, D. W. (1969). *A law and social science curriculum based on the analysis of public issues* (Final report). Cambridge, MA: Graduate School of Education, Harvard University.

Lipman, M. (1985). Thinking skills fostered by philosophy for children. In J. W. Segal, S. F. Chipman, & R. Glaser (Eds.), *Thinking and learning skills: Vol 1. Relating instruction to research* (pp. 83–108). Hillsdale, NJ: Lawrence Erlbaum Associates.

Lipman, M., Sharp, A. M., & Iscanyan, F. S. (1980). *Philosophy in the classroom* (2nd ed.). Philadelphia, PA: Temple University Press.

Mayer, R. E. (1983). *Thinking, problem solving, cognition.* New York: W. H. Freeman.

McNeil, L. M. (1986). *Contradictions of control: School structure and school knowledge.* New York: Routledge & Kegan Paul.

McPeck, J. E. (1981). *Critical thinking and education.* New York: St. Martins.

Metcalf, L. E. (1963). Research on teaching the social studies. In N. L. Gage (Ed.), *Handbook of research on teaching* (pp. 929–965). Chicago: Rand McNally.

Morrissett, I. (Ed.). (1967). *Concepts and structure in the new social science curricula.* New York: Holt, Rinehart & Winston.

Morrissett, I. (Ed.). (1982). *Social studies in the 1980s: A report of project SPAN.* Alexandria, VA: Association for Supervision and Curriculum Development.

Mosher, R. L. (Ed.). (1980). *Moral education: A first generation of research and development.* New York: Praeger.

Newmann, F. M. (1988). Can depth replace coverage in the high school curriculum? *Phi Delta Kappan, 69*(5), 345–348.

Newmann, F. M. (1990). Qualities of thoughtful social studies classes: An empirical profile. *Journal of Curriculum Studies, 22*(3), 253–275.

Nickerson, R. S. (1988). On improving thinking through instruction. In E. Z. Rothkopf (Ed.) *Review of Research in Education, 15,* (Washington, DC: American Educational Research Association), 3–57.

Nickerson, R. S., Perkins, D. N., & Smith, E. E. (1985). *The teaching of thinking.* Hillsdale, NJ: Lawrence Erlbaum Associates.

Norris, S. P. (1985). Synthesis of research on critical thinking. *Educational Leadership, 42*(8), 40–45.

Oliver, D. W., & Shaver, J. P. (1966). *Teaching public issues in the high school.* Logan, UT: Utah State University Press.

Palincsar, A. S., & Brown, A. L. (1984). Reciprocal teaching of comprehension-fostering and comprehension-monitoring activities. *Cognition and Instruction, 1,* 117–175.

Passmore, J. (1967). On teaching to be critical. In R. S. Peters (Ed.), *The concept of education* (pp. 192–211). London: Routledge & Kegan Paul.

Patterson, J. H., & Smith, M. S. (1986). The role of computers in higher-order thinking. In *Microcomputers and Education* (85th Yearbook of the National Society for the Study of Education, Part 1; pp. 81–108). Chicago: University of Chicago Press.

Paul, R. (1982, May). Critical thinking in the strong sense: A focus on self-deception, world views, and a dialectical mode of analysis. *Informal Logic Newsletter,* p. 2–7.

Perkins, D. N. (1984). Creativity by design. *Educational Leadership, 42*(1), 18–24.

Perkins, D. N. (1986, April). *Reasoning as it is and could be: An empirical perspective.* Paper presented at the annual meeting of the American Educational Research Association, San Francisco, CA.

Perrone, V. & Associates. (1985). *Portraits of high schools: A supplement to high school: A report on secondary education in America.* Princeton, NJ: Carnegie Foundation for the Advancement of Teaching.

Powell, A. G., Farrar, E., & Cohen, D. K. (1985). *The shopping mall high school: Winners and losers in the educational marketplace.* Boston: Houghton Mifflin.

Resnick, L. B. (1987). *Education and learning to think.* Washington, DC: National Academy Press.

Rest, J. R., in collaboration with Barnett, R., Bebeau, M., Deemer, D., Getz, I., Moon, Y., Schlaefli, A., Spickelmier, J., Thoma, S., & Volker J. (1986). *Moral development: Advances in research and theory.* New York: Praeger.

Schrag, F. (1988). *Thinking in school and society.* New York: Routledge & Kegan Paul.

Segal, J. W., Chipman, S. F., & Glaser, R. (Eds.). (1985). *Thinking and learning skills: Vol 1. Relating instruction to research.* Hillsdale, NJ: Lawrence Erlbaum Associates.

Shaver, J. P., & Larkins, A. G. (1973). Research on teaching social studies. In R. M. W. Travers (Ed.), *Second handbook of research on teaching* (pp. 1243–1262). Chicago: Rand McNally.

Siegel, H. (1985, Spring/Summer). Educating reason: Critical thinking, informal logic, and the philosophy of education. *American Philosophical Association Newsletter on Teaching Philosophy,* pp. 10–13.

Sizer, T. R. (1984). *Horace's compromise: The dilemma of the American high school.* Boston: Houghton Mifflin.

Sizer, T. R. (1986). Rebuilding: First steps by the coalition of essential schools. *Phi Delta Kappan, 68*(1), 38–42.

Sorenson, A. B. & Hallinan, M. T. (1977). A reconceptualization of school effects. *Sociology of education, 50,* 273–289.

Stake, R. E. & Easley, J. A. (1978). *Case studies in science education.* Washington, DC: National Science Foundation.

Sternberg, R. J. & Bhana, K. (1986). Synthesis of research on the effectiveness of intellectual skills programs: Snake-oil remedies or miracle cures? *Educational Leadership, 44*(2), 60–67.

Sternberg, R. J., & Wagner, R. K. (Eds.) (1986). *Practical intelligence: Nature and origins of competence in the everyday world.* New York, NY: Cambridge University Press.

Voss, J. F. (1989). Problem solving and the educational process. In R. Glaser & A. Lesgold (Eds.), *Foundations for a psychology of education.* Hillsdale, NJ: Lawrence Erlbaum Associates.

Walsh, D., & Paul, R. W. (1987). *The goal of critical thinking: From educational ideal to educational reality.* Washington, DC: American Federation of Teachers.

Wiggington, E. (1985). *Sometimes a shining moment: The foxfire experience.* Garden City, NY: Anchor Press/Doubleday.

Wiggins, G. (1988). *Student as worker: Towards engaging and effective curricula.* Providence, RI: Brown University, Coalition of Essential Schools.

Willis, P. E. (1977). *Learning to labour.* Lexington, MA: D. C. Heath.

20 Informal Reasoning and Writing Instruction

Arthur N. Applebee
State University of New York at Albany

For the past 2 decades, research on writing has focused primarily on reasoning and problem solving processes—a focus that would seem ideally relevant to the present concern with fostering students' informal reasoning processes. In this chapter, I review the major trends in these studies of writing, and their implications for our current concerns. Rather than delivering an optimistic message about the ease with which we can refocus instruction, my major themes concern the difficulties involved: in calling for more attention to reasoning processes, we are really calling for a redefinition of the goals and philosophy of education in most classrooms. And while I heartily endorse this call, I expect such changes to be neither simple to formulate nor easy to implement.

TRENDS IN INSTRUCTION AND ACHIEVEMENT

A New Direction for Writing Instruction

Until the 1970s, research in writing sought primarily to describe the nature of written texts (Braddock, Lloyd-Jones, & Schoer, 1963), specifically, the conventions and structures that give writing a particular shape and effectiveness. The results of this research are familiar to most of us. They provided the content for traditional composition programs in high school and college, taking the shape of admonitions about the use of topic sentences, formulas for paragraph construction, and exercises in the traditional modes of discourse (description, narration, persuasion, exposition, and sometimes poetry).

The concern with reasoning and problem solving in writing research, however, has been part of a general focus on the processes that writers engage in while they write. The underlying notion is simple enough: However final the words on a page may look, they gain their shape through an extended process of drafting and revision. Such studies began in large part because of frustration with the earlier studies of written texts (usually, of the classics), which were not yielding satisfactory instructional procedures. If we can describe the writing processes of good writers, the argument ran, then we can use this description to specify what we should teach novice writers. And expert writers, they found, seemed to use an elaborate process of problem solving.

The instructional approaches that derived from these studies are usually called *process oriented,* because they rely on techniques meant to lead novices through processes similar to those used by expert writers. While there are many variations on process-oriented approaches, they typically emphasize the notion that any piece of writing has a history, and that a writer's ideas develop during the process of writing, rather than being fully formed before writing begins. In instructional, this approach leads to an emphasis on multiple drafts; planning and revising; the use of journals, learning logs, and brainstorming activities; postponing of editing until the final draft; and the provision of multiple audiences through peer response groups and publishing of student work.

Process-oriented writing instruction, because it treats writing as a problem-solving process and a way of clarifying one's own ideas, is also an attempt to integrate the teaching of thinking and writing. It contrasts sharply with more product-oriented writing instruction, where the writer's task is usually treated as one of shaping a known message to a specific audience, and where the emphasis is on the accuracy and structure of the final text.

How widespread have process-oriented approaches become? The National Assessment of Educational Progress has been examining achievement and instruction in literacy-related areas since the 1969–1970 academic year. On the one hand, responses to its questions about writing instruction suggest that process approaches have increased somewhat over the past decade (Applebee, Langer, & Mullis, 1986a). Students report that they spend more time on individual writing assignments than in the past and are more likely to write multiple drafts. These trends mirror the emphases in journals on the teaching of writing, which have been dominated by process-oriented approaches. On the other hand, though process-oriented approaches are more widespread than in the past, they are far from universal. Even at Grade 11, only 59% of the students sampled by the National Assessment reported that they usually wrote more than one draft of their papers, even for an English class.

Effects on Student Achievement

If there is a greater emphasis in writing instruction on the development of problem-solving and reasoning skills, to what extent are students learning these processes? Overall, the results from the National Assessment studies of literacy suggest that there has been some improvement in reading skills during the past 15 years, but none in writing (although writing achievement seems to have recovered after a dip in performance during the 1970s) (Applebee, Langer, & Mullis, 1985, 1986a). Such patterns are puzzling, given the emphasis that has been placed on writing instruction during the past decade and the variety of new instructional approaches that have been suggested.

Much of the writing that students do for school is writing about reading, and the National Assessment has consistently examined tasks that ask for performance of this sort. Performance on these tasks involves four steps: (a) initial comprehension, leading to (b) preliminary interpretations, followed by (c) a reexamination of the text in light of the initial interpretation, which may, in turn, result in (d) a more accurate or fuller final interpretation (Applebee et al., 1981). These steps provide a convenient framework for examining student achievement. Results across a variety of National Assessment studies suggest that students have well developed skills at the level of initial interpretation. They do quite well on multiple-choice tests of comprehension of age-appropriate reading passages, and they have at least a minimal understanding of the elements of various types of writing. In the most recent assessment at Grade 11, 81% of the students demonstrated a general understanding of the elements of informative writing, 66% to 90% (depending on the task) showed a similar understanding of imaginative writing, and 60% or more understood at least the basic elements of persuasive writing (Applebee, Langer, & Mullis, 1986a, 1986b). Students seem quite comfortable, in other words, with the first two steps in the model, those being initial comprehension and preliminary interpretations.

But they have considerable difficulty in moving on to steps 3 and 4: Rather than being able to use the text or their own ideas to extend their initial interpretations, most students do very poorly at such tasks. They seem puzzled when called upon to explain or defend the interpretations they have reached, and they lack strategies for thinking about either their own ideas or the texts they are discussing.

As an example, we can consider a set of tasks that asked students to evaluate a literary selection they had read. (Similar results were obtained for questions asking about mood, point of view, and theme.) At age 9, 79% were able to make an initial evaluation, a proportion that rose to 95% by age 17. When students were then asked to give evidence for their judgment, only 8% at age 9 were able to do so satisfactorily, and this rose hardly at all (to 13%) by age 17 (Applebee et al., 1981).

That does not mean that there were no differences between the results at ages 9 and 17. What students did seem to be learning was a received point of view, that is, a belief about what one should say, rather than a set of analytic, problem-solving skills. Among the 9- and 13-year-olds, this was reflected in the first glimpses of an English-class vocabulary. For example, Applebee et al. (1981) reported this evaluation by a 9-year-old: "It was a little silly with a good ending" (p. 28). A 13-year-old wrote, "The story didn't have any suspense like a good one would have, also, it would have been better if the main character was a first-person story teller. This would have made the story more interesting" (p. 28). This approach had been honed to perfection by age 17. Consider this explanation, written by a 17-year-old, of a positive evaluation of a short story:

> The story was full of suspense and kept the reader in doubt as to the outcome. The author uses much description in revealing the characters and the setting. There is a hidden meaning running throughout the story and this definitely intrigues the reader. Together with the suspense, the extraordinary description, and the underlying motive, the author has created an interesting story. (p. 28)

Such a response is cast in perfectly acceptable prose, but it is essentially unthinking. It is little more than a boilerplate that can be moved unchanged from one story to another, with its careful litany of literary terms (suspense, outcome, characters, setting, hidden meaning, underlying motive). There is no evidence of real analysis or engagement on the writer's part; it is a perfect example of what Macrorie (1976) has called "Engfish": a kind of fluent but vapid writing that is encouraged by too much focus on form at the expense of content.

The National Assessment data are also useful in looking at relationships between student achievement and other variables, such as students' approaches to writing and the kinds of instruction that they report that they have received. The results of the 1984 assessment indicate a clear relationship between students' writing achievement and their use of a variety of process strategies. Students who report spending more time on such strategies as planning, revising, and sharing their work-in-progress with others write noticeably better than their peers who spend less time on such processes. These results are fully consistent with results from the many smaller-scale studies that have examined novice and expert performance during the past 15 years (see Hillocks, 1986, for a review of these studies).

On the other hand, the assessment data show no relationship between the extent to which teachers emphasize such processes and the writing achievement of their students. Students from classrooms where a variety of process-oriented approaches had been introduced did no better than students from classrooms without such approaches, and sometimes they did worse (Applebee, Langer, & Mullis, 1986b).

Thus we have a paradox: Students who use process strategies in their own writing write better than do students who do not, but teaching those strategies is unrelated to student performance.

RESEARCH ON WRITING INSTRUCTION

Studies of Process-Oriented Writing Instruction

To begin to understand these results, it is helpful to look more carefully at recent studies of writing instruction. One of the anomalies in research in this field has been that while there have been many studies of the processes of individual writers, there have been few studies of the processes of instruction that are most effective in teaching writing skills. Most instructional studies have followed old paradigms, contrasting alternative treatments on a variety of outcome measures. Some of these studies, however, have examined some of the particular techniques that have become part of process-oriented instruction, such as the use of student journals or of peer response groups. Hillocks' (1986) metaanalysis of the past 20 years of such studies provides a good synthesis of the results. Hillocks examined a variety of alternatives to traditional models of lecture and recitation. Of those alternatives, two are particularly relevant to our present concerns. One of these Hillocks' called "natural process" approaches, which are characterized by any of a variety of techniques meant to encourage students' involvement in the writing process. The other represents "structured process" approaches (Hillocks called them "environmental"), which are characterized by the same teaching techniques but introduced in structured, problem-solving contexts. (One of the major differences between the two approaches is that natural process instruction places more emphasis on students' choosing their own task, developing their own approaches to revision, and developing their own strategies for problem solving. In structured process approaches, on the other hand, the strategies to be practiced are planned and structured by the teacher.) Hillocks found that structured process approaches were more than twice as effective as natural process ones, even though they were made up of the same component techniques (such as prewriting activities, multiple drafts, and revisions).

For our purposes, the most important interpretation of Hillock's results is that effective instruction does not emerge simply from a large repertoire of effective teaching techniques; it requires the careful orchestration of those techniques toward a particular end. Rather than emphasizing freewriting, peer response, or multiple drafts for their own sake, we need to conceptualize such approaches as contexts for teaching students strategies for solving particular problems. Such an interpretation parallels results of recent studies of reading comprehension, which suggest that students need to know not only what to do, but also when and why they should do it (e.g., Brown, 1978). Process-oriented instruction, then, may work best if it focuses on the purposes of the activities that students are asked to do, rather than solely on the procedures or activities themselves.

What then, does writing instruction look like in American schools today?

Studies of Current Uses of Writing in the Classroom

In spite of the increasing attention that has been given to process-oriented instruction, much of the writing that students do for school is limited in its scope and purpose. During the National Study of Writing in the Secondary School (Applebee, 1981, 1984), we found that the typical writing assignment for high school students in all subject areas consisted of a first-and-final draft, a page or less in length, completed in less than a day, and graded by the teacher. One of my favorite examples of such writing, which was collected during the National Study, is an assignment that was given in a 9th-grade social studies class:

> Western Europe on the eve of the Reformation was a civilization going through great changes. In a well written essay describe the political, economic, social, and cultural changes Europe was going through at the time of Reformation. (23 points)

In the form in which it was given, this is clearly an impossible assignment: Books could easily be written in response to it. But students find such topics very easy to write about. Although the assignment *seems* to require extended discussion and careful reasoning and analysis, students quickly learn that assignments such as this one demand only a recitation of material presented earlier in the textbook or in class. The several parts of the assignment serve merely as an index of topics that have been covered and that should be included in the students' responses.

This assignment provides a good transition into a consideration of problems in process-oriented instruction. The assignment provided no process supports to help the students with the task—and none were needed by the students. In fact, activities such as brainstorming, peer response, or guided revision would have been inappropriate had they been suggested, because the purpose of the assignment was clearly to test what students had learned, not to help them learn something new.

This pattern reflects the role that writing plays in most American classrooms. There is a well established model of curriculum in which we test students to diagnose what they need to know, teach them the missing information, and retest to see what they have learned, in a never-ending cycle of teaching and testing (Langer, 1984). Writing assignments very easily slip into the testing slots in this model—as did the assignment on Europe at the eve of the Reformation. When writing is used for such purposes, process-oriented techniques are inappropriate: at best they will be trivialized, divorced from the process of transformation of knowledge and experience that they were originally meant to encourage. Yet because the model of testing and teaching is so deeply ingrained in American schools, such trivialization of process-oriented writing techniques is quite widespread.

Altering the Uses of Writing in the Classroom

This problem became very apparent in a series of studies that Judith Langer and I concluded recently (Langer & Applebee, 1987), examining the effects of introducing a wider variety of writing activities into high school classrooms in several subject areas (including history, science, literature, and home economics). In these studies, we worked collaboratively with classroom teachers, spending 6 months to 2 years in each classroom as we developed new activities and examined the process of implementation. Our data included interviews with students and teachers, classroom observations, transcripts of lesson-planning sessions, case studies of individual students, and analyses of student work. Our goals in these studies were to understand the principles governing instruction in each classroom and the ways in which new instructional techniques interacted with these principles. We were not looking for a "package" of writing techniques to suggest to content area teachers, nor did we find one.

One of the main findings of this research was that it was relatively easy to introduce new techniques into the participating classrooms, but it was extremely difficult to make these activities work in the ways taken for granted in most discussions of process-oriented instruction. Rather than using new writing activities to foster a "transformation of knowledge and experience" through the process of writing, the teachers most often assimilated each activity to their old goals and previous patterns of instruction, which were generally of the traditional test–teach–retest–reteach mode.

Learning Logs in Science.[1]   We can illustrate these processes by looking at one activity that was introduced into a 10th-grade biology class as part of our study (Langer & Applebee, 1987). The teacher, Julian Bardolini, had 22 years of experience at the time the study began, and confined writing primarily to note taking and end-of-chapter study questions. This approach had not been working particularly well: He graded the study questions perfunctorily and never reviewed the notes. Typically, there was considerable confusion by examination time. Connie, a case study student, described some of the problems:

> It's not very good writing at all. It's usually about what we're studying at that time. It's usually on a test. I don't like it at all 'cause I don't think it's helpful. It's kind of a waste of time, and it brings your grade down. No one can usually fit it together, what they want to say.

---

[1]The examples from the classrooms of Julian Bardolini and Kathryn Moss are taken from J. Langer and A. Applebee, 1978, pp. 45–48; 73–76.

During the project, we focused on ways to help students "fit it together" by writing about new material.

One activity that Julian introduced was an end-of-lesson learning log, which he asked students to complete each day. It was introduced carefully to the students, complete with special notebooks for the logs, sample topics to write about, and sample log entries. We also had extensive discussions with Julian about how to respond to the logs in order to encourage the students to use them as a learning rather than a testing situation. The guide questions were designed to focus on students' own understandings of a day's activities:

1. What was done?
2. What was learned?
3. What was interesting?
4. What questions remained?

The use of the logs showed a gradual evolution in Julian's class. Initially, most of the entries were very short, with some venting of frustration about the subject and about Julian's teaching in entries such as, "Mr. Bardolini got sidetracked into talking about sex, but that seems to happen every day," (p. 47) or, "I didn't like it at first, but I like it now because if Mr. Bardolini has done something in class I don't really like, I like putting it down here in the log" (Langer & Applebee, 1987, p. 47).

Julian took these comments gracefully, and the logs gradually shifted to a focus on the content of the lessons, becoming fully embedded in the instructional routine. When we returned to Julian's classroom 1 year later, we found that he had extended the learning logs to all three of his biology classes. He had even convinced the school to supply the special notebooks (a considerable investment). Though the logs were initially not graded, by the following June, Julian had assimilated them into the point system that he used for all other activities. He collected them two or three times each quarter and gave full points for completed entries. As Julian described it, the logs had become an expected part of his classroom routine: "They know what they have to do and most of them accept it as a way of getting a good grade other than testing. . . . [Doing the log] could guarantee a perfect score. They love it." (p. 48).

The learning logs worked in Julian's classroom because

1. They served an important pedagogical function: They helped to review and reinforce difficult material (a function that was served less well by the notetaking Julian had previously relied upon);

2. Julian had adapted them to the ongoing classroom culture; he used a system of points for the logs to fit them into a general classroom economy that was driven by evaluation;

3. Julian kept extra work to manageable proportions by collecting the logs only once a month or so.

As long as writing activities observed these three principles (serving an important pedagogical function, being adapted to the classroom culture, and keeping extra work manageable), teachers found it relatively easy to introduce them into their teaching. At this level, the project was clearly a success.

At another level, however, the process of implementation raised serious questions about the usefulness of the new activities. Although teachers broadened their repertoire of teaching techniques, they often reinterpreted the techniques based on their old notions of teaching.

This process is apparent if we return for a second look at Julian's learning logs. We had originally seen them as an opportunity for students to synthesize and recast what they were learning in biology, that is, a context for exploring the limits of their new understanding. Julian gradually reinterpreted the logs, however, as another way to check on what students remembered, placing the emphasis on evaluation rather than on the process of learning.

This transformation is particularly clear if we examine the writing that the students did. As part of the study, we collected the students' log entries and analyzed them in terms of the audience that the writers were implicitly addressing (Applebee, 1981; Britton, Burgess, Martin, McLeod, & Rosen, 1975). The contrast of interest is between writing cast as part of an instructional dialogue and writing directed to the teacher-as-examiner. The results were dramatic: In January when the logs were first introduced, 57 percent of the entries were cast as part of an instructional dialogue. By March, the emphasis had reversed, with 63% directed at the teacher-as-examiner; by May, this had increased to 83 percent being treated as an examination context. Connie, one of the case study students, expressed this point directly. Her description of the log writing late in the semester: "Today we had a pop quiz."

Julian had assimilated a new set of teaching techniques, but had not rethought the basic emphases in his classroom. As a result, the new techniques were simply adapted to serve those initial emphases. Although, by the end of the project, he was using a variety of process-oriented instructional activities, the activities were not providing contexts in which students were developing their reasoning and problem-solving skills. Instead, the activities had become simply another means of testing what students already knew.

Activities That Worked.   If many of Julian's new writing assignments failed to provide contexts that helped students think, what kinds of assignments "work" in academic classrooms? We found that this question could not be answered at the level of individual writing activities. Each of the teachers who worked with us developed a unique configuration of writing activities, and seemingly similar assignments worked differently in different classrooms. What we did find, however, were three broad pedagogical functions that the many different types of writing activities served: (a) to draw on relevant knowledge and experience in preparation for new activities, (b) to consolidate and review new information and experiences, and (c) to reformulate and extend knowledge (p. 41). These categories proved to be a much more useful way to think about writing than the traditional method of using school genres (e.g., journal writing, essays, freewriting), each of which could serve any of the three functions depending upon how it was introduced. For a task to work successfully in extending students' reasoning about a topic, it needed to be related to one of these general pedagogical functions, and be presented and evaluated in a way that respected students' own knowledge of the topic rather than requiring a recitation of previously presented material.

As one example of a successful incorporation of a new activity, we can look at another science teacher, Kathryn Moss, and her eleventh grade chemistry class. Kathryn began working in our project with enthusiasm for the general principle that writing could shape students' thinking and with a healthy skepticism about its application in chemistry. As she put it in an early interview, "I don't see a good way to get more writing from them, even though I think it is important."

Given this skepticism, Kathryn concentrated on activities that were simple and useful, and that built on procedures already in place. One of those procedures was a rapid-fire oral review session that Kathryn used regularly. These review sessions were an important technique for helping students consolidate new information, but Kathryn was concerned that many students were not participating.

Her solution as to develop a 5 minute freewriting activity in which students wrote "everything they knew" on the topic they had been studying. She was excited about this activity, because it helped to focus her review sessions and insured that all students would become involved. And this perception was reinforced by spontaneous comments from students about how they, too, found the activity helpful.

Once she had developed a notion of review writing, Kathryn incorporated it into her standard repertoire and began to explore several variations on it. In the earliest versions, students' freewriting was followed by class discussion, with important points summarized on an overhead projector. Later, she used review-writing tasks to focus students' attention before their quizzes (which came as often as twice a week); as the basis for class discussion; as a prelude to homework assignments; and by the end of the year as open-book notes that pupils could refer to during the quizzes that followed. Although she checked all of the other work in her class, she read none of these review writings, which formed instead the basis of many lively discussions.

Review writing worked well in Kathryn's classroom because it served a function that she valued—preparation for quizzes—and did so better than the activities she had used in the past. As it evolved, review writing did not supplant class discussion as a preparatory activity, but it did enrich the discussions that followed and insured that everyone was involved. Because it was a preparatory activity, Kathryn was willing to postpone evaluation, allowing the students to use these brief writings as a way to review and consolidate what they knew. She quickly integrated review writing into her teaching repertoire, in part because it was fulfilling her own goals so well. At the same time, it provided students with a comfortable context in which to consolidate what they were learning—a context in which they knew they would not be penalized for errors or inaccuracies as they grappled with new ideas.

For Kathryn Moss, the success of the review writing task was the beginning of a fundamental change in approach, a change that involved placing more emphasis on developing students' reasoning skills and less emphasis on recitation. Such changes are difficult. They require teachers to reconstrue their goals for instruction and their established systems of evaluating both student work and the success of their own teaching. They also require an increased tolerance for ambiguity (because there is no longer "one right answer").

Jane, a social studies teacher whom we worked with for 2 years, commented perceptively on the difficulties: "The textbook, the district competency test, the district objectives, all force me in a certain line of "This is where I have to be going." . . . . Having the right answer makes teaching easier 'cause I know what I'm looking for. Not having the right answers makes it more chancy" (p. 83). But Jane also came to believe that there were benefits in the ambiguity: "But they learned better things as a result of the writing: (1) They learned how to think a little better; (2) they learned how to organize a little better; and (3) they learned better how to raise questions and judge answers" (p. 147). For Jane, these benefits made the changes all worthwhile.

FOSTERING INFORMAL REASONING THROUGH SCHOOL WRITING ASSIGNMENTS: DIRECTIONS FOR THE FUTURE

The results from Hillocks' metaanalyses and from our own studies of classrooms in transition converge to suggest that discussions of process-oriented approaches to writing instruction may have given too much attention to instruction as a set of activities or techniques and too little attention to the purposes and structure of the activities. Simply using techniques associated with process-oriented instruction—all that the National Assessment studies (Applebee, Langer, & Mullis, 1986) asked about, for example—may not be enough to make a difference in what students are learning. Instead, these activities may need to be embedded in a classroom context that places a much greater value on students' learning and problem-solving processes, and much less emphasis than at present on accurate recitation of previous learning. Students themselves must be made aware of the purposes underlying the activities we ask them to undertake, so that they can eventually internalize effective strategies to use when they are asked to write on their own.

Effecting these changes, however, will not be simple. We are no longer asking for a shift in the surface curriculum, but for a fundamental realignment of what will count as effective teaching and learning. Compounding the difficulty, we are asking teachers to make changes that the profession has not fully clarified or examined. This is not a case of practice lagging lamentably behind theory but of theory that is not developed enough to guide practice. (For a fuller development of this argument, see Applebee, 1986.) We do not yet have clear guidelines on how activities should be structured, or on the signposts that teachers should look for to recognize that new learning has taken place.

What Counts as Learning

The issue of what should count as effective performance is an important one, for it interacts with a number of other problems. As long as effective performance is solely a matter of knowledge of specific content, rather than also one of using problem-solving and reasoning skills that are linked to that content, then the issues discussed so far are issues of English instruction. To the extent that they arise at all in other subjects, it will be only to help the English teacher do a better job in developing students' generic writing skills. But if effective writing involves context-specific thinking and problem-solving skills, then the issues are quite general and necessarily become the concern of teachers in all subject areas.

In another recent study, Langer and I examined this by looking more closely at the nature of academic learning in selected subject areas. We asked, in effect, what does doing well mean? In this study (Langer & Applebee, 1988), we examined conceptions of knowing in three disciplines (American history, American literature, and biology), examining in each subject (1) the scholarly discussions of the philosophy of the subject, (2) the pedagogical literature about instructional goals and approaches, and (3) high school and college teachers' conceptions of what their students should learn.

Our hypothesis was that knowing in each subject has two equally important components: 1) particular content knowledge, and 2) ways of knowing and thinking that are accepted as appropriate and necessary to the discipline. That there are differences in content is obvious and trivial; that there are differences in ways of knowing and thinking is less clear. There is a long tradition in American education of granting equivalent value to many academic subjects on the assumption that they demand discipline. And there is an equally long tradition of teaching generic modes of argument and exposition as part of English instruction.

On the other hand, the philosophy of each subject usually stresses the uniqueness of, for example, "historical perspective," "scientific objectivity," or "literary sensitivity." In general, our argument is that educators lack a clear conception of what is unique and what is generic, and that this in turn has led to an overemphasis on specific content (which is well defined and easily assessed) at the expense of ways of thinking and knowing (which are hardly defined at all).

To take a brief example, in the field of literature differing traditions focus on the importance of text (emphasizing strategies for analysis), reader (emphasizing explanations of reactions and responses), and message (emphasizing the moral lesson). Practitioners in these traditions differ profoundly over the skills that a good reader of literature can be expected to have, and over the value of literary studies in the first place. In the high school curriculum, these profound differences in philosophical stance have manifested themselves only in differences in the technical vocabulary (i.e., particular content) that students are expected to memorize. The texts that they are asked to read and the classroom approaches to those texts vary little in response to the different traditions.

Many problems in education may derive from this lack of attention to ways of knowing and from the concomitant overemphasis on specific content. Concern about the role of standardized testing, the new attention to writing skills, and the current emphasis on higher order thinking may all be reflections of the same underlying problem. Only by specifying the ways of knowing more clearly—articulating what is unique as well as what is generic about the types of knowledge that are valued in each subject—can we fundamentally alter the criteria teachers bring to their evaluations of student work. And in turn, unless we alter the criteria teachers bring to their evaluations, we are unlikely to alter the nature of student learning.

A final point: The recent history of writing instruction provides an object lesson for those who want schools to pay more attention to informal reasoning skills. It is likely to be very easy to introduce a new curriculum of "thinking activities" derived from one or another taxonomy of reasoning behaviors, either as a separate course or as part of other curricula. But such thinking activities will be easily trivialized, just as activities based on process-oriented approaches to writing instruction have been. We are unlikely to make a significant impact on student learning until the new activities are reconstrued as part of the essential knowledge of each subject, with concomitant changes in teachers' goals and in their methods of evaluating effective teaching and learning. Such changes will not be simple, for they involve fundamental patterns of expectations about the role of the teacher and the role of the student in classroom learning. But the changes are necessary if we are to move our students beyond the basic skills, which they now seem to be mastering, to higher levels of reasoning and problem solving, which, at present, few students seem to attain.

REFERENCES

Applebee, A. N. (1981). *Writing in the secondary school: English and the content areas* (Research Rep. No. 21). Urbana, IL: National Council of Teachers of English.

Applebee, A. N. (1984). *Contexts for learning to write: Studies of secondary school instruction.* Norwood, NJ: Ablex.

Applebee, A. N. (1986). Problems in process approaches: Toward a reconceptualization of process instruction. In A. Petrosky & D. Bartholomae (Eds.), *The teaching of writing* (pp. 95–113). 85th Yearbook of the National Society for the Study of Education. Chicago, IL: University of Chicago Press.

Applebee, A. N., Barrow, K., Brown, R., Cooper, C., Mullis, I., & Petrosky, A. (1981). *Reading, thinking, and writing*. Denver, CO: Education Commission of the States.

Applebee, A. N., Langer, J. A., & Mullis, I. V. (1985). *The reading report card*. Princeton, NJ: Educational Testing Service.

Applebee, A. N., Langer, J. A., & Mullis, I. V. (1986a). *Writing: Trends across the decade*. Princeton, NJ: Educational Testing Service.

Applebee, A. N., Langer, J. A., & Mullis, I. V. (1986b). *The writing report card*. Princeton, NJ: Educational Testing Service.

Braddock, R., Lloyd-Jones, R., & Schoer, L. (1963). *Research in written composition*. Champaign, IL: National Council of Teachers of English.

Britton, J. N., Burgess, T., Martin, N., McLeod, A., & Rosen, H. (1975). *The development of writing abilities (11–18)*. London: Macmillan Education.

Brown, A. (1978). Knowing when, where, and how to remember: A problem of metacognition. In R. Glaser (Ed.), *Advances in instructional psychology* (pp. 77–165). Hillsdale, NJ: Lawrence Erlbaum, Associates.

Hillocks, G., Jr. (1986). *Research on written composition*. Urbana, IL: National Conference on Research in English and the ERIC Clearinghouse on Reading and Communication Skills.

Langer, J. A. (1984). Literacy instruction in American schools. *American Journal of Equation, 93*, 107–132.

Langer, J. A., & Applebee, A. N. (1987). *How writing shapes thinking: A study of teaching and learning* (Research Rep. No. 22). Urbana, IL: National Council of Teachers of English.

Langer, J. A., & Applebee, A. N. (1988). Speaking of knowing: Conception of learning in academic subjects. Final Report to the U.S. Department of Education, Office of Educational Research and Improvement. Albany, NY: The University of Albany, State University of New York.

Macrorie, K. (1976). *Telling writing*. Rochelle Park, NJ: Hayden.

21

Structured Teaching for Critical Thinking and Reasoning in Standard Subject Area Instruction

Robert J. Swartz
University of Massachusetts at Boston

Conceptual and empirical research has revealed much about models of thinking, blocks to thinking, the capabilities of people to think well, and techniques that bring about good thinking in others. How, though, can these insights be implemented in formal educational settings, given traditional curricular and structural constraints on the work of the classroom teacher?

Although it is imperative that any such attempts be subjected to viable assessment techniques before we endorse them, it is equally important to have a clear conception of the ingredients that are to be designed into these attempts and their rationale based on what we already know about thinking, children, and classrooms. In this chapter, I discuss one such attempt that has evolved through the work of a number of classroom teachers. It represents an approach that I call the *conceptual-infusion approach* to teaching for critical thinking (Swartz, 1987-a). In it, the use of standard curricular content is restructured to teach in ways aimed at learning both this content and good thinking. The thinking that is the primary goal of this innovation is precisely what we ordinarily think of as informal reasoning: "reasonable reflective thinking directed at deciding what to believe and do" (Ennis, 1987). The skills involved in such thinking are the specific subgoals of this sort of teaching, skills we are all familiar with, such as engaging in well-founded forms of inference, judging the reliability and accuracy of the information on which such inferences are based, and exercising clarity and precision in the way we conceptualize these thoughts. The classroom teacher does this restructuring as part of his or her teaching style, and this teaching is reinforced across the curriculum and grade levels by other teachers in the same school or school system doing the same thing.

CAUSAL REASONING:
NATURE AND STRATEGIES

Processes Associated with Causal Reasoning:
The Mystery of the Dead Mouse

Suppose that as you left home today you noticed, lying on the floor of your garage, the following:

You wonder what killed the mouse. You have been trying to rid yourself of these pests for months, and if you can find out what caused this one to die, maybe you can exploit this knowledge and relieve your frustration. Some good thinking is needed here.

Conceptualizing Alternative Possibilities.   A natural thing to do at the outset is to ponder this question by thinking about what could have killed the mouse. This approach is, of course, useful when our information at the outset is *underdetermined.* If you see a board with a nail in it on the road, feel your car going over it, hear the tire blowing out, feel the car swerve, and then get out and are faced with a tire as flat as it could be, your inference to the best explanation requires no pondering. But when the information you have is underdetermined, as it is in a great many situations in which we are interested in what caused something, this pondering is a natural and important first step. Here are some possibilities that occur to people when they ponder the cause of death of the mouse: (a) poison, (b) the cat got it, (c) asphyxiation, (d) car ran over it, (e) freezing, (f) disease, (g) mouse trap that it broke free of, or (h) dehydration. These are somewhat commonplace explanations. When pushed to list some unusual possibilities, many people add possibilities such as the following to the list: (a) fright, (b) suicide, (c) old age, (d) it was not really a dead mouse but a plastic copy, put there to fool you, (e) AIDS, or (f) fell from a great height.

This approach, of course, is like open brainstorming but with a crucial difference. Although we do not yet make critical judgments about which of these groups offers the most reasonable explanation, we are usually constrained by thinking of them as possible causes of death. Of course, we still have much latitude in our thinking, given the underdetermined nature of our information. But this point suggests that characterizations of the sort of thinking we do when we use the technique of brainstorming as free of judgment are in error; critical judgment plays a role even in this kind of thinking. The natural contexts in which our primary concern is to generate a multiplicity of ideas for critical reflection are usually contexts in which, at some broader level, other forms of critical judgments are involved.

416

Thinking about farfetched explanations is not always frivolous. Sometimes it pays off, and we find that the most reasonable explanation is a farfetched one. Thinking of some at the outset can perhaps save us time, frustration, and a lot of blind alleys.

Looking for Good Evidence.   Nevertheless, it is a good idea to check out the more commonplace possibilities first if we want to find out what has really caused the death of the mouse. Thinking that involves only this type of brainstorming might be fun, but it serves little purpose by itself in trying to figure out what has really happened. We must shift to some hard-nosed thinking that involves calling up, gathering, and using evidence to make a reasonable judgment about what caused the death of the mouse. A natural way to move to this type of thinking is to take some of the more commonplace possibilities and think about what we might find that would count in favor of them. So, for example, people challenged to think about the possibility of poisoning list the following: (a) an empty poison box, (b) a poison box chewed through by the mouse, (c) remembering putting out mouse poison, (d) a little bit of mouse poison found around the corpse, (e) an autopsy finding poison in the mouse's stomach, or (f) the mouse looking shriveled and convulsed on close inspection.

Any good research project attempting to find a causal explanation usually involves some preliminary thinking of this sort. It helps guide us about what to look for in gathering evidence. We do not usually just mess around in the garage. Thinking beforehand about what may count in favor of an explanation helps us to figure out what we should look for. Any good detective writer knows this; preliminary thinking about what we could find that would build suspicion that the butler did it may help us to find relevant evidence while not precluding our stumbling on other relevant information that we do not expect to find.

It is also important to note the scope of what we are thinking about. Good evidence is not just what we could find if we looked; it also includes what we already know. Prompts that help us think about relevant dormant knowledge that we have already are important. In fact, in limiting cases we may already have all the evidence we need but not be aware of it. Thinking in terms of what we can call up that is relevant as well as what we can gather is a technique that we often use ourselves to prompt the recall of relevant information.

In both cases—recalling and gathering relevant information—it is, of course, important to make sure that we have an accurate rendering of this information. Critical judgment is necessary here, and if we really want to fine-tune this example, we should make sure that important factors that contribute to accurate observational reports, such as favorable conditions of observation, and accurate recollections, are present.

The Need to Rule Out Competing Hypotheses.   Good detective writers also exploit something we know only too well: the tendency to jump to a conclusion about what the cause of something is the minute we find some evidence in favor of a hypothesis. The butler was seen leaving the scene of the crime and had threatened the deceased (the mouse)—the butler did it!

Of course, later we may find out that this evidence is not conclusive and is perfectly consistent with the hypothesis that the uncle is the murderer. In fact, we may find that there is also pretty strong evidence that the butler did not do it. He may have also been seen entering the room after the murder was committed, and the fingerprints on the gun may not match up with his at all, not to mention, let us say, his inability to use his trigger finger because of an old war wound. Finding the hypothesis that is the best explanation involves a combination of finding pretty strong evidence in favor of it and finding evidence that tends to rule out the other competing hypotheses. Knowing this, we also may want to reflect on what we could find that would count against the mouse poison theory. Such reflections may lead to things like (a) there was no sign of poison, (b) the cat was seen leaving the scene of the crime, or (c) there was no poison in the mouse after an autopsy.

Repeating this procedure with a number of possibilities before looking and calling up relevant information can help us keep in mind the need for a good mixture of evidence, pro and con, in advancing a judgment about the most reasonable explanation. As a good thinker, you would want to use this process as well. The fine discriminations we make here between relevant and strong evidence and evidence that supports and counts against a hypothesis, of course, depend on our background knowledge, as they do in any good investigative work that involves the use of evidence. These discriminations are part of the use of very important critical thinking skills that play themselves out in this sort of reasoning about what caused something. It is important to note how they go hand in hand with the type of generative thinking that plays an important role in an earlier stage in this process of reasoning.

So far, we have been thinking about commonplace possibilities. We should not leave out fanciful—even farfetched—possibilities. It is often important to note the evidence that may count in favor of or against these possibilities, for noting such evidence in a real case is what usually leads us to reject such fanciful explanations or to consider them as more likely than we might have initially thought. Even the hypothesis that a neighbor put a mock-up of a dead mouse in the garage to get you thinking is one that deserves a dignified bit of thought. Sometimes people do try to fool us, perhaps even more often than we would like. But we should not be overly concerned about these possibilities. Knowing what we could find that counts in favor of or against such possibilities helps us make reasonable judgments about their likelihood. Usually, we hope, we have plenty of reason for rejecting them.

Collecting and Assessing Evidence.   What remains, of course, is to gather accurate information and call up relevant bits of knowledge we already have so that we can make a reasonable judgment. This evidence should, of course, be certified as accurate, and this is a matter that calls for the use of another cluster of basic critical thinking skills focusing on, among other things, the reliability of the sources of information, including our own observational capacities. When we have made a good stab at collecting all the reliable and relevant information we can, given whatever practical constraints we may be under, our job then is to weigh the evidence and make a judgment about what the best explanation is. This is our thinking goal. We strive to assess the reasonableness of ideas we ourselves generate or, in a social context, that others suggest as providing the best causal explanation. Indeed, this is the heart of the critical processes we use in making well-supported inferences and judgments. Belief in and affirmation of a particular causal explanation are what we are ultimately after.

Suppose now that, instead of just a dead mouse, what you found in the garage was the following:

Assessing the force of this additional information is part of the process of critical judgment that we are engaging in. What will this additional information—that the dead mouse was found in a sealed jar—tell us? Which possibilities are ruled out by this new information?

A quick reaction usually brings out the following responses, which are not atypical of what we ourselves usually think (a) The cat is ruled out, (b) the mouse trap is ruled out, (c) the mouse's being run over by the car is ruled out, and (d) the mouse's falling from the rafters is ruled out.

Actually, none of the possibilities is ruled out. The mouse could have died in any of the ways indicated in the initial brainstormed list and could then have been put in the jar, and the jar could then have been sealed up. By thinking that some of these possibilities are ruled out, we make an assumption that the mouse was put in the jar alive and died in the jar. The information we now have does not yet support this assumption.

When we recognize that we are making an assumption, this recognition immediately suggests other information that we might want to look for to narrow down the field of viable possibilities. This is a crucially important technique in sorting out the strength of our evidence and in leading us to the most reasonable explanation. We want to avoid unwarranted judgments. We should recognize that, in aiming at making such reasonable judgments, we may have to say, "I can't yet make a reasonable judgment. I don't have enough evidence." The virtues of not forcing ourselves into premature closure of an issue cannot be underscored enough. Suspension of judgment can be as legitimate at the end of a reasoning process as it is prior to such a process. It can also spur us on to get what we need to make a reasonable affirmation.

Solving The Mystery of the Dead Mouse as a Paradigm of Causal Reasoning

Thinking through what killed the mouse is a clear example that can lead to a well-thought-out judgment about the best explanation. This approach contrasts with examples of sloppy reasoning, in which we jump to conclusions based on sparse or no evidence. It operates when we begin with information we identify as underdetermined about some event we identify as an effect and when there is an interest in finding out what has happened that caused this event. It is easily represented by a process outline that highlights key ingredients that have been stressed. Four stages are present, which we undertake in roughly this order:

1. Listing a number of possible causal explanations of the event.
2. Considering what evidence one could find that counts in favor of and against these explanations.
3. Calling up and gathering such relevant evidence.
4. Weighing the pros and cons, and making a judgment of the most likely explanation.

As we engage in these considerations, each one involves skillful thinking of various sorts that could itself be further analyzed. Details of the brainstorming that are involved in listing possibilities, our assessment of the relevance and strength of evidence, the observational skills used in gathering accurate evidence, the effective recall of relevant facts, and the ultimate assessment of the hypotheses through this information all should play themselves out in systematic, careful, and thorough ways.

I consider this characterization of the nonformal processes of causal reasoning an example of an *instructional model* of causal thinking. Other models of causal thinking may be perfectly consistent with this one but may emphasize other features of such thinking for other purposes. This is an instructional model because it attempts to look at causal reasoning in a way that isolates components that can serve as the basis for an instructional design.

But deeper than that, this model also emphasizes the components in causal reasoning that need to be stressed to counter tendencies that we all have toward sloppy thinking, which yields hasty judgments. Such judgments are more likely than not to be in error. If my car does not start on a cold winter morning, and I think the source of the problem is the battery, I may call the local garage and buy a new battery. I might then get into my car after the battery is installed and find that the car still does not start. These types of hasty judgments are commonplace and sometimes very costly. We minimize their frequency by first considering alternatives: The problem might be the battery, but it also might be a broken wire, or the starter, and so forth. Usually, when we reason this way, we realize that there is little evidence that the battery is the cause. So, one thing we want to emphasize in developing a paradigm of good causal reasoning is that alternatives should be considered. For this procedure there are ready-made techniques, such as brainstorming.

Another problem we often have is that the minute we find a little evidence in favor of one of the hypotheses we are considering—especially if we have a predisposition to think that this one is the correct one—we latch on to it and think that it proves the hypothesis. Our thinking about causes often exhibits a *confirmation bias*. I might say to myself: "I won't make a hasty judgment, because I know that there are a number of possibilities. So I'll test to see if it really is the battery. One thing I could do is to try the lights." When I try the lights and they do not go on, it is easy to say: "It must be the battery!" But the problem could also still be a broken wire. Knowing this tendency not to think about what counts against a hypothesis—what negative evidence we might find—makes it important to stress looking for evidence *against* these hypotheses, as well as evidence in favor of them, until we have one that stands out as well supported and others that are rendered unlikely by the evidence. This process is structured into the model for explanatory reasoning by stressing the need to look for evidence against the hypotheses as well as in favor of them and to weigh cons as well as pros before making a judgment of the best explanation.

Use of These Processes in Other Causal Reasoning Problems

We can see the way these ingredients play themselves out in a more serious piece of reasoning that is now part of our recent history. In 1985, the space shuttle Challenger was destroyed by a disastrous explosion that shocked the world. The entire crew was killed. The cry immediately went out: What caused the disaster?

There were, of course, some quick and hasty responses. Someone said that it was sabotage: The space shuttle had been blown up by a terrorist group. Many of us remembered that someone had threatened to blow up the space shuttle, and I daresay it was easy for many people to believe this explanation, but at the time there was no evidence for it. The response was a rush to hasty judgment; so was the immediate offering of the famous O-ring hypothesis even though that turned out to be the one that we all now accept. The space commission that was set up to ascertain what happened, however, did try to manifest some more careful and thorough thinking about what caused the disaster. That is not to say that the ultimate conclusions of the commission about the intricacies of the causal connections were not challenged; but the process was a more thorough reasoning process. For example, the commission initially considered a number of possibilities. There was the O-ring hypothesis, at that time still a hypothesis. But there was also the possibility that someone could have left one of the vents open between segments of the rocket. This could have caused the disaster as well.

In addition, the commission was careful to think through what it could find as evidence for or against these hypotheses. For example, it speculated that it might find segments of the rocket at the bottom of the ocean (it had not yet found any parts of the Challenger) and said that if it found the segment of the rocket in question with the O-rings intact, it would rule out the O-ring hypothesis, however initially appealing it might have been.

We recognize the reasoning of the commission as involving the systematic interplay of ingredients in our paradigm of good causal reasoning. Similarly, we recognize the judgments of detectives like Hercule Poirot as being founded on a similar sensitivity to the interplay between the generation and consideration of hypotheses and the gathering and weighing of relevant evidence, which are directed toward the most reasonable explanation of what led to the death of the latest victim in an Agatha Christie murder mystery.

KEY INSTRUCTIONAL FEATURES OF THE CONCEPTUAL-INFUSION APPROACH

Engaging Students in Thinking Versus Teaching Them How to Think Well

Bringing the mystery of the dead mouse into the classroom is one of those activities that can get students thinking at any grade level. It has its virtues as a piece of instruction designed to teach thinking. This lesson contrasts with instructional techniques that prompt much thinking in the classroom but that are not focused on a specific sort of thinking, such as causal explanation. Issue-oriented instruction that prompts student discussion of such problems as the acid rain issue, hazardous waste, or even a parking ban at certain hours on city streets can generate much thinking. But this thinking is of all different sorts and comes in varying patterns. In such discussions, many students become familiar with the depth of some of these issues and the interplay between positions and counterpositions on them through this thinking. But there may be no one kind of thinking that they employ, and the issues rather than the thinking hold their attention. In contrast, solving the dead mouse mystery is structured in a way that is derived from the model we just discussed, in which a very specific sort of thinking is the target. The stage is set for this thinking by creating a thought-provoking situation: the discovery of a dead mouse. Subsequent thinking is then structured by a series of prompts in the form of specific questions raised at the right time and in the right order, according to our instructional model. Thus, the question, "What could have caused the death of the mouse?" is raised before the question, "What evidence can you find for and against each of these possibilities?".

To be sure, issue-oriented teaching that prompts thinking in the classroom and thinking skills instruction, such as that in solving the dead mouse mystery, share a feature that is very important in teaching thinking. Students are not just told about causal explanation; they are given an example in which they participate in active thinking themselves. If our goal is to help students develop some good habits of thought, such active thinking is necessary in good instructional design.

In the dead mouse exercise, active thinking is structured on the basis of an overall instructional "map" for this kind of thinking. This deliberate structure, based on a previously developed thinking map, differentiates it from what happens in typical issue-oriented instruction. Although active thinking and even a spirit of open thought are laudable in most issue-oriented instruction, structures used to teach specific thinking skills are usually not part of the instructional process. To put this another way, when we teach thinking by teaching thinking skills, students are not only offered practice in reasoning about cause–effect relationships, but they are also taught to use strategies for reasoning effectively and criteria for making the critical judgments that are the products of such reasoning.

Stand-Alone Versus Infused Lessons

Any number of other activities with a different content focus that involve causal reasoning can be introduced in the same way as the lesson about the dead mouse. Instead of the dead mouse, one could substitute a plane crash, a strike at a local factory, or the anger of a friend. Although these activities can be brought into a school classroom to teach skills in causal explanation, there are reasons for not doing this or, at least, for not doing only this. All of these activities have a curricular disadvantage. They must be brought into a school classroom in addition to whatever else is being taught. The problems here are not just problems of time. If the activities we bring to our classrooms to help students learn better thinking habits are always added on to the curriculum, we run the risk of giving students a seriously mixed message about the importance of good thinking. In the limiting case, imagine an add-on thinking program stressing specific directed thinking, such as that about the dead mouse and offered to students from 10:00 to 10:50 a.m. on Fridays. Students are bound to pick up the idea that this is the time for thinking, whereas during the rest of the school week we do other things.

Actually, the mystery of the dead mouse is part of a lesson that does not stand alone. Rather, it is an attempt to infuse teaching for skill in causal reasoning into

Causal Explanation

Whenever you draw a conclusion about why something happened based on evidence, you have come up with a causal explanation. Think, for example, of an automobile that won't start on a cold morning. Why has this happened? Some possible causes may be a lack of gas, a low battery, or ice in the gas line. Some of these explanations may be unlikely because of information you already have. For example, if the gas gauge doesn't read empty, it would be unlikely that you are out of gas. You might then try to gather evidence that would help you find the most likely cause. You might turn on the lights in the car to find out whether or not the battery is low, or you might seek the advice of a neighbor who had a similar experience the day before.

In this example, the car owner has sought to explain why a car won't start based on evidence that has been collected. Scientists often use this type of thinking when they investigate scientific problems. Sometimes, scientists are able to obtain strong enough evidence to establish a cause, as in the case of polio. Prior to the 1950s, scientists did not know what caused this disease. Through their research, however, they gained conclusive evidence that polio is caused by one of three viruses, and were then able to develop a vaccine for the disease. Other times, scientists are unable to gather enough evidence to explain why something happened. For example, scientists still cannot explain why dinosaurs became extinct.

THINK CRITICALLY

1. Here is an example of something that you might discover inside a barn or garage. As you examine the illustration of the dead mouse, list some possible causal explanations for its death.

2. What kind of evidence might you find that would support each of the possible causes for the mouse's death? What evidence would tend to rule out certain of these causes?

3. In 1772 Joseph Priestley, an English educator and chemist, did an experiment in which a dead mouse also played a role. To perform his experiment, Priestley first placed a live mouse in a completely sealed jar. Examine the illustration of Priestley's first experiment. List some possible explanations for why the mouse died. Are any of these explanations more likely than the others? Why?

Experiment 1

4. In a second experiment, Priestley placed a plant in another sealed jar. As you examine the illustration on the next page, list some possible explanations for the plant's death. Is there any evidence in this experiment that makes one cause more likely than the others?

FIG. 21.1

Experiment 2

5. In a third experiment, Priestley placed a mouse and a plant together in a closed jar, as illustrated below. What are some possible explanations why the mouse and the plant survived in this experiment? What evidence or information can you derive from the series of three experiments that would tend to support one of these explanations more strongly than the others?

Experiment 3

6. What could have been done in the second experiment that might have enabled the plant to survive? How would this have worked?

THINK ABOUT THINKING

7. How did you decide what to list as possible explanations for each of the experimental results?

8. Describe the sequence of your thinking as you attempted to explain why the plant and the mouse survived in the last experiment.

APPLY WHAT YOU HAVE LEARNED

9. Can you think of some examples from your own life in which you would like to find out why something happened? Describe one example.

10. There are many animals today that have been classified as endangered species, such as the Siberian tiger, the California condor, and the sea otter. List some possible explanations for why a particular species might have become endangered. How could you determine which of these causes is correct?

FIG. 21.1 (cont.)

a high school biology course by restructuring the way traditional biology content is used (Schraer & Stolze, 1987, pp. CCT 39–40). The lesson presented is a published lesson designed by a group of biology teachers with whom I served as a consultant. It is, of course, for students who are taking the biology course. But it is also designed as a model for biology teachers to use to develop their own infused lessons to teach for this type of thinking.

The way this lesson evolved is instructive. I worked on this project with a group of biology teachers. Our mission was to find biology content that is ordinarily designed for factual learning but that could be used as raw material for thinking skills lessons. We were attempting to design infused lessons, the use of which would be aimed at students learning the original content and specific forms of thinking. (I comment shortly on the overall thinking skills framework we used for this project.) In this case, we were grappling with how we could develop infused lessons on causal explanation.

One of the biology teachers found an illustration of Priestley's famous 1772 experiment, in which he demonstrated and verified the carbon dioxide/oxygen interchange between plants and animals. This is the illustration:

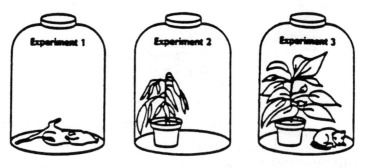

FIG. 21.2   In 1772 Joseph Priestley, an English educator and chemist, conducted three experiments in which he demonstrated that plants give off something (oxygen) that animals need for survival, and animals give off something (carbon dioxide) that plants need.

(Notice the full caption giving the facts and the horizontal line-up of the diagrams for Experiments 1–3.) The teacher who found this illustration thought that it would make good raw material for a causal explanation lesson. All that had to be done, he suggested, was to remove the upshot of the experiments from the caption and ask the students, "What is the explanation for these experimental results?".

Our goal was to structure a lesson in a way that students would be actively involved in the thinking processes we had isolated in our instructional model of causal explanation. It seemed to me, however, that asking "What is the causal explanation?" or even "Why did these things happen?" might prompt this kind of thinking in some students, but it probably would not in most. These questions would more likely prompt students to look up the explanation in the book or to ask someone—if they cared at all. If they did not care, they would probably guess. It is unlikely that this approach would activate the kind of thinking we were concerned about, despite our use of such key terms as *causal explanation* and *why?*.

What is lacking in this idea is a structure for the thinking that would both isolate the different ingredients we wanted to stress and give students a chance to go through a process like the one we felt it was important for them to internalize (see p. 420). Very specific prompting questions can lead students through this process. The key to a better lesson design for causal reasoning is to pull the content of this example apart to fit this structure. This approach means, first, taking the mouse out of the jar so that there would be something to be explained that was underdetermined. Asking students to list ways that the mouse could have died can then prompt some open thinking about possible explanations. Then, given that our goal is to give students material on the basis of which they can reflect on which hypotheses are rendered likely by the evidence, we realized that we should not give students the evidence of all three experiments at once. Rather, we should ask them to take the preliminary step of thinking about what evidence they can obtain that might count in favor of or against these hypotheses and then give them the evidence from these experiments bit by bit. Hence, the structure of this lesson. In its final stages, the lesson is intended to help students reflect discretely on what the evidence shows as it is accumulated, as in a good detective story, until students get the results of the last experiment and, given the right background knowledge, have what they need to support the hypothesis of the interchange of gases (CO_2 and O_2) that Priestly verified. The result is that they end up with the same information that the original diagram was designed to help them learn and, at the same time, have gone through a directed process of thinking that is a specific example of the general model of organized thinking on which we wanted to base the lesson.

This is a paradigm of what I mean by an infused thinking skill activity. It is intended to bring teaching for thinking into mainstream instruction and not treat it as an add-on to the regular curriculum (Swartz, 1987a).

Interweaving Content Knowledge and Reasoning Skills Instruction

It is well worth noting that, for students to be able to work through this thinking activity, more is needed than is explicitly given in the lesson. The final stages in this lesson work, as we have said, "given the right background knowledge." In particular, additional information is needed for students to be able to use the evidence given in the activity as supportive of inferences about the lack of oxygen and carbon dioxide in Experiments 1 and 2, and the interchange of these gases in Experiment 3 as the most reasonable explanations of the deaths and survival, respectively, of the mouse and plant. For example, to be able to claim that the interchange of carbon dioxide and oxygen is taking place, information about the composition of the air in the jars must be used as must a certain amount of basic information about respiration.

This requirement does not yet mean that students must know all about air and respiration before they start this activity (although they may). They can be given this information as explicit background information at the start of this activity. Figure 21.3, for example, contains a similar activity for elementary school students in which they are asked to think about the extinction of the dinosaurs based on the same instructional model of causal reasoning (Barman et al., 1989). Note that this activity is structured the same way as the dead mouse activity to take students through the same organized pattern of thinking, although this time at the fifth-grade level with entirely different content. In this case, they are all given the relevant background information about dinosaurs quite explicitly at the beginning of the lesson. This provision is to make sure that they have it available so that the inferential relationships between the type of evidence given in the activity and the hypothesis about extinction that it directs them toward—diminution in the food supply of the plant eaters, thereby reducing the food of the meat eaters—are relatively easy to notice and that students are not hampered from doing the kind of thinking called for by ignorance about dinosaurs.

In a more challenging version of this activity, students can be helped to recognize that they need such background information (e.g., the feeding habits of dinosaurs) to solve the problem and then be aided by the teacher in finding it. This process can involve them in reflecting on different sources of information about dinosaurs (stories, science texts, adventure magazine articles, science articles) and then thinking systematically about which sources may be the most reliable, and why. In so doing, these students become attuned to the need for thinking in a systematic way about such factors as the purpose of a piece of writing, the expertise of the author, and so forth before they accept information from what they have read. Thinking carefully about the reliability of sources of information as a route to making discriminating critical judgments about their accuracy is another important critical-thinking skill. It contrasts, of course, with accepting information uncritically, a bad habit that is hard to resist in a world in which we are constantly bombarded with information offered for immediate consumption. Thus, activities like thinking about the dead mouse or the extinction of the dinosaurs can segue very neatly into instruction in another, equally important critical thinking skill, through which students have access to the important background information in a field needed to make these lessons work.

The activities I have described herein show how we can exploit the relationship between basic content knowledge in a field and its use in important thinking activities to counter an extreme position about the relationship between content-oriented instruction and thinking-oriented instruction. The need for background knowledge in a field to make lessons such as those concerning the

Causal Explanation

Critical Thinking

Scientists are not just interested in things like floods that happen today. They are also interested in major changes that happened to the Earth a long time ago. One thing that has puzzled scientists for a long time is what happened to the dinosaurs at the end of the Mesozoic Era. No one knows why they became extinct, but it's worth thinking about what could have caused their extinction and how we could find out.

1. Dinosaurs lived for a very long time, there were lots of them, and even though they were huge animals not one survives today. Some were plant eaters only, others ate meat and hunted other animals. List as many different possible ways that you can think of that things could have changed on the Earth to cause the Dinosaurs to become extinct.

2. Pick three of these and write a story about how these things could have happened in a way that killed the dinosaurs.

3. Suppose you were looking for clues about which of these three possibilities was what really happened. What sorts of things might you find today that could give you evidence in favor of each, and what could you find that would count against each?

4. Imagine that while looking for clues you find the following things in various sedimentary rocks:

lots of dinosaur tracks at one level, fewer at another, and then none

fossilized leaves and plants at one level, and then very few

more mammal tracks and bones in some levels than in others

When you bring these to a laboratory for Carbon 14 dating you find that the plants and leaves coincided with a lot of dinosaur tracks and then the layers with fewer plants came just before there were fewer, and then no other dinosaur tracks. The increase in mammal bones came as the dinosaur tracks were diminishing.

What possible explanations does this evidence count in favor of?

FIG. 21.3   From Barman et al. (1989).

dead mouse or the extinction of the dinosaurs work as thinking skills lessons does not prescribe that students be taught a body of information first (e.g., in elementary and/or high school) and then, at some later time (e.g., in college), be introduced to thinking skills. This position is represented in item 1 in the following list; items 2 and 3 represent the approaches I have just described. These last two positions provide a window of opportunity for teachers to introduce students to thinking skills early in their educational careers in any of the standard subject areas and, at the same time, to teach them a body of basic information:

1. Teach the basic facts first in students' early educational careers; then introduce students to thinking-skills activities in which they use these facts later.

2. Provide students with the basic information needed to do thinking-skills activity concomitantly, as part of individual lessons on these skills.

3. Teach thinking skills in ways that challenge students to learn basic facts that they will need to do the thinking activities through the use of other relevant thinking skills that are related to the credibility of basic information.

I do not wish to suggest that it is never appropriate to teach a body of content knowledge directly to students. Obviously, there are many other possible instructional configurations between those described in items 1 and 2, and some may make sense in certain circumstances. For example, in highly specialized courses, such as advanced courses in science or in various professionally oriented courses in fields such as accounting, nursing, and engineering, it may well make sense to expose students to a body of basic noncontroversial information prior to structuring it into one's teaching infused activities, in which this information is used in playing out the application of specific thinking skills in the particular field. One hopes that this is done in ways that make this information meaningful and do not rely on rote memorization. This approach is a far cry from the position stated in item 1, and it shades into that stated in item 2. But, to reiterate, it is through the approaches represented in items 2 and 3 that we have models that provide an opportunity to blend the teaching of thinking skills with subject area instruction anywhere in a student's career. From my perspective, when there is no complex set of technical or highly specialized information that is basic to a field, the earlier this blending occurs, the better.

Fostering Metacognition

There is more than just thinking about why the mouse died to this lesson. Even structured thinking of the kind students go through in this activity may not yield what we teachers have as our goal: a modification of thinking habits so that this sort of thinking is what is done in similar circumstances, especially outside the classroom, when a causal explanation is called for. As teachers, we want students to integrate the forms of thinking that we help them use in the classroom into their ways of thinking in general. When this happens, real learning takes place.

The point here is that just one instance of such thinking does not counter the bad thinking habits we may have about what the causes are of things we are concerned about. A number of structured examples leading to the same sort of thinking are not a remedy. In lessons like the dead mouse lesson, there is a deliberate attempt to incorporate at least two additional ingredients to enhance learning and assimilation. First, there is an important *metacognitive* component built into this lesson. Including this component is based on the ample research that demonstrates improved learning when metacognition is involved (Bransford, Sherwood, Vye, & Reiser, 1986).

In the primary metacognitive section of the dead mouse lesson, students are prompted to reflect on the thinking that they have done by analogous, appropriate questions. It is our intention to let students know the purpose of these questions and how they are distinguished from what they have just done, so we title this section "Thinking About Thinking."

Metacognitive activities, by and large, fall into three categories. Sometimes students are brought to a level of awareness of the thinking they are doing by the use of an *appropriate thinking term to categorize* this type of thinking. This is a stage-setting activity that appears in the preamble of the lesson. There, students are told of the importance of explanatory inference, given some examples of such inferences going awry, and given some indication of what this form of reasoning is about. This type of labeling and categorizing, however, does not yet bring students to a very important level of understanding of the thinking that they are doing. Thus, a second level of awareness is introduced, which involves students in *describing the thinking that they are doing*. This process occurs through the questions raised in the "Thinking About Thinking" section. Students are asked to reflect on and describe what they do when they generate alternative explanations, and then they are asked to describe, in their own words, the steps in the thinking they do. Sometimes, students are asked to think out loud, in pairs, while a third student records the thinking strategies used (Lockhead, 1985).

Finally, students can be asked to make *critical judgments about the best strategies to use in thinking through the issues* with which they are presented. This type of normative judgment can lead to the development of normative principles of thinking, such as suggested thinking strategies, by the students. In the lessons accompanying the dead mouse lesson, students are sometimes asked what advice they would give to others who had to think through issues that involve predictions or accurate observational reports. Or, they are asked to do some planning of their predictions or observations to render them as accurate as possible. Both tactics prompt such reflective judgments.

The effectiveness of metacognitive awareness of one's thinking has been amply researched, and metacognitive elements are structured into these activities by teachers in part because of their awareness of this research. If students develop the principles of their thinking out of reflection on their own thinking, this approach seems a powerful vehicle toward providing them with basic principles of thinking that they can draw upon again and again.

From the Dead Mouse to Endangered Species: The Role of Varied Practice in Thinking Skills Instruction

There is a third component to the dead-mouse lesson. It caps off this lesson but paves the way to further extensions. It is based on the idea that, once students are armed with a metacognitive understanding of the thinking that they are doing, their learning will be enhanced by repeated and deliberate practice using the same form of thinking with different examples (Swartz, 1987-b). Teachers who utilize this structure for their teaching feel that repeated practice with the same sort of thinking furthers the habitual integration of this type of thinking into the lives of their students, provided that it is based on students' reflective understanding of the thinking they do. In this lesson on endangered species, another science example and a nonacademic example are introduced. This section of the lesson is headed "Apply What You have Learned."

Repeated practice for transfer is also a well-researched tactic, and it is the research that lies behind the frequent use of this tactic in classrooms (Perkins, 1987). Teachers using this lesson are urged to continue this repeated practice by introducing other examples for students to think about in the same way, as they go through the school year. For this practice to be effective, it should be done in a way that helps students not only to practice the skill often but also to learn to identify the type of example they are working on as one that calls for the skill in question—causal reasoning—and the way they think through the issues as following the specific instructional model of the skill that the original lesson was based on. In teaching for transfer, therefore, teachers design into their instruction the use of key terms that signal the need for a specific skill (e.g., "cause") and that can help students to think through the variety of issues that call for causal reasoning and ways to identify them.

The goal of thinking-skills instruction is for students to integrate the forms of thinking we are concerned about into their lives. This goal means that they develop habits of thought shaped by the organizational patterns that we discern specific thinking skills to involve. When these are critical thinking skills, the result should be well-founded critical judgment, something that maximizes one's chances of gaining accurate insight into the way the world works. Teaching for transfer to achieve this ability to judge is crucial: It is as important as the way in which the initial pattern of thinking is established through such examples as that of the dead mouse. In fact, even in cases in which students already know, for instance, about the carbon dioxide/oxygen interchange and in which going through an activity like thinking about the dead mouse might seem somewhat tedious to them, the benefits of learning such patterns of thought when there are problems like that of endangered species can be impressed on them. "Applying What You Have Learned" is the last component in these lessons but by no means the least important.

Summary of Basic Instructional Principles

A Thinking Skill Lesson Format.   The overall structure of the dead mouse lesson on causal explanation can be summarized by this format:

I. *Preamble*
   Commenting to students about what the skill is and why it is important to use it.
II. *Activities*
   A. *Thinking Critically*—Structured activities prompting component processes in the thinking you want students to do.
   B. *Thinking About Thinking*—Distancing activities, prompting students to stand back from the thinking they are doing to describe it and to reflect on effective ways to do it.
   C. *Applying Your Thinking*—Other examples calling for the same kind of thinking about which students are prompted to deliberately think in the same way.

This format shows how three basic ingredients in thinking-skills instruction can be woven together into a coherent lesson structure. It should not be interpreted as a rigid lesson structure. Although it is important to sequence the three phases of the activities, because each phase is built on the preceding one, flexibility is used by classroom teachers who employ this format in how they design the separate activities, how they emphasize each, and when they return to stress points.

It is also important to note that this is a format for start-up lessons on a thinking skill. Follow-up work on the same skill looks more like the activities described under the application section, preceding.

Some Principles About Thinking and About Teaching Thinking.   Causal explanation is not the only form of thinking that provides the instructional basis of teaching for thinking. In fact, any instructional program for teaching thinking ought to be based on a viable comprehensive conception of good thinking, in which different forms of thinking as well as other dimensions of good thinking are isolated, and similar maps are developed to provide structure for the cognitive activities in the lessons. There are three basic principles about good thinking in general that lie behind the programmatic approach I am explicating in this chapter; they are:

T1. Good thinking can be analyzed into component thinking skills, activities, and dispositions.

T2. These component mental processes have use in various natural thinking contexts.

T3. Usually, a multiplicity of these components blend together in strategic ways to yield good thinking in these contexts.

Three imperatives of teaching thinking result:

TT1. Emphasize specific skills, activities, and dispositions as educational goals.

TT2. Teach these goals in natural thinking contexts.

TT3. Teach strategies for using these skills, activities, and dispositions in these contexts.

A fourth follows if infusion is the approach adopted:

TT4. Find natural thinking contexts in the present curriculum.

The Priestley experiment, of course, illustrates the fourth imperative, and I have commented on the way this is one case among many that it is quite natural and indeed often important for us to think through in the same way (a matter related to the second imperative). Furthermore, my brief discussion of the thinking strategy for causal reasoning used in the dead mouse lesson provides an example of the upshot of the third imperative. In fact, this approach to an explication of the thinking we want to teach students is perfectly generalizable and applies both to broad thinking activities, such as making decisions, and to narrower, skill-related components, such as judging the accuracy of the information we get from our own observations and from others.

The sense in which learning good thinking involves learning a cluster of important skills useful in natural thinking activities, like causal reasoning and decision making, is discussed in the next section. However, a word about the attitudes and dispositions referred to in the first imperative is necessary here. Most explications of critical thinking refer to skills, such as reasoning skills, and attitudes and/or dispositions of thought, such as seeking reasons, being open minded, and suspending judgment until all the evidence is in (Beyer, 1987-b; Dewey, 1933; Ennis, 1987). Such dispositions are referred to in the first imperative to remind us that teaching good thinking is not just a matter of teaching thinking skills such as causal inference. Lessons like that of the dead mouse lesson must also be taught in ways that reinforce learning and help students develop these crucial attitudes and dispositions. The spirit of openness, exploration, and sensitivity to what the evidence does or does not show that I have tried to communicate earlier in this chapter must remain a meager attempt to capture a classroom atmosphere in which such attitudes and dispositions can be nurtured. (For more discussion of these issues see Beyer [1987-a, 1987-b], A. Swartz [1987], and R. Swartz [1987-a, in press].)

INFUSING TEACHING FOR THINKING
ACROSS THE CURRICULUM

The Science Process Approach: A Comprehensive Framework for Thinking Within a Subject Area

In science instruction in which there is a process orientation, the norm in setting educational goals is to try to develop a taxonomy of thinking activities used in the field. The chart reproduced in Figure 21.4 from the California State Department of Education (1986) on science instruction is a well-articulated and not atypical example of what has come to be called the science process approach to teaching science.

Separate thinking activities that clearly play a role in science are isolated and listed under various broader categories down the center of the diagram. This chart also includes what many now view as a problematic superimposition of Piagetian developmental categories on this list of processes and an equally problematic superimposition of all of this on different grade levels. It is just the central list of processes that I call attention to.

This list has two important features: (a) It is an attempt at a comprehensive listing of thinking processes used in science, and (b) many of the processes are identified in terminology that is drawn from the sciences. The use of such terminology as *experimenting, controlling and manipulating variables,* and so forth, exemplifies the second point. The alleged completeness of the listing referred to in the first item is clearly implied by the heading.

In California, there are similar listings for social studies and history, mathematics, English, and other fields of study. In the various thinking process charts developed for use in curriculum design in these fields, there is no common vocabulary employed from field to field. Rather, like in the California science listing, the terminology is often drawn from within the field (e.g., "controlling and manipulating variables"). Furthermore, in some cases—for example, in the Social Studies framework, which approaches thinking as problem solving—an entirely different way of conceptualizing the categories of thinking is employed from that used in science.

Some have, of course, argued for the domain-specificity of thinking skills and processes (McPeck, 1981). It is not this conviction that has generated this plurality of conceptions of good thinking in traditional academic fields in states such as California, however; rather, the fragmentation of instruction into separate

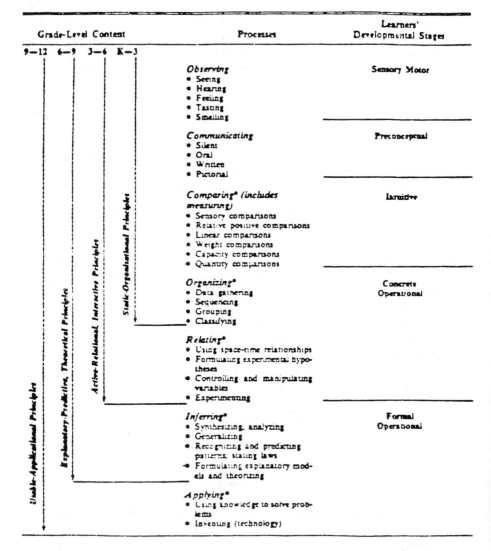

FIG. 21.4   Chart summarizing science process content and developmental stages.

subject areas taught by specialists in these subject areas is the pragmatic basis of this result. Each list was developed by people working in these fields of study.

The approach to teaching thinking that I am explicating in this chapter turns this way of developing a basic conception of good thinking to teach from on its head. Rather than start from separate conceptualizations that come from each field, a general root conception of good thinking is used, and thinking in the fields is defined in terms of it. The rationale for this approach is an instructional concern. For the teaching of thinking to be successful, transfer must be accomplished. The more students become aware of contexts for the use of specific thinking skills and activities, and the more they use them in new contexts, the more transfer is facilitated. Reinforcement of the type of reasoning identified in the dead mouse example in a specific subject area—biology, for example,— seems to be a technique that contributes to this type of learning. Reinforcement across the curriculum is an even more powerful tool. Yet, this process is frustrated if the basis for thinking-oriented instruction is fragmented in the ways represented by a subject-by-subject approach, in which not only is a different terminology used to capture the same processes but the basic categories of thinking are identified in entirely different ways.

Teaching Thinking Across the Curriculum: A Conceptual Model

The motivation for attempting to develop and use a general conception of good thinking that has application across the disciplines and in nonacademic work is clear. In fact, we have examples of such approaches to developing conceptions of good thinking that can provide general educational goals in the early work of Bloom (1961) and in more recent work by Baron and Glatthorn (1985) and Ennis (1962, 1987). It is a blending of the core of work like that found in Ennis's work and Bloom's overall conceptualization of thinking that serves as the basis of the science project in which the dead mouse lesson appears.

Bloom's categories of thinking—(a) knowledge (recall), (b) comprehension, (c) application, (d) analysis, (e) synthesis, and (f) evaluation—are now generally recognized as too broad to provide an instructional basis for teaching specific forms of thinking (Ennis, 1987). Think of the different types of reasoning processes that we engage in when we evaluate something, for example. Such taxonomies as Ennis's typically provide a large number of skills and subskills and are usually viewed as ideal at best and unmanageable at worst. Culling out of a taxonomy like Ennis's a smaller core of important skills and then treating specific skills and processes as subskills under certain of Bloom's broader categories can yield an instructionally manageable approach to articulating at least the basic types of thinking that should be stressed across the curriculum in appropriate thinking contexts drawn from the different fields of study.

Here is one root notion of thinking skills and activities that emerges when this blending is attempted:

I. SKILLS AT GENERATING IDEAS
    1. *Generating Alternative Possibilities*
        A. Multiplicity of Ideas
        B. Varied Ideas

      C. New Ideas
      D. Detailed Ideas
  II. SKILLS AT CLARIFYING IDEAS
    1. *Analyzing the Meaning of Words and Statements*
      A. Ambiguity/Equivocation
      B. Classifying/Definition
    2. *Analyzing Arguments*
      A. Finding Conclusions/Main Idea
      B. Finding Reasons
      C. Uncovering Assumptions
 III. SKILLS AT ASSESSING THE REASONABLENESS OF IDEAS
    1. *Support of Basic Information*
      A. Accurate Observation
      B. Reliable/Unreliable Secondary Sources
    2. *Inference*
      A. Use of Evidence
        1. Well/Ill-supported Explanation (Cause)
        2. Well/Ill-founded Prediction (Effect)
        3. Well/Ill-founded Generalization
      B. Deductions
        1. Valid/Invalid Conditional Arguments
        2. Valid/Invalid Syllogistic Arguments

This way of cutting up the skill-oriented ingredients in good thinking attempts to group these subskills into broad goal-directed categories: related to generating ideas, clarifying ideas, and assessing the reasonableness of ideas. Note that this schema is not intended as a comprehensive listing of thinking activities but as a way of capturing and organizing a root conception of the skills of the good thinker that can be added to when applied to different fields of study.

The particular application of this notion of the skills of the good thinker, when applied to science, has yielded the chart shown in Figure 21.5 (Schraer & Stolze, 1987, p. 27).

This is elaborated in a fleshed-out version in Appendix A (see pp. 443–6). Included in this version is an attempt to provide clear examples of how these different skills break out in use with content from the specific field of study—in this case, the sciences. Similar attempts to superimpose the same root conception on other fields of study have yet to be developed.

The value of using this conceptualization of good thinking as an instructional basis for reshaping curriculum to infuse teaching specific forms of thinking is inestimable. On the basis of the same conception of good thinking, teachers in history have used the same model of explanation to help students grapple with the causes of major historical events; English teachers have used it to reshape how they approach what they teach to help students think about the motivation of

I. RECALL OF FACT

II. COMPREHENSION

III. CRITICAL THINKING

A. Collecting Evidence and Judging Reliability
  1. Firsthand Observations
  2. Secondhand Sources

B. Analysis, Grouping, and Classification
  1. Analyzing Parts-Whole Relationships
  2. Comparing and Contrasting
  3. Ordering Information
  4. Classifying
  5. Identifying Reasons
  6. Identifying Assumptions

C. Inference (Reasoning)
  1. Induction
    a. Generalization
    b. Causal Explanation
    c. Reasoning by Analogy
    d. Predicting Consequences

  2. Deduction
    a. Categorical Arguments
    b. Conditional Arguments

D. Making Value Judgments
  1. Judgments of Usefulness
    a. Judging Things and Ideas
    b. Ranking Things and Ideas
  2. Ethical Judgments

E. Making Decisions

IV. CREATIVE THINKING

FIG. 21.5   Outline of thinking skills in science.

characters in a story or novel; teachers in the elementary school grades have also used this model in a variety of ways in language arts and social studies. One notable example, now much quoted in the literature on teaching thinking (Skowron, 1987; Swartz, 1986), is the use of the Chicken Little story in the first grade to help students think about what they would have done to think better than Chicken Little about what caused the bump she received on the head.

Similar work has been done using the conceptual infusion approach to teach for other important skills, activities, and attitudes of good thinking. (I refer to some of these in other published works [Swartz, 1986, 1987-a].) These examples are symptomatic of a basic conviction in the viability of a final imperative for the effective teaching of thinking: Use a general conception of the skills, activities, and attitudes of good thinking that has application across the curriculum, whenever possible, to set the goals of teaching thinking.

The Role of Teachers and Teacher Training in Implementing the Model

The lesson on the dead mouse is a written lesson in a textbook program that is designed for high school biology courses. (In fact, it is one of a series of lessons on each of the skills mentioned in the chart in Appendix A.) Although it is not included directly in the textbook that the lessons are to be used with, it is keyed into topics and material from the text. Having such thinking skills lessons available in textbook packets or structured directly into the text itself, as in the elementary science program from which the extract on the extinction of the dinosaurs comes (Barman et al., 1989), is an important innovation that provides much-needed incentive and support for individual teachers who are grappling with how to teach students in ways that improve their thinking and reasoning.

Even as a written lesson, the dead mouse lesson is designed to have a major impact on biology teachers as well as students (Schraer & Stolze, 1987). In addition to regular classroom use, it also serves as a model for similar lessons that teachers can construct with other pieces of curriculum. In fact, in both science projects from which the lessons in this chapter have been extracted, there are explicit suggestions included to guide teachers in constructing their own lessons on these models as well as in using a variety of specific teaching techniques directed toward the goal of teaching good thinking. (A sample from the teacher's notes that go along with the dead mouse lesson is included in Appendix B, and a sample from similar teacher-oriented notes from a fourth-grade lesson in the elementary science program referred to earlier is included in Appendix C [pp. 449–50].)

Written materials have more potential of reaching people than word of mouth. But their effectiveness depends on more than just their availability. In this case, the effectiveness of the dead mouse lesson and that of the others included in this particular packet will depend on whether these lessons communicate a spirit of curricular change and are not just treated as another lesson for students.

Working directly with teachers in staff development in-service programs seems, at the outset, an effective vehicle for the kind of reorientation to curriculum and classroom teaching that the conceptual infusion approach aims at. But there are trade-offs. The large-scale effectiveness of this approach depends on time and the availability of consultants who know the field and can work with groups of teachers over extended periods. When this approach has been attempted, the results have been promising although no formal assessment of this approach has been attempted (see Swartz & Perkins, 1989).

I mention these points here because in thinking about what can be done in a school setting, with all the constraints that are on teachers, one must take these trade-offs into account. The best program that could be devised for teaching thinking may not be workable because the preconditions for its implementation may not be present due to these constraints.

This chapter is a report on and an explication of what I have found to be a powerful approach to implementing the concerns that many have expressed about how we can translate what we know about reasoning, children, and learning into a viable program that has promise of yielding some real modification in the way our students think. Although this programmatic approach has yet to be formally assessed, it is based on enough solid research to make it well worth serious consideration as a vehicle to achieve these goals.

I conclude this chapter with a challenge: Given the institutional constraints on teaching and schooling, how can we bring this approach to teachers so that we have a chance of modifying their classroom behaviors to implement it on a large scale in the classroom? I daresay that the hope of helping our students become better thinkers, whether through the techniques I have described in this chapter or others that are equally well founded on solid research, depends on our being able to provide an answer to this crucial question.

REFERENCES

Barman, C., DiSpezio, M., Guthrie, V., Leyden, M., Mercier, S., & Ostlund, K. (1989). *Science*. Menlo Park, CA: Addison Wesley.

Baron, J., & Glatthorn, J. (1985). The good thinker. In A. Costa (Ed.), *Developing Minds* (pp. 49–53). Alexandria, VA: Association for Supervision and Curriculum Development.

Beyer, B. (1987-a). Teaching dispositions as well as skills. *Cogitare, 2*(1), 3–4.

Beyer, B. (1987-b). *Practical strategies for the teaching of thinking*. Needham, MA: Allyn & Bacon.

Bloom, B. (1961). *Taxonomy of educational objectives*. New York: Longmans, Green.

Bransford, J., Sherwood, R., Vye, N., & Reiser, J. (1986). Teaching thinking and problem solving: Research foundations. *American Psychologist, 41*, 1078–1089.

California State Department of Education. (1986). *Science curriculum framework addendum*. Sacramento, CA: Author.

Dewey, J. (1933). *How we think*. Boston: D. C. Heath.

Ennis, R. (1962). A concept of critical thinking. *Harvard Education Review. 32*, 81–111.

Ennis, R. (1987). A taxonomy of critical thinking abilities and dispositions. In J. Baron & R. Sternberg (Eds.), *Teaching thinking skills: Theory and practice* (pp. 9–26). New York: W. H. Freeman & Co.

Lockhead, J. (1985). On learning the basic skills underlying analytical reasoning: Teaching intelligence through pair problem solving. In S. Chipman, R. Glaser, & J. Segal (Eds.), *Thinking and learning skills* (Vol. 1, pp. 109–131). Hillsdale, NJ: Lawrence Erlbaum Associates.

McPeck, J. (1981). *Critical thinking and education*. London: St. Martin's Press.

Perkins, D. (1987). Thinking frames: An integrative perspective on teaching cognitive skills. In J. Baron & R. Sternberg (Eds.), *Teaching thinking skills: Theory and practice* (pp. 41–61). New York: W. H. Freeman & Co.

Schraer, R., & Stolze, J. (1987). *Biology: The study of life*. Newton, MA: Allyn & Bacon.

Skowron, C. (1987). Is Chicken Little a reliable source? *Cogitare, 2*(1), 2–3.

Swartz, A. (1987). Critical thinking dispositions and the transfer question. In M. Heiman & J. Slomnienko (Eds.), *Thinking skills instruction: Concepts and techniques* (pp. 58–68). Washington, DC: National Education Association.

Swartz, R. (1986). Restructuring curriculum for critical thinking. *Educational Leadership*, XX, 43–44.

Swartz, R. (1987-a). Teaching for thinking: A developmental model for the infusion of thinking skills into mainstream instruction. In J. Baron & R. Sternberg (Eds.), *Teaching thinking skills: Theory and practice* (pp. 106–126). New York: W. H. Freeman & Co.

Swartz, R. (1987-b). Critical thinking, the curriculum, and the problem of transfer. In D. Perkins, J.

Lockhead, & J. Bishop (Eds.), *Thinking; The second international conference* (pp. 261–284). Hillsdale, NJ: Lawrence Erlbaum Associates.

Swartz, R. (in press). Making good thinking stick. In D. Topping, D. Perkins, & J. Lockhead (Eds.), *Thinking: The third international conference*. Hillsdale, NJ: Lawrence Erlbaum Associates.

Swartz, R., & Perkins, D. (1989). *Teaching thinking: Issues and approaches*. Pacific Grove, CA: Midwest Publications.

APPENDIX A

THINKING SKILLS IN SCIENCE

SKILL	SUBSKILL	DESCRIPTION	EXAMPLE OF USE	DEVELOPMENT AND APPLICATION IN THE PROGRAM
I. RECALL OF FACT		Remembering items of information learned or experienced.	Q. Which human organ absorbs digested food? A. The small intestine.	• Chapter Reviews: Section Questions and Know the Facts • *Teacher's Resource Book*: Review Activities
II. COMPREHENSION		Understanding received ideas well enough to express them in one's own words. (Neither analysis (see III.B) nor inference (see III.C) is required.)	Q. List and explain the stages of the process of digestion in humans. A. (An explanation of the major events in one's own words.)	• Chapter Reviews: Understand the Concepts • *Teacher's Resource Book*: Review Activities
III. CRITICAL THINKING		The use of rational thought to make a decision or form an opinion. (The skills and subskills are discussed below.)	(See A-E below for examples of use for each subskill.)	• Chapter Reviews: Think Critically • Unit Features: Issues in Biology • *Teacher's Resource Book*: Critical Thinking Worksheets • Societal Issues • Chapter and Unit Tests
	A. Collecting Evidence and Judging Reliability	Collecting evidence is obtaining information on a subject. Judging reliability is forming an opinion about its accuracy and objectivity.		
	1. Firsthand Observations	Using one or more of the senses, either unaided or aided by instruments, to obtain information. Reliability varies with the experience, attentiveness, etc., of the observer, as well as with the quality of any instruments used.	Q. An observer described an animal rushing toward him as ferocious. What criteria could you use to accept or reject this description? A. E.g.: accept it, if the observer is an animal expert; reject it, if he has a fear of animals.	(Firsthand observation skills are developed and applied in laboratory activities and on field trips.)
	2. Secondhand Sources	Any reports, such as those in newspapers and magazines, that are not firsthand observations.	Q. How reliable is a magazine article? A. (Reliability depends on such factors as the author's bias or expertise, reasoning, and sources.)	

B. Analysis, Grouping, and Classification	Analysis is the breaking down or separating a whole into its parts in order to examine them. Grouping and classification involve the assignment of the parts to various groups or classes according to some system.	
1. Analyzing Parts-Whole Relationships	Consideration of the parts in relation to the whole or in relation to one another.	Q. Explain the relationship between a nerve and a neuron. A. A nerve (whole) is a bundle of neurons (parts).
2. Comparing and Contrasting	Comparing is examining things in order to identify similarities and differences. Contrasting is comparing in order to emphasize differences. When the things compared are similar, patterns may be detected.	Q. Compare and contrast the digestive systems of the hydra, earthworm, and grasshopper. A. (List of the similarities and differences.)
3. Ordering Information	Establishing a sequence according to size, weight, time, or some other characteristic.	Q. Rank three primates by brain size. A. Chimpanzees, orangutans, and monkeys, in decreasing order.
4. Classifying	Arranging into groups according to some system or organizing principle.	Q. Which of the following invertebrates are insects? Why? a. ant b. earthworm c. bee d. spider e. centipede f. beetle A. a, c, and f are insects because they have 3 body parts (head/thorax/abdomen) and 3 pairs of legs. b has no legs. d and e have *more than* 6 legs.
5. Identifying Reasons	Identifying ideas people use to justify thoughts, actions, or statements. A reason is distinct from a *cause*, which is what makes something happen.	Q. Why do food companies add iodine to some table salt? A. Salt is widely used and iodine prevents thyroid disease.
6. Identifying Assumptions	Recognizing ideas that are accepted as true without proof or examination.	Q. Before Darwin's time, what assumption was generally held about species of living organisms? A. Most people assumed that species did not change over time.
C. Inference (Reasoning)	Drawing a conclusion by the use of logic—induction or deduction.	
1. Induction	Drawing a conclusion from empirical data. *Induction produces only probable —not certain—conclusions.*	

SKILL	SUBSKILL	DESCRIPTION	EXAMPLE OF USE	DEVELOPMENT AND APPLICATION IN THE PROGRAM
III. **CRITICAL** **THINKING** *Continued*	**a. Generalization**	Drawing a conclusion about all cases, based on information or evidence of only some cases (called a sample).	Q. Water samples from a reservoir were tested. All were found to be safe to drink. Is the water from the reservoir safe to drink? A. Yes, it probably is, provided that the sample was sufficiently representative, random, and large.	
	b. Causal Explanation	Drawing a conclusion about a probable cause (that is, about why something happened), based on evidence.	Q. What could have caused the damage to the cotton crop? A. Since boll weevils were found on some of the plants, it is probable that they caused the damage.	
	c. Reasoning by Analogy	Extending a conclusion about one class to another class judged to be similar.	Q. Does drug X cause cancer in humans? A. No. From experiments in which drug X is fed to rats, it can be concluded that drug X does not cause cancer in rats. Since the response of humans is judged to be similar to that of rats, the conclusion can be extended from rats to humans.	
	d. Predicting Consequences	Drawing a conclusion, based on evidence, about the probable effects of a given cause whose effects have not yet occurred.	Q. Will the tomato plants survive the first frost of the war? A. Yes, they probably will, because they are healthy and hardy enough to endure exposure to cold that will not penetrate fully.	
	2. Deduction	Drawing a conclusion that necessarily follows from one or more statements (called premises). *Through deduction you can achieve certainty if the premises are certain.*		
	a. Categorical Arguments	Applying deductive methods to determine whether or not something belongs to a particular class or category.	Q. Are kangaroos mammals? A. All animals that nurse their young are mammals. Kangaroos nurse their young. Therefore kangaroos are mammals.	
	b. Conditional Arguments	Applying deductive methods to draw conclusions from conditional, or "if-then," statements and given information.	Q. Will this tree lose its leaves in the winter? A. If it is a deciduous tree, it will lose its leaves. It is deciduous. Therefore, it will lose its leaves.	

445

Category	Description	Example
D. Making Value Judgments	Assessing whether something is desirable or undesirable.	
1. Judgments of Usefulness	Assessing how well, or badly, some thing, action, idea, etc., serves a particular purpose or functions in a particular situation.	
a. Judging Things and Ideas	Applying judgments of usefulness to individual things and ideas.	Q: Is this knife a good tool for dissecting this specimen? A: (Answer depends on researcher's skill, need for accuracy, characteristics of the specimen, and so on.)
b. Ranking Things and Ideas	Comparing and ordering according to how well a particular function or purpose is served.	Q: Which plant is better adapted to life in the desert—a cactus or an oak? A: A cactus, with its special ability to absorb and store water.
2. Ethical Judgments	Assessing how well something accords with ideals such as justice, respect for human life, and truth.	Q: Should a dying person be told that he or she is dying? A: Answers will vary, depending on the weight given to values such as truth, respect for the dying person's wishes, etc.
E. Making Decisions	Using rational thought and value judgments to choose between two or more reasonable options. *Making a decision is the ultimate end-product of critical thinking.*	Q: What kinds of foods should you eat? A: (Nutritional requirements, personal preference, budget, and so on should be weighed.)
IV. CREATIVE THINKING	Generating ideas, or combining ideas in new ways. (synthesis)— Creative thinking is *divergent* ("to go in different directions") thinking, rather than convergent, because it generates several possible ideas or hypotheses. It may involve the generation of many ideas of a single type (*fluency*) and/or of different types (*flexibility*)	Q: How can we protect food crops from destructive insects? A: (*flexibility*) I. Reduce the insect population with (a) traps, (b) reproductive controls, (c) poisons, (d) predation. II. Enhance plant resistance. (*fluency*) I. (a) mechanical, electrical, hormonal lures, etc. (b) sterilization, elimination of breeding sites, destruction of eggs by fire or chemicals, etc. (c) natural plant poisons, synthetic nerve poisons, etc.

• Chapter Reviews:
  Think Creatively
• *Teacher's Resource Book:*
  Open-ended laboratory
  Experiments
  Creative Thinking
  Skills Worksheets

From Schraer & Stolze (1987). Thinking Skills in Science. *Biology: The Study of Life* (Teacher's Edition, pp. TG 30–33). Newton, MA: Allyn & Bacon.

446

APPENDIX B

For the Teacher

Causal Explanation (III.C.1.b.), p. CCT-39

Introduction

A causal explanation is a conclusion about why something has happened. In order to come up with a causal explanation, a person must:

1. generate a list of *all* possible explanations (including those that may be farfetched), and then

2. narrow this list, based on evidence collected from a variety of sources.

The person is then left with the most likely cause of why something has happened.

This activity can function as a model for thinking about causes in science as well as in everyday matters. Sometimes, students neglect to think through questions of causality; they simply jump to conclusions. Often, students do not give themselves a chance to think about the realm of possible explanations. They may just use evidence they already have or they may gather new evidence only to support a preconceived idea. The purpose of this activity is to help students avoid this type of sloppy thinking.

Answers and Notes

THINK CRITICALLY

1. The purpose of this question is to give students a chance to generate a list of possible causes for the mouse's death. Since the text provides only minimal information about the cause of death, students are free to brainstorm a number of possibilities: lack of food, lack of oxygen, poison, no water, disease, or a cat's meal. At this point students should list all possible explanations, even those that are only remotely possible. The point here is not only to think about the likely cause, but for students to think about the entire array of possibilities. Each of these could then be further investigated. If students get stuck and come up with only one or two possibilities, ask them to think about all the different things that could kill any living organism and to list whatever comes to mind.

2. In this question students must make a judgment about which of the possible causes of the mouse's death are likely and which are unlikely. This judgment requires skill at identifying relevant evidence that supports or refutes each possibility. The point here is for students to think about what kind of evidence they can find to support or refute each of the hypotheses they generated in question 1.

The following are possible answers: If the mouse had been poisoned, there might be a jar of mouse poison or some poisoned food nearby. If the mouse had been killed by a cat, the dead mouse might have tell-tale marks on it, or a cat might have been seen running away. The presence of cheese or other food in the area would suggest that the mouse had not died of starvation. It is important to give students ample time to generate as many of these pieces of evidence as they can. If students have trouble with this kind of reasoning, you could try to make things more concrete by asking them to imagine that they are detectives investigating the mouse's death. You might use the following line of questioning: What could you find by snooping around that would help you determine the cause of death? What would convince you that a cat killed the mouse? That the mouse was poisoned?

3. This question introduces an actual scientific experiment in which a causal explanation was sought. As in question 1, students should generate a list of hypotheses for why the mouse has died. Some possible answers include lack of food or water, lack of oxygen, disease, or poison. It may be helpful to point out to the students that there are fewer possible explanations for the mouse's death in this case than in question 1. This is because there is more evidence in this case (i.e., the mouse was alive before it was put in the sealed jar). This would make it highly unlikely that a cat killed the mouse. However, without any further evidence, it would not be possible to rule out any of the other hypotheses. By accumulating additional evidence, these hypotheses could be either supported or refuted. Note: Even if students tend to look ahead at the illustrations of the other experiments, encourage them to restrict their observations to Experiment 1 as they answer this question; this will allow them to do some specific focused thinking.

4. The purpose of this question is to give students a chance to generate a list of possible causes for the plant's death (lack of sunlight, lack of proper nutrients from the soil, lack of carbon dioxide, lack of water). As students brainstorm the possibilities, they should rely only on their own knowledge and the information provided in the text. Although some students will know that plants need carbon dioxide, not oxygen, to survive, it is important not to give them this fact at the outset. If they become stuck, help them by suggesting that they refer to a reliable source to find out about what can kill a plant. The important thing at this point is not so much what

BIOLOGY: The Study of Life

the right answer is but that students are engaged in the process of generating a list of possible causes.

5. This question gives students a chance to put together the clues from previous questions and to think through Priestley's experiment in its entirety. You may want to have students work together in groups of three or four or to have them compare their responses and think through the complexities of the experiment together. The importance of this exercise is not to ascertain the correct explanation but to gain an understanding of the thinking process that goes into arriving at an explanation. You can help students think through this question by creating a structure they can work with. For example, you might put a chart of Priestley's experiments on the board; under each experiment make a column for relevant information and the hypotheses this information supports or refutes. Then have students fill in the chart together, focusing on which hypotheses are supported by the evidence and which are not. Remember that in Experiments 1 and 2 more than one hypothesis is supported by the evidence even though, in the end, one set of causes (i.e., the mouse died from lack of oxygen; the plant died from lack of carbon dioxide; the mouse and the plant survived together because oxygen and carbon dioxide were somehow being generated and used when the two organisms were together) best explains the evidence from the cluster of experiments.

6. The purpose of this question is for students to see the importance of causal explanations in the development of solutions. They should realize that a solution to a problem cannot be found until the cause of the problem is understood. In this example students are asked to come up with possible ways that the plant's death could have been prevented. Possible answers include puncturing the filament that seals the jar, pumping carbon dioxide into the jar, and putting a mouse in the jar. Students should be made aware that these solutions could not have been found without first knowing what caused the plant's death.

THINK ABOUT THINKING

7. The purpose of this question is strictly to elicit a description of what students actually did in thinking through the problem. No evaluation of one scheme as better than another should be made here. It is important to let students share their responses with one another. To help students focus on their thought processes, you may want to ask questions like: What was your first thought when you read question 3? What did you think next?, etc. This would enable

students to compare the sequence of their thoughts with one another. You may wish to point out differences in the thinking that led one student to propose many possible explanations and the thinking that led another student to propose few explanations.

8. This question functions in exactly the same way as question 7.

APPLY WHAT YOU HAVE LEARNED

9– 10. These questions give students a chance to think about how they may use similar thinking processes to solve problems in their own lives. In question 9, some everyday examples include identifying the cause of: a headache or other health problem, the malfunctioning of a piece of equipment, receiving a certain grade in a class or on a report card, and a feeling of happiness or sadness.

In question 10, some possible causes would be: increased hunting by humans or other predators, a decreased availability of food, and the occurrence of a natural event that destroyed or altered the species' habitat. To determine which of these causes is correct, it would be necessary to conduct scientific studies or consult experts in order to gain evidence that one cause is more likely than the others.

Applications in the Textbook

Suggestions for reinforcing this thinking skill with specific content throughout the program *Biology: The Study of Life* are provided below. In using these suggestions to structure activities that effectively teach and exercise the thinking skill, the teacher should refer to page CCT-iii for suggested procedures and then be further guided by the format of the student worksheet provided.

Chapter 4 After students have read Sections 4-16— 4-18 (pp. 59–62), pose the following scenario: A scientist has isolated an enzyme in a test tube and then added the substrate. The reaction proceeded at a much slower rate than expected. List all possible causes for the slow reaction rate. How could the scientist find out the actual cause?

Chapter 9 After students have read Section 9-8 (pp. 152–153), ask them to list all possible explanations for a high blood pressure reading. Then, have students suggest a way that each of these explanations could be tested.

Chapter 17 Before students read section 17-3 (pp. 287–288), ask them to list some possible explanations for why most leaves change colors from summer to autumn. How would they attempt to determine the actual cause?

CCT-42   BIOLOGY: The Study of Life

From "Causal Explanation" in Schraer & Stolze (1987). *Biology: The Study of Life* (Teacher's Resource Book, pp. CCT 41–42). Newton, MA: Allyn & Bacon.

APPENDIX C

Finding Causes

The critical thinking skill of finding causes is a basic skill of reasoning or inference. In using this skill, we try to determine what caused some event, based on given evidence.

Many of the inferences based on evidence in science relate to causes. Once we know the cause of something, we can try to manipulate that cause. For example, we might manipulate the cause in order to prevent diseases or to make crops grow faster.

Students in the early grades are often asked to identify and differentiate between causes and effects, and to arrange them in causal sequences. In the upper elementary grades, however, there is more of an emphasis on the process of making a critical judgment about what is a cause.

💡 Thinking Critically

Finding Causes

Did you ever try to find out why something happened, so that you could make sure it would not happen again? Suppose you cannot hear what your friend is saying because the television is on too loud. Not hearing what is being said is the effect of the television being on too loud. You know the cause of this effect and you can turn the television down.

Sometimes it is not so easy to find out what the cause of an effect is. To make sure you find the right cause you have to find good evidence for it. Finding the right cause is like doing good detective work.

1 Practicing the Skill

When Jimmy got home from school, he found that his fish had died. He asked his brother Bob to help him find the cause of this effect before he got new fish. Jimmy and Bob came up with these possible causes.

1. Maybe the water was dirty.

2. Maybe the fish were sick.

Can you think of other possible causes to explain why the fish died? List your ideas.

What evidence could you find that would show you which of these causes was the most

104

Practicing the Skill

Students are first asked to brainstorm possible causes of the death of the fish. They are given two possibilities to start with. Avoid favoring these possibilities; instead, use them as a springboard from which students might see other possibilities. Accept all ideas without judging them. Students will evaluate their own responses later. Assist students by listing their responses on the board. (Some other possibilities might be: the water got

too cold, there was not enough oxygen in the water, the fish were old.) The next question encourages students to think about what evidence they could find to help them accept or reject the proposed causes. They should list evidence in favor of (as well as evidence against) each possible cause. Suggest that they consider "experiments" that could be conducted to gather evidence. For example, if the fish were sick, they could be examined for bacteria, and so on. Again, allow students to express all of their ideas, but question them by asking, "Why do you think this would be evidence?"

Next, students are given some evidence: the fish ate too much food. Fish that eat too much sometimes choke to death. This is one possibility rendered likely by the new evidence provided. Don't tell the students this. Rather, take them through each of the possibilities. Ask them if this new evidence suggests another possibility not on their list. Then ask them whether there is other evidence that they could find that would make them more sure that this is the cause. This will give them a sense of what further investigation could reveal to get better evidence.

Finding Causes (cont.)

In the critical thinking activity in the student text on pages 104–105, students will brainstorm possible causes, then consider what evidence must be found to determine the actual cause, and then proceed gathering such evidence. Based on the evidence, one explanation will appear to be more likely than the others.

The structure and sequence of this sort of thinking, as well as what goes into each of these component steps, define the skill of finding causes, or causal explanation.

In the final step of the process, discriminating critical judgment derives from the need for evidence—not only evidence in favor of one of the possibilities, but evidence that weighs against the others. Otherwise, the thinker is unable to select one explanation as the best one.

likely? What evidence could you find that would count against their causes and in favor of one of yours?

Later that day, Jimmy remembered that he had forgotten to feed his fish the day before, so he fed them twice as much food this morning. How could this new information help solve the mystery?

 Thinking About Thinking

What did you do to figure out which of the explanations about the fish was the best one? Why would you reject some possible causes and accept others?

3 Using the Skill

Scientists are concerned about some of the earth's animals. The populations of these animals are becoming so small that the animals might become extinct. What are some things that could cause this effect? Some endangered species are tigers, orangutans, whales, sea otters, and whooping cranes. Pick one of these and see what evidence you can find to help you decide which possible cause is the most likely one.

105

Thinking About Thinking

Metacognition (thinking about thinking) is crucial to learning the critical thinking skill identified. This portion of the exercise makes it possible for students to develop an understanding of how the skill works, so they can monitor and direct their own thinking. Here, we ask students to describe their own thinking, or to give advice to others about ways to think about something.

The goal in this section is to have students identify different steps in the process related to the thinking skill of finding causes. A critical thinker first considers possible causes, then thinks about the

evidence that he or she might find to support such causes, and so on.

If students have difficulty with this portion of the exercise, stimulate their thinking by asking, "What did you do first when you tried to think of the actual cause? Then what process did you follow?"

Using the Skill

In this section, students are given another example that requires the same thinking structure they used in the previous example. Some possible causes students might name for animal species becoming endangered are predators (including

people), diseases and running out of food. Encourage students to research the endangered species they choose. Make sure they look at each hypothesis they isolate and decide whether there is evidence in favor of that hypothesis.

"Thinking Critically: Finding Causes" from Barman, et al. (1989). *Science,* Teacher's Edition, Grade 4, pp. 104–105. Menlo Park, CA: Addison Wesley.

22

Informal Reasoning Assessment: Using Verbal Reports of Thinking to Improve Multiple-choice Test Validity

Stephen P. Norris
Memorial University of Newfoundland

It is commonly accepted that informal reasoning is characterized by multiple reasoning approaches and multiple solutions to problems. This diversity of approaches and outcomes creates problems for informal reasoning assessment. These problems are particularly acute for multiple-choice assessments, because they show examinees' answers but not the reasoning that led to them. If answers that are different from those keyed correct can be justified, it is difficult to infer the quality of examinees' reasoning from their answers alone. If an examinee chooses the keyed answer, how justified is it to infer that some acceptable reasoning process was followed? Alternatively, if an examinee chooses an unkeyed response, how sound is it to infer that an unacceptable reasoning process was followed?

Despite their shortcomings for informal reasoning assessment, multiple-choice tests are popular and likely to remain so. They are a major component of elementary and secondary school education and one of the best means available for assessing some aspects of informal reasoning competence (Tomko & Ennis, 1980). This is not to say that multiple-choice tests can be used for all purposes. Constructed-response tests in essay or short-answer format, interviewing individual students, and direct classroom observation can serve purposes and yield information that multiple-choice tests cannot. For instance, all three seem better suited than multiple-choice tests for assessing informal reasoning dispositions (Norris & Ennis, 1989). But using multiple-choice tests is probably the best way to develop student profiles on the many specific abilities that comprise informal reasoning, such as the ability to use the many criteria that are needed for judging the credibility of sources.

We are thus torn by two facts: (a) informal reasoning competence generally refers to the ability to use sound reasoning processes rather than to the provision of adequate answers to tasks; and (b) multiple-choice tests, which provide no direct evidence on the reasoning processes used to accomplish tasks, are a popular and important approach for assessing informal reasoning competence. These facts raise two questions: Can existing multiple-choice tests of informal reasoning adequately support inferences about the quality of reasoning processes? If not, can test construction practices be improved so that future multiple-choice tests will be more valid?

This chapter begins by challenging the validity of existing multiple-choice tests of informal reasoning. The methodologies used to design these tests generally provide no direct evidence to counter the challenges. The second section proposes that eliciting verbal reports of thinking from examinees on trial test items is a way to obtain the direct evidence required. Research on the use of verbal reports in testing is sparse and provides little clear guidance on their usefulness for multiple-choice test validation. Some relevant research on verbal reporting in nontesting areas is described, but there are still unresolved issues concerning the use of verbal reports of thinking for test validation. The third section reports a study that was designed to test the relevance of the evidence in verbal reports of thinking for validating multiple-choice tests of informal reasoning. The results strongly suggest that the evidence is relevant. Several implications for informal reasoning assessment are discussed in the final section.

DIFFERENCES AMONG EXAMINEES AFFECT VALIDITY OF MULTIPLE-CHOICE INFORMAL REASONING TESTS

When using multiple-choice tests of informal reasoning, it is necessary to infer examinees' reasoning processes from the answers they select. Several ways in which examinees differ can influence the reasoning processes they use, however, and raise questions about the accuracy of such inferences. Consider, for example, differences in the following four areas: (a) degree of informal reasoning sophistication, (b) background empirical beliefs, (c) assumptions that examinees make about test items, and (d) political and religious ideologies. Although these four areas overlap, it is useful to distinguish them to highlight different aspects of the overall problem of validating multiple-choice informal reasoning tests.

Degree of Informal Reasoning Sophistication

Multiple-choice items typically allow for only one correct answer. This restriction can create problems when testing reasoners with different degrees of sophistication in informal reasoning. Different degrees of sophistication does not merely mean different competence. A Grand Master is so superior to me at chess that comparisons of our competence are almost meaningless; we are in entirely different reference groups. The point here is that the advertised audience for many multiple-choice informal reasoning tests is so broad that one wonders whether entirely different reference groups are being considered.

Let us examine an item from Section I of the Cornell Critical Thinking Test Level X (Ennis & Millman, 1985-a), a popular multiple-choice test that assesses several aspects of informal reasoning competence. The test is aimed primarily at high school and undergraduate college students, but it is recommended for use as low as the fourth grade. Items are cast in the context of a story of a team of explorers that has just arrived on the newly discovered planet Nicoma. The explorers are searching for other explorers who arrived on Nicoma 2 years previously but who have not been contacted since. Each item in Section I presents some information discovered by members of the second team, and examinees are to decide whether the information is evidence for, evidence against, or neither evidence for nor against the hypothesis that all the members of the first team are dead. The first item reads: "You go into the first hut. Everything is covered by a thick layer of dust" (p. 1). The keyed answer is that the item presents evidence for the hypothesis that the members of the first group are all dead. However, judgments of the evidence can vary legitimately with examinees' informal reasoning sophistication. Suppose, reasoning in the following manner, that an examinee concluded that the information in Item 1 was evidence neither for nor against the hypothesis that all the members of the first team are dead: *I conclude that the information in Item 1 is evidence neither for nor against the hypothesis that all the members of the first team are dead. There are just too many ways to explain the information, and we do not have sufficient information to choose among the possibilities. Maybe the first team stopped using this hut. Maybe they are using the hut for activity that raises a lot of dust. Maybe they have moved to another place on Nicoma. Maybe, in fact, they are all dead. Given that all of these possibilities can explain the information and given that there is insufficient information to choose among the possibilities, my theory of evidence says that the information is evidence neither for nor against any of the possibilities, including the hypothesis that all the members of the first team are dead.*

There may be reason to disagree with the reasoning of this examinee. However, the reasoning could not be considered bad. In fact, the person's reasoning is quite sophisticated, and this very sophistication led to choosing an answer for Item 1 other than the one keyed correct. Concurring with the key and marking the examinee's answer incorrect would not do justice to the level of the person's thinking. On a multiple-choice test, where choice of answer is all that is recorded, this is exactly what would happen.

The same point can be illustrated using an item from the Cornell Critical Thinking Test Level Z (Ennis & Millman, 1985-b), a test aimed at more sophisticated reasoners than Level X. The item is in Section II of the test and portrays two people debating whether or not the drinking water of Gallton ought to be chlorinated. Some thinking in the debate is faulty, and, for each item, examinees are to choose from a list the best reason why the thinking is faulty:

11. DOBERT: I hear that you and some other crackpots are trying to get Gallton to chlorinate its water supply. You seem to think that this will do some good. There can be no doubt that either we should chlorinate or we shouldn't. Only a fool would be in favor of chlorinating the water, so we ought not to do it.

    ALGAN: You are correct at least in saying that we are trying to get the water chlorinated.

Pick the one best reason why some of this thinking is faulty.

A. Dobert is mistakenly assuming that there are only two alternatives.
B. Dobert is using a word in two ways.
C. Dobert is using emotional language that doesn't help to make his argument reasonable. (p. 3)

Alternative A appears to be true, because there are many alternatives, from not chlorinating at all to chlorinating using different concentrations of chlorine. Alternative B does not seem to be true. Alternative C, however, also appears to be true. There is thus a problem of deciding whether A or C offers the best reason for saying that some of Dobert's thinking is faulty. The keyed answer is C on the grounds that, compared to the objection in C, it is insignificant to object that there are more than the two alternatives that Dobert considers. However, a sophisticated informal reasoner might choose A on the grounds that it is Dobert's misunderstanding of chlorination that leads to his emotional outcry. The person might reason that if Dobert had an understanding that chlorination can occur in different degrees, then Dobert might have concluded that some level of chlorination is tolerable and not have become emotional. A sophisticated reasoner is more likely to see how people's beliefs, even about technical matters such as levels of chlorination, can affect their emotional responses. But this very sophistication can lead to being marked wrong on multiple-choice tests.

Problems can arise in other ways, too, because of the different degrees of sophistication of examinees. Some items used to test for informal reasoning ask examinees to choose a level of endorsement for conclusions. However, examinees with different degrees of sophistication can justifiably choose different levels of endorsement, leading again to the possibility of examinees choosing unkeyed answers even though they thought well. There is an example of such an item in the Watson-Glaser Critical Thinking Appraisal (Watson & Glaser, 1980), a test designed primarily for the junior high school level and up. In the item, examinees are instructed to read a passage and assume that it is true. They then read a statement and judge, based on the information in the passage, whether it is True, Probably True, Probably False, False, or that there is Insufficient Data to decide. The analysis that follows is derived from Ennis and Norris (1990) and Norris and Ennis (1989).

Mr. Brown, who lives in the town of Salem, was brought before the Salem municipal court for the sixth time in the past month on a charge of keeping his pool hall open after 1 a.m. He again admitted his guilt and was fined the maximum, $500, as in each earlier instance.

    6. On some nights it was to Mr. Brown's advantage to keep his pool hall open after 1 a.m., even at the risk of paying a $500 fine. (Watson & Glaser, 1980, p. 3)

The answer keyed correct is Probably True, which means, according to the test manual, that it is more likely to be true than false that on some nights it was to Mr. Brown's advantage to keep his pool hall open after 1:00 a.m.. However, a sophisticated informal reasoner might be able to imagine several alternative explanations of the facts. Mr. Brown might not have kept the pool hall open, but his son, whom Mr. Brown had recently put in charge of the business, kept it open. Mr. Brown was willing to take the blame and pay the fines for his son's offenses because he felt guilty for having neglected his son for many years. Maybe Mr. Brown had not kept the pool hall open but had admitted he did so that the fine could fall into the hands of corrupt municipal authorities as payment for giving him a license. Perhaps Mr. Brown had suffered a severe personal shock that resulted in his doing things that were not to his advantage. Perhaps Mr. Brown was protesting the discriminatory laws of his town that allowed some businesses to remain open later than 1:00 a.m., even though there were no principled reasons for doing this; he was protesting on principle, not because he thought the protest would be to his advantage. A sophisticated informal reasoner could conceive of possibilities such as these, and, if a number of possibilities occur to a person when there is not enough information to adjudicate among them, the person can justifiably choose Insufficient Data.

As another possibility, imagine a less sophisticated person who had learned that business people often break the law to their advantage if the fines are small enough. Suppose the person also believes that a fine of $500 is sufficiently large that the only explanation of a business person's repeatedly acting so as to be levied such a fine is that the action is to the person's advantage. This examinee might justifiably choose True. Either way, examinees reasoning justifiably according to their level of sophistication would be marked wrong on a multiple-choice test.

Background Empirical Beliefs

Examinees bring different background beliefs to bear on multiple-choice informal reasoning tasks. The effect of such differences can be illustrated using a question from Section II of the Cornell Critical Thinking Test Level X. Recall that a team of explorers has landed on Nicoma to search for a team that has not been contacted in 2 years. The second team is exploring the area around their landing site and has found some water. In the item, the task is to choose which, if either, of two underlined statements is more believable.

27. A. The health officer says, "This water is safe to drink."
    B. Several others are soldiers. One of them says, "This water is not safe."
    C. A and B are equally believable. (Ennis & Millman, 1985a, p. 4)

The keyed answer is that the health officer's statement is more believable, because the health officer should be more expert than the soldier on the potability of water and because experts speaking in their own fields tend to be more believable than nonexperts. Suppose, however, that an examinee believes that the training of soldiers and the apparatus they carry equips them to make as dependable tests of water safety as health officers. Such an examinee would choose C as the answer, because the health officer and soldier are equally expert, but would be wrong according to the key. However, the examinee would have known that expertise in a field tends to make one more credible and would have used that criterion for choosing C. This is precisely the informal reasoning competence that the item is designed to reward. But the person choosing A would be rewarded and the person choosing C penalized, even though the difference between them would have been their background empirical beliefs about the relative expertise of soldiers and health officers and not their informal reasoning competence.

Consider another example, based on the Test on Appraising Observations (Norris & King, 1983). Items are set in the context of a traffic accident, and various witnesses and people involved in the accident are reporting to police what they observed happening. In Item 9, Ms. Vernon and Martine, two witnesses, are reporting on cars they had seen going through a stop sign. The task for examinees is to judge which of the underlined reports is more credible.

9. Ms. Vernon then says, "I also remember that a fancy blue sports car went through the stop sign."
   Martine says, "A car with twin headlights went right through the stop sign."
   (Item 9)

This item is designed to test the principle of observational salience: Observations of more salient features of events tend to be more believable than observations of less salient features. Features of an event are salient to the extent that they are extraordinary, colorful, novel, unusual, and interesting and not salient to the extent that they are routine, commonplace, and insignificant. The keyed answer, based on the empirical belief that being a fancy blue sports car is more salient than having twin headlights, is that there is more reason to believe Vernon's statement.

A student reasoning as follows would use the principle of observational salience but would not choose the keyed answer.

A fancy blue sports car is something which would stand out, but blue is not as noticeable a color as red, and there are a lot of fancy blue sports cars around nowadays. Twin headlights aren't as popular as they were in the past when just about every car had them, so they would stand out, too. I believe neither would stand out more than the other, so the statements are equally believeable.

This student knew the principle of informal reasoning being tested but would have been marked wrong because of holding the empirical belief that having twin headlights is as salient a feature these days as being a fancy blue sports car.

Assumptions

Different examinees make different assumptions while working on the same multiple-choice informal reasoning items. Moreover, there are different assumptions that can lead *justifiably* to different choices of answers. Consider the following items from the Interpretation subtest of the Watson-Glaser test (Watson & Glaser, 1980). The task is to decide whether or not the numbered statements follow beyond reasonable doubt from the information given in the paragraph.

> Pat had poor posture, had very few friends, was ill at easy in company, and in general was very unhappy. Then a close friend recommended that Pat visit Dr. Baldwin, a reputed expert on helping people improve their personalities. Pat took this recommendation and, after three months of treatment by Dr. Baldwin, developed more friendships, was more at ease, and in general felt happier.
> 55. Without Dr. Baldwin's treatment, Pat would not have improved.
> 56. Improvements in Pat's life occurred after Dr. Baldwin's treatment started.
> 57. Without a friend's advice, Pat would not have heard of Dr. Baldwin. (p. 6)

The keyed answers are that the statement in Item 56 follows beyond reasonable doubt from the information in the paragraph and that the other two statements do not follow beyond reasonable doubt. In fact, the statement in Item 56 follows beyond *all* doubt, because the given information includes the fact that the improvements occurred after three months of treatment by Dr. Baldwin. This indicates a serious problem with the items, because it seems that the standards for being beyond *reasonable* doubt are taken by the test developers to be the same as those for being beyond all doubt.

However, imagine an examinee who understands "beyond reasonable doubt" in its everyday sense and ponders Item 55 as follows, making the assumptions indicated: *The statement is ambiguous between "would not have improved ever" or "would not have improved during the three month period." It is obvious that there is insufficient information to say beyond reasonable doubt that Pat would never have improved without the help of Dr. Baldwin, so the statement must mean "would not have improved during the three month period." But is it beyond reasonable doubt that he would not have improved during this three month period had he not received Dr. Baldwin's treatment? Well, from the description, I assume that Pat had been suffering in this way for a long time. Problems such as this typically do not occur overnight, nor typically do they go away quickly, by themselves, without professional help. I therefore assume that Pat's problem was not one that would have gone away quickly on its own. Given these assumptions, the most plausible explanation of Pat's improved condition is that it was brought about by the treatment, and, therefore, although I cannot be certain, it seems beyond reasonable doubt that without Dr. Baldwin's treatment there would not have been such an improvement during the three months.*

Such an examinee would be thinking well but would choose other than the keyed answer and be penalized for that on a multiple-choice test. The person made justified assumptions that were different from those of the test developers, and these different assumptions, coupled with sound informal reasoning, led to a choice of answer that would receive no credit on a multiple-choice test.

Ideologies

Conceptions of informal reasoning competence do not incorporate or presuppose any political or religious ideology. Being subject to reason might be considered an ideology, but, if so, it is not a political or religious one. However, political ideology can influence choices of answers on some informal reasoning items. Consider, for example, Items 65 and 67 from the Watson-Glaser test (Watson & Glaser, 1980). Examinees are presented with the question, "Would a strong labor party promote the general welfare of the people of the United States?" Possible answers to the question and reasons defending those answers are provided:

65. No; a strong labor party would make it unattractive for private investors to risk their money in business ventures, thus causing sustained large-scale unemployment.
67. No; labor unions have called strikes in a number of important industries. (p. 8)

Examinees are to assume that the reasons are true and to decide whether they provide strong or weak arguments for the answers given. They are told that strong arguments are those that are both important and directly related to the question.

Item 65 is keyed as giving a strong argument. However, for a laissez-faire examinee, the prospect of sustained large-scale unemployment might not be important, compared to the interference required to suppress a labor party. So, although the argument in 65 might be directly related to the question, it is considered unimportant by the examinee and is, therefore, judged weak. On the other hand, a social activist examinee might also mark Item 65 as weak, but for different reasons. The person might, for example, believe that sustained large-scale unemployment would be a good thing because it would arouse the general public to revolt against the existing economic system. For this person, the reasons given in the item would not support the "No" answer to the question.

Item 67 is keyed as giving a weak argument. However, a political conservative might consider the argument both important and directly related to the question and, therefore, mark the item as strong. The conservative might believe that a strong labor party would encourage unions, which would lead to strikes in important industries, and that such strikes would be detrimental to the general welfare of the people of the United States. Given these beliefs, the person could, while reasoning well, decide that the argument is strong.

Section Summary

Multiple-choice tests of informal reasoning provide only examinees' choices of answers to tasks, even though it is the reasoning that led to the choices and not the choices themselves that is of greatest interest. There is no direct evidence for the reasoning followed, so it must be inferred from the choices of answers. Several differences among examinees can make such inferences untrustworthy: different levels of informal reasoning sophistication, different background empirical beliefs, different assumptions made while taking tests, and different political and religious ideologies. Using examples from existing multiple-choice informal reasoning tests, this section has illustrated how each of these differences can lead to incorrect inferences about examinees' informal reasoning competence. These examples are not anomalies; they are indicative of a widespread problem in multiple-choice tests of informal reasoning.

The popularity and usefulness of multiple-choice informal reasoning tests call for research into methods to increase their validity, namely, to ensure that good informal reasoning leads to responses keyed correct and that poor reasoning leads to responses keyed incorrect. One plausible way to collect evidence on the relationship between examinees' answers and their reasoning is to ask them to think aloud while working on trial items, a widely accepted research approach that is rarely used in validating multiple-choice informal reasoning tests. The following section examines the usefulness of verbal reports of thinking for improving multiple-choice informal reasoning tests.

USING VERBAL REPORTS OF THINKING TO VALIDATE TESTS

Verbal reports of examinees' thinking while answering test questions contain information on the knowledge, strategies, and principles of reasoning that lead to their choices of answers. Verbal reports are not a means of observing reasoning processes directly, but they enable more trustworthy inferences about reasoning than just an examination of answers chosen.

Verbal reports are important tools in the construction of theories of human mental abilities, because they provide direct evidence for hypothesizing reasoning processes. The construct validation of ability tests has also been linked to theory construction (Cronbach, 1971). If construct validation includes the identification of the mental processes that underlie task performance, as argued by Embretson (1983) in her conception of *construct representation,* then verbal reports have relevance to construct validation (see also Haney & Scott, 1987). A multiple-choice informal reasoning test would have construct validity to the extent that good performance, defined in terms of number of items answered correctly, could be explained by examinees' following sound thinking, and poor performance could be explained by unsound thinking. Verbal reports can thus provide direct evidence for the construct validity of a test.

For verbal reports to be useful in the validation of an informal reasoning test, there must be a systematic procedure for collecting the reports, extracting information from them, and using that information for judging the quality of the test. The reports must be elicited in a manner that interferes as little as possible with examinees' reasoning. There must be a means to use the reports to judge examinees' reasoning independently of their answers to the test items while being sensitive to different levels of sophistication of informal reasoning, different background beliefs, different assumptions, and different political and religious ideologies. Finally, there must be a way to compare answers to quality of reasoning and to determine the extent to which good and poor reasoning lead, respectively, to answers keyed correct and answers keyed incorrect.

There are several ways to elicit verbal reports of examinees' thinking. They might be asked simply to say everything that comes to their minds as they work on a task. Alternatively, they might be asked to justify their answers. They might be probed with questions about the specifics of their reasoning by being asked whether such-and-such had anything to do with their thinking and, if so, what role it played in selecting their answer. Finally, some combination of these approaches might be used.

Whatever the specifics, it is not clear whether different elicitation approaches yield similar information on examinees' reasoning, or whether any approach yields trustworthy information on thinking. For a test validation methodology to rely on verbal reports, these issues must be clarified.

Verbal reports are relevant to the validation of multiple-choice informal reasoning tests only if the information on examinees' thinking that the reports contain is an accurate reflection of the thinking that would have taken place had the examinees taken the test in normal paper-and-pencil format. Verbal reports require that subjects relate the progress of their thinking or the reasons for their performance, often in the presence of an investigator. It is not known how such requirements influence thinking, and the small number of testing studies that have used verbal reports (Bloom & Broder, 1950; Connolly & Wantman, 1964; Kropp, 1956; McGuire, 1963; Schuman, 1966) have ignored the question. There is some relevant research from nontesting contexts, such as information-processing research on the use of verbal reports as data and memory research on eyewitness testimony. I thus briefly review the research in each of these areas.

Verbal Reports as Data

Research on the trustworthiness of verbal reports of mental processes points to conflicting conclusions. On the one hand, Nisbett and Wilson (1977) concluded that people have little or no introspective access to the things that stimulate their cognitive processes. On the other hand, Ericsson and Simon (1980, 1984) and Smith and Miller (1978) claimed that people do have dependable access to their mental processes *in certain situations.*

To support their conclusion, Nisbett and Wilson reviewed evidence from the cognitive dissonance, self-perception attribution, learning without awareness, and problem-solving literatures. Based on this evidence, they concluded three things: (a) people often cannot accurately report the effects of certain stimuli on their responses to problems requiring higher order thinking; (b) when people do report on such stimuli, they often do not search their memories to discover what the stimuli were, but rather appeal to plausible hypothetical mechanisms that they accept a priori; and (c) when people are correct about the stimuli affecting their responses, they have coincidentally appealed to a hypothesis that happens to be correct.

Smith and Miller (1978) criticized Nisbett and Wilson's reliance on results of controlled experiments in drawing their conclusions. They argued that controlled experiments are situations in which the influential stimulus is "systematically and effectively [hidden] from [subjects] by [the] experimental designs" (p. 356). The influential stimulus can be ascertained only by comparing the treatment and control groups and, of course, subjects in an experiment cannot do this. Therefore, Smith and Miller argued that Nisbett's and Wilson's conclusions apply only to experimentally controlled situations in which subjects' lack of awareness of what is influencing their thinking is a natural consequence of the experimental setup. They claimed that these experimental findings are not generalizable to people's attempts to report on their mental processes outside of experimental settings. Reports of thinking on test items might thus fall outside the scope of Nisbett's and Wilson's conclusions, because testing does not usually attempt to hide influential stimuli from examinees.

Ericsson and Simon (1980, 1984) discussed the trustworthiness of verbal reports of thinking from an information-processing perspective. They concluded that instructions to verbalize slow down but do not change the course of cognitive processing when subjects are verbalizing information that would normally be available to them in short-term memory. Specific and directive probes alter cognitive processing, however, as do requests to supply motives and reasons. This conclusion is particularly relevant for test validation contexts where reasons for answers might be sought. The conclusion suggests that some verbal reports of thinking on test items might not be applicable to testing contexts in which verbal reporting is not done.

Ericsson and Simon made specific hypotheses about how different types of requests to think aloud can affect the trustworthiness of verbal reports. In particular, they hypothesized that the less leading the probe employed, the more accurate the information obtained and that more information with an overall lower trustworthiness can be obtained with more leading probes. These hypotheses need to be tested.

It is not legitimate to assume that the research on verbal reports as data answers all the questions relevant to the use of verbal reports of thinking in testing situations. Testing contexts are sufficiently different from experimental and information-processing research contexts that it is reasonable to expect that memory retrieval and information processing demands might also differ. In particular, test takers make specific assumptions about how they should try to perform and how the results reflect on them that are probably different from those made when involved in a psychological study.

Eyewitness Testimony Research

Eyewitness testimony is often contained in verbal reports given in response to questions. Verbal reports of thinking on tests are similar. In one situation, people try to remember what they observed; in the other, they try to remember what they thought. The remembering processes are probably related, though not identical. Thus, research on the factors that affect the accuracy of eyewitness testimony is pertinent to the question of the accuracy of verbal reports of thinking on tests. The degree of pertinence is tempered by dissimilarities between the two contexts: In one, the memory is of an external event, whereas in the other, it is of an internal event; in one, the memory is of events in the more distant past, whereas in the other, the memory is of events in the very recent past.

The eyewitness testimony research most relevant to the present study explores the effect of different types of questioning on the accuracy of observation reports. Three categories of questions have been studied (Loftus, 1979, p. 90): (a) those eliciting *free* reports (e.g., "Tell us all that you saw"); (b) those eliciting *controlled* reports (e.g., "Give us a description of what your assailant was wearing"); and (c) those eliciting *alternate-choice* reports (e.g., "Did your attacker have dark or light hair?"). Two general conclusions can be drawn on the basis of many independent studies of these types of questioning techniques (Clifford & Scott, 1978; Dale, Loftus, & Rathbun, 1978; Harris, 1973; Hilgard & Loftus, 1979; Lipton, 1977; Loftus & Palmer, 1974; Marquis, Marshall, & Oskamp, 1972). The first is that free reports tend to be more accurate than any other type of report; controlled reports rank next in accuracy; and alternate-choice reports have the lowest degree of accuracy. The second is that the amount of information obtained increases in the opposite direction: Free reports contain the least amount of information; controlled reports contain somewhat more information; and alternate-choice reports contain the most information. Hence, free reports give a relatively lesser amount of relatively more accurate information, and alternate-choice reports give a relatively greater amount of relatively less accurate information. The results are consistent with the hypotheses offered by Ericsson and Simon.

As with the research on verbal reports as data, it is not legitimate to assume that the results of eyewitness testimony research can be applied directly to testing. Eliciting reports of thinking on tests is different from eliciting recollections of observed events, and there is no research that explores how these differences affect the accuracy of both types of report.

An Unresolved Problem

To summarize, the evaluation of informal reasoning competence makes demands that traditional multiple-choice tests are not equipped to meet. Problems requiring informal reasoning for their solution often admit of more than one solution, but multiple-choice tests usually have only one correct answer. Evaluators of informal reasoning are usually more interested in the process of examinees' reasoning than the product, but multiple-choice tests typically give no direct evidence on reasoning processes.

Despite these problems, multiple-choice tests are likely to continue to be used and to have considerable influence. Therefore, it would be worthwhile to have a way to validate the tests that can provide some direct evidence on the reasoning processes they elicit. One way to gain direct evidence on reasoning is to ask people to think aloud. Applied to the validation of multiple-choice informal reasoning tests, tests could be examined by asking samples of examinees to work on them and to report verbally on their thinking. Judgments could be made of whether or not good and poor informal reasoning led, respectively, to keyed and unkeyed answers. Specifically, the evidence could indicate whether differences in performance across an intended audience for the test was significantly affected by such factors as differences in reasoning sophistication, background empirical beliefs, assumptions made, and religious or political ideologies.

The idea is sound in the abstract. But there is still much to learn about how thinking aloud affects thinking itself. More particularly, there is virtually no research on the use of verbal reports of thinking in testing contexts, and the literature on verbal reports as data and eyewitness testimony is only suggestive of what to expect in testing. The use of verbal reports of thinking to validate tests would be justified only if their elicitation does not alter significantly the course of examinees' thinking from what it would have been had they worked on the tests in paper-and-pencil format. If a significant alteration occurs, then information on the validity of tests derived from the verbal reports would not provide evidence on the validity of the tests for paper-and-pencil sittings. It is, therefore, worth exploring whether verbal reports of thinking on multiple-choice informal reasoning tests can provide relevant evidence on the validity of those tests.

RELEVANCE OF THE EVIDENCE IN
VERBAL REPORTS OF THINKING

An investigation of the relevance of verbal reports of thinking to validating multiple-choice tests of informal reasoning considered two research questions:

1. Do different ways of requesting verbal reports from examinees yield different information on their thinking?
2. Does the act of verbally reporting thinking alter examinees' test performance?

The first question pertains to the role of the interview procedure. As stated earlier, slight changes in the wording of interrogations of eyewitnesses can cause different accounts of events to be given. Is the same true when asking examinees to verbally report their thinking? The second question addresses the issue of how verbally reporting one's thinking alters the course of that thinking. If significant alterations occur, they should be revealed in different test performances between examinees who verbally report their thinking and those who do not.

Description of the Study

To help answer these questions, 343 senior high school students from four high schools participated in an experiment. Verbal reports of their thinking were elicited as they worked through Part A of the Test on Appraising Observations (Norris & King, 1983). It is a multiple-choice test focused on one aspect of informal reasoning competence: the ability to judge the credibility of reports of observations. In Part A, items are cast in the context of a traffic accident. In each item, two people, either witnesses or individuals involved in the accident, provide accounts of what happened. Examinees are to judge which, if either, of the accounts is more credible. Judgments should be based on characteristics of either the observers, the observation conditions, or the statement of observation itself.

A completely randomized factorial design was used. Students were randomly assigned to one of five groups:

1. *No Probe Group:* Students were not interviewed and worked alone on the test in a paper-and-pencil format.
2. *Think Aloud Group:* Students were instructed to report all they were thinking as they worked through the items.
3. *Immediate Recall Group:* Students were asked to choose their answers to each question and to justify their choices immediately after each was made.
4. *Criteria Probe Group:* While working on each question, students' attention was drawn to a particular piece of infor-

mation in it. They were asked whether that information made any difference to the answers they chose and, if so, to explain the difference.

5. *Principle Probe Group:*   Students were treated as in the criteria probe group, except that they were asked an additional question aimed at determining whether their choices were based on particular general principles.

The no-probe group simulated conditions under which the test would normally be given. Students worked alone at a desk and marked their answers on an answer sheet. In the think-aloud group, students had considerable leeway to think and report as they saw fit because only the general instruction to think aloud was given. In the last three groups, students' responses were constrained by leading requests for particular information. The degree of leadingness of the probes varies analogously to those studied in eyewitness testimony research. If the results of eyewitness testimony research generalize to testing situations, then students' verbal reports of thinking should vary depending on their probing group.

Following is an illustration of how the system would proceed for each of the groups working on a given item, using item 3 as an example:

A policeman has been asking Mr. Wang and Ms. Vernon questions. She asks Mr. Wang, who was one of the people involved in the accident, whether he had used his signal.

   Mr. Wang answers, "Yes, I did use my signal."

   Ms. Vernon had been driving a car which was not involved in the accident. She tells the officer, "Mr. Wang did not use his signal. But this didn't cause the accident."

Students were to choose which, if either, of the underlined statements is more credible. In addition, the following instructions were given to students in each interviewed group:

Interviewed Group	Instructions to Examinees
Think Aloud	Try to tell me all that comes to your mind as you think about this question.
Immediate Recall	Which answer do you choose? . . . . Can you tell me why you chose that answer?
Criteria Probe	Which answer do you choose? . . . . Did the fact that Mr. Wang was involved in the accident affect your choice?
Principle Probe	Which answer do you choose? . . . . Did the fact that Mr. Wang was involved in the accident affect your

choice? . . . . (If "No") Go on to the next item. (If "Yes") What difference did it make to your thinking that he was involved?

Students' verbal reports were tape recorded and transcribed verbatim. All students were assigned performance scores equal to the number of items answered correctly according to the key provided with the test (Norris & King, 1985). Students who had given verbal reports were also assigned thinking scores. These scores indicated the quality of thinking displayed in the verbal reports on a scale of 0–3 for each item. They were assigned without regard to whether or not examinees chose correct answers according to the key.

Quality of thinking was judged by comparing students' verbal reports to ideal models of thinking developed for each item. The models were based on a set of principles for assessing the credibility of observations, knowledge of which the test was designed to measure. For example, in Item 3, the ideal model was based on the principle that people in a conflict of interest tend to be less credible than those not in a conflict of interest: *Mr. Wang was involved in the accident, but Ms. Vernon was not. Mr. Wang is less credible because his involvement would give him reason to say he used his signal even if he did not. Wang is in a conflict of interest. People in a conflict of interest, that is, people who have something to gain by events being cast as they described them, tend to be less credible than those who are not in such a situation.*

According to the model, an examinee first needs to identify the relevant information in the text about Wang's and Vernon's involvement. The text is simple enough that reading ability would not impede this identification for most high school students. Second, an examinee must remember from experience that not using a turn signal can cause an accident and that being held responsible for an accident can be troublesome. High school students should have ready access to such common knowledge. Finally, an examinee has to recognize that being in a conflict of interest is an accuracy-reducing factor and apply this principle to make a credibility judgment.

For Item 3, thinking scores were assigned according to the following scale:

1 point: The examinee points out that Mr. Wang was involved in the accident.
2 points: The examinee points out that Mr. Wang was involved in the accident and compares Mr. Wang's involvement to Ms. Vernon's being a bystander.
3 points: The examinee points out that Mr. Wang was involved in the accident, compares this with Ms. Vernon's noninvolvement, and shows that this is an instance of a more general phenomenon in which people stand to profit or lose, depending on what they say.
0 points: The examinee points out none of the above information or does not respond.

Generalizing to all items, students were assigned one point toward their thinking scores for each of the following: (a) citing the relevant facts in the text that can be used to compare the underlined statements for their credibility; (b) using these facts together with any relevant background knowledge to make a comparative evaluation of the credibility of the statements; and (c) showing how the evaluation is based on a generalized accuracy-reducing factor.

To illustrate the procedure more clearly, consider a transcript of one student's verbal report of thinking on Item 3: "The second one 'cause, ah, 'cause he'd say that he used the signal so he wouldn't have nothing to do with the accident. Probably afraid he'd have . . . he'd be questioned by the police or something." This student would be assigned a thinking score of 2, because she clearly recognized the accuracy-reducing role of Wang's involvement in the accident. She did not explicitly state that Wang was involved and Vernon was not, but these were clearly implicit in her thinking. She would not be given a 3, because no general principle was cited.

Results

The verbal reports, the thinking scores, and the performance scores were analyzed quantitatively and qualitatively (for more details, see Norris, 1990) to determine whether different ways of requesting examinees' verbal reports yielded different information on their thinking and whether the act of verbally reporting thinking altered examinees' test performance. The results of the quantitative analysis of thinking scores showed no statistically significant differences across the four groups that were interviewed. Whatever other effects the different types of probes might have had, they did not affect the quality of students' thinking as measured by the thinking score scale.

A qualitative analysis further supported this conclusion. It was conducted on a random sample of 40 (stratified by interview group) of the total sample of 271 interviews. The following coding scheme was devised to describe a variety of reasoning acts in the reports:

1. Citing Factual Details. Recalling a factual detail given in an item prior to the one currently being done, recalling such a prior detail incorrectly, or stating a detail in the current item.

2. Asking Rhetorical Questions. Posing questions that appear to be directed to the examinee rather than to the interviewer.

3. Making Evaluations. Evaluating previously stated judgments or conclusions or evaluating unspoken ones.

4. Constructing Supporting Assumptions. Making detailed factual assumptions specific to the current item or making more generalized assumptions of broad principles of appraisal or causal laws that cover more than the current situation.

5. Using Attention Control Devices. Commenting on progress of reasoning in the problem ("Let's see . . . Where was I?") or commenting on the direction in which reasoning should proceed ("Wait, now!").

6. Interacting with the Experimenter. Directing comments or questions to the experimenter.

7. Pausing. Making verbal inflections ("Ahhh!" "Mmmm!") or being silent.

The 40 verbal reports were coded according to these seven categories and the frequencies of reasoning acts calculated. (See Table 22.1.) Although these data were not systematically analyzed, the general trends indicate clear differences in the frequencies of reasoning act categories. However, there are no glaring differences in trends across the interview groups, supporting the conclusion of the quantitative analysis that there was no difference in quality of thinking across the four interviewed groups.

Both the quantitative and qualitative results strongly suggest that subjects' thinking, rather than the method by which that thinking was elicited, controlled what they reported. If this conclusion can be substantiated in other studies and for other tests, the accuracy of verbal reports of thinking on multiple-choice informal reasoning tests seems not to be as influenced by type of probing as research on verbal reports in other contexts indicates. Testing may be a context whose demands are sufficiently unique that the use of verbal reports of thinking to assess test validity deserves further study.

Analysis also showed that there are no statistically significant differences in performance scores between any of the interviewed groups and the group who took the test in the paper-and-pencil format. This result suggests that probing did not alter thinking, because if the course of examinees' thinking had been altered by giving verbal reports on their thinking, they would have performed differently. It is hard to imagine how their thinking could have differed in a systematic fashion while their performance stayed precisely the same.

TABLE 22.1
Frequency of Reasoning Acts by Interview Group

	Interview Group			
Reasoning Acts	Thinking Aloud	Immediate Recall	Criteria Probe	Principle Probe
Citing Factual Details	104	139	99	139
Asking Rhetorical Questions	16	9	2	5
Making Evaluations	45	24	39	43
Constructing Assumptions	178	228	214	227
Using Attention Control Devices	26	25	15	19
Interacting with Experimenter	19	9	12	13
Pausing	499	387	424	380

DISCUSSION AND CONCLUSIONS

Whenever no differences between treatments is the result of an experiment, the power of the experiment to detect differences that actually exist becomes an important concern. Was this experiment sufficiently powerful to detect any differences that existed among the groups? There are a number of reasons to believe that differences would have been detected had they been present in the population. First, the treatments were considerably different from one another. It is quite different for high school students to work alone on a test than to work in the presence of a stranger who is probing their thinking. If eliciting verbal reports tends to alter the course of thinking, alterations should have been revealed in differences in performance between the interviewed and uninterviewed groups.

Second, the interview treatments themselves were considerably different. The leading probes were quite leading, because they made explicit suggestions to students about what could have affected their choices of answers. It would have been an easy matter for students to conform to these suggestions by altering their answer choices and their way of thinking about items. Instead, students denied regularly that a suggested factor had anything to do with their thinking and proceeded to explain how their choices were made. That is, they tended to maintain whatever interpretation made sense to them.

Third, effects were sought from a number of different directions but were found in none of them. The quantitative analysis showed no differences in thinking scores across the four interviewed groups and no differences in performance scores across all five groups. The qualitative analysis showed that the same patterns of reasoning acts were used by students in each of the interviewed groups. It is plausible to conclude that, if the verbal reporting altered students' thinking, it would have been detected by at least one of these methods.

Fourth, eyewitness testimony research uncovers consistent effects using similar sorts of treatments. This does not mean that differences should have been found in this study, but it does suggest that *if* differences existed, they should have been detected.

Finally, an analysis of the statistical power of the experiment showed less than a 15% chance that real differences existed among the groups but were not detected.

This research points to a useful technique for validating multiple-choice tests of informal reasoning. Eliciting verbal reports of examinees' thinking is a plausible way to gather data on the quality of tests. This study bolsters confidence in the technique by showing that there is no need to be overly cautious about the leadingness of questions used to elicit reports of thinking. Examinees' thinking is not altered by requests to report on their thinking, so the information in the reports is relevant evidence for the validity of tests. Such evidence can show whether sophistication, background empirical beliefs, ideologies of reasoners, assumptions reasoners make, and other factors affect performance on multiple-choice informal reasoning tests.

Collecting verbal reports of thinking on existing multiple-choice informal reasoning tests should give important evidence on the validity of those tests. Because of doubts about their validity raised by criticisms discussed in the first section of this chapter, such evidence is needed. It is important to know, one way or the other, whether or not existing multiple-choice informal reasoning tests are valid.

The results of such validation studies might be mixed. For instance, whereas many multiple-choice informal reasoning tests are advertised for wide ranges of audiences, verbal reports of thinking from subjects across the entire range may indicate that the advertised applicability of a given test should be narrower. As a consequence, the advertised range of a test's applicability might be altered, or, using the information gathered from verbal reports of thinking, versions suitable for more narrowly defined audiences might be designed. These versions may differ considerably from each other, or they may only differ in keyed responses. It might be possible, for instance, to tailor answer keys to different audiences to take account of such factors as sophistication, empirical beliefs, ideologies, and so on.

Using verbal reports of thinking to tailor answer keys to different audiences suggests a developmental (in addition to validation) role for verbal reports. Further, verbal reports of thinking on trial items of a test under development can provide evidence for retaining, modifying, or discarding items. With a systematic procedure for quantifying and using this evidence to judge individual items and the test as a whole (Norris, 1988; 1989), validity can be built into a test from the item level on up. Verbal reports of thinking thus open the prospect of developing valid multiple-choice tests to do the sorts of informal reasoning assessment for which they are most suited.

However, not all informal reasoning assessment can be served by multiple-choice testing. The Test on Appraising Observations, used as an example in this chapter, assesses the ability to apply criteria one at a time to appraise credibility. But in a real-world context of appraising the credibility of a witness, several of the criteria would be likely to apply simultaneously. Some of the criteria might push the appraisal in one direction, others in another direction. The criteria would have to be weighed and balanced, and there are no strict rules for doing this. Judgment based on experience would have to be used. Multiple-choice tests are not useful for assessing how well people use their judgment to orchestrate a number of informal reasoning skills to work on ill-defined, real-world problems. Other assessment methods must be developed.

Informal reasoning dispositions also pass through the mesh of multiple-choice informal reasoning tests, but reasoning dispositions are as important to assess as reasoning abilities. Disposition assessment is logically a two-stage process, because failure to perform well (e.g., to give alternative hypotheses when appropriate) could be explained by lack of knowledge that giving alternatives is appropriate, by lack of ability to generate alternatives, or by lack of disposition (given the knowledge) to provide alternatives. The possibilities of lack of knowledge and ability must be ruled out before lack of disposition can be accepted as the explanation. Assessment of dispositions is doubly complex, and there are no adequate techniques for assessing dispositions to be open-minded, to seek reasons, to seek alternatives, to seek critical feedback, and so on. Furthermore, it is not clear how these assessments might best be done. Essay testing, interviewing individuals, and direct classroom observation are approaches with promise (Norris & Ennis, 1989), but considerable research is needed.

Because teaching reasoning has become an increasingly desired educational goal, many traditional assessment practices will have to change, or be dismissed, or be replaced. Practices that are adequate for assessing instruction focused primarily on learning factual knowledge are inadequate for assessing informal reasoning competence. Although the problems of informal reasoning assessment are large and have persisted because educators only recently have taken seriously instruction in reasoning, they are surmountable. In particular, the use of verbal reports of thinking to assess multiple-choice tests promises to be a useful analytical tool in providing the information needed to design reliable tests of informal reasoning ability.

ACKNOWLEDGMENT

This research was supported by a grant from the Social Sciences and Humanities Research Council of Canada, Grant No. 410-83-0697. The views expressed herein are those of the author and not the funding agency. I thank Robert Barcikowski, Robert Crocker, Susan Embretson, David Perkins, Linda Phillips, and Judith Segal for helpful comments.

REFERENCES

Bloom, B. S., & Broder, J. L. (1950). *Problem-solving processes of college students.* Chicago, IL: The University of Chicago Press.

Clifford, B. R., & Scott, J. (1978). Individual and situational factors in eyewitness testimony. *Journal of Applied Psychology, 63,* 352–359.

Connolly, J. A., & Wantman, M. J. (1964). An exploration of oral reasoning processes in responding to objective test items. *Journal of Educational Measurement, 1,* 59–64.

Cronbach, L. J. (1971). Test validation. In R. L. Thorndike (Ed.), *Educational measurement* (2nd ed.) (pp. 443–507). Washington, DC: American Council on Education.

Dale, P. S., Loftus, E. F., & Rathbun, L. (1978). The influence of the form of the question on the eyewitness testimony of preschool children. *Journal of Psycholinguistic Research, 7,* 269–277.

Embretson (Whitely), S. (1983). Construct validity: Construct representation versus nomothetic span. *Psychological Bulletin, 93,* 179–197.

Ennis, R. H., & Millman, J. (1985-a). *Cornell critical thinking test, level X.* Pacific Grove, CA: Midwest Publications.

Ennis, R. H., & Millman, J. (1985-b). *Cornell critical thinking test, level Z*. Pacific Grove, CA: Midwest Publications.

Ennis, R. H., & Norris, S. P. (1990). Critical thinking evaluation: Status, issues, needs. In J. Algina & S. M. Legg (Eds.), *Cognitive assessment of language and math outcomes*. New York: Ablex.

Ericsson, K. A., & Simon, H. A. (1980). Verbal reports as data. *Psychological Review, 87*, 215–251.

Ericsson, K. A., & Simon, H. A. (1984). *Protocol analysis: Verbal reports as data*. Cambridge, MA: MIT Press.

Haney, W., & Scott, L. (1987). Talking with children about tests: An exploratory study of test item ambiguity. In R. O. Freedle and R. P. Duran (Eds.), *Cognitive and linquistic analyses of test performance* (pp. 298–368). Norwood, NJ: Ablex.

Harris, R. J. (1973). Answering questions containing marked and unmarked adjectives and adverbs. *Journal of Experimental Psychology, 97*, 399–401.

Hilgard, E. R., & Loftus, E. F. (1979). Effective interrogation of the eyewitness. *The International Journal of Clinical and Experimental Hypnosis, 27*, 342–357.

Kropp, R. P. (1956). The relationship between process and correct item responses. *Journal of Educational Research, 49*, 385–388.

Lipton, J. P. (1977). On the psychology of eyewitness testimony. *Journal of Applied Psychology, 62*, 90–95.

Loftus, E. F. (1979). *Eyewitness testimony*. Cambridge, MA: Harvard University Press.

Loftus, E. F., & Palmer, J. C. (1974). Reconstruction of automobile destruction: An example of the interaction between language and memory. *Journal of Verbal Learning and Verbal Behavior, 13*, 585–589.

Marquis, K. H., Marshall, J., & Oskamp, S. (1972). Testimony validity as a function of question form, atmosphere, and item difficulty. *Journal of Applied Social Psychology, 2*, 167–186.

McGuire, C. (1963). Research in the process approach to the construction and analysis of medical examinations. *National Council on Measurement in Education Yearbook, 20*, 7–16.

Nisbett, R. E., & Wilson, T. D. (1977). Telling more than we can know: Verbal reports on mental processes. *Psychological Review, 84*, 231–259.

Norris, S. P. (1988). Controlling for background beliefs when developing multiple-choice critical thinking tests. *Educational Measurement, 7*(3), 5–11.

Norris, S. P. (1989). Can we test validly for critical thinking? *Educational Researcher, 18*(9), 21–26.

Norris, S. P. (1990). Effect of eliciting verbal reports of thinking on critical thinking test performance. *Journal of Educational Measurement, 27*, 41–58.

Norris, S. P., & Ennis, R. H. (1989). *Evaluating critical thinking*. Pacific Grove, CA: Midwest Publications.

Norris, S. P., & King, R. (1983). *Test on appraising observations*. St. John's, Newfoundland: Institute for Educational Research and Development, Memorial University of Newfoundland.

Norris, S. P., & King, R. (1985). *Test on appraising observations manual*. St. John's, Newfoundland: Institute for Educational Research and Development, Memorial University of Newfoundland.

Schuman, H. (1966). The random probe: A technique for evaluating the ability of closed questions. *American Sociological Review, 31*, 218–222.

Smith, E. R., & Miller, F. D. (1978). Limits on perception of cognitive processes: A reply to Nisbett and Wilson. *Psychological Review, 85*, 355–362.

Tomko, T. N., & Ennis, R. H. (1980). Evaluation of informal logic competence. In J. A. Blair & R. Johnson (Eds.), *Informal logic: The first international symposium* (pp. 113–144). Inverness, CA: Edgepress.

Watson, G., & Glaser, E. M. (1980). *Watson-Glaser critical thinking appraisal*. Cleveland, OH: The Psychological Corporation.

23 Informal Reasoning and Instruction: A Commentary

Larry Cuban
Stanford University

I come to the task of commenting on these seven chapters with two sets of biases. The first is anchored in a quarter-century service as a high school history teacher, a director of staff development, and superintendent of a middle-sized school district. Since 1955, when I began teaching history to eleventh graders, through 1981, when I left the superintendency, I have either taught courses that had within them a large component of what the authors call "informal reasoning" or actually tried to introduce systematic instruction in thinking skills in a school system of 20,000 students (and more than 1,000 teachers).

These experiences, then, have made me very sensitive to the complexities of schooling and its embeddedness, that is, to the entanglement of daily classroom and school practices within larger contexts of the district organization and the surrounding communities. These sensitivities surface when I work with those who design changes in what teachers and administrators do, yet have had limited or no previous experience in schools.

The other set of biases arises from my historical research. To historians, a sense of the particular and the unique combine with a sense of time and place to produce a singular perspective on both events and their causes. If my experience as a practitioner yielded an awareness of how practice is complex and embedded in a context, my historian's nose and intuition reinforced that experiential knowledge through my researches into how teachers have taught over the last century, teachers' use of machine technology since 1920, and the history of school reform. Practice and research intersect for me to underscore the complexities of classroom and school affairs and how those complexities are entangled in unique contexts (Cuban, 1984-a; 1986).

These biases come into play as I comment on these chapters. I want readers to be fully aware of the attitudes I have about instruction and informal reasoning.

BRIEF SUMMARIES

I divide the seven chapters into two categories: The first includes research into how experts and novices use informal scientific reasoning (Clement) and research into what teachers have done in writing and math (Applebee, Schoenfeld); the second includes designs based on research and experience that aim to improve how teachers teach informal reasoning in science and social studies, as well as through the use of tests (Swartz, O'Reilly, Norris, Newmann).

Briefly, Clement studied how 10 experts (doctoral students and professors) spontaneously used analogies in problem solving. He connects how his experts used analogical reasoning and images with other researchers' findings in mathematical thinking. Clement also investigated how these reasoning processes occurred in high school physics classes, where novices' misconceptions frequently interfered with conceptual understanding. Seven lessons aimed at combatting such misconceptions (for example, the notion that static objects cannot exert force) were taught to "experimental classes" using "anchoring examples" and "bridging analogies." In the absence of detailed information on the nature of the experimental and control groups, who the teachers were, or the degree of consistency in the instruction, I found it difficult to assess the design of the experiment. Nonetheless, Clement was encouraged by the pre- and post-test results to urge further research using this approach with high school students. Such research into the processes of reasoning may help generate new theories or enhance current ones guiding instructional and curricular practices.

To go from the laboratory into the school, however, is to go from theory-making to theories-in-action. Clement's account of a modest foray into schools was broadened considerably by Applebee's and Schoenfeld's examinations of informal reasoning in writing and math as they are taught in classrooms and schools.

Applebee presents us with a few puzzles. While the teaching of writing has come to concentrate, in the last two decades, on developing reasoning skills through drafting and revision of written work, the results of the National Assessment of Educational Progress (NAEP) over the same period reveals little improvement in writing. Moreover, the NAEP data show few linkages between teachers' emphasis on reason in writing and student performance; that is, students from classrooms where reasoning skills in writing were *not* stressed did as well as students who came from classrooms where writing and problem solving were emphasized. Yet, the very same NAEP data also show that students who reported that they spend more time on planning what they write, revising it, and letting others comment on the work clearly write better than peers who spend less time on those activities. Hence, Applebee offers another puzzle: Students who *use* process strategies in their own writing seem to write better than students who do not, but *teaching* those strategies seems to be unrelated to student performance.

To answer these puzzles, Applebee and Judith Langer studied what teachers and students do in classrooms. They found that teachers who are deeply interested in teaching reasoning skills through the writing process eagerly introduced to their students a repertoire of new teaching tasks. Over time, however, the researchers discovered that, rather than the students' writing being transformed, these novel teaching approaches evaporated, to be replaced by such common practices as covering content and testing students to determine if they knew the subject. Getting teachers to teach the right stuff about writing and reasoning was not enough; the right stuff became the old stuff. Applebee provides us with some clues to why this occurred by discussing teachers' belief systems about knowledge and the nature of the classroom and school as learning environments. But the puzzles remain.

For Schoenfeld, there are no puzzles. The problem is clear, and the solutions, though tough to achieve, are doable. Where Applebee argues that even changing teacher practices in writing instruction does not assure improvements in how students write, and where he cautiously tip-toes around the issues of teachers' beliefs and the nature of schooling as a process, Schoenfeld plunges forward to attack what he sees as the enemy of reasoning in mathematics: how teachers teach mathematics. Citing numerous studies, he argues that the curriculum delivered by teachers in the formal ways sanctioned by schools is divorced from life. Students are trained to see mathematics in ways that bury reasoning: "Teachers give you rules for solving problems, which you memorize and use. Those rules don't have to make sense, and they may not, but if you do what you're told you will get the right answer, and then everybody will be happy" (see Chapter 16, this volume). Schoenfeld doesn't tell us why teachers teach this way; they just do.

Schoenfeld sees the solution to this lack of sense-making in teaching mathematics as exploration, false starts, trial and error, and real-life problem solving— in short, teaching math as a process, rather than a product. Drawing from personal examples and the efforts of a teacher a half-century ago in a laboratory school, he argues that such classes can exist. These classes develop into cultures of "mathematical sense-making." Conceding that making such changes in teaching would be revolutionary, the author, nonetheless, dispenses with anger about a mindless classroom culture and launches a vigorous argument for a new kind of classroom, created by thoughtful teachers who understand the essence of mathematics.

This upbeat ending to Schoenfeld's chapter leads to the next four chapters which focus on improving existing teacher practices. The language of change and implementation dominates these discussions, although theory, conceptual frameworks, and models appear also. Swartz concentrates on science curriculum materials. O'Reilly describes the results of changing how he taught American history. Norris focuses on the inevitability of multiple choice tests and on how they can be improved to cultivate informal reasoning. Newmann develops a conceptual framework and extends it with an analysis of factors that inhibit classroom instruction in reasoning while proposing a curriculum, pedagogy, and organizational changes aimed at improving the level of student and teacher reasoning in social studies classrooms. These practicing educators take the here-and-now of classroom practices and ask how they can be improved. They seek to implement incremental, not fundamental, changes.

Drawing on his appraisal of many revealing examples of science materials, Swartz claims that good thinking can be introduced into classrooms, even in the face of organizational obstacles, through improved textbook content and teachers' use of enriched lessons and units across the curriculum. Based on his experience and that of a number of teachers with whom he has worked, Swartz has constructed a "conceptual-infusion approach" for the teaching of reasoning. Underlying this approach is a view of reasoning as a set of general skills that can be applied in all areas of the school curriculum, along with guidelines for teaching these skills in content domain courses. Swartz anchors his conceptual framework in a number of researchers' models of reasoning and in the assumption that transfer of learning will occur. He believes (and acts on his beliefs by helping teachers create materials) that each classroom teacher can reorganize the subject matter taught along the lines he suggests and thereby cultivate good thinking.

O'Reilly lays out, in substantial and illuminating detail, what an American history course that stresses reasoning might look like. In addition, he points out a range of constraints that face any teacher wishing to introduce a new style of teaching: a teacher load of over 150 students in five classes daily; lack of time to develop classroom materials; and the gap between theoretical models and daily classroom practice. Leaning heavily on the work of Barry Beyer, a professor of social studies education, O'Reilly shows how a taxonomy of skills can be woven into conventional content in an imaginative way. Here is a remarkable display of both creativity, in the tradition of Harold Fawcett, whom Schoenfeld admiringly describes in his chapter, and the inquiry approach to social studies teaching that was adopted by some teachers between the mid-1960s and mid-1970s.

Like Swartz and Schoenfeld, O'Reilly believes that individual teachers can restructure what they teach to incorporate reasoning skills in such a manner as to engage students intellectually. But even intellectually engaged students are tested in today's schools. Do tests, especially those aimed at assessing how well students reason, reveal much about the reasoning that goes on in students' heads when answering multiple-choice items?

According to Norris, current multiple-choice items on standardized and teacher-made tests aimed at assessing informal reasoning seldom get at that process. Like Swartz and O'Reilly, Norris acknowledges that there are organizational barriers to applying reasoning in the existing curriculum and instructional practices; yet Norris argues that testing practices are here to stay, but that the items can be improved to better assess informal reasoning.

Norris' examples of multiple-choice items drawn from current tests of thinking skills demonstrate convincingly that one cannot tell from students' answers what processes of reasoning they used—the outcome that is far more important to the writers of these chapters than the answer. As it now stands, a teacher can only infer what those reasoning processes were. Norris points out clearly that those inferences are unreliable, in light of students' varying background beliefs, ideologies, and assumptions about knowledge.

To improve the quality of inferences about students' informal reasoning, Norris advocates getting students to talk aloud about how they thought through answers to test questions. He describes a study that he conducted using special questioning techniques to generate verbal reports from students on the reasoning underlying their responses to multiple-choice test items. He suggests that information gathered from such verbal reports can produce a "more scientifically and morally defensible multiple-choice informal reasoning test."

If Norris is hopeful that further research can enhance existing tests of reasoning, Newmann is cautiously optimistic about changes in social studies teachers' classrooms that might result from linking theories more tightly to existing practices. Newmann constructs a conceptual framework for higher order thinking skills and connects that framework to the special challenges inherent to the social studies. He suggests what would need to be done in curriculum, pedagogy, school organization, and professional development of teachers for higher order reasoning to become part of teachers' routine repertoires. More than any of the other chapters, Newmann links existing theories to what teachers say about practicing their craft, while acknowledging the many organizational and personal factors involved in changing the existing system of social studies instruction.

Writing these brief summaries (I acknowledge that authors may wince in reading them) has suggested to me three issues of particular significance and revealed a blind spot in the chapters. First, the blind spot: The discussions raised in these chapters are ahistorical. Systematic efforts to introduce reasoning and problem solving into schools began at the turn of the century. Inspired by John Dewey, educators tried to create classrooms where reasoning was cultivated (Dewey, 1933). The "Eight-Year Study," in which 30 high schools participated, was specifically geared to the cultivation of thinking skills (Tyler & Smith, 1942). Schoenfeld's resurrection of a teacher in one of the schools is the lone instance of the writers, not being blissfully unaware of any effort that occurred before they put pen to paper. Moreover, in the 1960s and 1970s, a movement flourished in social studies, science, and mathematics to introduce formal and informal reasoning in classrooms (National Science Foundation, 1978). The general absence of references to previous efforts is a sign of a crippling amnesia that seriously handicaps researchers in this field; it allows them to ignore or skirt complex problems suggested or acknowledged in earlier work.

Then, it is troubling as well that there is no apparent consensus among these writers as to what informal reasoning is, what models of thinking (much less instruction or learning) are appropriate for use in classrooms, and what research strategies might be pursued to produce either a definition or a model. This conceptual anarchy mirrors the absence of consensus generally in the field and underscores the gap that exists between the enthusiasts for teaching informal reasoning and those responsible for putting into practice curricular packages or new programs in thinking skills. Without a narrowing of theoretical models to those that might be explored within schools or some general agreement on the significant variables to be examined, scholars can offer little guidance to policymakers and practitioners. That conceptual anarchy exists in these chapters should inspire caution in those hellbent on telling practitioners what they ought to do in classrooms to nourish informal reasoning (Cuban, 1984-b).

A second issue is the authors' views on the linkage between reasoning and content, or, in the awkward phrase of psychologists, domain-specific knowledge. O'Reilly, Swartz, Schoenfeld, and Newmann explicitly recognize the entanglement of subject matter and reasoning. The others either implicitly acknowledge the linkage or ignore its existence in preference for a skills approach that is generic to all subject matters.

A final issue that emerges from the Applebee, Schoenfeld, Swartz, O'Reilly, and Newmann chapters—with varying degrees of explicitness—is the need to acknowledge that both cultural and organizational factors influence what occurs in classrooms. The issue of the embeddedness of teaching is suggested by the practical awareness among the authors of the enormous complexity involved in adopting and implementing efforts to alter what teachers do in their classrooms to increase the chances of students engaging in informal reasoning in and out of school. Except for Newmann and O'Reilly, however, the authors display a perilous innocence of organizational realities in changing teaching practices.

This theme of the embeddedness of teaching in an organization and culture and the inherent difficulties of altering routine school and classroom practices deserves close attention. I concentrate on this because many researchers who look for applications to education are closet-reformers. If this claim is correct, attention to the embeddedness of teaching and process of change become primary issues.

COMMENTARY

A fundamental instructional question faces any informed policymaker, practitioner, or researcher interested in trying to get teachers to teach informal reasoning systematically and well: How can they teach, in a limited time, groups of 30 to 150 students (who are compelled to be in classes) a process of reasoning that must be individually understood, applied, and assessed through each students' words and behaviors, while simultaneously meeting other school, district, state, and community requirements? Within the present organizational framework of public schooling, it is a nearly impossible task. Few ever achieve success, yet all teachers are expected to do so daily (Cuban, 1984-b; Schrag, 1988).

Analysis of the growing body of classroom descriptions of what teachers actually do bleakly supports the view that the task is nearly impossible. According to these studies, the bulk of instructional time finds students listening to teachers talk, seldom asking questions, and working on tasks (homework, worksheets, multiple-choice items on achievement tests) that require little application of concepts, imagination, or serious inquiry. Applebee's studies of teachers who use innovative methods, yet slip back into the familiar syndrome of teach, test, reteach, test find familiar company in studies that show a remarkable continuity in teachers' practices. Schoenfeld's observations that math teachers teach in ways that are hostile to sense making are also supported in these studies (Boyer, 1983; Cohen, 1988; Cuban, 1984-a; Goodlad, 1984; National Science Foundation, 1978; Powell, Farrar, & Cohen, 1985).

What keeps teachers teaching in familiar ways, year in and out? For answers, one can look at individuals and the choices they make as independent professionals; one can look at the organizational structures that shape the workplace conditions; one can look at the institutional and larger cultures in which certain norms and beliefs exercise subtle but substantial influence on individual behavior; or one can create some mix of these perspectives. The authors chose liberally from all of these.

Applebee is puzzled by the ways teachers persisted in almost trivializing innovative techniques in the teaching of writing, and he has begun to look at teacher beliefs about knowledge and how those beliefs would need to be altered. Schoenfeld and Swartz see teachers as both the problem and the solution to the teaching of informal reasoning. Schoenfeld's sensitivity to the power of a classroom culture that shaped how teachers used content and pedagogy to divorce school math from life has not prevented his joining Swartz in looking for solutions to this mind-bending culture in individual teachers' willingness to restructure their classrooms. While not discounting the power of what an individual teacher can do once the classroom door is closed, both Newmann and O'Reilly see substantial organizational barriers to teachers cultivating reasoning in their classrooms.

How classrooms are organized, staffed, and governed, wedded to what teachers believe about knowledge and the diverse goals pursued by district and state authorities, creates an architecture of schooling. This architecture drives most teachers, but by no means all, toward pedagogies that prize content coverage, recall of information, facile performance on multiple-choice test items, and few student questions—approaches that seemingly run counter to the development of reasoning. Fifty-minute periods, self-contained classrooms, letter grades, and mandated tests, for example, are less than congenial arrangements for cultivating an active, holistic, and inquiring process of reasoning. Can teachers cultivate reasoning, much less the attitude of thoughtfulness, when they are bound by institutional arrangements and conflicting cultural demands over which they have little influence? The question suggests the embeddedness of teaching within overlapping organizations and cultures and the complexity of the task of altering classrooms.

Some teachers, of course, overcome this embeddedness and make substantial changes in their classrooms. They are uncommon. O'Reilly is one, of course, in the long line of maverick teachers who have invested great amounts of energy, time, and imagination to counter the strong undertow of organizational influence in order to create subject matter and pedagogies that nourish reasoning. In the tradition of Herb Kohl (1967), Elliot Wigginton (1985), Sylvia Warner (1963), and Patrick Welsh (1986), O'Reilly's beliefs about historical knowledge and work suggests exactly how difficult it is to overcome the organizational and cultural barriers that all teachers face. Can we expect ordinary teachers, with little available time, to undertake such ventures as O'Reilly undertook to create whiz-bang materials, despite the organizational disincentives that narrow teacher initiative or imagination, much less autonomy?

What about Harold Fawcett? Here was another gifted teacher whose beliefs about mathematical knowledge and whose independence in creating lessons and units engages the reader. But Schoenfeld neglects to tell us that Harold Fawcett, whom he rescues so nicely from the past, taught at the Ohio State Lab School when it and 29 others participated in the "Eight-Year Study," an experiment sponsored by the Progressive Education Association (1943) between 1934–1942. Participating high schools did not have to worry about college entrance requirements and could invent curricula quite different from those usually expected. I offer this additional information not to diminish the substantial achievements of Harold Fawcett but to place the school in a unique organizational context of the late 1930s.

O'Reilly and Fawcett are exceptions. One could easily argue that the workplace structures within which teachers teach today would have to be more hospitable to trial and error and reasoning processes like those used by O'Reilly and Fawcett for more teachers to do what Newmann, Schoenfeld, and Swartz desire. Currently, inhospitality reigns.

Newmann understands the organizational and cultural complexities of teaching. He sees the need for researchers to provide a path out of the conceptual swamp that characterizes discussions about informal reasoning. Recognizing the enormous complexity of trying to change individual behavior within organizational and cultural contexts, he sees the need for researchers' help in constructing conceptual maps for policymakers and practitioners to follow in figuring out both what to do and how to carry it off.

In his sensitivity to the complexities of the change process, Newmann calls our attention to an often ignored ingredient in any effort to introduce reasoning skills into classrooms systematically and durably: direct involvement of teachers in the change effort, conceiving what needs to be done, executing it, and, finally, assessing its worth. The direction of his research in five schools and his restrained language in arguing for teachers themselves as key participants in the process of organizational change goes beyond calling for teachers' responsibility for restructuring their own classrooms. This call has been popular among policymakers, who end up bashing teachers for failing to make the right changes.

The point that Newmann underscores is that altering classroom behavior requires an enormously complex series of interactions between teachers, administrators, and policymakers (with researchers sitting on the sidelines offering advice and counsel), within a place called school. Newmann's suggestions of what a restructured school that nourishes, not disables, reasoning can be offers modest hope to those still interested in the goal of improved reasoning skills for all children.

I say "hope" because my commentary on the chapters could easily be construed as deeply pessimistic—even despairing—about the potential for improving instruction in informal reasoning. By stressing, in these chapters, the embeddedness of teaching within organizational and cultural contexts and the complexities of the change process, readers could easily throw up their collective hands and say, "Forget it." The work that has to be done requires far more than individual teachers getting advice from policymakers and researchers as to what should be done and doing it. It will take much time, sustained effort, and imagination, wedded to resources. The complexities overwhelm. Hence, the potential for despair.

But Newmann's effort to drawn a conceptual map of both the substantive questions (e.g., What are the essential components of reasoning in the social studies that need to be taught?) and the procedural issues (e.g., What are the key elements and conditions necessary for change to occur?) offers a way out of the swamp. He has listened to teachers. He respects teachers and the tough working conditions they face daily in an effort meet impossible, conflicting obligations. He combines theory and an awareness of organizations and classroom practices to create potential paths to pursue in cultivating imaginative uses of reasoning in classrooms.

As an academic who has spent a quarter of a century in classrooms and administrative offices and been deeply involved in many instructional and curricular reforms, I need maps to pick my way through difficult terrain. The better the map, the better the chance of getting where I wish to go. In the midst of what many could easily label as a sad situation that is not amenable to improvement, Newmann offers us an initial map, one that is certainly full of errors yet is sensitive to the embeddedness of teaching and the complicated change process.

My cautious optimism is only that. The puzzle that Applebee wrestles with, the school culture of formal math that Schoenfeld rails at, and the organizational barriers that Newmann and O'Reilly list suggest that we need more and better maps of schooling, teaching, and student learning. What directions might I suggest to the mapmakers?

To policymakers and researchers, I offer the following:

1. *Acknowledge openly the inhospitality of schools to reasoning.* Current goals, school organization, governance, and staffing diminish possibilities for instruction in reasoning.

2. *Acknowledge openly that using research to improve schools is a severely limited tool.* As research is presently practiced, the use of findings to inform policy is, at best, of modest benefit to policymakers. At worst, it misleads.

3. *Continue those promising lines of research that have substantial policy implications for districts.*

A. Focus on elementary schools as relatively accessible targets for improvement by contrast to secondary schools. Fewer bureaucratic mechanisms, large chunks of student contact time, teacher beliefs that express sensitivity to human development, and fewer external demands in the lower grades provide more hospitable organizational conditions for strengthening reasoning skills (Cuban, 1984-a).

B. For all of its flaws, school effectiveness research, most of which has occurred in elementary schools, has affirmed that the local school, rather than the classroom or district, is the primary unit of change. The roles of the principal and of staff collaboration and the sense of mission and concern with group problem-solving offer promising avenues for exploring further how adults might model reasoning in order to make critical thought real in the teacher's classroom (David, 1982; Little, 1982).

C. Cognitive research that tries to uncover the mental processes by which teachers solve classroom problems, determine pacing, use questioning tactics, and decide when to improvise needs to be pursued. How do teachers think in classrooms while teaching and before they teach? How do they interpret the meaning of what happened in the classroom, and how does that meaning shape instructional behavior, or does it? Some researchers have explored these questions. Far more is necessary to map how teachers think and provide policymakers with a stronger conceptual basis for understanding teacher practice (Doyle & Ponder, 1977; Clark & Petersen, 1986; Lampert, 1984, 1986; Schrag, 1988).

D. Little is known of what students at various ages in different subjects think during lessons. How do students make sense out of what the teacher is saying or grasp the meaning of the tasks assigned by the teacher? If teachers formally teach critical thinking skills, what mental processes occur in students? Research on students' misconceptions in science is a beginning. As difficult as it is to capture patterns of thinking, researchers' ingenuity in the use of videotapes, interviews, and simulations might unlock these important puzzles.

E. What are the promising ways to prepare teachers to teach reasoning? Should there be logic courses in teacher-education curricula or better teacher preparation in questioning skills? What about the existing teacher population? Tests given to teachers to establish competency avoid reasoning; the state-of-the-art is primitive in this area. What, then, are some directions to pursue? A number of researchers and policymakers have suggested a focus on creating schools where both teacher and student learn. Teachers would do research or engage in school-based problem solving while teaching. Such activity would help satisfy the deep hunger that teachers express for opportunities to learn and grow. Researchers and policymakers talk and write about schools as places where professional renewal can occur, even while teachers are nurturing learning, but little research has occurred (Thelen, 1960; Sarason, 1972).

The direction of my suggestions is toward more descriptive and analytic school and classroom research. Until we understand the world of the teacher and student in the classroom and school, policies containing views of their worlds from the academy, state capitol, or superintendent's office that are aimed at improving informal reasoning will have little more effect than a passing knock on the classroom door.

REFERENCES

Boyer, E. L. (1983). *High school: A report on secondary education in America*. New York: Harper & Row.

Clark, C., & Petersen, P. (1986). Teachers' thought processes. In M. Wittrock (Ed.), *Third handbook of research on teaching* (pp. 255–296). Washington, DC: American Educational Research Association.

Cohen, D. (1988). Teaching practice, plus que ca change . . . . In P. Jackson (Ed.), *Contributing to educational change* (pp. 27–84). Berkeley, CA: McCutchan.

Cuban, L. (1984-a). *How teachers taught*. New York: Longman.

Cuban, L. (1984-b). Policy and research dilemmas in the teaching of reasoning: Unplanned designs. *Review of Educational Research, 54*(4), 655–681.

Cuban, L. (1986). *Teachers and machines: The classroom use of technology since 1920*. New York: Teachers College Press.

David, J. (1982). *School-based strategies: Implications for government policy*. Palo Alto, CA: Bay Area Research Group.

Dewey, J. (1933). *How we think*. Lexington, MA: D. C. Heath.

Doyle, W., & Ponder, G. (1977–1978). The practicality ethic in teacher decision-making. *Interchange, 8*(3), 1–12.

Goodlad, J. (1984). *A place called school*. New York: McGraw-Hill.

Kohl, H. (1967). *36 children*. New York: American Library.

Lampert, M. (1984). Teaching about thinking and thinking about teaching. *Journal of Curriculum Studies, 16*(1), 1–18.

Lampert, M. (1986). Knowing, doing, and teaching multiplication. *Cognition and Instruction, 3*(4), 305–342.

Little, J. (1982). Norms of collegiality and experimentation: Workplace conditions of school success. *American Educational Research Journal, 19*(3), 325–340.

National Science Foundation. (1978). *Report of the 1977 national survey of science, mathematics, and social studies education.* Washington, DC: National Science Foundation.

Powell, A. G., Farrar, E., & Cohen, D. K. (1985). *The shopping mall high school.* Boston, MA: Houghton Mifflin.

Progressive Education Association. (1943). *Thirty schools tell their story.* New York: Harper & Brothers.

Sarason, S. (1972). *The creation of settings and the future societies.* San Francisco, CA: Jossey-Bass.

Schrag, F. (1988). *Thinking in school and society.* New York: Routledge.

Thelen, H. (1960). *Education and the human quest.* New York: Harper & Brothers.

Tyler, R., & Smith, E. (1942). *Appraising and recording student progress.* New York: Harper & Brothers.

Warner, S. A. (1963). *Teacher.* New York: Simon and Schuster.

Welsh, P. (1986). *Tales out of school.* New York: Viking.

Wigginton, E. (1985). *Sometimes a shining moment.* New York: Anchor Press.

Author Index

Boden, M., 295, *308*
Bonham, G. M., 37, 39, 47, *56*
Borak, J., 26, *33*
Borgatta, E. F., 88, *104*
Boyer, E. L., 479, *483*
Braddock, R., 401, *414*
Bransford, J. D., 363, *378,* 387, *398,* 431, 441
Brewer, W. F., 176, *186*
Britton, J. N., 409, *414*
Broder, J. L., 460, *471*
Bronowski, J., 295, *308*
Brown, A. L., 97, *104,* 250, *262,* 383, 387, *398, 399,* 405, *414*
Brown, D., 358, *361*
Brown, J. S., 336, *342*
Brown, R., 403, 404, *414*
Brown, S. I., 333, *342*
Bruner, J. S., 22, *33*
Buchanan, B. G., 22, 24, *34, 35*
Burgess, T., 409, *414*
Burton, L., 339, *343*
Bushey, B., 96, *105*

C

California State Department of Education, 435, *441*
Camp, C., 358, *361*
Campbell, N. R., 346, *361*
Campione, J. C., 387, *398*
Cantor, G. N., 6, 7, *14*
Carbonell, J. G., 195, *207*
Carey, S., 252, 259, *262*
Carnap, R., 132, *150*
Carpenter, T. P., 316, *342*
Carr, E. H., 368, *378*
Casscels, W., 26, *33*
Cattell, R. B., 83, 84, *104*
Champagne, A., 357, *361*
Chan, S., 37, 39, *56*
Chance, P., 382, *398*
Chase, W. C., 93, *104*
Chase, W. G., 21, *33, 35,* 251, *262*
Cheng, P. W., 158, *168,* 304, *308*
Cherniak, C., 298, 299, *308*
Chi, M. T. H., 70, 79, *80,* 240, *246,* 391, *398*
Chipman, S. F., 382, *398, 400*
Chittenden, G. F., 273, 274, *289*
Christensen, C., 31, *32*
Christensen-Szalanski, C. M., 25, *33*

Christensen-Szalanski, J. J., 25, *33*
Clancey, W. J., 22, 24, 30, *33, 35*
Clark, C., 482, *483*
Clement, J., 349, 355, 356, 357, 358, 360, *361*
Clifford, B. R., 462, *471*
Cohen, D. K., 384, 393, *400,* 479, *483, 484*
Cohen, L. J., 299, *308*
Cohen, S. N., 24, *35*
Cole, M., 111, 112, 113, 114, *129, 130*
Collins, A., 336, *342,* 356, *361*
Collins, R. C., 191, *208*
Colomb, G., 229, *246*
Connolly, J. A., 460, *471*
Cooper, C., 403, 404, *414*
Cornbleth, C., 383, 387, *398*
Corsini, R. J., 88, *104*
Cosmides, L., 277, *289*
Costa, A., 382, *398*
Covington, M. V., 383, *398*
Cox, J. R., 304, *308*
Cronbach, L. J., 460, *471*
Crosswhite, F. J., 341, *342*
Cuban, L., 384, 391, 397, *398,* 473, 478, 479, 482, *483*
Curley, 19
Curly, S. P., *33*

D

Dale, P. S., 462, *471*
Daling, J. R., 19, *35*
Damon, W., 276, *289*
Darden, L., 346, *361*
Dasen, P. R., 112, *129*
Dauphinee, W. D., 30, *35*
David, J., 482, *483*
Davis, J., 61, *80*
Davison, M. L., 176, *186*
Davy, H., 6, *14*
Dawes, R. M., 31, *32,* 218, *223*
Day, M. C., 368, *378*
de Bono, E., 387, *398*
DeDombal, F. T., 30, *33*
deGroot, A. D., 21, *33*
Denham, C., 291, *398*
De Sanchez, M., 382, 387, *398*
Dewey, J., 434, *441,* 477, *483*
Diamond, S. S., 60, *80*
Diesing, P., 47, *57*
diSessa, A. A., 255, *262,* 353, *362*
DiSpezio, M., 428, 429, 440, *441,* 450

Subject Index

A

abstraction, 389, 394, 397
analogical reasoning, 250, 259, 295, 299,
    345-347, 349-351, 360, 474
analogy, 42, 43, 48, 142, 166, 167, 253,
    254, 295, 296, 347, 349, 354, 355,
    358, 474
analogy relation, 348-350
analogous case, 348-351
anchoring example, 358, 359, 474
anchoring, 26
"and," 293
argument, definitions of, 89, 265, 266, 274,
    305
argumentation, debate model of, 50, 51
Aristotle, 153-163
atmosphere effect, 160

B

base rates, 26, 30, 44
Bayes' theorem, 26, 31, 299
behavioral decision theory, 24
belief evaluation, 42
beliefs, 40, 42-46, 52, 175-178, 183, 184,
    258-260, 302, 303, 307
bias, 25-28, 90, 136, 138-141, 169, 172,
    174, 175, 191, 260
bottom up/top down reasoning, 24, 140

bounded rationality, 22, 47, 142
bridging analogies, 358, 359, 474

C

case building, 306
case-based reasoning (CBR), 190, 194-196,
    202, 203, 206
causal reasoning, models of, 258, 261, 420,
    423, 428
causal explanation, 417, 425, 427, 433
causal relations, 257
cause-and-effect reasoning, 372, 373, 376
characteristic-to-defining shift (C/D shift),
    249-251, 253, 254, 260
"chunking," 21, 140
cognitive complexity, 51
common ratio effect, 214
common consequence effect, 214
conceptual-infusion approach, 415, 476
confirmation bias, 44, 45, 421
confirming and disconfirming evidence, 11,
    42
conjunction fallacy, 216
connectionism, 195
constrained example generation, 197
construct representation, 460
context of demonstration, 346
context of discovery, 346
context typicality, 110